# HUMAN DEVELOPMENT

# ACADEMIC REVIEWERS

Nancy Hamblen Acuff, East Tennessee State University

Ira H. Bernstein, University of Texas at Arlington

Barbara L. Biales, The College of St. Catherine

James A. Blackburn, University of Wisconsin at Milwaukee

Kyle Ann Campos, Des Moines Area Community College

David Corsini, University of Connecticut

David Cuevas, El Paso Community College

Lisa Elliot, State University of New York at Geneseo

Juanita L. Garcia, University of South Florida

Susan W. Goodwyn, University of California at Davis

Harry W. Hoemann, Bowling Green State University

Frank H. Hooper, University of Wisconsin at Madison

Peg Hull-Smith, University of Toledo

Janet Kalinowski, Ithaca College

Thomas Mackie, Kellogg Community College

Pennie A. Medina, Bee County College

Charles D. Miron, Catonsville Community College

Barbara Morgan, Abraham Baldwin College

John M. Nash, Worcester State College

Yolanda Flores Niemann, University of Houston

Joanne Ramberg, Washburn University

Paul Retzlaff, University of Northern Colorado

Cynthia Scheibe, Ithaca College

Gail S. Scott, Briar Cliff College

Frank Sjursen, Shoreline Community College

Marcia Summers, Ball State University

Dennis Thompson, Georgia State University

Garry Whitehead, Darton College

# HUMAN DEVELOPMENT

FIFTH EDITION

## DIANE E. PAPALIA
## SALLY WENDKOS OLDS

McGRAW-HILL, INC.

New York   St. Louis   San Francisco   Auckland   Bogotá
Caracas   Lisbon   London   Madrid   Mexico   Milan
Montreal   New Delhi   Paris   San Juan
Singapore   Sydney   Tokyo   Toronto

HUMAN DEVELOPMENT

4 5 6 7 8 9 0 VNH VNH 9 0 9 8 7 6 5 4 3 2

ISBN 0-07-048557-7

This book was set in Century Expanded by York Graphic Services, Inc.
The editors were Jane Vaicunas and Susan Gamer;
the designer was Rafael Hernandez;
the production supervisor was Annette Mayeski.
The photo editor was Inge King.
The permissions editor was Barbara Hale.
Von Hoffmann Press, Inc., was printer and binder.

Permissions and credits appear on pages 605–608, and on this page by reference.
Photo of Sally Wendkos Olds, © 1985, Thomas Victor.
Cover illustration by Steve Karchin.

Library of Congress Cataloging-in-Publication Data

Papalia, Diane E.
    Human development / Diane E. Papalia, Sally Wendkos Olds.—5th ed.
        p.      cm.
    Includes bibliographical references and index.
    ISBN 0-07-048557-7
    1. Developmental psychology.      2. Developmental psychobiology.
    I. Olds, Sally Wendkos.      II. Title
BF713.P35      1992                                    91-19187
155—dc20

# ABOUT
# THE AUTHORS

**DIANE E. PAPALIA** is a professor who has taught thousands of undergraduates at the University of Wisconsin–Madison. She received her bachelor's degree, majoring in psychology, from Vassar College, and both her master's degree in child development and family relations and her Ph. D. in life-span developmental psychology from West Virginia University. She has published numerous articles in such professional journals as *Human Development, International Journal of Aging and Human Development, Sex Roles, Journal of Experimental Child Psychology,* and *Journal of Gerontology.* Most of these papers have dealt with her major research focus, cognitive development from childhood through old age. She is especially interested in intellectual development and factors that contribute to the maintenance of intellectual functioning. She is a Fellow in the Gerontological Society of America.

**SALLY WENDKOS OLDS** is an award-winning professional writer who has written more than 200 articles in leading magazines and is the author or coauthor of six books addressed to general readers, in addition to the three textbooks she has coauthored with Dr. Papalia. Her books *The Complete Book of Breastfeeding* and *The Working Parents' Survival Guide* have both been issued in completely updated and expanded editions. She is also the author of *The Eternal Garden: Seasons of Our Sexuality* and the coauthor of *Raising a Hyperactive Child* (winner of the Family Service Association of America National Media Award) and *Helping Your Child Find Values to Live By.* She received her bachelor's degree from the University of Pennsylvania, where she majored in English literature and minored in psychology. She was elected to Phi Beta Kappa and was graduated summa cum laude.

To our husbands
Jonathan L. Finlay
and
David Mark Olds
Our loved and loving partners
in growth and development

# CONTENTS

# LIST OF BOXES

# PREFACE

In the prefaces to the previous four editions of *Human Development,* we spoke of change as a principle that governs all our lives. As we said then, people change, grow, and develop throughout life. We, the authors, have known many changes in our own lives since we began writing together in 1973. Our life experiences, as much as our professional background (described in "About the Authors" on page v), have enabled us to become more sensitive to a number of the issues covered in this book.

When we launched our collaboration—and our friendship—with the first edition of *A Child's World,* our textbook about child development, Diane Papalia was a single, childless assistant professor at the University of Wisconsin in Madison. Sally Olds, a professional writer, was a married mother of three children—one in high school, one in junior high, and one in elementary school. Both parents of both authors were living, and we dedicated our first textbook to them.

Since then, as both of us have moved from young adulthood into midlife, our lives have changed in many ways. Diane took on more academic responsibilities as she became first an associate professor, then a dean, and then a full professor. Her personal life changed dramatically when she married, moved to California, and later came back to Wisconsin, where she and her husband adopted a baby girl. Since then, other career changes took her and her family to New York City, where they now live. Meanwhile, Sally's children grew up, went to college, chose careers, and left the nest; her husband retired; she knew the grief of losing first her father and then her mother; and then she knew the joy of celebrating a daughter's marriage and the birth of two grandchildren.

As we and our lives have changed, this book, *Human Development,* has reflected some of what we have learned along the way. The fifth edition retains much of the flavor of earlier editions, especially in its emphasis on interrelationships among the different stages of the life span and among physical, intellectual, social, and personality development. There are, however, a number of differences. The changes in this revision continue to represent growth and development in our own thinking, as we present human development from the moment of conception until that moment at the other end of the life span when death ends the continuing process.

## THE FIFTH EDITION

## OUR AIMS FOR THIS EDITION

The goal of this fifth edition is the same as that of the first four—to emphasize the continuity of development throughout the life span; to show how experiences at one time of life affect future development; and to understand how people are influenced by their genes, their families, and the world they live in. We continue to look at the findings of scientific research and the theories of social scientists. We continue to apply these to our understanding of humankind. And we continue to ask the same basic questions: What influences have made people living in the final decades of the twentieth century the way they are? What factors are likely to affect all of us in the future? How much control do people have over their lives? How are people like each other? How is each person unique? What is normal? What is cause for concern?

For this new edition, we also ask some new questions and come up with some new answers. This revision again updates the literature, as we discuss new research studies and new theories, a number of which have been published in the 1990s. As before, we synthesize research findings and help students to interpret them and to think critically about controversial issues. Our continuing work on two other college textbooks, *A Child's World* (for courses in child development) and *Psychology* (for introductory courses), has helped us refine and sharpen our thinking about life-span development. The changes in this revision, then, represent growth and development in our own ideas.

## ORGANIZATION

There are two major approaches to writing about and teaching human development. The chronological approach looks at the functioning of all aspects of development at different stages of life, such as infancy and late adulthood. The topical approach traces one aspect of development at a time. We have chosen the *chronological* approach, which provides a sense of the multifaceted sweep of human development, as we get to know first the infant and toddler, then the young child, the schoolchild, the adolescent, the young adult, the adult at midlife, and the person in late adulthood. As we discuss the ages and stages of human beings, we provide evenhanded treatment of *all* periods of the life span; we have taken special pains not to overemphasize some and slight others.

In line with our chronological approach, we have divided this book into eight parts. We begin with introductory material in Chapter 1. Then we discuss physical, intellectual, and social and personality development at each stage of the life span: Part One (Chapters 2 through 5) covers prenatal development, infancy, and toddlerhood; Part Two (Chapters 6 and 7), early childhood; Part Three (Chapters 8 and 9), middle childhood; Part Four (Chapters 10 and 11), adolescence; Part Five (Chapters 12 and 13), young adulthood; Part Six (Chapters 14 and 15), middle adulthood; and Part Seven (Chapters 16 and 17), late adulthood. In Part Eight (Chapter 18), we examine death—the end of life—and bereavement.

Readers who prefer a topical approach may read the book in this order: Chapters 1, 2, and 3 (general theories and issues, and prenatal and early physical development); the first sections of Chapter 6, 8, 10, 12, 14, and 16 (physical development); the second sections of these chapters, plus Chapter 4 (intellectual functioning); then Chapters 5, 7, 9, 11, 13, 15, and 17 (social and personality development); and finally Chapter 18 (death and bereavement).

## CONTENT

This new edition, like the earlier editions, provides comprehensive coverage of development from the crucial prenatal period through late adulthood. There are full descriptions of each stage of the life span, drawing on the most up-to-date information available about physical, intellectual, and social and personality development. The text integrates theoretical issues, issues related to research, and practical concerns for every stage of life, reflecting our belief that all stages of life are important, challenging, and full of opportunities for growth and change.

While we have retained the scope, emphasis, and level of the previous editions of *Human Development,* we have made a number of significant changes in this fifth edition.

- *Personal examples.* We communicate our own personal involvement with the issues we have written about. The book presents many personal examples from the authors' own lives, which relate to the material and personalize it. Perhaps the most dramatic example is the story of Anna's (Diane Papalia's daughter) language development, which serves as a springboard for the discussion of many issues.
- *Photographs.* Our photo program has evolved and is now even more committed than ever before to diversity—in ethnicity, race, age, gender, and ability (or disability). We have carefully chosen our illustrations to be teaching tools—for points in the text and for the demographic diversity of the United States and the world.
- *Updating and reorganization.* As in previous editions, we have updated the text whenever new findings or interpretations have been available, added tables and figures, and updated statistics. We have also reorganized some of the material to make it more effective.
- *New sections.* There are new sections on prenatal and infant care in various countries; the psychological implications of crawling; the mutual-regulation model of emotional communication between babies and parents; AIDS; homelessness; only children in China; comparisons between eastern and western learning styles; relationships between young adults and their parents; the impact of race on health; adults' reactions to their parents' death; cross-cultural patterns of aging among American minorities and in other countries; and the impact of religion on emotional well-being in late adulthood.
- *Important revisions.* Several of the discussions have been significantly revised: the contribution of heredity to intelligence; the prenatal environment, includ-

ing the effect of a pregnant woman's use of cocaine; language development, both normal and delayed; attachment research using the "strange situation" (which is now receiving extensive criticism); stranger and separation anxiety; memory; Piaget's cognitive stages; the transition to parenthood; characteristics of mature thinkers; the midlife crisis; stage theories of adult development (we emphasize these less and criticize them more); and patterns of grieving.

## SPECIAL FEATURES IN THIS EDITION

This edition of *Human Development* includes three kinds of boxed material:

- *"Window on the World."* These boxes have been increased, so that there is now one in every chapter of the book. They give readers glimpses of human development in a variety of societies other than our own, showing that people grow up, live, and thrive in many different kinds of cultures, under many different influences. The discussions treat such issues as cross-cultural differences in acquiring physical, intellectual, and social skills; in education and learning styles; and in moral reasoning.
- *"Practically Speaking."* The "Practically Speaking" boxes build bridges between academic study and everyday life by showing ways to apply research findings on various aspects of human development. They cover such topics as talking with babies and dealing with them when they're fussy; helping children make friends, do well in school, and cope with being on their own without adult supervision; enhancing marriage in midlife; visiting people in nursing homes; helping to prevent suicides; easing the lives of older adults; and evoking memories for a "life review."
- *"Thinking Critically."* These boxes explore important research issues, many of which are quite controversial. They include discussions of how a mother's depression affects her baby; the transition to junior high or high school; the role of rock music in adolescents' lives; and wisdom in late adulthood.

## LEARNING AIDS IN THE TEXT

We continue to provide a number of basic teaching aids:

- *Part overviews.* At the beginning of each part, an overview provides the rationale for the chapters that follow.
- *Chapter-opening outlines.* At the beginning of each chapter, an outline clearly previews its major topics.

- *"Ask Yourself" questions.* At the beginning of each chapter, a few key questions are given to highlight the most important issues that will be addressed in the chapter.
- *Key terms.* Whenever an important new term is introduced in the text, it is highlighted in **boldface italic** and defined. At the end of every chapter, the key terms are listed in order of appearance, and page references are provided. These terms also appear in the end-of-book glossary.
- *Chapter summaries.* At the end of every chapter there is a series of brief statements, organized by the major topics in the chapter, clearly restating the most important points.
- *Recommended readings.* Annotated lists of readings (classic works and lively contemporary treatments) are provided for students who want to explore issues in greater depth than is possible within these covers.
- *Glossary.* The extensive glossary near the end of the book repeats the definitions of key terms and indicates the pages on which they first appear in the text.
- *Bibliography.* A complete listing of references enables students to evaluate the sources of major statements of fact or theory.
- *Indexes.* Separate indexes, by subject and by author, appear at the end of the book.
- *Illustrations.* Many points in the text are underscored pictorially through extensive and carefully selected drawings, graphs, and photographs. The illustration program includes new figures and many full-color photographs.

## SUPPLEMENTARY MATERIALS

A complete package of supplements is available to instructors and students using *Human Development,* fifth edition.

- *Study Guide with Readings* by Thomas Crandell of Broome Community College and George Bieger of Indiana University of Pennsylvania. For each chapter of the text, the study guide provides a brief *chapter summary,* a *chapter outline,* a list of *key terms* cross-referenced by page to the text, *learning objectives* with space for notes, and an engaging *reading* from the popular press accompanied by questions for thought or discussion. A *self-test* for each chapter includes a mix of multiple-choice, true-false, and completion questions. The new edition of the study guide includes a revised and expanded section on how to study and take tests.

- *Instructor's Manual* by Corinne Crandell and Thomas Crandell of Broome Community College. For each chapter of the text, the instructor's manual provides a *chapter outline,* a list of *chapter objectives,* a *chapter summary,* a list of appropriate *audiovisual materials, lecture outlines,* a *student debate topic, discussion questions, student projects and class exercises,* and suggested *essay questions* with answer guidelines. A general resources section includes suggested background readings, a list of audiovisual distributors, and teaching tips.
- *Test Bank* by Ruth Duskin Feldman. The test bank includes a mix of factual and conceptual multiple-choice items indexed to the text, for a total of over 2000 items. Approximately 25 true-false questions are also provided for each chapter. *Computerized versions* of the test bank are available for IBM-compatible PCs (5¼″ and 3½″ disk sizes) and Macintosh PCs.
- *Overhead Transparencies.* This package of over 70 acetates, many in full color, illustrates all the stages and facets of development across the life span. The figures and tables are taken from several sources, including the text itself.
- *Films and videos.* Films and videos are available on a rental basis through several major distributors. A complete listing is available through your McGraw-Hill representative.
- *Newsletter.* The text will be supplemented regularly by a newsletter highlighting recent research and current issues, including the theme of *cultural differences,* within the United States and around the world.

## ACKNOWLEDGMENTS

We would like to express our gratitude to the many friends and colleagues who, through their work and their interest, helped us clarify our thinking about human development. We are especially grateful for the valuable help given by those who reviewed the published fourth edition of *Human Development* and the manuscript drafts of the fifth; their evaluations and suggestions helped greatly in the preparation of this new edition. These reviewers, who are affiliated with both two- and four-year institutions, are listed on page ii.

We appreciate the strong support we have had from our publisher and would like to express our special thanks to Jane Vaicunas, editorial sponsor of this book; to our meticulous and conscientious production editor, Susan Gamer; and to Renee Leonard and Beth Kaufman, both of whom helped in innumerable ways. Inge King—the photo editor for all five editions of *Human Development*—has again used her sensitivity, her interest, and her good eye to find outstanding photographs. Rafael Hernandez, our designer, produced a creative, unique book and text typography noteworthy for aesthetics, as well as for the rendering of concepts. Marthe Grice provided valuable help with the glossary, bibliography, and suggested readings; Jean Yanega keyboarded the entire manuscript onto computer disks; and Dorri Olds conceived graphic representation of some information.

*Diane E. Papalia*
*Sally Wendkos Olds*

Diane E. Papalia and Sally Wendkos Olds are the coauthors of *A Child's World* (in press for its sixth edition) and *Psychology* (in its second edition).

# HUMAN DEVELOPMENT

## CHAPTER 1

# ABOUT HUMAN DEVELOPMENT

There is nothing permanent except change.

HERACLITUS, FRAGMENT
(SIXTH CENTURY B.C.)

- What can you gain from the study of human development, and how does this book approach the subject?
- How has the study of human development developed?
- What are the major changes in the course of human life, and what common and individual influences affect people?

- How do social scientists study people, and what are some ethical considerations about their methods?
- What major theoretical perspectives try to explain human development, and what are their strengths and weaknesses?

The study of human development is endlessly fascinating because it is the study of real lives—yours, the reader's; ours, the authors'; and those of millions of people around the world. To introduce the subject matter of this book, we'd like to introduce one very small, real person, Anna Victoria Finlay. By focusing on one aspect of her life, her early language development, we can better understand some of the reasons for studying human development, and some of the ways it is studied.

At the time of this writing Anna—who was born in Santiago, Chile—is a bright-eyed, cheerful, lively 5-year-old. When she was 8 weeks old, Jonathan Finlay, her adoptive father, flew to Santiago and brought her home, to the waiting arms of her adoptive mother, a developmental psychologist and a professor at the University of Wisconsin—Madison named Diane E. Papalia.*

Anna was already cooing—making happy squeals, gurgles, and vowel sounds—when she came to Diane and Jonathan, and in the manner of parents around the world they began to coo back and to talk to their baby in dozens of daily "conversations." At about 6 months Anna added consonants to her "speech" and began to babble. And at 11 months, she toddled over to a next-door neighbor and said her first word—"Hi." Basking in the excited response she received from both her mother and her neighbor, Anna immediately repeated her first word six more times. She added three more words to her vocabulary over the next month and a few

more soon after her first birthday. A favorite word was "glee"—which originally meant Gregory, the family cat, and then came to mean all furry animals. Anna seemed to be right on schedule in becoming a speaker.

But then Anna's progress slowed down, and by the time she was 2½, Diane and Jonathan had begun to worry. Anna seemed to understand what was said to her, but she spoke only a few words and was not putting them together in two-word sentences—though the average child does this considerably earlier, at about 18 months of age. They mentioned their anxieties to their pediatrician, who suggested a language assessment at a nearby speech clinic. There, the speech pathologist told Diane and Jonathan that their daughter understood what a child her age was expected to, but that at 30 months, she had the expressive language of a 15-month-old.

"Was it something I did?" Diane asked, guilt-ridden and struck by the possible irony that she, a psychologist who writes about child development, might have contributed to Anna's language delay. The speech pathologist assured both parents that they did not seem to be to blame. Speech, she told them, may be late in developing for a number of reasons, unrelated to the child's intelligence or the environment provided by the parents. She then recommended a two-part program to bring Anna's speech up to normal for her age.

One aspect of the program, which began just before Anna's third birthday, was language stimulation. A trained speech therapist "played" with Anna, using toys to teach such concepts as *up-down*, *soft-hard*, and *big-little*. The therapist helped Anna to articulate her words more clearly and communicate more effectively—to use speech the way most people use it (or try to use it) much of the time—to get what she wanted.

---

*Diane Papalia is, of course, one of the two authors of this textbook; the other is Sally Olds. Throughout, we will use a first name—Diane or Sally—whenever we are referring to only one of us.

Besides being an enjoyable shared activity, reading with a child—as Anna's father is doing with her—is an important way to help language skills develop.

By age 4, Anna was chattering away constantly, making requests, giving orders, asking questions, issuing comments. She would tell her mother, "Do your happy face, Mommy. Do your crying face. Do your mean face." She could name her favorite books and videotapes, sing "Eentsy Weentsy Spider," and use pronouns and the future and past tenses correctly. One evening, Anna strode over to the window of the family's New York apartment, looked up into the night sky, and sang in clear, piping tones, "Twinkle, Twinkle, Little Star." When Diane and Jonathan looked at one another, each saw tears glistening in the other's eyes.

In many ways, language is a good illustration of the study of human development: it involves both the changes and the consistency that are typical of development, and it lends itself to study by all the basic methods of developmentalists. In this chapter, then, we focus on the study of language ability to show how learning about human development can enable us to understand and help children and adults.

As we describe our own approach to the study of human development, we will chart some major changes in the course of human life, and some influences on development. We will also touch on the history of the field, methods of social science, and ethical considerations in research. Finally, we will outline the major theoretical perspectives that try to explain human development.

The other part of Anna's speech therapy rested with her parents. Since her infancy, Diane and Jonathan had taken great joy in talking and reading to Anna, and they had generally spoken to her in "motherese," a simplified type of speech that most adults use almost automatically with babies. Now they were encouraged to simplify their speech even further. Instead of asking Anna, "Want to get up on Mommy's lap?" for example, they were to ask, "Want up?" Diane and Jonathan carried out this suggestion, gradually moving to more advanced levels of language as Anna's own speech improved. They also expanded on whatever Anna said and talked about whatever she showed interest in; and they used some new reading routines, as we'll see later (page 17).

After 4 months of speech therapy, Diane and Jonathan received good news: at the age of 3 years, 4 months, Anna now had the usual vocabulary for her age level. By 3 years, 9 months of age, her vocabulary was at an *advanced* level—4 years, 4 months. In addition, she was speaking sentences that averaged 5 to 7 words each and included some of up to 10 words.

## HUMAN DEVELOPMENT: THE SUBJECT AND THE TEXT

### WHAT IS HUMAN DEVELOPMENT?

**Human development** is the scientific study of how people change and how they stay the same over time.

Change is most obvious in childhood but occurs throughout life. It takes two forms, quantitative and qualitative. **Quantitative change** is a change in the number or amount of something, such as height and weight—or the increase in the number of words, phrases, and sentences that Anna uses. **Qualitative change** is a change in kind, structure, or organization, such as the nature of a person's intelligence, the way the mind works—or Anna's development from a nonverbal infant to a child who understands and speaks a language. Like the emergence of a butterfly from a cocoon, qualitative change is marked by the appearance of new phenomena that could not have been predicted from earlier functioning. Speech is one such phenomenon.

In some ways, people show an underlying continuity, or consistency, from one time of life to another. In other ways, they change. One area with aspects of both continuity and change is personality development. According to recent research, for example, about 10 to 15 percent of children are consistently shy, while another 10 to 15 percent are, by and large, sociable. (Most children fall between these extremes.) Although various factors in a child's life can modify these traits to some degree, the psychologist Jerome Kagan (1989) has found that they persist moderately through at least the first 7½ years, especially in children at one extreme or the other. Some characteristics—like outgoingness, neuroticism, and openness to new experiences—seem to persist through adulthood. But some others change in adulthood: at midlife, for instance, women typically become more assertive, men become more intimate and nurturing, and both sexes tend to become more introspective (that is, to think more about their lives).

Students of development are interested in factors that affect everyone. But since each member of the human species is unique, developmentalists also want to know why one person turns out different from another. Because human development is so complex, scientists cannot always answer that question. But by examining how people develop throughout life, they have learned much about what people need to develop normally, how they react to the many influences upon and within them, and how they can best fulfill their potential as individuals and as a species.

## HOW THIS BOOK APPROACHES HUMAN DEVELOPMENT

Before introducing the study of human development, we will introduce some of our own ideas on the subject— the assumptions and beliefs that underlie this book—so that you may keep them in mind as you read it.

### We Celebrate the Human Being

We are interested in what theory and research have to tell us, specifically, about human beings. Whenever possible, we cite research that was done with people rather than animals. Sometimes, of course, we have to refer to studies of animals—in cases where ethical standards preclude research on humans. When we present conclusions based on animal research, we do so with caution, since we cannot assume that they apply equally to humans.

More important, our interest is in uniquely human qualities. So that you can explore this rich diversity, every chapter in this book has at least one "Window on the World" box, focusing on some aspect of a culture other than the dominant one in the United States. We will also examine cross-cultural differences at appropriate points in the main body of the text.

### We Respect All Periods of the Life Span

We are convinced that people have the potential to change as long as they live. As we have pointed out, the changes of early life are especially dramatic, as almost helpless newborns transform themselves into competent, exploring children. Change in childhood normally involves increased size and improved abilities, but change in adulthood occurs in more than one direction. Some abilities, like vocabulary, continue to grow; others, like strength and reaction time, diminish. Still other capacities may emerge for the first time in adulthood, like the synthesis of knowledge and experience into wisdom. Very old people can show growth, and even the experience of dying can be a final attempt to come to terms with one's life—in short, to develop.

### We Believe in Human Resilience

We believe that people can often bounce back from difficult early circumstances or stressful experiences to make a good adaptation to life. A traumatic incident or a severely deprived childhood may well have grave emotional consequences; but the stories of countless people, some of whom researchers have followed from childhood into at least their sixties, show that a single experience—even one as painful as the death of a parent in childhood—is not likely to cause irreversible damage (Vaillant & Vaillant, 1990). A nurturing environment can often help a child overcome the effects of early deprivation or trauma.

### We Recognize That People Help Shape Their Own Development

People are not passive sponges, soaking up influences. They actively shape their own environment, and then they respond to the environmental forces that they have helped bring about. You can see this bidirectional influence over and over. When infants babble and coo, they encourage adults to talk to them, and this talk in turn stimulates the babies' language development. Teenagers' burgeoning sexuality may evoke their parents' fears of growing older and regrets for lost youth; the parents' reactions, in turn, may affect the teenagers' attitudes toward the changes they are undergoing. Older adults also shape their own development; for example, by deciding when to retire from paid work, by taking up new activities, and by forming new relationships.

Oprah Winfrey is an example of human resilience. Sexually molested as a child and rebellious as a teenager, she blossomed when she went to live with her father, who encouraged her to learn. Today, as host of a nationwide television talk show, she is one of the most successful entertainers in the country.

### We Believe That Knowledge Is Useful

As people who live in the real world, we are concerned with how research findings can be used to solve practical problems. There are two kinds of research, which complement each other. *Basic* research is launched in the spirit of intellectual curiosity with no immediate practical goal in mind; and *applied* research addresses immediate problems. Whenever possible, we extract from both kinds of research findings and theories with practical implications for everyday life.

Each chapter contains many examples and guidelines for action, some of them highlighted in the "Practically Speaking" boxes. The "Thinking Critically" boxes call attention to cutting-edge research or to controversial issues, encouraging the reader to analyze and draw conclusions about the information presented.

Now that you know something about how we approach human development, we introduce the study itself, sketching its outline and summarizing its history. Then we describe various ways of studying human development, their advantages, and their pitfalls. And finally, we present the perspectives of the field's most influential thinkers.

## HUMAN DEVELOPMENT: THE STUDY AND ITS HISTORY

The study of human development originally focused on *describing* behavior in order to derive age norms. Today, developmentalists also want to *explain* why be-

haviors occur by looking at the factors that influence development; their next step is to *predict* behavior and, in some cases, to try to *modify* or *optimize* development thorugh training or therapy.

We can see the interrelationship of these four steps by looking at language development. *Description* leads to establishing norms for language at various ages. *Explanation* involves trying to uncover how children acquire language and get better at using it. *Prediction* entails determining what "language status" at a given age can tell us about later behavior: does a delay at age 2½, for example, predict reading problems in second grade? *Modification* involves finding ways to change behavior, such as speech therapy to stimulate language growth. Of course, these four activities work together. Before starting language therapy, for instance, you need to know what is normal; to design a program, a therapist has to know how people acquire language skills.

The study of human development has very practical implications. After noting Anna's delayed speech development, her parents could, with the proper knowledge, be reassured that she was basically normal and could also learn how to help her overcome this specific problem. Similarly, understanding adult development helps professionals and laypersons alike to prepare for life transitions: a woman returning to work after maternity leave; a 50-year-old man who realizes that he will never be a company president; a person about to retire; a widow or widower; a dying patient.

Students of development draw on many disciplines, including psychology, sociology, anthropology, biology, education, and medicine. These disciplines are all reflected in the materials in this book.

## ASPECTS OF DEVELOPMENT

One reason for the complexity of human development is that growth and change occur in different aspects of the self. In this book we talk separately about *physical, intellectual,* and *personality and social* development at each period of life, but actually these strands are intertwined. Each aspect of development affects the others.

### Physical Development

Changes in the body, the brain, sensory capacities, and motor skills are all part of physical development. They exert a major influence on both intellect and personality. For example, much of an infant's knowledge of the world comes from the senses and from motor activity. A child who has a hearing loss is at risk of delayed language development. In late adulthood, physical changes in the brain, as in Alzheimer's disease—which has been estimated to affect about 10 percent of people over the age of 65 (Evans et al., 1989)—can result in intellectual and personality deterioration.

### Intellectual Development

Changes in mental abilities—such as learning, memory, reasoning, thinking, and language—are aspects of intellectual development. These changes are closely related to both motor and emotional development. A baby's growing memory, for example, is related to *separation anxiety,* the fear that the mother will not return once she has gone away. If children could not remember the past and anticipate the future, they could not worry about the mother's absence. Memory also affects babies' physical actions. For example, a 1-year-old boy who remembers being scolded for knocking down his sister's block tower may refrain from doing it again.

### Personality and Social Development

Personality—the unique way in which each person deals with the world, expresses emotions, and so on—and social development (relationships with others) affect both the cognitive aspects and the physical aspects of functioning. For example, anxiety about taking a test can impair performance; and social support from friends helps people cope with the negative effects of stress on their physical and mental health. On the other hand, the physical and the intellectual also affect the social: children who do not speak well may hit people to try to get what they want or have temper tantrums because of frustration over their inability to express their needs.

## PERIODS OF THE LIFE SPAN

In this book we divide the human life span into eight periods: (1) prenatal, (2) infancy and toddlerhood, (3) early childhood, (4) middle childhood, (5) adolescence, (6) young adulthood, (7) middle age, and (8) late adulthood. These age divisions are approximate and somewhat arbitrary—especially in adulthood, when there are no clear-cut social or physical criteria like those in childhood (such as starting school and entering puberty) to signal a shift from one period to another.

Each period has its own characteristic events and issues, some of which are described in Table 1-1 (on pages 7–8).

## INDIVIDUAL DIFFERENCES IN DEVELOPMENT

Although people typically proceed through the same general sequence of development, there is a wide range of individual differences in the timing and expression of developmental changes. Throughout this book, we talk about *average* ages for the occurrence of certain phenomena: the first word, the first menstruation, the development of abstract thought. In all cases, these ages are *merely* averages. Only when deviation from these norms is extreme is there cause to consider a person's development exceptionally advanced or delayed. (Was Anna's language delay, for example, a problematic deviation from established norms or merely a normal individual difference? Would she eventually have reached her age level without speech therapy?)

The range of individual differences increases as people grow older. Normal children pass the same milestones in development at nearly the same ages because many changes of childhood are tied to maturation of the body and brain. Later in life, experiences and environment exert more influence, and since we undergo different experiences and live in different kinds of worlds, it is natural that we should reflect these differences.

Not only rates but also results of development vary. People differ in height, weight, and body build; in constitutional factors like health and energy level; in comprehension of complex ideas; and in emotional reactions. Their lifestyles differ too: the work they do, how well they do it, and how much they like it; the homes and communities they live in, and how they feel about them; the people they see and the relationships they have; and how they spend their leisure time.

## INFLUENCES ON DEVELOPMENT

Development is subject to many influences: the characteristics people are born with plus the effects of the experiences they have. Some experiences are purely

**TABLE 1–1**
MAJOR DEVELOPMENTS IN EIGHT PERIODS OF THE LIFE SPAN

| Age Period | Major Developments |
|---|---|
| Prenatal stage (conception to birth) | Basic body structure and organs form. Physical growth is most rapid of life span. Vulnerability to environmental influences is great. |
| Infancy and toddlerhood (birth to age 3) | Newborn is dependent but competent. All senses operate at birth. Physical growth and development of motor skills are rapid. Ability to learn and remember is present, even in early weeks of life. Attachments to parents and others form toward end of first year. Self-awareness develops in second year. Comprehension and speech develop rapidly. Interest in other children increases. |
| Early childhood (3 to 6 years) | Family is still focus of life, although other children become more important. Strength and fine and gross motor skills improve. Independence, self-control, and self-care increase. Play, creativity, and imagination become more elaborate. Cognitive immaturity leads to many "illogical" ideas about the world. Behavior is largely egocentric, but understanding of other people's perspective grows. |
| Middle childhood (6 to 12 years) | Peers assume central importance. Children begin to think logically, although largely concretely. Egocentrism diminishes. Memory and language skills increase. Cognitive gains improve ability to benefit from formal schooling. Self-concept develops, affecting self-esteem. Physical growth slows. Strength and athletic skills improve. |
| Adolescence (12 to 20 years) | Physical changes are rapid and profound. Reproductive maturity is attained. Search for identity becomes central. Ability to think abstractly and use scientific reasoning develops. Adolescent egocentrism persists in some behaviors. Peer groups help to develop and test self-concept. Relationships with parents are generally good. |
| Young adulthood (20 to 40 years) | Decisions are made about intimate relationships. Most people marry; most become parents. Physical health peaks, then declines slightly. Career choices are made. Sense of identity continues to develop. Intellectual abilities assume new complexity. |

*(Continued)*

**TABLE 1–1**
(CONTINUED)

| Age Period | Major Developments |
| --- | --- |
| Middle age (40 to 65 years) | Search for meaning in life assumes central importance.<br>Some deterioration of physical health, stamina, and prowess takes place.<br>Women experience menopause.<br>Wisdom and practical problem solving skills are high; ability to solve novel problems declines.<br>Double responsibilities of caring for children and elderly parents may cause stress.<br>Time orientation changes to "time left to live."<br>Launching of children typically leaves empty nest.<br>Typically, women become more assertive, men more nurturant and expressive.<br>For some, career success and earning powers peak; for others, "burnout" occurs.<br>For a minority, there is a midlife "crisis." |
| Late adulthood (65 years and over) | Most people are healthy and active, although health and physical abilities decline somewhat.<br>Most people are mentally alert. Although intelligence and memory deteriorate somewhat, most people find ways to compensate.<br>Slowing of reaction time affects many aspects of functioning.<br>Need to cope with losses in many areas (loss of one's own faculties, loss of loved ones).<br>Retirement from work force creates more leisure time but may reduce economic circumstances.<br>Need arises to find purpose in life to face impending death. |

individual, while others are common to certain groups—age groups, generations, or people who live in or were raised in particular societies and cultures. People's own behavior and lifestyle also influence their development.

## Types of Influences: Sources and Effects

### Internal and external influences

Internal influences on development originate with *heredity*—the inborn genetic endowment that people receive from their parents. External influences, or *environmental influences*, come from people's experiences with the world outside the self.

But this distinction soon blurs: we change our world even as it changes us. A baby girl with a cheerful disposition, for example, brings out positive reactions from other people, which in turn strengthen her trust that her efforts will be rewarded. With this self-confidence, she is motivated to try to do more—and is likelier to succeed than a child who lacks such trust.

### Normative and nonnormative influences

The effects of certain major events have led some researchers to distinguish between normative and nonnormative influences on development (Baltes, Reese, & Lipsitt, 1980).

Something is "normative" when it occurs in a similar way for most people in a given group. *Normative age-graded influences* are biological and environmental influences on development that are highly similar for people in a particular age group, no matter when and where they live. These influences include biological events like puberty and menopause, as well as cultural events like entry into formal education (at about age 6 in most societies) and retirement from paid employment (usually between age 55 and age 70).

*Normative history-graded influences* are biological and environmental influences common to a particular generation, or *cohort* (people growing up at the same time in the same place). These influences include the worldwide economic depression of the 1930s, the political turmoil in the United States during the 1960s and 1970s in reaction to the Vietnam war, the massive famines in Africa during the 1980s, and the Persian Gulf war of the early 1990s. They also encompass such cultural factors as the changing roles of women, the use of anesthesia during childbirth, and the impact of television and computers.

*Nonnormative life events* are unusual events that have a major impact on individual lives—typical events that happen to a person at an atypical time of life or events that do not happen at all to most other people.

Normative history-graded influences, like the worldwide economic depression of the 1930s, can affect an entire cohort. Americans like these Missouri children who grew up in poverty were profoundly affected by the experience.

Such events include the death of a parent when a child is young, life-threatening illnesses, and birth defects. They can also, of course, be happy events, like being offered an exciting job. Whether such an event is positive or negative, it is likely to cause stress when a person does not expect it, is not prepared for it, and needs special help in adapting to it.

People often help create their own nonnormative life events—by, say, applying for a challenging job or taking up a risky hobby like sky-diving. Thus they are active participants in their own development.

## Contexts of Influences: An Ecological Approach

Both normative and nonnormative influences occur at particular "levels" of the environment. In his **ecological approach** to development, Urie Bronfenbrenner (1979) identifies four different levels of environmental influence, extending from the most intimate environment to the most global. Thus, to understand individual development, we must understand each person within the context of multiple environments.

First, the *microsystem* is the everyday environment of home or school or work, including relationships with parents, siblings, caregivers, classmates, and teachers. How, for example, does a new baby affect the parents' lives? How do teachers' attitudes affect a child's peformance in school?

Second, the *mesosystem* is the interlocking of various systems a person is involved with—the linkages between home and school, home and work, work and

community, and so on. How does a parent's unhappiness on the job affect the parent-child relationship? How does the birth of sibling affect an older child's progress at school?

Third, the *exosystem* is to the larger environment of institutions, like school, church, media, and government agencies. How does being on welfare affect a person's ambitions? How does does television affect a person's gender attitudes?

Finally, the widest-ranging environment is the *macrosystem*—overarching cultural patterns of government, religion, education, and the economy. How is an individual affected by the way a nation shows its values, such as commitment or lack of commitment to the family, child care, health care, and the like?

This approach, emphasizing systems in and beyond the family that affect individuals, enables developmentalists to see the variety of influences upon human development. To isolate these influences from each other, many developmentalists do cross-cultural research, studying people who live in different societies or in different cultural groups within the same society (see Box 1-1 on page 10).

## Timing of Influences: Critical Periods

A **critical period** is a specific time during development when a given event has its greatest impact. For example, if a woman receives x-rays, takes certain drugs, or contracts certain diseases at specific times during pregnancy, the fetus may show specific ill effects; the

## BOX 1-1    WINDOW ON THE WORLD

# THE PURPOSE OF CROSS-CULTURAL RESEARCH

When Kpelle adults (people from central Liberia in Africa) were asked to sort 20 objects, they consistently did so on the basis of "functional" categories (that is, knife with orange or potato with hoe). Western psychologists associate functional sorting with a low level of thought; but since the subjects kept saying that this was the way a "wise man" would do it, the experimenter finally asked, "How would a fool do it?" He then received the "higher-order" categories he had originally expected—four neat piles with food in one, tools in another, and so on (Glick, 1975, p. 636).

This story illustrates one important reason why psychologists conduct research among different cultural groups—to recognize biases in traditional western theories and perspectives that often go unquestioned until they are shown to be a product of cultural influences. "Working with

people from a quite different background can make one aware of aspects of human activity that are not noticeable until they are missing or differently arranged, as with the fish who reputedly is unaware of water until removed from it" (Rogoff & Morelli, 1989, p. 343).

By looking at people from different cultural and ethnic groups, researchers can learn which aspects of development are universal (and thus seem an intrinsic part of the human condition), and which are culturally determined. For example, no matter where children live, they learn to speak in the same sequence, going from cooing and babbling to single words and then to simple combinations of words. The words vary from culture to culture, but the sentences of toddlers around the world are structured similarly. Findings like this suggest that there is an inborn capacity for learning language. On the

other hand, culture can exert a surprisingly large influence on such seemingly basic aspects of functioning as babies' early motor development. African babies tend to sit and walk earlier than American babies, apparently because of cultural practices. For example, Africans often prop infants in a sitting position and bounce them on their feet (Rogoff & Morelli, 1989).

This book presents several examples of influential theories developed from research on western subjects which do not hold up when tested on people from other cultures—theories about gender roles, abstract thinking, moral reasoning, and a number of other concepts. We also look briefly at people in cultures other than the dominant one in the United States, to show how closely human development is tied to culture and society and to understand normal development in a variety of settings.

---

amount and kind of damage to the fetus will vary, depending on the nature of the "shock" and on its timing.

The concept of critical periods has been applied to psychological as well as physical development. For example, Lenneberg (1969) has suggested that there is a critical period for language development, before puberty. This might explain why, when Sally's daughter Jennifer moved with her husband and son from the United States to Germany, 5-year-old Stefan quickly learned to speak German with no accent at all; though Jennifer also became quite fluent, she was immediately recognizable as a foreigner.

Some of the evidence for critical periods of *physical* development, particularly fetal development, is undeniable. For other aspects of development, however, the concept of critical periods and irreversible effects is very controversial and seems too limiting. In these areas, although the human organism may be particularly sensitive to certain experiences at certain times of life, later events can often reverse the effects of early ones.

## HOW THE STUDY OF HUMAN DEVELOPMENT HAS EVOLVED

Human development has, of course, been going on as long as human beings have existed; but ideas about it have changed drastically. This is an exciting time to study it, since formal *scientific study* of human development is relatively new, and changes in the way adults look at children are particularly dramatic.

### Studies of Childhood

People have long held different ideas about what children are like and how they should be raised. According to the French historian Philippe Ariès (1962), not until the seventeenth century were children seen as qualitatively different from adults; before that, children were considered simply smaller, weaker, and less intelligent. Ariès based his opinion on such historical sources as old paintings, documents showing that children worked long hours and left their parents at early ages for ap-

This seventeenth-century painting by Georges de La Tour captures a tender moment between mother and baby, suggesting that—contrary to one widely held view—the recognition and appreciation of children's special nature is not a recent phenomenon.

prenticeships, and statistics showing high infant mortality rates. He also concluded that parents, afraid that their children would die young, were reluctant to love them wholeheartedly.

Ariès's view has been widely accepted, but more recent analyses suggest a different picture. The psychologist David Elkind (1987a) finds recognition of children's special nature in the Bible and in the works of the ancient Greeks and Romans. And after examining autobiographies, diaries, and literature going back to the sixteenth century, Linda A. Pollock (1983) makes a strong argument that children have always been seen and treated differently from adults.

But books of advice for parents did not appear until the sixteenth century. In most of them, physicians expressed their pet theories, telling mothers not to nurse their babies right after feeling anger, lest their milk prove fatal; to begin toilet training at the age of 3 weeks; and to bind babies' arms for several months after birth to prevent thumb-sucking (Ryerson, 1961).

By the nineteenth century, several important trends had prepared the way for the study of child development. Scientists had unlocked the mystery of conception and were beginning to argue about the relative importance of heredity and environment (discussed in Chapter 2). The discovery of germs and immunization

allowed parents to protect their children from the plagues and fevers that had made survival so uncertain. Adults also came to feel more responsible for the way children turned out, instead of simply accepting misfortune or misbehavior as fated. Moreover, new laws protecting children from long hours of labor meant that they could spend more time in school. The spirit of democracy filtered into home and classroom, as parents and teachers rejected the old, autocratic methods and focused on identifying and meeting children's needs. And the new science of psychology held that people could understand themselves by learning what influences had affected them during childhood.

## Studies of Adolescence, Adulthood, and Aging

Adolescence was not considered a stage of development until the twentieth century, when G. Stanley Hall, a pioneer in child study, formulated a theory of adolescence. His two-volume work *Adolescence*, published in 1904, was popular and provoked much thought and discussion; but it had very little scientific basis, serving mainly as a platform for his own ideas.

Hall was also one of the first psychologists to become interested in aging. In 1922, when he was 78, he published *Senescence: The Last Half of Life*. Six years later, Stanford University opened the first major scientific research unit devoted to aging. Not until a generation later, though, did this area of study blossom. By 1946, the National Institutes of Health (NIH) had established a large-scale research unit, and specialized organizations and journals were reporting the newest findings—at first mainly on such topics as intellectual ability and reaction time, and later on emotional aspects of aging.

Since the late 1930s, a number of long-term studies have focused on adults, beginning with the Grant Study of Adult Development, which followed its subjects from the time when they were 18-year-old Harvard University students into middle age. In the mid-1950s Bernice Neugarten and her associates at the University of Chicago began their studies of middle-aged people, and K. Warner Schaie launched his ongoing study of adult intelligence. These studies and others, discussed in this book, add to our understanding. We still, however, know much more about children and the elderly than we do about young and middle-aged adults, although a growing emphasis on studies about these age groups should yield fruit in coming years.

### Life-Span Studies

Today most psychologists recognize that human development is a lifelong process, and that each period of a person's life span is influenced by what has already occurred and will affect the periods that follow.

Life-span studies in the United States grew out of programs designed to follow children over a period of years, through adulthood. The Stanford Studies of Gifted Children (begun in 1921 under the direction of Lewis Terman) continue to focus on the development of people who were identified as unusually intelligent children. Other major studies that began around 1930—the Berkeley Growth Study, the Oakland Growth Study, and the Fels Research Institute Study—have also yielded information on long-term development.

These and other studies have drawn on a wide variety of research tools; often, several different methods are used in the same study. Let's see what some of these methods are.

## HUMAN DEVELOPMENT: RESEARCH METHODS

Researchers in different branches of the physical and social sciences use different methods. But the term *scientific method* refers to certain underlying principles that characterize scientific inquiry in any field:

careful observation and recording of data; testing of alternative hypotheses, or different explanations for data; and widespread public dissemination of findings and conclusions so that other observers can learn from, analyze, repeat, and build on the results. Only when developmentalists stick to these principles can they produce sound conclusions that explain and predict human behavior.

As we describe the research methods used to study human development, we'll illustrate each one with a real study. Many of these studies are on development of language in young children, but the methods can be applied to other aspects of development and to people of any age. Table 1-2 compares the various methods.

### NONEXPERIMENTAL METHODS

Nonexperimental techniques fall into four categories: case studies, observations, interviews, and correlational studies.

### Case Studies

*Case studies* are studies of a single case or individual. Much of the data for psychoanalytic theories comes from case studies—careful notes and interpretations of what patients have said under psychoanalysis.

Our earliest sources of information about infants' development are case studies called *baby biographies,* journals in which parents recorded children's day-by-day development. The first that we know about was begun in 1601; one of the most famous was Charles Darwin's, about his son; and perhaps the most influential were those of Jean Piaget, whose theories about how children learn drew extensively on observations of his own three children.

An important, more recent case study is the poignant story of "Genie" (Curtiss, 1977; Fromkin, Krashen, Curtiss, Rigler, & Rigler, 1974; Pines, 1981). From the age of 20 months until she was discovered at age 13½, "Genie" had been confined in a small room where no one spoke to her. When found, she weighed only 59 pounds, could not straighten her arms or legs, and did not speak. She recognized only her own name and the word *sorry*. Over the next 9 years Genie received intensive therapy that helped her learn many words and string them together in primitive sentences. Yet at last report, her language was still not normal.

Case studies offer useful, in-depth information, giving a rich description of an individual. But these studies have shortcomings. From studying Genie, for instance, we learn much about the development of a single child. However, like any case study, this one does not yield

**TABLE 1–2**
CHARACTERISTICS OF MAJOR RESEARCH METHODS

| Type | Main Characteristics | Advantages | Disadvantages |
|---|---|---|---|
| **NONEXPERIMENTAL METHODS** | | | |
| Case study | Study of single individual in depth. | Provides detailed picture of one person's behavior and development. | May not generalize to others; may reflect observer bias. |
| Naturalistic observation | Observation of people in their normal setting with no attempt to manipulate behavior. | Provides good description of behavior. Does not subject people to unnatural settings (such as the laboratory) that may distort behavior. Is a source of research hypotheses. | Lack of control; inability to explain cause-and-effect relationships. Observer bias. |
| Laboratory observation | Observation of people in the laboratory with no attempt to manipulate behavior. | Provides good descriptions, and greater control than naturalistic observation. Is a source of research hypotheses. | Inability to explain cause-and-effect relationships. Observer bias. |
| Interview | Participants asked about some aspect of their lives; ranges from highly structured to more flexible questioning. | Goes beyond observation in getting information about a person's life, attitudes, or opinions. | Interviewee may not remember information accurately or may distort responses in a socially desirable way. How question is asked may affect answer. |
| Correlational studies | Measure direction and magnitude of a relationship between variables. | Allow predictions from one variable about another variable. | Do not determine cause-and-effect relationships. |
| **EXPERIMENTAL METHODS** | | | |
| Experiment | Controlled procedure in which an experimenter manipulates the independent variable to determine its effect on the dependent variable; may be conducted in the laboratory or field or make use of naturally occurring events. | Establishes cause-and-effect relationships; is a highly controlled procedure that can be repeated by another investigator. Degree of control is strongest in the laboratory experiment and least in the natural experiment. | Findings, especially when derived from laboratory experiments, may not generalize to situations outside the laboratory. |

information about causes and effects. Even though it seems reasonable that Genie's severely deprived environment caused her deficiency in language, we cannot make this connection with certainty. Furthermore, case studies do not explain behavior, and if they try to, there is no way to test the validity of their explanations.

Also, case studies may be affected by "observer bias"; that is, the recorder may emphasize some aspects of a person's development and minimize others. While case studies may tell a great deal about individuals, then, it is questionable how well the information applies to people in general.

## Observation

Observation can take two forms. Both naturalistic observation and laboratory observation provide good descriptions of behavior.

### Naturalistic observation

In **naturalistic observation,** researchers observe and record people's behavior in real-life settings (like preschools or nursing homes). They do not manipulate the environment or alter behavior. To gain normative information, researchers observe people; record data about their development at various ages; and derive average ages, or norms, for growth and for the appearance of various skills and behaviors.

One type of naturalistic observation is *time sampling,* a technique used to determine how often a particular behavior (like aggression, babbling, or crying) occurs during a given period of time. One researcher used this method to study how infants and their parents act with each other. He went into the homes of forty 15-month-old babies and looked around during two typical 2-hour periods on separate days, without giving the parents any guidance or instructions. He recorded the presence or absence of 15 parental behaviors and 8 infant behaviors during alternating 15-second observe-record periods. He found that the mothers and fathers were more alike than different in the ways they treated their babies, that a parent paid slightly more attention to a child of his or her own sex, that a parent did more with a baby when he or she was alone with the baby than when the other parent was also present, and that the babies were more sociable when alone with one parent (Belsky, 1979).

### Laboratory observation

In **laboratory observation,** researchers observe and record behavior in settings that have been designed to place all the subjects in the same basic situation and to yield information on the subjects' behaviors in this experimental situation.

One research team, for example, looked at how mothers and fathers spoke to their babies of two different ages, either 2½ to 3½ months or 8½ to 9½ months (Kruper & Uzgiris, 1987). There were 40 mother-baby pairs and 32 father-baby pairs, equally divided between older and younger infants. Each parent-child pair was videotaped for about 10 minutes as the parent sat on a stool facing the baby. The parent had been asked to remain seated unless the baby needed attention, and to play with the baby without toys as he or she would at home. Even though there were some differences between mothers' and fathers' speech to their infants, by and large fathers and mothers spoke similarly to their babies, asking many questions and repeating often. These parents treated their children as "communicating partners" from a very early age, as they asked questions, interpreted the babies' actions as answers, sometimes responded for the babies, and commented on the babies' thoughts and feelings.

Observational studies cannot explain behavior or determine its causes and effects. The laboratory study described above does not tell us *why* mothers and fathers talk to babies the way they do—why, for example, they seem to explain more to boy babies or try harder to get the attention of older babies. Furthermore, the very presence of an observer can alter the behavior being

Playing with babies is work for the psychologist Tiffany Field, who studies children by laboratory observation. At a child development center affiliated with a university medical school and hospital, Field follows up high-risk infants to assess the effects of early social interactions.

observed. Observers sometimes station themselves behind one-way mirrors or try to "blend in" with the background. Still, older children and adults often know that they are being observed and, realizing this, may act differently.

## Interviews

In an *interview,* researchers ask questions about people's attitudes or opinions or some other aspect of their lives. By interviewing a large number of people, investigators get a picture of what people *say* they believe or do or have done.

An exploratory study of symbolic gestures—movements often used by toddlers to communicate before they can say words—was based largely on interviews with 38 mothers of 16- to 18-month-olds (Acredolo & Goodwyn, 1988). The researchers first sent the mothers a letter outlining the kind of gestures they were interested in (like those in Anna's repertoire, such as waving her hands up and down with small, quick motions to ask Jonathan to turn on the light, or waving a piece of paper sideways to tell Diane that the wind was blowing). Interviewers then asked each woman about any gestures her child used and other information about the child. From the interviews, the researchers learned that many children use such gestures as a transitional kind of communication—showing that even before they can talk, they understand that objects and concepts have names and that they can use symbols to refer to a variety of things and happenings in their lives.

A problem with interviews is that the memory and accuracy of interviewees may be faulty. Some subjects forget when and how certain events actually took place. Others distort their replies to make them more acceptable to the questioners or to themselves. Finally, the wording of a question can influence how people answer it. (Thus to corroborate the mothers' reports, these researchers followed up with a longitudinal study of 11-month-old babies for 9 months. Since this interview study had been inspired by a case study of a toddler who used 13 different gestures, we see how three methods can work together, each contributing to our understanding.)

## Correlational Studies

Suppose that we want to determine the relationship between two factors: for example, between a parent's intelligence and a child's language ability. By carefully measuring both factors—which are called *variables,* because they vary among members of a group or can be varied for purposes of an experiment—we might find that the higher a parent scores on an intelligence test, the larger a child's vocabulary is at a given age. If so,

we have found a positive correlation between the parent's intelligence and the child's vocabulary.

*Correlational studies* show the direction and magnitude of a relationship between variables. That is, they can tell us whether two variables are related *positively* (that is, both increase together or decrease together) or *negatively* (as one increases, the other decreases), and to what degree. Correlations are reported as numbers ranging from −1.0 (perfect negative, or inverse, relationship) to +1.0 (a perfect positive, or direct, relationship). The higher the number (whether + or −), the stronger the relationship (either positive or negative). A correlation of zero shows that there is no relationship between the variables. Knowing the correlation (or relationship) between variables allows researchers to make predictions about development.

However, correlational studies do not give information about cause and effect; only experiments (which we discuss below) can do that. A strong positive correlation does not tell us that, say, a parent's intelligence level *causes* the size of a child's vocabulary. A child's large vocabulary might have resulted from a third factor: a shared favorable environment that helped the parent to do well on an intelligence test and encouraged the child to develop a large vocabulary.

In fact, one study of infants' communicative development, which compared adopted 1-year-olds with a control group of babies living with their biological parents, suggests that both genetic and environmental factors influence language ability (Hardy-Brown & Plomin, 1985). (A study like this is of special interest to parents like Jonathan and Diane; they do not know Anna's genetic endowment, but they do have some control over her environment.) Researchers measured frequency and kinds of the babies' speech sounds, frequency and levels of gesturing, and other means of communication. They also noted the scores on cognitive tests of the parents raising the children, and information about the socioeconomic status and education of both adoptive and biological parents. Moderate positive correlations appeared between babies' use of language and control biological parents' cognitive scores, but not between babies' language and adoptive parents' scores, suggesting some genetic influence. However, the researchers also discovered environmental relationships: both adoptive and control mothers of the most advanced babies were most likely to imitate their babies' sounds, perhaps encouraging them to make more sounds. Of course, it is possible that the more advanced babies' precocity motivated their parents to imitate them more, but other research has also shown that such feedback from parents does encourage language development (C. E. Snow, 1977).

**TABLE 1–3**
DESIGN FOR AN EXPERIMENT

| Procedures | Rationale |
| --- | --- |
| 1 Frame your research question: "Does speech therapy improve the rate of expressive language acquisition?" | You have chosen a problem that interests you and is relevant for either basic or applied research. |
| 2 Review the literature on the topic. | You want to know what other work has been done, and you want a basis for formulating your hypothesis. |
| 3 State your hypothesis: "Speech therapy improves the rate of expressive language acquisition." | This is the statement you will seek to support or not support. |
| 4 Specify your operational definition of language acquisition: score on a standardized test of expressive language (that is, vocabulary). | You need an objective way to measure your findings. |
| 5 Specify your independent and dependent variables: the independent variable is the speech therapy; the dependent variable is the score on the test of expressive language. | You have developed a systematic framework for arriving at your data. |
| 6 Identify the population you're concerned with: 3-year-olds with a delay of 1 year in expressive language. (Let's say there are 1000 children with this diagnosis at a certain speech clinic.) | This is the group that might ultimately be affected by your findings, but it is probably so large that you could not include everyone in your experiment. |
| 7 Choose a sample, a subgroup of the population. You could do this by picking 50 children at random, say every twentieth child with this diagnosis at this speech clinic. | If the sample is chosen randomly so that each member of the population has an equal chance of being selected, you can generalize your results from the sample to the population. |
| 8 Assign the subjects randomly to either the experimental or the control group, so that each group has 25 3-year-olds with a 1-year language delay. | Random assignment of subjects to control for differences such as IQ, sex, geographic background, and learning ability. |
| 9 Manipulate the independent variable by exposing only the experimental group to the treatment (6 months of speech therapy given two times a week in 30-minute sessions), while the control group does not receive the treatment. | All other conditions are the same for the two groups. |
| 10 Measure the dependent variable; after 6 months give members of both groups a test of expressive language. | All subjects receive the same evaluation. |

**TABLE 1–3**
(CONTINUED)

| Procedures | Rationale |
|---|---|
| **11** Determine your results: calculate the test scores for both groups and perform a statistical analysis to see whether there is a significant difference in scores between the experimental and control groups. | Statistical techniques are used to determine whether the two groups differ significantly in average test scores. |
| **12** Analyze your findings: "Children in the experimental group scored significantly better on average on the expressive language test than those in the control group." | Because of the various objective, systematic controls, we can conclude that exposure to the treatment caused the statistical difference (higher scores on the test of expressive language), which probably represents greater linguistic progress. |
| **13** Draw your conclusion: "The findings support the hypothesis that speech therapy is effective in improving expressive language acquisition." | Because of this evidence, you may decide to apply your findings by offering speech therapy to all 3-year-olds with a 1-year expressive language delay. |

## EXPERIMENTAL METHODS

An **experiment** is a rigorously controlled procedure in which the investigator, called the *experimenter,* manipulates variables to learn how one affects another. Scientific experiments must be conducted and reported in such a way that another investigator can replicate (repeat) them to verify the results and conclusions.

Before recommending a program of speech therapy for a child like Anna, for example, a speech pathologist would want evidence that the program would be effective in helping children with expressive language delay. Such evidence could come from an experiment specifically designed to assess such therapy. Table 1-3 shows how such an experiment might be designed.

One actual team of researchers designed an experiment to examine the influence on children's language and vocabulary skills of a certain kind of reading by parents. The parents read picture books to their children, encourage the children's active participation, and respond with frequent, age-based feedback (Whitehurst, Falco, et al., 1988). The researchers compared two groups of middle-class children aged 21 to 35 months: in one group, the parents adopted the new reading routines (this was the *experimental group*); in the other, the parents continued their usual routines (this was the *control group*).

The parents of the children in the experimental group asked the children challenging open-ended questions rather than questions calling for simple yes-no answers. (Instead of asking, "Is the cat asleep?", they would ask, "What is the cat doing?") They expanded on the children's answers to their questions, corrected wrong answers, gave alternative possibilities, and bestowed praise. After 1 month of the program, the children in the experimental group were 8.5 months ahead of the control group in level of speech and 6 months ahead in vocabulary; 9 months later, the experimental group was still 6 months ahead of the controls. It is fair to conclude, then, that the new reading routines can help improve children's language and vocabulary skills. (One of the steps that Diane and Jonathan took in Anna's speech therapy was to adopt these new reading routines.)

### Variables and Groups

In the experiment just described, the parents' new reading approach was the *independent variable* and the children's language skills were the *dependent variable.* An **independent variable** is something over which the experimenter has direct control. A **dependent variable** is something that may or may not change as a result of changes in the independent variable (it *depends* on the independent variable). In an experiment, we manipulate the independent variable to see how changes in it will affect the dependent variable.

To conduct an experiment, we need two types of subjects: one or more experimental groups and one or more control groups. An **experimental group** is composed of people who will be exposed to the experimental manipulation or *treatment* (such as being read to in a new way). Following exposure, the effect of the treat-

Experiments use strictly controlled procedures that manipulate variables to determine how one affects another. To study how quickly young children assign new words to semantic categories, researchers showed them a blue tray and an olive-colored one, and asked them to hand over "the chromium tray, not the blue one." One week later, after one exposure, the children, who had originally called "olive" either "green" or "brown," now knew that it was neither of those.

ment on the dependent variable is measured one or more times. A **control group** is composed of people who are similar to the experimental group but do not receive the treatment whose effects we want to measure.

## Sampling and Assignment

If experimental results show a cause-and-effect relationship between two variables, how do we know that this relationship is true *generally,* and not just for the subjects of the experiment? And how can we be sure that the relationship is not due to some third factor? The answers hinge on how subjects are selected and on how they are assigned to experimental and control groups.

First of all, we must make sure that our **sample** (the group of subjects chosen for the experiment) is representative of the entire population under study (that is, all the members of the larger group we want to generalize about). We generally cannot study an entire population (this would be too costly and time-consuming); but only if the sample is representative of the larger group can we generalize the results of the experiment to the population as a whole.

Experimenters ensure representativeness by random sampling. In a **random sample,** each member of the population has an equal chance of being selected. For example, if we want a random sample of the students in a human development class, we might put all

their names into a hat, shake it, and then draw out the number of names we want.

Next, we should randomly *assign* these subjects to experimental and control groups. If the sample is large enough, differences in such factors as age, sex, race, IQ, and socioeconomic status will be evenly distributed so that the groups are as alike as possible in every respect except for the independent variable, the one to be tested. Random assignment *controls* for all other variables—that is, it prevents them from affecting the results. Thus the results of our experiment will reflect only the impact of the independent variable and not some other factor.

We could, of course, try to control for any and all factors we could think of that might have an effect, by deliberately matching the experimental and control groups. But no matter how carefully we match groups for certain characteristics, we will probably miss others that may turn out to be just as important. Therefore, the best way to control for unforeseen factors is to assign subjects randomly to the experimental and control groups, so that each subject has an equal chance of being assigned to either group.

Note that in the reading experiment described above, although the researchers did not select a sample from a larger population, they did divide their subjects randomly into experimental and control groups.

## Types of Experiments

There are three types of experiments: those conducted in the laboratory; those conducted in the "field," a setting that is part of the subject's everyday life; and those that make use of naturally occurring events.

### *Laboratory experiments*

In a *laboratory experiment* the subject is brought to a specific place and experiences conditions under the experimenter's control. The researcher records the subject's reaction to these conditions, possibly contrasting it with the same person's behavior under different conditions or with the behavior of people who experience a different set of conditions. In the first type of laboratory experiment, parents and children, for example, might be brought into a room so that researchers can measure the strength of parent-child attachment by seeing what happens when the mother leaves the child, when the father leaves the child, or when a stranger leaves the child. In the second type of laboratory experiment, some children might see a person acting aggressively while other children do not; then both groups of children would be measured on the degree to which they act aggressively themselves.

Laboratory experiments permit the greatest control over the situation and are the easiest studies to replicate (that is, they are the easiest for other researchers to carry out in exactly the same way). But because of the artificiality of the situation, the subjects may not always act as they would in real life.

### Field experiments

In a *field experiment,* experimenters make a change in a familiar setting, like school or home. The experiment in which parents adopted new reading routines was a field experiment.

### Natural experiments

A *natural experiment* compares people who have been accidentally divided into separate groups by circumstances of life—one group who were exposed to some naturally occurring event and another group who were not. Natural experiments are not true experiments, because they do not try to manipulate behavior; but they provide a way of studying events that cannot be created artificially. For example, it would be unethical to separate identical twins at birth just to do an interesting experiment, but if we discover identical twins who *did* happen to be separated at birth and raised in different circumstances, we can compare the effects of different environments on people with the same heredity.

### Comparing Experimentation with Other Methods

Experiments have several advantages over nonexperimental methods. Only experiments can tell us about cause-and-effect relationships. In addition, as we have noted, the rigor of the experimental method allows studies to be replicated by other researchers with different groups of subjects, to check the reliability of results.

Experiments also have drawbacks. For one thing, they may be designed so narrowly that they focus on one or two aspects of development and miss the overall picture. A second problem arises from the differences in the three types of experiments. Laboratory experiments, which allow the greatest control and thus tend to be the most reliable, are typically the *least* generalizable. That is, we cannot be sure that conclusions drawn from the laboratory apply to real life. Experimental manipulation shows what *can* happen if certain conditions are present: for example, that children who watch violent television shows in the laboratory *can* become more aggressive in that setting. It does not tell us what actually *does* happen in the real world: *do* children who watch a lot of "shoot-'em-ups" hit their little brothers or

sisters more than children who watch a different kind of show?

Greater understanding of human development may well result from combining nonexperimental and experimental approaches. Researchers can observe people as they go about their everyday lives, determine what correlations exist, and then design experimental studies of apparent relationships to assess cause and effect.

As we have seen in our examples of studies of language development, there is no one "right" way to examine an issue. Many questions can be approached from several different angles yielding different kinds of information. Very often one type of study leads into another. For example, the case study of Genie might suggest the importance of language stimulation, and an experiment could then be designed to test how different kinds of stimulation promote language development. And observations of the way parents talk to their children, as well as information gleaned from interviews, can generate hypotheses and inspire experiments to test them.

## METHODS OF DATA COLLECTION

Information about development is most commonly gathered by *cross-sectional* or *longitudinal* studies (see Figure 1-1). In some cases *sequential* designs are used.

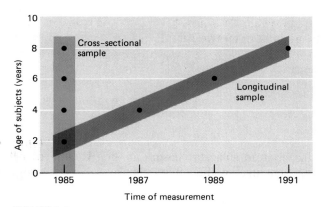

**FIGURE 1-1**

The two most important ways to obtain data about development. In a *cross-sectional* study, people of different ages are measured at one time. Here, groups of 2-, 4-, 6- and 8-year-olds were tested in 1985, to obtain data about age differences in performance. In a *longitudinal* study, the same people are measured more than once. Here, a sample of children were first measured in 1985 when they were 2 years old; follow-up testing was done in 1987, 1989, and 1991, when the children would be 4, 6, and 8, respectively. This technique shows age changes in performance.

## Cross-Sectional Studies and Longitudinal Studies

In a **cross-sectional** study, people of different ages are assessed on one occasion. This kind of study provides information about *differences* in development among different age groups, rather than *changes* with age in the same person (which longitudinal studies show).

In one cross-sectional study, people in six different age groups from age 6 to old age took a battery of cognitive tests. Age differences in performance appeared: middle-aged subjects scored highest, and young children and older people scored lowest (Papalia, 1972). You could not conclude from these findings, however, that when the younger subjects in this study became older themselves, their scores would drop to the lower levels of the older people in the original sample. The older subjects may, as a cohort, have had poorer education or other experiences that affected their performance so that they may *never* have scored as well as the middle-aged subjects. The only way to see whether or not change occurs over time in the same person is to conduct a longitudinal study.

In a **longitudinal study,** researchers measure the same people more than once to see changes in development over time. The researchers may measure one characteristic, such as vocabulary size, IQ, height, or aggressiveness. Or they may look at several aspects of development, to find interrelationships among factors. Since the same people are measured more than once, this design gives a picture of the *process* of development.

One classic longitudinal study of gifted children, started by Terman, followed young schoolchildren with high IQs into old age, and found that their intellectual, scholastic, and vocational superiority held up over time. Also, looking at differences within the group itself, researchers identified factors other than intelligence that seem to foster success in life (P. Sears & Barbee, 1978; Terman & Oden, 1959).

Cross-sectional studies, then, look at *differences* among groups of people; longitudinal studies assess *changes* undergone by one or more persons. Each design has strengths and weaknesses.

The advantages of the cross-sectional method include speed and economy: it is faster and cheaper than the longitudinal method. In addition, it does not lose subjects who drop out. Among its drawbacks is its masking of differences among individuals, since it looks at group averages. Its *major* disadvantage is that it cannot eliminate cohort, or generational, influences on subjects born at different times. Cross-sectional studies are sometimes misinterpreted as yielding information about developmental *changes* in groups or individuals; but such information is often misleading and may contradict longitudinal research. For example, it would be incorrect to conclude from the cross-sectional study described above that intellectual functioning declines in later years. This may be so, but longitudinal data would be needed to determine whether there were actual age changes. All that the cross-sectional method can show is that there were age *differences* in performance.

The great strength of *longitudinal* studies is their sensitivity to individual patterns of change, since data about individuals can be tracked. Also, they avoid cohort effects *within* a study—although longitudinal studies done on one particular cohort may not apply to a different cohort. (A study done with people born in 1930 may not apply to subjects born in 1980.) Longitudinal studies, however, are time-consuming and expensive. Another shortcoming is probable bias in the sample: people who volunteer tend to be of higher-than-average socioeconomic status and intelligence, and those who stay with the project over time tend to be more competent than those who drop out. Also, the results can be affected by repeated testing: people tend to do better in later tests because of a "practice effect."

### Sequential Studies

The **cross-sequential study** is one of several strategies designed to overcome the drawbacks of longitudinal and cross-sectional studies. This method combines the other two: people in a cross-sectional sample are tested more than once, and the results are analyzed to determine the differences that show up over time for the different groups of subjects.

Some important research on intellectual functioning in adulthood employs sequential techniques. As we will see in Chapter 16, these techniques seem to provide a more realistic assessment than either the cross-sectional method (which tends to overestimate the drop in intellectual functioning in later years) or the longitudinal method (which tends to underestimate it).

## ETHICS OF RESEARCH

### Ethical Issues

Some years ago, a doctor recommended giving psychological tests to young underprivileged children in the hope of predicting which ones might someday become delinquent. These children could then be watched and given social support to forestall their criminal tendencies. Many people—justifiably, we believe—attacked the proposal, pointing out that the test results might be a "self-fulfilling prophecy": the children who were labeled as potential delinquents and were therefore treated differently might actually *become* delinquent as a result.

Should research like this—research that might harm its subjects—ever be undertaken? Might it be undertaken if the risk of harm is small and the likelihood of gaining valuable knowledge is great? How can we balance the possible benefits to humanity against the risk of intellectual, emotional, or physical injury to individuals? Researchers confront many such ethical questions, among them questions about consent, deception, self-esteem, and privacy.

### Informed consent

When parents consent to a child's participation in research, can we assume that they are acting in the child's best interests? According to one panel on ethics, children aged 7 or over should be asked for their own consent and should be overruled only if the research promises some direct benefit to the child, as in the use of an experimental drug (National Commission for the Protection of Human Subjects of Biomedical and Behavioral Research, 1978).

Informed consent can also be an issue with adults; for example, we need to make sure that institutionalized older subjects are competent to give consent and are not being exploited.

### Deception

An issue that is often linked with consent is deception. How much do subjects need to know about an experiment before their consent can be considered informed? Suppose that children are told they are trying out a new game when they are actually being tested on their reactions to success or failure? Suppose that adults are told they are participating in a study on learning when they are really being tested on their willingness to inflict pain? Experiments like these, which cannot be carried out without deception, have been done—and they have added significantly to our knowledge, but at the cost of the subjects' right to know what they are getting involved in.

### Self-esteem

Subjects may also be affected by their own behavior in an experiment. For instance, research on the limits of children's capabilities has a built-in "failure factor": the investigator keeps presenting questions or problems until the child is unable to answer. How seriously might such failure affect subjects' self-confidence? Also, when researchers publish findings that middle-class children are academically superior to poor children, unintentional harm may be done to the latter's self-esteem. Furthermore, such studies may become self-fulfilling prophecies, affecting teachers' expectations and students' performance.

### Privacy

Is it ethical to use one-way mirrors and hidden cameras to observe people without their knowledge? How can we protect the confidentiality of personal information (for example, about income or family relationships or even about illegal activities, like smoking marijuana or shoplifting) that subjects may reveal in interviews or questionnaires?

## Ethical Standards

Since the 1970s, federally mandated committees have been set up at colleges, universities, and other institutions to review proposed research from an ethical standpoint. In 1982 the American Psychological Association adopted guidelines covering such points as protection of subjects from harm and loss of dignity, guarantees of privacy and confidentiality, informed consent, avoidance of deception wherever possible, subjects' right to decline or withdraw from an experiment at any time, and the responsibility of investigators to correct any undesirable short-term or long-term effects of participation. Still, specific situations often call for hard judgments. Everyone in the field of human development must accept the responsibility to try to do good and, at the very least, to do no harm.

## HUMAN DEVELOPMENT: THEORETICAL PERSPECTIVES

### THEORIES AND HYPOTHESES

How people explain development depends on how they view the fundamental nature of human beings. Different thinkers, looking through different lenses, have come up with different explanations, or theories, about why people behave as they do.

A *theory* is a set of related statements about *data,* the information obtained through research. Scientists use theories to help them organize, or make sense of, their data and then to predict what data might be obtained under certain conditions. Theories are important in helping scientists to *explain, interpret,* and *predict* behavior.

**TABLE 1–4**
FOUR PERSPECTIVES ON HUMAN DEVELOPMENT

| Perspective | Important Theories | Basic Belief | Technique Used |
|---|---|---|---|
| Psychoanalytic | Freud's psychosexual theory | Freud: Behavior is controlled by powerful unconscious urges. | Clinical observation |
| | Erikson's psychosocial theory | Erikson: Personality develops throughout life in a series of stages. | |
| Mechanistic | Behaviorism, or traditional learning theory (Pavlov, Skinner, Watson)<br><br>Social-learning theory (Bandura) | Behaviorism: People are responders; concern is with how the environment controls behavior.<br>Social-learning theory: Children learn in a social context, by observing and imitating models; person is an active contributor to learning. | Rigorous and scientific (experimental) procedures |
| Organismic | Piaget's cognitive-stage theory | There are qualitative changes in the way children think that develop in a series of four stages between infancy and adolescence. Person is an active initiator of development. | Flexible interviews; meticulous observation |
| Humanistic | Maslow's self-actualization theory | People have the ability to take charge of their lives and foster their own development. | Discussion of feelings |

Both research and theory are essential. Painstaking research adds, bit by bit, to the body of knowledge. Theories help researchers to find a coherent structure in the data—to go beyond isolated observations and make generalizations.

Theories guide future research by suggesting hypotheses to be tested. A **hypothesis** is a possible explanation for a phenomenon and is used to predict the outcome of an experiment. Sometimes research confirms a hypothesis, providing support for a theory. At other times, scientists must modify theories to account for unexpected facts that emerge from research.

The perspectives from which theorists look at development are important because they shape the questions researchers ask, the methods they use, and the way they interpret their results. Today human development is studied from at least four perspectives: psychoanalytic, mechanistic, organismic, and humanistic. Each has its dedicated supporters and its equally impassioned critics, and each has made important contributions to our understanding of human development.

In this book we examine and evaluate some of the more influential theories, and we emphasize the interplay between theory and research. The following brief overview summarizes the four perspectives (including their strengths and weaknesses), and Table 1-4 compares them. We present and analyze age-related aspects of the theories more fully throughout the book.

## PSYCHOANALYTIC PERSPECTIVE

Do you ever try to analyze your dreams? Do you believe that people often act in response to unconscious feelings—that is, feelings they are not aware of? If so, you are taking the *psychoanalytic perspective,* which is concerned with the unconscious forces motivating human behavior. This view originated at the beginning of the twentieth century, when a Viennese physician named Sigmund Freud first developed psychoanalysis, a therapeutic approach based on giving people insights into unconscious conflicts, stemming from childhood, that affect their behavior and emotions.

### Sigmund Freud: Psychosexual Theory

Freud (1856–1939), the oldest of eight children, believed that he was his mother's favorite, and he expected to accomplish great things (E. Jones, 1961). His initial goal was medical research, but limited funds and barriers to academic advancement for Jews forced him into the private practice of medicine.

One of his main interests was neurology, the study of the brain and treatment of disorders of the nervous system—a branch of medicine then in its infancy. To relieve symptoms with no apparent physical cause, Freud began to ask questions designed to summon up his patients' long-buried memories. He then concluded that the source of emotional disturbances lay in traumatic experiences of early childhood which people repressed.

Freud theorized that powerful unconscious biological drives, mostly sexual and aggressive, motivate human behavior, and that these natural urges put people into conflict with the constraints of society, producing anxiety. To combat such anxiety, according to Freud, people unconsciously distort reality through *defense mechanisms.* Everyone uses defense mechanisms at times; only when they are so overused that they interfere with healthy emotional development are they pathological.

Table 1-5, below, describes some common defense mechanisms.

**TABLE 1–5**
SOME FREUDIAN DEFENSE MECHANISMS

| Mechanism | Description and Examples |
| --- | --- |
| Regression | Return to behavior characteristic of an earlier age, during trying times, to try to recapture remembered security. A girl who has just entered school may go back to sucking her thumb or wetting the bed. Or a young man in college may react to his parents' recent separation by asking them to make decisions for him as they did when he was a child. When the crisis becomes less acute or the person is better able to deal with it, the inappropriate behavior usually disappears. |
| Repression | Blocking from consciousness those feelings and experiences that arouse anxiety. Freud believed that people's inability to remember much about their early years is due to their having repressed disturbing sexual feelings toward their parents. (See the discussion of the Oedipus and Electra complexes in Chapter 7.) |
| Sublimation | Channeling uncomfortable sexual or aggressive impulses into such socially acceptable activities as study, work, sports, and hobbies. |
| Projection | Attribution of unacceptable thoughts and feelings to another person. For example, a little girl talks about how jealous of her the new baby is, when she herself is jealous of the baby; or a husband who entertains fantasies of having an affair accuses his wife of being unfaithful. |
| Reaction formation | Saying the opposite of what one really feels. Buddy says, "I don't want to play with Tony, because I don't like him," when the truth is that Buddy likes Tony a lot but is afraid that Tony doesn't want to play with *him.* |

**TABLE 1–6**
DEVELOPMENTAL STAGES ACCORDING TO VARIOUS THEORIES

| Psychosexual Stages (Freud) | Psychosocial Stages (Erikson) | Cognitive Stages (Piaget) |
|---|---|---|
| *Oral (birth to 12–18 months).* Baby's chief source of pleasure is mouth-oriented activities like sucking and eating. | *Basic trust versus mistrust (birth to 12–18 months).* Baby develops sense of whether world can be trusted. Virtue: hope. | *Sensorimotor (birth to 2 years).* Infant changes from a being who responds primarily through reflexes to one who can organize activities in relation to the environment. Uses sensory and motor abilities to comprehend world. |
| *Anal (12–18 months to 3 years).* Child derives sensual gratification from withholding and expelling feces. Zone of gratification is anal region. | *Autonomy versus shame and doubt (12–18 months to 3 years).* Child develops a balance of independence over doubt and shame. Virtue: will. | *Preoperational (2 to 7 years).* Child develops a representational system and uses symbols such as words to represent people, places, and events. |
| *Phallic (3 to 6 years).* Time of the "family romance": Oedipus complex in boys and Electra complex in girls. Zone of gratification shifts to genital region. | *Initiative versus guilt (3 to 6 years).* Child develops initiative when trying out new things and is not overwhelmed by failure. Virtue: purpose. | |
| *Latency (6 years to puberty).* Time of relative calm between more turbulent stages. | *Industry versus inferiority (6 years to puberty).* Child must learn skills of the culture or face feelings of inferiority. Virtue: skill. | *Concrete operations (7 to 12 years).* Child can solve problems logically if they are focused on the here and now. |
| *Genital (puberty through adulthood).* Time of mature adult sexuality. | *Identity versus identity confusion (puberty to young adulthood).* Adolescent must determine own sense of self. Virtue: fidelity. | *Formal operations (12 years through adulthood).* Person can think in abstract terms, deal with hypothetical situations, and think about possibilities. |
| | *Intimacy versus isolation (young adulthood).* Person seeks to make commitments to others; if unsuccessful, may suffer from sense of isolation and self-absorption. Virtue: love. | |
| | *Generativity versus stagnation (middle adulthood).* Mature adult is concerned with establishing and guiding the next generation or else feels personal impoverishment. Virtue: care. | |
| | *Integrity versus despair (old age).* Elderly person achieves a sense of acceptance of own life, allowing the acceptance of death, or else falls into despair. Virtue: wisdom. | |

*Note:* All ages are approximate.

Freud's ideas shocked Victorian society, in which sexuality was something "nice" people did not discuss or even (supposedly) think about. Although his theory was at first rejected by the European medical establishment, it eventually achieved worldwide attention. But it remained controversial, particularly in its emphasis on sex and aggression as motivators of human behavior, and some of Freud's most prominent followers ultimately broke away or developed their own variations on psychoanalytic theory.

Freud's daughter, Anna Freud, carried on his work and developed psychoanalytic methods for use with children. (See Chapter 11.)

### Freud's stages of psychosexual development

Freud believed that personality is decisively formed in the first few years of life, as children deal with conflicts between their biological, sexually related urges and the requirements of society.

As Table 1-6 (opposite page) shows, he believed that these conflicts occur in an unvarying sequence of stages of **psychosexual development,** in which gratification, or pleasure, shifts from one zone of the body to another—from the mouth to the anus and then to the genitals. At each stage, the behavior that is the chief source of gratification changes, from feeding to elimination and then to sexual activity. Although the order of these stages is always the same, a child's level of maturation determines when the shifts will take place. (These stages will be discussed in turn in the appropriate chapters.)

*Fixation,* an arrest in development, may occur if children receive too little or too much gratification at any of these stages; they may become emotionally fixated, or stuck, at that stage and may need help in order to move beyond it. For example, a baby who is weaned too early or is allowed to suck too much may become an excessively distrustful or dependent adult. (However, Freud was vague about what constituted "too early" or "too much.")

### Id, ego, and superego

Freud saw the human personality as made up of three elements, which he called the *id,* the *ego,* and the *superego.*

Newborns are governed by the **id,** an unconscious source of motives and desires that is present at birth and seeks immediate gratification under the *pleasure principle.* At first, infants are egocentric in that they do

The Viennese physician Sigmund Freud developed an original, influential, and controversial theory of emotional development in childhood, based on his adult patients' recollections. His daughter, Anna, shown here with her father, followed in his professional footsteps and constructed her own theories of development.

not differentiate themselves from the outside world. All is there for their gratification, and only when it is delayed (as when they have to wait for food) do they develop an ego and begin to tell themselves apart from their surroundings.

The **ego** represents reason, or common sense. According to Freud, the ego develops during the first year of life and operates under the *reality principle* as it strives to find acceptable and realistic ways to obtain gratification.

The **superego,** which develops by about age 5 or 6, represents the values that parents and other adults communicate to the child. Largely through the child's identification with the parent of the same sex, the superego incorporates socially approved duties and prohibitions—"shoulds" and "should nots"—into the child's own value system.

The psychoanalyst Erik H. Erikson departed from Freudian thought in emphasizing societal, rather than chiefly biological, influences on personality. Erikson sees development as proceeding through eight significant turning points at different times throughout life.

## Erik Erikson: Psychosocial Theory

Erik Erikson (b. 1902), a German-born psychoanalyst who trained under Anna Freud in Vienna, fled from the threat of Nazism (which eventually forced the breakup of Sigmund Freud's entire circle) and came to the United States in 1933. His personal and professional experience—far broader than Freud's—led him to modify and extend Freudian theory.

### Erikson's approach

Erikson was of mixed Danish and Jewish parentage; after his parents' divorce, he had no contact with his father; as a youth he floundered before settling on a vocation; and when he came to America, he needed to redefine his identity as an immigrant. All these issues found echoes in the "identity crises" he observed among disturbed adolescents, soldiers in combat during the Second World War, and members of minority groups (Erikson, 1968, 1973; R. I. Evans, 1967). He concluded that the quest for identity is a major theme in life.

Erikson was influenced by his work with children. Before becoming a psychoanalyst, he taught art in a small progressive school in Vienna. He was also trained in the Montessori method of educating young children which stresses learning through play. His later studies ranged from child-rearing practices of Native Americans to social customs in India.

Erikson believed that Freudian theory undervalued the influence of society on the developing personality. For example, a girl growing up on a Sioux Indian reservation, where females are trained to serve their hunter husbands, will develop different personality patterns and different skills from a girl who grew up in a wealthy family in turn-of-the-century Vienna, as most of Freud's patients did. Erikson also felt that Freud's view of society was too negative. Freud saw civilization as a source of discontent, an impediment to biological drives; Erikson, on the other hand, sees society as a potentially positive force, which shapes the development of the ego, or self.

### Erikson's eight crises

Erikson's **psychosocial-development theory** traces personality development across the life span, stressing societal and cultural influences on the ego at each of eight "ages" (Erikson, 1950). Each stage involves a turning point, a crisis in personality having to do with a specific major conflict—one that is particularly critical at the time, though it remains an issue to some degree throughout life.

The eight Eriksonian crises emerge in a predetermined order according to a timetable that is in turn determined by maturation. Healthy ego development involves making adjustments to the demands of the particular crisis that characterizes each stage in the life span. If the conflict is not satisfactorily resolved, the person will continue to struggle with it and healthy ego development will be impeded. Success in each stage lays the groundwork for resolving the crises of later stages.

Successful resolution of each of the eight crises (which are listed in Table 1-6 on page 24, and discussed throughout this book) requires balancing a positive trait and a corresponding negative trait, such as (in the first crisis) trust and mistrust during infancy. Although the positive quality should predominate, some element of the negative is needed, too. Healthy people, for example, basically trust their world, but they need to learn some mistrust to be prepared for dangerous or uncomfortable situations. The successful outcome of each crisis includes the development of a particular "virtue"—in this first case, the "virtue of hope." According to Erikson, conflict and challenge over each of the psychosocial issues are needed for healthy growth and development.

## Critique of Psychoanalytic Theory

Freud's original and creative thinking has made immense contributions to our understanding of children and has had a major impact on child-rearing practices. He made us aware of infantile sexuality, the nature of unconscious thoughts and emotions, defense mechanisms, the significance of dreams, the importance (and ambivalence) of parent-child relationships, and many other aspects of emotional functioning. He also founded the psychoanalytic method of psychotherapy.

Yet Freud's theory grew out of his own place in history and in society, and today much of it seems to patronize or demean women, no doubt because of its roots in the social system of a culture convinced of male superiority. Also, Freud based his theories about normal development not on average children but on his clientele of upper-middle-class adults in therapy. His concentration on the resolution of psychosexual conflict as the key to healthy development seems too narrow; and—although the subjective way in which he phrased his theories has made them hard to test—research has questioned or invalidated many of his concepts.

Erikson's theory has stood up much better. One strength is its emphasis on social and cultural influences on development, which takes it beyond Freud's narrow focus on biological and maturational factors. Also, it covers the entire life span, while Freud's theory stops at adolescence. But Erikson too has been criticized for an antifemale bias, since he uses the male as the norm for healthy development. Some of his concepts are also hard to assess objectively or to use as a basis for research; and there is no real evidence that his stages unfold in the sequence he proposes (Chiriboga, 1989).

## MECHANISTIC PERSPECTIVE

The *mechanistic perspective* views human development primarily as a response to events, discounting not only unconscious forces but also purpose, will, and intelligence. According to this perspective, if we can identify all the significant influences in a person's environment, we can predict how that person will act.

Mechanistic theorists see development as quantitative (that is, as changes in amount rather than kind) and continuous (allowing prediction of later behaviors from earlier ones). Mechanistic research tries to identify and isolate environmental factors that make people behave in certain ways. It focuses on how experiences affect later behavior and tries to understand the effects of experience by breaking down complex stimuli and complex behaviors into simpler elements.

The mechanistic model includes two related theories: behaviorism and social-learning theory.

## Behaviorism: Learning through Conditioning

It would be hard to imagine two views more at odds than psychoanalysts' and behaviorists'. Whereas psychoanalysts dig for unconscious motives driving human behavior, *behaviorism* is interested only in behaviors that can be seen, measured, and recorded. Behaviorists look for immediate, observable factors that determine whether a particular behavior will continue. Although they recognize that biology sets limits on what people do, they see the environment as much more important in directing behavior.

Behaviorism—also called *traditional learning theory*—holds that *learning* is what changes behavior and advances development. It maintains that human beings learn about the world the same way as other animals: by reacting to features of their environments that they find pleasing, painful, or threatening.

Since behaviorists are interested only in quantitative change, they do not describe stages of development. Instead, they describe conditioning, the mechanism by which learning takes place. There are two kinds of conditioning: classical and operant.

### Classical conditioning

Ivan Pavlov (1849–1936), a Russian physiologist, taught dogs to salivate upon hearing a bell by repeatedly offering them food immediately after the bell sounded. Because the dogs had learned to associate the sound of the bell with the food, the bell eventually induced salivation even when no food appeared. Pavlov's experiment demonstrated *classical conditioning*—a kind of learning in which a person or animal learns a response to a stimulus that did not originally elicit it, after the stimulus is repeatedly associated with another stimulus that *does* ordinarily evoke the response.

Figure 1-2 (page 28) shows the three steps in classical conditioning:

1 *Before conditioning.* The dog does not salivate at the sound of the bell but salivates only when the food appears. The food is an *unconditioned stimulus (UCS),* a stimulus that automatically elicits an unlearned (unconditioned) response. The salivation is the *unconditioned response (unconditioned reflex) (UCR),* an automatic, unlearned response to a particular stimulus (food). The sound of the bell is a *neutral stimulus,* one that does not ordinarily elicit a reflex response.

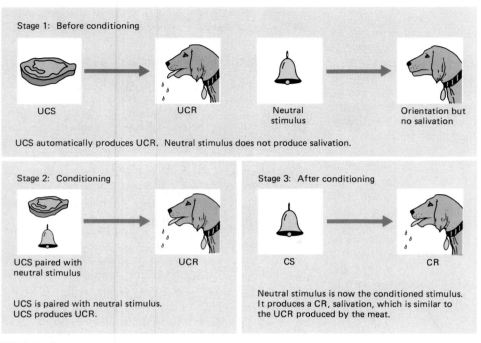

Stage 1: Before conditioning

UCS          UCR          Neutral          Orientation but
                          stimulus          no salivation

UCS automatically produces UCR.  Neutral stimulus does not produce salivation.

Stage 2: Conditioning

UCS paired with          UCR
neutral stimulus

UCS is paired with neutral stimulus.
UCS produces UCR.

Stage 3: After conditioning

CS          CR

Neutral stimulus is now the conditioned stimulus.
It produces a CR, salivation, which is similar to
the UCR produced by the meat.

FIGURE 1-2
Classical conditioning occurs in three stages. The neutral stimulus eventually
produces a conditioned response.

2  *During conditioning*. The experimenter repeatedly
pairs the neutral stimulus (the bell) with the unconditioned stimulus (food). Every time the bell rings,
food appears and the dog salivates in response to the
food.

3  *After conditioning*. The dog salivates at the sound
of the bell alone. The dog has learned to associate
the bell with food and to respond in the same way to
both stimuli. The bell has become a **conditioned
stimulus (CS),** an originally neutral stimulus that,
after repeated pairings with an unconditioned stimulus (food), elicits a response (salivation) similar to
that elicited by the unconditioned stimulus. The salivation has become a **conditioned response (CR),**
a response evoked by a conditioned stimulus (the
bell).

John B. Watson (1878–1958) was the first behaviorist to apply stimulus-response theories of learning to
the study of child development. We will see in Chapter
4 how he conditioned a child known as "Little Albert" to
fear furry objects.

### Operant conditioning

The American psychologist B. F. Skinner (1904–1990)
developed a type of conditioning that parents, teachers,
animal trainers, and others often use to shape desired
behavior. Skinner (1938) taught pigeons to respond to
bars of different colors by reinforcing them with food
when they pressed the correct bar. He then showed
how the principle underlying the animals' responses
could also be used to control human behavior: the principle is that an organism will tend to perform a behavior
to obtain a desired response. A pigeon will perform the
behavior of pressing the correct bar to obtain the desired response of getting food.

This principle is the basis of **operant conditioning,** a kind of learning in which an animal or person
continues to make a response because the response
has been reinforced, or suppresses a response because
it has been punished. A reinforcer is a stimulus that
follows a behavior and *increases* the likelihood that the
behavior will be repeated. **Reinforcement** is the process by which a behavior is strengthened. **Punish-**

FIGURE 1-3
Operant, or instrumental,
conditioning.

***Reinforcement and punishment***   Reinforcement is most effective when it is immediate. If a response is no longer reinforced—if the pigeon presses the red bar several times and gets no food—then the response will eventually no longer be repeated, or at least will be no more likely to appear than it was in the first place. This process, whereby a response that is no longer reinforced returns to its original (baseline) level, is called **extinction.**

Reinforcement can be either *positive* or *negative.* Positive reinforcement consists of giving a reward like food, gold stars, money, or praise. Negative reinforcement involves taking away something that the individual does not like, such as a bright light or a loud noise (known as an *aversive event*).

Negative reinforcement is sometimes confused with punishment, but they are different. Negative reinforcement encourages repetition of a behavior by *taking away* an aversive event, whereas punishment suppresses a behavior by *bringing on* an aversive event (like spanking a child or giving an electric shock to an animal), or by *withdrawing* a positive event (like watching television).

Intermittent reinforcement—reinforcing a response at some times but not at others—produces more durable behaviors than reinforcing a response every time. Because it takes longer for the individual to realize that intermittent reinforcement has ended, the behavior tends to persist. Thus, parents who only sometimes give in to a child's temper tantrums strengthen that kind of behavior even more than if they gave in every time. If they had been reinforcing every tantrum, once they stopped doing so, the child would realize almost at once that the tantrum was not producing the desired result.

Operant conditioning is a powerful tool that has been used in programmed learning and other efforts to train or change adults' and children's behavior. Desired actions are encouraged by reinforcement; undesired ones are punished or ignored. The choice of an effective stimulus depends on the individual being trained: one person's reinforcement may be another's punishment.

***Shaping***   What can be done if there *is* no "desired behavior" to encourage (for example, if a child consistently refuses to talk)? ***Shaping*** is a way to bring about a *new* response by reinforcing responses that are progressively more like the desired one. When the person does something that is "on the right track" because it is similar to the response being sought, a reinforcement is given. When that reinforcement has taken hold, the

**ment** is a stimulus that follows a behavior and *decreases* the likelihood that the behavior will be repeated. Operant learning is also called *instrumental conditioning,* because the learner is instrumental in changing the environment in some way—that is, in bringing about either reinforcement or punishment.

Figure 1-3 shows how operant conditioning occurs. A pigeon happens to press a red bar. This random or accidental response is reinforced by a grain of food. Since the reinforcement strengthens the response, the pigeon keeps pressing the red bar. The originally accidental response has now become a deliberate response.

shaper continues to reward responses that are closer and closer to the desired behavior. For example, the parent of a little boy who refuses to talk might first give him a toy after he makes any sound at all, then give the toy only after he says a word, and then give it only after he says a sentence.

Shaping is often part of *behavior modification,* a form of operant conditioning that is used to eliminate some behaviors or to teach others, as in toilet training. It is most often used for children with special needs, like retarded or emotionally disturbed youngsters, but its techniques are also effective in the day-to-day management of normal children.

## Social-Learning Theory: Learning through Modeling

*Social-learning theory* is a modern offshoot of traditional learning theory which today is more influential than the original version. It holds that children, in particular, learn by observing and imitating models (like their parents). The theory—of which Albert Bandura (b. 1925) is the most prominent advocate—is mechanistic in its stress on response to the environment. But it sees the learner as more active than behaviorism does and acknowledges the role of thought in human learning.

Social-learning theorists, like traditional behaviorists, emphasize rigorous laboratory experimentation but believe that human behavior cannot be explained by theories based on animal research. People learn in a social context, and human learning is more complex than simple conditioning allows for.

In social-learning theory, children's identification with their parents, who shape their behavior through reinforcements and punishments, is the most important element in the way they learn a language, deal with aggression, develop a sense of morality, learn socially expected behaviors for their gender, and so on. (A boy may be praised for acting "like Daddy," a girl for acting "like Mommy.")

Children take an active part in their own learning, partly by choosing the models they want to imitate, and the child's own characteristics influence the choice of models. For example, a boy with aggressive tendencies will be more likely to imitate Rambo than to imitate Mister Rogers.

The kinds of behavior people imitate depends, of course, on what kinds of behavior exist and are valued in their culture. In a tropical climate, where there are no reindeer, children will not learn to hunt them.

Behaviorists see the environment as molding the

These aspiring football players demonstrate the social-learning theory that children who spend many hours watching television tend to imitate dress, speech, and other behavior of models they see on the screen.

child, but social-learning theorists believe that the child also acts upon the environment—in fact, *creates* the environment to some extent. For example, a girl who spends hours at a time watching television rather than playing with other children is likely to take her models from people on the screen.

Social-learning theory also differs from behaviorism in recognizing the influence of cognitive processes, which (as we shall see) are the main concern of the organismic perspective. According to social-learning theorists, people observe models, learn "chunks" of behavior, and mentally put the chunks together into complex new behavior patterns. Thus, a woman may try to model her tennis serve on Martina Navratilova's and her backhand on Chris Evert's. Cognitive factors like the ability to pay attention and mentally organize sensory information affect the way a person will incorporate observed behavior. Children's developing ability to use mental symbols to stand for a model's behavior enables them to form standards for judging their own behavior.

### Critique of Mechanistic Theory

Both behaviorism and social-learning theory have helped to make the study of human development more scientific by their insistence on two things—defining terms clearly and designing rigorous experiments. But they have neglected the study of human behavior in natural settings. They also tend to underestimate biological and hereditary factors and fail to acknowledge internal motivation, free choice, and unconscious factors in behavior. Further, these theories are not developmental: they pay little attention to what children and adults are like at different periods of life.

The greatest contribution of behaviorism is in programs or therapies designed to effect rapid changes in behavior (like giving up smoking) or to teach new behaviors (like toilet training) without a long search for deep-seated emotional conflicts. But psychoanalysts charge that this failure to consider the causes of symptoms is a basic flaw of behaviorist theory. They argue that eliminating one undesirable behavior (like stealing) through punishment may merely result in the substitution of some other negative behavior (like bed-wetting), leaving the basic problem unresolved. Also, some people object to behaviorism on ethical grounds; they say that behaviorists "play God" and control other people's behavior.

The distinguishing features of social-learning theory—its focus on the social context of learning, its recognition that people actively influence their own development, and its acknowledgment of cognitive influences on behavior—are improvements on traditional learning theory.

## ORGANISMIC PERSPECTIVE

The third major theoretical perspective views people as living, growing beings with their own internal impulses and patterns for development. The **organismic perspective** sees people as active agents in their own development and sees development as occurring in qualitative stages. Let's examine each of these two points—people as actors and development as a series of stages:

1 *People are active organisms.* According to this view, people initiate acts; they do not just react to events. Although internal and external forces interact, the *source* of developmental change is within the person. Organicists see life experiences not as the cause of development but as factors that can speed it up or slow it down. These theorists do not try to determine, as mechanists do, how external reinforcements shape a person's responses. Nor do they focus, as psychoanalysts do, on underlying motivational forces of which a person is unaware. Instead, they look at human beings as doers who actively construct their worlds.

2 *Development occurs in qualitative stages.* Organicists focus on qualitative change. Like some other "stage" theorists,* they describe development as occurring in a set sequence of qualitatively different stages. At each stage, people develop different kinds of abilities and cope with different kinds of problems. Each stage builds on the previous one and lays the foundation for the next. Because thought and behavior at each stage are qualitatively different from what existed before, it is only by knowing the common course of development that we can anticipate (in broad outline) what a person will be like later in life. All people go through the same stages in the same order, but the timing varies, making any cutoff age only approximate.

## Jean Piaget: Cognitive-Stage Theory

The Swiss theoretician Jean Piaget (1896–1980) was the most prominent advocate of the organismic perspective. Much of what we know about the way children think is due to his creative inquiry.

When he was a boy, Piaget's wide-ranging curiosity led him to observe and write about such diverse topics as mechanics, mollusks, and an albino sparrow he saw in a park. As an adult, he applied his broad knowledge of biology, philosophy, and psychology to meticulous observations of children. He built complex theories about **cognitive development:** changes in children's thought processes that result in a growing ability to acquire and use knowledge about their world.

By the time of his death in 1980, Piaget had written more than 40 books and more than 100 articles on child psychology as well as works on philosophy and education, many of them with his long-time collaborator, Barbel Inhelder. Piaget's theory influenced other organicists like Lawrence Kohlberg, whose theory of moral development we discuss later in this book.

Piaget came to many of his conclusions by combining observation with flexible, individualized questioning in what he called the *clinical method.* To find out how children think, Piaget followed up their answers to his questions by asking more questions. In this way he discovered, for example, that a typical 4-year-old believed that pennies or flowers were more numerous when arranged in a line than when heaped or piled up. He individualized each interview, probing further when he received interesting responses, using language that he

---

*Although Freud and Erikson describe qualitative stages, they do not, to the extent that true organismic theorists do, view human beings as active initiators of development.

The influential Swiss psychologist Jean Piaget studied children's cognitive development by observing and talking with his own youngsters and others.

thought the child would understand, and even changing to the language that a child was using spontaneously.

Let's look at some of the principal features of Piaget's theory.

### Piaget's cognitive structures

Piaget believed that the core of intelligent behavior is an inborn tendency that people have to adapt to their environment. Children build on the foundation of their sensory, motor, and reflex capacities to actively construct their knowledge of the world—from feeling a pebble, say, or exploring the boundaries of a living room. They learn from their experiences and develop more complex mental structures, which help them progress through a series of four stages of cognitive development. (Piaget's stages, summarized above in Table 1-6, are discussed in Chapters 4, 6, 8, and 10.)

The cognitive structures of infants are called schemes. A *scheme* is an organized pattern of behavior that a baby uses to interact with the environment in a certain way. An infant has, for example, a scheme for sucking, a scheme for seeing, and a scheme for grasping. Schemes gradually become differentiated; for example, babies develop different ways to suck at the breast, a bottle, or a pacifier. Schemes also become

coordinated; for example, infants learn to grasp what they see.

As children develop the ability to think, their schemes become organized patterns of thought that correspond to particular behaviors. The cognitive structures of older children enable them to perform different kinds of mental operations—first in concrete situations involving things that they can see, hear, smell, taste, or feel, and later through abstract thought.

### Piaget's principles of cognitive development

How do people's cognitive structures advance from the simple behavioral schemes of infancy to the formal logic of adolescence? Piaget's answer lies in three interrelated principles of development, which he believed to be inborn, inherited tendencies and which he called *functional invariants* because they operate at all stages of cognitive growth. These three principles are organization, adaptation, and equilibration.

Cognitive *organization* is a tendency to create systems that bring together all of a person's knowledge of the environment. At all stages of development, people try to make sense of their world. They do this by systematically organizing their knowledge, at whatever level of complexity they are capable of. Development progresses from simple organizational structures to more complex ones. At first, for example, infants' schemes of looking and grasping operate independently. Later, the infants integrate, or organize, these separate schemes into a single more complex scheme that allows them to look at an object while holding it—to coordinate eye and hand—and thus to better understand that particular part of their environment.

More complex organization comes about as children acquire more information. *Adaptation,* Piaget's term for how a person deals with new information, is the second functional invariant. It occurs through the dual processes of assimilating new information and accommodating to it. *Assimilation* is the attempt to fit new information into an existing cognitive structure. When breastfed babies begin to suck on a rubber nipple, they are showing assimilation; that is, they are using an old scheme to deal with a new object or situation. *Accommodation* is a change in an existing cognitive structure to cope with new information or a new situation. For example, when babies discover that sucking on a bottle requires somewhat different tongue and mouth movements from those used to suck on a breast, they accommodate by modifying the old scheme. They have adapted their original sucking scheme to deal with a new experience—the bottle. Assimilation and accommodation work together to produce cognitive growth.

***Equilibration,*** the third functional invariant, is a tendency to strive for a state of mental balance (equilibrium), both between a person and the outside world and among the cognitive elements within a person. The need for equilibrium leads a child to shift from assimilation to accommodation. When children cannot handle new experiences with their existing structures, they organize new mental patterns, thus restoring a state of mental balance.

### Critique of Piaget's Theory

Piaget was the forerunner of today's "cognitive revolution" in psychology, with its emphasis on internal cognitive processes as opposed to the emphasis of learning on outside influences and overt behaviors. Although American psychologists were slow to accept his ideas, Piaget has inspired more research on children's cognitive development than any other theorist.

Piaget's careful observations have provided a wealth of information, including some surprising insights. Who, for example, would have thought that before age 5 or 6, even very bright children do not realize that a ball of clay that has been rolled into a "worm" before their eyes still contains the same amount of clay, or that an infant might think that a person who has left a room no longer exists? Piaget pointed out unique elements of children's thought and made us aware of how different it is from adult thought. Further, by describing what children can do and understand at various stages of cognitive development, Piaget gave valuable guidance to all who deal with children.

Yet critics fault Piaget on several counts. He spoke primarily of the "average" child and took little notice of individual differences among children or of the ways in which education and culture affect performance. Many of his ideas emerged from his highly personal observations of his own three children and from his idiosyncratic way of interviewing children, rather than from established, standardized experimental procedures. Also, he seems to have underestimated the abilities of young children.

On a more basic level, many modern developmentalists question the idea of clearly demarcated stages of cognitive growth. Today, psychologists generally view cognitive growth as gradual and continuous rather than as changing abruptly from one stage to the next.

It also seems that many people do not reach Piaget's highest level of thought, formal logic, even in adulthood. And formal logic (or abstract thinking) may not even be the best model of mature thought, since it fails to acknowledge practical problem-solving ability or the development of wisdom.

## HUMANISTIC PERSPECTIVE

In 1962, a group of psychologists founded the Association of Humanistic Psychology. Protesting against what they considered the essentially negative beliefs underlying behaviorist and psychoanalytic theory, they maintained that human nature is either neutral or good and that any bad characteristics are the result of damage that has been inflicted on the developing self.

Like organicism, the ***humanistic perspective*** views people as able to take charge of their lives and foster their own development. Humanistic theorists emphasize the potential for positive, healthy development and the distinctively human capacities of choice, creativity, and self-realization.

The humanistic approach is not truly developmental, since its proponents generally do not distinguish stages of the life span but make a broad distinction only between the periods before and after adolescence. We mention it here because it offers an influential view of the development of personality.

### Abraham Maslow: Self-Actualization and the Hierarchy of Needs

One important humanistic psychologist, Abraham Maslow (1908–1970), identified a hierarchy of needs that motivate human behavior (see Figure 1-4 on page 34). According to Maslow (1954), only when people have satisfied the most basic needs can they strive to meet higher needs.

The first need is physiological survival. Starving persons will take great risks to get food; only when they have obtained it can they worry about the next level of needs, those concerning personal safety and security. These needs, in turn, must be met (at least in part) before people can seek love and acceptance, esteem and achievement, and finally self-actualization, or the full realization of potential.

Maslow's ideal, a self-actualized person, shows high levels of all the following characteristics (Maslow, 1968): perception of reality; acceptance of self, of others, and of nature; spontaneity; problem-solving ability, self-direction; detachment and the desire for privacy; freshness of appreciation and richness of emotional reaction; frequency of peak experiences; identification with other human beings; satisfying and changing relationships with other people; democratic character structure, creativity, and a sense of values. Only about 1 person in 100 is said to attain this lofty ideal (R. Thomas, 1979). But no one is ever completely self-actualized; the healthy person is always moving up to levels that are even more fulfilling.

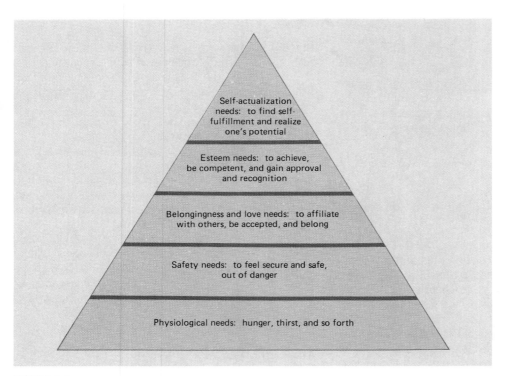

**FIGURE 1-4**
Maslow's hierarchy of needs. According to Maslow, human needs have different
priorities. First comes survival (base of pyramid). Starving people will take great risks
to obtain food; once they know they will not die of starvation, they start to worry
about safety. Then the need for security must be met, at least in part, before people
think about the need for love. As each level of needs is met, a person looks to the
needs at the next higher level. This progression is not invariant, however; for
example, self-sacrifice would be an exception. (*Source:* Maslow, 1954.)

On first impression, Maslow's hierarchy of needs
seems to be grounded in human experience. But the
priorities he outlined do not invariably hold true. For
example, history is full of accounts of self-sacrifice, in
which people give up what they need for survival so
that someone else (a loved one or even a stranger) can
live.

### Critique of Humanistic Theory

The humanistic outlook offers a positive, optimistic
model of humankind and its potential for development,
as opposed to the negative Freudian viewpoint; and it
goes deeper than learning theory by considering internal factors, like feelings, values, and hopes. Humanistic
theories have made a valuable contribution by promoting child-rearing approaches that respect the child's
uniqueness.

Its limitations as a scientific theory have to do largely
with its subjectiveness: since its concepts are not
clearly defined, they are hard to communicate and to
use as the basis for research designs. Furthermore,

since humanistic theories do not focus on issues at different times of life, they do not provide insights into the
process of development. However, since humanists are
more interested in bettering the human condition than
in increasing scientific knowledge about it, they make
no apologies for the approach.

## A WORD TO STUDENTS

Our final word in this introductory chapter is that this
entire book is far from the final word. While we have
tried to incorporate the most important and the most
up-to-date information about how people develop, developmentalists are constantly learning more. As you
read this book, you are certain to come up with your
own questions. By thinking about them, and perhaps
eventually conducting research to find answers, it is
possible that you yourself, now just embarking on the
study of human development, will someday add to our
knowledge about the interesting species to which we all
belong.

## SUMMARY

### HUMAN DEVELOPMENT: THE SUBJECT AND THE TEXT

■ Human development is the scientific study of the quantitative and qualitative ways people change over time. Quantitative change is change in number or amount, such as height, weight, and vocabulary. Qualitative change is change in kind, structure, or organization, such as in the nature of intelligence. Qualitative change is marked by the appearance of new phenomena that cannot be predicted from earlier functioning.

■ This book emphasizes human research, appreciates the lifelong capacity for change, acknowledges human resilience, recognizes that people help shape their own development, and is practically oriented.

### HUMAN DEVELOPMENT: THE STUDY AND ITS HISTORY

■ The study of human development focuses on describing, explaining, predicting, and modifying development.

■ Although we can look separately at various aspects of development (such as physical, intellectual, and personality and social development), we must remember that these do not occur in isolation. Each affects the other.

■ Although we have divided the human life span into eight periods, the age ranges are often subjective. Individual differences must be taken into account.

■ Influences on development are both internal (hereditary) and external (environmental). Influences that affect large groups of people are called either *normative age-graded* or *normative history-graded. Nonnormative* life events are those that are unusual in themselves or in their timing; they often have a major impact.

■ According to the ecological approach, environmental influences on development occur at four levels: microsystem, mesosystem, exosystem, and macrosystem.

■ The concept of a critical period, or time when an event has its greatest impact, seems more applicable to physical (and especially prenatal) development than to psychological development.

■ Attitudes about children were quite different in the past and affected how children were studied. As researchers became interested in following children's development over a longer period, into adulthood, life-span development expanded as a subject for study.

### HUMAN DEVELOPMENT: RESEARCH METHODS

■ There are four major nonexperimental techniques for studying people: case studies, observation, interviews, and correlational studies. Each approach has strengths and weaknesses.

1 Case studies are studies of individuals.
2 Observation is of two types, naturalistic and laboratory. Each provides a good description of behaviors.
3 In an interview, researchers ask questions about peoples' attitudes, their opinions, or some other aspect of their lives.
4 Correlational studies show the direction and magnitude of a relationship between variables.

■ Controlled experiments are the only method of discovering cause-and-effect relationships. The three principle types are laboratory, field, and natural experiments.

■ The two major methods of collecting data about development are the cross-sectional and the longitudinal. Cross-sectional studies describe age differences; longitudinal studies describe age changes. Each method has strengths and weaknesses. Sequential strategies have been developed to overcome the weaknesses of the other two designs.

■ Studies of people must reflect certain ethical considerations. In a carefully designed study, researchers consider its effect on the participants, as well as its potential benefit to the field.

### HUMAN DEVELOPMENT: THEORETICAL PERSPECTIVES

■ A theory is a set of related statements about data, the information obtained from research. Theories are important in explaining, interpreting, and predicting behavior and in guiding future research. We consider four theoretical perspectives: psychoanalytic, mechanistic, organismic, and humanistic.

■ The psychoanalytic perspective focuses on unconscious forces motivating behavior. Sigmund Freud's psychosexual theory and Erik Erikson's psychosocial theory are the two most influential examples of this approach.

■ The mechanistic perspective views human development primarily as a response to events, and change as quantitative. Its focus is on observable behaviors. Behaviorism and social-learning theory reflect the mechanistic perspective. Behaviorists are interested in shaping behavior through conditioning. Social-learning theory, which stresses imitation of models, incorporates some elements of the this perspective.

■ The organismic perspective sees people as active contributors to their own development and views development as occurring in a series of qualitatively different stages. The cognitive-developmental theory of Jean Piaget is the most important example of this perspective.

■ The humanistic perspective, represented by Abraham Maslow, views people as fostering their own development through choice, creativity, and self-realization.

## KEY TERMS

human development (page 3)
quantitative change (3)
qualitative change (3)
heredity (8)
environmental influences (8)
cohort (8)
ecological approach (9)
critical period (9)
scientific method (12)
case studies (12)
naturalistic observation (14)
laboratory observation (14)
interview (15)
correlational studies (15)
experiment (17)
independent variable (17)
dependent variable (17)
experimental group (17)
control group (18)

sample (18)
random sample (18)
cross-sectional study (20)
longitudinal study (20)
cross-sequential study (20)
theory (21)
data (21)
hypothesis (22)
psychoanalytic perspective (23)
defense mechanisms (23)
psychosexual development (25)
id (25)
ego (25)
superego (25)
psychosocial-development theory (26)
mechanistic perspective (27)
behaviorism (27)
classical conditioning (27)
unconditioned stimulus (UCS) (27)

unconditioned response
    (unconditioned reflex) (UCR) (27)
neutral stimulus (27)
conditioned stimulus (CS) (28)
conditioned response (CR) (28)
operant conditioning (28)
reinforcement (28)
punishment (28)
extinction (29)
shaping (29)
social-learning theory (30)
organismic perspective (31)
cognitive development (31)
scheme (32)
organization (32)
adaptation (32)
assimilation (32)
accommodation (32)
equilibration (33)
humanistic perspective (33)

## SUGGESTED READINGS

**Chudacoff, H. P. (1990).** *How old are you? Age consciousness in American culture.* Princeton, NJ: Princeton University Press. The historian author of this lively book traces the development of age consciousness in urban middle-class culture from its beginnings in the late 1800s and discusses both advantages (policy makers can better identify groups that need special help) and disadvantages (ageism, or discrimination against certain age groups, most often the elderly).

**Erikson, E. H. (1963).** *Childhood and society.* New York: Norton. A collection of Erikson's writings that includes the classic "Eight Ages of Man," in which he outlines his theory of psychosocial development from infancy through old age.

**Kagan, J. (1984).** *The nature of the child.* New York: Basic Books. A beautifully written and compelling argument against the idea of the irreversibility of early experience. Kagan believes that people have the ability to change throughout life and that later events transform early childhood experiences.

**Pryor, K. (1985).** *Don't shoot the dog: The new art of teaching and training.* New York: Bantam. A fascinating and practical explanation of the way principles of operant conditioning can be used to change the behavior of children, adults, and animals. The author, a trainer of dolphins, uses humor and a wealth of anecdotes to make her points.

# ONE

# BEGINNINGS

Life is change. From the moment of conception to the moment of death, human beings undergo many complex processes of development. Throughout life, people have the potential to grow, to change, to develop.

The study of human development will help you to understand yourself and the people you know. You will become aware of influences and choices that have made you the person you are, and of forces that can affect the person you will become. In Part One—Chapters 2, 3, 4, and 5—you will read about the dramatic changes that occur during the earliest stages of human development, changes broader in scope and faster in pace than any that you have experienced since then or will ever experience.

■ **Chapter 2** begins our discussion of the exciting human journey. We examine how conception occurs and which of the forces that guide development are already present through the mechanisms of heredity. We then trace the growth of the new life in the womb and see what factors influence it, for both good and ill, during gestation. We touch on the revolutionary techniques now being used to intervene in the natural process of prenatal development. And finally, we focus on the complex process of birth itself.

You will then learn some fascinating things about the impressive capabilities of newborn babies, and their even more impressive potential for future growth. In the rest of Part One, you will follow human development through the first 3 years of life, the stages known as *infancy* and *toddlerhood*.

■ In **Chapter 3,** we see how newborns make the transition from the womb to the outside world, how their body systems function, and how their brains develop. We explore low birthweight and some other issues. Then, we go on to look at typical, normal sensory and motor development and at important health concerns during the first 3 years of life.

■ In **Chapter 4,** we cover intellectual growth. We see how babies learn and how social scientists study and measure their learning and their cognitive functioning. We pay particular attention to language skills, which are specifically human capabilities. And we explore competence—what it is and how it develops early in life.

■ In **Chapter 5,** we see how babies begin to show their unique personalities right from birth. We examine prominent theories about personality and social development, as we seek to explain why each child develops in his or her own way. Helping to explain this are such influences as inborn temperament and the family, which affect the development of sociability and of babies' ability to regulate their own behavior.

As in the rest of this book we see, right from the beginning, how the various kinds of development—physical, intellectual, and personality—overlap and affect each other.

# CONCEPTION THROUGH BIRTH

If I could have watched you grow as a magical mother might, if I could have seen through my magical transparent belly, there would have been such ripening within. . . .

ANNE SEXTON, 1966

- How does human life begin?
- How do heredity and environment affect a new human being's sex, appearance, health, intelligence, and personality?
- How does a baby develop inside the mother's body?

- How does the prenatal environment influence development?
- What happens during birth, and how can medical intervention affect the natural birth process?

The beginning of human life has always inspired wonder and curiosity, and over the years both scientists and laypersons have held some surprising notions about it. Even today, when we know much more about the origin of life, an element of awe remains. The beginning for you, as for everyone, came long before you gave your first yell after leaving your mother's womb. In this chapter we will explain that beginning. We will then talk about the influences of what you inherited from your parents and of what you have experienced, both before and after birth. We also discuss the birth process itself, choices about childbirth, and the role of medical intervention.

Your true beginning was a split-second event when a single spermatozoon, one of millions of sperm cells from your father, joined an ovum (egg cell), one of the several hundred thousand ova produced and stored in your mother's body during her lifetime.

Which sperm meets which ovum has tremendous implications for the new person: for sex, appearance, susceptibility to disease, and even personality. The sperm and the ovum are partial microcosms of the two human beings, man and woman, who bring the new life into existence. There are also environmental influences. Who the mother and father are, what talents they have, where and how they live, how they feel about each other and their child—these and many other factors profoundly affect the child's development. Let us see how this important union takes place and what occurs during the 9 months when the new life grows inside the womb until birth.

## FERTILIZATION

*Fertilization,* or conception, the process by which sperm and ovum fuse to form a single new cell, is most likely to occur about 14 days after the beginning of a woman's menstrual period. The new single cell formed by the two *gametes,* or sex cells—the ovum and the sperm—is called a *zygote.* Once conceived, this zygote duplicates itself again and again by cell division.

### HOW DOES FERTILIZATION TAKE PLACE?

At birth, a human female has about 400,000 immature ova in her two ovaries, each ovum in its own small sac, or follicle. The ovum—though only about one-fourth the size of the period that ends this sentence—is the largest cell in the human body. From the time a female matures sexually until menopause, *ovulation* occurs about once each menstrual cycle (for most women, every 28 days): a mature follicle in one ovary ruptures and expels its ovum. The ovum is swept along through the fallopian tube by tiny hair cells called *cilia,* toward the uterus, or womb. It is in the fallopian tube that, if the ovum meets a sperm cell, fertilization normally occurs (see Figure 2-1 on page 42, showing the female and male reproductive systems).

The sperm—shaped like a tadpole but only $1/600$ inch from head to tail—is one of the smallest cells in the body. Sperm are produced in the testicles (testes), or reproductive glands, of a mature male at a rate of several hundred million a day and are ejaculated in the semen at sexual climax.

The sperm enter the vagina and begin to swim up through the opening of the cervix, the neck of the uterus. From the uterus they head into the fallopian tube, but only a few sperm actually get that far. The protective layer around the ovum needs to be worn down so that one, and only one, sperm cell will actually penetrate the membrane. About 20 million sperm cells must enter a woman's body at one time to make fertilization likely, but only one of them can fertilize an ovum to conceive a new human being.

From the time of ejaculation, sperm maintain their ability to fertilize an ovum for up to 48 hours; and ova can be fertilized for about 24 hours after release from the ovary. Thus there is a "window" of about 48 hours during each menstrual cycle when sexual intercourse can result in fertilization. Sperm that reach a woman's reproductive tract up to 24 hours before or after an ovum is released are capable of fertilizing that ovum. If fertilization does not occur, the ovum and any sperm cells in the woman's body die. The sperm are absorbed by the woman's white blood cells, and the ovum passes into the uterus and exits through the vagina (see Figure 2-2, page 42). If sperm and ovum do meet, they conceive a new life and endow it with a rich genetic legacy.

## WHAT CAUSES MULTIPLE BIRTHS?

Unlike most animals, the human baby usually comes into the world alone. Exceptions—multiple births—occur in two different ways.

One mechanism occurs when the woman's body releases two ova within a short time of each other, and both are fertilized. The two babies that are conceived are called *fraternal, two-egg,* or **dizygotic twins.** Since they are created by different ova and different sperm cells, they are no more alike in genetic makeup than any other siblings. They may be of the same sex or different sexes.

The other mechanism is the division in two of a single ovum after fertilization. *Identical, one-egg,* or **monozygotic twins,** who result from this cell division, have the same genetic heritage. Any differences they will later show must be due to the influences of environment. They are always of the same sex.

Triplets, quadruplets, and other multiple births result from either one of these processes or a combination of both.

Identical twins seem to be the result of an accident in prenatal development, unrelated to either genetic or environmental influences. They account for one-fourth to one-third of all twins.

Fraternal twins are more common in some ethnic groups and under some circumstances. More are being

Fertilization takes place when a sperm cell unites with an ovum to form a single new cell. The fertilized ovum shown here has begun to grow by cell division. It will eventually differentiate into 800 billion or more cells with specialized functions.

born these days because of fertility drugs that stimulate ovulation and often cause the release of more than one ovum. These twins are more likely to be born in third and later pregnancies, to older women, in families with a history of fraternal twins, and in various ethnic groups (Vaughan, McKay & Behrman, 1979). Twin births are most common among African Americans (1 in 70 births), East Indians, and northern Europeans, and least common among Asians other than East Indians (1 in 150 births among the Japanese and 1 in 300 among the Chinese). These differences are probably due to hormonal differences in women.

Multiple births are more common today than they used to be because of the increased use of fertility drugs. The infants have a better chance of survival because of advances in caring for small babies. These Chicago quintuplets are 7 years old.

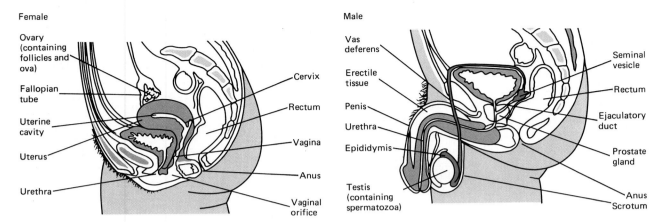

Female

Ovary (containing follicles and ova)

Fallopian tube

Uterine cavity

Uterus

Urethra

Cervix

Rectum

Vagina

Anus

Vaginal orifice

Male

Vas deferens

Erectile tissue

Penis

Urethra

Epididymis

Testis (containing spermatozoa)

Seminal vesicle

Rectum

Ejaculatory duct

Prostate gland

Anus

Scrotum

**FIGURE 2-1**
*Above:* Human reproductive systems.

**FIGURE 2-2**
*Below:* Fertilization. Spermatozoa can live for 48 hours in a woman's reproductive tract. If a live sperm is present during the 24-hour period after an ovum has been released, fertilization may occur. If it does not, both ovum and sperm die, and fertilization cannot occur until another ovum is released, usually about 28 days later.

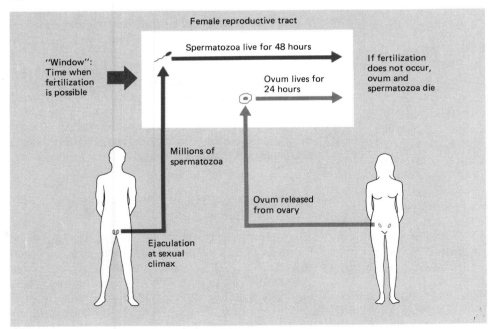

Female reproductive tract

Spermatozoa live for 48 hours

Ovum lives for 24 hours

"Window": Time when fertilization is possible

If fertilization does not occur, ovum and spermatozoa die

Millions of spermatozoa

Ovum released from ovary

Ejaculation at sexual climax

## WHAT DETERMINES SEX?

Henry VIII of England divorced Catherine of Aragon because (among other reasons) she had borne him a daughter rather than the son he desperately wanted. It is ironic that this basis for divorce has been recognized in many societies, since we now know that the sperm cell—that is, the father—determines the sex of a child.

At conception, the zygote receives 23 chromosomes (segments of hereditary materials, described below) from the sperm and 23 from the ovum. They align themselves in pairs: 22 pairs are **autosomes,** or non-sex chromosomes; the twenty-third pair are **sex chromosomes,** which determine whether the new human being will be male or female.

In a female, the two sex chromosomes—called *X*

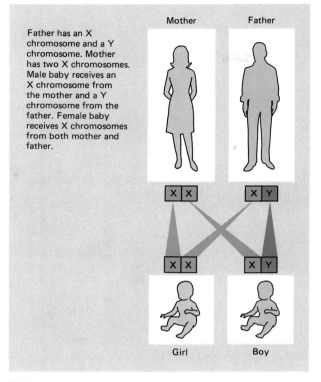

Father has an X chromosome and a Y chromosome. Mother has two X chromosomes. Male baby receives an X chromosome from the mother and a Y chromosome from the father. Female baby receives X chromosomes from both mother and father.

Mother    Father

X X    X Y

X X    X Y

Girl    Boy

**FIGURE 2-3**
Determination of sex. All babies receive an X chromosome from the mother; therefore, sex is determined by whether an X or a Y chromosome is received from the father.

*chromosomes*—are the same. In a male, an X chromosome is paired with a smaller *Y chromosome.* An ovum can carry only an X chromosome, but sperm can carry either an X or a Y. When an ovum is fertilized by an X-carrying sperm, the resulting zygote has the pair XX, which makes it female. When an ovum is fertilized by a Y-carrying sperm, the zygote has the pair XY and so is male (see Figure 2-3 above). Thus, the sex of the child depends entirely on whether the sex chromosome carried by the sperm cell that fertilized the ovum was X or Y.

Differences between the sexes begin to appear at conception. About 120 to 170 males are conceived for every 100 females, but since males are more likely to be spontaneously aborted or stillborn, only 106 are born for every 100 females (U.S. Department of Health and Human Services, USDHHS, 1982). Boys' births average 1 hour longer than girls' births, which is one reason why more boys have birth defects (Jacklin, 1989). More males die early in life, and at every age males are more susceptible to many disorders, so that there are only 95 males for every 100 females in the United States (USDHHS, 1982). Furthermore, the

male develops more slowly than the female from early fetal life into adulthood. At 20 weeks after conception, males are, on average, 2 weeks behind females; at 40 weeks they are 4 weeks behind; and they continue to lag behind till maturity (Hutt, 1972).

Why are males more vulnerable throughout life? The X chromosome may contain genes that protect females, the Y chromosome may contain harmful genes, or there may be different mechanisms in the sexes for providing immunity to various infections and diseases. One controversial hypothesis suggests that the mother's body produces damaging antibodies against a male fetus (Gualtieri & Hicks, 1985).

## HEREDITY AND ENVIRONMENT

### WHAT IS THE ROLE OF HEREDITY?

Do you ever read horoscopes? These popular but unreliable predictions are based on an ancient pseudo science, astrology. Astrologers claim that a new life is influenced or controlled by the positions of heavenly bodies at the moment of birth. If we want to understand the true sources of our physical, intellectual, and emotional makeup, however, the best place to look is, as Shakespeare put it, "not in our stars, but in ourselves."

The science of *genetics* is the study of *heredity*—the inborn factors, inherited from our parents, that affect our development. Genetics tells us that it is the meeting of ovum and sperm, not the crossing of heavenly orbits, which determines much of our future course. When two gametes unite to form a zygote, they give the new life a unique genetic makeup.

### Mechanisms of Heredity: Genes and Chromosomes

The basic unit of heredity is the *gene,* a bit of *deoxyribonucleic acid (DNA).* Genes determine inherited characteristics. DNA carries the "program" that tells each cell in the body what specific functions it will perform and how it will perform them—a program that is unique for every person. Human beings have as many as 100,000 genes distributed among 46 *chromosomes,* larger segments of DNA that carry the genes. Each gene seems to be located, by function, in a definite position on a particular chromosome. Half the chromosomes come from each parent: 23 from the ovum and 23 from the sperm. At conception, then, the zygote has all the biological information needed to guide its development into a complete human being.

This single cell develops into a complex organism, with billions of cells specializing in different functions.

Body cells of women and men contain 23 pairs of chromosomes.

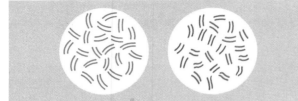

At maturity, each sex cell has only 23 single chromosomes. Through meiosis, a member is taken randomly from each original pair of chromosomes.

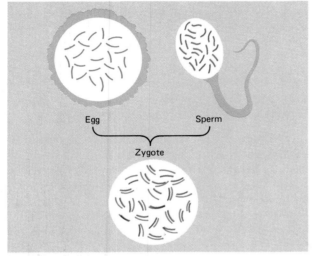

At fertilization, the chromosomes from each parent pair up so that the zygote contains 23 pairs of chromosomes—half from the mother and half from the father.

**FIGURE 2-4**
Hereditary composition of the zygote.

Through a process of cell division called *mitosis,* each cell except the sex cells will have 46 chromosomes identical to those in the original zygote. Thus each has the same genetic information, which remains stable throughout life. Mature gametes, as we have seen, contain only 23 chromosomes each—the result of *meiosis,* a form of cell division in which the number of chromosomes is reduced by half (see Figure 2-4). This special type of division, which implies an almost unlimited variety of combinations of chromosomes and genes in ova and sperm, accounts for the differences in genetic makeup of children of the same parents.

## Patterns of Genetic Transmission

Why does one person have blue eyes and another brown? Why is one person tall and another short? What causes such defects as color blindness? To answer questions like these, we need to see how the genes transmit hereditary characteristics.

### Mendel's laws

Gregor Mendel, an Austrian monk, experimented with plants during the 1860s and laid the foundation for our understanding of inheritance in all living things. He cross-pollinated purebred pea plants that produced only yellow seeds with pea plants that produced only green seeds. All the resulting plants—hybrids—produced yellow seeds. But when he bred those hybrids, 75 percent of their offspring had yellow seeds, and the other 25 percent had green seeds.

Mendel explained his findings by what he called the law of ***dominant inheritance:*** when an organism inherits competing traits (like green and yellow coloring), only one of the traits will be expressed. The expressed trait is called the *dominant* one, and the trait that is not revealed is called *recessive.*

Mendel also tried breeding for two traits at once. Mating pea plants that produced round yellow seeds with plants that produced wrinkled green seeds, he found that color and shape were transmitted independently of each other. In the first generation of hybrids, all the seeds were yellow and round—dominant traits. When the hybrid plants self-fertilized, most of the offspring still produced seeds that were yellow and round; but some (less than half) were either yellow and wrinkled, or green and round; and the smallest number were green and wrinkled. Thus Mendel proved that hereditary traits are transmitted as separate units. He called this principle the law of ***independent segregation.***

### Dominant and recessive inheritance

How do dominant inheritance and recessive inheritance work? Genes that govern alternative expressions of a characteristic (like the color of seeds) are called **alleles.** A plant or animal receives a pair of alleles for a given characteristic, one from each parent. When both alleles are the same, the organism is **homozygous** for the characteristic; when they are different, the organism is **heterozygous.** In a heterozygous situation, the dominant allele is expressed. ***Recessive inheritance*** occurs only when a homozygous organism has received the same recessive allele from each parent; it is then that the recessive trait shows up.

Mendel's original purebred plants were homozygous—each had two alleles for either yellow or green seeds. The crossbred plants were heterozygous, having inherited alleles for both colors. Since yellow is dominant and green recessive, the crossbred plants all had yellow seeds. When those hybrids reproduced, one-fourth of the offspring had two yellow alleles, half had yellow and green, and one-fourth had two green alleles. Because of the law of dominance, three out of

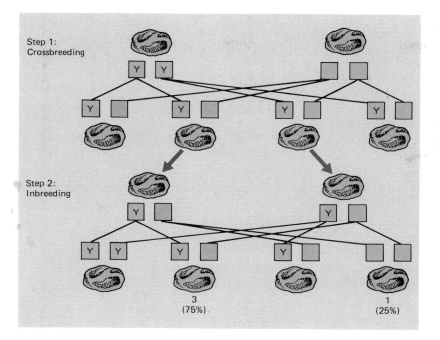

**FIGURE 2-5**
Mendel's experiments with colors of pea seeds. Mendel's experiments with peas established the pattern of dominant inheritance. When the plants are crossbred, the dominant characteristic (yellow seeds) is expressed. When the offspring breed, dominant and recessive characteristics show up in a 3:1 ratio. Because of dominant inheritance, the same observable phenotype (in this case, yellow seeds) can result from two different genotypes (yellow-yellow and yellow-green). However, a phenotype expressing a recessive characteristic (like green seeds) can have only one genotype (green-green).

four plants in the third generation bore yellow seeds and one bore green seeds (see Figure 2-5).

An observable trait (like the color of seeds) is called a **phenotype;** the underlying, invisible genetic pattern that causes certain traits to be expressed is a **genotype.** Organisms with identical phenotypes may have different genotypes, since (because of the principle of dominant inheritance) the same observable trait (like yellow seeds) can result from different genetic patterns.

The difference in genotypes explains why Mendel's first generation of homozygous yellow-seeded plants could have only yellow-seeded offspring, while the heterozygous second generation—just as consistently bearing yellow seeds—could produce some green-seeded offspring when mated with other hybrids of that generation. This difference also explains why recessive traits, like albino skin in humans, may "skip" several generations and then suddenly show up when two people carrying the recessive gene happen to mate. Also, phenotypes may be modified by experience. For example, illness or malnutrition can make a person whose genetic "blueprint" calls for tallness shorter than his genes would dictate.

### Sex-linked inheritance and other forms

Dominance and recessiveness are not always absolute. *Incomplete dominance* is seen, for example, when red and white snapdragons are crossbred and pink flowers result; and in people with blood type AB, who have alleles for types A and B.

In **sex-linked inheritance,** certain recessive genes carried on a sex chromosome—usually the X chromosome—are not counteracted by a gene on the male's Y chromosome and thus are expressed more often in males. Red-green color blindness is a recessive trait that usually shows up only in males.

The genetic picture in humans is far more complex than Mendel imagined. It is hard to find a normal trait that people inherit through simple dominant transmission—other than the ability to curl the tongue lengthwise! Some genes, like those for blood types A, B, and O, exist in three or more alternative forms known as **multiple alleles.** Most characteristics—like height, weight, and intelligence—are probably affected by many genes as well as environmental factors, through a pattern called **multifactorial inheritance.**

Scientists have recently discovered *genetic imprinting,* a process that contradicts one aspect of Mendel's theory—that genes from each parent behave the same way. Instead, some genes can be imprinted, or chemically altered, by either the mother or the father, and an imprinted gene will dominate one that has not been imprinted. For example, people who inherit the gene for Huntington's disease (a progressive degeneration of the nervous system) from their fathers seem to develop it more severely and earlier than those who inherit the gene from their mothers (Merz, 1989).

It is in genetic defects and diseases (Table 2-1) that we see most clearly the operation of dominant, recessive, and sex-linked transmission in humans.

**TABLE 2-1**
BIRTH DEFECTS

| Problem | Effects |
|---|---|
| Alpha$_1$ antitrypsin deficiency | Enzyme deficiency that can lead to cirrhosis of the liver in early infancy and pulmonary emphysema and degenerative lung disease in middle age. |
| Alpha thalassemia | Severe anemia that reduces ability of the blood to carry oxygen. Nearly all affected infants are stillborn or die soon after birth. |
| Beta thalessemia (Cooley's anemia) | Severe anemia resulting in weakness, fatigue, and frequent illness. Usually fatal in adolescence or young adulthood. |
| Cystic fibrosis | Body makes too much mucus, which collects in the lungs and digestive tract. Children do not grow normally and usually do not live beyond age 30, although some live longer. |
| Down syndrome | Minor to severe mental retardation caused by an extra 21st chromosome. |
| Duchenne's muscular dystrophy | Fatal disease found only in males, marked by muscle weakness. Minor mental retardation is common. Respiratory failure and death usually occur in young adulthood. |
| Fragile X syndrome | Minor to severe mental retardation. Symptoms, which are more severe in males, include delayed speech and motor development, speech impairments, and hyperactivity. Considered one of the main causes of autism. |
| Hemophilia | Excessive bleeding affecting only males. In its most severe form, can lead to crippling arthritis in adulthood. |
| Neural tube defects<br>Anencephaly<br><br>Spina bifida | Absence of brain tissue. Infants are stillborn or die soon after birth.<br>Incompletely closed spinal canal, resulting in muscle weakness or paralysis and loss of bladder and bowel control. Often accompanied by hydrocephalus, an accumulation of spinal fluid in the brain, which can lead to mental retardation. |

*Source:* Adapted from Fahey, 1988, pp. 68–69.

| Who Is at Risk | Tests and Their Accuracy | What Can Be Done |
|---|---|---|
| 1 in 1000 Caucasians | Amniocentesis, CVS (chorionic villus sampling). Accuracy varies, but can sometimes predict severity. | No treatment |
| Primarily families of Malaysian, African, and southeast Asian descent | Amniocentesis, CVS. Accuracy varies; more accurate if other family members tested for gene. | Frequent blood transfusions |
| Primarily families of Mediterranean descent | Amniocentesis, CVS; 95% accurate. | Frequent blood transfusions |
| 1 in 2000 Caucasians | Amniocentesis, CVS. Accuracy varies; more accurate if other family members tested for gene. | Daily physical therapy to loosen mucus Antibiotics for lung infections; enzymes to improve digestion |
| 1 in 350 women over age 35; 1 in 800, all women | Amniocentesis, CVS; nearly 100% accurate. | No treatment, although programs of intellectual stimulation are effective |
| 1 in 7000 male births | Amniocentesis, CVS; 95% accurate. | No treatment |
| 1 in 1200 male births; 1 in 2000 female births | Amniocentesis, CVS; 95% accurate. | No treatment |
| 1 in 10,000 families with a history of hemophilia | Amniocentesis, CVS; 95% accurate. | Frequent transfusions of blood with clotting factors |
| 1 in 1000 | Ultrasound, amniocentesis; 100% accurate. | No treatment |
| 1 in 1000 | Ultrasound, amniocentesis. Test works only if the spinal cord is leaking fluid into the uterus or is exposed and visible during ultrasound. | Surgery to close spinal canal prevents further injury; shunt placed in brain drains excess fluid and prevents mental retardation |

(Continued)

### Defects transmitted by recessive inheritance

Diseases transmitted by recessive genes are often fatal in infancy. An example is Tay-Sachs disease, a degenerative disease of the central nervous system that occurs mainly among Jews of eastern European ancestry.

Some apparently healthy people act as carriers of such diseases and defects. Recessive traits show up only if a child has received the same recessive gene from each parent. When only one parent—for instance, the father—has the faulty recessive gene, none of the children will show the defect. Each child, though, will have a 50-50 chance of being a carrier like the father and of passing the recessive gene on to his or her own children. Sometimes both parents carry the faulty gene, and though both may be unaffected, they are capable of passing it on to their children. In such cases, a child has a 25 percent chance of a birth defect and a 50 percent chance of being a carrier (see Figure 2-7).

Inbreeding—marriage of close relatives—used to be common among the European upper classes. Today, such marriages are usually prohibited by law, to lower the risk of children's inheriting a disease passed on through recessive genes that both parents may have inherited from a common ancestor.

### Defects transmitted by sex-linked inheritance

Hemophilia, a blood-clotting disorder, used to be called the "royal disease," because it was prevalent among the highly inbred ruling families of Europe. Hemophilia is a sex-linked condition transmitted by a recessive gene.

Because they are carried on one of the X chromosomes of an unaffected mother, sex-linked recessive traits almost always show up only in male children, who do not have a countermanding dominant trait on the Y chromosome.

The sons of a normal man and a woman with one abnormal gene will have a 50 percent chance of inheriting the abnormal X chromosome and thus inheriting the disorder, and a 50 percent chance of inheriting the mother's normal X chromosome and being unaffected. Daughters will have a 50 percent chance of being carriers. (See Figure 2-8 on the opposite page.) An affected father can never pass on such a gene to his sons, since he contributes a Y chromosome to them; but he can pass the gene on to his daughters. The daughters can become carriers or, if the mother is a carrier and passes on the recessive gene, they may inherit the disease themselves.

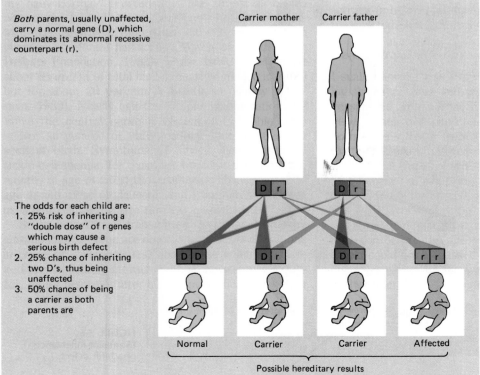

*Both* parents, usually unaffected, carry a normal gene (D), which dominates its abnormal recessive counterpart (r).

Carrier mother    Carrier father

The odds for each child are:
1. 25% risk of inheriting a "double dose" of r genes which may cause a serious birth defect
2. 25% chance of inheriting two D's, thus being unaffected
3. 50% chance of being a carrier as both parents are

Normal    Carrier    Carrier    Affected

Possible hereditary results

FIGURE 2-7
Recessive inheritance of a birth defect.

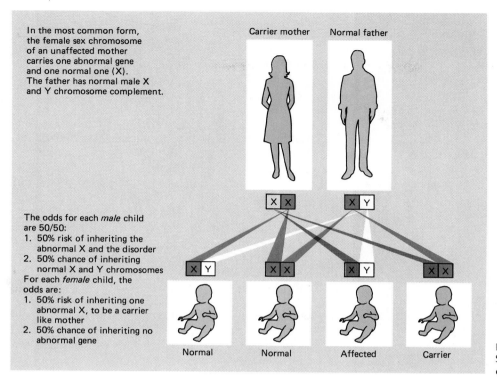

In the most common form, the female sex chromosome of an unaffected mother carries one abnormal gene and one normal one (X). The father has normal male X and Y chromosome complement.

Carrier mother    Normal father

The odds for each *male* child are 50/50:
1. 50% risk of inheriting the abnormal X and the disorder
2. 50% chance of inheriting normal X and Y chromosomes

For each *female* child, the odds are:
1. 50% risk of inheriting one abnormal X, to be a carrier like mother
2. 50% chance of inheriting no abnormal gene

Normal    Normal    Affected    Carrier

FIGURE 2-8
Sex-linked inheritance of a birth defect.

## Chromosomal abnormalities

Usually, chromosomal development proceeds normally, but when something does go wrong, serious abnormalities may develop. Some chromosomal defects are inherited; others result from accidents that occur during development. Accidental abnormalities are not likely to recur in the same family.

Some relatively rare chromosomal disorders are caused by either a missing (O) or an extra sex chromosome (either X or Y). Examples are Klinefelter's syndrome (with the pattern XXY), Turner's syndrome (with the pattern XO, and thus missing a second sex chromosome), and the XYY and XXX syndromes. The most obvious effects are sexually related characteristics (underdevelopment, sterility, or secondary sex characteristics of the other sex). Children with these disorders, while not usually seriously retarded, often have reading problems and general learning disabilities ("Long-term outlook," 1982).

**Down syndrome** is the most common chromosomal disorder. Its most obvious symptom is a downward-sloping skin fold at the inner corners of the eyes. Other signs are a small head, a flat nose, a protruding tongue, mild to severe mental and motor retardation, and defective heart, eyes, and ears. Down syndrome is caused by an extra twenty-first chromosome or the translocation of part of the twenty-first chromosome onto another chromosome.

About 1 in every 800 babies born alive has Down syndrome. The risk is greatest with older parents: the chances rise from 1 such birth in 2000 among 25-year-old mothers to 1 in 40 for women over 45. The risk also rises with the father's age, especially among men over 50 (Abroms & Bennett, 1981).

More than 90 percent of cases of Down syndrome are caused by an accident, a mistake in chromosome distribution during development of the ovum, sperm, or zygote (D. W. Smith & Wilson, 1973). But among mothers under age 35, the disorder is more likely to have a hereditary cause. A clue to its genetic basis is the recent discovery of a gene on chromosome 21; this gene expresses a brain protein that seems to lead to Down syndrome (Allore et al., 1988).

Many children with Down syndrome can be taught skills with which they can support themselves as adults, and these children's progress has caused educators to revise their expectations upward (Hayden & Haring, 1976). Because of medical advances, more than 70 percent of people with the syndrome live at least until age 30 (Baird & Sadovnick, 1987). Support groups help many parents learn about the condition and deal with it.

This lively little girl has Down syndrome. Although her intellectual potential is limited, loving care and patient teaching are likely to help her achieve much more than was once thought possible for such children.

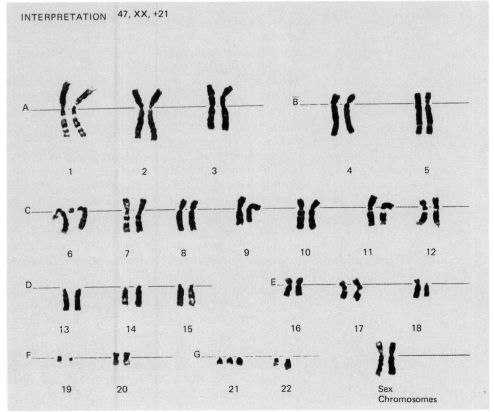

INTERPRETATION    47, XX, +21

**FIGURE 2-9**
Karyotype. Chromosomes of a child with Down syndrome, showing three chromosomes on number 21. (In the normal pattern, there are two chromosomes on number 21.) Since pair 23 consists of two X's, we know that this is the karyotype of a girl. (*Source:* Vanderbilt University and March of Dimes.)

## Genetic Counseling

*Genetic counseling* helps couples who believe that they may be at high risk of bearing a child with a birth defect. People who have already borne one handicapped child, who have a family history of hereditary illness, or who suffer from conditions known or suspected to be inherited can get information about their likelihood of producing affected children.

After giving a thorough family history, both parents and any children in the family are examined physically. They may also take tests that identify carriers of genetic defects. One test involves laboratory investigations of blood, skin, urine, or fingerprints. Chromosomes prepared from body tissue are analyzed and photographed. Enlarged photographs of the chromosomes are then cut out and arranged according to size and structure on a chart called a *karyotype* to demonstrate any chromosomal abnormalities (see Figure 2-9 on the opposite page).

On the basis of such tests, the genetic counselor calculates the mathematical odds for having an affected child but does not advise a couple on whether to take the risk. Rather, the counselor helps couples understand the implications of particular diseases and defects and makes them aware of what they can do. Sometimes counseling can show that a risk is either very slight or nonexistent. If a risk is high, one partner may choose to be sterilized or the couple may consider adoption or artifical insemination by donor (see Chapter 13). If a disorder is not extremely disabling or is treatable, a couple may take a chance. (An analogous type of help for prospective parents is assessment of fetal development and well-being before birth; see Box 2-1 on pages 54–55.)

Geneticists hope that in the future they will be able to do much more to help parents. Many advances may come from current progress in locating defective genes on chromosomes. Investigators use complex instruments to identify and locate specific genes; so far they have mapped more than 1500 human genes. They determine what proteins are made by these genes and detect the presence or absence of proteins associated with particular disorders. Such knowledge can lead to new predictive tests, both before and after birth; to drugs to prevent or treat disease; and to "gene therapy"—technology for repairing abnormal genes.

A new treatment for one rare genetic disease involves implanting normal genes into the blood cells of affected people to alter defective genetic instructions that would eventually destroy their immune system (Angier, 1990). If this treatment proves successful, it might point the way to repairing thousands of hereditary disorders.

## HOW DO HEREDITY AND ENVIRONMENT INTERACT?

From what you have read so far, you might have the impression that almost everything about human beings—how we look, how our minds work, and how we feel—is determined at conception. Heredity, of course, is only part of the story. Environment also plays a critical role in making us what we are and what we will become.

### "Nature versus Nurture": Hereditary and Environmental Factors

Which has more effect—nature or nurture, heredity or environment?

People have asked this question for years, and the answer differs for different traits. Some physical characteristics, like eye color and blood type, are clearly inherited. But more complex traits having to do with health, intelligence, and personality are subject to an interplay of both hereditary and environmental forces. (For example, the different-shaded bands in Figure 2-10, below, show how these two forces, in varying degrees, can cause or contribute to mental retardation.) How much is inherited? How much is environmentally influenced?

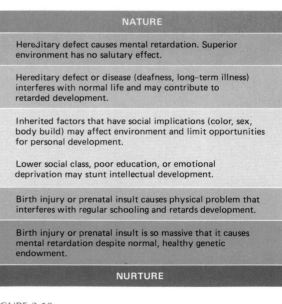

| NATURE |
|---|
| Hereditary defect causes mental retardation. Superior environment has no salutary effect. |
| Hereditary defect or disease (deafness, long-term illness) interferes with normal life and may contribute to retarded development. |
| Inherited factors that have social implications (color, sex, body build) may affect environment and limit opportunities for personal development. |
| Lower social class, poor education, or emotional deprivation may stunt intellectual development. |
| Birth injury or prenatal insult causes physical problem that interferes with regular schooling and retards development. |
| Birth injury or prenatal insult is so massive that it causes mental retardation despite normal, healthy genetic endowment. |
| NURTURE |

**FIGURE 2-10**
How nature and nurture can contribute to intellectual retardation. As colors can be mixed to different shades and intensities, so heredity and environment interact to varying degrees to shape a trait like intellectual retardation. (*Source:* Adapted from Anastasi, 1958.)

BOX 2–1    PRACTICALLY SPEAKING

# PRENATAL ASSESSMENT

Not long ago, almost the only decision parents had to make about their babies before birth was the decision to conceive; most of what happened in the intervening 9 months was beyond their control. But we now have an array of new tools to assess fetal development and well-being.

## AMNIOCENTESIS

In *amniocentesis,* a sample of the fluid in the amniotic sac is withdrawn and analyzed to detect the presence of various genetic defects. This fluid, in which the fetus floats in the uterus, contains fetal cells. The procedure can be done in the fifteenth or sixteenth week of pregnancy; it takes about 2 weeks to get the results. Amniocentesis can also reveal the sex of the fetus, which may be crucial in the case of a sex-linked disorder like hemophilia.

Amniocentesis is generally recommended for pregnant women if they are at least 35 years old, if they and their partners are both known carriers of Tay-Sachs disease or sickle-cell disease, or if they or their partners have a family history of such conditions as Down syndrome, spina bifida, Rh disease, or muscular dystrophy. One analysis of 3000 women who had the procedure indicated that it was "safe, highly reliable and extremely accurate" (Golbus et al., 1979, p. 157). But another study of 4600 women found a slightly higher risk of miscarriage in women who had the procedure (Tabor et al., 1986).

## CHORIONIC VILLUS SAMPLING

*Chorionic villus sampling (CVS)* consists of taking tissue from the end of one or more villi—hairlike projections of the membrane around the embryo, which are made up of fetal cells. These cells are then tested for the presence of various conditions. This procedure can be performed earlier than amniocentesis (in the first trimester), and it yields results sooner (within about a week). CVS has a higher risk of procedural failure and loss of the fetus than amniocentesis (Rhoads et al., 1989); and these and other problems are raising some doubts about its use (E. Rosenthal, 1991).

## MATERNAL BLOOD TESTS

Blood taken from the mother between the fourteenth and twentieth weeks of pregnancy can be tested for the amount of alpha fetoprotein (AFP) it contains. This *maternal blood test* is appropriate for women at risk of bearing children with defects in the formation of the brain or spinal cord (like anencephaly or spina bifida), which may be detected by high AFP levels. Low AFP levels may suggest Down syndrome (DiMaio, Baumgarten, Greenstein, Saal, & Mahoney, 1987). To confirm or refute the presence of suspected conditions, ultrasound or amniocentesis, or both, may be performed.

Blood tests can also identify carriers of sickle-cell disease (a blood disorder seen mostly in black people), Tay-Sachs disease, and thalassemia (a blood disorder that affects people of Mediterranean origin). And they can reveal the sex of a fetus, which can be of help with sex-linked disorders (Lo et al., 1989).

## ULTRASOUND

Some parents see their baby for the first time in a *sonogram,* a picture of the uterus, fetus, and placenta that is created by high-frequency sound waves directed into the woman's abdomen. The technique of *ultrasound* provides the clearest images yet obtained of a fetus in the womb, with little or no discomfort to the woman. Ultrasound is used to measure a baby's head size, to judge gestational age, to detect multiple pregnancies, to evaluate uterine abnormalities, to detect major structural abnormalities in the fetus, and to determine whether a fetus has died, as well as to guide other procedures like amniocentesis. Although some obstetricians administer ultrasound routinely, it has been in use for only a short time, and so its long-term effects are as yet unknown (Kleinman, Cooke, Machlin, & Kessel, 1983). Because animal studies have suggested possible harmful effects, the National Institutes of Health (1984b) recommend ultrasound only for a specific medical reason.

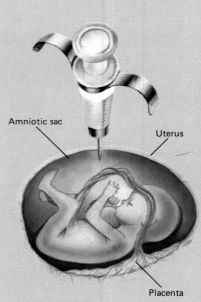

Amniotic sac

Uterus

Placenta

Amniocentesis. A sample of amniotic fluid can be withdrawn (by inserting a needle through the mother's abdominal wall) and analyzed for the presence of several birth defects. Analysis of the sampled fluid generally takes 2 to 4 weeks. (*Source*: F. Fuchs, 1980.)

## BOX 2–1 (CONTINUED)

This 6-month-old baby is shown next to an ultrasound picture taken during his fourth month of gestation. Ultrasound is a popular diagnostic tool that presents an immediate image of the fetus in the womb.

### UMBILICAL CORD ASSESSMENT

By threading a needle into tiny blood vessels of the umbilical cord under the guidance of ultrasound, doctors can take samples of a fetus's blood. They can then get a blood count, examine liver function, and assess various other body functions. This procedure can test for infection, anemia, certain metabolic disorders and immunodeficiencies, and heart failure, and it seems to offer promise for identifying still other conditions. The technique is associated with such occasional problems as bleeding from the umbilical cord, early labor, and—most serious—infection (Chervenak, Isaacson, & Mahoney, 1986; Kolata, 1988).

These techniques for prenatal diagnosis of birth defects, coupled with the legalization of induced abortion, have encouraged many couples with troubling medical histories to take a chance on conception. For example, a couple who know that they both carry a recessive gene for a disorder may conceive and then take tests to learn whether the fetus has the condition. They may be reassured that their baby will be normal, or, if the fetus is affected, they may terminate the pregnancy or plan for the special needs of a handicapped child.

These questions matter because (among other reasons) they affect the way people act toward children. For example, if it is possible to enhance a baby's intelligence through environmental factors, we can try to make the environment as favorable as possible. On the other hand, if a child's activity level is set mainly by heredity, parents and teachers need to have realistic expectations. And as we have seen, knowing which birth defects are hereditary makes genetic counseling possible.

The answer to the question "Nature or nurture?" is rarely "either-or." Which of the two has the greater influence may depend on many factors.

### Hereditary and environmental influences on traits

Some traits governed by genes (like eye color) do not seem to be affected by the environment or by a person's own behavior. But many traits are subject to variation, within the limits set by the genes. Genetic influences are not necessarily all-powerful, then; they may set up a range of possible reactions among people living in a particular range of environmental conditions. Also, genes are not expressed directly as behavior; thus they may be expressed differently in different environments. How our genetic inheritance shows itself depends to a considerable extent on our specific environment.

For example, genes have a strong effect on weight and height, but actual body size can depend on what a person does. A genetic tendency for "fatness" does not make a person eat a lot, but someone who does take in more calories than his or her body needs will be fatter than another person with a similar genetic tendency who eats less. In societies where nutrition improves, an entire generation of people may tower over their parents. The children have inherited their parents' genes, but within the range those genes allow, the second generation has responded to its healthier world. And as we saw in discussing phenotypes, illness or malnutrition may stunt growth.

## *Maturation*

One reason it is so hard to untangle the relative effects of heredity and environment is that human beings keep changing throughout life, and some of these changes seem to be caused by the environment whereas others are clearly programmed by the genes. (For example, crawling, walking, and running develop in that order at certain approximate ages.) *Maturation* is the unfolding of a biologically determined, age-related sequence of behavior patterns. Behaviors that depend largely on maturation generally appear when the organism is ready—not before, and rarely afterward.

Yet environmental forces can affect this hereditary timetable, particularly in extreme cases like long-term deprivation. This was seen in infants in Iranian orphanages who received little attention and had no exercise. These babies did not sit up or walk until quite late, compared with well-cared-for Iranian children (Dennis, 1960). But even under these extreme conditions, maturation did occur, at a slowed pace.

The balance between nature and nurture seems most complex in the development of intellect and personality. Consider language. The genetic timetable dictates that before children can talk, they have to reach a certain level of neurological and muscular maturation. No 6-month-old could speak this sentence, no matter how enriched his or her home life might be. Yet environment plays a large part in language development. If parents encourage babies' first sounds by talking back to them, children will start to speak earlier than they would if their early vocalizing had been ignored. Heredity, then, draws the blueprint for development, but environment affects the pace at which "construction" proceeds and even the specific form of the structure.

## Studying the Relative Effects of Heredity and Environment

Researchers use a number of methods to assess the relative influences of heredity and environment on various traits. These include:

- *Selective breeding of animals*. If animals can be bred for a certain characteristic (like an ability to run mazes or a tendency to become obese), we conclude that the trait is at least partly hereditary. In some cases, we can generalize the findings to human beings.
- *Studies of twins*. If a trait is basically hereditary, identical twins, who have the same genetic legacy, should be more *concordant* (similar) for that trait than fraternal twins, who are no more alike genetically than any siblings. Identical twins who were

Identical twins separated at birth are sought after by researchers who want to determine the impact of genes on personality. These twins, adopted by different families and not reunited till age 31, both became firefighters. Was this coincidence or heredity?

raised in different homes are valuable as subjects of research attempting to distinguish hereditary and environmental factors. But such people are hard to find, and often their environments turn out to be similar.
- *Consanguinity studies*. By examining as many blood relatives as possible in one family, we can discover the degree to which they share certain traits and whether the closeness of the relation affects the degree of similarity. This is also called the *pedigree* method.
- *Adoption studies*. When adopted children are more like their biological parents and siblings, we see the influence of heredity; when they resemble their adoptive families more, we see the influence of environment.
- *Prenatal studies*. By investigating relationships between conditions in offspring and their mothers' experiences during pregnancy, we can often pinpoint the cause of a specific condition.
- *Comparisons of actual histories*. By interviewing parents about their child-rearing practices (if we discount the effects of faulty and distorted memories) and by comparing other life-history factors, researchers can sometimes isolate specific environmental influences on specific characteristics.
- *Manipulating the environment*. By changing diet, opportunities for exercise, intellectual enrichment, and sensory stimulation in one group of animals or people and then comparing this group with a control group, we can draw conclusions about the effects of such environmental differences.

Our ability to manipulate either the heredity or the environment of human beings is, of course, limited by both ethical and practical considerations. We cannot, for example, mate human beings for selective characteristics, and we would not separate identical twins, make adoption placements, institutionalize children, or prescribe questionable drugs to pregnant women for experimental purposes. Therefore we often have to rely on animal studies or after-the-fact observations of events that have occurred naturally.

## Some Characteristics Influenced by Heredity and Environment

### *Physical and physiological traits*

When Robert Shafran went away to college, students he had never met greeted him like an old friend and called him "Eddy." After seeing a snapshot of Eddy Galland, who had attended the same school the year before, Robert said, "What I saw was a photograph of myself." When a third look-alike turned up, the youths learned that they were identical triplets who had been separated at birth (Battelle, 1981).

The carbon-copy physical appearance of identical twins is well known. They are also more concordant than fraternal twins in other traits, such as blood pressure; rates of breathing, perspiration, and pulse; height and weight (Jost & Sontag, 1944) and age of first menstruation (Petri, 1934).

Obesity is strongly influenced by heredity. It is twice as likely that both identical twins will be overweight as that both fraternal twins will be (Stunkard, Harris, Pedersen, & McClearn, 1990). This does not mean that environment has no effect; it means that people genetically at risk of obesity must work harder not to get fat.

Even our days on earth may be numbered by our genes, since senescence (the process of growing old) and death occur at more similar ages for identical twins than for fraternal twins (Jarvik, Kallmann, & Klaber, 1957). In one study, adopted children (born in the 1920s) whose biological parents died before age 50 were twice as likely to have died young as adopted children whose biological parents were alive at 50 (T. Sorensen, Nielsen, Andersen, & Teasdale, 1988).

### *Intelligence*

Researchers in behavioral genetics have focused more on intelligence than on all other characteristics combined, generally using IQ scores as its measure. What have they found? Heredity seems to exert a major influence on intelligence, more clearly so with age (Plomin, 1989).

Since genes do not direct specific behaviors, how do they affect intellectual performance? Apparently, many genes—each with its own small effect—combine to create an overall influence on intelligence. Genes establish a range of possible reactions to a range of possible experiences (Weinberg, 1989).

There is *no* evidence that differences in IQ scores between cultural, ethnic, or racial groups are due to hereditary factors. But many studies point to a strong genetic influence on differences between individuals *within a group*. About 50 percent of the difference in intelligence between persons in a group is believed to be genetically determined, with the remaining variation due to each person's experiences (Weinberg, 1989). This has clear implications for social policy, since the half of the variance that is environmentally determined is responsive to a number of strategies that help children with low IQ scores do better both academically and socially. Changes in environment seem to be able to affect IQ by a range of 20 to 25 points (Weinberg, 1989).

Evidence for the role of heredity in intelligence has emerged from several adoption and twin studies. Adopted children's IQs have been compared with those of their adoptive siblings and parents, and with either the IQs or the educational levels of their biological mothers (from whom they had been separated since the first week of life). Resemblances have been consistently higher to the biological mothers than to the family members children have lived with. (J. Horn, 1983; Scarr & Weinberg, 1983).

Also, heredity seems to become more important as people grow older. In the adoption studies, young siblings scored similarly, whether related by blood or adoption; but adolescents' scores had zero correlation with those of their adoptive siblings. Furthermore, the adolescents' IQs correlated more highly with their biological mothers' levels of schooling than with their adoptive parents' IQs. Scarr and Weinberg (1983) concluded that family environment is more important for younger children, but that older adolescents find their niches in life on the basis of inborn abilities and interests.

Longitudinal studies have also found the influence of heredity on intelligence increasing with age. Among 500 pairs of twins, identical twins became more and more alike in IQ from infancy to adolescence, while fraternal twins became less alike. And individual children followed their own distinct patterns of "spurts and lags" in mental development. The home environment had some impact, but genetic factors had more (Plomin, Pedersen, McClearn, Nesselroade, & Bergeman, 1988). An adoption study found similar effects into late adulthood (R. S. Wilson, 1983).

We have to remember, however, that genetics accounts only in part for variations in intelligence; changing the environment can have considerable impact. Black children adopted into upper middle-class white families performed better than average on IQ and school achievement tests and better than black and interracial children not raised in the culture assessed by the tests (i.e., the white majority culture) (Scarr & Weinberg, 1976). The fact that much of intelligence seems to be inherited does not mean that it cannot be changed, given a better (or worse) environment.

### Personality

**Personality** is a person's overall pattern of character, behavioral, temperamental, emotional, and mental traits. Something so complicated cannot be ascribed to any one major influence, either hereditary or environmental. But specific aspects of personality appear to be inherited, at least in part.

In 1956, two psychiatrists and a pediatrician (A. Thomas & Chess, 1984; A. Thomas, Chess, & Birch, 1968) launched the New York Longitudinal Study

(NYLS), following 133 children from infancy into adulthood. These researchers concluded that **temperament,** or a person's basic style of approaching and reacting to situations, seems to be inborn. They looked at how active children were; how regular they were in hunger, sleep, and bowel habits; how readily they accepted new people and situations; how they adapted to changes in routine; how sensitive they were to noise, bright lights, and other sensory stimuli; whether they tended to be cheerful or sad; how intensely they responded; and whether they persisted at tasks or were easily distracted. The children varied enormously in all these characteristics, almost from birth, and the variances tended to continue. But many children changed their behavioral style, apparently reacting to special experiences or parental handling (see Chapter 5).

Other researchers have found evidence for genetic influence on a wide range of personality characteristics (see Figure 2-11). These include extroversion and introversion, emotionality, and activity (Vandenberg, 1967); depression, psychopathic behaviors, and social introversion (Gottesman, 1962; Inouye, 1965); neuroticism (Eysenck & Prell, 1951; Slater, 1953); shyness

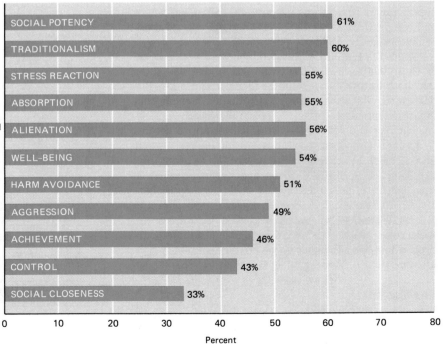

**FIGURE 2-11**
Roots of personality: degree to which 11 personality traits are estimated to be inherited, on the basis of tests with twins. Traits were measured by the Multidimensional Personality Questionnaire, developed by Auke Tellegren at the University of Minnesota. (*Source:* Tellegren et al., 1988.)

According to findings of longitudinal research, the basically cheerful mood of a baby like 10-month-old Maika seems to be the result of inborn temperament. However, life experiences can influence, for good or ill, the way a person approaches life.

(Daniels & Plomin, 1985; Kagan, 1989—see Box 2-2 on page 60); fears (R. J. Rose & Ditto, 1983); and leadership ability (Tellegren et al., 1988). Hyperactivity, sleepwalking, bed-wetting, nail biting, and car sickness (Bakwin, 1970, 1971a, 1971b, 1971c, 1971d) also seem to have a genetic base.

## Some Disorders Influenced by Heredity and Environment

### Alcoholism

Alcoholics may be largely born, not made. There is considerable evidence that alcoholism runs in families and that a heightened risk results from the interaction of genetic and environmental factors (Plomin, 1989). Identical twins are significantly more concordant for alcoholism than fraternal twins. Sons of alcoholic men are 4 times as likely as sons of nonalcoholic men to develop alcoholism themselves, even when they are adopted at birth, and regardless of whether their adoptive parents are alcoholic. Children do not seem to be at unusual risk if their adoptive parents are alcoholic but their biological parents are not (Schuckit, 1985, 1987).

No one is predestined to develop alcoholism. But since genetic factors seem to make some people more vulnerable, children of alcoholic parents should be warned that they may not be able to handle liquor the way their peers do.

### Schizophrenia

**Schizophrenia** is a group of mental disorders marked by a loss of contact with reality and by such symptoms as hallucinations, delusions, and other thought disorders. Many studies suggest that it has a strong genetic element. The biological children of women with schizophrenia are more likely than people in the general population to suffer from the disorder themselves; identical twins are more likely than fraternal twins to be concordant for it; and the closer a person's biological relation to someone with schizophrenia, the more likely the person is to develop it (Plomin & Rende, 1991).

Although there is, then, strong evidence of biological transmission of schizophrenia, we have to ask why not all identical twins are concordant for this disorder. One answer may be that it is not the illness itself that is transmitted, but a predisposition toward it. If certain environmental stresses occur in the life of someone who is genetically predisposed, that person may develop schizophrenia.

### Infantile autism

**Infantile autism** is a rare developmental disorder involving an inability to communicate with or respond to other people. It develops within the first 2½ years of life, sometimes as early as the fourth month, when a baby may lie in the crib, apathetic and oblivious to other people. The child does not cuddle; does not make eye contact with caregivers; either treats adults as interchangeable or clings mechanically to one person; and may never learn to speak but may be able to sing a wide repertory of songs. Boys are 3 times more likely than girls to be afflicted.

Many autistic children are retarded; only 30 percent have an IQ of 70 or more. They often, however, do well on tasks of manipulative or visual-spatial skill, and may perform unusual mental feats (like memorizing entire train schedules). They may scream when their place at the table is changed, insist on always carrying a particular object (like a rubber band), clap their hands constantly or repeat some other behavior, or be fascinated by moving objects—staring for hours, for example, at an electric fan.

Although "cold and unresponsive" parents have been blamed for causing autism, it is now recognized as

## BOX 2–2    THINKING CRITICALLY

# SHYNESS

At age 4, Jason went with his parents to an office Christmas party. For the first hour he didn't say a word; for the next hour he clung to his mother's side as he stared wide-eyed at the other children, the strange adults, and the array of toys. By the time he felt comfortable enough to venture away from her, the party was over.

Vicky, also 4, was at the same party. She had barely burst into the room when she ran up to the Christmas tree, grabbed the nearest brightly wrapped package, asked a strange man standing nearby if he could help her open it, and hardly gave her parents a backward glance.

Which of these two children do you think will have an easier time in our society?

Classical psychoanalytic thought has held for years that such differences between children are created by early experience—perhaps Jason is wary of the world because he has not learned to trust, while Vicky's experiences have been more positive. A major body of recent research, however, strongly suggests that shyness and boldness are inborn characteristics, which are related to various physiological functions and which tend to stay with people throughout life. These traits do not seem related to sex or socioeconomic class (Plomin, 1989).

Jerome Kagan, a professor of psychology at Harvard University, has led a series of longitudinal studies of some 400 children who were followed for over 5 years, starting at just under 2 years of age (Garcia-Coll, Kagan, & Reznick, 1984; Kagan, 1989; Kagan, Reznick, Clarke, Snidman, & Garcia-Coll, 1984; Reznick et al., 1986). Shyness, or what these researchers call "inhibition to the unfamiliar," was marked in about 10

Shyness seems to be inborn, to be related to various physiological functions, and to persist into adulthood. Should parents try to help a shy child, like this boy, become more outgoing; or should they try to help the child accept his or her personality as it is? Or should they try to do both?

to 15 percent of the children, first showing up at 21 months of age and persisting in most cases at 7½ years. The opposite trait, "boldness," or comfort in strange situations, was also especially strong in about 10 to 15 percent. Most of the children fell between the two extremes.

Both the genetic influence and the stability of the trait were strongest for the children at either extreme, whose personality characteristics were associated with various physiological signs that may give clues to the heritability of the traits. When asked to solve problems or learn new information, the very shy children had higher and less variable heart rates than the middle-range and bolder children, and the pupils of the shy children's

eyes dilated more. The shy children seemed to feel more anxious in situations that the other youngsters did not find particularly stressful.

A genetic factor in shyness also showed up in another study. Two-year-olds who had been adopted soon after birth closely resembled their biological mothers in terms of shyness. However, these babies also resembled their adoptive mothers, showing an environmental influence as well (Daniels & Plomin, 1985). The parents of shy babies tended to have less active social lives, exposing neither themselves nor their babies to new social situations. This was true for the adoptive parents, and even more so for biological parents raising their own children.

Thus, there is an intertwining of factors. While a *tendency* toward shyness may be inherited, some shy children become more outgoing and spontaneous, apparently in response to parents' efforts to help them become more comfortable with new people and situations.

In some societies children are encouraged to stay close to their parents, not to speak, and to hold back in the presence of strangers. Our society, however, values boldness. Therefore, parents are often advised to help shy children become more outgoing, by protecting them from as much stress as possible, by teaching them coping skills for stressful situations, and by bringing other children into the home. "Parents need to push their children—gently and not too much—into doing the things they fear" (Kagan, in J. Asher, 1987). In the long run, though, would it perhaps be better if society itself changed to place more value on all types of personalities? If so, how could this be done?

a biological disorder of the nervous system, sometimes associated with epilepsy (*Diagnostic and Statistical Manual of Mental Disorders,* 3d ed., rev., DSM III-R, 1987). New research has revealed that the brain of an autistic person is not fully developed and that the interference with development seems to occur either during early prenatal life or during the first or second year after birth (Courchesne, Yeung-Courchesne, Press, Hesselink, & Jernigan, 1988). Since concordance between identical twins is 96 percent, compared with 23 percent for fraternal twins, autism is probably inherited, perhaps through a recessive gene, and the impact of the environment is minimal (Ritvo, Freeman, Mason-Brothers, Mo, & Ritvo, 1985).

Some autistic children have been helped to develop social and language skills through operant conditioning techniques (McDaniel, 1986), and the drug fenfluramine reduces symptoms in some children (DuVerglas, Banks, & Guyer, 1988). Overall, 1 in 6 adjust adequately and are able to do some kind of work as adults, 1 in 6 make a fair adjustment, and 4 in 6 remain severely incapacitated for life (Geller, Ritvo, Freeman, & Yuwiler, 1982). Fortunately, the disorder is very rare (about 3 cases per 10,000 people).

### Depression

The serious clinical syndrome called **depression** is different from normal temporary sadness. It is an affective disorder (a disorder of mood) in which a person feels unhappy and often has trouble eating, sleeping, or concentrating. It is not a single disease, but rather one that seems to involve a variety of causes, mechanisms, and symptoms. Some 6 percent of American adults are depressed in any 6-month period (J. K. Myers et al., 1984). Children—even infants—may also become depressed (see Chapter 9).

Since 1950, studies in the United States, Sweden, Germany, Canada, and New Zealand have shown increasing rates of depression (Klerman & Weissman, 1989). Depression affects more people and strikes earlier, in adolescence and young adulthood. Women are 2 to 3 times as likely as men to be depressed, but this imbalance is narrowing as more young men are affected. These trends have not, however, shown up in studies of Koreans, Puerto Ricans, or Mexican Americans.

Clearly, depression has a strong genetic basis. It is 2 to 3 times higher in close relatives of depressed people than in the general population (Klerman & Weissman, 1989). Identical twins have a 70 percent concordance rate, while fraternal twins, other siblings, and parents and children have only a 15 percent concordance rate (USDHHS, 1981b).

However, heredity cannot be the entire story, or we would not have seen significantly higher rates of depression over the past 40 years—genes are not likely to change in such a short time. Apparently, many forms of depression result from interaction between an inherited biochemical sensitivity and life stresses. Some stresses are physical, like bodily illness, changes in the chemistry of the central nervous system, and effects of various drugs. Others, however, are psychological, including changes in family stucture, shifts in male and female roles, increasing urbanization, and greater geographic mobility that disrupts networks of relationships (Klerman & Weissman, 1989). Because of hereditary factors, different people respond to the same environment in different ways.

### The Importance of the Environment

The power of heredity is great—but so is the power of environment. Recent efforts to acknowledge the role of genetics may have gone too far, attributing too much human outcome to our genes. According to one team of behavioral geneticists, research indicates that environmental factors are at least as important as genetic factors (Plomin & Rende, 1991). Since the heritability of a trait generally does not exceed 50 percent, there is a great deal of room for environmental influences.

One particularly important force is a person's *individual* environment, within the family as well as outside it. Even within the same family, every child grows up in a different environment. For example, Sally's daughter Nancy was a first baby, born to a 23-year-old mother who had worked in an advertising agency until 3 weeks before the birth, had been married just over 1 year, and lived 500 miles from any relatives. Her second child, Jennifer, had an older sibling and a family that was better established in the community and living in a suburban house rather than an apartment. Dorri, the third daughter, had two older sisters, a mother who was restless and wanted to go back to work, a father who had recently taken a new job in New York, and loving grandparents who lived nearby.

These are just a few of the obvious differences within one family. In addition, there were, of course, differences in the way the same parents reacted to each child's personality. (Diane's daughter, Anna, has a very different environment, as the only child of parents who were both in their thirties when they adopted her.)

Moreover, other events in these children's lives—illnesses, injuries, the schools they went to, the friends they made, and other individual experiences—also became environmental influences. It is easy to see, then, why even children growing up in the same family are not very similar. Usually, in fact, siblings are more different than alike. For instance, correlations among siblings are only about .40 for cognitive abilities, and only about .20 for personality (Plomin, 1989).

**TABLE 2–2**
DEVELOPMENT OF EMBRYO AND FETUS

| Approximate Date | Description |
| --- | --- |

1 month

During the first month, the new life grows more quickly than at any other time during its life, achieving a size 10,000 times greater than the zygote. It now measures from ¼ to ½ inch in length.

Blood is flowing through its tiny veins and arteries. Its minuscule heart beats 65 times a minute. It already has the beginnings of a brain, kidneys, a liver, and a digestive tract. The umbilical cord, its lifeline to its mother, is working. By looking very closely through a microscope, it is possible to see the swellings on the head that will eventually become its eyes, ears, mouth, and nose. Its sex cannot yet be distinguished.

2 months

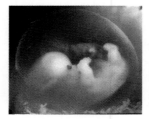

The embryo is less than 1 inch long and weighs only 1/13 ounce. Its head is one-half its total body length. Facial parts are clearly developed, with tongue and teeth buds. The arms have hands, fingers, and thumbs, and the legs have knees, ankles, and toes. It has a thin covering of skin and can even make hand and foot prints.

The embryo's brain impulses coordinate the function of its organ systems. Sex organs are developing; the heartbeat is steady. The stomach produces digestive juices; the liver, blood cells. The kidneys remove uric acid from the body. The skin is now sensitive enough to react to tactile stimulation. If an aborted 8-week-old embryo is stroked, it reacts by flexing its trunk, extending its head, and moving back its arms.

3 months

The developing person, now a fetus, weighs 1 ounce and measures about 3 inches in length. It has fingernails, toenails, eyelids (still closed), vocal cords, lips, and a prominent nose. Its head is still large—about one-third its total length—and its forehead is high. Its sex can be easily determined.

The organ systems are functioning, so that the fetus may now breathe, swallow amniotic fluid in and out of the lungs, and occasionally urinate. Its ribs and vertebrae have turned to cartilage, and its internal reproductive organs have primitive egg or sperm cells.

The fetus can now make a variety of specialized responses: it can move its legs, feet, thumbs, and head; open and close its mouth; and swallow. If its eyelids are touched, it squints; if its palm is touched, it makes a partial fist; if its lip is touched, it will suck; and if the sole of the foot is stroked, the toes will fan out. These reflex behaviors will be present at birth but will disappear during the first months of life.

4 months

The body is catching up to the head, which is now only one-fourth the total body length, the same proportion it will be at birth. The fetus now measures 6 to 10 inches and weighs about 7 ounces. The umbilical cord is as long as the fetus and will continue to grow with it. The placenta is now fully developed, and all organs are formed.

The mother may be able to feel the fetus kicking, a movement known as *quickening*, which some societies and religious groups consider the beginning of human life. The reflex activities that appeared in the third month are now brisker, because of increased muscular development.

5 months

The fetus, now weighing about 12 ounces to 1 pound and measuring about 1 foot, begins to show signs of an individual personality. It has definite sleep-wake patterns, has a favorite position in the uterus (called its *lie*), and becomes more active—kicking, stretching, squirming, and even hiccuping. By putting an ear to the mother's abdomen, it is possible to hear the fetal heartbeat. The sweat and sebaceous glands are functioning. The respiratory system is not yet adequate to sustain life outside the womb; a baby born at this time is not expected to survive.

Coarse hair has begun to grow on the eyebrows and eyelashes, fine hair is on the head, and a woolly hair called *lanugo* covers the body.

**TABLE 2–2**
(CONTINUED)

| Approximate Date | Description |
| --- | --- |
| 6 months  | The rate of fetal growth has slowed down a little—the fetus is now about 14 inches long and weighs 1¼ pounds. It is getting fat pads under the skin; the eyes are complete, opening and closing and looking in all directions. It can maintain regular breathing for 24 hours; it cries; and it can make a fist with a strong grip.<br><br>If the fetus were to be born now, it would have an extremely slim chance of survival because its breathing apparatus is still very immature. There have been instances, however, when a fetus of this age has survived outside the womb, and these are becoming more common. |
| 7 months 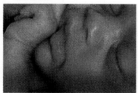 | The fetus, about 16 inches long and weighing 3 to 5 pounds, has fully developed reflex patterns. It cries, breathes, swallows, and may suck its thumb. The lanugo may disappear at about this time, or it may remain until shortly after birth. Head hair may continue to grow.<br><br>Survival chances for a fetus weighing at least 3½ pounds are fairly good, provided it receives intensive medical attention. It will probably have to live in an isolette until a weight of 5 pounds is attained. |
| 8 months 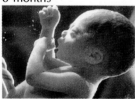 | The fetus is now about 18 to 20 inches long and weighs between 5 and 7½ pounds. Its movements are curtailed because it is fast outgrowing its living quarters. During this month and the next, a layer of fat is developing over the fetus's entire body, to enable it to adjust to varying temperatures outside the womb. |
| 9 months  | About a week before birth, the baby stops growing, having reached an average weight of about 7½ pounds and a length of about 20 inches, with boys tending to be a little longer and heavier than girls. Fat pads continue to form, the organ system is operating more efficiently, the heart rate increases, and more wastes are expelled. The reddish color of the skin is fading. On its birth day, the fetus will have been in the womb for approximately 266 days, although gestation age is usually estimated at 280 days, since doctors date the pregnancy from the mother's last menstrual period. |

*Note:* Even in these early stages, individuals differ. The figures and descriptions given here represent averages.

## PRENATAL DEVELOPMENT

Many overlapping influences, then—both hereditary traits and environmental factors—affect everyone from the moment of conception onward. Some of the most far-reaching of these numerous influences come to bear during the prenatal period, long before an infant leaves the womb.

## STAGES OF PRENATAL DEVELOPMENT

Prenatal development proceeds according to genetic instructions, from a single cell to an extremely complex being. This development before birth, called *gestation,* takes place in three stages: germinal, embryonic, and fetal. A month-by-month description is given in Table 2-2. Let's look at some of the highlights of each stage.

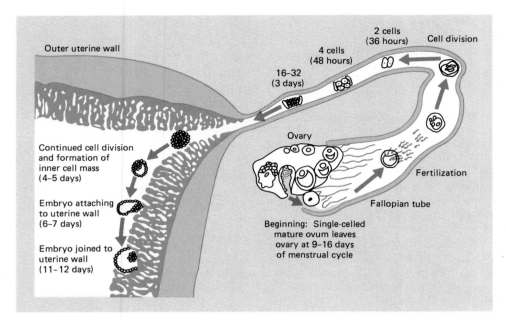

FIGURE 2-12
How an ovum becomes an
embryo.

**Germinal Stage (Fertilization to about 2 Weeks)**

During the **germinal stage,** the organism divides, becomes more complex, and is implanted in the wall of the uterus.

Within 36 hours after fertilization, the single-cell zygote enters a period of rapid cell division. Seventy-two hours after fertilization, it has divided into 32 cells; a day later it has divided into 64 cells. Cell division continues until the original cell has become the 800 billion or more cells that make up the adult human body.

While the fertilized egg is dividing, it is also making its way down the fallopian tube to the uterus, a journey of 3 or 4 days. Meanwhile, its form has changed into a fluid-filled sphere, a *blastocyst,* which then floats freely in the uterus for a day or two. Some cells around the edge of the blastocyst cluster on one side to form the *embryonic disk,* a thickened cell mass from which the baby will develop. This mass is already differentiating into two layers. The upper layer, the *ectoderm,* will become the nails, hair, teeth, sensory organs, the outer layer of skin, and the nervous system, including the brain and spinal cord. The lower layer, the *endoderm,* will develop into the digestive system, liver, pancreas, salivary glands, and respiratory system. Later, a middle layer, the *mesoderm,* will develop and differentiate into the inner layer of skin, muscles, skeleton, and excretory and circulatory systems.

During the germinal stage, other parts of the blastocyst develop into the nurturing and protective organs: the *placenta,* the *umbilical cord,* and the *amniotic sac.* The placenta, which has several important functions, is connected to the embryo by the umbilical cord, through which it delivers oxygen and nourishment to the embryo and removes its body wastes. The placenta also helps to combat internal infection and protects the unborn child from various diseases. It produces the hormones that support pregancy, prepare the mother's breasts for lactation, and eventually stimulate the uterine contractions that will expel the baby from her body. The amniotic sac, a fluid-filled membrane, encases the baby, protecting it and giving it room to move.

The *trophoblast,* the outer cell layer of the blastocyst, produces tiny threadlike structures that penetrate the lining of the uterine wall. In this way, the blastocyst burrows into the wall of the uterus until it is implanted in a nesting place where it will receive nourishment from the mother's body. Upon implantation, the blastocyst has about 150 cells; when it is fully implanted in the uterus, it is an embryo (see Figure 2-12).

**Embryonic Stage (2 to 8–12 Weeks)**

During the **embryonic stage**—the second stage of gestation—the major body systems (respiratory, alimentary, nervous) and organs develop.

Because of its rapid growth and development, the embryo is very vulnerable to environmental influences. Almost all developmental birth defects (like cleft palate, incomplete or missing limbs, blindness, and deafness) occur during the critical first 3-month period, or *trimester,* of pregnancy. The most severely defective embryos usually do not survive beyond this time and are aborted spontaneously.

A ***spontaneous abortion,*** commonly called a *miscarriage,* is the expulsion from the uterus of a conceptus (prenatal organism) that cannot survive outside the womb. Three out of four spontaneous abortions occur within the first trimester, affecting an estimated 31 percent of all pregnancies (Wilcox et al., 1988). A woman's risk of dying from a spontaneous abortion, while quite small, is greater after the first trimester (S. M. Berman, MacKay, Grimes, & Binkin, 1985).

In ancient times, people believed that miscarriage could be brought on by the pregnant woman's fear of a sudden loud thunderclap, for example, or by jostling when her chariot hit a rut in the street. Today we realize that the *normal* conceptus is well protected from almost all such jolts. About half of all spontaneous abortions are associated with chromosomal abnormalities (Ash, Vennart, & Carter, 1977). Most other miscarriages result from a defective ovum or sperm, an unfavorable location for implantation, a breakdown in the supply of oxygen or nourishment caused by abnormal development of the umbilical cord, or some physiological abnormality of the mother.

### Fetal Stage (8–12 Weeks to Birth)

With the appearance of the first bone cells at about 8 weeks, the embryo begins to become a fetus, and by 12 weeks it is fully in the ***fetal stage,*** the final stage of gestation. From now until birth, the finishing touches are put on the various body parts, and the body changes in form and eventually grows about 20 times in length.

The fetus is far from being a passive passenger in its mother's womb. It kicks, turns, flexes its body, somersaults, squints, swallows, makes a fist, hiccups, and sucks its thumb. It responds to both sound and vibrations, showing that it can hear and feel.

Even within the womb, each of us is unique. Fetuses' activity varies in amount and kind, and their heart rates vary in regularity and speed. Some of these patterns seem to persist into adulthood, supporting the notion of inborn temperament.

### THE PRENATAL ENVIRONMENT

Only recently have we become aware of some of the myriad environmental influences that can affect the developing fetus. The role of the father, for example, used to be almost ignored. Today we know that various environmental factors can affect a man's sperm—and the children he conceives. While the mother's role has been recognized far longer, we are still discovering many elements that can affect her fetus. (Box 2-3 on page 66 suggests what prospective mothers can do to have a healthy pregnancy.)

### Maternal Factors

Most of our knowledge about prenatal hazards comes from animal research or from studies in which mothers reported on such factors as what they had eaten while pregnant, what drugs they had taken, how much radiation they had been exposed to, and what illnesses they had contracted. Both these methods have limitations: it is not always accurate to apply findings from animals to human beings, and people do not always remember what they did in the past.

Various influences in the prenatal environment affect different fetuses differently. Some environmental factors that are ***teratogenic,*** or birth-defect-producing, in some cases have little or no effect in others. Research suggests that the timing of an environmental event, its intensity, and its interaction with other factors are all relevant.

#### *Prenatal nourishment*

***Why is prenatal nutrition important?*** Babies develop best when their mothers eat well. A woman's diet *before* as well as during pregnancy is crucial to her child's future health.

Well-nourished mothers bear healthier babies, while mothers with inadequate diets are more likely to bear premature or low-birthweight infants or babies who are stillborn (born dead) or die soon after birth, or babies whose brains do not develop normally (J. L. Brown, 1987; Read, Habicht, Lechtig, & Klein, 1973; Winick, Brasel, & Rosso, 1972). In low-income families, other kinds of deprivation may aggravate the effects of poor nutrition.

Giving dietary supplements to malnourished pregnant women results in bigger, healthier, more active, and more visually alert infants (J. L. Brown, 1987; Read et al., 1973; Vuori et al., 1979). In addition, better-nourished mothers tend to breastfeed longer, and this is a practice that benefits their babies (Read et al., 1973).

A favorable environment after birth may also help to counteract the damaging effects of fetal malnutrition. In one study of babies who had been malnourished as fetuses, researchers randomly assigned some infants with developmental problems to an intellectually enriching program at a day care center before 3 months of age; others remained at home. When the children took intelligence tests 3 years later, those who had been part of the enrichment program tested higher (Zeskind & Ramey, 1981). Proper prenatal nourishment, though, is far easier, surer, and more effective than postnatal action in safeguarding a child's development.

## BOX 2–3   PRACTICALLY SPEAKING

# REDUCING RISKS DURING PREGNANCY

Following are some guidelines for reducing risks during pregnancy:

- *Eat properly.* A well-balanced diet increases the odds of a successful pregnancy and a healthy baby. It may also help to prevent various disorders of pregnancy.
- *Gain weight sensibly.* A gradual, steady, moderate weight gain (26 to 35 pounds for a woman of average weight) may help prevent a variety of complications, including diabetes, hypertension, varicose veins, hemorrhoids, and a difficult delivery due to an overly large fetus.
- *Keep fit.* Regular exercise contributes to a more comfortable pregnancy and an easier, safer delivery by preventing constipation and improving respiration, circulation, muscle tone, and skin elasticity. Exercise should be moderate—not pushing to the limit, keeping the heart rate below 150, and tapering off rather than stopping abruptly (Carpenter et al., 1988).
- *Don't smoke.* Quitting smoking as early in pregnancy as possible reduces many risks to mother and baby, including prematurity and low birthweight.

- *Don't drink alcohol.* Abstaining from alcohol will reduce the risk of birth defects, particularly of fetal alcohol syndrome, which results from high alcohol intake.
- *Avoid drugs.* It is best to avoid taking any drugs during pregnancy that are not absolutely essential and prescribed by your doctor.
- *Get good medical care.* Even an otherwise low-risk pregnancy is put at high risk if prenatal care is lacking or poor. Seeing a qualified practitioner regularly, beginning as soon as you suspect you might be pregnant, is vital. Use an obstetrician experienced with your particular condition if you are in a high-risk category. Be an active participant in your medical care—ask questions, report symptoms—but don't try to be your own doctor.
- *Prevent or promptly treat infections.* All infections—from common flu to urinary tract and vaginal infections to sexually transmitted diseases—should be prevented if possible. If contracted, infection should be treated

promptly by a physician who knows you are pregnant.
- *Beware the "superwoman syndrome."* Getting enough rest during pregnancy is far more important than getting everything done, especially in high-risk pregnancies. Don't wait until your body starts pleading for relief before you slow down. If you work and your doctor recommends that you begin maternity leave earlier than you had planned, take the advice. Some studies have suggested a higher incidence of premature delivery among women who work until term, particularly if their jobs entail physical labor or long periods of standing.
- *If you are going through an especially stressful time, seek special counseling.* Although stress during pregnancy has not been proven to harm the baby, it can interfere with a mother's ability to nurture the baby once it is born.

*Source:* Adapted from A. Eisenberg, Murkoff, & Hathaway, 1986, p. 52.

***What should pregnant women eat?*** A well-balanced daily diet for pregnant women includes foods from each of the seven basic groups: protein (meat and meat alternatives), dairy products, bread and cereals, fruits and vegetables rich in vitamin C, dark-green vegetables, other fruits and vegetables (including yellow ones rich in vitamin A), and fats and oils. Women need to eat more than usual when pregnant: typically, 300 to 500 more calories a day, including extra protein (Winick, 1981). Teenagers, women who are ill or undernourished or under stress, and those who took birth control pills until shortly before pregnancy need extra nutrients (J. E. Brown, 1983).

Pregnant women should gain between 26 to 35 pounds; gaining less than this seems riskier than gaining more (National Center for Health Statistics, 1986). A study of 16,000 pregnancies showed that women who gain in the prescribed range have significantly less chance of stillbirths or late miscarriages or of low-birth-weight babies, regardless of the mother's weight before pregnancy.

### Maternal drug intake

Practically everything the mother takes in makes its way to the new life in her uterus. Drugs may cross the placenta, just as oxygen, carbon dioxide, and water do.

Each year as many as 375,000 infants may be affected by their mothers' drug abuse during pregnancy (Silverman, 1989). The organism is especially vulnerable in its first few months, when development is most rapid. Thus drugs taken early in pregnancy have the strongest effects.

***Medical drugs*** Drugs known to be harmful include the antibiotics streptomycin and tetracycline; the sulfanomides; excessive amounts of vitamins A, $B_6$, C, D, and K; certain barbiturates, opiates, and other central nervous system depressants; several hormones, including birth control pills (Bracken, Holford, White, & Kelsey, 1978), progestin, diethylstilbestrol (DES), androgen, and synthetic estrogen; Accutane, a drug often prescribed for severe acne (Lott, Bocian, Pribram, & Leitner, 1984); and even ordinary aspirin (Stuart, Gross, Elrad, & Graeber, 1982). The American Academy of Pediatrics (AAP) Committee on Drugs (1982) recommends that *no* medication be prescribed for a pregnant or breastfeeding woman unless it is absolutely essential for her health or her child's.

The effects of taking a drug during pregnancy do not always show up immediately. In the late 1940s and early 1950s, the synthetic hormone diethylstilbestrol (DES) was widely prescribed (ineffectually, as it turned out) to prevent miscarriage. Years later, when the daughters of women who had taken DES during pregnancy reached puberty, about 1 in 1000 developed a rare form of vaginal or cervical cancer (Melnick, Cole, Anderson, & Herbst, 1987). "DES daughters" also have had more trouble bearing their own children, with higher risks of miscarriage or premature delivery (A. Barnes et al., 1980), and "DES sons" seem to show a higher rate of infertility and reproductive abnormalities (Stenchever et al., 1981). Therefore, all children of women who took DES during pregnancy should get regular medical checkups.

Let's look at the effects of some other drugs.

***Alcohol*** Each year in the United States, more than 40,000 babies are born with alcohol-related birth defects. About 1 infant in 750, according to American and European studies, suffers from **fetal alcohol syndrome (FAS),** a combination of slowed prenatal and postnatal growth, facial and bodily malformations, and disorders of the central nervous system. Central nervous system problems can involve poor sucking response, brain-wave abnormalities, and sleep disturbances in infancy; and, throughout childhood, a short attention span, restlessness, irritability, hyperactivity, learning disabilities, and motor impairments.

For every child with this full cluster of alcohol-related characteristics (about 6 percent of the offspring of alcoholic mothers), as many as 10 others may be born with *fetal alcohol effects,* a less severe condition that can include mental retardation, retardation of intrauterine growth, and minor congenital abnormalities.

Some of the problems of FAS recede after birth; but learning disabilities and hyperactivity persist, and some malformations require surgery (Charness, Simon, & Greenberg, 1989). FAS is one of the three leading causes of mental retardation (along with Down syndrome and neural-tube defects) and the only preventable one (Barr, Streissguth, Darby, & Sampson, 1990; Ioffe, Childiaeva, & Chernick, 1984; National Institute on Alcohol Abuse and Alcoholism, NIAAA, 1986; Shaywitz, Cohen, & Shaywitz, 1980; Spiegler, Malin, Kaelber, & Warren, 1984; Streissguth et al., 1984).

Even moderate drinking may harm the fetus. A study of nearly 32,000 pregnancies found that having even one or two drinks a day can raise the risk of growth retardation. The effect increased sharply with heavier alcohol intake; taking less than one drink a day had a minimal effect (Mills, Graubard, Harley, Rhoads, & Berendes, 1984). Another study found that 4-year-old children of mothers who had 3 or more drinks a day in the first month of pregnancy scored an average of 5 points less on IQ tests than the average for the other children in the study (Streissguth, Barr, Sampson, Darby, & Martin, 1989). But not all the children were affected.

Because *no* level of drinking has been clearly established as "safe," women should avoid alcohol completely during pregnancy—better yet, from the time they begin *thinking* about becoming pregnant until they stop breastfeeding, since one study showed that breastfed babies of mothers who have one or two drinks a day are slightly slower learning to crawl and walk (Little, Anderson, Ervin, Worthington-Roberts, & Clarren, 1989).

***Marijuana*** Evidence is mounting that heavy marijuana use by pregnant women can lead to birth defects. Researchers analyzed the cries of newborns in Jamaica (where marijuana use is common) and concluded that a mother's heavy use affects her infant's nervous system (Lester & Dreher, 1989). A Canadian study found transient neurological disturbances, like tremors and startles, as well as higher rates of premature and small-for-date infants (Fried, Watkinson, & Willan, 1984). And another study found a link between marijuana use just before and during pregnancy and a childhood cancer—acute lymphoblastic leukemia—possibly because of pesticide contamination of the cannabis leaves (Robison

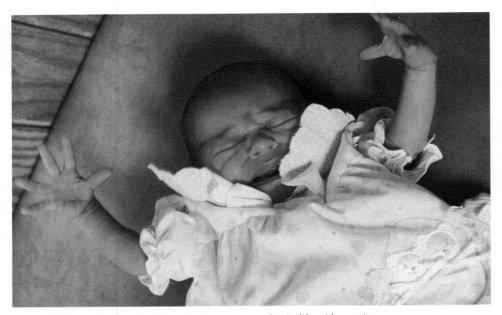

Babies whose mothers used cocaine during pregnancy begin life with massive problems. Many are preterm and small, many have neurological problems, and many, like this one-month-old baby girl, cry for long periods of time and cannot be comforted.

et al., 1989). In sum, women of childbearing age should not use marijuana.

***Nicotine*** Smoking during pregnancy is probably the single most powerful cause of poor fetal growth in the developed world (Nieburg, Marks, McLaren, & Remington, 1985). Pregnant smokers tend to bear small babies (Landesman-Dwyer & Emanuel, 1979; Sexton & Hebel, 1984). Also, maternal smoking is linked to complications ranging from bleeding during pregnancy to death of the fetus or newborn. A Swedish study found that children whose mothers smoke 10 or more cigarettes a day during pregnancy run a 50 percent greater risk than other children of contracting a childhood cancer (Stjernfeldt, Berglund, Lindsten, & Ludvigsson, 1986). The impact may be even greater in the future, since the first big cohort of people whose mothers smoked during pregnancy is just now reaching the age when cancer commonly occurs (D. H. Rubin, Krasilnikoff, Leventhal, Weile, & Berget, 1986).

Smoking in pregnancy seems to have some of the same effects on school-age children as drinking in pregnancy: poor attention span, hyperactivity, learning problems, perceptual-motor and linguistic losses, social maladjustment, poor IQ scores, low grade placement, and minimal brain dysfunction (Landesman-Dwyer & Emanuel, 1979; Naeye & Peters, 1984; Streissguth et al., 1984; Wright et al., 1983). Of course, since women

who smoke during pregnancy also tend to smoke after the birth, it is hard to separate the effects of fetal and postnatal exposure.

***Opiates*** Women addicted to such drugs as morphine, heroin, and codeine are likely to bear premature, addicted babies who show effects until at least age 6. Addicted newborns are restless and irritable and often have tremors, convulsions, fever, vomiting, and breathing difficulties; they are twice as likely to die soon after birth as nonaddicted babies (Cobrinick, Hood, & Chused, 1959; Henly & Fitch, 1966; Ostrea & Chavez, 1979). As older babies, they cry often and are less alert and less responsive (Strauss, Lessen-Firestone, Starr, & Ostrea, 1975). And in early childhood—from ages 3 to 6—they weigh less, are shorter, are less well adjusted, and score lower on perceptual and learning tests (G. Wilson, McCreary, Kean, & Baxter, 1979). Although long-term follow-up studies on these children have been few and inconclusive, researchers have found educational deficits, excessive anxiety in social situations, and poor socialization in later childhood (Householder, Hatcher, Burns & Chasnoff, 1982).

***Cocaine*** An apathetic, lethargic baby who in early childhood will have trouble loving his or her mother, making friends, and playing normally: this is a typical description of a child whose mother used cocaine during pregnancy. These women have a higher rate of spontaneous abortions and their babies have a greater risk of developing neurological problems, possibly because cocaine seems to interfere with the flow of blood through the placenta and may act on fetal brain neurotransmitters to bring about behavioral change.

The babies are not as alert as other babies; they do not respond as well to various stimuli; and they are more likely to be born preterm and to weigh less, to be shorter and have smaller heads at birth, and to have urinary tract defects (Chasnoff, Griffith, MacGregor, Dirkes, & Burns, 1989; Chavez, Mulinare, & Cordero, 1989; Hadeed & Siegel, 1989; Zuckerman et al., 1989). Although babies whose mothers stopped using cocaine early in pregnancy grew just as normally as babies of drug-free mothers, many of them were less alert and responsive.

The effects of cocaine are especially frightening, since this drug—especially in its smokable form, crack—appeals to young women more than many other hard drugs. Women should stop using the drug for the sake of their children's well-being, as well as their own.

**Caffeine**   When pregnant rats were force-fed huge doses of caffeine, their offspring developed birth defects. Can the caffeine that a pregnant woman swallows in coffee, tea, cola, or chocolate cause trouble for her fetus? We are not certain. Because questions remain, the U.S. Food and Drug Administration recommends that pregnant women avoid or use sparingly any food, beverages, or drugs that contain caffeine.

### Other maternal factors

**Illness**   A number of illnesses—including German measles and AIDS—can have serious effects on the developing fetus, depending partly on *when* a pregnant woman gets sick.

Rubella (German measles) before the eleventh week of pregnancy is almost certain to cause deafness and heart defects in the baby; but the chance of these consequences drops to about 1 in 3 between 13 and 16 weeks of pregnancy and is almost nil after 16 weeks (E. Miller, Cradock-Watson, & Pollock, 1982). The syndrome can be prevented by immunizing women before pregnancy—ideally, by immunizing girls before puberty.

AIDS (acquired immune deficiency syndrome) may be contracted by a fetus if the mother has the disease or even has the virus in her blood. An infant or young child who was infected in utero (that is, before birth) with the AIDS virus may have a small head, a prominent boxlike forehead, a flat nasal bridge, a short nose, a "scooped-out" profile, slanting eyes, fat lips, and growth failure (Iosub, Bamji, Stone, Gromisch, & Wasserman, 1987; Marion, Wiznia, Hutcheon, & Rubinstein, 1986). Premature babies are more susceptible, perhaps because they miss the protection of antibodies that may not appear until the third trimester (Goedert et al., 1989).

Diabetes, tuberculosis, and syphilis have also led to problems in fetal development, and both gonorrhea and genital herpes can have harmful effects on the baby at the time of delivery.

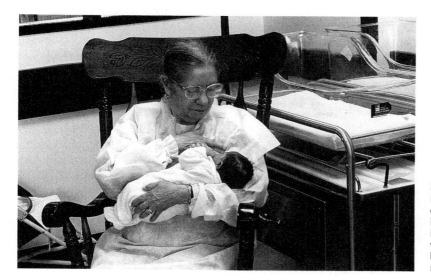

Newborns afflicted with AIDS, like this infant, thrive better when they can be cuddled, fed, and cared for in loving arms, like those of the volunteer Monserrate Bones. Infants with AIDS are often "boarder babies," who have to remain in the hospital either because they are sick or because they have no one to care for them.

***Incompatibility of blood types*** A problem resulting from the interaction of heredity with the prenatal environment is incompatibility of blood type between mother and baby. When a fetus's blood contains the *Rh factor*—a protein substance—but the mother's blood does not, antibodies in the mother's blood may attack the fetus and possibly bring about spontaneous abortion, stillbirth, jaundice, anemia, heart defects, mental retardation, or death. Usually the first Rh-positive baby is not affected, but with each succeeding pregnancy the risk becomes greater. A vaccine can now be given to an Rh-negative mother which, when administered within 3 days after childbirth or abortion, will prevent her body from making antibodies. Babies already affected with Rh disease can be treated by repeated blood transfusions, sometimes even before birth.

***Medical x-rays*** We have known for more than 60 years that radiation can cause gene mutations, minor changes that alter a gene to produce a new, often harmful characteristic (D. P. Murphy, 1929). Although we don't know what exact dosage of x-rays will harm a fetus, the greatest potential for harm seems to occur early in pregnancy. Radiation exposure should be avoided, especially during the first 3 months (Kleinman, Cooke, Machlin, & Kessel, 1983). With the availability of ultrasound (see Box 2-2 on pages 60–61) medical x-rays are less necessary and less prevalent today than they were in the past.

***Environmental hazards*** Anything that affects a pregnant woman can affect her fetus—chemicals, radiation, extremes of heat and humidity, and other hazards of modern life. For example, babies whose mothers ate fish contaminated with PCBs (chemicals widely used in industry before they were banned in 1976) weighed less at birth, had smaller heads, and showed weaker reflexes and more jerky movements than infants whose mothers did not eat the fish; and they showed poor visual-recognition memory at 7 months and poor memory for words and numbers at 4 years (J. L. Jacobson, Jacobson, Fein, Schwartz, & Dowler, 1984; J. L. Jacobson, Jacobson, & Humphrey, 1990; S. W. Jacobson et al., 1985).

Infants exposed to high levels of lead prenatally scored lower on intelligence tests than those exposed to low or moderate levels (Bellinger, Leviton, Watermaux, Needleman, & Rabinowitz, 1987; Needleman & Gatsonis, 1990).

Radiation is especially dangerous. It affected Japanese infants after the atomic bomb explosions in Hiroshima and Nagasaki (Yamazaki & Schull, 1990) and German infants after the spill-out at the nuclear power plant at Chernobyl in the Soviet Union (West Berlin Human Genetics Institute, 1987). In utero exposure to radiation has been linked to greater risk of mental retardation, small head size, chromosomal malformations, Down syndrome, seizure, and poor performance on IQ tests and in school. The critical period seems to be 8 through 15 weeks after fertilization (Yamazaki & Schull, 1990).

### Paternal Factors: Environmental Influences Transmitted by the Father

The father, too, can transmit environmentally caused defects. Exposure to lead, marijuana and tobacco smoke, large amounts of alcohol and radiation, DES, and certain pesticides may result in the production of abnormal sperm (R. Lester & Van Theil, 1977). Associations have appeared between nervous system tumors in children and such occupations of their fathers as electrical or electronic worker, auto mechanic, miner, printer, paper or pulp mill worker, and aircraft industry worker (M. R. Spitz & Johnson, 1985).

A harmful influence on both mother and baby is nicotine from a father's smoking. In one study, babies of fathers who smoked were lighter at birth by about 4 ounces per pack of cigarettes smoked per day by the father (or the cigar or pipe equivalent) (D. H. Rubin et al., 1986). Another study found that children of men who smoked were twice as likely as other children to contract cancer in adulthood (Sandler, Everson, Wilcox, & Browder, 1985). In both studies, however, it was difficult to distinguish between prebirth and childhood exposure to smoke.

A later paternal age (average in the late 30s) is associated with increases in several rare conditions, including one type of dwarfism; Marfan's syndrome (deformities of the head and limbs); and a kind of bone malformation (G. Evans, 1976). Advanced age of the father may also be a factor in about 5 percent of cases of Down syndrome (Antonarakis, 1991).

## BIRTH

Birth is both a beginning and an end: the climax of all that has happened from the moment of fertilization through 9 months (266 days) of growth in the womb.

The uterine contractions that expel the fetus begin as mild tightenings of the uterus, each lasting 15 to 25 seconds. A woman may have felt similar contractions from time to time during the final months of pregnancy, but she can often recognize birth contractions as the "real thing" because of their greater regularity and intensity.

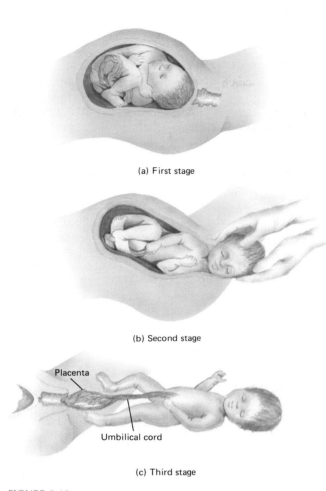

(a) First stage

(b) Second stage

Placenta

Umbilical cord

(c) Third stage

**FIGURE 2-13**
Birth of a baby. (a) During the first stage of labor, a series of stronger and stronger contractions dilates the cervix, the opening to the mother's womb. (b) During the second stage, the baby's head moves down the birth canal and emerges from the vagina. (c) During the brief third stage, the placenta and umbilical cord are expelled from the womb. Then, the cord is cut. (*Source:* Adapted from Lagercrantz & Slotkin, 1986.)

## STAGES OF CHILDBIRTH

Childbirth, or labor, takes place in three overlapping stages (see Figure 2-13 above). The *first stage,* which is the longest, lasts an average of 12 to 24 hours for a woman having her first child. During this stage, uterine contractions cause the cervix to widen until it becomes large enough for the baby's head to pass through, a process called *dilation.* At the beginning of this stage, the contractions occur about every 8 to 10 minutes and last 30 seconds. Toward the end of labor they may come every 2 minutes and last 60 to 90 seconds. Women who have prepared for childbirth through spe-

cial classes learn certain breathing techniques to make labor more comfortable.

The *second stage,* which typically lasts about 1½ hours, begins when the baby's head begins to move through the cervix into the vaginal canal, and it ends when the baby emerges completely from the mother's body. During the second stage, the "prepared" mother bears down hard with her abdominal muscles during each contraction, helping the baby in its efforts to leave her body. At the end of this stage, the baby is born. The umbilical cord, which is still attached to the placenta, is cut and clamped.

During the *third stage,* which lasts only a few minutes, what is left of the umbilical cord and the placenta are expelled.

## METHODS OF CHILDBIRTH

Babies are delivered in a variety of ways. Historically, two concerns have been primary during delivery: the baby's safety and the mother's comfort. Another concern, growing sensitivity to the emotional needs of family members, has more recently resulted in efforts to bring the father and sometimes the other children into the experience.

### Medicated Delivery

Most societies have evolved techniques to hasten delivery, make the mother's work easier, and lessen her discomfort. Most western women expect some pain relief during labor and delivery, usually a **medicated delivery**—that is, a delivery involving anesthesia. Anesthesia can be general, rendering the woman completely unconscious; or regional (local), blocking the nerve pathways that would carry the sensation of pain to the brain. Or the mother can receive a relaxing analgesic. All these drugs pass through the placenta to enter the fetal blood supply and tissues.

A number of studies have emphasized that obstetric medication involves dangers for the baby. Children have shown the effects of such medication as early as the first day of life, in poorer motor and physiological responses (A. D. Murray, Dolby, Nation, & Thomas, 1981); and through the first year, in slower development in sitting, standing, and moving around (Brackbill & Broman, 1979).

In one study, the babies had caught up by 1 month of age, but their mothers felt differently about them (A. D. Murray et al., 1981). This could be for one of two reasons. Many professionals believe that there is no such thing in human beings as a "maternal instinct." According to this theory, much of a woman's motherly

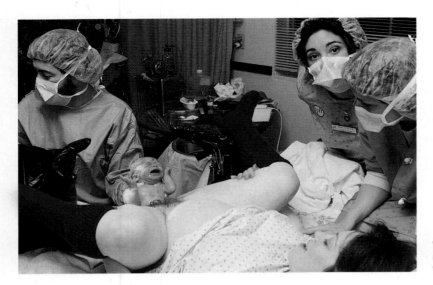

Women who choose natural rather than medicated childbirth can remain alert enough to participate fully in the birth process.

feeling comes about because of her baby's behavior. An infant who nurses eagerly and acts alert sets up positive feelings in the mother. On the other hand, if the first encounters between mother and baby do not draw a strong reaction from the baby, the effects of this early impression may remain. It is also possible that mothers who choose unmedicated deliveries may feel more positive about parenting and that this attitude affects how they act with their babies.

However, in contradiction to these findings, one team of researchers compared babies born to medicated and nonmedicated mothers on several characteristics: strength and tactile sensitivity, activity and irritability, and sleep. They found *no* evidence of *any* drug effect (Kraemer, Korner, Anders, Jacklin, & Dimiceli, 1985). These investigators charge that research in this area has been poorly designed and misleading; that it may keep appropriate drugs from some mothers, making them suffer unnecessary pain and discomfort; and that it may cause others, who did receive drugs, to feel guilty.

Because the woman is the only person who can gauge her pain and is the most personally concerned about her child's well-being, she should have a strong voice in decisions about obstetric medication. The American Academy of Pediatrics (AAP) Committee on Drugs (1978) recommends the minimum dose for relief of the mother's pain.

Alternative methods of childbirth, which we'll consider next, seek to minimize the use of harmful drugs while maximizing the parents' satisfaction as participants.

## Natural and Prepared Childbirth

In 1914 a British physician, Dr. Grantly Dick-Read, claiming that fear causes most of the pain in childbirth, put forth the theory of **natural childbirth.** This method aims to eliminate fear by educating women in the physiology of reproduction and delivery and training them in breathing, relaxation, and physical fitness. By midcentury, Dr. Fernand Lamaze was using the psychoprophylactic method—**prepared childbirth**—substituting new breathing and muscular responses to the sensations of uterine contractions for the old responses of fear and pain.

The Lamaze method of prepared childbirth instructs women in anatomy to remove fear of the unknown, and trains them to vary their patterns of breathing to match the strength of contractions and to concentrate on sensations other than the contractions. The mother learns to relax her muscles as a conditioned response to the voice of her "coach" (usually the father or a friend). Social support is also a factor. The coach attends classes with the expectant mother, takes part in the delivery, and helps with the exercises—enhancing her sense of self-worth and reducing her fear of being alone at the time of birth (Wideman & Singer, 1984).

## Cesarean Delivery

A **cesarean delivery** is a medical procedure in which the baby is removed surgically from the uterus. Almost 1 in 4 babies are delivered in this way in the United States, an increase from 5.5 percent in 1970 to 24.4 percent in 1987 (Stafford, 1990).

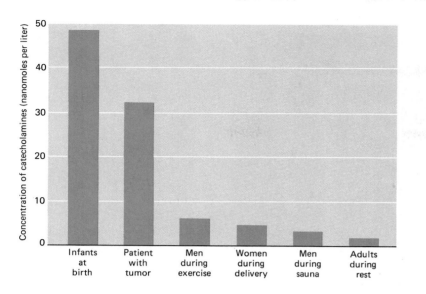

**FIGURE 2-14**
Stress hormones in newborn babies and adults. Umbilical samples from newborns show a level of stress hormones 20 times higher than that in resting adults. The surge of hormones during birth is also greater than that found in adults who are exercising or under great physical stress. (*Source:* Adapted from Lagercrantz & Slotkin, 1986.)

The operation is commonly done when labor is not progressing as quickly as it should, when the baby seems to be in trouble, or when the mother is bleeding through the vagina. It is often needed when the baby is in the breech (head last) or the transverse position (lying crosswise in the uterus), or when the baby's head is too big to pass through the mother's pelvis.

Cesarean deliveries have a superior safety record in delivering breech babies (Sachs et al., 1983). But there is little evidence that they improve the overall survival of very low-birthweight infants (Malloy, Rhoads, Schramm, & Land, 1989). And in some circumstances the benefits need to be weighed against the risks, one of which is depriving the infant of the experience of labor. It now seems that the birth struggle may help the baby adjust to life outside the uterus (Lagercrantz & Slotkin, 1986). The stress of being born apparently stimulates the production in the infant's body of huge amounts of hormones called *catecholamines* (see Figure 2-14). This burst of catecholamines clears the lungs for breathing, mobilizes stored fuel for cell nourishment, and sends blood to the heart and brain. By sharpening the newborn's alertness, it may even foster early bonding between mother and child. An infant delivered by elective cesarean, before the onset of labor, misses this normal hormonal surge, which seems to be triggered by uterine contractions. (Babies delivered by emergency cesarean, after labor has begun, show catecholamine levels almost as high as babies delivered vaginally.) The breathing problems that cesarean-delivery babies often suffer may be traceable to this lack of catecholamines, which help absorb liquid in the lungs.

Cesarean deliveries have other drawbacks. For the mother, there is a greater risk of infection and a longer hospital stay and recovery period, besides the physical and psychological impact of any surgery (Sachs et al., 1983). Cesarean sections have saved the lives of mothers and babies who could not have managed traditional deliveries, but many critics assert that too many cesareans are now being performed in the United States when they are not strictly necessary (deRegt, Minkoff, Feldman, & Schwartz, 1986). Rates in this country are the highest in the world (see Figure 2-15, page 74), and women with median family incomes of over $30,000 a year have cesarean deliveries at nearly twice the rate as women with median incomes under $11,000 (Gould, Davey, & Stafford, 1989).

## Medical Monitoring

In *electronic fetal monitoring,* machines monitor the fetal heartbeat throughout labor and delivery. This procedure provides valuable information (especially in detecting a lack of oxygen) for high-risk deliveries, including those of premature and low-birthweight babies and fetuses who seem to be in distress.

Routine monitoring in low-risk pregnancies, on the other hand, is costly, is uncomfortable for the mother, and results in twice as many deliveries by the riskier cesarean method, without corresponding improvements in outcome (Leveno et al., 1986; Lewin, 1988). Therefore it is best *not* to perform continous, routine monitoring when a pregnancy seems to be uncomplicated.

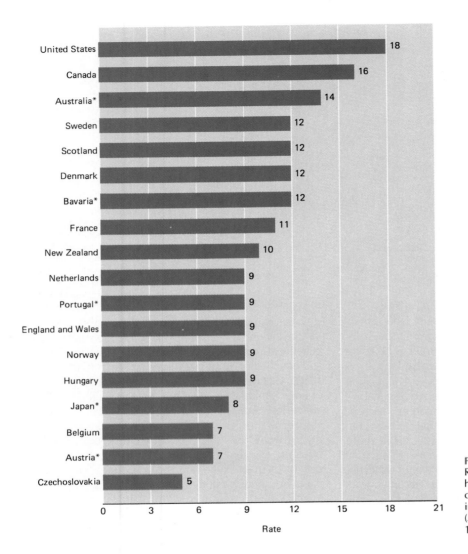

**FIGURE 2-15**
Rates of cesarean delivery per 100 hospital deliveries in selected countries, 1981. (Note: Asterisks indicate incomplete information.) (*Source*: Notzon, Placek, & Taffel, 1987.)

## SETTINGS FOR CHILDBIRTH

More than 99 percent of the 3.91 million babies born in 1988 in the United States were delivered in hospitals, and 96 percent were attended by a physician, usually an obstetrician, who specializes in delivering babies (Wegman, 1989). But a small but growing number of women with good medical histories and normal pregnancies are opting for more intimate, less impersonal settings. Some mothers elect to have their babies in the comfort and familiarity of their homes or in small, homelike birth centers and to be attended by midwives. In 1987 almost 114,000 births were attended by midwives, nearly 4 times the number in 1975 (Wegman, 1989).

If a pregnancy is of low risk and the birth is uncomplicated, almost any of these arrangements can work

well. It is often impossible to predict a sudden emergency during childbirth, however, and so it is vital to have backup plans in case of trouble. A good birth center has a contract with an ambulance service, an agreement with a nearby hospital, and on-premises emergency equipment for resuscitation and for administering oxygen. Provisions for a home birth should include arrangements for emergency transportation to a hospital no more than 10 minutes away.

Many hospitals *are* big and impersonal, with rules that seem designed for the smooth functioning of the institution rather than for the benefit of the patients. Others, though, cater to the comfort of their patients. In recent years, as hospitals have competed for maternity cases, they have become more responsive to the desires of patients. Many now have birthing centers,

## BOX 2–4   WINDOW ON THE WORLD

# MATERNITY CARE IN WESTERN EUROPE AND THE UNITED STATES

Why do proportionately more babies die at or soon after birth in the United States compared with a number of western European countries? Why has this nation's rate of infant mortality risen over the past several decades in the world rankings? An answer may lie in differences in various levels of health care (Behrman, 1985; C. A. Miller, 1987).

Suppose you are a woman in one of ten western European countries that have high standards of maternity care and entitlements to health services and social support (Belgium, Denmark, Germany, France, Ireland, Netherlands, Norway, Spain, Switzerland, and Great Britain). While the specific services you received would vary depending on which country you lived in, in any one of them you would receive either free or very low-cost prenatal and postnatal care, including a paid maternity leave from work (ranging from 9 to 40 weeks).

You would want to seek prenatal care early because only after your pregnancy was confirmed and officially registered would you begin to get benefits like transportation privileges and preferential hospital booking for delivery. You would probably go first to a general practitioner, who would coordinate your care with a midwife and an obstetrician. The midwife would give you most of your prenatal care and attend the birth—unless your pregnancy was considered high-risk, in which case a doctor would assist you.

The number of your prenatal visits would vary—from 4 if you were Swiss to 12 if you were Dutch, British, or Norwegian. If you missed an appointment or had a complicated

pregnancy, your midwife would visit you at home, and in some countries you would receive one such visit routinely. If you lived in Norway, you would be reimbursed for up to 10 days' worth of travel and living expenses, so that you could be near a hospital at time of delivery.

After the baby was born, you would probably receive at least one home visit to get counseling about infant care, family planning, and your own health. If you were a single mother, you would get extra help; if you were an employed mother or the mother of a large family, you would get priority for day care and public housing. You would receive a monthly family allowance for each child, usually until adulthood or completion of education. And you would get a financial bonus at time of delivery (unless you were Danish) to help pay for baby supplies and equipment. This bonus might hinge on the number of prenatal visits you made, and it might be larger if you breastfed.

In the Netherlands you could pay a token fee for a trained helper to stay with you for up to 8 hours a day for 10 days, helping you shop, cook, and take care of the baby and your other children. In Germany either you or your husband could take paid child-care leave, and unpaid leave might last for 3 years.

The bottom line is that as a pregnant woman in Europe, you would never need to ask how or where you would receive care or who would pay for it. As a pregnant woman in the United States, you would face a very different situation. You would not get the benefits of uniform national standards for maternity care,

and thus you would not be ensured of consistent, high-quality care. Furthermore, you could not count on financial coverage.

Nationwide, 16 percent of pregnant women get inadequate prenatal care, and those most at risk of bearing low-birthweight babies—teenage, minority, and unmarried women, and women with little education—get the least (S. S. Brown, 1985; Ingram, Makuc, & Kleinman, 1986; Singh, Forrest, & Torres, 1989). In 1987, 21 percent of white mothers and about 40 percent of African American, Hispanic, and Native American mothers did not receive prenatal care in the first trimester; and 5 percent of white mothers and 11 percent of black mothers had none at all or none until the third trimester (U.S. Department of Health and Human Services, USDHHS, 1990; Wegman, 1989). Hispanic women are 3 times as likely as other groups to receive no prenatal care at all (Council on Scientific Affairs of the American Medical Association, 1991).

This bleak picture might change if local and federal governments linked prenatal care to comprehensive social and financial benefits. There is need for a wide range of educational, social, and medical services (including outreach workers to identify women in need and help with transportation, baby-sitting, and housing problems). The state of New Jersey has launched a new program offering a full range of prenatal health services to all women in the state (J. F. Sullivan, 1989). If more states follow suit, the future should be brighter for many American babies.

where fathers or other birth coaches may remain with the mother during labor and delivery, and rooming-in policies, so that babies can stay in the mother's room for much or all of the day.

Freestanding maternity centers are usually staffed principally by nurse-midwives, with one or more physicians and nurse-assistants; they are designed for low-risk, uncomplicated births; and they offer prenatal care and birth in a homelike setting, with discharge the same day.

What are the psychological implications of the new ways of giving birth? First, techniques that minimize drugs provide a better start in life for the baby. Second, the active participation of both parents reinforces close family attachments between mother, father, and infant.

Last, women's insistence on assuming a strong role in the birth of their children has helped spur a general movement in which people take active responsibility for their own health rather than sitting back passively and relying on doctors. Of course, there are many ways to have a healthy baby, and many healthy, well-adjusted adults have been born in traditional hospital settings. One of the best guarantees of a healthy pregnancy and delivery is good prenatal care—something that is, unfortunately, not received by a significant number of American women (see Box 2-4).

In view of the importance of feeling in control of one's life, the availability of alternative means and sites of childbirth is a healthy trend. Choice is the crucial element. Children born in a variety of ways and places can grow up physically and psychologically healthy.

## SUMMARY

### FERTILIZATION

▪ Fertilization is the process by which sperm and ovum unite to form a one-celled zygote. The zygote duplicates by cell division.

▪ Although conception usually results in single births, multiple births can occur. When two ova are fertilized, fraternal (dizygotic) twins will be born; these have different genetic makeups and may be of different sexes. When a single fertilized ovum divides in two, identical (monozygotic) twins will be born; they have the same genetic makeup and therefore are always of the same sex. Larger multiple births result from either one of these processes or a combination of the two.

▪ At conception, each normal human being receives 23 chromosomes from the mother and 23 from the father. These align into 23 pairs of chromosomes—22 pairs of autosomes and 1 pair of sex chromosomes. Chromosomes carry the genes that determine inherited characteristics.

▪ A child who receives an X chromosome from each parent will be a female. But if the child receives a Y chromosome from the father, a male will be conceived.

### HEREDITY AND ENVIRONMENT

▪ The science of genetics is the study of heredity. The basic unit of heredity is the gene.

▪ The chief patterns of genetic transmission are dominant, recessive, sex-linked, and multifactorial inheritance. Various birth defects and diseases can be transmitted through each of these patterns.

▪ Chromosomal abnormalities can also result in birth defects. Down syndrome is the most common.

▪ Through genetic counseling, prospective parents can receive information about the mathematical odds of having children with certain birth defects.

▪ Amniocentesis, chorionic villus sampling, maternal blood testing, and umbilical cord assessment are procedures used to determine if a fetus is developing normally or is affected by certain abnormal conditions.

▪ It is hard to disentangle the relative contributions of heredity and environment from development. Today, developmentalists look at the interaction of heredity and environment rather than attributing development exclusively to one factor or the other. However, certain aspects of development are influenced more by heredity and others more by environment.

### PRENATAL DEVELOPMENT

▪ Prenatal development occurs in three stages. The germinal stage is characterized by rapid cell division, increased complexity of the organism, and implantation of the organism in the wall of the uterus. The embryonic stage is characterized by rapid growth and differentiation of major body systems and organs. The fetal stage is characterized by the appearance of bone cells, rapid growth, and changes in body form.

▪ Nearly all birth defects and three-quarters of all spontaneous abortions occur during the critical first trimester of pregnancy.

▪ The conceptus is affected by its prenatal environment. Important dangers include maternal nutrition, maternal drug intake, maternal illness, incompatibility of blood type with the mother's blood type, medical x-rays, and external environmental hazards. Paternal factors are also important.

## BIRTH

- Birth normally begins 266 days after conception and occurs in three stages: (1) dilation of the cervix; (2) descent and emergence of the baby; (3) expulsion of the umbilical cord and the placenta.
- Excessive anesthesia in medicated deliveries may have a harmful effect on the newborn.
- Natural and prepared childbirth can offer both physical and psychological benefits.

- In recent years the rate of cesarean deliveries has risen to almost 25 percent in the United States.
- Electronic fetal monitoring is widely used during labor and delivery, especially in high-risk births, to detect signs of fetal distress.
- Delivery at home or in birth centers is an alternative to hospital delivery for some women with normal, low-risk pregnancies.

## KEY TERMS

fertilization (page 40)
gametes (40)
zygote (40)
ovulation (40)
dizygotic twins (41)
monozygotic twins (41)
autosomes (42)
sex chromosomes (42)
genetics (43)
heredity (43)
gene (43)
deoxyribonucleic acid (DNA) (43)
chromosomes (43)
dominant inheritance (44)
independent segregation (44)
alleles (44)
homozygous (44)

heterozygous (44)
recessive inheritance (44)
phenotype (45)
genotype (45)
sex-linked inheritance (45)
multiple alleles (45)
multifactorial inheritance (45)
Down syndrome (51)
genetic counseling (53)
karyotype (53)
amniocentesis (54)
chorionic villus sampling (CVS) (54)
maternal blood test (54)
ultrasound (54)
maturation (56)
concordant (56)

personality (58)
temperament (58)
schizophrenia (59)
infantile autism (59)
depression (61)
germinal stage (64)
embryonic stage (64)
spontaneous abortion (65)
fetal stage (65)
teratogenic (65)
fetal alcohol syndrome (FAS) (67)
medicated delivery (71)
natural childbirth (72)
prepared childbirth (72)
cesarean delivery (72)
electronic fetal monitoring (73)

## SUGGESTED READINGS

DeFrain, J., Montens, L., Stork, J., & Stork, W. (1986). *Stillborn: An invisible death*. Lexington, MA: Heath. A sensitive study of the effects of stillbirth on families, based on data from 300 questionnaires and 25 in-depth interviews, the book provides concrete information about the reactions of parents, family, and friends to this experience and gives suggestions for coping.

Dorris, M. (1990). *The broken cord*. New York: Harper-Collins. A moving account of the struggles of a child with fetal alcohol syndrome, written by his adoptive father.

Eisenberg, A., Murkoff, H. E., & Hathaway, S. E. (1991). *What to expect when you're expecting* (rev. 2d ed.). New York: Workman. An excellent, comprehensive description of pregnancy, month to month, that incorporates research on care for both mother and baby.

Nilsson, L., Ingelman-Sundberg, A., & Wirsen, C. (1990). *A child is born* (2d ed.). New York: Delacorte. A completely new edition of this classic depiction of fetal development. The material about the parents' experience of pregnancy has been updated but the beautiful photographs of the developing fetus are unchanged.

Tannenhaus, N. (1988). *Pre-conceptions*. Chicago: Contemporary Press. Up-to-date information on the effects of all aspects of one's lifestyle on an unborn child's health and development.

## CHAPTER 3

# PHYSICAL DEVELOPMENT IN INFANCY AND TODDLERHOOD

The experiences of the first three years of life are almost entirely lost to us, and when we attempt to enter into a small child's world, we come as foreigners who have forgotten the landscape and no longer speak the native tongue.

SELMA FRAIBERG,
*THE MAGIC YEARS*, 1959

- How do newborn infants adjust to life outside the womb, and how can we tell whether they are healthy and are developing normally?
- What conditions can complicate newborn babies' adjustment and even endanger their lives?
- What can infants do at birth, and how do they acquire more sophisticated sensory and motor capabilities over the first 3 years?
- What can and should be done to foster infants' and toddlers' physical growth and development?

Suppose that after a rough voyage, you are cast ashore alone and without possessions in an unknown land. You are cared for by giants, who act strangely and speak gibberish. What's more, you are physically helpless and unable to tell anyone what you need or want.

You have been through just such an experience—at birth. A newborn baby is, in an extreme sense, an immigrant. After struggling through a difficult passage, the infant is faced with much more than the task of learning a language and customs. A baby has to start to breathe, eat, adapt to the climate, and respond to confusing surroundings. This is a mighty challenge for beings who weigh but a few pounds and whose organ systems are still not fully mature. But as we'll see, infants normally come into the world with body systems and senses all working to some extent and ready to meet that challenge.

In this chapter we see what newborn babies look like, how their body systems work, and how the brain develops, permitting reflex behaviors to operate. We describe some ways to evaluate newborns, and we discuss how birth trauma and low birthweight affect development. Then we go on to chart some aspects of development during the first 3 years of life—basic principles, states of arousal, the importance of nutrition, early sensory and motor development, and similarities and differences between boys and girls.

As you read this chapter, it is important to bear in mind that because human beings live and behave as whole persons, all aspects of their development are intimately connected. When we try to separate these aspects (as in a textbook), we find ourselves making arbitrary divisions, as if we were cutting the person into jigsaw pieces.

For example, although we usually think of learning as a mental function, infants learn a great deal by action. Babies cannot tell themselves apart from their surroundings until they begin to explore their environment and learn from their own movements where the body ends and the rest of the world begins. As they drop toys, splash water, and hurl sand, they learn how their bodies can alter their world. Physical gestures also accompany a baby's first attempts to speak. As Maika says "Bye-bye," she opens and closes her hand. When Darryl says "Up," he raises his arms, showing Grandpa where he wants to go. Even more to the point, if Maika and Darryl had not developed the motor coordination needed to form certain sounds, they would not be able to speak at all. Because the brain itself—the center of intellectual as well as much of emotional functioning—is a physical organ, intelligence, learning, and personality are linked with the physical aspects of growth and development.

Thus as we look at early physical growth and sensory and motor development of infants and toddlers in this chapter, and at their personality and social development in Chapter 5, we should remember that these categories are arbitrary.

## THE NEONATE

The first 4 weeks of life are the **neonatal period,** a time of transition from intrauterine life—when a fetus is supported entirely by a mother's body—to an independent existence. In this section, we'll consider neonates. Who are these newcomers to the world? What do they look like? What can they do?

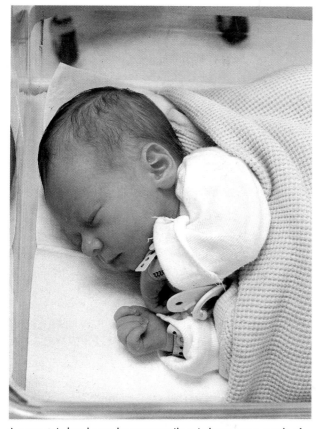

A neonate's head may be temporarily misshapen as a result of the passage through the birth canal. Neonates spend most of their time sleeping, but they awaken, hungry, every 2 to 3 hours.

## PHYSICAL CHARACTERISTICS

An average **neonate,** or newborn, is about 20 inches long and weighs about 7½ pounds. At birth, 95 percent of full-term babies weigh between 5½ and 10 pounds and are between 18 and 22 inches long (Behrman & Vaughan, 1983). Size at birth is related to such factors as race, sex, parents' size, maternal nutrition, and maternal health. Boys tend to be slightly longer and heavier than girls, and a firstborn child is likely to weigh less at birth than later-borns. Size at birth is related to size during childhood (Behrman & Vaughan, 1983).

In their first few days, neonates lose as much as 10 percent of their body weight, primarily because of a loss of fluids. They begin to gain weight again at about the fifth day and are generally back to birthweight by the tenth to the fourteenth day. Light full-term infants lose less weight than heavy ones, and firstborns lose less than later-borns (Behrman & Vaughan, 1983).

The neonate's head may be long and misshapen because of the "molding" that eased its passage through the mother's pelvis. This temporary molding was possible because the baby's skull bones are not yet fused; they will not be completely joined for 18 months. The places on the head where the bones have not yet grown together—the soft spots, or *fontanels*—are covered by a tough membrane. Since the cartilage in the baby's nose is also malleable, the trip through the birth canal may leave the nose looking squashed for a few days.

Newborns are quite pale; even black babies who will later be very dark have a light complexion at birth. But newborns have a pinkish cast because of the thinness of their skin, which barely covers the blood flowing through their capillaries. The **vernix caseosa** ("cheesy varnish"), an oily covering that protects new babies against infection, dries in a few days' time. Some neonates are very hairy, covered with **lanugo,** a fuzzy prenatal hair that drops off within a few days.

"Witch's milk," a secretion that sometimes issues from the swollen breasts of both female and male newborns, was believed during the Middle Ages to have special healing powers. Like the blood-tinged vaginal discharge of some baby girls, this fluid emission results from high levels of the hormone estrogen, which is secreted by the placenta just before birth.

## BODY SYSTEMS

Before birth, the fetus's blood circulation, respiration, nourishment, elimination, and temperature regulation are all accomplished through its connection with the mother's body. After birth, infants must perform these functions on their own. The transition from intrauterine life to life on the outside makes major demands on all body systems (see Table 3-1 on page 82).

### Circulatory System

Before birth, mother and baby have independent circulatory systems and separate heartbeats; but the fetus's blood is cleansed through the umbilical cord, which carries blood to and from the placenta. At birth, the baby's own system must take over. The neonate's heartbeat is still fast and irregular, and blood pressure does not stabilize until about the tenth day.

### Respiratory System

The fetus gets oxygen through the umbilical cord, which also carries away carbon dioxide. The newborn, who needs much more oxygen, must now get it independently. Most infants start to breathe as soon as they

**TABLE 3–1**
A COMPARISON OF PRENATAL AND POSTNATAL LIFE

| Characteristic | Prenatal Life | Postnatal Life |
| --- | --- | --- |
| Environment | Amniotic fluid | Air |
| Temperature | Relatively constant | Fluctuates with atmosphere |
| Stimulation | Minimal | All senses stimulated by various stimuli |
| Nutrition | Dependent on mother's blood | Dependent on external food and functioning of digestive system |
| Oxygen supply | Passed from maternal bloodstream via placenta | Passed from neonate's lungs to pulmonary blood vessels |
| Metabolic elimination | Passed into maternal bloodstream via placenta | Discharged by skin, kidneys, lungs, and gastrointestinal tract |

*Source:* Timiras, 1972, p. 174.

emerge into the air. A baby who is not breathing within 2 minutes after birth is in trouble; if breathing has not begun in 5 minutes or so, some degree of brain injury from **anoxia**—lack of oxygen—may result. Infants' lungs have only one-tenth as many air sacs as adults'; thus infants are susceptible to respiratory problems.

### Gastrointestinal System

The fetus relies on the umbilical cord to bring food and carry body wastes away. The newborn has a strong sucking reflex to take in milk and has gastrointestinal secretions to digest it. **Meconium** (stringy, greenish-black waste matter formed in the fetal intestinal tract) is excreted during the first 2 days or so after birth. When the neonate's bowels and bladder are full, the sphincter muscles open automatically. Many months will pass before the baby can control these muscles.

Three or four days after birth, about half of all babies—and a larger proportion of babies born prematurely—develop *physiologic jaundice:* their skin and eyeballs look yellow. This kind of jaundice is caused by the immaturity of the liver; usually it is not serious and has no long-term effects. In some cases, it is treated by putting the baby under fluorescent lights.

### Temperature Regulation

The layers of fat that develop during the last months of fetal life enable healthy full-term infants to keep their body temperature constant despite changes in air temperature. Newborn babies also maintain body temperature by increasing their activity in response to a drop in air temperature.

### THE BRAIN AND REFLEX BEHAVIOR

What makes newborns respond to the touch of a nipple? What tells them to start the sucking movements that allow them to control their intake of milk?

These are functions of the nervous system, which consists of the brain, the spinal cord (a bundle of nerves running through the backbone), and a network of nerves that eventually reaches every part of the body. Through this network, sensory messages travel to the brain and motor commands travel back. This complex communication system governs what a person can do both physically and mentally. Normal growth of the brain, before and after birth, is fundamental to future development.

### Growth and Development of the Brain

We can think of brain development by using an analogy—sculpture. A sculptor starts with a block of stone and chisels away the unwanted pieces. This is roughly what happens in the brain (Kolb, 1989). Starting in the womb, the brain produces more cells than it needs, and those that do not function well die out after birth. This removal of excess cells helps to create an efficient nervous system; in fact, some neurobiologists believe that certain disorders are caused by the persistence of extra cells (I. Feinberg, 1982).

The human brain grows fastest prenatally and soon after birth. In the uterus an estimated 250,000 brain cells form every minute through cell division (mitosis), and by birth most of the 100 billion cells in a mature brain are already formed (Cowan, 1979; see Figure 3-1).

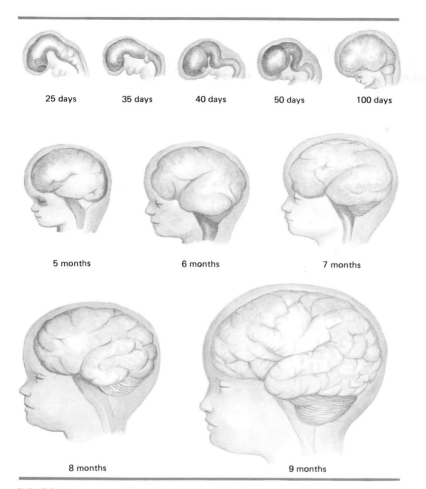

25 days      35 days      40 days      50 days      100 days

5 months        6 months        7 months

8 months                    9 months

**FIGURE 3-1**
Fetal brain development from 25 days of gestation through birth. As the brain
develops, the front part expands greatly to form the cerebrum (the large, convoluted
upper mass). Specific areas of the cerebral cortex (the gray outer covering of the
brain) have specific functions, such as sensory and motor activity; but large areas
are "uncommitted" and thus are free for higher intellectual activity, such as
thinking, remembering, and problem solving. The subcortex (the brain stem and
other structures below the cortical layer) handles reflex behavior and other lower-
level functions. The newborn's brain contains most of the cells it will eventually
have, but it is only about 25 percent of its adult weight. A rapid increase in cortical
connections during the first 2 years of life results in a dramatic weight gain (to four-
fifths of adult brain weight) and in the capacity for thought. (*Source*: Restak, 1984).

A spurt in the formation of brain cells comes just
before birth and shortly afterward. Within 2 months
after birth, practically no new cells are forming (Lipsitt,
1986), though existing cells continue to grow in size.
The cells sort themselves out by function, migrating to
their proper positions either in the **cerebral cortex**
(the upper level of the brain) or in the subcortical levels
(below the cortex). In a newborn infant, the subcortical
structures (which regulate such basic biological func-

tions as breathing and digestion) are the most fully developed; cells in the cortex (which is responsible for
thinking and problem solving) are not yet well connected. Connections between cortical cells increase
astronomically as the child matures, allowing more flexible, higher-level motor and intellectual functioning.

The development of the cortex occurs in several
stages. The innermost layers develop first; then the
outer layers develop. This is why the timing of prenatal

**TABLE 3–2**
HUMAN PRIMITIVE REFLEXES

| Reflex | Stimulation | Behavior |
|--------|-------------|----------|
| Rooting | Baby's cheek is stroked with finger or nipple. | Baby's head turns; mouth opens; sucking movements begin. |
| Darwinian (grasping) | Palm of baby's hand is stroked. | Baby makes strong first; can be raised to standing position if both fists are closed around a stick. |
| Swimming | Baby is put into water face down. | Baby makes well-coordinated swimming movements. |
| Tonic neck | Baby is laid down on back. | Baby turns head to one side, assumes "fencer" position, extends arms and legs on preferred side, flexes opposite limbs. |
| Moro (startle) | Baby is dropped or hears loud noise. | Baby extends legs, arms, and fingers; arches back: draws back head. |
| Babinski | Sole of baby's food is stroked. | Baby's toes fan out; foot twists in. |
| Walking | Baby is held under arms, with bare feet touching flat surface. | Baby makes steplike motions that look like well-coordinated walking. |
| Placing | Backs of baby's feet are drawn against edge of flat surface. | Baby withdraws foot. |

Rooting reflex.

Darwinian reflex.

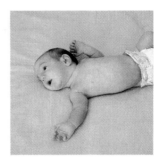

Tonic neck reflex.

Moro reflex.

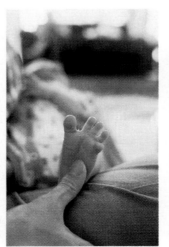

Babinski reflex.

Walking reflex.

"insults" (from drugs or other causes) makes such a difference in the kind of defect that may result. An "insult" may block the formation of an entire cell group. On the other hand, if an "insult" damages the brain after new cells have stopped forming, the remaining cells often change to compensate for the injured ones (Kolb, 1989).

The brain, which is only 25 percent of its adult weight at birth, reaches about two-thirds of its eventual weight during the first year and four-fifths by the end of the second year. It continues to grow more slowly until, by age 12, it is nearly of adult size. An infant's neurological growth permits development in motor and intellectual activities. Although programmed by the genes, this development is also affected by environmental influences.

Until the middle of the twentieth century, the established scientific view was that brain development followed an unchangeable pattern. Now we know that the brain is—figuratively speaking—plastic, especially while it is developing rapidly: it can be easily molded. Experiences of early life may have lasting effects, for better or worse, on the capacity of the central nervous system to learn and store information (Wittrock, 1980). For example, chronic malnutrition during either the prenatal period or the critical period shortly after birth can result in brain damage.

Furthermore, when rats and other animals were raised in "enriched" cages with stimulating apparatus, they developed heavier brains with thicker cortical layers, more connective cells, and higher levels of neurochemical activity (which helps to form connections between brain cells) than littermates raised in "standard" cages or in isolation (Rosenzweig, 1984; Rosenzweig & Bennett, 1976). And the brain's plasticity seems to continue to a lesser degree throughout most of the life span; similar neural differences appeared when older animals were exposed to different environments.

Such findings have sparked successful efforts to maximize the functioning of children with Down syndrome, to keep aging people mentally fit, and to help victims of brain damage recover. Brain plasticity can also help some infants with birth complications to develop normally.

## A Newborn's Reflexes

When babies (or adults) blink at a bright light, they are acting involuntarily. Such automatic responses to external stimulation are called ***reflex behaviors.***

Human beings have an array of reflexes, many of which are present before birth, at birth, or very soon after birth (see Table 3-2). Some of them seem to promote survival or offer protection. These "primitive" reflexes—or their absence—are early signs of brain development. Normally, the primitive reflexes disappear during the first year or so; for example, the Moro, or "startle," reflex drops out at 2 to 3 months, and rooting for the nipple at about 9 months. Such protective reflexes as blinking, yawning, coughing, gagging, sneezing, and the pupillary reflex (dilation of the pupils in the dark) remain. (Reflexes vary somewhat, however, according to culture; see Box 3-1 on page 86).

Because the subcortex controls the primitive reflexes, their disappearance indicates development of the cortex and a shift to voluntary behavior. Since there is a timetable for shedding these reflexes, their presence or absence in the first few months of life is a guide to evaluating neurological development. Testing for normal reflexes immediately after birth is one of many ways to assess a baby's health and functioning.

## THE NEWBORN'S HEALTH

How can we tell whether a neonate's systems are functioning normally? What can be done to help infants who suffer from complications of birth, who are born prematurely, or whose birthweight is dangerously low? In short, how can we ensure that babies will live, grow, and develop as they should?

### Medical and Behavioral Screening

Because the first few weeks, days, and even minutes after birth are crucial for development, it is important to know as soon as possible whether a baby has any problem that needs special care. To find out, doctors and psychologists use such tools as the Apgar and Brazelton scales and screen for certain medical conditions.

#### Immediate medical assessment: The Apgar scale

One minute after delivery, and then again 5 minutes after delivery, infants are evaluated using the ***Apgar scale*** (see Table 3-3 on page 87). The name of this scale commemorates its developer, Dr. Virginia Apgar (1953), and also helps us remember its five subtests: *a*ppearance (color), *p*ulse (heart rate), *g*rimace (reflex irritability), *a*ctivity (muscle tone), and *r*espiration (breathing).

The infant receives a rating of 0, 1, or 2 on each measure, for a possible maximum of 10. Ninety percent of normal infants score 7 or better. A score below 7 generally means that the baby needs help to establish breathing. A score below 4 means that the baby is in danger and needs immediate life-saving treatment. In

## BOX 3–1    WINDOW ON THE WORLD

# HOW UNIVERSAL IS "NORMAL" DEVELOPMENT?

What happens if you briefly press a baby's nose with a cloth? Western babies will normally turn their heads away or swipe at the cloth. But Chinese babies will probably open their mouths promptly to restore breathing, without a fight. What happens if you lift a baby's body, supporting its head, and then release the head support, allowing the head to drop? Typical white newborns show the Moro reflex: they extend both arms and legs, cry persistently, and move about in an agitated way. Navajo infants, however, typically respond with a reduced reflex extension of the limbs. They rarely cry and almost immediately stop any agitated behavior. These differences suggest that some reflex behaviors are not universal, as we might expect (D. G. Freedman, 1979).

Are motor skills universal? When the Denver Developmental Screening Test (described on page 102) was given to southeast Asian children (V. Miller, Onotera, & Deinard, 1984), the youngsters failed on three standard measures of normal development: they did not play pat-a-cake, they did not pick up raisins, and they did not dress themselves at the usual ages. But we cannot jump to the conclusion that these youngsters were backward in development. In their culture, children do not play pat-a-cake; raisins look like a medicine they are taught to avoid; and Asian parents do not expect children to dress themselves as early as American parents do. Because the test was devised for American children, it may be biased against children in cultures with different customs.

Even for universal behaviors like sitting and walking, what is "normal" or "typical" in one culture may not

be in another. Black African babies seem to be more precocious in gross motor skills, and Asian infants less so, than infants of European origin. These differences may be related to cultural differences in temperament. Asian infants, for example, are typically more docile and thus may tend to stay closer to their parents (Kaplan & Dove, 1987).

Although short-term experiments suggest that it is difficult (and not necessarily desirable) to speed up or modify a child's motor development, certain child-rearing practices that are widespread in a culture may advance or retard it. The anthropologist Margaret Mead saw that Arapesh infants in New Guinea could stand while holding on to something before they could sit alone. The reason, Mead reported, was that these infants were often held in a standing position, "so that they can push with their feet against the arms or legs of the person who holds them" (1935, p. 57).

At 3 months of age, babies from the Yucatan peninsula in Mexico are ahead of American babies in manipulative motor skills; yet by 11 months the Yucatecan babies are far behind in locomotive skills—so much so that the same pattern in an American child might be taken as an indication of neurological disease (Solomons, 1978). The Yucatecan babies' manipulative precocity may result from their having no toys and thus discovering and playing with their fingers sooner. Their delayed skills in moving about may have to do with their being swaddled as infants and restrained in various ways as they get older. However, Navajo babies—who are also swaddled for most of the day—begin to walk at about the

same time as other American babies (Chisholm, 1983).

Some cultural differences in motor development may reflect genetic differences among peoples, which have arisen through the process of natural selection. This evolutionary process occurs as individuals who adapt successfully to their environment survive and reproduce, passing on their hereditary traits to their offspring. This may explain why Ache children in eastern Paraguay show delays in gross motor skills, walking about 9 months later than American babies (Kaplan & Dove, 1987). Until the mid-1970s, the Ache economy relied on hunting and foraging. Natural selection may have favored more cautious, less exploratory individuals. Another explanation may lie in the tendency of Ache mothers to pull their babies back when they begin to crawl away, to protect them from danger. Perhaps when mothers spend less time in direct child care, children become independent sooner because their caretakers are less vigilant—an observation that may be relevant today, when day care is prevalent and some aspects of development seem to be occurring at earlier ages than they did previously.

Children in other cultures who show early developmental lags often catch up to American children later. Ache 8- to 10-year-olds climb tall trees, chop branches, and play in ways that enhance their motor skills. Development, then, may be viewed "as a series of immediate adjustments to current conditions as well as a cumulative process in which succeeding stages build upon earlier ones" (Kaplan & Dove, 1987, p. 197).

Some observers have suggested that babies from the Yucatan develop motor skills later than American babies because they are swaddled. But Navajo babies, like this one, are also swaddled for most of the day, and they begin to walk at about the same time as other American babies. Another explanation for such developmental variations might be hereditary differences.

that case, the test is repeated at 5-minute intervals to check on the effectiveness of resuscitation. If the effort succeeds and the score rises to at least 4, there are usually no serious long-term consequences. A score of 0 to 3 at 10, 15, and 20 minutes suggests a greater risk of neurological damage, particularly cerebral palsy (American Academy of Pediatrics, AAP, Committee on Fetus and Newborn, 1986).

A low Apgar score does not always indicate that a baby is suffocating. An infant's tone and responsiveness may be affected by the amount of sedation or pain-killing medication the mother received. Neurological and cardiorespiratory conditions may interfere with one or

more vital signs. Premature infants may score low simply because of their physiological immaturity.

Recently, there has been some criticism of the Apgar test, partly because it is not as sensitive as more recent physiological measures (one new test, for instance, measures the oxygen in the newborn's blood). Another important charge is that the Apgar has little predictive value, mostly because of sloppy administration. However, since the Apgar test is inexpensive and easy to administer, it should probably not be abandoned; rather, hospital workers should be taught to perform it better and to act quickly on the basis of its results.

**TABLE 3–3**
APGAR SCALE

| Sign* | 0 | 1 | 2 |
|---|---|---|---|
| Appearance (color) | Blue, pale | Body pink, extremities blue | Entirely pink |
| Pulse (heart rate) | Absent | Slow (below 100) | Rapid (over 100) |
| Grimace (reflex irritability) | No response | Grimace | Coughing, sneezing, crying |
| Activity (muscle tone) | Limp | Weak, inactive | Strong, active |
| Respiration (breathing) | Absent | Irregular, slow | Good, crying |

*Each sign is rated in terms of absence or presence from 0 to 2; highest overall score is 10.
*Source:* Adapted from Apgar, 1953.

### Neonatal screening for medical conditions

Children who inherit the enzyme disorder phenylketon-uria (PKU) will become mentally retarded unless they are fed a special diet beginning in the first 3 to 6 weeks of life. Screening tests that can be administered imme-diately after birth can often discover such correctable defects. Routine screening of all newborn babies for such rare conditions as PKU (1 case in 14,000 births), hypothyroidism (1 in 4250), and galactosemia (1 in 62,000)—or other, even rarer disorders—is, of course, expensive. Yet the cost of detecting one case of a rare disease is often less than the cost of caring for a mentally retarded child for a lifetime. Almost all states require routine screening for PKU, and about half of the states require screening for one or more other condi-tions.

### Assessing responses: The Brazelton scale

The **Brazelton Neonatal Behavioral Assessment Scale** is a neurological and behavioral test used to mea-sure neonates' responses to their environment (Brazel-ton, 1973). The Brazelton scale assesses four dimen-sions of infants' behavior:

1 *Interactive behaviors,* like alertness and cuddling
2 *Motor behaviors* (reflexes, muscle tone, and hand-mouth coordination)
3 *Physiological control,* like the ability to quiet down after being upset
4 *Response to stress* (the startle reaction)

The Brazelton test takes about 30 minutes, and scores are based on a baby's best performance rather than an average. Testers try to get babies to do their best, sometimes repeating an item and sometimes ask-ing the mother to alert her baby. The Brazelton scale may be a better predictor of future development than the Apgar scale or standard neurological testing (Behr-man & Vaughan, 1983).

### Effects of Birth Trauma

For a small minority of babies, the passage through the birth canal is a particularly harrowing journey. A study of more than 15,000 births over a period of 6 years at an outstanding medical school (A. Rubin, 1977) found that although fewer than 1 percent of the infants suf-fered **birth trauma**—injury sustained at the time of birth—such trauma was still the second most common cause of neonatal death (after suffocation because of

failure of the lungs to expand). Birth trauma may be caused by anoxia (oxygen deprivation at birth), neonatal diseases or infections, or mechanical injury; some trau-mas leave permanent brain damage, causing mental re-tardation or behavior problems.

Often, however, the effects of birth injuries can be counteracted by a favorable environment. In a longitu-dinal study of almost 900 children born on the island of Kauai, Hawaii, those whose births had been difficult, whose birthweight had been low, or who had been sick when born were examined at age 10, at age 18, and in their early thirties. The findings were clear: "Perinatal complications were consistently related to later im-paired physical and psychological development *only* when combined with persistently poor environmental circumstances" (E. E. Werner, 1985, p. 341). Unless the damage was so severe as to require institutionaliza-tion, these children—when their environment was sta-ble and enriching—did better in school and had fewer language, perceptual, and emotional problems than chil-dren who had not experienced unusual stress at birth but who had suffered "environmental trauma" in poor homes where they received little intellectual stimula-tion or emotional support (E. E. Werner, 1989; E. E. Werner et al., 1968).

We see, then, that children are remarkably resilient, and even very alarming one-time events can be less important than day-to-day experience.

### Low Birthweight and Infant Mortality

We have made great strides in protecting the lives of new babies. Today in the United States the **infant mortality rate**—the proportion of babies who die within the first year of life—is the lowest in our history. In 1988, for every 1000 live births there were about 10 deaths during the first year—an improvement of more than 60 percent since 1960 (Wegman, 1989).

Even so, the nearly 40,000 infants who died before their first birthday represented the largest number of deaths in any single year of life up to age 65. Almost two-thirds of those babies died in their first 4 weeks (U. S. Department of Health and Human Services, USDHHS, 1990).

Birth defects are the leading cause of infant mortality (Morbidity and Mortality Weekly Report, MMWR, 1989b). But **low birthweight**—a weight of 5½ pounds or less at birth—follows closely as a major fac-tor in infant death and in the poorer chances American babies have for survival than babies in 21 other industri-alized countries (Wegman, 1989) (see Figure 3-2, oppo-site, and Figure 3-3 on page 90).

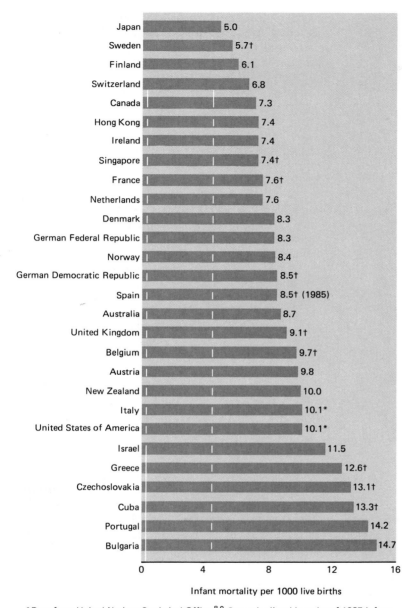

Infant mortality per 1000 live births

*Data from United Nations Statistical Office.[8,9] Countries listed in order of 1987 infant mortality rate. Birth rate per 1000 population. Infant mortality rate per 1000 live births.
†Provisional data.

**FIGURE 3-2**
Infant mortality rates in industrialized countries as of 1987. A nation's infant mortality rate is one indicator of its health status. The United States is only twenty-second among 28 industrialized nations with populations of 2.5 million or more, largely because of its very high rate for minority babies. The overall infant mortality rate in the United States was 10.4 per 1000 births, but the rate for white babies was only 8.9 while the rate for black babies was 18. (*Sources:* U.S. Department of Health and Human Services, USDHHS, 1990; Wegman, 1989.)

About 7 percent of babies born in the United States —1 in 14—have low birthweights (USDHHS, 1990). According to government statistics, these babies are at least 5 times more likely to die during the first 4 weeks of life than are those weighing 6½ pounds or more; and babies weighing 3⅓ pounds or less are 90 times more likely to die. These figures are better than they used to be because of improved ways of keeping these babies alive, but public health authorities are concerned because the rate of low birthweight itself is rising.

An overall improvement in infant survival may result from such factors as centers for prenatal and postnatal care, early identification of high-risk pregnancies, and spacing of pregnancies to reduce the danger of high-risk

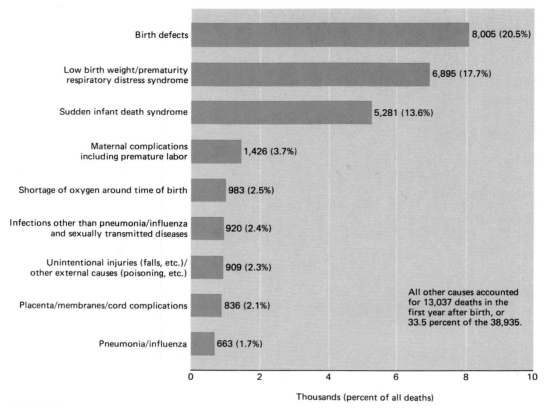

Birth defects — 8,005 (20.5%)
Low birth weight/prematurity respiratory distress syndrome — 6,895 (17.7%)
Sudden infant death syndrome — 5,281 (13.6%)
Maternal complications including premature labor — 1,426 (3.7%)
Shortage of oxygen around time of birth — 983 (2.5%)
Infections other than pneumonia/influenza and sexually transmitted diseases — 920 (2.4%)
Unintentional injuries (falls, etc.)/ other external causes (poisoning, etc.) — 909 (2.3%)
Placenta/membranes/cord complications — 836 (2.1%)
Pneumonia/influenza — 663 (1.7%)

All other causes accounted for 13,037 deaths in the first year after birth, or 33.5 percent of the 38,935.

Thousands (percent of all deaths)

**FIGURE 3-3**
Leading causes of infant mortality in the United States in 1986. Birth defects are the most common cause of death in infancy, but low birthweight and sudden infant death syndrome (SIDS) followed closely as major factors. (*Sources*: Morbidity and Mortality Weekly Report, MMWR, 1989b; *New York Times.*)

births (AAP Task Force on Infant Mortality, 1986; C. A. Miller, 1985). But the rate of improvement seems to be slowing, possibly because of a rise in deaths *after* the neonatal period. Also, these factors have not brought the same benefits to the African American community. About twice as many black babies die as white babies; and while the survival rate of black infants has improved, it has not kept pace with the dramatic overall improvement.

The main difference is in black and white babies' birthweights. Government data show that black newborns are more than twice as likely as white newborns to have low birthweights and 3 times as likely to have very low birthweights. The average baby from a socioeconomically disadvantaged group weighs ½ pound less at birth than the average middle-class baby. Yet, as one pediatric nutritionist notes, "Pound for pound, the poor baby does as well as the rich baby; black babies do as well as white babies" (Winick, 1981, p. 80).

## Types of low birthweight

All very small infants used to be considered "premature"; that is, it was assumed that they had not completed the full term of a normal gestation. Doctors now assign very small babies to one or both of the following two categories:

- ■ ***Preterm (premature) babies*** are born before the thirty-seventh gestational week, dated from the first day of the mother's last menstrual period. (Normal gestation, as we saw in Chapter 2, is 40 weeks.) Babies in this category typically weigh less than 5½ pounds. They account for 60 percent of low-birthweight babies.
- ■ ***Small-for-date babies,*** who weigh less than 90 percent of all babies of the same gestational age, may or may not be preterm. For babies in this category, low birthweight has resulted from slowed fetal growth.

Because the distinction between the two types of low-birthweight babies has evolved only within the past decade or so, it has not been considered in most studies of the effects of "prematurity." Therefore we do not know whether most studies of low-birthweight babies yield information about babies who were born early, about babies who were small for their gestational age, or about both.

The risks for both types of babies are similar, but premature babies are more likely to die in infancy than small-for-date babies are (Behrman, 1985). The shorter the gestation period (if it is less than 36 weeks), the more problems the baby is likely to have. The neonatal transition takes longer for preterm babies because they enter the world with less fully developed body systems.

### Risk factors in low birthweight

Women in certain categories are statistically more likely than others to give birth to underweight infants (see Table 3-4). Low birthweight is associated with the following factors (S. S. Brown, 1985):

- *Demographic factors,* like race, age, education, and marital status
- *Medical factors predating the pregnancy,* like previous abortions, stillbirths, or medical conditions
- *Medical factors associated with the current pregnancy,* like bleeding or too little weight gain
- *Prenatal behavioral and environmental factors,* like poor nutrition, inadequate prenatal care, smoking, use of alcohol and drugs, and exposure to toxic substances

How can these risk factors be reduced? Women, of course, should stop smoking, eat better, give up drugs and alcohol, get treatment for chronic illness, and obtain early and regular prenatal care. In addition, public information programs and prepregnancy counseling for women who have previously lost low-birthweight infants can be of help.

### Consequences of low birthweight

Very small babies suffer from many potentially fatal complications. Because the immune system is not fully developed, they are more vulnerable to infection, and infectious diseases are an increasing cause of death (Jason, 1989). Their reflexes are not mature enough to perform some of the functions basic to survival; they may, for example, be unable to suck and have to be fed

**TABLE 3–4**
PRINCIPAL MATERNAL RISK FACTORS FOR DELIVERING UNDERWEIGHT INFANTS

| Category | Risks |
|---|---|
| Demographic risks | Age (under 17 or over 34)<br>Race (black)<br>Low socioeconomic status<br>Unmarried<br>Low level of education |
| Medical risks predating current pregnancy | No children or more than four<br>Low weight for height<br>Genital or urinary abnormalities or past surgery<br>Diseases such as diabetes or chronic hypertension<br>Lack of immunity to certain infections, such as rubella<br>Poor obstetric history, including previous low-birth-weight infant and multiple spontaneous abortions<br>Genetic factors in the mother (such as low weight at her own birth) |
| Medical risks in current pregnancy | Multiple pregnancy<br>Poor weight gain (less than 14 pounds)<br>Less than 6 months since previous pregnancy<br>Low blood pressure<br>Hypertension or toxemia<br>Certain infections, such as rubella and urinary infections<br>Bleeding in the first or second trimester<br>Placental problems<br>Anemia or abnormal hemoglobin<br>Fetal abnormalities<br>Incompetent cervix<br>Spontaneous premature rupture of membranes |
| Behavioral and environmental risks | Smoking<br>Poor nutritional status<br>Abuse of alcohol and other substances<br>Exposure to DES and other toxins, including those in the workplace<br>High altitude |
| Risks involving health care | Absent or inadequate prenatal care<br>Premature delivery by cesarean section or induced labor |

*Source:* Adapted from S.S. Brown, 1985.

intravenously. Because they have less fat to insulate them and to generate heat, it is harder for them to maintain normal body temperature, and so it is especially important to keep them warm. Low-birthweight babies have a higher incidence of low blood sugar, jaundice, and bleeding in the brain than babies of normal size, and their lungs may not be strong enough to sustain breathing.

A common disorder is respiratory distress syndrome (also called *hyaline membrane disease*). Babies with respiratory distress syndrome lack an essential lung-coating substance and therefore breathe irregularly or stop breathing altogether and die. Fortunately, medical progress had caused such deaths to decline by almost 45 percent between 1979 and 1987 (Wegman, 1989).

In the past, even when low-birthweight babies survived the dangerous early days, they were often left with various disabling conditions. Now, however, not only are more low-birthweight babies surviving, but most of the survivors are doing fairly well.

Still, low birthweight may have long-term consequences. In an analysis of 80 studies published since 1979, for example, about a 6-point difference in IQ was found between low-birthweight infants and normal controls (97.7 versus 103.78—both in the average range) (Aylward, Pfeiffer, Wright, & Verhulst, 1989). This difference is statistically significant, although it may not have affected the children's lives. The differences in IQ scores did not show up until after age 2; this is the age when verbal ability becomes more important and when scores are more predictive of later scores; but it is also the age when the environment makes more of a difference. (All these factors are discussed in Chapter 4.)

IQ measures, however, may not pick up subtle dysfunctions that may cause learning disabilities and that are more common in low-birthweight babies. More specific assessments are needed to predict later academic and behavioral problems. For example, 7-month-olds who had been born early did not do as well as full-term babies of the same age on tests of attention and visual-recognition memory; and their poorer performance persisted in intelligence test scores at age 5 (S. A. Rose, Feldman, Wallace, & McCarton, 1989; S. A. Rose & Wallace, 1985). The kinds of homes children grow up in affect outcomes; children in higher socioeconomic circumstances are better able to overcome the early disadvantage of low birthweight (Aylward et al., 1989; Beckwith & Cohen, 1989; McCormick, 1989).

## Treatment of low birthweight

Much of the increase in neonatal survival is due to improved care. The low-birthweight baby is placed in an *isolette*—an antiseptic, temperature-controlled crib (formerly called an *incubator*)—and is fed through tubes. Jaundiced babies are placed under special lights, anemic babies get iron supplements, and babies with low blood sugar are fed glucose intravenously (through the veins).

Hospitals used to maintain a "hands off" policy in the belief that these delicate creatures were best left undisturbed once their basic needs were met, as if they were still in the womb. But life in the womb, where sounds and motion reach the fetus, is more interesting than life in an isolette. It now seems that isolation and its resulting sensory impoverishment may cause problems for both infant and parents.

Parents tend to view a low-birthweight baby negatively and are likely to be anxious about the baby's health. Afraid that the baby may die, they may also be afraid of becoming too attached (Jeffcoate, Humphrey, & Lloyd, 1979). This makes them treat the child differently, perhaps touching the baby less, offering less mature toys, and feeling less comfortable around the baby (Stern & Hildebrandt, 1986).

Frequent visits can give parents a more realistic idea of how the baby is doing, and perhaps a more optimistic attitude. In addition, babies who are visited frequently seem to recover more quickly and leave the hospital sooner (Zeskind & Iacino, 1984). Parents who get extra counseling tend to care for their babies better afterward (Minde et al., 1980), unless the mothers are so overwhelmed by other life stresses that they can barely get through each day (J. Brown et al., 1980). In such cases, intervention and support from professional agencies are especially important.

Other efforts to help low-birthweight babies show promising results. In the first large-scale study of a development program for such babies, significant gains in intelligence and social functioning appeared (Infant Health & Development Program, 1990). In this study, 985 babies were divided into two groups. The babies, mostly from poor families living in inner cities, all weighed less than 5½ pounds at birth. The parents of the babies in the experimental group received group counseling every 2 weeks. Every week they were visited by researchers, who gave them information about health and development and taught them games and activities to improve their children's cognitive, language, and social skills. At 1 year, these babies entered an educational day care program.

The tiniest babies thrive on human touch. This nurse's holding and stroking of a low-birthweight baby will help the baby grow and be more alert.

What were the results? By age 3, these children scored higher on IQ tests and functioned better than the control group, who had not received the intervention. The heavier babies (4.4 to 5.5 pounds at birth) in the special program had IQs 13.2 points higher than the controls, and the lighter babies (less than 4.4 pounds at birth) had IQs 6.6 points higher than the controls. The controls were almost 3 times more likely to show mental retardation. In addition, fewer mothers in the experimental group reported behavior problems in their children, possibly because the mothers had learned what to expect of their children and how to manage them effectively. Follow-up studies will see whether these effects will hold up over the years.

Other research has confirmed the value of touch stimulation (massage) in fostering growth, behavioral organization, weight gain, motor activity, and alertness (T. M. Field, 1986; Schanberg & Field, 1987).

## Sudden Infant Death Syndrome (SIDS)

One kind of death in infancy follows a typical, sad scenario: a baby falls asleep peacefully, but a parent comes in later and finds the baby dead. ***Sudden infant death syndrome (SIDS)*** is the sudden death of an apparently healthy infant under 1 year of age, which remains unexplained after a complete postmortem examination. Some 7000 babies a year, or about 2 out of every 1000 babies born, die of SIDS, which is the leading cause of deaths in infants from 1 to 12 months old. SIDS occurs most often between 2 and 4 months of age, but it occurs very rarely before 3 weeks or after 9 months (Zylke, 1989).

We know little about SIDS. The death is not caused by suffocation, vomiting, or choking. It is most common in winter. It is not contagious. There is no known way to predict or prevent it.

Several risk factors are related to sudden infant death syndrome. Babies who succumb to SIDS are more likely to be of low birthweight, black, and male. Their mothers are more likely to be young, unmarried, and poor; to have received little or no prenatal care; to have been ill during pregnancy; to smoke or abuse drugs or both; and to have had another baby less than 1 year before the one who has died. The fathers are are also more likely to be young (Babson & Clark, 1983; C. E. Hunt & Brouillette, 1987; Kleinberg, 1984; D. C. Shannon & Kelly, 1982a, 1982b; USDHHS, 1990; Valdes-Dapena, 1980). The problems of such babies are worsened by living in poor socioeconomic circumstances. However, SIDS also strikes infants in advantaged families.

New theories about the cause of sudden infant death syndrome are constantly being proposed, including such possibilities as respiratory or neurological dysfunction and abnormal brain chemistry. A recent review concluded that the most compelling hypothesis about SIDS relates it to a brain abnormality involving control of breathing (C. E. Hunt & Brouillette, 1987). One controversial study questioned the attribution of some infant deaths to SIDS, suggesting that these deaths may actually have been caused by accidents (Bass, Kravath, & Glass, 1986).

The bereaved families suffer greatly. In studies of SIDS families, all the parents considered SIDS the most severe family crisis they had ever experienced (DeFrain & Ernst, 1978; DeFrain, Taylor, & Ernst, 1982). The parents felt guilty and under criticism from society. Siblings often reacted with nightmares and school problems. It usually took almost a year for the families to recover.

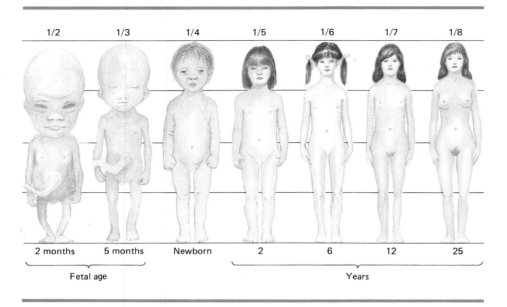

| 1/2 | 1/3 | 1/4 | 1/5 | 1/6 | 1/7 | 1/8 |

| 2 months | 5 months | Newborn | 2 | 6 | 12 | 25 |

Fetal age                    Years

**FIGURE 3-4**

Changes in proportions of the human body during growth. The most striking change is that the head becomes smaller relative to the rest of the body: the fractions indicate head size as a proportion of total body length at several ages. More subtle is the stability of the trunk proportion (from neck to crotch). The increasing leg proportion is almost exactly the reverse of the decreasing head proportion.

## DEVELOPMENT DURING THE FIRST 3 YEARS OF LIFE

Fortunately, 990 out of 1000 children do *not* die in the first year of life but go on to develop normally, as we'll now see.

### PRINCIPLES OF DEVELOPMENT

Development is not haphazard or idiosyncratic. Rather, it progresses along logical lines that are similar for all human beings. Three guiding principles are at work in growth and development both before and after birth.

### Top-to-Bottom Development

Babies develop head first. The ***cephalocaudal principle*** ("head to tail," from Greek and Latin roots) dictates that development proceeds from the head to the lower parts of the body. As we saw in Table 2-1, an embryo's head, brain, and eyes develop earliest; the head of a 2-month-old embryo is half the length of the

entire body. By the time of birth, the head is only one-fourth the length of the body but is still disproportionately large; it becomes less so as the child grows (see Figure 3-4).

Furthermore, infants learn to *use* the upper parts of the body before the lower parts. Babies can see objects before they can control the trunk, and they can use their hands to grasp long before they can walk.

### Inner-to-Outer Development

Before infants can use their hands purposefully, they are quite adept at moving their arms. This is evidence of a second principle of development that is at work beginning in the womb. According to the ***proximodistal principle*** ("near to far," from Latin roots), development proceeds from the central part of the body to the outer parts. The embryonic head and trunk develop before the limbs, and the arms and legs before the fingers and toes. Babies first develop the ability to use their upper arms and upper legs (which are closest to the central axis), then their forearms and forelegs, then their hands and feet, and finally their fingers and toes.

### Simple-to-Complex Development

Although Kim was able to sit up at 6 months and Julio not until 11 months, both could sit with support before they could sit alone. The third rule of development is obvious yet profound: in acquiring practically all skills, physical or other, we progress from the simple to the complex.

Maturation follows an apparently predetermined course. The times when individual babies reach specific milestones vary widely—there is no "right" age for being able to stand or speak. But almost all children progress in a definite order from simpler movements and activities to more complicated ones. (Only with specific kinds of stimulation, like those sometimes found in mother-child interactions in certain nonwestern cultures, is the sequence altered noticeably; refer back to Box 3-1).

We now look at specific aspects of physical development during the first 3 years of life. Let's first see how babies spend their time—noting the increasing wakefulness that allows them to develop in response to the world around them. We'll then consider their dramatic physical growth; after that, we'll examine their increasing sensory capacities and their increasing motor capabilities.

## STATES: THE BODY'S CYCLES

The human body has an inner "clock" that regulates cycles of eating, sleeping, elimination, and perhaps even mood. These patterns of timing, which seem inborn, govern the various *states* of infants—the periodic variations in their daily cycles of wakefulness, sleep, and activity (see Table 3-5).

**TABLE 3–5**
STATES IN INFANCY

| State | Eyes | Breathing | Movements | Responsiveness |
|-------|------|-----------|-----------|----------------|
| Regular sleep | Closed | Regular | None, except for sudden, generalized startles | Cannot be aroused by mild stimuli. |
| Irregular sleep | Closed | Irregular | Muscles twitch, but no major movements | Sounds or light bring smiles or grimaces in sleep. |
| Drowsiness | Open or closed | Irregular | Somewhat active | May smile, startle, suck, or have erections in response to stimuli. |
| Alert inactivity | Open | | Quiet; may move head, limbs, and trunk while looking around | An interesting environment (with people or things to watch) may initiate or maintain this state. |
| Waking activity and crying | Open | | Much activity | External stimuli (such as hunger, cold, pain, being restrained, or being put down) bring about more activity, perhaps starting with soft whimpering and gentle movements and turning into a rhythmic crescendo of crying or kicking, or perhaps beginning and enduring as uncoordinated thrashing and spasmodic screeching. |

*Sources:* Adapted from information in Prechtl & Beintema, 1964; and Wolff, 1966.

Neonates sleep more than they do anything else, but each baby's sleep pattern is different. The average is about 16 hours of sleep a day, yet one healthy baby may sleep only 11 hours while another sleeps 21 (Parmelee, Wenner, & Schulz, 1964). This sleep, of course, is not continuous. The next time you say "I slept like a baby," remember that new babies usually wake up every 2 to 3 hours around the clock.

To the heartfelt relief of parents, this pattern soon changes. At about 3 months, babies grow more wakeful in the late afternoon and early evening and start to sleep through the night. By that age, most babies "sleep through" without eating or crying; by 6 months, babies do more than half their sleeping at night. Their increasing daytime wakefulness, alertness, and activity are accompanied by rapid physical, intellectual, and emotional development.

Sleep patterns change, too. Newborns have about six to eight sleep periods, which alternate between quiet and active sleep. Babies cannot tell us if they dream, but active sleep (probably the equivalent of rapid eye movement or REM sleep, which in adults is associated with dreaming) appears rhythmically in cycles of about 1 hour and accounts for 50 to 80 percent of a newborn's total sleep time. During the first 6 months, the amount of this active sleep diminishes until it accounts for only 30 percent of sleep time, and the lengths of the cycles become more consistent (Coons & Guilleminault, 1982).

Babies' states give us clues to how their bodies work and how they are responding to what goes on around them. A baby in a state of deep sleep responds to stimulation very differently from an alert baby or a drowsy one. And parents' reactions to a baby who is almost always sleepy or who spends a great deal of time in a state of interested, quiet wakefulness are different from their reactions to a baby who is often awake and crying. Thus infants' states influence how their parents treat them, which in turn influences what kinds of people they will turn out to be.

Parents try to change a baby's state when they pick up or feed a crying infant or soothe a fussy one to sleep. In most cases, crying is more distressing than serious. But for low-birthweight babies, crying interferes with maintenance of weight. The age-old way to soothe crying babies involves steady stimulation—rocking or walking them, wrapping them snugly, or letting them hear rhythmic sounds or suck on pacifiers. A baby who is easy to soothe enhances a caregiver's sense of competence and self-worth, thereby helping to set up a mutually reinforcing cycle.

Beginning at birth, babies show unique behaviors during wakeful periods. Jenny sticks her tongue in and out; Davey makes rhythmic sucking movements. Some infants smile often; others do not. Some boys have erections frequently, others rarely.

The level and kind of activity a newborn shows can also provide a glimpse into the child's future. One study, which followed up children at ages 4 and 8 whose movements had been electronically monitored during the first 3 days of life, shows the continuity in development we noted in Chapter 1. The most vigorous newborns tended to become highly active children who welcomed new experiences; the least vigorous newborns tended to be the least active when they got older (Korner et al., 1985).

## GROWTH AND NOURISHMENT

Growth is faster during the first 3 years—and especially during the first few months—than it ever will be again (see Figure 3-5). Children's early physical growth and muscular development make possible the rapid motor advancements of this period.

At 5 months, the typical baby's birthweight has doubled. This brings a baby who weighed 7½ pounds (the average birthweight) to about 15 pounds. By 1 year, babies weigh 3 times their birthweight—on average, about 22 pounds. During the second year, this rapid growth tapers off; the child gains 5 or 6 pounds and by the second birthday weighs about 4 times his or her birthweight. During the third year, the gain is even less: about 4 to 5 pounds, for an average weight of 31 or 32 pounds.

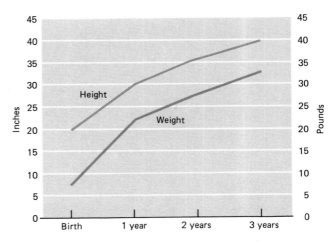

FIGURE 3-5
Growth in height and weight during infancy and toddlerhood. Babies grow most rapidly in both height and weight during the first few months of life, then taper off somewhat by age 3.

The same pattern holds true for height, which increases by about 10 to 12 inches during the first year, making the typical 1-year-old about 30 inches tall. The average 2-year-old has grown about 6 inches and is 3 feet tall; another 3 to 4 inches will be added in the third year.

As young children grow in size, their shape also changes. The rest of the body catches up with the head, which becomes proportionately smaller until full adult height is reached (as was shown in Figure 3-4). Most children become leaner; the 3-year old is slender, compared with the chubby, potbellied 1-year-old.

Teething usually begins around 3 or 4 months (when infants begin grabbing almost everything in sight to put into their mouths), but the first tooth may not arrive until sometime between 5 and 9 months of age or even later. By the first birthday, babies generally have 6 to 8 teeth; by age 2½, they have a mouthful—20 (Behrman & Vaughan, 1983).

### Influences on Growth

The genes that babies inherit have the biggest say in shaping the body: whether it will be tall and thin, short and stocky, or in between. Gender and racial differences exist. Boys are slightly longer and heavier than girls at birth and remain larger throughout adulthood, except for a brief time during puberty (when girls' earlier growth spurt causes them to overtake boys). The bones of black children harden earlier than those of white children, and their permanent teeth appear sooner. Black children mature earlier than white children, and they tend to be larger (AAP, 1973).

Height and weight are also affected by health and by such environmental factors as nutrition, living conditions, and medical care. Well-fed, well-cared-for children tend to grow taller and heavier than children whose care and nutrition are inadequate; they mature sexually and attain their full height earlier, and their teeth erupt sooner. Differences in growth usually show up by the first year and remain consistent throughout life (AAP, 1973).

Certain illnesses can have grave effects on growth and development. Although some children who are ill for a long time catch up later, others may never achieve their genetically programmed stature. Depending on the circumstances, they may not be able to make up for the growth time lost while they were sick.

We see, then, how heredity and environment interact in the process of physical growth. Let's now look specifically at nourishment, considering feeding practices that can influence babies' growth and development.

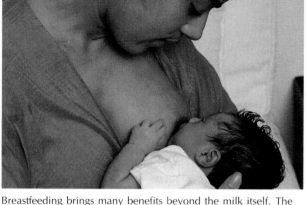

Breastfeeding brings many benefits beyond the milk itself. The close, warm contact helps to establish bonding between mother and baby. More than 60 percent of contemporary American mothers choose this natural method of feeding.

### Breastfeeding

After a 50-year decline in popularity, breastfeeding has made a strong comeback, especially among better-educated, high-income women. In 1971, only 25 percent of new mothers breastfed their babies. When Sally was growing up, she never saw a child being nursed, but when she first became a mother, she decided to breastfeed her baby—and found the experience so gratifying that she went on to nurse her other two children (and was inspired to write both her first published article and her first book about breastfeeding). Today, more than half of new mothers breastfeed, and at least 5 times as many mothers now (as compared with 1971) continue to nurse their babies until at least the fifth or sixth month (AAP, 1989a; Eiger & Olds, 1987).

These increases have occurred across socioeconomic and educational levels (Martinez & Kreiger, 1985), but breastfeeding is still less popular than bottle feeding among younger, poorer, and minority women (Fetterly & Graubard, 1984; Rassin et al., 1984). The rate of nursing dropped somewhat from 1980 to 1988 (AAP, 1989a), partly because many hospital practices discourage it and many doctors are not knowledgeable enough about it to help and encourage new mothers.

Even though today's excellent infant formulas approximate human milk, breast milk is still almost always the best food for newborns. It has been called the "ultimate health food," because it offers so many benefits (Eiger & Olds, 1987, p. 26). Breast milk is a complete source of nutrients for young infants, more digestible than cow's milk and less likely to produce allergic reactions. Because the way babies suck at the breast is different from the way they suck on a bottle, their teeth and jaws develop better when they are breastfed (Labbok & Hendershot, 1987). Breastfed children get varying degrees of protection against diarrhea and respiratory infections like pneumonia and bronchitis (Fallot, Boyd, & Oski, 1980; Forman et al., 1984; Howie et al., 1990; Wright, Holberg, Martinez, Morgan, & Taussig, 1989). Low-birthweight infants digest and absorb the fat in breast milk better than that in cow's milk formula; and the milk of mothers of premature babies has a different composition from that of mothers of full-term infants, which may be "nature's way" of meeting premature babies' needs (Alemi, Hamosh, Scanlon, Salzman-Mann, & Hamosh, 1981).

Breastfeeding is an emotional as well as a physical act. The warm contact with the mother's body fosters bonding, or emotional linkage, between mother and baby, although such bonding also, of course, takes place with bottle feeding. A mother's health, her emotional state, her lifestyle, and her attitude toward breastfeeding affect her ability to nurse her child. A very small proportion of women are physically unable to nurse; other women have strong feelings against it or are prevented by work or travel. Women are more likely to breastfeed if they begin within the first 10 hours after birth, have had a vaginal rather than a cesarean delivery (because a surgical delivery demands a longer recovery time), and do not return to work soon after the baby's birth (Romero-Gwynn & Carias, 1989).

To encourage new mothers to consider breastfeeding, doctors, nurses, expectant parents, and schoolchildren need information about nutrition and lactation; hospitals should make it possible for mothers to nurse on "demand" rather than restrict babies' feedings to rigid 3- or 4-hour schedules; and employers should provide child care centers near the workplace.

## Bottle Feeding

Babies who are fed with properly prepared formula and raised with love also grow up healthy and well adjusted. Most bottle-fed babies receive a formula based on either cow's milk or soy protein. These formulas are manufactured to resemble mother's milk as closely as possible, but they contain supplemental vitamins and minerals that breast milk does not have. Breast milk or formula is the only food most babies need till about 4 to 6 months of age.

Long-term studies that have compared breastfed and bottle-fed children have found no significant differences (McClelland, Constantian, Regalado, & Stone, 1978; M. H. Schmitt, 1970). The quality of the relationship between mother and child seems to be more important than the feeding method.

## Cow's Milk and Solid Foods

Because infants who were fed plain cow's milk in the early months of life were found to suffer from iron deficiency (Sadowitz & Oski, 1983), the American Academy of Pediatrics (AAP, 1989b) recommends that babies receive breast milk or formula until they are at least 6 months old, and ideally until 1 year. Then they can switch to cow's milk if they are getting a balanced diet of supplementary solid foods providing one-third of their caloric intake. They should get homogenized whole milk fortified with vitamin D—not skim milk, since babies need the calories in whole milk for proper growth (Fomon, Filer, Anderson, & Ziegler, 1979). They do not need specially blended follow-up, or "weaning," formulas (AAP, 1989b).

Although the AAP recommends waiting to start solid foods until 4 to 6 months of age, many infants begin getting solids—usually cereal or strained fruits—by the age of 2 months. This practice results from aggressive marketing of baby food, parents' competitiveness, and the belief that solid food will help babies sleep through the night. Some nutritionists condemn early feeding of solids as a form of "forced feeding" (Fomon et al., 1979, p. 54), because babies who cannot sit without support or control their heads and necks cannot effectively communicate when they have had enough. (See Box 3-2 for a discussion of obesity in infants, a possible consequence of overfeeding.)

Of course, children need a good diet beyond infancy. After 1 year, they need a varied diet drawn from all the major food groups. Those from families with histories of high cholesterol should be screened after age 2 to see whether they need special diets or medicine, and some physicians are now recommending routine cholesterol screening after age 3 for *all* children (Garcia & Moodie, 1989). Current trends toward consumption of less saturated fat, less cholesterol, and less salt should be followed in moderation: "Diets that avoid extremes are safe for children for whom there is no evidence of special vulnerability" (AAP Committee on Nutrition, 1986, p. 524).

# WHEN DOES OBESITY BEGIN, AND WHAT SHOULD BE DONE ABOUT IT?

Obesity is a major problem among American children today. The latest studies suggest that the tendency to get fat is mainly genetic, and it is possible that some people inherit more subcutaneous fat or a more sluggish metabolism.

The belief that people may become obese later in life from being overfed in infancy rests on research in rats (Jelliffe & Jelliffe, 1974; Mayer, 1973). Feeding rat pups too many calories makes them develop too many fat cells, which persist through life (Hirsch, 1972). Recent research has cast doubt, however, on the long-term effects of how much food human babies eat.

Roche (1981) found almost no correlation between obesity before age 6 and at age 16. But after age 6 there was an increasingly strong correlation: children who were fat at age 6 or later were more likely to be fat as adults. A 40-year follow-up of Swedish children found that whether obese infants became obese adults depended very much on obesity in the family, especially in the mother. If she was fat, her child was likely to remain fat, even on a recommended diet (Mossberg, 1989). This seems to confirm a genetic basis for obesity.

Because we have no evidence that fatness hurts babies, and because children have critical growth needs, the AAP Committee on Nutrition (1981) warns against putting young children on any kind of weight-loss diet. As usual, moderation seems to be the safest course. Babies should be fed as much as they reasonably seem to need—neither more nor less.

What, then, should be done for children with a genetic heritage of fatness? Obese people are subject to more physical illness and tend to die sooner than people of normal weight. Starting in childhood, they begin to suffer from our society's negative and judgmental reactions to fatness. How soon should efforts be made to control children's weight? Or should our society spend more efforts on changing our image of the more abundantly endowed among us?

## THE SENSES

"The baby, assailed by eyes, ears, nose, skin, and entrails at once, feels that all is one great blooming, buzzing confusion," wrote the psychologist William James in 1890. We now know that this is far from true. From birth, the normal infant's senses all operate to some degree, and the sensory capacities develop rapidly.

### Touch

Touch seems to be the earliest sense to develop. If you stroke a hungry newborn's cheek near the mouth, the infant will respond by trying to find and connect with the nipple. (Early signs of this rooting reflex show up in 2-month-old fetuses, and by 32 weeks of gestation, all body parts are sensitive to touch.) Infants' sensitivity to touch—and particularly to pain—increases during the first 5 days after birth (Haith, 1986).

Parents have suffered as their tiny infants cried out in apparent pain from various medical procedures. But for years physicians shied away from giving newborn babies anesthesia during surgery because of a persistent belief that neonates do not feel pain and because of the known side effects of many pain relievers.

However, recent reports state unequivocally that even 1-day-old babies can and do feel pain. Preterm and full-term newborns undergoing circumcision and such procedures as heel lancing (to obtain blood samples) cry more, have higher heart rates and blood pressure, and sweat more during and after the procedures. They also react to pain through body movements, like pulling a leg away from a pinprick, grimacing, and crying (Anand & Hickey, 1987). Evidently, the nervous system of a newborn is more highly developed than we used to think.

These findings have had important practical consequences, such as the following:

■ *Changes in some neonatal surgical procedures, and concern for safe levels of pain medication.* A newer mechanical method of heel lancing, for example, seems less painful than the manual method. Furthermore, the AAP Committee on Fetus and Newborn (1987), noting the availability of new, relatively safe pain relievers, recommends their use in most surgery on infants and urges that decisions on use be based on medical criteria rather than on patients' age.

▪ *Reconsideration of routine circumcision.* Routine nonritual circumcision—surgical removal of the foreskin of the penis—was at one time performed on almost 90 percent of newborn boys in the United States. It is now done on about 60 percent (Lindsey, 1988; National Center for Health Statistics, 1987). The rate may rise again in response to a report by the AAP Task Force on Circumcision (1989) that circumcision prevents several penile conditions, lowers the rate of cancer of the penis in adults, and may protect against urinary tract infection. The procedure is fast and usually safe when done by an experienced practitioner, but it should be performed only on stable, healthy babies. Although complications rarely arise, parents should understand both benefits and risks before choosing the procedure.

## Taste

Newborns can discriminate between different tastes. They reject bad-tasting food, and they seem to prefer sweet tastes to sour or bitter ones. The sweeter a fluid, the harder they suck and the more they drink (Haith, 1986). When pure water or a sweet glucose solution is placed on a newborn's tongue, the baby moves the tongue to the side; the higher the concentration of glucose, the greater the response (Weiffenback & Thach, 1975).

## Smell

Newborns are sensitive to smell. Their facial expressions seem to show that they like the aroma of vanilla and strawberries and do not like the odor of fish or rotten eggs (Steiner, 1979). They can also tell where smells are coming from. When babies from 16 hours to 5 days old are dabbed on one side of the nose with an ammonium compound, the babies turn their noses to the other side (Rieser, Yonas, & Wilkner, 1976).

Very young infants can make subtle discriminations based on smell; like touch, this sensitivity increases during the first few days of life. Six-day-old breastfed infants show a preference for their mother's breast pad over that of another nursing mother, but 2-day-old infants do not, suggesting that babies need a few days' experience to recognize the mother's scent (Macfarlane, 1975).

## Hearing

The inner ear and middle ear reach nearly adult size and shape in the womb (Aslin, Pisoni, & Jusczyk, 1983; Haith, 1986). Newborns turn their heads toward sounds (Haith, 1986); even premature infants appear to respond to auditory stimulation (A. Starr, Amlie, Martin, & Sanders, 1977).

Infants' hearing is often studied through a phenomenon called **habituation**—a simple type of learning in which a baby becomes used to a stimulus and stops responding to it. When a new stimulus is presented, the response (like sucking hard on a pacifier) resumes, showing that the infant has perceived a difference between the two stimuli. From habituation experiments, researchers have learned that as early as 3 days after birth, infants can already tell new speech sounds from those they have already heard: in one study, babies stopped responding to familiar words but became more attentive when they heard new words (L. R. Brody, Zelazo, & Chaika, 1984).

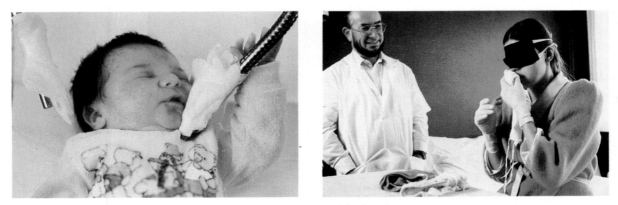

The nose knows. Three-day-old infants, like this one, act more peaceful when they smell pieces of gauze that their mothers have worn than when they smell cloth worn by other women. And blindfolded mothers can distinguish by smell between shirts their own babies have worn and shirts worn by other babies.

In another study, 1-month-old babies discriminated between two sounds as close as *bah* and *pah* (Eimas, Siqueland, Jusczyk, & Vigorito, 1971). The babies were given special nipples, which, when sucked, could turn on a recording. At first the infants sucked vigorously to hear the *bah* sound; but after they got used to it, their sucking slowed down. When the *pah* sound replaced the *bah* sound, they started to suck strongly again, showing that they could recognize this minor difference in sound. (We will discuss habituation further in Chapter 4.)

In another study, based on a method called *discriminative sucking,* infants less than 3 days old showed that they could tell their mothers' voices from that of a stranger (DeCasper & Fifer, 1980). By sucking on a nipple, the babies (at different times) were able to turn on recordings of the mother or another woman reading a story. As young as they were, the babies sucked about 24 percent more when they heard their own mothers' voices. Apparently, knowing the mother's voice, they had more interest in producing it. This early preference may be important for initiating bonding between mother and child.

No matter how enticing a mother's arms are, this baby is staying away from them. As young as she is, she can perceive depth and wants to avoid falling off what looks like a cliff.

### Sight

The eyes of neonates are smaller than those of adults, the retinal structures are incomplete, and the optic nerve is underdeveloped. Still, newborn babies blink at bright lights and shift their gaze to follow a moving light or target (Behrman & Vaughan, 1983).

Infants seem to have relatively mature color perception within the first few months of life. The cones, or receptors, in the retina that perceive red and green are functioning by about 2 months of age, and the cones for blue are working by about 3 months (Haith, 1986). By 4 months, infants (like adults) show a preference for red and blue (Teller & Bornstein, 1987).

Peripheral vision, which is very narrow at birth, more than doubles between 2 and 10 weeks of age (Tronick, 1972). The baby's eyesight becomes progressively more acute, approaching adult acuity by age 3 (Behrman & Vaughan, 1983).

Very young babies seem to have some depth perception, which is either inborn or learned during the first few months. To study early depth perception, E. J. Gibson and Walk (1960) constructed a **visual cliff** consisting of a clear glass surface with a checkered cloth draped underneath to give the illusion of a ledge ending at a sudden drop-off. In an experiment measuring differences in heart rate, 2- to 3-month-old babies placed on their stomachs on the "deep" side of the visual cliff

had slower heart rates than infants placed on the "shallow" side. The slower heart rate probably showed that the infants on the "deep" side were responding to the illusion of depth (Campos, Langer, & Krowitz, 1970).*

How much time babies spend looking at different sights tells us about their **visual preferences,** which depend on the ability to distinguish one sight from another. Research shows that this ability to view things selectively is present from birth.

Using an apparatus that lets an observer watch an infant's eyes and time fixations on a visual stimulus, researchers have found that babies less than 2 days old show definite preferences. Babies prefer curved lines to straight lines, complex patterns to simple patterns, three-dimensional objects to two-dimensional objects, pictures of faces to pictures of other things, and new sights to familiar ones (Fantz, 1963, 1964, 1965; Fantz, Fagan, & Miranda, 1975; Fantz & Nevis, 1967).

In one experiment, 1- and 2-month-old babies saw three expressionless faces: the mother's, a strange woman's, and a strange man's (Maurer & Salapatek, 1976). The 1-month-olds tended to look away from the faces, perhaps because the lack of expression was dis-

---

*Babies of this age are not likely to show *fear* of the drop-off. Fear would probably have resulted in a *faster* heart rate.

turbing to them. The 2-month-olds looked longer, possibly because they had become more familiar with a variety of expressions. The 1-month-olds turned away particularly from the faces of their own mothers, showing that they already recognized their mothers and—apparently—that they did not like to see their mothers without expression. The babies' eyes focused on the borders of the faces, suggesting that their recognition of their mothers was probably based on the chin or hairline. This observation is consistent with findings that infants less than 6 weeks old tend to fix on a small part of a visual stimulus rather than on the whole (Leahy, 1976; Salapatek & Kessen, 1966). The 2-month-olds gazed especially at eyes; other studies have shown that by this age, babies look longer at a face if the eyes are open and that they smile at it only if they can see both eyes.

## MOTOR DEVELOPMENT

Newborn babies are busy. They turn their heads, kick their legs, flail their arms, and display an array of reflex behaviors. Even fetuses move around in the womb; they turn somersaults, kick, and suck their thumbs. But neither fetuses nor neonates have much conscious control over their movements.

By about the fourth month, voluntary, cortex-directed movements largely take over. Motor control, the ability to move deliberately and accurately, develops rapidly and continuously during the first 3 years, as babies begin to use specific body parts consciously. The order in which they acquire this control follows the three principles of development outlined earlier: head to toe, inner to outer, and simple to complex.

Two of the most distinctively human motor capacities are the precision grip, in which thumb and index finger meet at their tips to form a circle; and the ability to walk on two legs. Neither of these capacities is present at birth, and both develop gradually. First, for example, Anna picked things up with her whole hand, with her fingers closing against her palm; then she began to use neat little pincer motions with her thumb and forefinger to pick up tiny objects. First she gained control of separate movements of her arms, legs, and feet; then she was ready to put these movements together to manage walking.

### Milestones of Motor Development

Babies do not have to be taught the basic motor skills; they just need freedom from interference. As soon as the central nervous system, muscles, and bones are mature enough, they need only room and freedom to move in order to keep showing new abilities. They are persistent, too; as soon as they acquire a new skill, they usually keep practicing and improving it. Parents soon grow tired of picking up a small object that a baby keeps dropping over the side of a high chair, only to cry for it and drop it again once it is retrieved; but this repetition is an important part of mastery and social interaction. Each newly mastered skill prepares a child to tackle the next one in the preordained sequence. And the proliferation of motor skills gives a child more of a chance to explore and manipulate the environment, and thus to obtain sensory and mental stimulation.

Motor development is marked by a series of milestones: achievements that signal how far development has come. The *Denver Developmental Screening Test* was designed to identify children who are not developing normally (Frankenburg, Dodds, Fandal, Kazuk, & Cohrs, 1975), but it may also be used as a benchmark for normal development between the ages of 1 month and 6 years. The test covers such gross motor skills as rolling over and catching a ball and such fine motor skills as grasping a rattle and copying a circle. It also covers language development (for example, knowing the definition of words) and personal and social development (like smiling spontaneously and dressing).

The Denver Developmental Screening Test provides norms for the ages at which 25 percent, 50 percent, 75 percent, and 90 percent of children show each skill (see Table 3-6 for selected milestones). A child who fails to show a skill at an age when 90 percent of children ordinarily show it is considered developmentally delayed. A child with two or more delays in two or more sectors is thought to need special attention.

In the following discussion, when we talk about what the "average" baby can do, we'll be referring—for convenience—to the 50 percent Denver norms. There is, however, no "average" baby. Normality covers a wide range; about half of all babies master these skills before the ages given and about half afterward. Anna, for example, didn't roll over from back to front (see "Locomotion" below) until she was about 8 months old, considerably later than the average. By age 4, however, she was exceptionally agile and well coordinated.

### Head control

At birth, most newborns can turn the head from side to side while lying on the back. While lying chest down, many can lift the head enough to turn it. Within the first 2 to 3 months, they lift the head higher and higher. By 4 months of age, almost all infants can keep the head erect while being held or supported in a sitting position.

**TABLE 3–6**
MILESTONES OF MOTOR DEVELOPMENT

| Skill | 25 percent | 50 percent | 90 percent |
|---|---|---|---|
| Rolling over | 2 months | 3 months | 5 months |
| Grasping rattle | 2½ months | 3½ months | 4½ months |
| Sitting without support | 5 months | 5½ months | 8 months |
| Standing while holding on | 5 months | 6 months | 10 months |
| Grasping with thumb and finger | 7½ months | 8½ months | 10½ months |
| Standing alone well | 10 months | 11½ months | 14 months |
| Walking well | 11 months | 12 months | 14½ months |
| Building tower of two cubes | 12 months | 14 months | 20 months |
| Walking up steps | 14 months | 17 months | 22 months |
| Jumping in place | 20½ months | 22 months | 36 months |
| Copying circle | 26 months | 33 months | 39 months |

*Note:* This table shows the approximate ages when 25 percent, 50 percent, and 90 percent of children can perform each skill.

*Source:* Adapted from Frankenburg, 1967.

### Hand control

Newborns are born with a grasping reflex. If the palm of an infant's hand is stroked, the baby automatically closes the hand tightly. At about 3½ months, most infants can grasp an object of moderate size, like a rattle, but have trouble holding a small object. Next they begin to grasp objects with one hand and transfer them to the other, and then to hold (but not pick up) small objects. Sometime between 7 and 11 months, their hands become coordinated enough to pick up a tiny object like a pea with pincer-like motion. After that, hand control becomes increasingly precise. At 14 months, the average baby can build a tower of two cubes. About 3 months before the third birthday, the average toddler can copy a circle fairly well.

### Locomotion

After 3 months, the average infant begins to roll over purposefully, first from front to back and then from back to front. (Before this time, however, babies sometimes roll over accidentally, and so even the youngest ones should never be left alone on a surface they might roll off.)

Babies sit either by raising themselves from a prone position or by plopping down from a standing position. The average baby can sit without support by 5 months to 6 months and can assume a sitting position without help 2 months later.

At about 6 months, most babies begin to get around under their own power, in several primitive ways. They wriggle on the belly and pull the body along with their arms, dragging their feet behind. They hitch or scoot by moving along in a sitting position, pushing forward with their arms and legs. They bear-walk, with hands and feet touching the ground. And they crawl on hands and knees with the trunk raised, parallel to the floor. By 9 or 10 months, babies get around quite well by such means, and so parents have to keep a close eye on them.

This kind of locomotion has important psychological implications. Did you ever drive for the first time to a place where you had gone only as a passenger? When you first had to find your own way, you probably saw landmarks you had never noticed, were aware of turns you had never felt, and—after getting there on your own—felt much more familiar with the entire route. The same kind of thing happens when babies begin to get around on their own, after having been carried or wheeled everywhere. "Self-produced locomotion" seems to be a turning point in the second half of the first year of life, influencing many aspects of physical, intellectual, and emotional development.

Between 7 and 9 months of age, babies show vast changes. They show a new understanding of concepts like "near" and "far"; they imitate more complex behaviors; they show new fears; and, on the other hand, they show a new sense of security around their parents or other caregivers. All these changes may result from a major reorganization of brain function, initiated by the new ability to crawl (Bertenthal & Campos, 1987; Bertenthal, Campos, & Barrett, 1984).

Crawling, a physical development, has social and emotional implications—showing the intertwining of all aspects of development. Being able to go after something she wants helps Lydia develop a sense of mastery over her environment.

Crawling gives children a new view of the world. They become very sensitive to where and how big objects are, whether objects are rooted or movable, and how objects are positioned relative to each other (Campos, Bertenthal, & Benson, 1980). In one study, babies were more successful at finding a toy hidden in a box when they had crawled around the box than when they had been carried around it (Benson & Uzgiris, 1985).

The ability to move from one place to another also has social implications. Crawling babies seem to be better able to tell themselves apart from the rest of the world: they see that people and objects around them can look different, depending on distance and closeness. Also, being able to get around means that a child is no longer a "prisoner" of a particular location. If Milly wants to be close to her mother and far away from a strange dog, for example, she can move toward the one and away from the other. This is an important step in developing a sense of mastery over the world, which enhances self-confidence and self-esteem.

Crawling babies get into new situations, and they learn to look for clues as to whether an ambiguous situation is secure or frightening, showing growth in a skill known as *social referencing*. Crawling babies look at ("socially reference") their mothers more than babies who have not yet begun to crawl, apparently to try to pick up emotional signals from their mothers' faces or gestures, which in turn influence the babies' behavior (Garland, 1982). The physical milestone of crawling seems to have far-reaching effects in helping babies see their world and themselves in a new way.

The next milestone is standing. By holding onto a helping hand or a piece of furniture, the average baby can stand at a little less than 6 months of age, but will only occasionally stand erect. About 4 months later, after dogged practice in pulling themselves up to an upright posture, babies can at last let go and stand alone. The average baby can stand well about 2 weeks or so before the first birthday.

All these developments are milestones along the way to the major motor achievement of infancy: walking. For some months before they can stand without support, babies practice walking while holding onto furniture—sitting down abruptly when they reach table's end, and crawling or lurching from chair to sofa. Soon after they can stand alone well, most infants take their first unaided steps, tumble, go back to crawling, and then try again. The average baby is walking regularly, if shakily, within a few days after that, and within a few weeks—soon after the first birthday—is walking well and thus achieves the status of toddler.

During the second year, children begin to climb stairs one at a time. (They can crawl upstairs before that—and tumble down long before; vigilance and baby gates are needed.) At first they put one foot and then the other on the same step before going on to the next higher one; later they will alternate feet. Going down the stairs comes later. In their second year, toddlers are running and jumping; their parents, trying to keep up with them, are running out of energy. At age 3, most children can balance briefly on one foot, and some begin to hop.

## Environmental Influences on Motor Development

Human beings seem to be genetically programmed to sit, stand, and walk. Motor skills like these unfold in a regular, largely preordained pattern. Children must reach a certain level of physiological maturation before they are ready to exercise each ability.

The role of the environment in this timetable is usually quite limited, although early experience can affect maturation rates in some areas, like vision (Lipsitt, 1986). In general, when children are well fed and well cared-for, and have physical freedom and the chance to practice motor skills, their motor development will be normal (Clarke-Stewart, 1977). When the environment is grossly deficient in any of these areas, development can suffer—as in a classic study of three orphanages in Iran.

In this study, the overworked attendants in two of the orphanages hardly ever handled the children. The younger babies spent almost all their time on their backs in cribs. They sucked from propped-up bottles. They were never put in a sitting position or placed on their stomachs. They had no toys and were not taken out of bed until they could sit without help (often not till 2 years of age, as compared with 5½ months for the average American child). And once a child who could sit did reach the floor, there was no child-sized furniture or play equipment. These children were delayed in their motor development because of the deficient environment, which kept them from moving around and provided little stimulation. By contrast, the children in a third orphanage were fed in the arms of trained attendants, were placed on their stomachs and propped up to sit, and had many toys. These children showed normal levels of motor development.

When the children in the first two orphanages did start to get about, they scooted (moved around in a sitting position, pushing the body forward with their arms and feet), rather than crawling on hands and knees. Since they had never been placed on their stomachs, they had no opportunity to practice raising their heads or pulling their arms and legs beneath their bodies—the movements needed for crawling. Also, since they had never been propped in a sitting position, they had not practiced raising the head or shoulders to learn how to sit at the usual age. Surprisingly, however, these delays seemed temporary. Older children in one of these two institutions, who presumably had also been delayed as toddlers, worked and played normally (Dennis, 1960).

Fortunately, such severe environmental deprivation is rare. But it is clear that the environment can play a part in motor development, and that the more restricted a child's environment is, the greater its effect will be.

## Can Motor Development Be Speeded Up?

A number of researchers have tried to train children to walk, climb stairs, and control the bladder and bowels earlier than usual.

In a classic experiment, Gesell (1929) studied a pair of identical twins. He trained twin T, but not twin C, in climbing stairs, building with blocks, and hand coordination. With age, however, twin C became just as expert as twin T; Gesell therefore acknowledged the powerful influence of maturation on infants' behavior. Even though this study was conducted more than 50 years ago—and on only two infants—Gesell's conclusion still stands.

Toilet training, for example, is often begun long before babies can control their sphincter muscles. When a child seems to be successfully trained at a very early age, it is usually because the *parent* has been trained to recognize the child's readiness and can get the child to a potty or toilet in time. Before children can really control elimination, they have a lot to learn. Initially, elimination is involuntary: when an infant's bladder or bowels are full, the sphincter muscles open automatically. To control these muscles, children have to know that there is a proper time and place to allow them to open. They have to become familiar with the feelings that indicate the need to eliminate, and they have to learn to tighten the sphincter muscles until seated on the potty, and only then to loosen them.

In a study of another pair of twins, McGraw (1940) measured the effects of very early toilet training. She put one twin on the toilet every hour of every day starting at 2 months of age; the other twin was not put on the toilet until 23 months of age. The first twin did not begin to show some control until about 20 months and did not achieve consistent success until about 23 months; and the other twin quickly caught up. This shows that maturation has to occur before training can be effective.

While it is usually not advisable to attempt to speed up motor development for an individual child (see Box 3-3 on page 106), developmental ages for certain skills do, as we've seen, appear to vary somewhat from one culture to another.

## BOX 3–3    PRACTICALLY SPEAKING

### ARE "WALKERS" WORTH THE RISK?

A 6-month-old baby died in a Toronto hospital of a head injury suffered after falling down 14 steps onto a concrete floor. The infant had been sitting in a "walker"—a seat in a collapsible frame on wheels. In 1984, in that one hospital, 139 children were treated for walker-related injuries, most resulting from falls (Rieder, Schwartz, & Newman, 1986).

During the past decade, walkers have become very popular; it is estimated that 55 to 86 percent of babies are placed in them at some time before they begin to walk. About 1 million walkers were bought in the United States in 1980, a year in which nearly 24,000 walker-related injuries are estimated to have occurred.

Most of the injuries in the Toronto study took place in the home and were caused by falls down stairs; in one-third of the cases, stair gates had been in place but were improperly attached or left unlatched. In 10 cases, the baby fell from the walker itself. In 21 cases, no one was in the room with the baby.

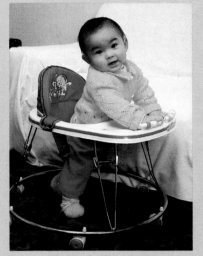

Despite a high risk of injury, many babies spend part of their time in infant walkers. Although walkers are designed to give greater mobility, they do not help babies learn to walk any faster than they would on their own.

Surprisingly, 2 months after the accidents, nearly one-third of the babies were still being placed in their walkers; another one-third had stopped being placed in walkers only after learning to walk. The parents' most frequently stated reasons for using the walkers were that they made the babies happier by helping them get around, that they served as "baby-sitters," and that they encouraged early walking.

Ironically, a study of twins found that infant walkers do not speed up independent walking (Ridenour, 1982). One twin in each pair was placed in a walker for 1 hour a day from 4 months of age until walking began; the other twin was not. Twins in the two groups walked at about the same average age.

These findings reinforce others, cited in this chapter, that motor control and coordination generally develop at a natural pace (Gesell, 1929; McGraw, 1940). Efforts to hurry the process are likely to be useless or even harmful. At the very least, walkers should be used only when a parent or caretaker is within arm's reach—and never near open stairs.

### HOW DIFFERENT ARE BOYS AND GIRLS?

Males are physically more vulnerable than females from conception throughout the life span. And baby boys are slightly larger than baby girls. Aside from these two differences, however, infant boys and infant girls are very similar.

Although some research has found baby boys to be more active than baby girls (Maccoby & Jacklin, 1974), other studies have found the two sexes equally active during the first 2 years of life (Maccoby, 1980). Gender differences do not show up in sensitivity to touch, and very little difference appears in strength (although males may be slightly stronger). Further, girls and boys are more alike than different in reaching such maturational milestones as sitting up, teething, and walking. Recently a surge of interest in possible differences between the male and the female brain has led to attempts to explain girls' earlier language acquisition (see Chapter 4) and boys' greater problems in learning how to read (see Chapter 8). Close analysis of the brains of babies who died at birth or soon afterward, however, has yielded no evidence for any marked gender difference in the readiness of the newborn's brain for language acquisition (Maccoby, 1980).

In personality and social development, however, gender differences are more pronounced (see Chapter 5).

By the time small children—of either sex—can run, jump, and play with toys requiring fairly sophisticated coordination, they are very different from the neonates that we described at the beginning of this chapter. The changes that have taken place in their intellectual capacity and activity while this physical development has gone on are equally dramatic, as we'll see in Chapter 4.

## SUMMARY

### THE NEONATE

■ The neonatal period, the first 4 weeks of life, is a time of transition from intrauterine to extrauterine life. At birth, the neonate's circulatory, respiratory, gastrointestinal, and temperature-regulation systems become independent of the mother's.

■ A newborn baby's brain is one-fourth the weight of an adult's brain and grows to 80 percent of adult weight by the end of the second year. Primitive reflexes drop out as involuntary (subcortical) control of behavior gives way to voluntary (cortical) control. The brain can be molded by experience.

■ At 1 minute and 5 minutes after birth, the neonate is assessed medically by the Apgar scale, which measures five factors (appearance, pulse, grimace, activity, and respiration) that indicate how well the newborn is adjusting to extrauterine life. The neonate may also be screened for one or more medical conditions.

■ The Brazelton Neonatal Behavioral Assessment Scale may be given to assess a newborn's responses to the environment and to predict future development.

■ Birth trauma and low birthweight can influence early adjustment to life outside the womb and may even exert an influence on later development. A supportive postnatal environment can often improve the outcome.

■ Low birthweight is a major factor in infant mortality. Although the infant mortality rate in the United States has improved, it is still disturbingly high, especially for African American babies.

■ Sudden infant death syndrome (SIDS) is the leading cause of death in infants between 1 month and 1 year of age, affecting some 7000 infants each year in the United States. There are many theories about the cause of SIDS, and none is universally accepted, although the most important one relates it to a brain abnormality.

### DEVELOPMENT DURING THE FIRST 3 YEARS OF LIFE

■ Normal physical growth and motor development proceed in a largely preordained sequence, according to three principles:

1  According to the cephalocaudal principle, development proceeds from the head to lower body parts.
2  According to the proximodistal principle, development proceeds from the center of the body to the outer parts.
3  Development usually proceeds from simple to complex behavior.

■ Newborn babies alternate between states of sleep, wakefulness, and activity, with sleep taking up the major (but diminishing) amount of their time. State patterns are indicators of how an infant is responding to the environment.

■ A child's body grows most dramatically during the first year of life; growth proceeds at a rapid but diminishing rate throughout the child's first 3 years.

■ Breastfeeding seems to offer physiological benefits to the infant and facilitates formation of the mother-infant bond. However, the quality of the relationship between parents and the infant is more important than the feeding method in promoting healthy development.

■ Sensory capacities—present from birth—develop rapidly in the first months of life. Very young infants show pronounced abilities to discriminate between stimuli.

■ During the first 3 months of life, infants gain control over their body movements. Motor skills normally develop when an infant is maturationally ready.

■ The Denver Developmental Screening Test is widely used to assess motor, linguistic, and personal and social development.

■ Environmental factors may retard motor development if deprivation is extreme. Environmental factors that are pervasive in a culture may affect the timetable of motor development, but short-term experiments aimed at accelerating specific types of motor development—such as stair climbing and toilet training—have generally had little effect.

■ Although infant boys are somewhat larger and more vulnerable than girls, researchers have found few other significant physical or maturational differences between the sexes in infancy.

## KEY TERMS

neonatal period (page 80)
neonate (81)
vernix caseosa (81)
lanugo (81)
anoxia (82)
meconium (82)
physiologic jaundice (82)
cerebral cortex (83)
reflex behaviors (85)

Apgar scale (85)
Brazelton Neonatal Behavioral
  Assessment Scale (88)
birth trauma (88)
infant mortality rate (88)
low birthweight (88)
preterm (premature) babies (90)
small-for-date babies (90)
sudden infant death syndrome (SIDS)
  (93)

cephalocaudal principle (94)
proximodistal principle (94)
states (95)
habituation (100)
visual cliff (101)
visual preferences (101)
Denver Developmental Screening
  Test (102)

## SUGGESTED READINGS

**DeFrain, J., Taylor, J., & Ernst, L. (1982).** *Coping with sudden infant death.* Lexington, MA: Heath. An investigation of the experiences and special problems of families who have lost a child to sudden infant death syndrome.

**Eiger, M. S., & Olds, S. W. (1987).** *The complete book of breastfeeding.* New York: Workman. A classic guidebook for nursing mothers that draws on research findings and incorporates many suggestions appropriate for the lifestyles of today's families.

**Jason, J., & van der Meer, A. (1989).** *Parenting your premature baby.* New York: Dell. The senior author of this book, a pediatrician and herself the mother of a premature baby, covers what to expect in neonatal intensive care units, how to meet the baby's special needs, finally taking the baby home from the hospital, and the long-term outlook for premature infants. The book contains a number of reassuring photos of healthy, normal-looking children who were once premature babies.

**Leach, P. (1990).** *Babyhood* (rev. ed.). New York: Knopf. A comprehensive look at the period of infancy, covering everything about a newborn baby. Although written for the layperson, the text covers the whole field of study about babies.

**Worth, C. (1988).** *The birth of a father.* New York: McGraw-Hill. A supportive book that answers new fathers' questions about their new world, using interviews with fathers taken during the first year of parenthood.

Because habituation is associated with normal development, its presence or absence, as well as the speed with which it occurs, can tell us a great deal about a baby's development. Since the capacity for habituation increases during the first 10 weeks of life, it is regarded as a sign of maturation (Rovee-Collier, 1987). Habituation studies show us how well babies can see and hear, how much they can remember, and what their neurological status is. Babies with low Apgar scores and those with brain damage, distress at the time of birth, or Down syndrome show impaired habituation (Lipsitt, 1986), as do neonates whose mothers were heavily medicated during childbirth (Bowes, Brackbill, Conway, & Steinschneider, 1970). Full-term neonates can habituate to stimuli in all sensory modalities (sight, hearing, touch, taste, and smell), while preterm newborns can generally habituate only to some stimuli in some circumstances (Rovee-Collier, 1987).

As we shall see in our discussion of information processing later in this chapter, speed of habituation shows promise as a predictor of intelligence, especially of verbal abilities. Poor habituation during the neonatal period often foreshadows slow development; a child who does not habituate at all is likely to have future learning problems (Lipsitt, 1986).

## Conditioning

### Classical conditioning

Anna's proud father often took pictures of her: Anna crawling, Anna waving bye-bye, Anna "dancing." Whenever a flashbulb went off, Anna blinked. One evening when Anna was about 11 months old, as Jonathan was about to snap her picture, she blinked *before* the flash. Anna had learned to associate the camera with the blinding light and no longer needed the flash itself to call forth the reflex of blinking.

Anna's behavior is an example of ***classical conditioning,*** which was introduced in Chapter 1 in connection with Pavlov's experiments on dogs. In this basic kind of learning, a person or animal learns to respond to a stimulus that originally was neutral (did not bring forth the response). Its significance is that it allows a person or animal to anticipate events instead of just reacting to them after they occur.

Let's analyze what happened in Anna's case. The flash was an ***unconditioned stimulus:*** it naturally caused her to blink. Her blinking after the flash was an ***unconditioned response:*** it came of its own accord. The camera was originally a ***neutral stimulus:*** it would not, by itself (without the flash), provoke blinking. After the two stimuli—camera and flash—were paired repeatedly, the camera became a ***conditioned stimulus:*** a stimulus that was neutral before the conditioning but now elicited the response of blinking. Anna's blinking at the camera was a ***conditioned response:*** it came only after repeated association of the camera with the flash.

A famous example of classical conditioning involved a baby known in the psychological literature as "Little Albert" (J. B. Watson & Rayner, 1920). When "Little Albert" was 9 months old, he showed no fear of any animal. Two months later, as he reached toward a white rat, laboratory experimenters sounded a loud

An Indian snake charmer's baby eagerly plays with a snake the father has trained, showing that fear of snakes is a learned response. Children can be conditioned to fear animals that are associated with unpleasant or frightening experiences, as "Little Albert" was in a classic study by John B. Watson and Rosalie Rayner.

noise, and he began to cry. This happened again and again. Eventually, Albert would whimper in fear as soon as he saw the rat.

How would we describe "Little Albert's" experience in psychological terms? The noise (a hammer struck against a steel bar just behind his head) was the unconditioned stimulus. The rat was originally a neutral stimulus. But after repeated pairing of the white rat with the loud noise, the rat became a conditioned stimulus. "Little Albert" would cry as soon as he saw the rat; he no longer needed the noise. The crying response that "Little Albert" now made to the rat (and later to other furry white things, including a rabbit and a Santa Claus mask) was a conditioned response: it arose only after repeated association of the rat with the loud noise.

The conditioning of "Little Albert" raises some controversial issues. The first, of course, is the moral one. This experiment would not be permitted today, under contemporary ethical standards. Also, critics of the conclusions say that this experiment was not pure classical conditioning but rather resembled operant conditioning (as defined in Chapter 1), since the frighteningly loud noise had some aspects of punishment (B. Harris, 1979). Yet this study is a classic in the field of human development and does suggest that fears can be learned through association.

How early can conditioning occur? The most recent research seems to show that there are ways to classically condition newborn infants. Newborns have learned to suck when they hear a buzzer or a tone; to show the Babkin reflex (turning the head and opening the mouth) when their arms are moved (instead of the traditional stimulus, pressure on the palm of the hand); to dilate and constrict the pupils of the eye; to blink; and to show a change in heart rate (Rovee-Collier & Lipsitt, 1982). When events are presented in a biologically meaningful context, conditioning can take place within hours after birth (Rovee-Collier, 1987). For example, babies only 2 hours old can be classically conditioned to turn their heads and suck if their foreheads are stroked at the same time they are given a bottle of sweetened water (Blass, Ganchrow, & Steiner, 1984, in Rovee-Collier, 1987).

### Operant conditioning

As early as 3 days after birth, infants will suck more on a nipple that activates a tape of their mother's voice than on a nipple that produces the voice of a strange woman (A. DeCasper & Fifer, 1980). They have learned two separate things: they can distinguish between their mother's voice and somebody else's, and

they have discovered an action that brings a pleasing sound. The second of these is an example of *operant* (or *instrumental) conditioning;* the infants learn to make a certain response in order to hear their mothers' voices.

When Tony's sucking results in hearing his mother's voice, he is being reinforced for the behavior of sucking; and this *reinforcement* encourages repetition of the behavior. Operant conditioning differs from classical conditioning in that the learner acts on the environment.

Neonates' ability to learn through operant conditioning allows us to learn things about *them.* In one study, 2-day-old infants were reinforced by hearing music as long as they sucked on a dry nipple. The babies would prolong their sucking when the music continued, but not when the sucking turned the music off (Butterfield & Siperstein, 1972). The researchers concluded that babies like music and that they can learn to do certain things in order to keep music playing. Such studies, which change babies' behavior by reinforcing them in various ways, show that operant conditioning "works" in the neonatal period—if the conditioning is based on a preexisting, biologically important behavior like sucking, rather than on an action that the baby would not ordinarily perform. Even newborns, then, quickly learn responses associated with feeding or responses associated with hearing their mothers (Rovee-Collier, 1987).

### Combinations of classical and operant conditioning

Classical and operant conditioning can be combined to produce increasingly complex learning. In one series of studies, researchers first taught infants as young as 1 week, through operant conditioning, to turn their heads left at the sound of a bell to receive milk. The babies who failed to learn in this way were given classical conditioning: the left corner of the baby's mouth was stroked when the bell sounded; these babies would then turn their heads and get the milk. By the age of 4 to 6 weeks, the babies had learned to turn their heads when they heard the bell. After that, the infants were trained to tell the bell from a buzzer. They were fed on the left when the bell rang and on the right when the buzzer sounded. At about 3 months of age, the babies had learned to turn to the appropriate side. Four-month-olds even learned to reverse the response to bell and buzzer, showing the remarkable complexity of babies' learning capacities (Papousek, 1959, 1960a, 1960b, 1961).

## What Do Scores on Intelligence Tests Mean?

Unfortunately, many people have the misconception that the score on an intelligence test represents a fixed quantity of intelligence that people are born with, rather than simply an indicator of relative intellectual functioning. While intelligence tests are often presumed to measure innate ability, what they actually measure is achievement and performance, which are affected by factors beyond "pure" intelligence. Although scores of school-age children and adults tend to be fairly stable, some people show marked changes, perhaps reflecting environmental circumstances (Kopp & McCall, 1982). Binet himself recognized the effects of nurturance when he urged that students who did poorly on his test be given special training to increase their intelligence (Kamin, 1981).

Indeed, test-takers on the whole have been doing better on the Stanford-Binet in recent years (Anastasi, 1988), forcing test developers to raise previously established norms. This improvement probably reflects exposure to educational television programs, preschools, better educated parents, and a wider variety of experiences—as well as exposure to the tests themselves—rather than genetic changes in the population.

Intelligence is difficult to define and even more difficult to measure. There undoubtedly are real differences in intellectual ability among children, but there is serious disagreement over how accurately psychometric tests assess those differences. We will continue to discuss issues concerning intelligence testing in Chapter 8, when we examine the intellectual development of school-age children. Right now, let's see why it's especially hard to gauge a baby's intelligence.

## Why Is It Difficult to Measure Infants' and Toddlers' Intelligence?

Though we now know that infants are intelligent, measuring their intelligence is another matter. For one thing, babies cannot talk. You can't ask them questions and get answers. They can't tell you what they know and how they think. The most obvious way to gauge their intelligence is by what they can do, but very young infants do not do very much. An experimenter may try to catch their attention and coax them into a particular behavior; but if they do not grasp a rattle, for example, it is hard to tell whether they do not know how, do not feel like doing it, or do not realize what is expected of them.

Not surprisingly, an infant's test scores are not very reliable; they tend to vary widely from one time to another. Their value in assessing a baby's *current* abilities is questionable; and they are almost useless for predict-

ing *future* functioning. It is next to impossible to predict adult or even childhood IQ from psychometric scores of normal children before age 2. A more useful predictor of childhood IQ is the parents' IQ or educational level (Kopp & Kaler, 1989; Kopp & McCall, 1982). Not until the third year of life do the child's own scores, along with these factors, increase the reliability of prediction.

Even for toddlers, predictions based on psychometric tests are highly unreliable. In one longitudinal study, individual IQs changed by an average of 28½ points between ages 2½ and 17, and the IQs of 1 in 7 children shifted by more than 40 points (McCall, Appelbaum, & Hogarty, 1973). As youngsters are tested closer to their fifth birthday, the relationship between their intelligence scores and those in later childhood becomes stronger (Bornstein & Sigman, 1986).

Why do early intelligence scores fail to predict later scores? One answer probably has to do with the fact that the tests traditionally used for babies (see the discussion of developmental testing below) are primarily sensory and motor whereas the tests used for older children are heavily verbal. This implies that the tests measure different and largely unrelated kinds of intelligence (Bornstein & Sigman, 1986). Even when we look at motor skills alone, children who are good at the large-muscle activities tested at an early age may not be as adept at fine motor, or manipulative, skills considered to be a sign of intelligence a little later on. For example, a child who at 1 year could build towers with blocks may not by the age of 7 be able to copy a design made from colored blocks.

It is somewhat easier to predict the future IQ of a handicapped infant. Yet some children born with mental and motor handicaps make impressive strides in tested intelligence as they grow older. A supportive environment can help such a child learn special ways to cope (Kopp & Kaler, 1989; Kopp & McCall, 1982). In addition, human beings seem to have what some observers call a "strong self-righting tendency" (Kopp & McCall, 1982). That is, given a favorable environment, infants will generally follow normal developmental patterns unless they have suffered severe damage. Sometime between the ages of 18 and 24 months, however, this self-righting tendency seems to diminish as children begin to acquire skills (like verbal abilities) in which there will eventually be great variations in proficiency. As these sophisticated skills develop, individual differences become more pronounced and more lasting.

## What Is Developmental Testing?

Despite the difficulties in measuring the intelligence of very young children, sometimes there are reasons for testing them. If parents are worried that a baby is not doing the same things as other babies of the same age, early testing may reassure them that their child's development is normal, though different—or it may alert them to abnormal development and to the need to make special arrangements for the child.

Developmental tests are tests specially designed to chart the progress of infants and toddlers. These tests are primarily nonverbal, because they are designed for a group who cannot be assessed by traditional verbal means (Anastasi, 1988). Many of these tests measure sensory and motor development.

Developmental tests are based on careful observations of large numbers of children. After determining what most infants or toddlers can do at particular ages, researchers develop standardized norms, assigning a developmental age to each specific activity. An individual child's performance is then evaluated in comparison to these standardized norms.

One important test for this purpose is the **Bayley Scales of Infant Development** (Bayley, 1933, revised 1969). This instrument, which is used to assess the developmental status of children from 2 months of age to 2½ years of age, has three parts:

1  *Mental scale.* This measures such abilities as perception, memory, learning, and verbal communication. Test items include turning the head to follow an object and imitating simple actions and words.
2  *Motor scale.* This measures gross motor skills (like standing and walking) and fine motor skills (like grasping a piece of paper or drinking from a cup).
3  *Infant behavior record.* This is a behavioral history completed by the examiner, which looks at such aspects of personality development as emotional and social behavior and persistence.

The separate scores calculated for each scale are useful for assessing current developmental status, but (as noted above) not for predicting later intelligence. They are most helpful for early detection of emotional disturbances and sensory, neurological, and environmental deficits (Anastasi, 1988).

### Can Children's Scores on Intelligence Tests Be Improved?

Improved parenting skills can apparently increase very young children's scores on intelligence tests.

From 1970 to 1975, federally sponsored Parent Child Development Centers tested the notion that the performance of low-income children on intelligence tests can be improved by influencing parents' attitudes and behavior during a child's first 3 years of life. Mothers of children in the centers' nursery school received

Developmental tests are designed to chart the progress of infants—like 7-month-old Adam—and toddlers.

information and training in child development, child-rearing practices, home management, nutrition, health, and other topics, along with a range of support services. In recognition of cultural differences, the centers let parents decide what was best for their children and hired staff members of the same ethnic and cultural backgrounds as the parents.

The results were striking. "Trained" mothers gave their children more instruction, information, and praise. They asked more questions, encouraged their children to think and talk, and gave them more appropriate play materials and more flexible routines. Also, they were more emotionally responsive, sensitive, and accepting; and less interfering and critical than mothers in control groups. Children of trained mothers did better on the Stanford-Binet at the age of 3 than the other children, and they maintained their gains a year later (Andrews et al., 1982).

These results show that what kind of care babies get and how their mothers treat them can affect their intellectual development.

## PIAGETIAN APPROACH: COGNITIVE STAGES

The Swiss psychologist Jean Piaget took a different approach from that of the psychometricians to children's *cognitive development*—the growth in thought processes that enables them to acquire and use knowledge about the world. Piaget, who initially worked in Binet's laboratory to help standardize the early IQ tests, concluded that standardized tests miss the special and interesting aspects of children's thought processes, which he set out to describe.

To learn how children think, Piaget asked them unusual questions, like "Is a rock alive?" and "Where do dreams come from?" Then—unlike the psychometricians, who look for *right* answers to questions—Piaget paid more attention to the *wrong* answers children gave. He drew out their reasons for their answers, to get clues to the way they thought. Their thinking, he concluded, was not merely a less developed level of adult thought; it was a different kind of thought from that of adults. As children mature, he said, their thought evolves in a sequence of stages. Whereas psychometricians are interested in the differences among individuals, Piaget was more interested in sequences of intellectual development in *all* normal children. The *Piagetian approach,* then, describes qualitatively different stages of cognitive development that characterize children from infancy through adolescence.

Although Piaget's theory begins with infancy, he obviously could not ask questions of babies. But he did carefully scrutinize his own three children, and his observations provided the basis for his theory of the first stage of development—the sensorimotor stage. They also inspired a great deal of research on infants' cognition and intelligence.

### Piaget's Sensorimotor Stage (Birth to About 2 Years)

Piaget's first cognitive stage is called the *sensorimotor stage.* It is a time when infants learn about themselves and their world through their own developing sensory and motor activity. (See Table 4-1.) During the first 2 years, babies change from creatures who respond primarily through reflexes and random behavior into goal-oriented toddlers. They now organize their activities in relation to their environment, coordinate information they receive from their senses, and progress from trial-and-error learning to using rudimentary insights in solving simple problems.

This change is very obvious in any bookshop with a good section of children's books. Many books for babies are made of cloth or heavy board or vinyl, reflecting the

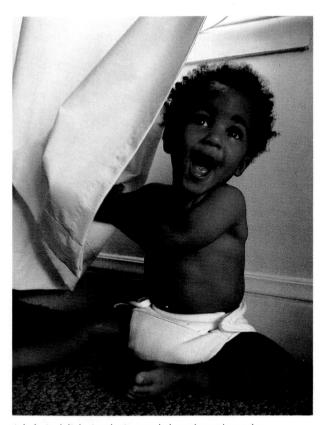

A baby's delight in playing peekaboo depends on the development of object permanence—the knowledge that a familiar face is still there, even when the baby cannot see it. Object permanence develops gradually over the first 18 months of life.

fact that a baby first reacts to books by banging them, chewing on them, and taking them into the bathtub—in short, using them as objects. Not until babies are well into the sensorimotor stage do they realize that the pictures in the books stand for objects in the real world, and not until still later do they understand that the black marks in books represent a world of ideas as well as things.

### Cognitive concepts of the sensorimotor stage

During the sensorimotor stage, children develop several important cognitive concepts. One is *object permanence:* the realization that an object or person continues to exist even when out of sight. Object permanence is the basis for children's awareness that they exist apart from objects and other people. It allows a child whose parent has left the room to feel secure in the knowledge that the parent continues to exist and will return. It is essential to understanding time, space, and a world full of objects.

Another important concept that emerges during this stage is **causality,** the Piagetian term for the recognition that certain events cause other events. In one study, babies saw films that showed physically impossible events, like a ball moving toward a second ball which then moved before the first ball touched it. Infants under 10 months of age showed no surprise, but older babies did. Evidently the older infants realized that a cause—such as something necessary for the movement of the second ball—was missing (Michotte, 1962, in Siegler & Richards, 1982).

It is not surprising that awareness of causality develops at about 10 months, since that is when many babies begin making their own experiments. They play with light switches and delight in making the light go on and off. Their favorite toys are those they can do something with—roll, drop, or make noise. By their actions, infants of this age show an understanding that *they* can cause things to happen.

While the roots of such important concepts as causality are taking hold now, infants cannot fully grasp them. The reason, according to Piaget, is that children of this age have limited **representational ability**—that is, a limited capacity to mentally represent objects and actions in memory. But this ability to remember and imagine things and events—largely through the use of symbols like words, numbers, and mental pictures—blossoms as children enter the next cognitive stage, the preoperational stage (discussed in Chapter 6).

**TABLE 4–1**

SIX SUBSTAGES OF PIAGET'S SENSORIMOTOR STAGE OF COGNITIVE DEVELOPMENT

| Substage | Description |
|---|---|
| Substage 1 (birth to 1 month): Use of reflexes | Infants exercise their inborn reflexes and gain some control over them. They do not coordinate information from their senses. They do not grasp an object they are looking at. They have not developed object permanence. |
| Substage 2 (1 to 4 months): Primary circular reactions | Infants repeat pleasurable behaviors that first occur by chance (such as sucking). Activities focus on infant's body rather than the effects of the behavior on the environment. Infants make first acquired adaptations; that is, they suck different objects differently. They begin to coordinate sensory information. They have still not developed object permanence. |
| Substage 3 (4 to 8 months): Secondary circular reactions | Infants become more interested in the environment and repeat actions that bring interesting results and prolong interesting experiences. Actions are intentional but not initially goal-directed. Infants show partial object permanence. They will search for a partially hidden object. |
| Substage 4 (8 to 12 months): Coordination of secondary schemes | Behavior is more deliberate and purposeful as infants coordinate previously learned schemes (such as looking at and grasping a rattle) and use previously learned behaviors to attain their goals (such as crawling across the room to get a desired toy). They can anticipate events. Object permanence is developing, although infants will search for an object in its first hiding place, even if they saw it being moved. |
| Substage 5 (12 to 18 months): Tertiary circular reactions | Infants show curiosity as they purposefully vary their actions to see results. They actively explore their world to determine how an object, event, or situation is novel. They try out new activities and use trial and error in solving problems. Infants will follow a series of object displacements, but since they cannot imagine movement they do not see, they will not search for an object where they have not observed it being hidden. |
| Substage 6 (18 to 24 months): Mental combinations | Since toddlers have developed a primitive symbol system (such as language) to represent events, they are no longer confined to trial and error to solve problems. Their symbol system allows toddlers to begin to think about events and anticipate their consequences without always resorting to action. Toddlers begin to demonstrate insight. Object permanence is fully developed. |

*Note:* Infants show enormous cognitive growth during Piaget's sensorimotor stage, as they learn about the world through their senses and their motor activities. Note their progress in problem solving, object permanence, and the coordination of sensory information.

### Substages of the sensorimotor stage

Let's look more closely at how development proceeds during the sensorimotor stage. We will see the enormous cognitive growth that occurs even before most babies can talk (see Table 4-1).

Much of this growth occurs through what Piaget called *circular reactions,* in which the child learns how to reproduce pleasurable or interesting events originally discovered by chance. The process has elements of operant conditioning. Initially, an activity produces a sensation so welcome that the child wants to repeat the activity. The repetition then feeds on itself in a continuous cycle in which cause and effect become almost indistinguishable (see Figure 4-2).

The sensorimotor stage consists of six substages, which flow from one to another as a baby's *schemes,* or organized patterns of behavior, become more elaborate. As we look at each substage, we will pay particular attention to what Piaget regarded as the single most important cognitive acquisition of the sensorimotor period: the development of object permanence.

#### Substage 1: Use of reflexes (birth to 1 month)   As neonates exercise their inborn reflexes, they gain some control over them. They begin to engage in certain behaviors even when the stimulus that elicits the behavior as an automatic reflex is not present. For example, newborn babies suck reflexively when their lips are touched. During the first month, infants learn to find the nipple even when they are not touched, and they begin to practice sucking when they are not hungry. Thus infants become energetic initiators of activity, not just passive responders. Their inborn schemes for sucking are modified and extended by experience.

Object permanence is completely lacking; the presence or absence of any object seems random and unpredictable.

#### Substage 2:  Primary circular reactions and acquired adaptations (1 to 4 months)   A baby lying in a crib blissfully sucking a thumb exemplifies what Piaget called a *primary circular reaction:* a simple, repetitive act, centered on the baby's own body, to reproduce a pleasant sensation first achieved by chance. One day Max exercises his sucking scheme while his thumb happens to be in his mouth. He likes the feeling and tries to recapture it through trial and error. Once successful, he makes deliberate efforts to put his thumb into his mouth, keep it there, and keep sucking. In so doing, he also makes his first *acquired adaptations:* he learns to adjust or accommodate his actions by sucking on his thumb differently from the way he sucks on a nipple. The result of this learning is a reorganized scheme for sucking.

At this time a baby also starts to coordinate and organize different kinds of sensory information—for example, vision and hearing. When Ashley hears her mother's voice, she turns toward the sound and eventually discovers that it comes from her mother's mouth. Her world is beginning to make sense.

Object permanence is still absent. Ashley can now follow a moving object with her eyes; but when something disappears, she does not look for it. However, she will continue to stare briefly at the spot where the object was last seen, as if passively watching for it.

#### Substage 3: Secondary circular reactions (4 to 8 months)   The third substage coincides with a new interest in reaching out to manipulate objects in the environment. The baby begins to engage in *secondary circular reactions:* intentional actions repeated not merely for their own sake, as in substage 2, but to get results beyond the infant's own body. Ahmed enjoys shaking a rattle to hear the noise it makes. He is learning ways to prolong interesting experiences; for example, he finds that by making a soft sound when a friendly face appears, he can make the face stay longer. However, his behavior is not fully goal-oriented; before he will pursue a goal, he must first discover it accidentally.

Object permanence is beginning to develop: Ahmed looks for an object which he has dropped or which is hidden from him, but only if he can see any part of it. If it is completely hidden, he acts as if it no longer exists.

#### Substage 4: Coordination of secondary schemes (8 to 12 months)   By the time they reach the fourth substage, infants have built on the few schemes they were born with, adapting and elaborating on them through experience with the environment. Babies now begin to separate schemes from the original context in which they were learned and recombine them to deal with new situations. In other words, they generalize from past experience, calling upon responses they have previously mastered in order to solve new problems. When an obstacle arises—as when Keiko's father playfully withholds an object she wants—Keiko may grab for the object, push her father's hand away, or hit his hand. The infant tries out, modifies, and coordinates previous schemes, searching for one that works in the new situation.

Object permanence is developing rapidly. Keiko looks for an object behind a screen if she sees it being hidden there. But if she sees it being moved from one hiding place to another, she will still look for it in the first hiding place.

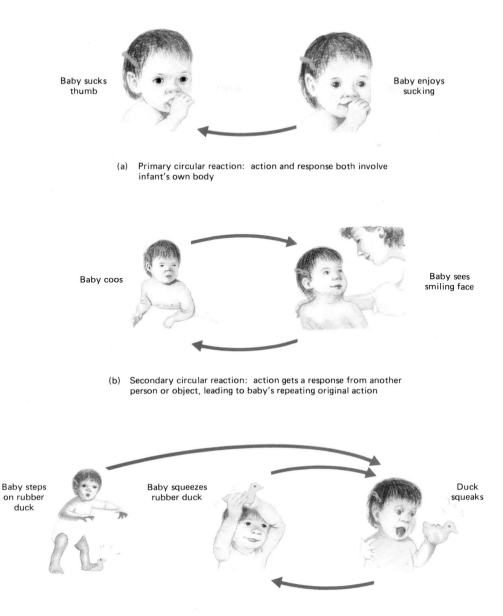

(a)  Primary circular reaction:  action and response both involve infant's own body

(b)  Secondary circular reaction:  action gets a response from another person or object, leading to baby's repeating original action

(c)  Tertiary circular reaction:  action gets one pleasing result, leading baby to perform similar actions to get similar results

FIGURE 4-2
Primary, secondary, and tertiary circular reactions. According to Piaget, infants learn to reproduce pleasing events they have discovered accidentally. (a) Primary circular reaction: A baby happens to suck a thumb, enjoys sucking, and puts the thumb back into the mouth or keeps it there. The stimulus (thumb) elicits the sucking reflex; pleasure then stimulates the baby to keep on sucking. (b) Secondary circular reaction: This involves something outside the baby's body. The baby coos; the mother smiles; and because the baby likes to see the mother smile, the baby coos again. (c) Tertiary circular reaction: The baby tries different ways to reproduce an accidentally discovered response. When the baby steps on a rubber duck, the duck squeaks. The baby then tries to produce the squeak in other ways, as by squeezing it or sitting on it.

***Substage 5: Tertiary circular reactions (12 to 18 months)*** In the fifth substage, babies begin to experiment with novel rather than purely repetitive behavior. Once they begin to walk, their curiosity focuses on many new objects, which they learn about through inspection. Babies now engage in **tertiary circular reactions,** varying their original actions to see what will happen rather than merely repeating pleasing behavior they have accidentally discovered, as before. For example, Noah might step on a rubber duck and hear it squeak. Then he might try pressing it, and after that, he might sit on the duck.

For the first time, children show originality in problem solving, which they do by trial and error. Rather than merely building on past responses, they try out new behaviors until they find the most effective way to attain a goal. When Rebecca, for example, wanted to get the Cheerios from her father's hand, she tried prying and holding his fingers open first with one hand, then with both hands, and finally by using her chin as an additional tool.

Object permanence has developed further. Infants look in the last place they have seen something being hidden rather than in the first place, as in substage 4. Still, they cannot imagine movement that they do not see. If Rebecca's father were to put a toy in his hand, put his hand behind a pillow, leave the toy there, and bring out his closed hand for her to examine, Rebecca would look for her toy in his hand. It would not occur to her that the toy might be behind the pillow, because she did not see him putting it there.

***Substage 6:   Beginning of thought—mental combinations (18 to 24 months)*** At about 18 months, according to Piaget, children become capable of symbolic thought. They make symbolic mental representations of events and thus can think about actions before taking them and can go beyond the action-oriented behavior of the sensorimotor stage. Since they now have some understanding of cause and effect, they no longer have to go through laborious trial and error to solve new problems. Rather, mental representations let them try out solutions in their minds and discard the ones that they decide will not work. Piaget's daughter Lucienne demonstrated this breakthrough—the development of insight—when she figured out how to pry open a partially closed matchbox to remove a watch chain from it, opening and closing her mouth to signify her idea of widening the slit in the box (Piaget, 1952).

The ability to manipulate symbols frees children from immediate experience and lets them use language. They can imitate actions even after whatever or whomever they are copying is no longer in front of them. They are now able to pretend, as Anna does at 20 months when she is given a tea set and immediately "serves tea" to Diane and Jonathan. This simple "pretend" play is the forerunner of the more elaborate dramatic play that occurs at age 3 and later, as symbolic abilities and behaviors become vastly enlarged during the preoperational stage (see Chapter 6).

Object permanence is now fully developed. When children see an object being moved from one place to another, they look for it in the last hiding place. They will also search for objects they have not witnessed being hidden. Thus, Rebecca would now look behind the pillow for the toy, even if she had not seen her father putting it there.

### Research based on the sensorimotor stage

While Piaget's theories are highly regarded and considered a basically sound way to chart children's cognitive growth, researchers testing them have questioned some of his claims. So far the sequences he outlined have held up fairly well, but follow-up studies have raised questions about the timing of various concepts. A body of recent research suggests that infants are able to conceptualize much earlier than Piaget proposed. Also, Piaget did not address the phenomenon of abilities that appear, disappear, and then reappear later.

Some researchers observing infants from 4 weeks of age to about 2 years have confirmed Piaget's unvarying order for the progression of sensorimotor stages (Uzgiris, 1972). Other investigators gave object permanence tasks to children aged 5 to 32 months (like finding partially and completely hidden objects, finding objects that had been moved and hidden several times, and finding objects hidden under three layers of cloth). These babies developed the concept of object permanence in the order outlined by Piaget (Kramer, Hill, & Cohen, 1975).

Researchers have developed tests based on Piaget's theories in order to measure intellectual development in children who have not begun to speak. Standardized tests of sensorimotor development, like the Infant Psychological Development Scales (IPDS) created by Uzgiris and Hunt (1975), combine the psychometric and Piagetian approaches. In one study 23 babies were tested on the IPDS every 3 months between 1 and 2 years of age, and at 31 months they were given the Stanford-Binet Intelligence Scale. A positive relationship showed up between the Stanford-Binet scores and the scores on each of the eight subscales of the IPDS. The age of attaining object permanence was the strongest predictor of later scores on intelligence tests

(Wachs, 1975). This seems to be a useful way to predict childhood intelligence from infants' abilities, a goal that, as we have seen, has been hard to achieve.

Piaget's thesis that children are active participants in their own learning, and that much of what they know comes about as the result of their own activity, has been supported in research that examines the impact of children's ability to get around on their own. As we saw in Chapter 3, 10-month-olds were more successful in finding toys hidden in a box after they had crawled around the box on their own than when their parents carried them around it (Benson & Uzgiris, 1985).

## Piaget's Timing: When Do Children Actually Attain Various Abilities?

A number of researchers studying cognitive concepts first described by Piaget have found them at earlier ages than he had proposed. It seems likely that Piaget underestimated children's abilities because of the way he tested them. Let's briefly consider some of the findings of recent innovative testing techniques.

### Object permanence

Piaget maintained that babies do not look for an object that they cannot see any part of, even if it has been hidden while they watched, until they are about 9 months old; before that age, if it is completely hidden, they act as if it does not exist. But new studies using different methods suggest that Piaget may have underestimated infants' understanding of object permanence because of how he tested them (Baillargeon, 1987). The new research underscores the point that the way an experiment is conducted can affect the results.

Young infants may fail to *search* for hidden objects because they are not yet able to perform sequences of actions—like moving a cushion to look for something hidden behind it. This does not necessarily mean they do not *know* that the objects are there. The phenomenon may be like toddlers' ability to understand speech before they can form words themselves.

### Invisible imitation

Piaget held that **invisible imitation**—imitation using parts of their own bodies that babies cannot see for themselves, like the mouth—begins at about 9 months. It follows a period of **visible imitation**—imitation using parts of their bodies (the hands and feet, for example) that babies *can* see.

But in some studies, 2- to 3-week-old babies imitated adults by sticking out the tongue, opening the mouth, and making their lips protrude—all of which ac-

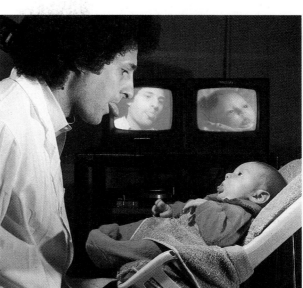

Does this baby's tongue express contempt for the researcher, A. N. Meltzoff? No; infants as young as 2 weeks old stick out their tongues after adults do, in what Meltzoff considers invisible imitation, which he maintains is present at birth. Other researchers, who found that only the youngest babies did this, suggest that the tongue movement may be a primitive reflex.

tions, of course, they could not see (Meltzoff & Moore, 1977). Even younger infants—newborns less than 72 hours old (including one who was only 42 minutes old!)—imitated an adult by opening the mouth and sticking out the tongue (Meltzoff & Moore, 1983). And still other babies, whose average age was 36 hours, imitated three different expressions—a smile, a pout, and the wide-open mouth and eyes that usually denote surprise (T. M. Field, Woodson, Greenberg, & Cohen, 1982). Nor is imitation limited to mouth movements: newborns less than 72 hours old copied adults' head movements (Meltzoff & Moore, 1989). These researchers concluded that the capacity to imitate is present at birth and does not need to be learned, and that newborn infants can, at some level, understand that body changes they can see in other people are the same kinds of changes they can produce themselves.

However, other researchers who studied infants aged 2 to 21 weeks, failed to find invisible imitation (Abravanel & Sigafoos, 1984; Hayes & Watson, 1981). Only the youngest infants stuck out their tongues, and not completely. It is possible that sticking out the tongue is a reflexive action that disappears in older infants, or that the previous presence of a pacifier in a baby's mouth may cause mouth movements that seem like imitation. Meltzoff and Moore (1983) suggest that procedures used by other researchers may have masked infants' imitative capacities. In any case, there is enough evidence to suggest that neonates do display invisible imitation.

### Deferred imitation

According to Piaget, *deferred imitation*—the ability to imitate an action that has been seen some time before—does not begin until at least 18 months of age. This ability shows that a baby has long-term memory for an event, and thus that the baby has a mental representation for it, a "picture" in the mind.

Research has found deferred imitation in infants aged 14 months (Meltzoff, 1985, 1988b) and even 9 months (Meltzoff, 1988a). In separate studies with babies at these two ages, adults performed specific actions (like pulling apart a two-piece wooden toy or shaking a plastic rattle) in front of the babies. Since the babies could not touch the toys, they could not imitate the actions right away; they went home and returned to the lab 24 hours later (or 1 week later in the most recent research). Upon seeing the same toys, more of the babies who had seen the adults' actions did the same things than a group of control babies (who had been in the lab the day before and had seen the toys but not the actions).

The actions the babies imitated were simple, and the research samples were small, but these studies still show that at least some babies as young as 9 months can remember several kinds of actions over a 24-hour period well enough to copy them—and that 14-month-olds can remember them as long as 1 week later. Older babies were more likely to reproduce the actions, perhaps showing a superior ability to receive and encode the information in memory. These findings suggest that deferred imitation occurs before Piaget theorized it did. Future research may establish how far deferred imitation extends in early infancy—whether it extends to more complex behaviors.

### Number concepts

According to Piaget, children do not begin to understand the concept of counting until the preoperational stage, which begins at about age 2, when they begin to use symbols like words and numbers. But newer research suggests that an understanding of number begins earlier. In one study, 7-month-old babies heard two or three drumbeats at the same time as they saw slides of either two or three common household objects (like a key, a pillow, and a drinking glass). Most of the infants looked longer at the displays that matched the number of beats they heard (that is, a photo of two objects accompanied by two drumbeats rather than

three drumbeats), suggesting that these babies had at least a primitive sense of number (Starkey, Spelke, & Gelman, 1983).

### Conservation

One of the first researchers to question Piaget's timetables, Bower (1976), suggested that certain abilities show up earlier than Piaget proposed, then disappear, and later reappear. Piaget said, for example, that children under 9 years old do not understand the principle of *weight conservation*—that an object weighs the same if nothing is added to it or taken away from it, even though its appearance may change. Bower, however, found that 18-month-old babies who picked up a piece of clay that was molded first into one shape and then into a different shape moved their arms in a way that showed that they knew the weight remained the same. But 2 years later, the same children no longer acted as if they understood this principle. Children seem to reacquire this concept at the age of 7 or 8, lose it again, and not develop a stable grasp of it until they are 9 or 10 (Bower, 1976).

Even though Piaget's theories are being modified in response to the work of other psychologists, his vast contributions to the entire field of developmental psychology will continue to hold a prominent place in the history of science. He was a pioneer in shedding light on the workings of the child's mind and in showing specific ways in which children's thinking differs from that of adults. If it had not been for his creative, prolific work, the experiments that questioned his theories might not have been conceived, let alone carried out.

## INFORMATION-PROCESSING APPROACH: PERCEPTIONS AND SYMBOLS

A smiling 6-week-old baby boy begins to make sucking noises as his mother approaches. It is clear that he recognizes her and is happy to see her; but just how does that recognition take place? What is going on in his head? Neither Piaget nor the psychometricians have answers for such questions.

The *information-processing approach* is a new way to explain how intelligence works. This approach sees people as manipulators of perceptions and symbols. Its goal is to discover what infants, children, and adults do with information from the time they perceive it until they use it. Like the psychometric approach, information-processing theory focuses on individual differences in intelligent behavior. But it concentrates on describing the processes that people go through in acquiring information or solving problems, rather than merely assuming differences in mental functioning from answers given or problems solved.

### Information Processing during Infancy as a Predictor of Intelligence

The popularity of the psychometric approach—along with the difficulty of assessing infants' intelligence psychometrically—has led to serious misconceptions about infants' intelligence. Because of discrepancies between scores on tests for infants (like the Bayley scales) and later IQ tests, many people have believed that the intellectual functioning of an infant has little in common with that of older children and adults—that there is a discontinuity in intellectual development. Today, discoveries about the ability of very young babies to process visual and auditory stimuli (see Chapter 3) cast doubt on this view. In fact, when we look at how infants process information rather than at how they perform on psychometric tests, we find that mental development is fairly continuous from birth into childhood (Bornstein & Sigman, 1986).

How *do* infants process information? Answers to this question are being provided by studies that use sensitive equipment to monitor such responses as eye movements, heart rate, and brain activity. For example, even very young infants show *visual-recognition memory,* the ability to remember and recognize something they have seen. If infants pay more attention to new patterns than to familiar ones, they can tell the new from the old; therefore, they must be able to remember the old. To compare new information with information they already have, they must be able to form mental images or representations of stimuli. Infants apparently acquire information, then, by forming such images, and the efficiency of their information processing depends on the speed with which they form and refer to them.

Researchers gauge the efficiency of infants' information processing by measuring variations in attention: how quickly different babies habituate to familiar stimuli, how fast their attention recovers when they are exposed to new stimuli, and how much time they spend looking at the new and the old (Bornstein, 1985; Bornstein & Sigman, 1986). As Rheingold (1985) observed, mental development is the process of transforming the novel into the familiar, the unknown into the known. It is not surprising, therefore, that efficient habituation correlates with other signs of advanced mental development, like a preference for complexity, rapid exploration of the environment, relatively sophisticated play, rapid problem solving, and an ability to match pictures.

Children who were more efficient as infants at taking in and interpreting what they saw, or at remembering what they saw or heard, do better on childhood intelligence tests. In a number of longitudinal studies, habituation and "attention recovery" during the first 6 months of life were moderately useful in predicting scores on psychometric tests taken between ages 2 and 8 (Bornstein & Sigman, 1986). Infants' attention is particularly related to language ability in childhood—surprisingly, more so than to later visual-recognition memory. Researchers have linked infants' visual recognition with their scores 4 and 7 years later on vocabulary tests (J. F. Fagan & McGrath, 1981).

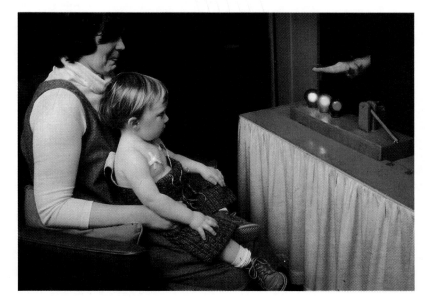

This 2-year-old is taking part in a new kind of intelligence test, especially effective with developmentally disabled babies. Electrodes attached to the child's chest measure changes in heart rate, which speeds up when events violate expectations. Here, light bulbs glow and darken in response to a wand. Testers estimate children's intelligence on the basis of how long it takes them to learn what to expect. This child was previously thought to be a slow learner, but the test indicated normal intelligence.

One line of research focuses on preterm infants. Predictions are particularly important for these babies, who are believed to be less capable than full-term infants of visually interpreting their world. The studies did not use habituation to measure visual-recognition memory but instead used a paired-comparison procedure, in which the babies first saw pictures of faces and abstract patterns and later saw some of the same pictures along with new ones. Assessment relied on how long they paid attention to the pictures, and on how much longer they spent looking at the new pictures rather than the familiar ones. ***Novelty preference***— the greater length of time babies spend looking at new stimuli rather than familiar ones—of 6-month-old preterm babies is consistently and significantly related to psychometric scores of cognitive development between ages 2 and 6 years. Novelty preference was an even better predictor of childhood IQ than parents' educational levels. The researchers, S. A. Rose and Wallace (1985), see in their results an "impressive continuity" between early information-processing capabilities and later cognition (p. 849).

In another study, 7-month-old preterm babies had poorer visual-recognition memory and were less able to "recruit," sustain, and shift attention than were full-term 7-month-old babies (S. A. Rose, Feldman, McCarton, & Wolfson, 1988). Also, scores of 7-month-old preterm babies on infant attention and memory tasks were good predictors of their later scores on the Bayley Mental Development Index, on the Stanford-Binet, and on the Wechsler Preschool and Primary Scale of Intelligence (WPPSI—see Chapter 6) (S. A. Rose, Feldman, Wallace, & McCarton, 1989). Although the 7-month Bayley scores were good predictors only for preterm (not full-term) babies and mostly at younger ages, the association does show evidence of continuity between competence in early infancy and later cognitive performance.

Infants' sensitivity to sounds, too, may allow us to estimate aspects of their later cognitive functioning. A highly significant positive correlation showed up between 4-month-old infants' ability to discriminate sounds and their IQ scores at 5 years of age (O'Connor, Cohen, & Parmelee, 1984).

Differences in how efficiently infants discriminate and remember stimuli seem to forecast aspects of childhood intelligence. But we still do not know what accounts for these differences or just how they affect cognitive development. In Rose and Wallace's study (1985), although both novelty preference and parents' educational levels were indicators of later IQ, the two factors were apparently unrelated to each other; in other words, both contributed independently to individual differences.

## Influences on Information Processing and Cognitive Development

One major influence on cognitive development is the way parents and other caregivers act toward children. This may sound obvious, but many beliefs that seem to be "common sense" do not withstand the test of well-designed research. This one has been confirmed by a number of well-designed experiments across cultures.

In several studies, researchers looked at how responsive American and Japanese mothers were to their babies, seen first when the babies were 2 to 5 months old, and then again at 1, 1½, 2½, or 4 years of age, when the children were assessed on various cognitive abilities (Bornstein & Tamis-LeMonda, 1989). Responsiveness was defined as behavior that promptly and appropriately followed some behavior of the baby. In other words, when the baby babbled or looked at the mother ("nondistress" activities) or cried (a sign of distress), did the mother smile at, talk to, pick up, pat, feed, or pay attention to the baby in some other way?

While almost all the mothers responded quickly when their babies were distressed, their rate of responsiveness to nondistress behavior varied greatly and was apparently unrelated to education or socioeconomic status. Although the responses mothers made to 2-month-old babies were not associated with the children's later development, the way the women acted when the babies were 4 or 5 months old was. The children of the most responsive mothers had more advanced representational abilities as toddlers, and as 4-year-olds scored higher on the WPPSI and other learning tasks. In other research, mothers' responsiveness to 4-month-old babies was associated with later cognitive achievements (in conjunction with the babies' abilities in processing information), but the way they acted with their 1-year-olds was not (Bornstein, 1985). These different findings, then, may point to a critical period for caregivers' impact on babies' intellectual growth.

Other research focused on mothers' responsiveness to preterm infants. The infants whose mothers were most sensitive, responsive, and positively involved with them scored higher on IQ tests as adolescents and considered themselves more competent than the teenage children of less responsive mothers (Beckwith & Cohen, 1989). Findings like these confirm other data showing that the environment a child grows up in can do a great deal to offset the negative effects of complications around the time of birth. Although most of these studies have been done with mothers, their findings are most likely just as relevant for fathers and other primary caregivers.

## BOX 4–1    WINDOW ON THE WORLD

# EASTERN AND WESTERN LEARNING STYLES

Benjamin, aged 1½ years, loved to play with the key to his family's hotel room in Nanjing, China. He liked to shake it vigorously, enjoying the sounds it made. He also liked to hold the plastic block attached to the key and liked to try to insert the key into the narrow slot at the front desk where guests dropped their keys. It did not seem to bother him at all that he usually failed to get the key into the slot, and his parents were happy to let him continue banging the key around.

But then his parents noticed something related to their mission, to investigate early childhood education and creativity in China. Benjamin's father, Howard Gardner, a professor of education at Harvard University, describes a typical scene:

"Any Chinese attendant nearby would come over to watch Benjamin and, noting his lack of initial success, attempt to intervene. He or she would hold onto Ben-

jamin's hand and, gently but firmly, guide it directly toward the slot, reorient it as necessary, and help him to insert it. The 'teacher' would then smile somewhat expectantly at Ellen or me, as if awaiting a thank you" (p. 54).

What did this experience tell Gardner? It illuminated a major difference in cultural attitudes toward helping children learn. Benjamin's American parents encouraged his exploratory behavior, wanting him to become self-reliant, to learn that he could solve problems on his own, and to come up with creative solutions to new problems. Chinese educators and parents, however, believe that molding children's behavior by guiding them gently into tasks that are beyond them will diminish their frustration, make them happy, and help them learn how to do one task so that they can then go on to a harder one.

Relating this to creativity, Gardner calls the Chinese view "evolution-

ary": children should be helped to become competent through approved means, and only then will they be in a position to deviate from the traditional approved forms. In contrast, the American view is "revolutionary": the young westerner makes bold departures first and gradually moves into tradition. Americans value originality and independence and worry that creativity will never emerge unless children acquire it early; the Chinese fear that children may never acquire skills if they do not learn them early.

Gardner recognizes that both cultures produce competent, creative people, but he asks, "Can we glean, from the Chinese and American extremes, a superior way to approach education, perhaps striking an optimal balance between the poles of creativity and basic skills?" (p. 56)

*Source:* Gardner, 1989.

How exactly does adults' responsiveness help children develop intellectually? It might raise their self-esteem and make them feel that they have some control over their lives. It might make them feel secure enough to explore and motivate them to persist in exploring. It might also help them regulate themselves so that they can pay attention and thus can learn.

Parents' involvement—or noninvolvement—in their children's learning is strongly affected by the culture or the subculture they live in, as illustrated in Box 4-1 above.

## DEVELOPMENT OF LANGUAGE

At 4½ months, Stefan chuckles out loud. He also says "Ngoo-ooo" and "Ngaaah." At 7 months he makes more sounds, mostly sounding like "Da" or "Ga." At 11 months he says "Dada," and at 14 months he points to everything, asking "What zis?" or saying "Da" for "I

want that." At 17 months he points to the right places when asked "Where is your nose? Tongue? Belly button?" and so forth. By 21 months he says, or tries to say, at least 50 words, and understands many more. He can now tell you exactly what he does or does not want, in his own language. When asked "Do you want to go to bed?" his answer is "Eh-eh-eh," accompanied by vigorous arm waving. In other words, "No!" He has also said his first three-word sentence: "Choo-choo bye-bye dada." (His mother translates, "The train went away, and now it's all gone.")

Aside from being a source of amusement, delight, and pride to his parents (and a source of information for Sally, his grandmother), Stefan's language ability is a crucial element in his cognitive growth. Once he knows the words for things, he can use a system of symbols to stand for the objects around him; he can reflect on people, places, and things in his world; and he can communicate his needs, feelings, and ideas in order to exert control over his life.

## THEORIES OF LANGUAGE ACQUISITION

Although both maturation and environment are important in the development of language, different linguists assign major importance to one or the other of these factors. *Learning theory* (introduced in Chapter 1) holds that learning (including learning of language) is based on experience; *nativism* maintains that there is an inborn capacity for learning language.

### Learning Theory

According to learning theory, children learn language in the same way that they learn other kinds of behavior— through reinforcement. Parents reinforce children for making sounds that resemble adult speech, and so children make more of these sounds, generalizing and abstracting as they go along. *Behaviorists* believe that children utter sounds at random, and that those which sound like adult speech are then reinforced. *Social-learning theorists* maintain that children imitate the sounds they hear adults making and then are reinforced for doing so; thus children in English-speaking countries learn English rather than another language. Imitation may explain why children generally outgrow incorrect usages even when their parents do not correct their grammar (R. Brown, Cazden, & Bellugi, 1969).

Learning theorists point to the fact that children reared at home, who presumably hear more adult speech and get more attention and more reinforcement than those who grow up in institutions, do babble more (Brodbeck & Irwin, 1946). However, learning theory does not account for children's marvelously imaginative ways of saying things they have never heard, like one girl's description of walking on her heels as "tip-heeling."

### Nativism

According to nativism, human beings have an inborn capacity for acquiring language and learn to talk as naturally as they learn to walk. Evidence for this viewpoint comes from several facts:

- Almost all children learn their native language, no matter how complex, mastering the basics in the same age-related sequence without formal teaching.
- Human beings, the only animals that have a spoken language, are also the only species in which the brain is larger on one side than the other and seems to have an inborn mechanism for language localized in the larger hemisphere (for most people, the left hemispehere).

- Newborns respond to language in sophisticated ways. They move their bodies in the rhythm of the adult speech they hear (Condon & Sander, 1974); they can tell their mother's voices from those of strangers (A. DeCasper & Fifer, 1980); and, in the first month of life, they can distinguish very similar sounds (Eimas, Siqueland, Jusczyk, & Vigorito, 1971).

One researcher suggests that neonates can put sounds into categories because all human beings are "born with perceptual mechanisms that are tuned to the properties of speech" (Eimas, 1985, p. 49). Contact with the sounds of a particular language leads children to "tune in" the corresponding preset "channels" and "tune out" unused ones. These perceptual mechanisms, along with the vocal cords and the specialized speech centers of the brain, let a child "join the community of language" quickly (p. 52).

How, after starting with simple recognition of sounds, do babies go on to create complex utterances that follow the specific rules of language in their society? Noam Chomsky (1972) proposes one answer to this question: that an inborn *language acquisition device (LAD)* programs children's brains to analyze the language they hear and to extract from it the rules of grammar. Using these rules, children can then make up original sentences.

Deaf children make up their own sign language when they do not have models to follow—and this is more evidence that internal mechanisms play a large role in a young child's growing linguistic capacity (H. Feldman, Goldin-Meadow, & Gleitman, 1979; Hoff-Ginsberg & Shatz, 1982). Still, the nativist approach does not explain why children differ so much in grammatical skill and fluency; nor does it explain how they come to understand the meanings of words, or why (as we will see) speech development depends on having someone to talk with.

Most developmentalists today draw on both nativism and learning theory; they believe that children enter the world with an inborn capacity to acquire a language, which is then activated and enhanced by learning through experience.

## STAGES IN LANGUAGE DEVELOPMENT

Table 4-2 lists language milestones during the first 3 years of life. Let's now examine four stages of language development: prespeech, the first words, the first sentences, and early syntax.

**TABLE 4–2**
LANGUAGE MILESTONES FROM BIRTH TO 3 YEARS

| Age | Development |
|---|---|
| Birth | Baby can perceive speech, cry, make some response to sound. |
| 1½ to 3 months | Coos and laughs. |
| 3 months | Plays with speech sounds. |
| 5 to 6 months | Makes consonant sounds, trying to match what she or he hears. |
| 6 to 10 months | Babbles in strings of consonants and vowels. |
| 8 to 10 months | Begins to understand words (usually "no" and baby's own name); imitates sounds. |
| 9 months | Uses gestures to communicate and plays gesture games. |
| 10 months | Loses ability to discriminate sounds not in own language. |
| 10 to 14 months | Says first word (usually a label for something); imitates sounds. |
| 13 months | Understands symbolic function of naming. |
| 14 months | Uses symbolic gesturing. |
| 16 to 24 months | Learns many new words, expanding vocabulary rapidly, going from about 50 words to up to 400; uses verbs and adjectives; speaks 2-word sentences. |
| 18 to 24 months | Says first sentence. |
| 20 months | Uses fewer gestures; names more things. |
| 24 months | Uses many 2-word phrases; no longer babbles; wants to talk. |
| 30 months | Learns new words almost every day; speaks in combinations of 3 or more words; understands very well; makes many grammatical mistakes. |
| 36 months | Says up to 1000 words, 80 percent intelligible; makes few mistakes in syntax; grammar is close to informal adult speech. |

*Sources:* Bates, O'Connell, & Shore, 1987; Capute, Shapiro, & Palmer, 1987; Lenneberg, 1969.

## Prespeech

The word *infant* is based on the Latin for "without speech." Before Stefan said "Dada" or Anna said "Hi," both, like all normal infants, made a variety of sounds that progressed in a fairly set sequence from crying to cooing and babbling, accidental imitation, and then deliberate imitation. These sounds are known as **prelinguistic speech.**

Babies can distinguish between sounds long before they can utter anything but a cry. In the first months of life, they can tell apart similar sounds like *bah* and *pah* (Eimas et al., 1971). This ability to differentiate sounds seems to be an inborn capacity that people lose as they hear the language spoken around them. Japanese infants, for example, can easily tell *ra* from *la,* but Japanese adults have trouble making this distinction (Bates, O'Connell, & Shore, 1987). Babies seem to lose this ability at about 9 or 10 months of age, when they begin to understand meaningful speech, but before they are physically mature enough to produce their own.

Crying is the newborn's first and only means of communication. To a stranger, a baby's cries may sound alike, but the baby's parents can often tell, for example, the cry for food from the cry of pain. Different pitches, patterns, and intensities signal hunger, sleepiness, or anger.

At anywhere from 6 weeks to 3 months of age, babies start to laugh and coo when they are happy, making squeals, gurgles, and vowel sounds like *ah.* A kind of "vocal tennis" begins at about 3 months, when they begin to play with speech sounds, producing a variety of sounds that seem to match the ones they hear from the people around them (Bates et al., 1987). Cross-cultural studies—like one that looked at babies growing up in

French-, Chinese-, and Arabic-speaking families—found that babies do not, as was once believed, "try out" all speech sounds in all human languages, but instead move in the direction of their own language (Boysson-Bardies, Sagart, & Durand, 1984).

Babbling—repeating consonant-vowel strings like *ma-ma-ma-ma*—occurs rather suddenly between 6 and 10 months of age, and these strings are often mistaken for a baby's first word. Early babbling is not real language, since it does not seem to have meaning for the baby, but it becomes more wordlike, leading into early speech. In this stage one kind of difference shows up between babies. "Word babies" seem to understand words earlier and produce word sounds in their babbling, whereas "intonation babies" babble in sentence-like patterns and tend not to break their babbling strings down into individual words (Dore, 1975).

At first babies accidentally imitate sounds they hear. Then they imitate themselves making these sounds. At about 9 to 10 months of age they deliberately imitate other sounds, without understanding them. Once they have this basic repertoire of sounds, they string them together in patterns that sound like language but seem to have no meaning (Lenneberg, 1967).

This prelinguistic speech can be rich in emotional expression. Starting at about 2 months, when infants' cooing begins to express contentment, the range of emotional tone increases steadily. Long before children can express any ideas in words, parents become attuned to their babies' feelings through the sounds they make (Tonkova-Yompol'skaya, 1973).

Babies understand many words before they can say them. The first words most babies understand are either their own names or the word *no*—which is not surprising, considering the fact that these are the two words an active baby is likely to hear most often. They also pick up other words with special meaning for them, and parents sometimes have to start spelling words in front of 14-month-olds if it is not time yet to give them their *b-a-n-a-n-a.*

Throughout the prespeech period, parents and other caregivers have been actively communicating with a baby in many different ways. By the end of the first year the baby has some sense of intentional communication, a primitive idea of reference, and a set of signals that serve to communicate with the baby's familiar caregivers (Bates et al., 1987). The linguistic stage is now set for speech.

## First Words

When Stefan said "Dada" and Anna said "Hi"—their first words—both were right on time. The average baby says his or her first word sometime between 10 and 14 months, initiating **linguistic speech**—the use of spoken language to convey meaning. Before long, the baby will use many words and will also show some understanding of grammar, pronunciation, intonation, and rhythm. At this point, though, the sum total of an infant's repertoire is likely to be "Mama" or "Dada." Or it may be a simple syllable that has more than one meaning, depending on what is on the baby's mind at the moment. As with Stefan, "Da" may mean "I want that," "I want to go out," "Where's Daddy?" and so forth. A word like this is called a **holophrase,** because it expresses a complete thought in a single word.

### Growth of vocabulary

Typically, by 15 months of age a child of either sex has spoken 10 different words or names (Nelson, 1973). Vocabulary continues to grow throughout the single-word stage (which tends to last until the age of about 18 months). There is also an increasing reliance on words. More and more occasions inspire the child to speak a word or a name. The sounds and rhythms of speech grow more elaborate, and even if much of the child's speech is still babbling (many children over the age of 1 year babble steadily), it does seem quite expressive.

In studying the first 50 words spoken by a group of 1- and 2-year-olds, Nelson (1973, 1981) found that the most common were *names* of things, either in the general sense ("oof-oof" for dog) or the specific ("Unga" for one particular dog). Others were *action* words ("bye-bye"), modifiers ("hot"), words that express *feelings or relationships* (the ever-popular "no"), and a few *grammatical* words ("for").

By 13 months most children seem to understand the symbolic function of naming; that is, they realize that a

This toddler is clearly communicating something—maybe saying "baby" as she points to the doll. The most common first words are names of things, either general ("baby") or specific (the doll's name).

word stands for a specific thing or event. They add words slowly to their vocabulary until a "naming explosion" occurs somewhere between 16 and 24 months, and the baby goes from saying about 50 words to saying about 400 within a few weeks (Bates, Bretherton, & Snyder, 1985, in Bates, O'Connell, & Shore, 1987).

### Symbolic gesturing

Just before or at about the same time that babies say their first words, they often develop a repertoire of nonverbal gestures (Anna did this, as we saw in Chapter 1). "Symbolic gestures" go beyond pointing and games like pat-a-cake, to represent specific objects, events, desires, and conditions. Not all children use such gestures. Those who do typically start to use them at about 14 months to make requests, at about 15 months to describe attributes (like blowing to mean "hot"), and about 2 weeks later to "name" objects. Symbolic gestures usually appear before children have a vocabulary of 25 words and drop out when the children learn the words for the ideas they were expressing in gestures. Among thirty-eight 17-month-olds, 87 percent used at least one such gesture, and the average child used four (Acredolo & Goodwyn, 1988).

More than half the children developed gestures as a result of routines with their parents; for instance, several bounced their torsos to mean "horse," a gesture that arises from being bounced on an adult's knee. While children make up most of these gestures themselves, the parents' role is important. It takes two to communicate, and if parents do not interpret and respond to the gestures, children are likely to drop them and try to get adults' attention in other ways—like grabbing or making sounds.

These gestures show that even before children can talk, they understand that objects and concepts have names and that they can use symbols to refer to the things and happenings in their everyday lives.

### Language and cognition in the first-word stage

During the one-word period, cognitive and linguistic achievements seem very closely related. Within a few weeks of learning complex object permanence tasks, babies tend to acquire words for disappearance (like *gone*); and after they learn how to solve problems (using a stick to obtain an object or putting a necklace into a bottle), they often use words associated with success or failure (like *there, did it,* and *uh-oh*). The babies in one study (Gopnik & Meltzoff, 1986) learned how to do the tasks and solve the problems between 15 to 22 months; and they used the associated words by 2 years. The cognitive-linguistic link was very specific; solving the object-permanence task did not lead to the use of success-failure words; and problem solving did not lead to acquisition of words for disappearance. This suggests that children are motivated to learn words that are important to them at the time.

## First Sentences

At 18 months, Sally's daughter Nancy first spoke two words to express one idea. "Shoe fall," she said to her father, who was pushing her along in her stroller. Her father paused, saw the shoe on the sidewalk, and picked it up. Nancy had spoken her first sentence, putting two words together to express a single thought.

The age at which children begin combining words varies, although the range is similar for children who learn spoken language and children of deaf parents who learn sign language. Generally they put words together between 18 and 24 months of age, about 8 to 12 months after the first word, but this is very variable. Although prelinguistic speech is fairly closely tied to chronological age, linguistic speech is not. Knowing a child's age tells us very little about his or her language development, according to Roger Brown (1973a, 1973b), who has studied this phase of language acquisition.

Nancy's first sentence was typical in that it dealt with everyday events, things, people, or activities (Braine, 1976; Rice, 1989; Slobin, 1973). This early speech, described as "telegraphic," was once thought to be universal, but now we know that children vary individually in the extent to which they use telegraphic speech (Braine, 1976) and that the form itself varies depending on the language being learned (Slobin, 1983).

## Early Syntax

Children's speech becomes increasingly complex. First, tense and case endings, articles, and prepositions are missing ("Shoe fall"); and, frequently, so are subjects or verbs ("That ball" and "Mommy sock"). Next the child may string two basic relationships together ("Adam hit" and "Hit ball") to get a more complicated relationship ("Adam hit ball").

Sometime between the ages of 20 and 30 months, children acquire the fundamentals of syntax. They begin to use articles (*a, the*), prepositions (*in, on*), plurals, verb endings, and forms of the verb *to be* (*am, are is*). By 3 years of age, their speech becomes longer and more complex; although they omit many parts of speech, they get their meaning across, and they are fluent speakers (R. Brown, 1973a, 1973b).

Language continues to develop, of course, and by late childhood, children are fully competent in grammar, although they continue to enlarge their vocabulary and improve their style.

## CHARACTERISTICS OF EARLY SPEECH

When Diane's nephew, Eddie, was 14 months old, he jumped in excitement at the sight of a gray-haired man on the television screen and shouted, "Gampa!" When Stefan was 15 months old, he saw a cow and squealed, "Oof-woof!" Both these toddlers were doing something common in early speech: *overgeneralizing concepts.* Apparently Eddie thought that because his grandfather had gray hair, all gray-haired men could be called "Grandpa." And Stefan seemed to think that because a dog has four legs and a tail, all animals with these characteristics are "oof-woofs."

Children's speech is not just an immature version of adult speech. It has a character all its own. These are some other characteristics of early speech:

- Children *simplify.* They say just enough to get their meaning across ("No drink milk!").
- Children *overregularize rules,* applying them rigidly, without knowing that some rules have exceptions. Having learned grammatical rules for plurals and past tense, they say "mouses" and "goed" instead of "mice" and "went."
- Children *understand grammatical relationships that they cannot yet express.* A child may understand that a dog is chasing a cat, but cannot string together enough words to express the complete action. The sentence comes out as "Puppy chase" rather than "Puppy chase kitty."

## INFLUENCES ON LANGUAGE ACQUISITION

What determines how quickly and how well a baby learns to speak? Again, we see nature and nurture.

### Heredity

A genetic influence is apparent in the moderate relationship between parents' intelligence and the rate at which their biological children develop communication skills during the first year of life. Such a relationship has been found for adopted children and their biological mothers, but not their adoptive parents. It also seems likely, however, that environmental factors, like parents' imitation of the sounds infants make, also affect the pace of linguistic learning (Hardy-Brown & Plomin, 1985; Hardy-Brown, Plomin, & DeFries, 1981).

### Environment

Other research attributes many, if not most, of the marked differences in language abilities that surface by the end of a child's second year to differences in children's surroundings (Nelson, 1981). One important environmental influence, of course, is how much and what kind of speech babies hear. A study in Bermuda found that 2-year-olds in day care centers where caregivers speak to them often (especially to give or ask for information rather than to control their behavior) are more advanced in language development than children who do not have such conversations with adults (McCartney, 1984). Conversely, when children with normal hearing grow up in homes with deaf parents who communicate only through sign language, the children's speech development is slowed (Moskowitz, 1978).

In order to speak and communicate, children need practice and interaction. Hearing speech on television is not enough; for example, Dutch children who watch German television every day do not learn German (C. E. Snow et al., 1976). Language is a social act. By talking to babies, parents and other caregivers show how to use new words, structure phrases, and express speech; and they give children a basic sense of how to carry on a conversation—how to introduce a topic, comment on and add to it, and take turns talking.

Unquestionably, conversation with babies is important. The question is, What sort of conversation? Too much direction—commands, requests, and instructions—is not helpful (Nelson, 1973). Among the most helpful things adults can do are to paraphrase what a child says, expand on it, talk about what interests the child, remain quiet long enough to give the child a chance to respond, and use reading-aloud sessions to ask specific questions (Rice, 1989). Box 4-2 gives practical suggestions for talking with babies and toddlers, and Box 4-3 (pages 136) discusses "motherese," a particular kind of infant-directed speech.

### Delayed Language Development

Albert Einstein did not start to speak until he was 3 years old, a fact that heartens the parents of other children—like Anna—whose speech develops later than usual. About 40 percent of late talkers have other problems, like hearing impairment or mental retardation. But Anna seems to be among the 3 percent of young children with delayed language skills whose sensory, motor, cognitive, and emotional abilities are on a par with or above those of their peers (Rice, 1989).

It is still unclear why these children speak later than others. They are not necessarily from homes where

## TALKING WITH BABIES AND TODDLERS

"Yes, you like this, don't you? . . . Yes, you do. . . . You love your bath. . . . And your mommy loves your little noises. . . . Now let's wash your little tummy. . . . Now . . . ." Although this typical commentary from a parent to a child may not sound as if it is on the highest intellectual plane, it is a vital influence on the baby's cognitive and emotional development.

Talking to babies comes naturally to most parents, who greet them when they first awaken, coo at them while changing their diapers, and so on. This beginning communication expands over the years, especially as babies assume a more active role—first imitating, then responding, and then initiating. Through talking, reading, and singing to babies, they learn the language, learn how to get along with other people, and learn that they are valued and special.

Here are some suggestions for talking with babies at different stages of language development:

■ *Prespeech.* When a baby babbles, repeat the syllables. Make a game of it, and soon the baby will repeat your sound. This kind of game gives a baby the idea that a conversation consists of taking turns, an idea they seem to grasp at about 7½ or 8 months of age. A round of stimulating chitchat like "dee, dee, dee; dah, dah, dah" helps babies to experience the social aspect of speech.

■ *First words.* At about 1 year, when babies say their first words, you can help them by going beyond repeating their sounds of "mama" or "da-da." Instead, repeat the word, pronouncing it correctly, or, if you can't understand what the baby is saying, smile in approval and say something yourself. Babies can understand many more words than they can say. Help them learn the names for the objects in their world. For example, point to Jason's doll and say, "Please give me Kermit." If Jason doesn't respond, reach over, pick up the doll, and say, "Kermit." Jason's ability to understand grows as he learns to discover through language what another person is thinking.

■ *First sentences.* Although it is not necessary to *teach* a child to talk, it is important to talk naturally. Help a toddler who has begun to string words together to make sentences by expanding on what the child says. For example, if Vicky says, "Mommy sock," you can reply, "Yes, that is Mommy's sock." Such paraphrasing and expansion has a strong social use, along with a linguistic one. Talk about what the child is interested in and provide pauses to give the child a chance to make his or her contributions to the conversation.

■ *Reading to young children.* Encourage your child's participation in reading-aloud sessions by asking challenging open-ended questions rather than questions that simply call for a yes-or-no answer. Instead of asking, "Is the cat asleep?" ask "What is the cat doing?" Start with easy questions ("Where is the ball?") and then pose more challenging ones ("What color is the ball?" "Who is playing with the ball?" "What is happening to the boy in the corner?"). Expand on the child's answers, correct wrong ones, give alternative possibilities, and bestow praise.

A study comparing methods like these with standard read-aloud practices found that 21- to 35-month-old children participating in this kind of reading session scored 6 months higher than control children in vocabulary and expressive language skills (Whitehurst et al., 1988).

Above all, talking and reading with a child should be fun. Not every conversation should be a lesson or a test. And the baby should be able to decline to play occasionally, because sometimes people of any age do not feel like talking. Most children who begin talking fairly late catch up eventually—and many make up for lost time by talking nonstop to anyone within range!

they do not get enough linguistic input. Even though some of their parents may be talking to them more in terms of what the children can say rather than in terms of what they can understand, this may be more the result than the cause of their delay. Current investigations focus on problems in information processing, or "fast mapping" new words, that is, absorbing the meaning of a new word on the basis of having heard it in conversation (Rice, 1989).

In any case, these children can often benefit from special teaching programs at home, at preschool, and from a qualified professional.

## Can Training Help Parents Improve Children's Competence?

Once the Harvard team had identified guidelines for successful parenting, they launched a pilot study with 11 sets of parents they considered to have "average child-rearing ability." The goal was to help the parents adopt practices to enhance children's competence and to avoid unhelpful practices.

While these children's progress more closely resembled that of the original A children than that of the C children, they did not, by and large, do as well as the A's. It may be that naturally effective parenting styles are hard to duplicate by training, or that personalities of both parents and children play a significant role. Thus, while we can learn from research on successful parenting, no one has yet found the perfect recipe for raising children. One important element, for example, which the researchers did not investigate in depth, was the children's own contributions to their parents' child-rearing styles. It is possible that the children of the A mothers had personality characteristics that made their mothers *want* to respond as they did. Perhaps these children showed more curiosity, more independence, and more interest than the C children in what their mothers said and did.

## HOME: THE HOME OBSERVATION FOR MEASUREMENT OF THE ENVIRONMENT

To look at the impact of a child's home surroundings in infancy and early childhood on later intellectual growth, researchers often use a measure called the *Home Observation for Measurement of the Environment (HOME)* (R. H. Bradley, 1989). This inventory now comes in a version for infants and toddlers, one for young children, and a third for schoolchildren; a fourth version, for young adolescents, is being developed. All three versions include scales of parental responsiveness, which, as we saw earlier, influences children's cognitive development. HOME gives credit to the parent of a toddler for caressing or kissing the child once during the examiner's visit; to the parent of a preschooler for spontaneously praising the child twice during the visit; and to the parent of an older child for answering the child's questions. Examiners evaluate how parent and child talk to each other, and they give high marks for a parent's friendly, nonpunitive attitude.

This measure also evaluates the number of books in the home, at the presence of challenging toys that encourage the development of concepts, and at parents'

involvement in children's play. High scores on all these factors are fairly reliable in predicting children's IQ; when combined with the parent's level of education, they are even more accurate.

In one study, researchers compared HOME scores for low-income 2-year-olds with the children's Stanford-Binet intelligence test scores two years later. The single most important factor in predicting high intelligence was the mother's ability to create and structure an environment that fostered learning (Stevens & Bakeman, 1985). This result supports the findings of the Harvard Preschool Project.

A longitudinal study in Little Rock, Arkansas, found positive correlations between how responsive parents were to their 6-month-old babies and how well the children did when they were 10 years old on IQ and achievement test scores and teachers' ratings of classroom behaviors (R. Bradley & Caldwell, 1982; R. Bradley, Caldwell, & Rock, 1988).

Again, although this research studied mothers, other people, too, can offer children the same kinds of benefits. Fathers and other caregivers can provide books and toys that encourage conceptual thinking and language development, can talk with and read regularly to children, can pay attention to and get involved in their play, and can use punishment sparingly.

The importance of what parents do can be seen in the findings of one study of children from three different ethnic groups. It found that day-to-day aspects of a child's home environment (like parental responsiveness and the availability of stimulating play materials) are more closely related to the child's development than are such aspects of the child's wider environment as socioeconomic status (R. H. Bradley et al., 1989). This conclusion emerged from a study in which researchers looked at 931 white, African American, and Mexican American children up to age 3. Across all the ethnic groups, a favorable home environment could offset problems in infancy, but when a child's early developmental status was low *and* his or her early home environment was poor, the chances for a good outcome for the child were much less than when only one of these measures was low.

Interaction is a key to much of childhood development—intellectual, social, and emotional. Children call forth responses from the people around them and they, in turn, react to those responses. In the next chapter—Chapter 5—we'll look more closely at these bidirectional influences as we explore early personality and social development.

## SUMMARY ▒▒▒▒▒▒▒▒▒▒▒▒▒▒▒▒▒▒

### HOW INFANTS LEARN

- Learning is a relatively permanent change in behavior that occurs as a result of experience. Learning and maturation interact to produce changes in cognitive abilities.

- Very young infants are capable of several kinds of simple learning, including habituation and classical and operant conditioning. Complex learning consists of combinations of several types.

- Infants exhibit some memory ability virtually from birth.

### STUDYING INTELLECTUAL DEVELOPMENT: THREE APPROACHES

- Intelligence involves both adaptive and goal-oriented behavior.

- Three major approaches for studying intelligence are the psychometric, Piagetian, and information-processing approaches.

    1 The psychometric approach seeks to determine and measure quantitatively the factors that make up intelligence. Psychometric testing for infants emphasizes motor skills, which may not measure the same thing as verbal tests do. Psychometric tests of infant intelligence are generally poor predictors of intelligence in later childhood and adulthood.

    2 The Piagetian approach is concerned with qualitative stages of cognitive development, or the way people develop the ability to acquire and use knowledge about the world. During the sensorimotor stage, infants develop from primarily reflexive creatures to goal-oriented toddlers capable of symbolic thought. A major development during the sensorimotor stage is object permanence, the realization that an object or person continues to exist even when out of sight.

    3 The information-processing approach is concerned with the processes underlying intelligent behavior, that is, how people manipulate symbols and what they do with the information they perceive. An important way to assess infants' ability to process information is by measuring their visual-recognition memory, which is related to attention and habituation. Such assessments show promise of predicting later intelligence.

### DEVELOPMENT OF LANGUAGE

- The major theories of language acquistion are learning theory (which emphasizes the role of reinforcement and imitation) and nativism (which maintains that people have an inborn capacity to acquire language). Today, most psychologists hold that children have an inborn language capacity that is activated and enhanced by certain environmental experiences.

- Development of language is a crucial aspect of cognitive growth.

    1 Prelinguistic speech, which precedes the first words, includes crying, cooing, babbling, and imitation. During the second year of life, the typical toddler begins to speak the language of his or her culture; that year seems to be particularly important for understanding language. Symbolic gestures may precede spoken language.

    2 Early speech is characterized by overgeneralizing concepts, simplicity, and overregularizing rules. The child can understand grammatical relationships before being able to express them in speech. Linguistic speech—the use of spoken language to convey meaning—is not closely tied to age.

- At least some communication between caregivers and children is important for children's linguistic growth. It is not clear whether hearing simple, direct language (''motherese'') is crucial to infants' language development. The causes of delayed language development are also unclear.

### DEVELOPMENT OF COMPETENCE

- Parents' child-rearing styles (especially during the first 2 years) affect children's intellectual, social, and emotional competence.

- Parents of the most competent children are those who are skilled at ''designing'' a child's environment, are available as ''consultants'' to a child, and use appropriate controls.

- Parental responsiveness is associated with optimal cognitive development.

## KEY TERMS

learning (page 112)
maturation (112)
habituation (113)
classical conditioning (114)
unconditioned stimulus (114)
unconditioned response (114)
neutral stimulus (114)
conditioned stimulus (114)
conditioned response (114)
operant (instrumental) conditioning
    (115)
reinforcement (115)
intelligent behavior (117)
psychometric approach (117)
intelligence quotient (IQ) tests (117)
standardized norms (117)

valid (117)
reliable (117)
Bayley Scales of Infant Development
    (119)
cognitive development (120)
Piagetian approach (120)
sensorimotor stage (120)
object permanence (120)
causality (121)
representational ability (121)
circular reactions (122)
schemes (122)
primary circular reaction (122)
acquired adaptations (122)
secondary circular reactions (122)
tertiary circular reactions (124)

invisible imitation (125)
visible imitation (125)
deferred imitation (126)
weight conservation (126)
information-processing approach
    (126)
visual-recognition memory (127)
novelty preference (128)
learning theory (130)
nativism (130)
language acquisition device (LAD)
    (130)
prelinguistic speech (131)
linguistic speech (132)
holophrase (132)

## SUGGESTED READINGS

**Bolles, E. B. (1982).** *So much to say.* New York: St. Martin's. A detailed description of children's speech from birth to 5 years of age, written for parents. The book presents the child as a poet discovering new things to say and new ways to say them.

**Brown, R. (1973).** *A first language: The early stages.* Cambridge, MA: Harvard University Press. A classic book that describes the language development of three young children: Adam, Eve, and Sarah.

**deVilliers, P. A., & deVilliers, J. (1979).** *Early language.* Cambridge, MA: Harvard University Press. An engaging discussion of early linguistic development, containing many examples of children's language.

**Ginsburg, H., & Opper, S. (1979).** *Piaget's theory of intellectual development.* (2d ed.). Englewood Cliffs, NJ: Prentice-Hall. A clear, readable discussion of Piaget's concepts. It includes outlines of Piaget's basic ideas, his early research and theory, his use of logic as a model for adolescents' thinking, and a discussion of the implications of his work.

**Piaget, J. (1952).** *The origins of intelligence in children.* New York: International Universities Press. Piaget's now classic presentation of the six substages of sensorimotor development. Based on abundant observations of his three children.

**White, B. L. (1985).** *The first three years of life* (rev. ed.). Englewood Cliffs, NJ: Prentice-Hall. A presentation for lay readers of White's findings on children's competence. It is a thorough treatment of cognitive changes during infancy and toddlerhood.

**White, B. L., Kaban, B. T., & Attanucci, J. S. (1979).** *The origins of human competence.* Lexington, MA: Heath. The final report of the Harvard Preschool Project focusing on the interrelationship between child-rearing practices and children's development of competence during the first few years of life.

## CHAPTER 5

# PERSONALITY AND SOCIAL DEVELOPMENT IN INFANCY AND TODDLERHOOD

I'm like a child
trying to do everything
say everything
and be everything
all at once

JOHN HARTFORD,
"LIFE PRAYER", 1971

- What are some common influences on personality and social development, and how do infants and toddlers develop distinct personalities?
- What do Freud and Erikson say about personality and social development in the first 3 years of life?
- What emotions do infants and toddlers have, and how do they show their emotions?

- What are the effects of differences in temperament and gender?
- How do family relationships contribute to personality and social development?
- What causes child abuse and neglect, and what can be done to combat these problems?

At 2 years, 10 months, Anna shouted, "No! Won't go!" running away from Jonathan as soon as she saw him walking over to the sandbox. Getting Anna to do anything her parents suggested had become harder and harder. Even though Diane and Jonathan knew that their daughter's constant "no's" were a normal and healthy aspect of this stage of life, it was sometimes hard for them to keep smiling through the "terrible twos."

This period—in which many children express their urge for independence by resisting almost everything they are told to do—is an important stage. Dependent, docile infants who trustingly accept what their parents want them to do are often transformed into strong-willed, sometimes ill-tempered creatures with minds of their own. Toddlers *have to* test the new notion that they are individuals, that they have some control over their world, and that they have new, exciting powers. "Me do" becomes the watchword in the relentless quest to do everything without guidance or help. No longer content to let someone else decide what they should do, they are now driven to try out their own ideas and find their own preferences. Because one of their favorite ways of testing is to shout "No!" this behavior is called **negativism**.

This period in a child's life—often ushered in before the second birthday and lasting well beyond it—dramatizes one of the most important aspects of early psychosocial development. When we look beyond the tears and the tantrums, the "no's" and the noise, we can appreciate that toddlers' emphatic expressions of what they want to do, as opposed to what *we* want them to do, signal the all-important shift from the dependency of infancy to the independence of childhood. Tracing the course of this shift is one major theme of this chapter.

The parent-child relationship is another theme. This chapter will explore the ways in which parents influence their children in infancy and toddlerhood—and how children influence their parents. It will also examine the development and measurement of emotions in infancy, when these emotions and their expression are highly organized and quite varied. We will pay close attention to the ways in which babies are like each other, and to the many ways they differ because of temperament, sex, birth order, and early experiences.

These issues underlie two psychoanalytic theories of early personality development, those of Sigmund Freud and Erik Erikson. They have also inspired research into the relationships between babies and their mothers and fathers, as well as their other caretakers, their siblings, and other babies. And they have spurred study of situations when parent-child relationships are disrupted by separation—or when they go tragically wrong, resulting in abuse and neglect. All these issues raise basic questions about the roots of personality. (See Table 5-1 for highlights of infants' and toddlers' personality and social development discussed in this chapter.)

## THEORETICAL APPROACHES TO EARLY PERSONALITY DEVELOPMENT

Among the most important approaches to early personality development are those proposed by the psychoanalytic theorists Sigmund Freud and Erik H. Erikson (both introduced in Chapter 1). Although parts of these theories have not held up under scrutiny (as we will show), both theories have had an impact on the study of child development and on child rearing. Erikson's theory in particular has led to research on such issues as the growth of self during the first 3 years of life.

**TABLE 5–1**

HIGHLIGHTS OF INFANTS' AND TODDLERS' PERSONALITY AND SOCIAL DEVELOPMENT, BIRTH TO 36 MONTHS

| Approximate Age, Months | Characteristics |
|---|---|
| 0–1 | Infants are relatively unresponsive, rarely reacting to outside stimulation. |
| 1–3 | Infants are open to stimulation. They begin to show interest and curiosity, and they smile readily at people. |
| 3–6 | Infants can anticipate what is about to happen and experience disappointment when it does not. They show this by becoming angry or acting wary. They smile, coo, and laugh often. This is a time of social awakening and early reciprocal exchanges between the baby and the caregiver. |
| 7–9 | Infants play "social games" and try to get responses from people. They "talk" to, touch, and cajole other babies to get them to respond. They express more differentiated emotions, showing joy, fear, anger, and surprise. |
| 9–12 | Infants are intensely preoccupied with their principal caregiver, may become afraid of strangers, and act subdued in new situations. By 1 year, they communicate emotions more clearly, showing moods, ambivalence, and gradations of feeling. |
| 12–18 | Babies explore their environment, using the people they are most attached to as a secure base. As they master the environment, they become more confident and more eager to assert themselves. |
| 18–36 | Toddlers sometimes become anxious because they now realize how much they are separating from their caregiver. They work out their awareness of their limitations in fantasy, in play, and by identifying with adults. |

*Source:* Adapted from Sroufe, 1979.

## PSYCHOSEXUAL THEORY: SIGMUND FREUD

Freud believed that personality is decisively formed in the first few years of life, as children deal with conflicts between their biological, sexually related urges and the requirements of society. As Table 1-6 (on page 24) shows, Freud proposed that these conflicts occur in a series of psychosexual stages, each of which centers on a particular part of the body and its needs. Two of these stages occur during the first 3 years of life.

### Freud's Oral Stage (Birth to 12–18 Months)*

Infants in the **oral stage** are "all mouth." Feeding is their main source of pleasure, as it stimulates the mouth, lips, and tongue. Infants also enjoy nipples, bottles, fingers, pacifiers, and anything else they can put into their mouths. At first they suck and swallow; when their teeth begin to erupt, biting and chewing become important.

Freud maintained that infants whose oral needs are not met may become fixated ("stuck") in the oral stage. Because they have not adequately resolved this stage, they will continue trying to meet oral needs throughout life, possibly becoming nail-biters or developing "bitingly" critical personalities. Infants who receive so *much* gratification at the oral stage that they do not want to abandon this pleasure may also become fixated. They may become compulsive eaters or smokers or perhaps gullible "swallowers" of whatever they are told. Infants who are neglected or people who are kept dependent too long also become fixated and develop dependent personalities. When they feel anxious and insecure, they may unconsciously long to return to infancy—or even to the womb.

*All ages are approximate.

According to Freud, babies are "all mouth." In Freud's oral stage, babies get pleasure from feeding—and even from gnawing on a wooden truck.

### Freud's Anal Stage (12–18 Months to 3 Years)

In the **anal stage,** the chief source of gratification shifts to the anus and rectum. Moving the bowels produces great relief and pleasure. Thus, toilet training is a decisive event because it forces the child to delay this gratification. The developing ego must come to terms with a major externally imposed curb on the id's instinctual impulses.

If methods of toilet training and attitudes toward it are too strict and threatening, the child may retaliate by holding back feces or by releasing them at inappropriate times. A person fixated in the anal stage may develop a "constipated" personality, becoming obsessively clean, neat, or precise—or rigidly tied to schedules and routines. Or the person may become defiantly messy. Some "anal personalities," fixated on the idea that their feces are a gift to their parents, may hoard possessions (as they once withheld feces) or may identify love with giving material goods.

## PSYCHOSOCIAL THEORY: ERIK ERIKSON

At each stage in Erikson's theory of psychosocial development (see Table 1-6), a crisis occurs that must be resolved with a satisfactory balancing of opposites, for healthy progress through the next stage. Two crises occur during the first 3 years, at times corresponding roughly to Freud's oral and anal stages.

### Erikson's Crisis 1: Basic Trust versus Basic Mistrust (Birth to 12–18 Months)

The first of Erikson's crises is **basic trust versus basic mistrust.** The infant comes to sense whether the world is or is not a place where people and things can be relied on. For good psychological health, an infant must achieve a proper balance of trust (which allows intimacy) over mistrust (which permits self-protection). If trust predominates, as it should, children develop what Erikson calls the *virtue of hope:* the belief that their needs will be met and their wishes can be attained. If mistrust dominates, children will see the world as unfriendly and unpredictable. Overwhelmed by disappointment, they will have trouble developing close relationships.

According to Erikson, it is in the feeding situation that this mixture of trust and mistrust is established; and the mother plays a principal role in resolving the crisis. Unlike Freud (who considered feeding a source of oral gratification), Erikson regards feeding mainly as an opportunity for interaction between mother and infant. Does the mother respond quickly and sensitively? Can the baby count on being fed when he or she is hungry and therefore trust the mother as the representative of the world? (More recent research goes well beyond the feeding situation and suggests that healthy development—including cognitive development, as discussed in Chapter 4—results from sensitive, responsive, *overall* parenting from the child's primary caregiver, who may or may not be the mother.)

Trust allows an infant to let the mother out of sight, "because she has become an inner certainty as well as an outer predictability" (Erikson, 1950, p. 247). The mother's sensitive care of her baby's needs lays the groundwork for the child's sense of self: in Erikson's words, "a sense of being 'all right,' of being oneself, and of becoming what other people trust one will become" (p. 249).

According to Erikson, toddlers need to develop autonomy. During this stage, parents need to ignore messy faces, bibs, tables, and floors, and let children learn how to master such basic tasks as feeding themselves.

### Erikson's Crisis 2: Autonomy versus Shame and Doubt (12–18 Months to 3 Years)

The second of Erikson's crises is ***autonomy versus shame and doubt.*** The push toward ***autonomy*** (independence, or self-determination) is related to maturation. Toddlers try to use their developing muscles to do everything themselves—to walk, to feed and dress themselves, and to expand the boundaries of their world. During this stage, the *virtue of will* emerges: children learn to make their own decisions and to use self-restraint. Having come through the first stage with a sense of basic trust in the world and an awakening sense of self, toddlers begin to trust their *own* judgment and to substitute it for the mother's. This often looks like negativism. A key issue during toddlerhood, then, is the development of self-regulation and self-control versus external regulation and control.

Shame and doubt have a place in toddlers' learning how to regulate themselves, Erikson holds, since unlimited liberty is neither safe nor healthy for them. They need a certain amount of self-doubt to recognize what they are not yet ready to do, and a sense of shame to help them learn to live by reasonable rules. Toddlers need important adults to set limits. Too few or too many may make children compulsive about controlling themselves; and fear of losing self-control may fill them with inhibitions, doubt, shame, and loss of self-esteem.

Erikson's theory has given rise to research on how children begin to regulate and control themselves. From birth, they move toward ***self-regulation,*** independent control of their own behavior to conform with understood social expectations (Kopp, 1982). As they process, store, and act on information about the behaviors approved by adults, a gradual shift from external to internal control takes place. At first they learn about specific situations—how to soothe themselves by sucking or what dangerous situations to avoid (like hot stoves). By 18 to 24 months, they think and remember well enough to connect what they do with what they have been told to do. At 2, they know (but do not always follow) the rules about what and how to eat, and how to dress for sleep or play.

***Self-control,*** then, is children's ability to adjust what they do to fit what they know is socially acceptable. However, when they want *very* badly to do something, they easily forget the rules—and will run into the street after a ball or take a forbidden cookie. Not until about age 3 do they attain the greater flexibility, conscious thought, and willingness to wait that helps them control themselves.

Toilet training, which Freud sees as the imposition of social control on a child's natural function, is for Erikson an important step toward self-control and autonomy. So is language; as children are better able to make their wishes understood, they become more powerful and independent.

### EVALUATING THE THEORIES

These theories have helped us understand how children's personalities develop. Freud made us aware that early experiences are important and that human beings are sensual creatures from birth. Erikson's theory is especially helpful in its description of the shift from the dependency of infancy to the autonomy of toddlerhood. But both theories have serious shortcomings. Both assign the major responsibility for the way a child turns out to the mother. Neither acknowledges the child's own contribution or the impact of other people and of life circumstances. Today, most developmentalists recognize that although the mother is an important influence, these other factors are also important (Chess & Thomas, 1982).

Furthermore, the theories of Freud and Erikson are

## HOW INFANTS SHOW THEIR EMOTIONS

Newborns plainly show when they are unhappy. They let out piercing yells, flail their arms and legs, and stiffen their bodies. It is harder to tell when they are happy. During the first month, they become quiet at the sound of a human voice or when they are picked up, and they smile when their hands are moved together to play pat-a-cake. With every passing day, infants respond more to people—smiling, cooing, reaching out, and eventually moving toward them. These signals, if we become adept at reading them, are fairly reliable clues to a baby's emotional state.

By expressing their feelings, babies gain a growing amount of control. When they want or need something, they cry; when they feel sociable, they break into a smile or laugh. When these early messages get a response, babies' sense of connection with other people is strengthened. Their sense of personal power grows as they see that their cries bring help and comfort and that their smiles and laughter elicit smiles and laughter in return.

The meaning of this emotional language changes as babies develop. At first, crying is a signal of physical discomfort (at 2 months, to an injection; at 4 months, to arm restraint); later it more often expresses psychological distress. The early smile comes spontaneously as an expression of internal well-being; later smiles express pleasure in other people—as early as 3 to 4 weeks of age in response to a high-pitched human voice, and at 4 to 6 weeks in response to a nodding face (Izard & Malatesta, 1987).

### Crying

Crying is the most powerful way—and sometimes the only way—in which young infants can communicate their vital needs. Babies have four patterns of crying (Wolff, 1969): the basic *hunger cry* (a rhythmic cry, which is not always associated with hunger), the *angry cry* (a variation of the rhythmic cry in which excess air is forced through the vocal cords), the *pain cry* (a sudden onset of loud crying without preliminary moaning, sometimes followed by holding the breath), and the *frustration cry* (two or three drawn-out cries, with no prolonged holding of the breath). Babies in distress cry louder, longer, and more irregularly than hungry babies and are more apt to gag and to interrupt their crying (Oswald & Peltzman, 1974).

Parents often worry that they will spoil a child by responding too much to crying, but research puts this fear to rest. Babies whose cries bring relief apparently gain a measure of confidence that their actions will produce a response. By the end of the first year, babies whose mothers have regularly responded to their crying with tender, soothing care cry less (Ainsworth & Bell, 1977; S. Bell & Ainsworth, 1972). By now they are communicating more in other ways—with babbling, gestures, and facial expressions—than the babies of more punitive or ignoring mothers, who cry more. Thus although parents do not need to leap to a baby's side at every whimper, it seems safe to err in the direction of responding more rather than less.

### Smiling

A baby's smile is almost irresistible. Parents usually greet a baby's first smile with great excitement, and adults who see a smiling baby will almost always smile back.

The early faint smile that appears soon after birth occurs spontaneously as a result of central nervous system activity. It generally appears without outside stimulation, often when the infant is falling asleep (Sroufe & Waters, 1976).

In their second week, babies often smile after a feeding, when they are drowsy and may be responding to the caregiver's sounds. After this, smiles come more often when babies are alert but inactive. At about 1 month, the smiles become more frequent and more social, directed toward people. Babies smile now when their hands are clapped together or when they hear a familiar voice (Kreutzer & Charlesworth, 1973; Wolff, 1963). During the second month, as visual recognition develops, babies respond more selectively, smiling more at people they know than at those they do not know.

Some infants smile much more than others (Tautermannova, 1973). Babies who generously reward caretaking with smiles and gurgles are likely to form more positive relationships with their caregivers than babies who smile less readily.

### Laughing

At about the fourth month of life, babies start to laugh out loud. They chortle at being kissed on the stomach, hearing various sounds, and seeing their parents do unusual things. In addition, some of their laughter may be related to fear. Babies sometimes react to the same stimulus (like an object looming toward them) with both fear and laughter (Sroufe & Wunsch, 1972).

As babies grow older, they laugh more often and at more things. A 4- to 6-month-old may respond to sounds and touch; a 7- to 9-month-old may delight in a game of peekaboo or howl with glee when a parent puts on a funny mask. This shift reflects cognitive development: the older baby has learned to recognize what is

This baby won't be "spoiled" by being picked up; instead, mother and child will improve their communication with each other. When a caregiver "reads" a baby's behaviors accurately and responds appropriately, the baby learns how to send signals. This is known as the *mutual regulation* model.

expected and to perceive an incongruity. Thus laughter is a response to the environment, which helps babies discharge tension in situations that otherwise might be upsetting, and represents "an important tie between cognitive development and emotional growth and expression" (Sroufe & Wunsch, 1972, p. 1341).

## HOW EMOTIONS ARE COMMUNICATED BETWEEN INFANTS AND ADULTS

### Mutual-Regulation Model

Matthew smiles at his mother, a signal she takes as an invitation to play; as she kisses his stomach, he goes into gales of giggles. But the next day, when she begins to kiss his stomach again, the baby looks at her glassy-eyed and turns his head away. His mother interprets this as a message saying, "I want to stay quiet now." Following this cue, she tucks him into a baby carrier and lets him rest quietly against her body.

This process, called the *mutual regulation model* (E. Z. Tronick & Gianino, 1986), illustrates how infants as young as 3 months of age take an active part in regulating their emotional states. Babies differ in the amount of stimulation they need or want: too little leaves them uninterested, too much overwhelms them. Overstimulation is a special danger for low-birthweight infants, but it can also affect other babies.

Babies and adults send a variety of signals to each other, and a healthy interaction occurs when a caregiver "reads" a baby's behaviors accurately and re-

sponds appropriately. Adults do not, of course, always receive or understand the babies' messages. When babies do not get the results they want, they may be upset at first, but they usually keep on sending signals so that they can "repair" the interaction. Normally, interaction moves back and forth between poorly regulated and well regulated states, and babies learn from these shifts how to send signals and what to do when the first signal does not bring what they want.

According to E. Z. Tronick (1989), when a baby's goals for connecting with people and objects and for retaining a comfortable emotional balance are met, the baby feels joyful or at least interested. But if someone taking care of a baby like Matthew either ignores his invitation to play or insists on playing after he has signaled that he does not feel like it just then, the baby would feel angry or sad. Both partners, then, are important to the outcome of these exchanges, and each stimulates the other.

Even very young infants can "read" emotions expressed by other people, and they adjust their own behavior accordingly. At 10 weeks of age, they meet anger with anger (Lelwica & Haviland, 1983). At 3 months, infants faced with a stony-faced, unresponsive mother will make faces, sounds, and gestures to get a reaction (Cohn & Tronick, 1983; E. Z. Tronick, 1980). And 9-month-olds show more joy, play more, and look longer when their mothers seem happy; and look sad and turn away when their mothers seem sad (Termine & Izard, 1988). This is one more example of the competence very young babies show. They do not just passively receive other people's actions; they do a great deal to act on and change the way people act toward them.

(See Box 5-2 on page 152 for an example of what can happen when this mutual-regulation model breaks down.)

### Social Referencing

If, at a formal dinner table, you have ever cast a sidelong glance to see which fork the person next to you was using, you have read another person's nonverbal signals to get information on how to act. Babies learn how to do this at a very early age.

Through **social referencing,** one person forms an understanding of an ambiguous situation by seeking out another person's perception of it. Babies are confronted by many situations that they neither understand nor know how to respond to. They learn to "read" other people's emotional and cognitive reactions sometime after 6 months of age, when they begin to judge the possible consequences of events, imitate complex behaviors, and distinguish among and react to various

---

BOX 5–2   THINKING CRITICALLY

# HOW A MOTHER'S DEPRESSION AFFECTS HER BABY

What happens when a baby's emotional signals to a caregiver are ignored or overridden? When this keeps happening, the system of mutual regulation breaks down. Babies of emotionally depressed mothers, who tend to be consistently unresponsive, often stop sending signals and try to comfort themselves by such behaviors as sucking or rocking. The babies will try for a while to repair the interaction; but with repeated failures, they will fall back on their own resources. If this defensive reaction becomes habitual, it can create major problems for the babies—who feel powerless to elicit responses from other people and who feel that their mothers are unreliable and the world is untrustworthy. The babies themselves then become sad, not as a reflection of the mother's depression but as the result of impaired interaction.

This cycle may explain why children of depressed mothers are at risk of various emotional and cognitive disturbances. They are more

likely to have been of low birthweight (this might contribute to a mother's depression), to be drowsy as infants, to show tension by squirming and arching the back, and to cry often. As toddlers they tend to engage in a low level of symbolic play; later they are likely to grow poorly and perform poorly on cognitive measures, to have accidents, and to have behavior problems that often last into adolescence (T. M. Field et al., 1985; B. S. Zuckerman & Beardslee, 1987).

Depressed mothers tend to be punitive, to consider their children bothersome and hard to care for, and to feel as if their lives are out of control (T. M. Field et al. 1985; Whiffen & Gotlib, 1989; B. S. Zuckerman & Beardslee, 1987). Some 12 to 20 percent of American mothers with children under age 5 suffer from *depression,* an emotional state characterized by sadness and such other symptoms as difficulties in eating, sleeping, and concentrating (W. T. Garrison & Earls, 1986). The risk is

higher for mothers who are poor, poorly educated, single, immigrants, and dissatisfied with their marriage or living conditions; and for those who have a temperamentally difficult or handicapped child and no family and friends to turn to (W. T. Garrison & Earls, 1986; B. S. Zuckerman & Beardslee, 1987). About 20 percent of new mothers suffer from postpartum depression, which lasts 6 to 8 weeks after birth (B. S. Zuckerman & Beardslee, 1987).

Most depressed mothers know that their feelings affect their children, and they often feel guilty. How can society help? How much should public agencies do to help them find the causes of their problems and to provide social services, counseling, or psychotherapy? Who can step in to give part-time care to their babies and to help their older children? Questions like these test a nation's commitment to the well-being of its youngest members and to the ultimate health of its citizenry.

---

emotional expressions. They show referencing by the way they look at their caregivers when they meet a new person or toy (Feinman & Lewis, 1983).

A study using the visual cliff (described in Chapters 3 and 4) found that when the drop looked very shallow or very deep, 1-year-olds did not look toward their mothers; they were able to judge for themselves whether to cross over or not. But when they were uncertain about the depth of the "cliff," they paused at the "edge," looked down, and then looked up to their mothers' faces. Meanwhile, the mother posed one of several expressions—fear, anger, interest, happiness, or sadness. The particular emotion shown influenced the babies' actions. Most of those whose mothers showed joy or interest crossed the "drop"; very few whose mothers looked angry or afraid crossed it; and an intermediate number of those whose mothers looked sad did (Sorce, Emde, Campos, & Klinnert, 1985). Apparently, babies turn to social referencing of facial expressions most often in puzzling situations.

## DIFFERENCES IN PERSONALITY DEVELOPMENT

Even in the womb each person begins to show a unique personality. As was pointed out in Chapter 2, before babies emerge into the world, differences like personal activity levels and favorite positions in utero already exist. After birth, individual differences become even more apparent. We'll look now at differences in emotional makeup and temperament, which seem to be largely inborn, though they are also influenced by the environment; and at differences between the sexes, which also seem to arise as a result of both biological and social influences.

### EMOTIONAL DIFFERENCES

Some infants are born cheerful. They smile and laugh often from an early age. Other babies cry often and seem to take less joy in living.

Very young infants' normal emotional responses seem to reflect patterns or traits that persist as they get older, suggesting that an infant's personality has a biological component. A 2-month-old who screams in outrage when given a shot is likely to become just as enraged at 19 months when a playmate takes away a toy, whereas a 2-month-old who takes the shot more calmly will probably put up with later indignities without much fuss. In other words, infants not more than 8 weeks old already show signs of emotional differences that form an important part of their personalities (Izard, in Trotter, 1987).

Such characteristic emotional reactions may stem from differences in temperament. Let's see what some of those differences are.

## TEMPERAMENTAL DIFFERENCES

Aretha, the eldest of three sisters, was a cheerful, calm baby who ate, slept, and eliminated at regular times. She greeted each day and most people with a smile, and the only sign that she was awake during the night was the tinkle of the musical toy in her crib. When Belinda, the second sister, woke up, she would open her mouth to cry before she even opened her eyes. She slept and ate little and irregularly; she laughed and cried loudly, often bursting into tantrums; and she had to be convinced that new people and new experiences were not threatening before she would have anything to do with them. The youngest sister, Clarissa, was mild in her responses, both positive and negative. She did not like most new situations, but if allowed to proceed at her own slow pace, she would eventually become interested and involved.

Each of these children was showing her own **temperament**—her characteristic style of approaching and reacting to people and situations. Temperament has been defined as the *how* of behavior: not *what* people do, or *why*, but how they go about doing it. Two toddlers, for example, may be equally able to dress themselves and equally motivated to do it, but the ways they approach the task may be different (A. Thomas & Chess, 1984).

### Components of Temperament

The New York Longitudinal Study (NYLS—introduced in Chapter 2) followed 133 people from early infancy into adulthood. The researchers identified nine aspects or components of temperament that showed up soon after birth. In many cases, these aspects remained relatively stable, though some people did show considerable change (A. Thomas & Chess, 1984; A. Thomas, Chess, & Birch, 1968). These nine components of temperament are:

1 *Activity level*—how and how much a person moves
2 *Rhythmicity, or regularity*—predictability of biological cycles like hunger, sleep, and elimination
3 *Approach or withdrawal*—how a person initially responds to a new stimulus, like a new toy, food, or person
4 *Adaptability*—how easily an initial response is modified in a desired direction
5 *Threshold of responsiveness*—how much stimulation is needed to evoke a response
6 *Intensity of reaction*—how energetically a person responds
7 *Quality of mood*—whether a person's behavior is predominantly pleasant, joyful, and friendly; or unpleasant, unhappy, and unfriendly
8 *Distractibility*—how easily an irrelevant stimulus can alter or interfere with a person's behavior
9 *Attention span and persistence*—how long a person pursues an activity and continues in the face of obstacles

### Three Patterns of Temperament

Almost two-thirds of the children studied fitted into one of three categories identified by these researchers (see Table 5-3 on page 154). Aretha, in our example, is an *easy* child (like 40 percent in the NYLS sample): generally happy, rhythmic in biological functioning, and accepting of new experiences. Belinda is a *difficult* child (like 10 percent in the sample): more irritable, irregular in biological rhythms, and more intense in expressing emotion. And Clarissa is considered a *slow-to-warm-up* child (like 15 percent in the sample): generally mild and slow to adapt to new experiences (A. Thomas & Chess, 1977, 1984).

Many children (like 35 percent of the NYLS sample) do not fit neatly into any of these three groups. A baby may have regular eating and sleeping schedules, yet be fearful of strangers. A child may be extremely easy or relatively easy most of the time but not always. Another child may warm up slowly to new foods but adapt quickly to new baby-sitters. All of these variations are normal (A. Thomas & Chess, 1984).

### Influences on Temperament

Temperament seems to be inborn and largely genetically determined (A. Thomas & Chess, 1977, 1984). Individual differences in basic temperament do not seem to be determined by parents' attitudes (A. Thomas & Chess, 1984) or by gender, birth order, or social class (Persson-Blennow & McNeil, 1981).

But unusual events or parents' handling of a child can *change* temperamental style. One "difficult" girl in the NYLS who was having a hard time in childhood sud-

**TABLE 5–3**
THREE TEMPERAMENTAL PATTERNS

| Easy Child | Difficult Child | Slow-to-Warm-Up Child |
| --- | --- | --- |
| Responds well to novelty and change | Responds poorly to novelty and change | Responds slowly to novelty and change |
| Quickly develops regular sleep and feeding schedules | Has irregular sleep and feeding schedules | Sleeps and feeds more regularly than difficult child; less regularly than easy child |
| Takes to new foods easily | Accepts new foods slowly | Shows mildly negative initial response to new stimuli (e.g., a first encounter with a bath; a new food, person, or place; entering school or another new situation) |
| Smiles at strangers | Is suspicious of strangers | |
| Adapts easily to new situations | Adapts slowly to new situations | |
| Accepts most frustrations with minimal fuss | Reacts to frustration with tantrums | |
| Adapts quickly to new routines and rules of new games | Adjusts slowly to new routines | Gradually develops liking for new stimuli after repeated, unpressured exposures |
| Has moods of mild to moderate intensity, usually positive | Has frequent periods of loud crying; also laughs loudly | Has mildly intense reactions, both positive and negative |
| | Displays intense and frequently negative moods | |

*Source:* Adapted from A. Thomas & Chess, 1984.

denly showed musical and dramatic talent at about age 10, leading her parents to see her in a new way and to respond differently to her, and by age 22 she was well-adjusted. Another "difficult" child was doing well with quiet and firm limit-setting by her parents—until she was 13, when her father died and her overwhelmed mother could not cope with the child's needs; this girl developed a severe behavior disorder. An "easy" child got into trouble at age 14 after experimenting with drugs; he gave up drugs a year later when he began following an Indian guru; several years later he broke with the guru; and in his early twenties he was doing well (A. Thomas & Chess, 1984).

Other evidence of the influence of environmental factors comes from a study of babies from three African cultures, which found differences across cultures in temperamental characteristics. The researchers attributed these differences to different child-rearing customs (like unconcern with "clock time" in a tribe whose babies have irregular biological rhythms), mothers' attitudes (expecting different behaviors from boys and girls), and ecological settings (M. W. DeVries & Sameroff, 1984).

While cross-cultural variations may result to some extent from genetic differences among the three groups, they do seem to reflect early life experiences. The NYLS researchers found the same thing—that children respond to the way their parents treat them.

One analysis of NYLS data found that the way mothers feel about their roles—whether they are happy or unhappy about either being employed or being at home full time—seems to affect their children's adjustment. Mothers who were dissatisfied either with their jobs or with their status as homemakers were more likely to be intolerant of, to disapprove of, or to reject their 3-year-olds' behavior, and the rejected children were likely to become "difficult" (J. V. Lerner & Galambos, 1985).

**Effects of Temperament on Adjustment: "Goodness of Fit"**

About one-third of the NYLS subjects developed behavior problems at some time. Most were mild disturbances that showed up between ages 3 and 5 and cleared up by adolescence, but some remained or grew worse by adulthood.

No temperamental type was immune to problems. Even easy children had them when their lives held too much stress. One kind of stress is being expected to act in ways contrary to basic temperament. If a highly active child is confined to a small apartment and expected to sit still for long periods, if a slow-to-warm-up child is pushed to adjust to many new people and situations, or if a persistent child is constantly taken away from absorbing projects, trouble may result. The key to healthy adjustment is "goodness of fit" between children and the demands made upon them.

"Goodness of fit" between parent and child—the degree to which parents feel comfortable with the child they have—is also important, because it affects parents' feelings toward their children. Thus, energetic, active parents may become impatient with a slow-moving, docile child, while more easygoing parents might welcome such a personality.

One of the most important things that parents can do is ride with a child's basic temperament instead of trying to cast him or her into a mold of the parents' design. For example, the parents of a rhythmic child can use a "demand" feeding schedule, letting the child set the pace; the parents of an irregular child can help by setting a flexible schedule. The parents of a slow-to-warm-up child need to give the child time to adjust to new situations and need to ask other people, like relatives and nursery school teachers, to do the same.

Recognition of inborn temperament relieves parents of some heavy emotional baggage. When they understand that a child acts a certain way not out of willfulness, laziness, or stupidity, but because of inborn temperament, they are less likely to feel guilty, anxious, or hostile, or to act rigid or impatient. They can focus on helping the child use his or her temperament as a strength, rather than seeing it as an impediment. In this way they can change "poorness of fit" to "goodness of fit" and make positive contributions to the child's development.

## GENDER DIFFERENCES

As we saw in Chapter 3, there are few physiological differences between baby boys and baby girls. Are there differences in personality?

Researchers have studied infants' activity levels, their responses to what they see as opposed to what they hear, how irritable they are, and how interested they are in exploring their surroundings as opposed to staying close to a parent. Some studies have found differences between the sexes, but these findings have not always held up when the studies were repeated by the same or other investigators. After reviewing the literature, Birns (1976) concluded that gender differences cannot be described clearly until after age 2.

Other studies have focused on the ways adults act toward infants. The findings of these studies are much clearer. A baby, even a newborn, who is identified as a female will be treated differently from one identified as a male. When strangers think that a crying baby is a male, they are likely to assume that "he" is crying from anger; when they believe that the baby is female, they think that "she" is afraid (Condry & Condry, 1974).

In one study, twenty-four 14-month-old children, 12 boys and 12 girls, were introduced to adults who did not know them. Sometimes the babies were identified according to their real sex, and sometimes they were said to belong to the other sex. In playing with the children, the adults were more likely to encourage the "boys" in active play and more likely to choose a ball rather than a doll for them to play with. The adults tended to talk more to the "girls" and to choose a doll or a bottle for them to play with. Interestingly, though, the children themselves did not show gender differences; the boys and girls played in very similar ways, even though they were treated differently by the adults (Frisch, 1977).

Parents' behavior toward babies is affected by the parent's own sex and by the age and personality of the infant, but there are some consistent findings. Baby boys get more attention in infancy, but the attention baby girls get is designed to make them smile more and be more social (Birns, 1976). Mothers' facial expressions show a wider range of emotion with baby daughters than with sons—which may explain why girls are better than boys at interpreting emotional expression (Malatesta, in Trotter, 1983).

Thus, although differences may not be present at birth, environmental shaping of boys' and girls' personalities begins very early in life. As we look more closely at the crucial influence of children's families, we will see other differences among children.

## THE FAMILY AND PERSONALITY DEVELOPMENT

Was your birth planned and welcomed? How old were your parents? Were they physically and emotionally healthy? Were they wealthy, comfortable, or poor? How did your personality mesh with theirs? How many people lived in your home?

Such early social factors had a major influence on the child you were and the person you are now. Furthermore, you yourself influenced your family in ways you may never have imagined. Your parents' feelings and actions toward you were influenced by your sex, your temperament, your health, and your birth order—whether you were the oldest child, the youngest, or somewhere in between.

The kind of family you grew up in was probably very different from what it would have been a century earlier; and family life will probably change even more in the future. A baby born today is likely to have only one

The family may well be the largest single influence on children's development, and children also influence other family members in many important ways. Research now focuses on relationships between children and their fathers and siblings, as well as their mothers.

sibling, a mother who works outside the home, and a father who is more involved in his children's lives than his own father was. An infant has a 40 to 50 percent chance of spending part of his or her childhood with only one parent, probably the mother and probably because of divorce (P. C. Glick & Lin, 1986a).

These changes in family life are revolutionizing research on *socialization*—how children learn the behaviors their culture deems appropriate. The relationships that are formed in infancy set the pattern for much of a child's early socialization. In the past, most research focused on the relationship between mothers and babies, but now we also recognize the importance of the relationships infants have with their fathers, their brothers and sisters, their grandparents, and other caregivers.

Another trend is a focus on how the entire family system operates. How does the marital relationship affect the relationship each spouse has with the baby? Do Joey's parents act differently with him when either one is alone with him and when they are all together? Questions like these have produced provocative answers. When both parents are present and talking to each other, for example, they pay less attention to their child. Some spouses' closeness to each other may detract from their ability to be close to their children; in other cases parenting itself either strengthens a marriage or strains it (Belsky, 1979). By looking at the

family as a unit, we get a fuller picture of the web of relationships among all its members.

The ability to form intimate relationships throughout life may well be affected by relationships formed in infancy. Let us see how babies influence and are influenced by the people close to them.

## THE MOTHER'S ROLE

Until recently most developmentalists seemed to agree with Napoleon that "the future good or bad conduct of a child depends entirely on the mother." Although we now recognize that mothers are not the only important people in babies' lives, they are still central characters in the drama of development.

### The Mother-Infant Bond

To find out how and when the special intimacy between mothers and their babies forms, some researchers have looked at animals. Newly hatched chicks follow the first moving thing they see—usually, but not always, the mother hen. Konrad Lorenz (1957), an ethologist who studied animal behavior in its natural setting, called this behavior *imprinting.* This is an instinctual form of learning in which, after a single encounter, an animal learns to recognize and follow a particular individual. Imprinting is said to take place automatically and irreversibly during a brief critical period in the animal's early life.

Among goats and cows, certain rituals occur right after birth. If these rituals are prevented or interrupted, mother and offspring will not recognize each other. The results for the baby animal can be devastating—abnormal development, or physical withering and death (Blauvelt, 1955; A. U. Moore, 1960; Scott, 1958). These findings raise questions about humans.

### Is there a critical period for mother-infant bonding?

In 1976, two researchers concluded that if mother and baby are separated during the first hours after birth, the **mother-infant bond**—the mother's feeling of close, caring connection with her newborn—may not develop normally (Klaus & Kennell, 1976). After comparing mothers and babies who had "extended contact" immediately after birth with those who were kept apart for long periods, these researchers reported differences in bonding that persisted over the first few years of life. This research inspired many hospitals to establish rooming-in policies, allowing mothers and babies to remain together. Although developmentalists have welcomed such humane changes, follow-up research has not confirmed the notion of a critical time for bonding (Chess & Thomas, 1982; M. E. Lamb, 1982a, 1982b; Rutter, 1979b). Although some mothers seemed to achieve closer bonding with their babies after early extended contact, no long-term effects were shown.

In 1982, Klaus and Kennell modified their original position; and in 1983, the researcher and psychiatrist Stella Chess wrote, "By now the whole 'critical period concept' has been generally discredited in human development theory" (p. 975). This finding relieved adoptive parents, and parents who had to be separated from their infants after birth, of much unnecessary worry and guilt. Concern with bonding is still a vital issue, however, and some developmentalists urge research on groups at risk of weak bonding (like poor, young, or single mothers and fathers) to find out what factors other than early contact affect parent-child bonds (Lamb et al., 1983).

### What do babies need from their mothers?

In one famous study, rhesus monkeys were separated from their mothers 6 to 12 hours after birth and raised in a laboratory. The infant monkeys were put into cages with one of two kinds of surrogate "mothers"—a plain cylindrical wire-mesh form or a form covered with terry cloth. Some monkeys were fed from bottles connected to the wire "mothers"; others were "nursed" by the warm, cuddly cloth ones.

In a series of classic experiments, Harry Harlow and Margaret Harlow showed that food is not the most important way to a baby's heart. When infant rhesus monkeys could choose whether to go to a wire surrogate "mother" or a warm, soft terry-cloth "mother," they spent more time clinging to the cloth mother, even if they were being fed by bottles connected to the wire mother.

When the monkeys were allowed to spend time with either kind of "mother," they all spent more time clinging to the cloth surrogates—even if they were being fed only by the wire ones. In an unfamiliar room, the babies "raised" by cloth surrogates showed more natural interest in exploring than those "raised" by wire surrogates—even when the appropriate "mothers" were there. Apparently, the monkeys also remembered the cloth surrogates better. After a year's separation, the "cloth-raised" monkeys eagerly ran to embrace the terry-cloth forms, whereas the "wire-raised" monkeys showed no interest in the wire forms (Harlow & Zimmerman, 1959). None of the monkeys in either group grew up normally, however (Harlow & Harlow, 1962), and none were able to mother their own offspring (Suomi & Harlow, 1972).

It is hardly surprising that a dummy mother would not provide the same kind of stimulation and opportunities for development as a live mother. These experiments show that (contrary to the Freudian emphasis on satisfaction of biological needs) feeding is *not* the most important thing mothers do for their babies. Mothering includes the comfort of close bodily contact and, in monkeys, the satisfaction of an innate need to cling. Surely, human infants also have needs that must be satisfied, or at least acted upon, if they are to grow up normally. A major task of psychology is to find out what those needs are.

Going beyond such one-way concepts as imprinting and the mother-infant bond, research over the past few decades has shifted its focus to the two-way process of *attachment* between babies and the important people in their lives.

## Attachment: A Reciprocal Connection

When Andrew's mother is near, he looks at her, smiles at her, talks to her, and crawls after her. When she leaves, he cries; when she comes back, he squeals with joy. When he is frightened or unhappy, he clings to her. Andrew has formed his first attachment to another person.

**Attachment** is an active, affectionate reciprocal relationship between two people. In unscientific circles, we call it *love*. The interaction between the two people continues to strengthen their bond. It may be, as Mary Ainsworth (1979), a pioneering researcher on attachment, has said, "an essential part of the ground plan of the human species for an infant to become attached to a mother figure" (p. 932)—who does not have to be the infant's biological mother but may be any primary caregiver.

### Studying attachment

Attachment research dramatically illustrates how scientists build on the work of those who have gone before. Ainsworth first studied attachment in the early 1950s as a junior colleague of John Bowlby (1951). Bowlby was convinced of the importance of the mother-baby bond, partly from examining ethological studies of bonding in animals and partly from seeing disturbed children in a psychoanalytic clinic in London. He recognized the baby's role in fostering attachment and warned against separating mother and baby.

Ainsworth was also influenced by studies of attachment in monkeys and research on the behavior of babies in a strange room. After studying attachment in Ugandan babies (1967), she tried to replicate her studies in Baltimore. But because of cultural differences between Africa and the United States, she changed her approach, which had relied on naturalistic observation in babies' homes, and devised the now famous **strange situation.** This laboratory technique, designed to elicit behaviors of closeness between an adult and a child, is now the most common way to study attachment.

In the eight-episode *strange situation,* (1) the mother and baby enter an unfamiliar room; (2) the mother sits down and the baby is free to explore; (3) an unfamiliar adult enters; (4) the mother goes out, leaving the baby alone with the stranger; (5) the mother comes back and the stranger leaves the room; (6) the mother leaves the baby alone in the room; (7) the stranger comes back instead of the mother; and finally, (8) the stranger goes out as the mother returns. The mother encourages the baby to explore and play again, and gives comfort if the baby seems to need it (Ainsworth, Blehar, Waters, & Wall, 1978).

### Patterns of attachment

When Ainsworth and her colleagues observed 1-year-olds in the strange situation and also at home, they found three main patterns of attachment: *secure attachment* (the most common category, into which 66 percent of the babies fell) and two forms of anxious attachment—*avoidant* (20 percent of the babies) and *ambivalent* (12 percent).

**Securely attached** babies (like Andrew) cry or protest when the mother leaves and greet her happily when she returns. When she is present, they use her as a base from which to explore; they leave her readily to go off and investigate their surroundings, returning from time to time for reassurance. They are usually cooperative and relatively free of anger. At 18 months they get around better on their own than anxiously attached toddlers (J. Cassidy, 1986). They are better at crossing open spaces and at reaching for, playing with, and holding on to toys; and they stumble and fall less. Perhaps, knowing that their mothers are available, they can pay more attention to their surroundings than babies who anxiously eye their mothers.

*Avoidant* babies rarely cry when the mother leaves, and they avoid her on her return. These babies do not reach out in time of need and tend to be very angry. They dislike being held, but dislike being put down even more.

*Ambivalent (resistant)* babies become anxious even before the mother leaves. They are very upset when she does go out; when she comes back, they show their ambivalence by seeking contact with her while at the same time resisting it by kicking or squirming. Resistant babies do little exploration and are harder to comfort than other babies (Egeland & Farber, 1984).

A fourth pattern, *disorganized-disoriented,* has recently been identified (Main & Solomon, 1986). Babies with this pattern often show contradictory behaviors, greeting the mother brightly when she returns but then turning away, or approaching without looking at her. They seem confused and afraid and may represent the least secure pattern (O'Connor, Sigman, & Brill, 1987).

### How attachment is established

According to Ainsworth, a baby builds a "working model" of what can be expected from the mother. As long as the mother continues to act in basically the same ways, the model holds up. But if she changes her behavior toward the baby—not just once or twice but consistently—the baby can revise the model, and the nature of attachment may well change.

A baby's own personality—the tendency to cuddle, cry, or adapt to new situations—also exerts an influence. Attachment is affected by what both mother and baby do and how they respond to each other.

**What the mother does**   Secure attachment thrives when the mother is affectionate, attentive, and responsive to her baby's signals. The amount of positive interaction between the two is more important than the mother's caretaking skills and the amount of time she spends with her baby (A. Clarke-Stewart, 1977).

Ainsworth and her colleagues (1978) found several important differences in the quality of mothering, which were related to babies' patterns of attachment. Mothers of securely attached babies were the most sensitive to their infants throughout the first year of life. They truly ob-

served "demand" feeding, taking their cues from their babies about when to feed them and responding to the babies' signals to stop, slow down, or speed up feeding (Ainsworth, 1979). More recent research also found that mothers of babies considered secure at 1 year of age had been more responsive to their infants at 1, 3, and 9 months—more likely to soothe the babies when they cried, to "answer" the babies' sounds, and to talk to the babies when they looked into the mothers' faces (Isabella, Belsky, & von Eye, 1989).

Furthermore, mothers of securely attached babies tended to hold them closer to the body than mothers in the other two groups. The value of body contact was confirmed by a study of 49 low-income mothers and infants in New York (Cunningham, Anisfeld, Casper, & Nozyce, 1987). Babies whose mothers had carried them on their bodies in soft baby carriers rather than in infant seats in the first months of life were more securely attached at 13 months of age.

Mothers of avoidant babies were the angriest of all three groups. They had trouble expressing their feelings and shied away from close physical contact with their babies. Babies subjected to such physical distancing and rebuffs became angry in turn.

In a group of low-income, mostly single mothers (Egeland & Farber, 1984), mothers of securely attached infants were responsive and skilled in caretaking and had positive feelings about themselves. Mothers of avoidant babies were tense, irritable, and lacking in confidence, and seemed uninterested in their babies. Mothers of resistant babies were well-meaning but less capable; they tended to score lower on IQ tests and understand less how to meet their babies' needs.

"Mother love" is not automatic, nor is love necessarily enough to guarantee nurturance and a sound mother-child attachment. Many factors affect the way a woman acts toward her baby. These include her reasons for having the baby, her experience and competence in child care, her emotional state and view of her life, her relationship with the baby's father, her interest in a job or other outside activities, her living circumstances, and the presence of other relatives in the home, like a supportive or intrusive grandmother (Egeland & Farber, 1984).

**What the baby does**   Infants actively influence the people who take care of them. Virtually any activity on a baby's part that leads to a response from an adult is an attachment behavior: sucking, crying, smiling, clinging, and looking into the caregiver's eyes (Bowlby, 1958; Richards, 1971; Robson, 1967).

Both Anna and her mother contribute to the attachment between them by the way they act toward each other. The way the baby molds herself to her mother's body shows her trust and reinforces the mother's feelings for her child, which she then displays through sensitivity to the baby's needs. Again we see how babies actively influence their world.

As early as the eighth week of life, babies direct some of these behaviors more to their mothers than to anyone else. Their overtures are successful when the mothers respond warmly, expressing delight and giving the babies frequent physical contact along with freedom to explore (Ainsworth, 1969). The babies gain a sense of the consequence of their own actions—a feeling of power and confidence in their ability to bring about results.

An infant's early characteristics may be a strong predictor of whether the baby is likely to become securely attached or anxiously attached. Many resistant babies, for example, have had problems as neonates—about half of such babies in one study (Ainsworth et al., 1978). Many showed developmental lags that may have made them harder to care for (Egeland & Farber, 1984). However, no infant is doomed to be anxiously attached; for example, very low birthweight is not associated with impaired attachment (Easterbrooks, 1989; Macey, Harmon, & Easterbrooks, 1987). "As in any relationship, the partner's responses are critical" (Egeland & Farber, 1984, p. 769). It is the interaction between adult and infant that determines the quality of attachment.

### Changes in attachment

Although attachment patterns normally persist, they can—and often do—change (Ainsworth, 1982). In one study, almost half of a group of 43 middle-class babies changed attachment pattern between ages 12 and 19 months (R. A. Thompson, Lamb, & Estes, 1982). The changes were associated with changes in the babies' everyday lives, including mothers' taking jobs outside the home and providing other kinds of care for their children. The changes were not all in one direction: some of the babies became less securely attached, but most who changed became more securely attached.

What accounts for this? Although a mother's caretaking skills are important in forming the initial attachment, her emotional expressions—the joy she shows in feeding or bathing her baby—may help the attachment pattern evolve, especially during the second year of life. Some initially resistant infants of young, immature mothers become more secure as their mothers gain experience, skill, and more positive attitudes (Egeland & Farber, 1984). Also, other people can make a difference in a child's life, allowing attachment to, say, a father, a grandmother, or another caregiver in place of the mother.

## Long-term effects of attachment

Common sense might suggest that infants who are securely attached to their mothers grow into children who are very dependent on adults, but research tells us that this is not so. In fact, the more secure a child's attachment is to a nurturing adult, the easier it is for the child to leave that adult. Children who have a secure base do not need to stay close to their mothers. Their freedom to explore lets them try new things, attack problems in new ways, and be more comfortable with the unfamiliar.

These effects may persist for at least 5 years after birth. When securely attached 18-month-olds were followed up at age 2, they turned out to be more enthusiastic, persistent, cooperative, and generally effective than children who had been insecurely attached as babies (Matas, Arend, & Sroufe, 1978). At age 3, securely attached children get more positive responses from their playmates than anxiously attached children (J. L. Jacobson & Wille, 1986). At age 3½, securely attached children are described as "peer leaders, socially involved, attracting the attention of others, curious, and actively engaged in their surroundings" (Waters, Wippman, & Sroufe, 1979). At 4 or 5 years, they are more curious and more competent (Arend, Gove, & Sroufe, 1979).

In one study, 4- and 5-year-olds who had been securely attached at 12 and 18 months were most likely to be independent, seeking help from preschool teachers only when they needed it. Children who had been anxiously attached earlier, however, were now more likely to be so dependent on the teacher that their needs for adult approval, contact, and attention made it harder for them to form relationships with other children and to learn how to do age-appropriate things (Sroufe, Fox, & Pancake, 1983).

## Effects of other caregivers

All mothers are, of course, "working mothers," since rearing children and caring for a family are valuable—though unpaid—forms of work. Here, however, we define *working mother* as one who works for pay, usually outside the home. A decade ago, most babies of working mothers were cared for in their own homes (Hofferth, 1979). Today, about 55 percent of such infants (including some as young as 3 weeks) receive care outside the home, most often in the homes of relatives or friends (Gamble & Zigler, 1986; U.S. Bureau of the Census, 1987; Young & Zigler, 1986).

What effects does such substitute care have on babies' attachment to their mothers? The effects may depend upon many factors, including the mother's satisfaction with her marriage; whether (and why) she works full time or part time; the child's age, sex, and temperament; and the kind and quality of care the baby gets. Early child care in itself does not seem to pose a risk; the risk lies in poor-quality care and poor family environments (Scarr, Phillips, & McCartney, 1989). The quality of child care tends to be higher outside the United States, as described in Box 5-3 (page 162).

The first year of life seems the most critical. When babies from stable families receive high-quality care, most studies report positive findings (L. W. Hoffman, 1989). On the other hand, when infants get unstable or poor-quality day care, they are more likely to avoid their mothers and to have emotional and social problems later on. These effects are worse when there is a poor fit between the mother's and baby's personalities, when the family is under great stress, and when the mother is not responsive to the baby (Gamble & Zigler, 1986; Young & Zigler, 1986).

Some controversial research suggests that extensive substitute care in the first year may affect some children negatively, especially boys (Belsky & Rovine, 1988). In one study, most (57 percent) of a group of children who had been cared for by someone else for 20 or more hours a week, beginning before age 9 months and through the first year, formed secure attachments to their mothers. But baby boys who received more than 35 hours a week of substitute care tended to be insecurely attached to both parents. The most vulnerable had been "difficult babies" at 3 months of age and had mothers who were dissatisfied with their marriages, insensitive to other people, and strongly career-motivated. Other research, however, has found that working mothers who are warm, accepting, and available when they are home do have securely attached 18-month-old sons (Benn, 1986). We cannot, then, make a blanket statement about day care without considering specific characteristics of the people, the care, and the situation.

The timing of the mother's first going out to work is related to quality of attachment. In one study, 18-month-old boys whose mothers started work in the second half of their first year of life were more likely to be insecurely attached than those whose mothers went to work when the babies were younger (Benn, 1986). This suggests that the second half of a child's (particularly a boy's) first year may not be the best time for a mother to return to work and that women who must, or choose to, go back to work by that time should try to do so before the baby is 6 months old (Benn, 1986).

However, after reviewing studies of parent-infant attachment, Lois W. Hoffman (1989) concluded that if there is a relationship between a mother's employment

## BOX 5–3    WINDOW ON THE WORLD

# CHILD CARE AND MATERNITY LEAVE IN INDUSTRIAL COUNTRIES

Infants and toddlers need a great deal of loving care. Most working parents of young children want to give it but are under stress because of conflicting demands and lack of time. To serve families, therefore, the governments of many nations provide paid, "job-protected" parental leave to let mothers or fathers (or both) be with their children in the important early months, and high-quality subsidized child care when the parents go back to work. In fact, of 100 industrialized countries, only one—the United States—has not established a national policy for parental leave and has a dismal record for child care (Kamerman, in Scarr, Phillips, & McCartney, 1989).

In Sweden, both parents can take a childbirth leave for 9 months, during which they receive 90 percent of one parent's wages. For the next 3 months, they receive smaller benefits; until the child is 18 months old, their leave is unpaid but job-protected; until the child is 8 years old, they may work a 6-hour day.

In Italy, women may take a job-protected leave for 6 months, during which they receive pay equal to the average wage of women workers. They may then take another leave, unpaid but job-protected, for 1 year. French women receive a job-protected maternity leave of 6 weeks before a baby is born and 10 weeks afterward.

Child care, too, is provided in these and many other countries. In 1986, almost 40 percent of Swedish preschoolers of working mothers were in subsidized child-care programs. And in France, Italy, Spain, and all the eastern European countries, more than half of all infants, toddlers, and preschoolers receive subsidized child care because their mothers are at work. France has a particularly good system of child care, which also offers preventive health services to virtually every child (Clinton, 1990).

In the United States, it is almost impossible to find figures for the number of children in subsidized child care, in itself an indication that in a country where politicians routinely talk about "family values," the family and children are undervalued. Our country accepts the principle of using tax funds for public schools to create an informed citizenry; if it wants a well-adjusted, productive citizenry, it will mandate high-quality child care, as well.

*Source*: Scarr, Phillips, & McCartney, 1989.

---

during her baby's first year of life and the baby's attachment security, it is weak. Most studies find that most babies of full-time employed mothers are securely attached. It is possible that a mother's working outside the home during the first few months of a baby's life may be a form of stress that, when combined with other stresses, can interfere with attachment, but that in itself it does not make a difference.

Also, as we will see below, the "strange situation" may not be the most appropriate measure of quality of attachment for children of working mothers. At least some babies who seem insecurely attached in the strange situation may really be showing independence. Because they are so used to their mothers' comings and goings, they are not anxious and are simply doing what works for them on a day-to-day basis—that is, showing an appropriate "avoidant" pattern (K. A. Clarke-Stewart, 1989).

### Critique of attachment research

Almost all the research on attachment is based on the strange situation. This research has yielded many findings that help us understand attachment, but a number of critics question its conclusions.

The strange situation *is* strange, and also artificial. It sets up a series of eight 3-minute staged episodes, asks mothers not to initiate interaction, exposes children to repeated comings and goings of adults, and expects the children to pay attention to them. Attachment cuts across a wide range of behaviors; thus a more complex method may be needed to measure it more sensitively, especially to see how mother and infant interact during natural, *non*stressful situations (T. M. Field, 1987).

Furthermore, the strange situation may be an especially poor way to study attachment in children who are used to routine separations from their mothers and to the presence of other caregivers (K. A. Clarke-Stewart, 1989; L. W. Hoffman, 1989). This point has special relevance for the children of employed mothers.

And finally, conclusions about long-term effects of attachment have been questioned. After reviewing the literature, M. E. Lamb (1987a) concluded that the association between attachment in infancy and development in childhood is weak and inconclusive. Differences among older children may stem from parent-child interaction after infancy. Because interaction patterns are often set early and remain consistent over the years, it is hard to tell when they are most influential. We will probably learn more about attachment as researchers use other measures besides the strange situation and as they integrate new attachment patterns into research designs.

While the mother-child attachment is important, it is not the only meaningful tie that babies form. The mother may be the only one who can suckle her infants, but other people—fathers, grandparents, siblings, friends, and caregivers—can also comfort and play with them, and give them a sense of security. Fathers are especially important.

## THE FATHER'S ROLE

Television commercials show fathers diapering and bathing their infants. Stores offer strollers with longer, man-sized handles and diaper bags with fewer frills. Psychologists have noticed the increasing presence of fathers in the nursery and are devoting more research to the father's role in a child's life—a role that has too often been ignored or minimized in the past.

The findings from such research underscore the importance of sensitive, responsive fathering to child development. Bonds and attachments form between fathers and babies during the first year of life, and fathers go on to exert a strong influence on their children's social, emotional, and cognitive development.

Fathers and children often form close bonds during the first year of life. Adam's father is likely to go on to exert a strong influence on his son's social, emotional, and cognitive development.

### Bonds and Attachments between Fathers and Infants

Many fathers form close bonds with their babies soon after birth. Proud new fathers admire their babies and feel drawn to pick them up. This reaction, called *engrossment,* is defined as a father's absorption in, preoccupation with, and interest in his infant (M. Greenberg & Morris, 1974). The babies contribute to the bond simply by doing the things all normal babies do: opening their eyes, grasping their fathers' fingers, or moving in their fathers' arms.

Babies develop attachments to their fathers and to their mothers at about the same time. In one study, babies 1 year old or older protested about equally against separation from both mother and father, while babies 9 months or younger did not protest against either parent's departure. When both parents were present, just over half of the babies were more likely to go to their mothers, but almost half showed as much or more attachment to their fathers (Kotelchuck, 1973).

Another study found that although babies prefer either the mother or the father to a stranger, they usually prefer their mothers to their fathers, especially when

upset (M. E. Lamb, 1981). This is probably because mothers typically care for them more often than fathers do. It will be interesting to see whether the nature of the father-infant attachment changes in families in which the father is the primary caregiver.

### How Do Fathers Act with Their Infants?

Despite a common belief that women are biologically predisposed to care for babies, research suggests that men can be just as sensitive and responsive to infants (M. E. Lamb, 1981). Fathers talk "motherese" (see Chapter 4); they adjust the pace of feeding to the baby's cues; and when they see crying or smiling infants on a television monitor, their physiological responses (changes in heart rate, blood pressure, and skin conductance) are similar to those of mothers.

Still, fathers are typically not as responsive as mothers. They usually take a less active role in child rearing, and the crucial factor in determining how sensitive an adult is to a baby's cues is the amount of care that the adult gives the baby (Zelazo, Kotelchuck, Barber, & David, 1977).

In our culture, fathers *care for* their babies less than they *play with* them (Easterbrooks & Goldberg, 1984). And they tend to do many things differently. Fathers videotaped face to face with 2- to 25-week-old infants typically provide a series of short, intense bursts of stimulation, whereas mothers tend to be more gentle and rhythmic. Fathers pat the babies; mothers talk softly to them (Yogman, Dixon, Tronick, Als, & Brazelton, 1977). Fathers toss infants up in the air and wrestle with toddlers; mothers typically play gentler games and sing and read to them (M. E. Lamb, 1977; Parke & Tinsley, 1981).

The father's involvement is influenced by many factors. One is the mother's attitude. She often serves as the "gatekeeper" of the father's involvement with the baby, both in her direct actions and in the way she talks about him (Yogman, 1984). Another factor is the mother's employment. Women who work full time stimulate their babies more than women who stay at home full time, and they play with their babies more than the fathers do. They still spend more time taking care of their babies, however, than the babies' fathers do (Pedersen, Cain, & Zaslow, 1982). A study of fathers who were their babies' primary caretakers found that these men behaved more like mothers than like "typical" fathers (T. M. Field, 1978).

It seems likely, then, that different roles and different societal expectations about what fathers and mothers are supposed to do influence their styles of interacting with their babies.

## What Is the Significance of the Father-Infant Relationship?

The differences between men and women, both biological and social, make each parent's role in the family unique—and each one's contribution special. For example, the physical way in which fathers typically play with babies offers excitement and a challenge to conquer fears. During the first 2 years, babies often smile and "talk" more to the father, probably because he is more of a novelty (M. E. Lamb, 1981).

In one study, a group of toddlers—two-thirds of whose mothers were employed outside the home—showed the benefits of the father's involvement in caring for and playing with them, especially when his attitude was sensitive and positive. The father's behavior had a particularly strong influence on competence in problem solving, and although the mother's behavior had more impact on attachment, the father's involvement helped to make boys' attachment to their mothers more secure (Easterbrooks & Goldberg, 1984).

Fathers, along with mothers, also seem to play an important part in helping toddlers become independent.

In a study of the interaction between forty-four 2-year-old boys and girls, their fathers, and their mothers (who were the primary caregivers), the parents were instructed to get the toddlers to put away toys and not touch a tape recorder. Since both parents dealt very similarly with their children, the researchers concluded that fathers do not play the part of family disciplinarian but act in far less stereotyped ways (Yogman, Cooley, & Kindlon, 1988).

As we noted earlier, adults act differently toward babies depending on whether they think the baby is a boy or a girl. Fathers act *more* differently toward boys and girls than mothers do, even during a baby's first year (M. E. Snow, Jacklin, & Maccoby, 1983). By the second year, this difference intensifies: fathers talk more and spend more time with sons than with daughters (M. E. Lamb, 1981). For these reasons, fathers, more than mothers, seem to affect the development of gender identity and *gender-typing*—the process by which children learn behavior that their culture considers appropriate for each sex (P. Bronstein, 1988).

Fathers may also influence their sons' cognitive development more than mothers do. The more attention a father pays to his baby son, the brighter, more alert, more inquisitive, and happier that baby is likely to be at 5 or 6 months (Pedersen, Rubenstein, & Yarrow, 1973). Baby boys raised without fathers tend to lag cognitively behind boys in two-parent families, even when the mother does not act differently (Pedersen, Rubenstein, & Yarrow, 1979). This finding may be further evidence of the father's importance in cognitive development (Radin, 1988)—or it may reveal the economic or social disadvantages of growing up in a single-parent family.

The very fact that a child's two parents have two different personalities—no matter what those personalities are—influences development in unknown ways. We don't know, for example, what effects stem from babies' learning that the same action will bring different reactions from mother and father. It seems clear, though, that anyone who plays a large part in a baby's day-to-day life will exert an important influence.

## STRANGER ANXIETY AND SEPARATION ANXIETY

Sophie used to be a friendly baby, smiling at strangers and going to them, continuing to coo happily as long as someone—anyone—was around. Now, at 8 months, she howls when a new person approaches her or when her parents try to leave her with a sitter. Sophie is experiencing both **stranger anxiety,** wariness of a person she does not know, and **separation anxiety,** distress when a familiar caregiver leaves her.

Separation anxiety and stranger anxiety used to be considered emotional and cognitive milestones of infancy, reflecting attachment to and recognition of the mother. Research over the past decade or so, however, suggests that these phenomena are very variable and depend largely on a baby's temperament and life circumstances.

Although Sophie's reaction is typical, it is not universal. That is, babies rarely react negatively to strangers before 6 months of age, commonly react negatively by 8 or 9 months, and react more and more negatively throughout the remainder of the first year (Sroufe, 1977). Even at these ages, however, a baby may react positively to a new person—especially if the person waits for a little while before approaching the baby and then approaches gradually, gently, and playfully. With this kind of approach, the infant's natural curiosity and inborn tendency to relate to other people can take over. But if a stranger reaches for a baby suddenly, or touches or picks him or her up before the baby has gotten used to the stranger's presence, the baby is more likely to cry.

One factor affecting a baby's reaction to a stranger is how the caregiver reacts to the new person (Dickstein & Parke, 1988; Klinnert, Emde, Butterfield, & Campos, 1986). In one study, the mothers of 10-month-old babies who were approached by an unfamiliar woman spoke to their babies either positively or neutrally about the woman, or spoke to the woman herself positively or neutrally, or remained silent (Feinman & Lewis, 1983). When the mothers spoke positively about the stranger, the babies—especially those with easy temperaments—were friendlier to her than in any of the other situations, and were more likely to lean toward her and offer her a toy. Apparently, the babies socially referenced their mothers in this ambiguous situation and acted accordingly. Sally saw this phenomenon in action when she visited her 9-month-old granddaughter, Maika, in Germany, after not having seen her for 7 months. Since Maika's mother (Sally's daughter) greeted Sally eagerly, the baby apparently decided that this was a person she could trust, and she soon went willingly into her grandmother's arms.

Today, neither early and intense fear of strangers nor intense protest when the mother leaves is considered to be a sign of secure attachment. As we saw in the discussion of attachment, researchers now measure attachment more by what happens when the parent returns than on how many tears the baby shed at departure time. And whether a baby cries when a parent leaves or someone new approaches may tell us more more about a baby's temperament than about the security of his or her attachment (R. J. Davidson & Fox, 1989).

## DISTURBANCES IN FAMILY RELATIONSHIPS

The attachments that infants form with their parents exert a major influence on physical, intellectual, personality, and social development. When these attachments are disrupted or impaired because children are separated from their parents or have painful relationships with them, the consequences can be grave.

### Loss of Parents

What happens to infants who are deprived of their parents very early in life, either permanently or temporarily? The answer may depend on a number of factors, including the reason for the separation, the kind of care the child receives, and the quality of the child's relationships before and after the separation.

#### Institutionalization

When orphanages were the most common way to care for children whose parents were dead or unable to care for them, many babies in these institutions died in the first year (R. A. Spitz, 1945). Children institutionalized for a long time often declined in intellectual functioning and developed major psychological problems.

A classic study by R. A. Spitz (1945, 1946) compared 134 children reared in two institutions (called "Nursery" and "Foundling Home") with 34 children reared in their own homes. At the end of a year, the children in "Nursery" and the children reared at home were healthy and normal. But those in "Foundling Home" were below average in height and weight, and their developmental quotients had deteriorated (from 124 at the outset to 75, and then to 45 in the second year). Also, they were highly susceptible to disease, often fatally. Paradoxically, many of the "Foundling Home" babies had favorable backgrounds, whereas those in "Nursery" had been born to delinquent girls, many of whom were emotionally disturbed or retarded. The most important difference between the two institutions turned out to be how much personal attention the babies got. In "Nursery," all babies received full-time care from their own mothers or from full-time substitutes; but in "Foundling Home," eight children shared one nurse—a typical situation in institutions.

By showing the need for care approximating good mothering, Spitz's work hastened a trend toward placement in foster homes and much earlier adoption. True, his study (and other studies) showed that children in well-run institutions—which provide plenty of conversation and active, meaningful experiences—suffer no impairment of intelligence. But even in these conditions, children remain at risk of social deprivation. The factor that causes damage does not seem to be separa-

Early research in child development brought out the need for sensitive, individualized care when children, like these Romanian orphans, need to be in an institution. One of the most important factors is stability of caregivers, letting children become attached to particular people.

tion from natural parents or having more than one caregiver, but frequent changes in caregivers, a situation that prevents the formation of "early emotional bonds to particular individuals" (p. 151).

The drop in intellectual and emotional responsiveness that infants in institutions typically show may be overcome by abundant attention and stimulation from a person to whom a baby becomes attached as a "substitute mother" (A. Clarke-Stewart, 1977). Dramatic gains, especially in talking, have appeared (Rheingold, 1956).

### Hospitalization

Even a short stay in a hospital can be disturbing to infants and toddlers. Unless they get a great deal of attention from substitute caregivers, their intellectual responsiveness tends to decline until they return home. Hospitalized babies 15 to 30 months old have been ob-

served to go through three stages of separation anxiety (Bowlby, 1960):

1 *Protest.* Babies try to get their mothers back by shaking the crib and throwing themselves about.
2 *Despair.* Babies become withdrawn and inactive, crying monotonously or intermittently. Because they are so quiet, it is often assumed that they have accepted the situation.
3 *Detachment.* Babies accept care from a succession of nurses and are willing to eat, play with toys, smile, and be sociable; but when their mothers visit, the babies remain apathetic and may turn away.

What can be done to reduce stress and fear when a baby or young child must be hospitalized? One parent can stay with the child, even sleeping overnight; and daily visits from other family members, familiar routines, and limits on the number of caregivers can relieve the strangeness of the situation (Rutter, 1979b).

Providing occasional happy separations ahead of time can make an impending hospital visit less stressful. Children who are used to being left with grandparents or sitters or who have stayed overnight at friends' houses are less likely to be upset by hospitalization (Rutter, 1971; Stacey, Dearden, Pill, & Robinson, 1970).

### Child Abuse and Neglect

Most parents try to do the best they can for their children, but some cannot or will not meet a child's most basic needs. Neglected children starve because their parents do not feed them; they freeze when they are left without enough clothing in frigid temperatures; and, left alone, they perish in fires. Emotionally neglected children may not grow properly. Other children are actively abused: kicked, beaten, burned, thrown against walls and radiators, strangled, suffocated, sexually molested, even buried alive. They are humiliated and terrorized by the people who are supposed to nurture them. The list of horrors seems endless.

Maltreatment of children can take several different forms. **Child abuse** involves physical injury. The typical pattern has been identified as the **battered child syndrome** (Kempe et al., 1962). **Sexual abuse** refers to any kind of sexual contact between a child and an older person. **Neglect** is withholding of adequate care, usually physical care such as food, clothing, and supervision. Emotional neglect also occurs, sometimes resulting in a syndrome called **nonorganic failure to thrive,** in which a baby fails to grow and gain weight at home despite adequate nutrition, but improves rapidly when moved out of the home and given emotional attention.

Even though such mistreatment of children is more widely recognized today than it was in the past, still the hideous maltreatment goes on. In the late 1980s, more than 2 million children a year in the United States were reported to be victims of abuse and neglect, and many of them were victims of sexual abuse. This represented a rise in reported cases, which may reflect an increase in mistreatment, or better reporting of mistreatment, or both.

### Causes of abuse and neglect

Why do adults hurt or neglect children? Researchers suggest various causes, including characteristics of the abuser or neglecter, the victim, the family, the community, and the larger culture (Belsky, 1980).

*Abusers and neglecters*   More than 90 percent of all child abuse occurs at home (Child Welfare League of America, 1986). In the past, the mother was usually the abuser, but recent analyses suggest that men are committing more child abuse, especially sexual abuse and serious and fatal injuries (Bergman, Larsen, & Mueller, 1986; Browne & Finkelhor, 1986). Over 90 percent of abusers are not psychotic and do not have criminal personalities; but many are lonely, unhappy, depressed, angry, dissatisfied, isolated, and under great stress, or they have health problems that impair their ability to raise their children. The power they exert over their children through abuse may be a misplaced effort to gain control over their own lives (B. D. Schmitt & Kempe, 1983; Wolfe, 1985). They may have been mistreated in their own childhood and may have felt rejected by their parents (Trickett & Susman, 1988).

Abusers often hate themselves for what they do and yet feel powerless to stop. Often deprived of good parenting themselves, they do not know how to be good parents to their own children. They do not know how to make a baby stop crying, for example, and will sometimes lose all control when they cannot get their children to do what they want them to do. They tend to be ignorant of normal child development, expecting children to be toilet-trained or to stay clean and neat at unrealistically early ages. Furthermore, they often expect their children to take care of them, and they become abusive when this does not happen. They have more confrontations with their children than nonabusive parents do and are less effective in resolving problems (J. R. Reid, Patterson, & Loeber, 1982; Wolfe, 1985). Abusive parents have trouble reading babies' emotional expressions; they may not be ignoring babies' needs but misinterpreting them. A parent may try to feed a child who is actually crying in pain, and then be frustrated when the baby spits out the food (Kropp & Haynes, 1987).

The death by beating of 6-year-old Lisa Steinberg aroused a nation and brought about changes in New York State adoption laws. The man convicted as her killer—an attorney who, with his companion, raised Lisa from infancy—had never legally adopted her.

Neglectful parents, on the other hand, are likely to be irresponsible and apathetic, and to ignore their children (Wolfe, 1985). Mothers of infants who fail to thrive tend to have been poorly nurtured themselves and to have had stressful relationships with the babies' fathers. These mothers tend to have more complications of pregnancy and childbirth than other mothers, gaining less weight, delivering earlier, and bearing smaller babies; they also have more trouble feeding their infants (Altemeir, O'Connor, Sherrod, & Vietze, 1985). They do not hug or talk to their babies, and they seem unable to organize a safe, warm home environment for these babies, whose presence they seem to resent (P. H. Casey, Bradley, & Wortham, 1984).

*Victims*   Abused children tend to need or demand more from their parents than other children, because of their personalities or for other reasons. They are more likely to have been low-birthweight infants; to be hyperactive, mentally retarded, or physically handicapped; or to show behavioral abnormalities (J. R. Reid et al., 1982). They cry more and show more negative behavior than other children—almost 50 percent more in one study (Tsai & Wagner, 1979). Babies who fail to thrive because of emotional neglect have often had medical problems at or soon after birth (Altemeir et al., 1985). Victims of sexual abuse seem to have a greater-than-average need for affection, which may make them easy prey to child molesters (Tsai & Wagner, 1979).

Babies and toddlers become closely attached to their older brothers and sisters, especially when, as with these Guatemalan children, the older siblings assume a large measure of care for the younger ones.

Finally, older siblings adjust better if their fathers give extra time and attention to them to make up for the mother's sudden involvement with the infant (M. E. Lamb, 1978).

### How Siblings Interact

Siblings have more to do with each other after the first 6 months of a baby's life. In many societies around the world, including our own, older siblings have some responsibility for taking care of babies (Dunn, 1985).

How do siblings get along? In one study of 34 pairs of same-sex middle-class siblings at home, the younger ones averaged 20 months of age. Their brothers and sisters, 1 to 4 years older, more often initiated both positive and negative behaviors, while the younger ones imitated more. Older boys were more aggressive; older girls were more likely to share, cooperate, and

hug. The sibling interaction was "rich and varied, clearly not based predominantly on rivalry" (Abramovitch, Corter, & Lando, 1979, p. 1003). Thus, although rivalry is often present, so is genuine affection.

Young children usually become quite attached to their older brothers and sisters. (At 1 year, Sally's daughter Dorri referred to her 4- and 6-year-old sisters as "my choo-jun" ("my children".) Babies become upset when their siblings go away, greet them when they come back, prefer them as playmates, and go to them for security when a stranger enters the room (Dunn, 1983; R. B. Stewart, 1983).

The environment that siblings create for each other affects not only their future relationship but each one's personality development as well (Dunn, 1983). For example, when little girls imitate their big brothers, they may take on some characteristics commonly thought of as masculine.

### SOCIABILITY

Although the family is the center of a baby's social world, infants and—even more so—toddlers show interest in people outside the home, particularly people their own size. Since more babies now spend time in day care settings in close contact with other babies, more researchers are studying how infants and toddlers react to each other.

Babies' interest in other children rises and falls. From the first days of life in a hospital nursery, infants who have been lying quietly in their cribs will start to cry when they hear another baby's cries (G. B. Martin & Clark, 1982; Sagi & Hoffman, 1976; Simner, 1971). During the first few months of life, they are very interested in other babies and respond to them in about the same way they respond to their mothers: they look, they smile, they coo (T. M. Field, 1978). From age 6 months till about 1 year, they increasingly smile at, touch, and babble to another baby, especially when they are not distracted by the presence of adults or toys (Hay, Pedersen, & Nash, 1982). At about 1 year, however, when the biggest items on their agenda seem to be learning to walk and to manipulate objects, they pay more attention to toys and less to other people (T. M. Field & Roopnarine, 1982).

In their second year, babies become more sociable again, and now they understand relationships better. A 10-month-old who holds out a toy to another baby pays no attention to whether the other's back is turned, but a child in the second year of life knows when the offer has the best chance of being accepted and how to respond to another child's overtures (Eckerman, Davis, & Didow, 1989; Eckerman & Stein, 1982).

# PUTTING RESEARCH FINDINGS TO WORK

If you are, or are about to become, a parent—or if you have occasion to care for infants or toddlers, you can put into practice important findings that have emerged from research in child development. The following recommendations are based on theories and findings discussed in Chapters 3, 4, and 5:

1 *Respond to babies' signals.* This is probably the single most important thing that caregivers can do. Meeting the needs of an infant—whether for food, cuddling, or comforting—establishes a sense of trust and gives the child a sense that the world is a friendly place. Answering cries or requests for help gives a baby a sense of having some control over his or her life, an important awareness for emotional and intellectual development. Adults often worry about spoiling children by reacting too quickly, but the children who have the most problems are those whose needs go unmet.

2 *Provide interesting things for babies to look at and do.* By first watching a mobile hanging over a crib and then handling brightly colored toys and simple household objects, babies learn about shapes, sizes, and textures. Playing helps them develop their senses and motor skills. And handling objects helps them realize the difference between themselves and things that are separate from them.

3 *Be patient.* When a baby keeps throwing toys or other objects out of the crib or high chair, the purpose is not to annoy but to learn. By throwing things, babies learn such concepts as space and distance, what hands can do, and the fact that objects remain the same even when they are moved to a different place. It may be easier on your back and disposition if you tie one or two items to a string that can be pulled up each time. Of course, you should not leave the string near an unattended baby—or leave a baby alone in a high chair.

4 *Give babies the power to make changes.* If you hang a mobile over the crib, make it possible for the baby to make the mobile move rather than depend on currents of air. Give toys that the baby can shake to make a noise, or can change in shape, or can make move. Babies need to learn that they have some control over their world and that they can have an effect on the things in it.

5 *Give babies freedom to explore.* It is better to baby-proof a room than to confine the baby in a playpen. Take away breakables, small things that can be swallowed, and sharp objects that can injure. Jam books so tightly into a bookcase that a baby cannot pull them out. But leave plenty of unbreakable objects around. Babies need opportunities to crawl and eventually to walk, to exercise their large muscles. They need to learn about their environment, to feel a sense of mastery over it. They also need freedom to go off on their own (under a caregiver's watchful eye) and develop a sense of independence.

Some people, of course, are more sociable than others. Readiness to accept new people, ability to adapt to change, and a person's usual mood seem to be inherited traits (A. Thomas et al., 1968) that remain fairly stable over time. But babies are also influenced by the attitudes of those around them. Sociable infants tend to have sociable mothers (M. Stevenson & Lamb, 1979). And children who spend time with other babies from infancy on seem to become sociable at earlier ages than those who spend all their time at home.

From just under 1½ years of age to almost 3, children show a growing interest in what their playmates do. They imitate each other—more in what they do than in what they say—like hiding, throwing something, knocking on a playhouse, or jumping off a box.

They also play more games like hide-and-seek and follow-the-leader. These strategies help them connect with other children and pave the way for the more complex games involving talking and symbolic play that take over during the preschool years (Eckerman et al., 1989). As children grow older, they enter more and more into the world beyond their own home, and their social skills become increasingly important.

Research has told us much about the way infants and toddlers develop physically, intellectually, emotionally, and socially (see Box 5-4 for ways to apply some of the findings discussed in Chapters 3, 4, and 5). In Part Three, we'll see how young children build on the foundation laid during their first 3 years.

## SUMMARY

### THEORETICAL APPROACHES TO EARLY PERSONALITY DEVELOPMENT

- According to Freud, certain events that occur during the first 3 years are among those having the greatest influence on adult personality.

  1. In the oral stage (birth to 12–18 months), an infant receives pleasure through oral stimulation.
  2. In the anal stage (12–18 months to 3 years), a toddler receives pleasure from moving the bowels.

- According to Erikson, infants and toddlers experience the first two crises in a series of eight that influence personality development throughout life.

  1. The first critical task, which an infant faces in the first 12 to 18 months, is to find a balance between basic trust and basic mistrust of the world. Like that of the Freudian oral stage, the resolution of this crisis is influenced greatly by events surrounding feeding and by the quality of the mother-infant relationship.
  2. The second crisis, which a toddler faces from 12–18 months to 3 years, is autonomy versus shame and doubt. As in Freud's anal stage, toilet training is a key event in resolving this crisis, which is greatly affected by help the child gets from parents.

### EMOTIONS: THE FOUNDATION OF PERSONALITY

- Recent research suggests that the expressions of different emotions are tied to brain maturation, although experiences and the development of self-awareness also affect the timing of their arrival.
- Babies communicate their feelings through tears, smiles, laughter, and a variety of facial expressions. Infants take an active part in emotional regulation.

### DIFFERENCES IN PERSONALITY DEVELOPMENT

- Early differences in emotional expression, which may stem from temperament, are indicative of future personality development.
- The New York Longitudinal Study identified nine fairly stable components of temperament, or a person's individual style of approaching people and situations. These traits appear to be largely inborn but may be affected by significant environmental changes. On the basis of these temperamental patterns, most children can be classified as easy, difficult, or slow to warm up.
- Significant physiological and behavioral differences between the sexes typically do not appear until after infancy. However, parents treat their sons and daughters differently from birth, and so some personality differences result.

### THE FAMILY AND PERSONALITY DEVELOPMENT

- Some research has suggested that the first few hours or days of life constitute a critical period for forming the mother-infant bond, but follow-up research has failed to support this conclusion. However, infants do have strong needs for closeness and warmth as well as physical care from one caregiver or a few caregivers.
- Mother-infant attachment, a reciprocal connection that forms and consolidates in infancy, is receiving considerable attention in research. Patterns of attachment seem to have long-term implications for development.
- When mothers work outside the home, babies' (especially boys') attachment patterns may be affected. Significant factors include the amount of time the baby spends away from the mother (unless the caregiver is the father); the child's age, sex, and temperament; the mother's attitude; and the quality of substitute care.
- Fathers and babies become attached early in a baby's life. Infants' and toddlers' experiences with mothers and fathers seem to differ, and the variety is valuable.
- Separation anxiety and stranger anxiety are normal phenomena that arise during the second half of the first year and appear to be related to a baby's temperament and life circumstances. Separation anxiety is a child's distress upon the departure of the caregiver. Stranger anxiety is wariness of strangers. There is considerable individual difference in the expression of both separation anxiety and stranger anxiety.
- Studies of parental deprivation—generally conducted among orphans in institutions in which considerable sensory deprivation is common—point to the need for consistent parenting or caregiving in a stimulating environment. Attempts at enriching institutional environments have dramatically benefited children's emotional and intellectual development.
- Effects of short-term separations, such as for hospitalization, depend on particular circumstances.
- Child abuse, including sexual abuse and neglect, has received widespread attention and medical documentation. Characteristics of victim, abusers or neglecters, families, the community, and the larger culture are associated with or contribute to child abuse and neglect.

### RELATIONSHIPS WITH OTHER CHILDREN

- Siblings influence each other both positively and negatively from an early age. Parents' actions and attitudes can help reduce sibling rivalry.
- Although infants' interest in other children fluctuates with their developmental priorities, individual differences in sociability tend to remain stable over time.

## KEY TERMS

negativism (page 144)
oral stage (145)
anal stage (146)
basic trust versus basic mistrust (146)
autonomy versus shame and doubt (147)
autonomy (147)
self-regulation (147)
self-control (147)
emotions (148)

self-awareness (149)
self-recognition (149)
social referencing (151)
depression (152)
temperament (153)
socialization (156)
imprinting (156)
mother-infant bond (157)
attachment (158)
strange situation (158)

securely attached (158)
avoidant (159)
ambivalent (resistant) (159)
stranger anxiety (164)
separation anxiety (164)
child abuse (166)
battered child syndrome (166)
sexual abuse (166)
neglect (166)
nonorganic failure to thrive (166)

## SUGGESTED READINGS

**Brazelton, T. B., & Cramer, B. G. (1990).** *The earliest relationship.* New York: Addison-Wesley. This book examines the parent-child relationship from its beginning in pregnancy to its further development after the child is born. It coordinates current research on infant behavior and parent-infant interaction with psychoanalytic theories about becoming a parent. The second half of the book consists of case studies which illustrate different types of parent-infant relationships.

**Lamb, M. E. (Ed.). (1981).** *The role of the father in child development* (2d ed.). New York: Wiley. A collection of writings on the impact of the father on the developing child, by leading researchers on paternal influences.

**Mahler, M., Pine, F., & Bergmann, A. (1975).** *The psychological birth of the human infant.* New York: Basic Books. This is the classic report on a longitudinal study of mother-child pairs during the separation-individuation process in which the child emerges from symbiotic fusion with the mother and begins to assume a unique identity of his or her own.

**Stern, D. N. (1990).** *Diary of a baby.* New York: Basic Books. A noted developmental psychologist describes what a baby sees, feels, and experiences in the first 22 months of life.

# EARLY CHILDHOOD

The years from 3 to 6 used to be called the *pre-school years*. Now, when most children attend some kind of school starting at age 3, and many go to day care centers even earlier, a more accurate term for this stage is *early childhood*.

■ In **Chapter 6,** we discuss physical and intellectual development during these years. Children now look different, as they lose their babyish roundness. They act differently, too. They become better at fine motor tasks like tying shoelaces (in bows instead of knots), drawing with crayons (on paper rather than on walls), and pouring cereal (into the bowl, not onto the floor). They improve in large motor abilities like running, hopping, skipping, jumping, and throwing balls. They also think differently, as they leap forward in their ability to han-

dle a wide range of intellectual concepts and to express their thoughts and feelings in the language of their culture.

■ In **Chapter 7** we see how critical these years are for personality development. Children's conceptions of themselves grow stronger. They know what sex they are—and they want everyone else to affirm their sense of maleness or femaleness. Their behavior becomes more socially directed—sometimes helping other people, sometimes hurting them. The number of important people in their lives expands, as friends and playmates become more important.

All aspects of development—physical, intellectual, emotional, and social—continue to intertwine to make each person unique.

## CHAPTER 6

# PHYSICAL AND INTELLECTUAL DEVELOPMENT IN EARLY CHILDHOOD

Children live in a world of imagination and feeling. . . .
They invest the most insignificant object with any form
they please, and see in it whatever they wish to see.

ADAM G. OEHLENSCHLAGER

- How do children's bodies and motor skills grow and develop during early childhood?
- How can young children be kept healthy?
- What sleep patterns and problems develop during early childhood, and how can they be handled?
- How do young children think and remember, and what does research tell us about their cognitive competence?

- How does language ability flower in early childhood?
- How can we assess intelligence in early childhood, and how do parents influence intellectual performance?
- What options are available for young children's care and schooling, and how important is the quality of care and education?

It is the day before Keisha's third birthday. "Pretty soon," she tells her mother, "I'll be big enough to sleep without sucking my thumb. And maybe tomorrow I'll be big enough to wear pajamas like Daddy's."

The big day dawns. Keisha leaps out of bed at her usual early hour and runs to the mirror. As she stands there, first on one foot and then on the other, she examines her mirror image closely; then she runs to her parents' room. "Mommy, Daddy!" she squeals into sleepy ears. "I'm 3!" But then a note of disappointment creeps into her voice as she acknowledges sadly, "But I don't look different."

Keisha's change from the day before may be infinitesimal, but in terms of what she was a year earlier, she is very different indeed. Her next 3 years of life will show greater changes.

Children who have celebrated their third birthday are no longer babies. They are capable of bigger and better things, both physically and intellectually. The 3-year-old is a sturdy adventurer, very much at home in the world and eager to explore its possibilities, as well as the developing capabilities of his or her own body. A child of this age has come through the most dangerous time of life—the years of infancy and toddlerhood—to enter a healthier, less threatening phase.

Youngsters grow more slowly in early childhood, between the ages of 3 and 6, than during the preceding 3 years; but they make so much progress in coordination and muscle development that they can do much more. Intellectual development, too, continues at a staggering pace. Children in this age group have taken huge leaps forward in their ability to remember, reason, speak, and think.

In this chapter, we'll trace all these developing capabilities and consider several important concerns. We'll also describe the profound effects of young children's expanding environment: at day care centers, preschool, and kindergarten.

# PHYSICAL DEVELOPMENT

## PHYSICAL GROWTH AND CHANGE

Physical changes may be less obvious during early childhood than during the first 3 years of life; but they are nonetheless important, and they make possible dramatic advances in motor skills and intellectual development.

### HEIGHT, WEIGHT, AND APPEARANCE

At about age 3, boys and girls begin to lose their chubbiness and begin to take on the slender, athletic appearance of childhood. As children's abdominal muscles develop, their potbellies slim down. The trunk, arms, and legs all grow longer. The head is still relatively large, but (in keeping with the cephalocaudal principle, described in Chapter 3) the other parts of the body continue to catch up as body proportions steadily become more adult.

Within that overall pattern, children show a wide range of individual and sex-related differences. Boys tend to have more muscle per pound of body weight than girls, while girls have more fatty tissue.

Although Keisha's growth has slowed now that she is 3, she is 4 inches taller than she was a year ago; she now measures almost 38 inches and weighs almost 32 pounds. Her friend Felipe, whose birthday is within a week of hers, is slightly taller and heavier. Each year for the next 3 years, both will grow about 2 to 3 inches and gain 4 to 6 pounds. Boys' slight edge in height and weight normally continues until puberty. (At puberty, girls suddenly surpass boys, but a year or two later boys again become taller and heavier than girls of the same age.)

## STRUCTURAL AND SYSTEMIC CHANGES

The changes in children's appearance reflect important internal developments. Muscular and skeletal growth progresses, making children stronger. Cartilage turns to bone at a faster rate than before, and bones become harder, giving the child a firmer shape and protecting the internal organs. These changes, coordinated by the maturing brain and nervous system, allow a proliferation of both large-muscle and small-muscle motor skills. In addition, the increased capacities of the respiratory and circulatory systems improve physical stamina and, along with the developing immune system, keep children healthier.

By the age of 3, all the primary, or deciduous, teeth are in place, and so children can chew anything they want to. The permanent teeth, which will begin to appear at about age 6, are developing; therefore, if thumb-sucking persists past the age of 5, it can affect how evenly the teeth come in.

## NUTRITION

Proper growth and health depend on good nutrition. As children's growth rate slows down, so does their appetite, and parents often worry that their children are not eating enough. Because caloric requirements per pound of body weight decline, children between ages 3 and 6 normally eat less in proportion to their size than infants do. A child who is energetic—with good muscle tone, bright eyes, glossy hair, and the ability to recover readily from fatigue—is unlikely to be suffering from inadequate nutrition, no matter how little she or he may be eating.

The nutritional demands of early childhood are satisfied quite easily. For example, a small child's daily protein requirement can be met with two glasses of milk and one serving of meat or an alternative (like fish,

cheese, or eggs). Vitamin A requirements can be met with modest amounts of carrots, spinach, egg yolk, or whole milk (among other foods); and vitamin C can be obtained from citrus fruits, from tomatoes, and from leafy dark-green vegetables (E. R. Williams & Caliendo, 1984).

If children do not get these and other essential nutrients, there is cause for concern. That commonly happens when children and their families succumb to seductive television commercials for foods heavy in sugar and fat. If children's diet includes a lot of sugared cereals, chocolate cake, other snacks low in nutrients, and fast foods, their small appetite will not allow them room to eat the foods they really need. Therefore the snacks they eat should have nutritional value.

## HEALTH

The early childhood years are basically healthy, especially since the major diseases that used to strike young children are now relatively rare because of widespread vaccinations.

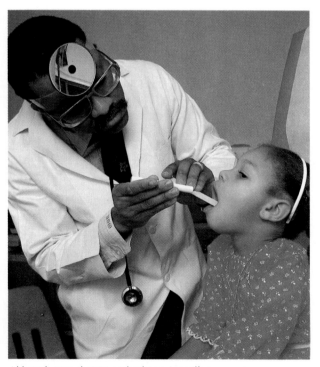

Although sore throats and other minor illnesses are common among 3- to 6-year-olds, they are usually not serious enough to require visits to the doctor. This 5-year-old will probably have fewer colds and sore throats in the next few years, as her respiratory and immune systems mature.

BOX 6–1    THINKING CRITICALLY

## IS ILLNESS GOOD FOR CHILDREN?

Nobody likes to be sick. But might the frequent minor illnesses of early childhood be blessings in disguise? Some observers maintain that common childhood illnesses help children by building up immunity to disease, and that they also confer certain cognitive and emotional benefits (Parmelee, 1986). Let's look at the reasoning that lies behind this viewpoint.

When children are ill, they often feel achey, feverish, weak, and depressed. When they recover, their usual sense of physical well-being bounces back. Repeated experiences with illness call children's attention to their various sensations and states and make them more aware of their physical selves. Illness helps children learn how to cope with physical distress, and the coping enhances their sense of competence.

When contagious illnesses spread, children see their brothers, sisters, playmates, and parents going through experiences similar to their own. Adam's bout with the flu teaches him empathy—the ability to put himself in someone else's place. He can understand how his little sister Bobbi feels when *she* catches the flu, and he can help give her the comfort and care he gets when he is ill.

During early childhood, Adam may, to some extent, confuse "feeling bad" when his throat hurts and "feeling bad" when he has hurt Bobbi. His confusion is natural, since speakers of English use the same expression for both physical and emotional upsets and regard both as unwanted states. Children are often convinced that they "feel bad" (are sick) because they "did something bad" (like disobey their parents). Illness gives parents a chance to deal with children's confusion and guilt and to reassure the child: "I know you feel bad because you're sick, but you'll soon be well."

## HEALTH PROBLEMS IN EARLY CHILDHOOD

### Minor Illnesses

Coughs, sniffles, stomachaches, and runny noses are part of early childhood. These minor illnesses typically last from 2 to 14 days but are seldom serious enough to require a doctor's attention. In fact, they may even have some cognitive and emotional as well as physical benefits (see Box 6-1).

Because the lungs are not fully developed, respiratory problems are common during these years, though less common than in infancy. Three- to five-year-olds average seven to eight colds and other respiratory illnesses a year; but later, during middle childhood, children average fewer than six such illnesses (Denny & Clyde, 1983), because of the gradual development of the respiratory system and natural immunity (resistance to disease).

### Major Illnesses

Until recently, immunization seemed to have banished the specter of such contagious diseases as measles, rubella (German measles), mumps, whooping cough, diphtheria, and poliomyelitis—illnesses that before the middle of the twentieth century were widespread and often fatal. But between 1980 and 1985 the proportion of children aged 1 to 4 who were immunized against the major childhood illnesses dropped. Since then, cases of whooping cough and measles have risen, and now 1 in 4 preschoolers and 1 in 3 poor children are not protected against measles, rubella, polio, and mumps (National Association of Children's Hospitals and Related Institutions, NACHRI, & American Academy of Pediatrics, AAP, 1990). Table 6-1 on the opposite page shows the current recommendations for immunizations during childhood.

Still, death rates from all kinds of illness have come down in recent years. Since 1950, deaths from influenza and pneumonia have dropped by 84 percent, although respiratory diseases are still the major cause of death among infants and children worldwide. The 5-year survival rate for cancer (which in medical terms is considered a cure) has risen dramatically for children under 15 diagnosed between 1977 and 1983, compared with children under 15 diagnosed between 1967 and 1973 (American Cancer Society, 1988).

During the 1980s, nearly 2000 children under age 12 were diagnosed with AIDS (acquired immune deficiency syndrome), and the rate is growing 200 percent per year. Currently the ninth leading cause of death for children aged 1 to 4, AIDS is expected to move into the five leading causes of childhood death over the next few years (NACHRI & AAP, 1990).

**TABLE 6–1**
RECOMMENDED CHILDHOOD IMMUNIZATIONS

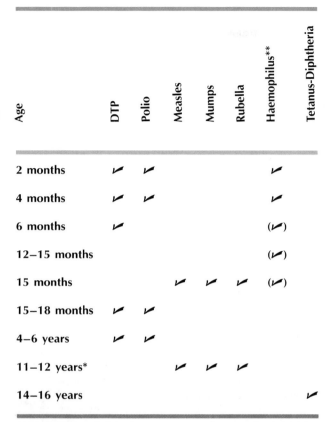

| Age | DTP | Polio | Measles | Mumps | Rubella | Haemophilus** | Tetanus-Diphtheria |
|---|---|---|---|---|---|---|---|
| 2 months | ✔ | ✔ | | | | ✔ | |
| 4 months | ✔ | ✔ | | | | ✔ | |
| 6 months | ✔ | | | | | (✔) | |
| 12–15 months | | | | | | (✔) | |
| 15 months | | | ✔ | ✔ | ✔ | (✔) | |
| 15–18 months | ✔ | ✔ | | | | | |
| 4–6 years | ✔ | ✔ | | | | | |
| 11–12 years* | | | ✔ | ✔ | ✔ | | |
| 14–16 years | | | | | | | ✔ |

*Notes:* DTP = diphtheria, tetanus, and pertussis (whooping cough). * = Except where public health authorities require otherwise. ** = As of March 1991, two vaccinations for *Haemophilus influenzae* infections have been approved for use in children younger than 15 months of age. ( ) = Indicated in many circumstances, depending on which vaccine for *Haemophilus influenzae* infections was previously given.
*Source:* American Academy of Pediatrics, AAP, 1991.

Aside from the devastating physical effects of this fatal disease, AIDS has severe psychological implications (Task Force on Pediatric AIDS of the American Psychological Association, 1989). For parents of a child with AIDS, who are themselves often limited in functioning because of drug use or lifestyle, caregiving is an even heavier burden. Most children with AIDS show developmental delays and often behave like younger, less competent children. Futhermore, the entire family may be stigmatized by the community, and the child may be shunned in the neighborhood or kept out of school, even though there is virtually no risk of infecting classmates. Infected preschoolers do not transmit the human immunodeficiency virus (HIV) to other people in the household, even when they share toys, toothbrushes, eating utensils, toilets, and bathtubs (Rogers et al., 1990).

### Accidental Injuries

Accidents are the leading cause of death in childhood, most often because of automobiles. All 50 states and the District of Columbia have laws requiring young children to be restrained in cars, either in specially designed seats or by standard seat belts (AAP, 1990). The *restraints* are effective: children who are *not* restrained are 11 times more likely to die in an automobile accident than children who are restrained (Decker, Dewey, Hutcheson, & Schaffner, 1984). However, the *laws* are not always effective. Active young children often rebel against the discomfort of wearing seat belts, and parents—to avoid argument—frequently give in. An Australian study found that educating preschoolers about the importance of wearing restraints was more effective than threatening parents with police checks and fines (Bowman, Sanson-Fisher, & Webb, 1987).

Most fatal accidents that do not take place in cars occur in and around the home: children are struck by cars, drown in bathtubs and pools (as well as in lakes, rivers, and oceans), are burned in fires and explosions, drink or eat poisonous substances, fall from heights, get caught in mechanical contrivances, and suffocate in traps like abandoned refrigerators.

Considering how many child-hours are spent at day care centers, it is not surprising that injury often occurs there, although day care poses no greater risk of injury than the home (Rivara, DiGuiseppi, Thompson, & Calonge, 1989). Almost half of all injuries at day care centers occur on playgrounds; 1 in 3 are from falls, often resulting in skull injury and brain damage (Sacks et al., 1989). Children would be protected somewhat by covering ground surfaces with impact-absorbing materials like wood chips, loose sand, or mats.

Children are naturally venturesome and unaware of danger. It is hard for parents and other caretakers to tread the delicate line between smothering children and exposing them to risk. A great deal of help is needed from society, in the form of laws like those requiring car restraints and "childproof" caps on medicine bottles.

## INFLUENCES ON HEALTH

Why do some children have more illnesses or injuries than others? Heredity contributes to some illness: some children seem to be predisposed toward some medical conditions. Such environmental factors as nutrition and physical care also make a difference. So does frequency of contact with other children, who may be harboring bacteria or viruses. Besides purely physical factors, family situations involving stress and economic hardship may make some children more prone to illness or injury than others.

### Exposure

Children in large families are sick more often than children in small families (Loda, 1980). And children in day care centers seem to pick up more colds, influenza, and other infections than children raised at home (Wald, Dashevsky, Byers, Guerra, & Taylor, 1988). They also have a higher risk of contracting more serious gastrointestinal diseases, hepatitis A, and meningitis (AAP, 1986c).

Caregivers can cut the rate of illness by more than half by teaching children how to wash their hands after using the toilet; washing their own hands frequently, especially after changing diapers; separating children in diapers from those who are toilet-trained; preparing food away from toilet areas; and discouraging children from sharing food. Safe playground equipment and supervision can help prevent falls and other injuries.

Children in high-quality day care (see Box 6-2 on page 201), where nutrition is well-planned and illnesses may be detected and treated early, tend to be healthier than those who are not in day care programs (AAP, 1986c).

### Stress

Stressful events in the family—like moves, job changes, divorce, and death—seem to increase the frequency of minor illnesses and home accidents. In one study, children whose families had experienced 12 or more such events were more than twice as likely to have to go into the hospital as children from families who had experienced fewer than 4 events (Beautrais, Fergusson, & Shannon, 1982).

Of course, such events also affect the adults in the family. Anything that reduces a parent's or caregiver's ability to cope may result in neglect of basic safety and sanitary precautions. A distraught adult is more likely than one who is not under stress to forget to put away a kitchen knife, fasten a gate, or make sure that a child washes before eating.

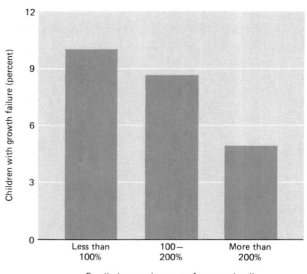

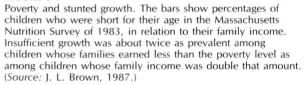

Family income (percent of poverty level)

**FIGURE 6-1**
Poverty and stunted growth. The bars show percentages of children who were short for their age in the Massachusetts Nutrition Survey of 1983, in relation to their family income. Insufficient growth was about twice as prevalent among children whose families earned less than the poverty level as among children whose family income was double that amount. (*Source:* J. L. Brown, 1987.)

### Poverty

Poverty is unhealthy. Income is the *chief* factor associated with ill health (J. L. Brown, 1987), and young children are the largest poverty group in the United States (NACHRI & AAP, 1990). Poor children often do not eat properly, do not grow properly, and do not get the immunizations or medical care they need. (Figure 6-1 shows the relationship between poverty and stunted growth.) Poor families often live in crowded, unsanitary housing, where parents are too busy trying to feed and clothe their children to supervise them adequately.

In 1989, in the relatively affluent United States, 1 in 4 children were poor, in terms of the official "poverty level" (about $12,500 a year for a family of four). In nearly half the states, children in two-parent homes did not qualify for welfare, no matter how poor they were (NACHRI & AAP, 1990). Minorities are especially at risk: about 43 percent of African American children and 40 percent of Hispanic children are poor, compared with fewer than 16 percent of white children.

The problems of poor children begin before birth. Poor mothers often do not eat well or receive adequate prenatal care, and their babies are likely to have low birthweight, to be stillborn, or to die soon after birth. Poor children are often malnourished, and malnourished children—and their mothers—tend to be weak and susceptible to disease. They are likely to suffer from such diverse maladies as lead poisoning, hearing and vision loss, and iron-deficiency anemia, as well as possibly stress-related conditions like asthma, headaches, insomnia, and irritable bowels. They also tend to have behavior problems, psychological disturbances, and learning disabilities (J. L. Brown, 1987; Egbuono & Starfield, 1982).

The United States lags behind Canada, France, Norway, England, and the Netherlands in rates of infant mortality, fatal childhood injuries, and immunization (Harvey, 1990). One solution for this would be a national children's health policy, which would include universal access to health care, computerized monitoring and tracking of immunizations, home visits from health professionals, enlightened policies of sex education, and networks of community services.

In view of the far-reaching effects of poverty and hunger on the bodies and minds of growing children, it is essential to make sure that every child has an adequate diet and adequate health care. All of society suffers when hunger and disease flourish.

### Homelessness

Children who do not even have a home to call their own are especially vulnerable. Families with children account for between one-third and three-fourths of the swelling ranks of the homeless in the United States today, whose number is estimated at from 350,000 to more than 3 million people (J. L. Bass, Brennan, Mehta, & Kodzis, 1990).

Most homeless children are under the age of 5. Since they are spending these crucial early years in an unstable, insecure, chaotic environment, it is not surprising that—both as preschoolers and as schoolchildren, they tend to have high rates of developmental delays, learning difficulties, and severe depression and anxiety. A study in Massachusetts found that about half the homeless children in 14 family shelters needed psychiatric referral (E. Bassuk & Rubin, 1987). Homeless youngsters showed more developmental and behavioral problems than poor children with homes, even though both groups had higher rates than children in general (E. L. Bassuk & Rosenberg, 1990).

The plight of homeless children is serious, but these families' very visible problem can be considered—and treated—as an "opportunity" to provide decent housing and adequate medical and social welfare services for them. If our government does not allocate enough resources to meet their needs, the prognosis for their individual futures and for the future of society is grave.

## MOTOR SKILLS

When we see what 3-year-olds can do, it's hard to realize that they were babes in arms just 3 years earlier and have been walking for only about 2 years. Tiffany puts on her older sister's tutu, stretches on tiptoe, and balances shakily on one foot; a few minutes later, she is back in overalls, riding her tricycle. With her stronger bones and muscles, greater lung power, and improved coordination between senses, limbs, and central nervous system, she can do more and more of the things she wants to do. Between the ages of 3 and 6, children continue to make important advances in motor development.

### LARGE-MUSCLE COORDINATION

At 3, David could walk a straight line and stand on one foot—but only for about 1 second. At 4, he could hop on one foot; and he could catch a ball his father bounced to him, with hardly any misses. On his fifth birthday, he could jump nearly 3 feet and was learning to roller-skate.

Such motor skills—advanced far beyond the reflexes of infancy—are required for sports, dancing, and other activities that begin during middle childhood and may last a lifetime. (See Table 6-2 on page 185 for a sampling of large-muscle skills that develop in early childhood.)

### SMALL-MUSCLE AND EYE-HAND COORDINATION

A few months ago, given a crayon and a large piece of paper, Winnie would cover the sheet with scribbles that only she could make sense of. Now, at age 3, she can draw a nearly straight line and a recognizable circle. At 4, Nelson can cut on a line with scissors, draw a person, make designs and crude letters, and fold paper into a double triangle. At 5, Juan can string beads and copy a square.

With their small muscles under control, children are able to tend to more of their own personal needs and so have a sense of competence and independence. By age 2 or 3, they use one hand more than the other (9 out of 10 are right-handed). At 3, Winnie can eat with a spoon and pour milk into her cereal bowl. She can button and unbutton her clothes well enough to dress herself without much help. She can use the toilet alone and can wash her hands afterward (with some reminding). By the time she starts kindergarten, she will be able to dress without supervision.

Children make significant advances in motor skills during the preschool years. As they develop physically, they are better able to make their bodies do what they want. Large-muscle development lets them run, jump, and hop, while increasing eye-hand coordination helps them to use scissors or chopsticks.

**TABLE 6–2**
LARGE-MUSCLE MOTOR SKILLS IN EARLY CHILDHOOD

| 3-Year-Olds | 4-Year-Olds | 5-Year-Olds |
|---|---|---|
| Cannot turn or stop suddenly or quickly | Have more effective control of stopping, starting, and turning | Start, turn, and stop effectively in games |
| Jump a distance of 15 to 24 inches | Jump a distance of 24 to 33 inches | Can make a running jump of 28 to 36 inches |
| Ascend a stairway unaided, alternating the feet | Descend a long stairway alternating the feet, if supported | Descend a long stairway unaided, alternating the feet |
| Can hop, using largely an irregular series of jumps with some variations added | Hop 4 to 6 steps on one foot | Easily hop a distance of 16 feet |

*Source:* Corbin, 1973.

## SLEEP: PATTERNS AND PROBLEMS

The baby who sleeps almost around the clock, waking up for feedings, grows into a toddler who sleeps 12 hours at night—plus 1 or 2 hours in the morning and afternoon; later, there is only one nap after lunch. By age 3, children often lie awake at nap time, but if they skip the nap altogether, they become fretful and cranky just before dinner. Food often perks them up for another couple of hours.

Sleep patterns change throughout life, and early childhood has its own distinct rhythms. Young children generally sleep deeply through the night—more so than they will later in life (Webb & Bonnet, 1979)—and they need a daytime nap or quiet rest until about age 5.

### NORMAL SLEEP PATTERNS

As children approach age 5, they try harder and harder to put off going to bed. They hate to part with a stimulating world full of people and be alone in their beds. Because of this, and because it now takes them longer to fall asleep, they often look for ways to postpone the inevitable. The elaborate bedtime routines that are common at this age also reflect children's increased mastery over the environment.

Children under age 2 will play quietly by themselves or with a sibling before falling asleep. Slightly older children are more likely to want a light left on in their rooms or to sleep with a favorite stuffed animal or blanket (Beltramini & Hertzig, 1983), and *everyone* loses sleep when a special "sleep pal" cannot go another day without being laundered—or is left behind when the family goes visiting. These **transitional objects** help

a child make the transition from the dependence of infancy to the independence of later childhood.

Anna falls asleep clutching her stuffed "Grover," but Diane and Jonathan are not worried that she will become too dependent on a *thing*. A longitudinal study found that children who had insisted on taking cuddly objects to bed at age 4 were outgoing, self-confident, and self-sufficient at age 11. They enjoyed playing by themselves and were not likely to be worriers; at 16, they were just as well adjusted as boys and girls who had not used transitional objects (Newson, Newson, & Mahalski, 1982).

### SLEEP DISTURBANCES

Sometimes more serious sleep problems develop during early or middle childhood. If they persist for a long time, they may be signs of emotional difficulties.

A child who demands a night-light may simply be trying to put off going to sleep. But many youngsters are afraid of being left alone in the dark, and it is important to know that bedtime fears can be treated. In one program, children who had had severe and chronic fears for an average of 5 years starting between the ages of 1 and 8 learned how to relax, how to substitute pleasant thoughts for frightening ones, and how to give themselves verbal instructions for coping with stressful situations (Graziano & Mooney, 1982).

Many children—from 20 to 30 percent of those in their first 4 years of life—engage in long bedtime struggles (lasting more than an hour) and wake their parents frequently at night. The problem tends to be at its worst between ages 2 and 4. These children have often gone through such stresses as an accident or illness in the family, a depressed or ambivalent mother, or a mother's sudden absence during the day. In addition, they often sleep in the same bed with their parents—though this may be a reaction to, rather than a cause of, disturbed sleep (Lozoff, Wolf, & Davis, 1985).

The most effective way to eliminate bedtime temper tantrums seems to involve setting a regular routine, in which the parents change the bedtime to coincide with the usual time the child falls asleep, and precede that with about 20 minutes of four to seven quiet activities, like brushing teeth, reading a story, and a goodnight kiss (L. A. Adams & Rickert, 1989).

About 1 in 4 children between ages 3 and 8 (most of them under age 6), have nightmares or night terrors (Hartmann, 1981). Nightmares are frightening dreams, often brought on by staying up too late, eating a heavy meal close to bedtime, or overexcitement. Upon awakening, a child can often recall the nightmare vividly. An occasional bad dream is no cause for alarm. Anna, at age 4, for example, went through a brief period of having nightmares about spiders, but they disappeared as suddenly as they had begun. Frequent nightmares, however, especially if they produce fear or anxiety during waking hours, may signal excessive stress.

Night terrors are not connected with dreams; they seem to result from waking suddenly from deep sleep. Children wake in an unexplained state of panic. They may scream and sit up in bed, breathing rapidly and staring ahead unseeing, yet they are not aware of any frightening dreams or thoughts. They go back to sleep quickly, and in the morning they remember nothing. These episodes, which alarm parents more than children, are rarely serious and usually stop by themselves.

*Sleepwalking*—literally, walking while asleep—is fairly common in children, is usually harmless, and is usually outgrown (T. Anders, Caraskadon, & Dement, 1980). Nothing needs to be done besides "sleepwalk-proofing" the home with gates at the top of stairs and in front of windows. *Sleeptalking*—talking while asleep—is also rarely related to any problem and rarely requires any corrective action.

### BED-WETTING

Most children stay dry, day and night, by the age of 3 to 5 years; but **enuresis,** repeated urination during the day or night in clothing or in bed, is common, especially at night. Enuresis is of concern if it occurs at least twice a month after age 5. About 7 percent of 5-year-old boys and 3 percent of girls wet the bed; by age 10, the proportion is 3 percent of boys and 2 percent of girls (*Diagnostic and Statistical Manual of Mental Disorders*, 3d ed., rev., DSM III-R, 1987). Most outgrow the habit

without any special help. Fewer than 1 percent of bed-wetters have any physical disorder; the causes in the other 99 percent are thought to be heredity and developmental delay, not psychological dynamics.

Enuresis runs in families. About 75 percent of bed-wetters have a close relative who also wet the bed, and identical twins are more concordant for enuresis than fraternal twins (DSM III-R, 1987). Among more than 1000 children in New Zealand, family history was the strongest predictor of childhood bed-wetting (Fergusson, Horwood, & Shannon, 1986). Biological factors also seemed crucial. Children who were small at birth, slept more at ages 1 and 2, and developed slowly in the first 3 years attained bladder control later, with boys slightly slower than girls. The only significant environmental influence was age of toilet training; when this began after 18 months, it took the child longer to attain bladder control. The only emotional factor in bed-wetting seems to be its tendency to recur in children who have already had the problem, especially at times of upset over such events as the birth of a sibling or entering school (DSM III-R, 1987).

Bed-wetting is common and not serious, and the child should not be blamed or punished. Parents need not do anything about it unless the child sees it as a problem. The most effective treatments include rewarding children for staying dry; waking them when they begin to urinate by using electric devices that ring bells or buzzers; administering drugs (as a last resort, no more than 6 months after the last occurrence, and then tapered off—McDaniel, 1986); and teaching children to practice controlling the sphincter muscles.

## INTELLECTUAL DEVELOPMENT

At the breakfast table, Terry, aged 3½, overhears his grandparents discussing the number of square feet of tile in their kitchen. In his small voice he pipes, "But then you'd need to have square shoes!" Later that morning he takes the P from his set of magnetic letters and puts it under his doll's mattress to find out whether the doll is a real princess. He defines spareribs as "sideways rectangle things with a bone in the middle."

Terry's growing facility with speech and ideas is helping him form his own unique view of the world—in ways that often surprise adults. From ages 3 to 6, Terry becomes more competent in cognition, intelligence, language, and learning. He is developing the ability to use symbols in thought and action, and to handle such concepts as age, time, and space more efficiently.

# ASPECTS OF INTELLECTUAL DEVELOPMENT

## DEVELOPMENT OF MEMORY: INFORMATION PROCESSING

When Anna was 3 years old, she went on a trip with her preschool class to pick apples. Months later, she would still talk about riding on the bus, visiting the farm, picking the apples, bringing them home, and eating them. She clearly had vivid memories of the event.

Until recently, the kinds of things children ordinarily remember were rarely studied. Before the mid-1960s, there was very little research on memory in children younger than 5; and until about the 1980s, most of that research was done in the artificial setting of the psychological laboratory rather than in the real world.

Now, with a recent surge in interest in the development of memory, we have a clear picture of the "remembering child." When young children are tested by methods that identify their abilities, they turn out to have better memories than was once thought. Their ability to remember continues to develop, becoming even more efficient in middle childhood. Let's now see what memory is like in early childhood.

### Types of Memory: Recognition and Recall

At all ages, people can recognize better than they can recall. **Recognition** is the ability to identify something that has been encountered before (like distinguishing in an array of pictures those you have seen before and those that are new). **Recall** is the ability to reproduce knowledge from memory (like describing pictures you have seen after they are no longer present). Two-year-olds average about 80 percent correct on recognition tasks, but on average they recall only just over 20 percent of nine items. Four-year-olds average about 90 percent correct on recognition tasks; they recall best the last item presented. Older children remember significantly more items in the other eight positions than younger ones do (N. Myers & Perlmutter, 1978).

### Influences on Children's Memory

#### "Mastery motivation" and study activities

Some researchers have proposed that older children recall better than younger ones because they have a larger base of information (N. Myers & Perlmutter, 1978). However, new studies suggest that older children remember better than younger ones, and that some children remember better than others of the same age, because of two other factors—a child's motivation to master skills in general and the child's way of approaching a specific task (Lange, MacKinnon, & Nida, 1989).

These conclusions emerged from studies of ninety-three 3- and 4-year-olds. During three sessions over a 4-month period, the children were tested on their knowledge of a variety of objects, were assessed on how reflective or impulsive they were, were videotaped to analyze how they did two tasks presented to them, and were rated by both preschool teachers and parents on such characteristics as "takes initiative in carrying out activities," "uses problem-solving strategies," and "tries to pursue difficult tasks." One of the two tasks involved putting together a picture puzzle. In the other, the children were shown an array of toys, which they were permitted to handle before the toys were taken away and replaced by a set of new toys; the children were asked to label these new toys before they too were removed. Finally, the children were asked to recall what the toys were. The videotapes showed what the children did with the toys—how much they looked at them, picked them up, and moved them around; how they grouped and named them; and whether they repeated the names of the toys to themselves. Not surprisingly, children varied considerably in these activities.

The best predictor of how well a child remembered the names of the toys was "mastery motivation," that is, a child's tendency to be independent, self-directed, and generally resourceful (as rated by the child's teacher, *not* the parents). The only other factor related to recall was the child's activities while studying the toys. Children who named the toys, grouped the toys, or spent time thinking about the names of the toys or repeating those names to themselves (in other words, used strategies to help them remember) recalled better than children who did less of these specific activities. These two factors did not seem to be related to each other—that is, "mastery motivation" did not seem to encourage use of particular study activities (Lange et al., 1989).

#### General knowledge

It stands to reason that the more familiar children are with items, the better they should be able to remember them. Early studies found that young children recalled material better when items bore an understandable relation to each other. When 3-year-olds and 4-year-olds in one study were shown pairs of pictures, they did much better recalling pairs that were related in some way than pairs that were unrelated (Staub, 1973). Also, children remembered pictures in which one member of the pair was a part of the other (like a tire and a car)

"Remember the giraffe?" Young children remember better events that are unique and new, and they may recall many details from a trip to the zoo for a year or longer.

better than those in which one item was the usual habitat of the other (like a fish and a lake), and they remembered to a lesser degree those in which the two items belonged to the same category (like a hat and a sock). This suggests that the more children know about the world and what is in it, the better are their tools for remembering.

### Unusual activities and new experiences

Anna's memory of picking apples is an example of a finding that children as young as 3 years remember events better that are unique and new, and may recall many details from, say, a trip to the zoo or to an unusual museum for a year or longer (Fivush, Hudson, & Nelson, 1983). They also remember events that recur regularly (having lunch, going to the beach, or attending a series of workshops), but one such occasion tends to blur into another.

The new trend toward naturalistic research has confirmed this. One study found that preschoolers tend to remember activities they took part in better than objects they saw (D. C. Jones, Swift, & Johnson, 1988). Sixty-five 3- and 4½-year-olds visited a child-size replica of a turn-of-the-century farmhouse, where they took part in five activities, including pretending to sew a blanket on a treadle sewing machine and chopping ice with a pick and hammer. Then they were interviewed— some later the same day, some 1 week later, and some 8 weeks later—to determine what they remembered. There were very few age differences in the children's memories of what they had *done*. However, the older

children were better at recalling objects they had seen and objects they had handled (like the blanket). The best-remembered objects were those that the children had used to *do* something (like the sewing machine).

### Social interactions

The way people talk with a child about an event also influences how well the child will remember it. In one field experiment, ten 3-year-olds and their mothers visited a natural history museum (Tessler, in Nelson, 1989). Half the mothers talked naturally with their children as they walked through the museum. The other half, as requested, did not open discussions but only responded to their children's comments. All the conversations were tape-recorded. A week later the researchers interviewed the mothers and children separately and asked 30 questions about objects seen the week before. The results were dramatic. The children remembered *only* those objects that they had talked about with their mothers. Furthermore, the children in the "natural conversation" group remembered better.

In this study, the mothers' styles of talking to the children also had an effect. Four of the mothers had a narrative style, reminiscing about shared experiences ("Remember when we went to Vermont and saw Cousin Bill?"); six mothers had a more practical style, using memory for a specific purpose like solving a problem ("Where does this puzzle piece go? You remember we did that one yesterday"). The children of the "narrative" mothers averaged 13 correct answers, compared with fewer than 5 for the children of the "practical" mothers.

## COGNITIVE DEVELOPMENT: PIAGET'S PREOPERATIONAL STAGE

Although Piaget made his observations of children's intellectual development long before the recent research on memory, the growth of recall is fundamental to his description of the way thought develops during early childhood. When children can recall events and objects, they can begin to form and use concepts—representations of things not present at the moment. Their communication improves as they become able to share their representational systems with others.

Children between ages 3 and 6 are in Piaget's second major stage of cognitive development, the preoperational stage. In western cultures, children enter this stage at about age 2, as they leave the sensorimotor stage; they enter the third stage, concrete operations, at about age 6 or 7. (Ages at which individual children move from one stage to another vary.)

As we saw in Chapter 4, Piaget held that symbolic thought begins in the sixth and last substage of the sensorimotor period, when toddlers begin to generate ideas and solve problems through mental representations. But he said that in the sensorimotor stage, such representations are limited to things that are physically present. In the **preoperational stage,** children can think about objects, people, or events that are absent, by using mental representations. (They cannot yet manipulate those representations through logic, however, as they will be able to do in the stage of concrete operations, which they reach in middle childhood; see Chapter 8.) The preoperational stage is a significant step beyond the sensorimotor period because preoperational children can learn not only by sensing and doing but also by thinking symbolically, and not only by acting but also by reflecting on their actions.

### The Symbolic Function

The major important development of the preoperational stage is the **symbolic function:** the ability to learn by using symbols. A **symbol** is a mental representation to which, consciously or unconsciously, a person has attached meaning. It is something that stands for something else. According to Piaget, symbolic thought begins at about 1½ to 2 years, but really comes into its own between ages 2 and 6.

Symbols allow us to think about objects or events without actually having them in front of us. An object can be a symbol, taking on in people's minds the qualities of whatever it stands for. (This is why there is such controversy about how a piece of cloth with stripes and stars on it is treated. It would not be such an emotional issue if, in people's minds, the flag did not symbolize

As Anna pretends to take Grover's blood pressure, she is showing a major cognitive achievement, deferred imitation—the ability to act out an action she observed some time before.

the United States of America.) But the most common symbol—and probably the most important one for thought—is the word, at first spoken and then written. When 2-year-old Cherie hears the word *apple,* she thinks of something round and red and good to eat, and runs to the kitchen; when Anna, 4, hears the word *apple,* she remembers the trip she took with her class. Knowing the symbols for things helps us to think about them, to incorporate their qualities, to remember them, and to communicate with other people about them. Symbolic thought is, therefore, a great advance over the sensorimotor stage.

Three ways in which children show the symbolic function are deferred imitation, symbolic play, and language. **Deferred imitation** is imitation of an observed action after time has passed. Keith, aged 3, sees his father shaving. Later, at his preschool, he heads for the housekeeping corner and begins to "shave." According to Piaget, Keith saw the shaving, formed and stored a mental symbol of it (probably a visual image), and later—when he could no longer see it—reproduced the behavior by calling up the stored symbol.

In **symbolic play,** children make an object stand for something else. Anna, 4, makes her finger stand for a bottle, and she "feeds" her doll by putting her finger to its mouth. Her laughter as she does this shows that she knows her finger is not really a bottle.

The symbolic function is most impressive in language. Preoperational children use language to stand for absent things and for events that are not taking place at the time. By using the words *apple tree* to stand for something that was not there, Anna invested an utterance with symbolic character.

## Achievements of Preoperational Thought

By using symbols based on recall, preoperational children think in new and creative ways. Although their thinking is not yet fully logical, it does show partial logic. Let us see how a child at this preoperational level of cognitive development thinks.

### Understanding of functions

Early in the preoperational stage, a child understands, in a general way, basic functional relationships between things and events. For example, Tanya, age 3, knows that when she pulls a cord, the curtain opens; and that when she flicks a switch, the light goes on. Although she does not yet understand fully how one action causes the other, she does perceive a connection between them.

### Understanding of identities

Rico, aged 5, now understands that certain things stay the same even though they may change in form, size, or appearance. For example, the day Pumpkin, his cat, was nowhere to be found, Rico suggested, "Maybe Pumpkin put on a bear suit and went to someone else's house to be their pet bear." When his baby-sitter questioned him about this possible turn of events, however, Rico showed that he still believed Pumpkin would, even underneath her disguise, continue to be his beloved cat.

Rico also knows that even though he has grown and changed since he was a baby, he is still Rico. In the early part of the preoperational stage, however, he may still believe he can change certain aspects of his identity that are in fact unchangeable. For example, at times he may believe that he will turn into a girl if he does "girlish" things like wearing girls' clothes, or if he *wants* to turn into a girl (R. DeVries, 1969).

## Limitations of Preoperational Thought

In some ways, of course, preoperational thinking is still rudimentary compared with what children will be able to do when they reach the stage of concrete operations in middle childhood. For example, preoperational children do not yet clearly differentiate reality from fantasy. What are some other ways in which, according to Piaget, children in this stage are intellectually different from older children?

### Centration

Preoperational children tend to **centrate:** they focus on one aspect of a situation and neglect others, often coming to illogical conclusions. They cannot **decenter,** or think simultaneously about several aspects of a situation.

A classic example is Piaget's most famous experiment. He designed it to test children's development of **conservation**—the awareness that two things that are equal remain so if their shape is altered so long as nothing is added or taken away. He found that children do not fully understand this principle until the stage of concrete operations, normally in middle childhood.

Let's consider a typical conservation experiment (see Figure 6-2). A child, Nils, is shown two identical clear glasses, both short and wide and holding the same amount of water. Then the water in one glass is poured into a third glass—say, a tall, thin one. Nils is now asked whether both glasses contain the same amount of water, or whether one contains more. In early childhood—even after watching an experimenter pour the water out of one of the short, fat glasses into a tall, thin glass or even after pouring it himself—Nils will say that the taller glass (or the wide glass) contains more water. When asked why, he says, "This one is bigger this way," stretching his arms to show height (or width). Preoperational children cannot consider height and width at the same time. They center on one aspect or the other and so cannot understand what is happening. Their logic is flawed because their thinking is tied to what they "see"; if one glass *looks* bigger, they seem to think it must *be* bigger.

### Irreversibility

Preoperational children's logic is also limited by **irreversibility:** failure to understand that an operation can go two ways. Once a child can conceptualize restoring the original state of the water by pouring it back into the other glass, he or she will realize that the amount of water in both glasses is the same. The preoperational child does not realize this.

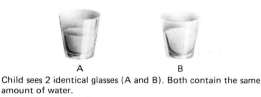

Child sees 2 identical glasses (A and B). Both contain the same amount of water.

As child watches, experimenter pours water from B into a different glass of a different shape (B¹). Or child does the pouring.

Experimenter asks child: "Do both glasses have the same amount of water, or does one glass have more?"

Preoperational child says, "B¹ has more." Asked why, child says, "It's taller." (Child is fooled by appearance.)

Concrete operational child says, "They're both the same." Asked why, child says, "You didn't add anything," or "B¹ is taller, but thinner." or "You can pour the water back from B¹ into B."

**FIGURE 6-2**
Piaget's most famous experiment: A test of conservation.

### Focus on states rather than on transformations

Preoperational children think as if they were watching a filmstrip with a series of static frames. They focus on successive states and are not able to understand the meaning of the transformation from one state to another. We saw this in the experiment with conservation (refer back to Figure 6-2). Preoperational children do not grasp the meaning of pouring the water from the original glass to the new one. That is, they do not understand the implication of transforming B into B¹—that even though the appearance changes, the amount does not.

### Transductive reasoning

Logical reasoning is of two basic types: deduction and induction. Deduction goes from the general to the particular: "Eating a lot of candy can make people sick. I ate a lot of candy today, and so I may get sick." Induction goes from the particular to the general: "Yesterday I ate a lot of candy and felt sick. Last week I ate a lot of candy and felt sick. The same thing happened to Emily and Bret. Therefore it looks as if eating a lot of candy can make people sick."

Preoperational children, said Piaget, do not think along either of these lines. Instead, they reason by **transduction:** they move from one particular to another particular without taking the general into account. This kind of reasoning leads Adam to see a causal relationship where none actually exists: "I had bad thoughts about my sister. My sister got sick. Therefore, I made my sister sick." Because the bad thoughts and the sister's sickness occurred around the same time, Adam assumes illogically that one caused the other (compare Adam's thinking here with his confusion in Box 6-1).

### Egocentrism

At age 4, Sally's daughter Jenny was at the beach. Awed by the constant thundering of the waves, she turned to her father and asked, "But when does it stop?" "It doesn't," he replied. "Not even when we're *asleep?*" asked Jenny incredulously. Her thinking was so egocentric, so focused on herself as the center of her universe, that she could not consider anything—even the mighty ocean—as continuing its motion when she was not there to see it.

**Egocentrism** is an inability to see things from another's point of view. A classic Piagetian experiment known as the *mountain task* illustrates egocentric thinking (see Figure 6-3 on page 192). A child would sit on a chair facing a table on which were three large mounds. The experimenter would place a doll on an-

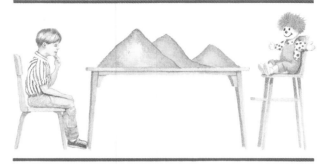

**FIGURE 6-3**
Piaget's mountain task. A preoperational child is unable to describe the "mountain" from the doll's point of view—an indication of egocentrism.

other chair, on the opposite side of the table, and would ask the child to tell or show how the "mountains" looked to the doll. Young children could not answer the question; instead, they persistently described the mountains from their own perspective. Piaget took this as proof that they could not imagine a different point of view (Piaget & Inhelder, 1967).

Egocentrism, to Piaget, is not selfishness but self-centered understanding, and it is fundamental to the limited thinking of young children. Egocentrism is a form of centration: these children are so centered on their own point of view that they cannot take in another's view at the same time. Three-year-olds are not as egocentric as newborn babies, who cannot distinguish between the universe and their own bodies; but young children still think that the universe centers on them. This inability to decenter helps explain why they have trouble separating reality from what goes on inside their own heads and why they show confusion about what causes what. When Adam believes that his "bad thoughts" have made his sister sick, he is thinking egocentrically. Egocentrism, for Piaget, explains why young children often talk to themselves or seem to "talk past" other people.

### Assessing Piaget's Theory

Did Piaget underestimate children's abilities? No thinker about cognitive development during early childhood has been more influential than Piaget. Yet recent research suggests that the cognitive abilities of children he would categorize as "preoperational" may be far greater than he supposed.

One problem seems to have been his tendency to *over*estimate young children's understanding of language. He assumed that wrong answers revealed faults

in thinking, when some of the errors may actually have arisen from the way he phrased the questions. In many of his experiments, children apparently misinterpreted tasks they were asked to do and answered questions that may not have been the ones the experimenter was asking.

### Do young children understand cause and effect?

Young children apparently have more understanding of cause and effect than Piaget thought. One psychologist, who looked up some of the stories Piaget had asked children to retell, found that she had trouble remembering them herself. When she simplified the stories to clarify cause-and-effect connections, first-graders had no trouble retelling them correctly (Mandler, in Pines, 1983).

To eliminate the complicating factor of language, other researchers asked 3- and 4-year-olds to look at pictures like those on the top in Figure 6-4, and then to choose the picture on the bottom that would tell "what happened" (Gelman, Bullock, & Meck, 1980). These children showed an understanding of causality, telling stories like: "First you have dry glasses, and then water gets on the glasses, and you end up with wet glasses."

Story A

Choices for A

**FIGURE 6-4**
Examples of sequences to test understanding of causality. A child is asked to look at pictures like those in the top row, to pick the one in the bottom row that would show what happened, and to tell a story about what happened. (*Source:* Gelman, Bullock, & Meck, 1980.)

When we listen to children talk, we hear them spontaneously using such words as *because* and *so*. "He's crying because he doesn't want to put his pajamas on—he wants to be naked," said Diane's niece Marie, 27 months old, watching her twin brother's bedtime struggle. Even at this early age, children seem to understand some causal relationships, long before they can answer adults' "why" questions.

### How animistic are young children?

**Animism** is a tendency to attribute life to objects that are not alive. When Piaget asked children about the sun, the wind, and clouds, the answers he received led him to think that young children are confused about what is alive and what is not. Piaget attributed this to egocentrism; one child, for example, said that the moon is alive "because we are."

However, when a later researcher questioned 3- and 4-year-olds about differences between a rock, a person, and a doll, the children showed that they understood that people are alive and rocks are not (Gelman, Spelke, & Meck, 1983). They did not attribute thoughts or emotions to rocks, and they talked about the fact that dolls cannot move on their own as evidence that dolls are not alive. The confusion Piaget observed may have been due to the fact that the objects he asked about are all capable of movement and, in addition, are very far away. Since children know so little about sun, wind, and clouds, they are less certain about the nature of these phenomena than about the nature of more familiar objects like rocks and dolls.

Even 3-year-olds realize that animals can go uphill by themselves and that statues (even statues that look like animals), wheeled vehicles, and rigid objects cannot, showing an understanding of which things are capable of independent movement (Massey & Gelman, 1988). When faced with an array of photos of such objects, children of this age are not always accurate in *saying* which ones are alive and which are not, but many know which ones can do things that live creatures can do and which cannot.

### How egocentric are young children?

Let's consider a variation on Piaget's mountain task. A child is seated in front of a square board, with dividers that separate it into four equal sectors. A figure of a police officer is put at the edge of the board. Then a doll is put into one of the sectors after another, and each time, the child is asked whether the police officer can see the doll. Another police officer is then brought into the action, and the child is told to hide the doll from both police officers. When 30 children between the ages of 3½ and 5 were given this task, they gave the correct answer or did the right thing 90 percent of the time (Hughes, 1975).

Why were these children able to take another person's point of view—in this case the police officer's—whereas children doing Piaget's classic mountain task were not? The difference may be that this task calls for thinking about more familiar, less abstract materials. Most children do not look at mountains and do not think about what other people might see when looking at a mountain, but even 3-year-olds know about dolls and police officers and hiding.

Another example—from real life rather than the laboratory—shows a similar ability to take another viewpoint. When Anna, 4, was going back to the United States with her parents after a family visit to England, she said, "Don't be sad, Grandma. We'll come see you again. And you can come see us in New York." Anna's grandmother had not cried or talked about feeling sad, but Anna imagined how she must have been feeling. When children are in situations that are familiar and important to them, they are likely to show *empathy*—the ability to put themselves into another's place. Even 10- to 12-month-old babies often cry when they see another child crying; by 13 or 14 months, they pat or hug a crying child; by 18 months, they may hold out a new toy to replace a broken one or give a bandage to someone with a cut finger (Yarrow, 1978).

### How well can young children classify?

Researchers today also differ with Piaget on children's ability to classify. Piaget identified three stages of classification (Inhelder & Piaget, 1964):

- *Stage 1 (2½ to 5 years)*. Children group items to form a design or figure (like a house); or they group them according to criteria that keep changing (like adding a blue square to a red square because they are both squares and then adding a red triangle to the group because it is red, like the red square).
- *Stage 2 (5 to 7 or 8 years)*. Children group by similarity but may switch criteria in midtask, sorting some groups by color and others by shape or size. They often subclassify: they may put all the red items into one group and then group the red squares, triangles, and circles.
- *Stage 3 (7 to 8 years)*. At the stage of concrete operations, children are truly classifying. They *start out* with a plan to group items by two criteria (like color and shape), showing that they understand the relationships between classes and subclasses.

These children's building of a tower shows that they can classify by at least two different attributes—in this case, by color and size.

- Level 1—Single-category grouping (average age 16.04 months). The child moves 4 objects of one kind and groups them together.
- Level 2—Serial touching (average age 16.39 months). The child touches first 4 items from one group and then 4 from the other group.
- Level 3—Two-category grouping (average age 17.24 months). The child moves all 8 objects and either sorts them into two distinct groups or establishes one-to-one correspondence (like putting each of the 4 dolls on top of a red car).

At about 18 months babies typically go through a "naming explosion" when they suddenly acquire many new words with which to label objects. This interest in naming things seems to show that babies now realize that objects belong to different categories. It is not surprising that they develop two-category classification at about the same time as they feverishly try to name all the objects in their world. They seem "to want to divide the world into 'natural kinds,' both in word and in deed" (Gopnik & Meltzoff, 1987, p. 1530).

### Can cognitive abilities be accelerated?

Programs to teach specific cognitive abilities do seem to work when a child is already on the verge of acquiring the concept being taught. However, certain kinds of training are more effective than others.

In one experiment to teach conservation (D. Field, 1981), 3- and 4-year-olds were shown various arrangements of such items as checkers, candies, jacks, sticks, and rods. The child was asked to pick the two rows that had the same number of items or to show which two objects were the same length. Then the objects were moved or changed in some way, and the child was asked whether they were the same as before (see Figure 6-5).

The child was then given one of three rules to explain why items that did not appear the same might *be* the same:

1 *Identity*—sameness of the materials. "No matter where you put them, they're still the same candies."
2 *Reversibility*—the possibility of returning the items to their original arrangement. "Look, we just have to put the sticks back together to see that they are the same length."
3 *Compensation*—showing that a change in one dimension was balanced by a change in the other. "Yes, this stick does go farther in this direction, but at the other end the stick is going farther, and so they balance each other."

Researchers after Piaget, however, have found that many 4-year-olds can classify by two criteria (Denney, 1972) and that children can begin to classify early in the second year of life (Gopnik & Meltzoff, 1987).

In one study, researchers brought 12 babies (whose average age was 15½ months at the beginning of the study) into the laboratory and set out three different sets of 8 objects, 4 of one kind and 4 of another. The sets included (1) 4 flat yellow rectangles and 4 brightly colored plastic people figures, (2) 4 clear pillboxes and 4 balls of red modeling clay, and (3) 4 rag dolls and 4 red cars. The children were told to "play with these things" or "fix them all up." The problems, posed at 3-week intervals and continuing until every baby had passed a series of cognitive tests, elicited an unvarying sequence of classification ability:

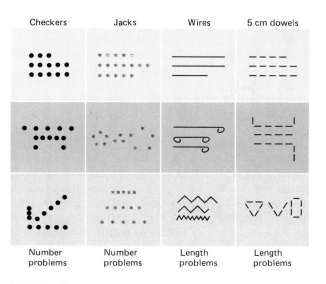

| Checkers | Jacks | Wires | 5 cm dowels |

Number problems | Number problems | Length problems | Length problems

**FIGURE 6-5**
Examples of conservation training problems. In these experiments, a child was shown arrangements of items like those in the top row, and then was shown rearrangements of the same objects (as in the second or third row) and asked whether they were the same. The child was then told why they were the same on the basis of identity, reversibility, or compensation. Identity was the strongest concept for teaching conservation. (*Source*: D. Field, 1977.)

The children who were given the identity rule made the most progress in learning the principle of conservation. Those who learned reversibility also advanced, but those who were taught compensation benefited little from the training.

The 4-year-olds (who presumably were closer to acquiring conservation on their own) were more apt than the 3-year-olds to learn the concept and to retain it up to 5 months later. The 3-year-olds were not able to conserve as many quantities and tended to lose whatever abilities they did gain. This kind of training seems, then, to benefit children only when their intellectual structures are well enough developed to handle the principle of conservation. The training then gives them a strategy for integrating it into their thought processes (D. Field, 1981).

Such experiments suggest that young children are more competent than Piaget believed. "Preoperational" children do, of course, have more cognitive limitations than children in the next higher phase of development, which Piaget identified as the concrete operations stage. However, when faced with tasks compatible with what they are familiar with and explained in language they understand, they show greater competence than they do on traditional Piagetian tasks. Our estimation of young children's intellectual abilities has changed for the better as a result of new, more age-appropriate research techniques.

## DEVELOPMENT OF LANGUAGE

"Why is the sky?" "When is tomorrow? "Where do clouds go?" Young children are interested in the whole wide world, and they ask questions about everything— partly because they are hungry for knowledge and partly because they quickly learn that asking "why" will almost always keep a conversation going. At the beginning of early childhood, children can give and follow commands that include more than one step, like "Pick up your toys and put them in the closet." And they can name familiar things like pets, body parts, and people. Their linguistic skills progress rapidly through early childhood.

### Using Words, Sentences, and Grammar

Speech becomes more adult once children pass the age of 3. Children over 3 use plurals and the past tense, and they know the difference between *I, you,* and *we.*

Between ages 4 and 5, children's sentences average four to five words. They can now deal with prepositions like *over, under, in, on,* and *behind.*

Between ages 5 and 6, children use longer and more complex sentences. They can define simple words, and they know some opposites. They use more conjunctions, prepositions, and articles.

Between 6 and 7 years of age, children's speech becomes quite sophisticated. They now speak in grammatically correct compound and complex sentences, and they use all parts of speech.

Although young children speak fluently, understandably, and fairly grammatically, they often make errors by failing to note exceptions to rules. A mistake like saying "holded" instead of "held" or "hurted" instead of "hurt" is a normal sign of progress in learning a language. Younger children correctly say, "I held the baby" or "I hurt myself," but at that point they are merely repeating expressions they have heard. When children begin to discover rules (like adding *-ed* for past tense), they tend to *overregularize*—that is, to use a rule on all occasions. This is appropriate most of the time, but not with, say, irregular verbs like *to hold* and *to hurt.* Eventually, as children hear people talking and take part in conversations themselves, they notice that *-ed* is not always used to form the past tense of a verb. Thus we might think of such "mistakes" as a case of taking one step backward in order to take two steps forward.

From a very early age, children communicate through social speech. They take into account other people's needs and use words to establish and maintain social contacts. Whatever these tots are talking about seems engrossing enough to interrupt their seesawing.

## Speaking to Others

The form and function of speech are linked. As children master words, sentences, and grammar, they communicate better. **Social speech** is intended to be understood by someone other than the speaker. It takes other people's needs into account and is used to establish and maintain communication with others. It must be adapted to the other person's speech patterns and behavior. It may take the form of questions and answers or other means of exchanging information, or it may involve criticism, commands, requests, or threats.

Piaget characterized most of young children's speech as egocentric (not adapted to the listener), but recent research suggests that children's speech is quite social from an early age (see Table 6-3). When 3- to 5-year-olds were asked to communicate their choice of a toy, they behaved very differently with a person who could see and with one who could not. They pointed to the toy for a sighted listener, but described it to a blindfolded listener (Maratsos, 1973). In addition, 4-year-olds use "motherese" (see Chapter 4) when speaking to 2-year-olds (Shatz & Gelman, 1973). And even 2-year-olds use social speech as they point out or show objects to others. Most of the time (almost 80 percent in one study), the feedback they get shows that they have captured their listeners' attention (Wellman & Lempers, 1977).

Children's general knowledge affects their ability to communicate. Asked to describe a variety of pictures, 4½-year-olds did very well with simple, familiar subjects like monkeys and people but not with abstract designs (Dickson, 1979). Even youngsters as old as 14 were unable to describe unusual designs clearly enough for others of their age to understand (Krauss & Glucksberg, 1977).

Children's ability to communicate is related to their popularity with their peers—one more example of the close tie between cognitive and emotional aspects of development. Well-liked preschoolers can start and keep up conversations better than less popular children, who are not as good at adapting the way they speak to the needs of a listener and the demands of a situation (Hazen & Black, 1989).

Research suggests, however, that when children do not communicate with others, it is usually not because they are unable to but because they do not intend to. In one study, 3- to 5-year-old lower- and middle-class urban children had little trouble making themselves understood when they *tried* to communicate with others (Berk, 1986). But sometimes children engage in *private speech*—they are not trying to communicate with anyone else.

**TABLE 6–3**
DEVELOPMENT OF SOCIAL SPEECH

| Age | Characteristics of Speech |
|---|---|
| 2½ | *Beginnings of conversation:* Speech is increasingly relevant to others' remarks. Need for clarity is being recognized. |
| 3 | *Breakthrough in attention to communication:* Child seeks ways to clarify and correct misunderstandings. Pronunciation and grammar improve markedly. Speech with children the same age expands dramatically. Use of language as instrument of control increases. |
| 4 | *Knowledge of fundamentals of conversation:* Child shifts speech according to listener's knowledge. Literal definitions are no longer a sure guide to meaning. Disputes can be resolved with words. |
| 5 | *Good control of elements of conversation.* |

*Source:* Adapted from E. B. Bolles, 1982, p. 93.

## Speaking to Oneself

As Sergei, 4 years old, picks up his friend Dorri's art book, he says quietly to himself, "Now I can use this—I washed my hands so now they're clean and I can hold this book." As he jumps on Dorri's bed, he says—also to himself—"I have to take my shoes off to do this. I took them off, so now I can jump."

*Private speech*—talking aloud to oneself with no intent to communicate with others—is normal and common in early and middle childhood. Twenty to sixty percent of what children say at these ages consists of private utterances, ranging from playful rhythmic repetition (something like babies' babbling) to the kind of "thinking out loud" Sergei does or barely audible muttering.

What is the function of private speech? Piaget considered it an egocentric inability to recognize another person's viewpoint and therefore an inability to communicate. He believed that young children talk while they do things because they do not yet fully differentiate between words, or symbols, and what the words represent.

On the other hand, the Russian psychologist Lev Vygotsky (1962) saw private speech as a special form of communication: communication with oneself. Like Piaget, he believed that private speech helps children integrate language with thought. But unlike Piaget, he believed that private speech *increases* through the early school years as children use it to guide and master their actions, and then fades away as they establish internal control through silent thought.

A number of studies support Vygotsky's position. Among nearly 150 middle-class children 4 to 10 years old, not only did private speech rise and then fall with age, but the most sociable children used the most private speech—apparently confirming Vygotsky's view that private speech is stimulated by social experience (Berk, 1986; Kohlberg, Yaeger, & Hjertholm, 1968). Private speech peaked earliest—around age 4—for the brightest children and between ages 5 and 7 for the average child; it was virtually nonexistent by age 9.

A similar but slower pattern appeared among low-income 5- to 10-year-olds in the Appalachian mountains of Kentucky; 25 percent of the children (especially boys) in this largely nonverbal culture still used private speech at age 10. These youngsters talked to themselves most when they were trying to solve difficult problems and no adults were around (Berk & Garvin, 1984). This suggests that private speech guides children's behavior and helps them think; if so, talking out loud in school is not necessarily "naughty," and forbidding such behavior may slow children's learning (Berk, 1986).

## DEVELOPMENT OF INTELLIGENCE

### Assessing Intelligence by Traditional Measures

Because the child of 3, 4, or 5 is quite proficient with language, intelligence tests can now include verbal items. As a result, from this age on tests produce more reliable results than the largely nonverbal tests used in infancy. As children approach age 5, there is more correlation between their scores on intelligence tests and the scores they will achieve later (Bornstein & Sigman, 1986; Honzik, Macfarlane, & Allen, 1948).

Children are now easier to test than infants and toddlers, but they still need to be tested individually. Let's look at two important individual tests of intelligence.

#### Stanford-Binet Intelligence Scale

The **Stanford-Binet Intelligence Scale,** the first individual childhood intelligence test to be developed, takes 30 to 40 minutes. The child is asked to define words, string beads, build with blocks, identify the missing parts of a picture, trace mazes, and show an understanding of numbers. The child's score is supposed to measure practical judgment in real-life situations, memory, and spatial orientation.

The fourth edition of the Stanford-Binet, revised in 1985, differs in several ways from previous editions. It is less verbal: there is an equal balance of verbal and nonverbal, quantitative, and memory items. It assesses patterns and levels of cognitive development instead of providing the IQ as a single overall measure of intelligence. The revamped standardization sample is well balanced geographically, over the United States; ethnically, in proportion to ethnic groups' representation in the population; and by gender, representing both sexes equally. Also, the corrected norms offer a socioeconomic balance and include handicapped children.

#### Wechsler Preschool and Primary Scale of Intelligence (WPPSI-R)

The **Wechsler Preschool and Primary Scale of Intelligence (WPPSI-R),** an hour-long individual test used with children aged 3 to 7, yields separate scores for verbal and performance IQs as well as a combined score, the "full-scale IQ." Its separate scales are similar to those in the Wechsler Intelligence Scale for Children (WISC), discussed in Chapter 8. The 1989 revision includes a number of new subtests and has new picture items. It too has been restandardized on a sample of children representing the population of preschool-age children in the United States. Because children of this age tire quickly and are easily distracted, the test may be given in two separate sessions.

## Assessing Intelligence by "Zone of Proximal Development" (ZPD)

A form of testing that has become popular in the Soviet Union and is now arousing interest in the United States is based on Vygotsky's theory (1978). Vygotsky argues that all higher planning and organizing functions in cognitive development appear twice: first as the result of interaction with other people (usually adults), and then after the child has internalized what these others have taught. At first, then, adults have to direct and organize a child's learning, and they do this most effectively in what Vygotsky calls the **zone of proximal development (ZPD).** The ZPD is a context in which children can almost—but not completely—perform a task on their own. With the right kind of tutoring, they can accomplish it successfully. A good tutor seeks out the ZPD and helps the child learn within it, then gradually reduces support until the child can perform the task independently.

To take stock not only of completed areas of development but also of areas still in the process of developing, testers using the ZPD approach give children test items up to 2 years above their level of actual development and help them to answer the items by asking leading questions and giving examples and demonstrations. The testers can then find the child's current ZPD (Rogoff & Wertsch, 1984).

## Parents' Influence on Children's Intelligence

How well children do on intelligence tests is influenced by many factors, including their temperament, the match between their cognitive style and the tasks they are asked to do, their social and emotional maturity, their ease or unease in the testing situation, and their socioeconomic status and ethnic background. (We'll examine the last two factors in Chapter 8.) One of the most important influences of all is a child's parents.

### Providing an environment for learning

Is there something special that parents who raise bright children do? On the basis of results of many studies (A. Clarke-Stewart, 1977), we can draw a picture of the parents of young children who score high on intelligence tests and whose IQs *increase* in early childhood. This research suggests a number of ways in which parents can help their children grow intellectually.

Parents of children with higher IQs are often sensitive, warm, and loving. They are very accepting of their children's behavior, letting them express themselves and explore. When they do want to change a child's behavior, they often use reasoning or appeals to feel-

A home full of books and toys is a key factor in this boy's intellectual growth. Parents who provide an enriched environment for learning are most likely to have children with high IQs.

ings rather than enforcing rigid rules. They use relatively sophisticated language and teaching strategies, and they encourage their children's independence, creativity, and growth by reading to them, teaching them to do things, and playing with them. The children respond by showing curiosity and creativity, exploring new situations, and doing well in school. Apparently, parents who provide challenging, pleasurable learning opportunities for the child can lay a foundation for optimum intellectual growth.

### "Scaffolding"

The metaphor of scaffolds—temporary platforms where building workers stand—has been applied to a way of teaching children based on the concept of ZPD (Wood, 1980; Wood, Bruner, & Ross, 1976). **Scaffolding** is the temporary support that parents give a child to do a task. There is an inverse relationship between the child's current ability and the amount of support needed. In other words, the less ability a child has in doing a task, the more direction the parent should give; and the more ability the child has, the less direction the parent should give. As the child becomes able to do more and more, the parent helps less and less. Once the job is done, the parent takes away the temporary support—or scaffold—that is no longer needed.

The importance of scaffolding is supported by research. In one study, parents worked with their 3-year-old children on three difficult tasks: copying a model made of blocks; classifying by size, color, and shape; and having the children retell a story they had heard. Both mothers and fathers tended to be guided by their child's level of competence. Parents gave more help when children had more trouble. Furthermore, the parents became more sensitive to their children's needs later in the experiment than they had been at first. This sensitivity was important, because the more finely tuned the parents' help was, the better a child did on the tasks (Pratt, Kerig, Cowan, & Cowan, 1988).

### The father's role

Although most studies have concentrated on the mother's role in children's intellectual development, research also shows the father's impact. The father influences his children through how he feels and acts toward them, the kind of relationship he has with their mother, and his position in the family. Probably because of sons' identification with their fathers (see Chapter 7), fathers influence their sons more than their daughters. As boys take on their fathers' attitudes, values, roles, gestures, and emotional reactions, they also pick up their fathers' styles of thinking, their problem-solving strategies—even the very words they use. Boys are especially likely to imitate fathers who are nurturant and approving and who are seen as strong but do not dominate or intimidate (Radin, 1981).

A father's influence on his daughter is more complex, but girls whose fathers show interest in their intellectual development and encourage independence seem to develop best. Neither boys nor girls develop as well intellectually when their fathers are strict, dogmatic, and authoritarian (Radin, 1981).

What happens when there is no father in the home? The father's absence seems to inhibit children's cognitive development. Boys who lose their fathers before age 5 do less well in mathematics than boys who have fathers (Shinn, 1978); so do girls who lose their fathers before the age of 9 (Radin, 1981). The mother's reaction to a father's absence is likely to affect her child's response. So will any changes in the family's financial situation. Economic hardship—often a direct result of loss of the father—can handicap children's development in many ways.

However, much of the research on the father's absence was done when single-parent families were rarer than they are today. Now that this lifestyle is more common, some of its disadvantages, like social stigma and the lack of male models and other support systems, may be diminishing. Sometimes a supportive stepfather, an older brother, a grandfather, or an uncle helps make up for the lack of a father.

### The mother's role: When mothers are employed

What happens when the mother works outside the home—as more than half of mothers of babies under 1 year of age now do in the United States? Overall, the cognitive, social, and emotional development of preschool children seems at least as good when mothers are employed as when they are not (L. W. Hoffman, 1989; Zimmerman & Bernstein, 1983).

Some research suggests that mothers' employment has a gender-related influence. Daughters of working mothers tend to be more independent and to have a more positive attitude toward being female than daughters of mothers who are at home (Bronfenbrenner, Alvarez, & Henderson, 1984). Other research has found that middle-class boys—but not girls, and not boys in lower-income families—do worse in school when the mother works, especially if she worked full time during their preschool years (D. Gold & Andres, 1978b; D. Gold, Andres, & Glorieux, 1979).

What accounts for these differences? Recent interviews with 152 parents of 3-year-olds suggest a possible explanation: that children's intellectual development may be affected by the way their parents view them. Working parents—when the mother is well educated and works full time—are likely to regard young girls more positively than young boys. Both mothers and fathers praised girls as competent and self-reliant but described boys as disobedient and aggressive. The parents' attitudes may reflect professional women's aspirations for their daughters, as well as boys' tendency to be more active and to need more supervision and control, which may cause extra stress for the parents (Bronfenbrenner et al., 1984; L. W. Hoffman, 1989).

Parents' view of a child—and thus, arguably, the child's intellectual progress—may be influenced by the mother's attitude toward her role. Both husbands and wives described their 3-year-olds (of both sexes) less favorably when a mother worked out of necessity rather than choice and she felt conflict between demands of work and home. This was particularly true for women with little education who worked full time. The more positive attitudes of mothers who worked part time toward both sons and daughters may reflect the fact that balancing work and child care was easier for them (Alvarez, 1985; L. W. Hoffman, 1989).

We have to be careful in interpreting such results, however. Although the attitudes the parents expressed toward their sons and daughters seem to mesh with the earlier findings about differences in boys' and girls' development when mothers work, the studies did not prove a link; further investigation is needed. (We will discuss gender-role differences more fully in Chapter 7, and the effects of both parents' work in Chapter 9.)

## THE WIDENING ENVIRONMENT

As important as parents are in a young child's life, they are far from the only influence on development. Today more young children than ever spend part or most of the day in day care, preschool, or kindergarten.

### DAY CARE

The difference between preschool and day care lies in their primary purpose. Preschool emphasizes educational experiences geared to children's developmental needs, typically in sessions of only 2 hours or so. Day care provides a safe place where children can be cared for, usually all day, while parents are at work or school. But the distinction has blurred: good day care centers seek to meet children's intellectual and emotional needs, and many preschools offer longer days in response to the growing number of working mothers.

Good day care is like good parenting. Children can thrive physically, intellectually, and emotionally in day care that has small groups, a high adult-to-child ratio,

and a stable, competent, highly involved staff. Caregivers should be trained in child development, sensitive to children's needs, authoritative but not too restrictive, stimulating, and affectionate (Belsky, 1984).

The need for good day care is reaching crisis proportions. About 60 percent of working mothers with children under the age of 5 use some form of day care outside the home, either in someone else's home or at group care centers (see Figure 6-6).

Much of what we know about the effects of day care comes from studies of high-quality, well-funded, university-based centers. A body of research shows that children in good day care programs do at least as well, both physically and cognitively, as those raised at home. High-quality day care seems to enhance emotional development, too, and may even improve relationships with parents. Parents may feel less stress because their child is well cared for while they earn the income they need and because they get some relief from the demands of parenting.

Children's language development can be greatly affected by day care, according to one of the few studies comparing care at different levels of quality. This research involved 166 children from nine different day care centers in Bermuda, where 84 percent of 2-year-olds spend most of the workweek in day care. When caregivers speak often to children—especially to give or ask for information rather than to control behavior—and encourage children to start conversations with them, the children do better on tests of language development than children who do not have such conversations with adults (McCartney, 1984).

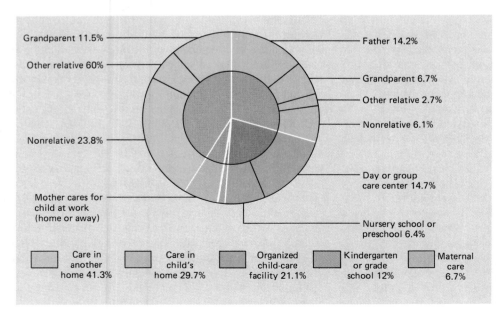

FIGURE 6-6
Primary child-care arrangements used by employed mothers for children under 5. About 60 percent of these mothers use some form of day care outside the home, either in someone else's home or at group centers. (*Source*: U. S. Bureau of the Census, 1989.)

# HOW TO CHOOSE A GOOD DAY CARE CENTER

What makes a day care center good? A number of factors are important. For one, children get the best care when small numbers of children interact with a few adults. When groups are too large, adding more adults to the staff does not help. It does not seem to matter how many years of formal education the caregivers have had. What does matter is how much they have specialized in a child-related field, like developmental psychology, early childhood education, or special education. Adults with such special training tend to give better care, and children in their care do better on tests of school readiness skills (Abt Associates, 1978).

A licensed center meets minimum state standards for health, fire, and safety (if it is inspected regularly), but many centers and home care facilities are not licensed or regulated. Furthermore, licensing does not tell anything about the program's quality (American Academy of Pediatrics, AAP, 1986c).

Here are some things to look for in deciding whether to use a particular day care facility (AAP, 1986c; Olds, 1989).

## DOES THE CENTER . . .

- Provide a safe, clean, setting?
- Have trained personnel who are warm and responsive to all the children?
- Promote good health habits?
- Offer a stimulating environment to help children master cognitive and communicative skills?
- Encourage children to develop at their own rate?
- Nurture self-confidence, curiosity, creativity, and self-discipline?
- Stimulate children to ask questions, solve problems, make decisions, and engage in a variety of activities?
- Foster social skills, self-esteem, and respect for others?
- Help parents improve their child-rearing skills?
- Promote cooperation between parents, personnel, public schools and private schools, and the community?

## BE WARY IF THE PROGRAM . . .

- Is not licensed or registered with the state
- Refuses to let parents visit unannounced
- Employs staff members who are not educated, trained, or experienced in child-related subjects
- Is overcrowded, unclean, or poorly supervised
- Does not have enough heat, light, or ventilation
- Has no written plans for meals or emergencies
- Has no smoke alarms, fire extinguishers, or first aid kit
- Does not set aside separate areas for playing, feeding, resting, and diapering
- Has no policy on managing injuries or infections, or managing sick children
- Does not have a medical consultant

A follow-up study (D. Phillips, McCartney, & Scarr, 1987) found that the children who talked often with their caregivers were also more sociable and considerate. In fact, the quality and amount of verbal stimulation seemed even more important for social development than the children's family background. Again we see the intertwining of different aspects of development and the connection between cognitive influences and personality.

Other studies have confirmed the importance of high-quality day care. Children develop best when they have access to educational toys and materials, when they are cared for by adults who teach them and accept them (are neither too controlling nor merely custodial), and when they have a balance between structured activities and freedom to explore on their own (K. A. Clarke-Stewart, 1987).

Children from low-income families or stressful home environments benefit the most from good day care. Although the average child in a good program is not much affected for better or for worse, disadvantaged children in good programs tend not to show the declines in IQ often seen when such children reach school age. Children in day care may be more motivated to learn (AAP, 1986c; Belsky, 1984; Bronfenbrenner, Belsky, & Steinberg, 1977).

These findings have to be seen in perspective, however. First, some studies had serious flaws in methodology and did not follow children long enough to determine long-range effects. Second, most of the research has focused on high-quality group care centers, but most American children are cared for in their own homes or other people's homes by relatives, neighbors, or paid caretakers; and the care they receive is often run-of-the-mill at best. (See Box 6-2 for suggestions on choosing a good day care program.)

## PRESCHOOL

One reason for the rapid growth of day care has been a scarcity of affordable preschools. Although preschools have flourished in the United States since 1919, when the first public nursery schools were established, many privately run preschools serve mainly well-educated, affluent families.

Today, however, more and more public schools are moving into preschool education. As a result, preschool enrollment has grown dramatically since 1970, despite a sharp decline in the birthrate.

### How Good Preschools Foster Development

When Sally's daughter Jenny was 4 years old, she broke her leg in a sledding accident. But 2 weeks later, she was back in school finger-painting, building block towers, and making paper placemats. She went to a good preschool—and she did not want to miss anything.

A good preschool helps children learn and grow in many ways and is fun, as well. Autonomy flourishes as children explore a world outside the home and choose from among many activities tailored to their interests and abilities, which let them experience many successes that build confidence and self-image. Preschool is particularly valuable in helping children from one- or two-child families (like most families today) learn how to get along with other children.

Some preschools stress social and emotional growth. Others, like those based on the theories of Piaget or the Italian educator Maria Montessori, have a strong cognitive emphasis. Teachers in a good preschool try to advance cognitive development in many ways. They provide experiences that let children learn by doing. They stimulate children's senses through art, music, and tactile materials like clay, water, and wood. They encourage children to observe, to talk, to create, and to solve problems—activities that lay a foundation for more advanced intellectual functioning.

Over the past decade, pressures have built to offer more formal education in preschool. The rising demand for day care, the recognition of the "head start" obtained by disadvantaged children in compensatory programs, the numbers of teachers put out of work by declining school enrollments, and the growing desire among parents to give their children a leg up on the educational ladder have all combined to bring the three R's into nursery school. Many educators and psychologists, however, maintain that the only children who benefit from early schooling are those from disadvantaged families—and that most middle-class children are better served by a relaxed preschool experience (Elkind, 1987a).

Not every preschooler wants to hear a story at the same time. Preschool provides a certain level of individual freedom, while it helps children to grow in many ways—physically, intellectually, socially, and emotionally.

One study compared children who had been enrolled in a heavily academic preschool with children from more relaxed (traditional) preschools. In the early grades the children from the academic preschool did better, but 10 years later the boys from the traditional preschools did better in reading and mathematics than boys from the academic preschool. The girls from the academic school did better in reading, but not in mathematics (L. B. Miller & Bizzel, 1983). Although children may learn more in the short term, an early academic emphasis may affect their interest in learning or their ability to learn over the long run.

Another study found that children who had gone to a traditional preschool did as well in kindergarten as those who had attended more academic programs. Furthermore, children from academically accelerated preschools were more anxious when taking tests, less creative, and more negative about school than those who went to low-key preschools (Hirsh-Pasek, Hyson, & Rescorla, 1989).

The most important contribution of preschool may well be the feeling children get there: that school is fun, that learning is satisfying, and that they are competent in a school setting. The answer to "What makes a good preschool?" depends on the values of particular cultures, which vary considerably, as indicated in Box 6-3 (page 204).

## Montessori Preschools

A remarkably successful system, designed originally by Dr. Maria Montessori to teach poor and retarded Italian children, spread rapidly in the United States during the 1960s, when Montessori schools became popular with affluent parents. Recently, public school administrators have turned to this approach because so many of its tenets coincide with proposals for reforming schools to help disadvantaged children.

The Montessori curriculum is child-centered, based on respect for the child's natural abilities. It focuses on motor, sensory, and language education. Children enter a "prepared environment," a carefully planned arrangement of surroundings, equipment, and materials in which they advance in a graduated sequence from the simple to the complex. Preschoolers learn from their own experiences, with the guidance, support, and help of skilled teachers. Students select their own materials, which are designed so that they can tell whether they are using them correctly. The method aims to foster moral development by emphasizing order, patience, self-control, responsibility, and cooperation.

## Compensatory Preschool Programs

Children from deprived socioeconomic backgrounds often enter school with a considerable handicap. Since the 1960s, large-scale programs have been developed to help such disadvantaged children compensate for the experiences they have missed and to prepare them for school.

### Project Head Start

The best known compensatory preschool program in the United States is **Project Head Start.** It was developed in 1965 as a major weapon in the federal government's war against poverty. Its goal is to improve the lives of children of low-income families by providing health care, intellectual enrichment, and a supportive environment. Today, more than 25 years later, Project Head Start has provided services to well over 8 million children and their families. Still, the program reaches fewer than 1 in 6 of the nation's poor 3- and 4-year-olds.

Has Head Start lived up to its name? Head Start children have shown substantial intellectual and language gains, with the neediest children benefiting most. One reason why Head Start children do as well as they do in school is that they are absent less than other youngsters from impoverished homes. They are healthier, are more likely to be of average height and weight, and do better on tests of motor control and physical development. Still, Head Start children have not equaled the average middle-class child in performance either in school or on standardized tests (R. C. Collins & Deloria, 1983).

The most successful Head Start programs have been those with the most participation by parents, as well as the best teachers, the smallest groups, and the most extensive services. In many cases the positive effects have gone beyond the children themselves; families report educational and financial gains and an increased sense of satisfaction with and control over their lives.

### Long-term benefits of compensatory preschool education

Compensatory preschool education can have a number of long-term benefits. Children enrolled in good programs show long-lasting gains that repay society's initial investment. Although increases in IQ have been short-lived, some of the positive effects of Head Start have held up through high school. Head Start students are less likely than other needy children to be held back and more likely to stay in school and to be in regular rather than special classes (L. B. Miller & Bizzel, 1983).

A number of studies have found long-term benefits for children enrolled in high-quality preschool programs, which incorporated many special services like those in Head Start (Haskins, 1989). Children who had preschool education were less likely than those who had no formal schooling until kindergarten or first grade to need special education for slow learners. They were also much more likely at age 19 to have finished high school, to have enrolled in college or vocational training, and to have jobs. They did better on tests of competence and were less likely to have been arrested, and the women were less likely to have become pregnant (Berrueta-Clement, Schweinhart, Barnett, Epstein, & Weikart, 1985; Haskins, 1989).

**BOX 6–3**   WINDOW ON THE WORLD

# PRESCHOOLS IN THREE CULTURES

It is morning in a Japanese preschool. After a half-hour workbook session— lively with talk, laughter, and playful fighting among the children— twenty-eight 4-year-olds sing in unison (in Japanese): "As I sit here with my lunch, I think of Mom. I bet it's delicious; I wonder what she's made?" The children speak freely, loudly, even vulgarly to each other for much of the day, but then have periods of formal, teacher-directed group recitations of polite expressions of greeting, thanks, and blessings.

In a Chinese preschool, twenty-six 4-year-olds sing a cheerful song about a train, acting out the words by hooking onto each other's backs and chugging around the room. They then sit down and for the next 20 minutes follow their teacher's direction to put together blocks, copying pictures she has handed out. They work in an orderly way, and their errors are corrected as the session proceeds. The teacher has taught the children to recite long pieces and sing complicated songs, emphasizing enunciation, diction, and self-confidence, but she discourages spontaneous talk as a possible distraction from work.

The eighteen 4-year-olds at an American preschool begin their day with a show-and-tell session in which they speak individually. Then they all sing a song about monkeys. For the next 45 minutes, they separate into groups for different activities, including painting, blocks, puzzles, a housekeeping corner, and listening to a story. The teacher moves around the room, talking with the children about their activities, mediating fights, and keeping order. She en-

courages children to express their own feelings and opinions, helps them learn new words to express concepts, and corrects their speech.

What makes a good preschool? Your answer to this question depends on what you regard as the ideal child, the ideal adult, and the ideal society. How schools reflect such values shows up in a comparison among preschools in Japan, China, and the United States (Tobin, Wu, & Davidson, 1989). This wide-ranging study involved videotaping preschool activities in the three countries; showing the tapes and discussing them with parents and educators, and asking 750 preschool teachers, administrators, parents, and child development specialists to fill out questionnaires. The classroom activities were consistent with the opinions expressed in the questionnaires from each cultural group. (Excerpts from the questionnaire data are given in Table 6-4.)

At a time when many American educators worry about a trend for preschools to teach children about science, computers, and foreign languages, as well as reading and arithmetic, it is noteworthy that one of the biggest differences was the importance given to the teaching of actual subject matter. Over 50 percent of the Americans who answered the questionnaires listed "to give children a good start academically" as one of their top three reasons for a society to have preschools. But only 2 percent of the Japanese gave this reason, since the Japanese tend to see preschools as a haven, before the academic pressure and competition that children will face in the years to come. Japanese preschoolers are

encouraged to develop more basic skills like concentration and the ability to function in a group, which will help them learn academic subjects later on. Teachers cultivate perseverance, for example, by refusing to help children dress and undress themselves.

The Chinese, on the other hand, emphasized academics even more than the Americans: 67 percent gave this reason. Their emphasis on early learning seems to have several sources: the Confucian tradition of early, strenuous study; the Cultural Revolution, which discouraged frivolous play and stressed such productive skills as reading, writing, working with numbers, and clear speaking; and the desire of parents to compensate through their children for their own disrupted educations. This early stress on academics is controversial, though, and a less academically oriented preschool curriculum is becoming more popular, especially among child development specialists.

By and large, then, although preschoolers in all three cultures do many of the same activities, China stresses academic instruction, Japan stresses play, and the United States presents a mixed picture. But in all three countries, parents often pressure preschools to give their children a strong educational start so that they will achieve prominent positions in the society. It would be interesting to follow today's children to find out whether those who work harder at ages 3 or 4 or 5 do in fact achieve more as adults.

*Source:* Tobin, Wu, & Davidson, 1989.

**TABLE 6–4**
CULTURAL ATTITUDES TOWARD PRESCHOOLS
IN CHINA, JAPAN, AND THE UNITED STATES

**Question 1: What Are the Most Important Things for Children to Learn in Preschool?**

**Top 3 answers in each country**
*China:*
1  Good health, hygiene, and grooming habits
2  Cooperation and how to be a member of a group
3  Creativity

*Japan:*
1  Sympathy, empathy, concern for others
2  Cooperation and how to be a member of a group
3  Good health, hygiene, and grooming habits

*United States:*
1  Self-reliance, self-confidence
2  Cooperation and how to be a member of a group
3  Sympathy, empathy, concern for others

**Question 2: Why Should a Society Have Preschools?**

**Top 3 answers in each country**
*China:*
1  To give children a good start academically*
2  To make young children more independent and self-reliant*
3  To free parents for work and other pursuits

*Japan:*
1  To give children experience being a member of a group
2  To make young children more independent and self-reliant
3  To give children a chance to play with other children

*United States:*
1  To make young children more independent and self-reliant
2  To give children experience being a member of a group
3  To give children a good start academically

*Note:* The two items marked with an asterisk were tied for first place.

*Source:* Tobin, Wu, & Davidson, 1989.

But a warning against too strong an academic emphasis in preschool came from one longitudinal study that compared low-income youngsters from three different types of preschool programs (Schweinhart, Weikart, & Larner, 1986). One program stressed social and emotional development and activities initiated by the child; the second was highly structured, emphasizing the teaching of numbers, letters, and words; and the third took a middle ground. Children from all three programs did better in elementary school than children with no preschool experience. The children from the academic program narrowly outperformed the others—but they had more behavior problems. And by 15 years of age, many had lost interest in school and developed serious social and emotional problems, such as vandalism and delinquency.

It seems, then, that early childhood education can help to compensate for deprivation and that well-planned programs produce long-term benefits that exceed their original cost (Haskins, 1989). However, we need to keep in mind the developmental needs of young children for play, exploration, and freedom from undue demands—and we need to look closely at particular programs. Today, similar questions are being raised about the benefits of different kinds of education for 5-year-olds.

## KINDERGARTEN

The typical 5-year-old gets a first taste of "real school" when she or he attends kindergarten, a traditional introduction to formal schooling, often situated in a neighborhood public school. Historically, kindergarten has been a year of transition between the relative freedom of home or preschool and the structure of the primary grades. During the 1970s and 1980s, however, it became more like first grade.

In fact, the pressures that have made preschools more academically oriented filtered down from kindergarten, where today many children spend less time on freely chosen activities that stretch their muscles and imaginations, and more time on worksheets and learning to read (Egertson, 1987).

Many kindergartners now spend a full day in school rather than the traditional half day. Results of studies on the effects of all-day kindergarten are mixed (Robertson, 1984; Rust, in Connecticut Early Childhood Education Council, CECEC, 1983). Advocates of full-day kindergarten stress its longer blocks of uninterrupted time for unhurried experiences and educational activities; its greater opportunities for pupil-teacher and parent-teacher contact, since a teacher is responsible for one rather than two classes; teachers' and childrens' higher energy levels, resulting from a structured morning start and a more relaxed afternoon. Opponents point to the fact that some 5-year-olds cannot handle a 6-hour day and a long separation from their parents, and to a danger of overemphasizing academic skills and sedentary activities.

Some educators and psychologists express alarm over "treating kindergarten like a miniature elementary school with a heavy cognitive-academic orientation" (Zigler, 1987, p. 258). Furthermore, they caution against sending children to kindergarten too early, pointing to studies showing the "age effect"—that the youngest children in a class do more poorly than the oldest (Sweetland & DeSimone, 1987). One alternative is a half-day kindergarten program taught by licensed, qualified teachers, followed by a half-day of care given by certified caregivers to children who need day care (Zigler, 1987). This gives some academic preparation and also all-day supervision for those who need it.

We know that many 5-year-olds—and even some younger children—can be taught that 2 times 2 equals 4, just as we know that 9-month-old infants can be taught to recognize words printed on flash cards. But unless motivation comes from the children themselves, and unless learning arises naturally from their experiences, their time might be better spent on the business of early childhood. Young children need concrete sensory activities that help them make sense of their world. They also need a widening network of social interactions that, as we'll see in Chapter 7, help them define their emerging identity.

## SUMMARY

### PHYSICAL GROWTH AND CHANGE

■ Physical growth increases during the years from 3 to 6, but more slowly than during infancy and toddlerhood. Boys are on average slightly taller and heavier than girls.

■ The muscular, skeletal, nervous, respiratory, circulatory, and immune systems are maturing, and all primary teeth are present.

■ Proper growth and health depend on nutrition. Children eat less than before and need a balanced diet.

### HEALTH

■ Minor illnesses help build immunity to disease and may also have cognitive and emotional benefits.

■ Major contagious illnesses are rare when children receive vaccinations.

■ Accidents, the leading cause of death in childhood, are most common in cars, at home, or at day care.

■ Factors such as exposure to other children, stress in the home, poverty, homelessness, and hunger increase children's risk of illness or injury.

### MOTOR SKILLS

■ Motor development advances rapidly during early childhood. Children progress in large- and small-muscle and eye-hand coordination.

■ By the time they are 6 years old, children can tend to many of their own personal needs.

### SLEEP: PATTERNS AND PROBLEMS

■ Sleep patterns change during early childhood. Young children tend to sleep through the night, take one daytime nap, and sleep more deeply than later in life.

■ It is normal for children close to age 5 to develop bedtime rituals that delay going to sleep. However, prolonged bedtime struggles and nighttime fears may indicate emotional disturbances that need attention.

■ Night terrors, nightmares, sleepwalking, and sleeptalking may appear in early childhood.

■ Bed-wetting is common, especially at night. It is a cause for concern when it occurs at least twice a month after age 5.

### ASPECTS OF INTELLECTUAL DEVELOPMENT

■ Studies of memory development indicate that recognition ability is better than recall ability in early childhood, but both increase during this period. Recall is required for the processing and use of information. Children's memory is influenced by mastery motivation, study strategies, general knowledge, unusual activities, and social interactions.

■ According to Piaget, the child is in the preoperational stage of cognitive development approximately from 2 years of age to 7 years. Because of the development of recall, thought is not limited to events in the immediate evironment as in the sensorimotor stage. But the child cannot yet think logically as in the next stage, concrete operations.

■ The symbolic function—as shown in deferred imitation, symbolic play, and language—enables children to mentally represent and reflect upon people, objects, and events.

■ Preoperational children can understand basic functional relationships and the concept of identity. However, they confuse reality and fantasy, they are unable to decenter, they reason transductively, and they do not understand reversibility and the implications of transformations. They are unable to conserve.

■ Research shows that in some ways, Piaget may have underestimated abilities of the children he described as "preoperational." They seem better able to understand causal relationships and classification than he thought, and they appear to be less animistic and egocentric. Researchers have been able to teach conservation when children are mature enough to grasp it.

■ During early childhood, speech and grammar become fairly sophisticated. Speech is of two main types: social and private.

  **1** Social speech is intended to communicate with others. Piaget characterized much of early speech as egocentric, but recent research indicates that young children engage in social speech more than was previously thought.

  **2** Private speech—children's talking aloud to themselves—is not intended to communicate but appears to help children gain control over their actions. It usually disappears by age 9 or 10.

■ Since psychometric intelligence tests for young children (such as the Stanford-Binet Intelligence Scale and Wechsler Preschool and Primary Scale of Intelligence) include verbal items, they are better predictors of later IQ than tests of infants are.

■ Intelligence test scores are influenced by factors such as social and emotional development and parent-child interaction.

## THE WIDENING ENVIRONMENT

■ Many children between 3 and 6 years of age attend day care centers, preschool, and kindergarten. Some of these programs are changing to meet the needs of working parents, as well as children's intellectual and other developmental needs.

■ Little is known yet about the effects of most day care. Studies of the highest-quality day care, however, do suggest that good day care can enhance children's development.

■ Preschool and kindergarten prepare children for formal schooling. Some programs focus more on structured cognitive tasks, others on activities initiated by the children. In the past 20 years, the academic content of the kindergarten curriculum has increased.

■ Evaluations of compensatory preschool programs demonstrate that they can have long-term positive outcomes. However, it is important not to put too much academic pressure on children 3 and 4 years old.

## KEY TERMS

transitional objects (page 185)
enuresis (186)
recognition (187)
recall (187)
preoperational stage (189)
symbolic function (189)
symbol (189)
deferred imitation (189)
symbolic play (190)

centrate (190)
decenter (190)
conservation (190)
irreversibility (190)
transduction (191)
egocentrism (191)
animism (193)
social speech (196)
private speech (197)

Stanford-Binet Intelligence Scale (197)
Wechsler Preschool and Primary Scale of Intelligence (WPPSI-R) (197)
zone of proximal development (ZPD) (198)
scaffolding (198)
Project Head Start (203)

## SUGGESTED READINGS

**Beardsley, L. (1990).** *Good day bad day: The child's experience of child care.* New York: Teachers College Press, Columbia University. The author introduces a group of fictional preschool-age children and contrasts their experiences through a hypothetical day in each of two very different child care situations. Although fictional, it is based on real observations in good and poor quality day care settings.

**Leach, P. (1990).** *Your baby and child from birth to age 5.* New York: Knopf. A *very* comprehensive book on child care, encompassing physical, cognitive, and emotional development in the first five years of a child's life.

**Schorr, L. & Schorr, D. (1988).** *Within our reach— Breaking the cycle of disadvantage.* New York: Doubleday. An optimistic book describing how the cycle of disadvantage can be turned around by large-scale social programs for children.

**Tobin, J. J., Wu, D. W. H., & Davidson, D. H. (1991).** *Preschool in three cultures: Japan, China, and the United States.* New Haven: Yale University Press. A thought-provoking study of preschools in three countries shows that the Japanese, Chinese, and Americans have very different ideas about how to train children for their future roles in society.

## CHAPTER 7

# PERSONALITY AND SOCIAL DEVELOPMENT IN EARLY CHILDHOOD

Children's playings are not sports and should be deemed as their most serious actions.

MONTAIGNE, *ESSAYS*

- How do various theories explain important personality developments of early childhood?
- How do boys and girls identify their sex, and how does this identification affect their personalities and standards of behavior?
- What accounts for common fears in early childhood, and what can be done about them?

- What makes young children act aggressively or altruistically?
- How do parents' child-rearing practices influence young children's personality development?
- How do young children get along with their siblings, and how do they begin to form friendships?
- What kinds of play do children engage in?

At 1 year of age, Anna loved to bang on the tiny red piano that she got for her birthday. At 2, she was climbing onto the bench at the big piano in the living room and enjoying the wider range of sounds she could produce on its keys. And by her third birthday, she would hum nursery tunes while her mother played them on the piano.

At 5, Anna usually gets along very well with her friend Danielle, as they build with wooden blocks or pretend to fix hot dogs for lunch. They do fight sometimes, though; one day Anna took Danielle's pail and shovel, and Danielle threw sand in Anna's face. On another day Danielle was crying; Anna said, "Danielle is upset," and kissed her "best friend." Danielle is an important presence in Anna's life. As they play and talk, and even as they fight, it is apparent how they have changed since infancy and toddlerhood. "They're becoming real people," Anna's father says.

What does it mean to become a real person? It means that Anna is developing a sense of herself as someone different from Danielle or anyone else, with her own traits, her own likes and dislikes, and her own ideas about what she wants to do and believes she ought to do. This uniqueness did not come to Anna overnight on her third, fourth, or fifth birthday; her basic temperament, for example, showed up quite early, soon after birth. Nor is the process anywhere near complete; Anna will not focus on some important issues about her identity until adolescence or later. But now, in early childhood, she has left behind the days of infantile dependence, she is coming out of the stage of saying "no" for its own sake, and she shows definite

signs of her singular personality. She is also becoming a more social being, defining herself through her relationships with others.

We'll begin this chapter by examining several theoretical views of these developments of early childhood. Then we'll look at various aspects of personality development during these years. Differences between the sexes begin to surface at this age, as children identify themselves and others as male or female; and so we'll first consider how gender affects personality. Next we'll examine fear, aggression, and altruism in young children; how parenting styles are related to children's competence; and how children get along with their brothers and sisters and form their first friendships. Young children work out many of these relationships through play—which is also a vehicle for expressing their budding personalities, social skills, and cognitive abilities—and so we end this chapter with a look at play.

## PERSONALITY IN EARLY CHILDHOOD: THEORETICAL APPROACHES

Four-year-old Timmy sometimes goes to the library with his grandfather. One afternoon the librarian teasingly asks, "Can you read?" and hands him an open volume of Shakespeare. Timmy is momentarily taken aback by this book without pictures, but then in perfect imitation of his grandfather he pats all his pockets and says, "I must have left my glasses at home."

Timmy's actions illustrate an important personality

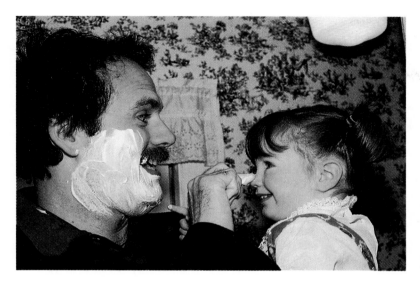

This little girl playfully interacting with her father is learning that males shave their faces but females do not. Awareness of what it means to be a girl or a boy shapes personality and behavior in many subtle and not-so-subtle ways.

development: *identification,* a child's adoption of the characteristics, beliefs, attitudes, values, and behaviors of another person or of a group. Between the ages of 3 and 6, a boy normally forms a strong identification with his father or another male, while a girl normally identifies with her mother or another female. Some psychologists believe that this identification shapes children's moral codes as well as their understanding of what is expected of members of each sex.

The sex we are born with is a key element of our identity. It is one of the first things people want to know about us at birth and one of the first things others notice about us throughout our lives. It affects how we look, how we move our bodies, and how we work, play, and dress. It influences what we think about ourselves and what others think of us. All those characteristics—and more—are included in what we refer to when we use the word *gender:* what it means to be male or female.

How do young children achieve *gender identity—* awareness of themselves as male or female? How do they develop *gender roles,* the behaviors that their society expects of males and females, as well as general standards of socially and morally correct behavior? And how do other important aspects of personality development take place? Let's see what insights several theoretical perspectives can give us. We'll look at them in chronological order, beginning with the psychoanalytic theories of Sigmund Freud and Erik Erikson, going on to the social-learning theories of Albert Bandura and others, and ending with the cognitive theories of Lawrence Kohlberg and Sandra Bem. Although none of these theories fully explains personality development, each contributes something to our understanding of it.

## PSYCHOANALYTIC THEORIES: BIOLOGY, SOCIETY, AND CULTURE

### Psychosexual Theory: Freud's Phallic Stage

Anatomic differences between girls and boys and between adults and children fascinate 3- to 6-year-olds. They want to find out how adults make babies, and they love "dirty" jokes. Freud said that children act this way at this age because they are in the *phallic stage,* when the chief source of biological gratification is in the genital area. (The fact that Freud named this stage for the phallus, or penis, shows his male orientation.)

Because children's feelings now have a sexual focus, the nature of their attachments changes. Freud believed that the Oedipus and Electra complexes are the central forces in male and female personality development, underlying the common anxieties and fears of this age. An important result of the phallic stage is the superego, the part of the personality that monitors behavior.

### Oedipus complex

Freud's concept of the *Oedipus complex*—a boy's sexual attachment to his mother and rivalry with his father—is named after an ancient Greek myth in which Oedipus kills his father and marries his mother. A boy in the phallic stage, said Freud, has sexual fantasies about his mother and murderous thoughts about his father, whom he sees as a competitor for her love. Unconsciously, the little boy wants to take his father's place. But the boy has conflicting feelings toward his father—real affection on the one hand, and hostility, rivalry, and fear on the other. Noticing that little girls do not have a penis, he wonders what happened to it. This observation and his guilt over his Oedipal feelings lead to **castration anxiety,** a fear that his father will castrate him. The boy represses his sexual strivings toward his mother, stops trying to rival his father, and begins to identify with him. This *identification with the aggressor* (as Freud called it) relieves the boy's anxiety: the powerful enemy is now an ally.

### Electra complex

The **Electra complex**—the female counterpart of the Oedipus complex—involves sexual attachment to the father and rivalry with the mother. In the original Greek story, Electra, a king's daughter, helps her brother kill their mother to avenge the murder of their father.

According to Freud, a little girl's desire for her father stems from **penis envy,** the desire for a penis, which she notices on her brothers or male playmates and recognizes as larger than, and superior to, her own clitoris. She assumes that she once had a penis but lost it, blames her mother for this imagined castration, and envies her father because he has a penis. Eventually the girl realizes that she cannot have a penis and wishes instead for a child; then, she sees her father as a love object and becomes jealous of her mother. Freud saw the desire for motherhood as the result of penis envy. The baby is a gift to the mother's own father, and when her baby is a boy, he brings the penis the mother has longed for.

According to Freud, a girl cannot win. If she succumbs to penis envy, she longs hopelessly to acquire a penis and become a man. If she denies her envy, she is likely to have emotional problems in adulthood. Either way, she feels inferior.

A girl eventually gives up the idea of replacing her mother. Instead, she identifies with her mother and vicariously achieves the coveted relationship with her father. But her attachment to her father and jealousy of her mother tend to persist.

In Freud's scenarios, identification results from repressing or abandoning the wish to possess the parent of the opposite sex. Achieving identification puts the child into the next stage, latency (discussed in Chapter 9).

### Development of the superego

The identification with the aggressor that occurs at about age 5 or 6 permits the creation of Freud's third aspect of personality, the **superego.** The superego represents the values communicated by parents and other agents of society. Operating unconsciously, and mostly through fear, the superego internalizes rules of right and wrong. Freud believed that girls cannot develop as strong a superego as boys because they do not fear castration.

The superego tries to prevent the id from acting on its impulses. The ego acts as a mediator. It tries to find ways to gratify the id while accommodating the demands of the superego. The superego has both positive and negative aspects. *Ego-ideal* defines the "shoulds": behavior we aspire to, receive approval for, and feel proud of. *Conscience* defines the "should-nots": behavior we are punished for and feel guilty or ashamed about.

In early childhood, the superego is rigid. For example, a child may feel guilty after having fought with a friend, even though his or her parents do not disapprove of harmless tussling. With maturity, the superego becomes more realistic and flexible, letting people consider their self-interest.

### Psychosocial Theory: Erikson's Crisis 3—Initiative versus Guilt

Erikson sees the central issues of early childhood as social rather than sexual. His first two crises— revolving around issues of trust (in infancy) and autonomy (in toddlerhood)—are followed by the crisis of **initiative versus guilt,** a conflict between children's urge to form and carry out goals and their moral judgments about what they want to do. When children do not succeed in meeting their goals, they feel guilty. Anna at 5, for example, likes to pour her own juice, make her own sandwich, and help clean house. If her attempts at initiative fail—if she spills her juice, gets jelly on her shorts, or breaks a vase—she experiences guilt.

Erikson also sees a moral faculty emerging as a result of identification with the powerful parents. A split occurs between the part of the personality that remains an exuberant child, eager to try new things and test new powers, and the part that is becoming an adult, constantly examining motives and actions for propriety and punishing the self for sexual fantasies and "bad" behavior. Thus, in playing house, a child may play the roles of both a naughty child and an admonishing father.

Children who resolve this third crisis well acquire the *virtue of purpose:* "the courage to envisage and pursue valued goals, uninhibited by the defeat of infantile fantasies, by guilt and by the foiling fear of punishment" (1964, p. 122). They can then develop into adults who combine spontaneous enjoyment of life with a sense of responsibility. Those who do not resolve the crisis well, however, may become guilt-ridden and repressed. They may become adults who inhibit their impulses and are self-righteously intolerant of others; in extreme cases they may suffer from psychosomatic illness, impotence, or paralysis. Or, if initiative is overemphasized, they may feel that they must constantly achieve.

Erikson urges parents to help children strike a healthy balance by letting them do things on their own, while providing guidance and setting firm limits. (This is the goal of "authoritative" child rearing, described later in this chapter.)

### Evaluating the Psychoanalytic Theories

After taking a bath with a boy cousin and noticing his penis, a little girl said to her mother at bedtime, "Isn't it a blessing he doesn't have it on his face?" (Tavris & Offer, 1977). Freudian thinkers would dismiss the girl's remark as a defense against her true feeling of penis envy.

Freud himself, however, has been accused of an elaborate defense mechanism. Initially, he theorized that his patients had actually been victims of sexual advances by their parents (Masson, 1984). The resistance and disbelief that this early "seduction" theory encountered apparently led him to look into the psyche for an explanation of the traumatic events his patients described. The Oedipus and Electra theories were the result; but in his letters, Freud later expressed doubts about having discarded his first theory.

Although parents often detect what might be considered Oedipal feelings (as when Stefan, at age 4, announced, "I'm going to marry Mommy"), there is little scientific evidence for Freud's concept of penis envy (Matlin, 1987). Further, contemporary views of female sexuality reject the idea that the penis is an ideal for both sexes. Karen Horney, once a disciple of Freud, contended that females envy the male's social status more than his anatomy and that males often feel "womb envy"—envy of a woman's ability to bear children.

Freud's theory is hard to test scientifically, and what research has been done does not support all its tenets (Stangor & Ruble, 1987). For example, both boys and girls are more like their mothers than their fathers, and people other than parents influence children's development. Bold and imaginative as Freud's ideas were for his time, today research psychologists consider them inadequate to explain personality issues of childhood.

Erikson's theory, too, is based not on scientifically controlled research but on his personal and clinical experience. He fails to consider the different effects of social and cultural influences on males and females.

Rather, he regards male development as the norm. Nevertheless, his broad life-span view of human development offers a helpful structure for interpreting behavior at different stages throughout life.

## SOCIAL-LEARNING THEORY: OBSERVING AND IMITATING MODELS

Freud stresses biology, and Erikson stresses society and culture, but they would agree that parents have a vital impact on a child's development. Social-learning theorists also emphasize the parents' role, but in a different way. These theorists hold that children *learn*, from watching their parents and other adults, what it means to be male or female and what kinds of behavior are right and proper.

### Identification

Social-learning theory sees identification as the result of observing and imitating a model. Typically, a child's model is a parent, but children can also model themselves after a grandparent, an older brother or sister, a teacher, a baby-sitter, an athlete, or a television personality. Children usually pick up characteristics from several different models, whom they choose on the basis of how much power a person seems to have and how nurturant, or caring, the person is (Bandura & Huston, 1961).

Music is a language all its own—and here it fosters an important aspect of growth. As this little girl plays and sings along with her father, she demonstrates identification, one of the most important personality developments of early childhood.

According to Jerome Kagan (1958, 1971), four related processes establish and strengthen identification:

1 *Wanting to be like the model.* Children may want to
be like a sports hero whose strength and agility they
would like to have.
2 *Acting like the model.* Children adopt the model's
mannerisms, voice inflections, and phrasing. Parents are often startled to hear their own words and
tone of voice come out of their children's mouths.
3 *Feeling what the model feels.* Children often experience emotions like those the model expresses. For
example, when Sally's 5-year-old daughter saw Sally
cry after her own brother's death, Dorri cried, too,
not for the uncle she barely knew but because her
mother's grief made her feel sad.
4 *Believing that they are like the model.* Children believe that they look like the model, tell jokes like the
model, walk like the model. Identification with a parent is often reinforced by other people's comments
("You certainly have your father's eyes!").

Through identification, then, children come to believe that they have the same characteristics as a
model. When they identify with a nurturant and competent model, children are pleased and proud. When the
model is inadequate, the child may feel unhappy and
insecure.

According to social-learning theory, young children
generally identify with the parent of the same sex; and
when they imitate that parent, they are reinforced. A
boy sees that he is physically more like his father than
like his mother. He imitates his father (especially when
he sees the father as nurturant, competent, and powerful) and is rewarded for acting "like a boy." An analogous process occurs for a girl. Children learn morally
acceptable behavior in the same way as gender identity,
by imitation and reinforcement. By the end of early
childhood, these lessons are largely internalized; a child
no longer needs frequent praise or punishment or the
presence of a model to act in socially appropriate ways.

### Evaluating Social-Learning Theory

Social-learning theory seems to make sense but has
been hard to prove. Children do imitate adults, but not
always those of the same sex. You may have seen a
little girl put on her father's hat or a little boy put on his
mother's shoes (Maccoby & Jacklin, 1974; Raskin &
Israel, 1981). Moreover, often children do not imitate a
parent at all. When children are tested for similarity to
their parents, most are found to be no more like them
than like other parents chosen at random. Those who
are similar to their own parents are no closer to the

same-sex parent than to the other parent (Hetherington, 1965; Mussen & Rutherford, 1963).

Also, studies cast doubt on the reinforcement aspect
of social-learning theory, at least as it applies to gender.
Although parents do treat their sons and daughters
somewhat differently, in some respects the difference
is not great. Many parents, for example, feel that it is
appropriate for boys to play with dolls and for girls to
play with trains. And parents of young children punish
fighting and reward helpfulness in both boys and girls
(Maccoby & Jacklin, 1974), though fathers are more
likely to encourage "masculine" or "feminine" behavior
(J. H. Block, 1978).

Social learning may underlie children's acquisition of
gender identity and behavioral standards. But simple
imitation and reinforcement do not seem to explain adequately how this occurs.

## COGNITIVE-DEVELOPMENTAL THEORY: MENTAL PROCESSES

Cindy learns that she is something called a "girl" because people call her a girl. She figures out the kinds of
things girls are "supposed" to do, and she does them.
In other words, she learns her gender in the same way
she learns everything else—by actively thinking about
her experience. This is the heart of the cognitive-developmental theory proposed by Lawrence Kohlberg
(1966).

### Gender Identity and Gender Constancy

To learn their gender, Kohlberg says, children do not
depend on adults as models or dispensers of reinforcements and punishments; instead, they actively classify
themselves and others as male or female and then organize their behaviors around their gender.

*Gender identity*—awareness of being male or
female—may begin at about age 2. By age 3, according
to Kohlberg, most children have a firm idea of which
sex they belong to. When Dorri, at age 3, had a very
short haircut, she indignantly corrected people who
thought she was a boy. But gender constancy comes
later, at about age 4 or 5. It is this that Kohlberg considers important in the behaviors that children adopt.

*Gender constancy,* or *gender conservation,* is
a child's realization that his or her sex will *always* be the
same. Three-year-old Eric, for example, told his
mother, "When I grow up, I want to be a mommy just
like you so I can play tennis and drive a car." But Anna,
at 4, said that she would always be a girl and that her
friend David would always be a boy—even if he played
with dolls. Eric had not achieved gender constancy;
Anna had.

According to Kohlberg, gender differences in behavior *follow* the establishment of gender constancy. Thus the reason Anna prefers dolls and dresses is not the approval she gets for those preferences (as in social-learning theory) but her cognitive awareness that such things are consistent with her idea of herself as a girl. Once children realize that they will *always* be male or female, they try to adopt "sex-appropriate" behaviors.

### Evaluating Cognitive-Developmental Theory

Research supports a link between gender concepts and cognitive development. Children as young as 2 years old can classify pictures as "boys" or "girls," or "mommies" or "daddies." And by age 2½, children can tell which pictures they themselves resemble, and they know whether they will be fathers or mothers when they grow up (S. K. Thompson, 1975).

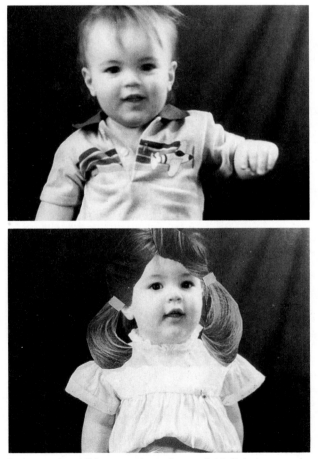

In one study, children saw three photos of this little boy—nude, dressed in boys' clothes, and dressed in girls' clothes. Preschoolers who identified the child's sex by genitals rather than by dress were more likely to show gender constancy—to know that they themselves would remain the sex they were.

But when Sandra Bem (1989) tested fifty-eight 3-, 4-, and 5-year-olds, she found that gender *constancy* was connected more to children's knowledge of genital sex differences than to their age. These children saw three photos of a male toddler and three of a female toddler—one showing each child nude, one showing each child dressed in clothes traditional for his or her sex, and one showing each child in clothes usually worn by the other sex (including, for the boy, a ponytail wig and barrettes). Preschoolers who identified the sex of the child in the photo by genitals rather than by dress were more likely to know that they themselves would remain the sex they were, and this association held across age levels. Forty percent of 3-, 4-, and 5-year-olds knew that sex remained constant; of the 60 percent who did not, 77 percent did not know the genital differences between the sexes. Girls knew more about this than boys did and achieved gender constancy earlier. Thus, factors other than chronological age influence the achievement of gender constancy.

Cognitive-developmental theory has its weaknesses. Children often act in "gender-appropriate" ways *before* they achieve gender constancy, contradicting Kohlberg's predictions. More important, the theory does not explain why—of all the differences among people—children pay so much attention to sex in setting up the classifications by which they make sense of their world. Gender-schema theory, which we'll consider next, tries to answer that question.

## GENDER-SCHEMA THEORY: A "COGNITIVE-SOCIAL" APPROACH

### Gender Schemata and Gender Roles

***Gender-schema theory*** is a "cognitive-social" approach with elements of both cognitive-developmental theory and social-learning theory. It is based on the concept of a ***gender schema*** (Bem, 1983, 1985). A schema (the plural is *schemata*) is a mentally organized pattern of behavior that helps a child sort out information. Bem maintains that children socialize themselves in their gender roles (we'll define and discuss gender roles more fully later in this chapter). First, they develop a concept of what it means to be male or female by organizing information around the schema of gender. They pick up this schema as they see that society classifies people more by gender than by anything else: males and females wear different clothes, play with different toys, use separate bathrooms, and line up separately in school.

As children see what boys and girls are supposed to be and do—the culture's gender schema—they adapt their own attitudes and behavior. From the full range of human attributes, they pick and choose those in their society's gender schema that fit them. In the United States, for example, boys learn that it is important to be strong and aggressive, while girls learn that it is important to be nurturant. Children then look at themselves: if they act "gender-appropriate," their self-esteem rises; if not, they feel inadequate.

This theory assumes that since gender-typing (which we'll define and discuss in more detail later in the chapter) is learned, it can be modified; and that stereotypes can be eliminated if children do one or more of the following:

- *Discard all schemata*—distinguishing the sexes only by anatomical and reproductive differences. (Young children usually fail to do this, basing their decision about a person's sex on other external signals like clothing or hairstyle.)
- *Learn the individual differences schema*—that there is great variation within groups. For example, while some girls do not like to play baseball, others do—and some boys do not.
- *Learn the cultural-relativism schema*—the understanding that people in different cultures and at different historical times hold different beliefs and customs about what is appropriate for males and females.
- *Learn the sexism schema*—the conviction that gender-stereotyped roles are not only different but wrong, no matter how common they are.

We are living through a real-life test of gender-schema theory. In many countries around the world today, the gender schema is undergoing change. Both official and informal standards for gender-appropriate behavior have changed considerably over the past several decades, with mixed results.

### Evaluating Gender-Schema Theory

Gender-schema theory is supported by the fact that very little evidence directly links children's acquisition of gender constancy to their gender-related behavior, as Kohlberg's theory predicts. Rather, research shows that children who have not yet developed gender constancy still know a good deal about what is "appropriate" for males and females (G. D. Levy & Carter, 1989). Instead of saying, as Kohlberg does, that acquisition of gender roles depends on a single essential cognitive factor, like gender constancy, it therefore seems reasonable to look at a number of different factors. These can include how much children know about

gender-role stereotypes and how likely they are to categorize various activities or objects by gender, two factors that G. D. Levy and Carter (1989) found important in children's gender-typing.

Bem's idea that a culture's gender schema should be deliberately changed is a reasonable goal. But we have to realize that change in ingrained attitudes about basic aspects of human behavior is slow. As early as 1910, for instance, the founders of kibbutzim (communal settlements) in Israel tried to do away with special roles for men and women by changing family structure and assigning chores without regard to sex. But today, work on the kibbutz generally follows traditional gender lines, with men doing, say, agricultural and mechanical work and women cooking, laundering, and caring for children (Tiger & Shepher, 1975). Also, while the past several decades have brought major changes in the way American men and women—and boys and girls—think, feel, and act about gender, many of the old patterns persist. Women, even those with full-time jobs, still do most of the child care and housework; and men are still, by and large, more career-oriented.

## ASPECTS AND ISSUES OF PERSONALITY DEVELOPMENT

### GENDER

Two 4-year-olds, Wendy and Michael, are neighbors. They were wheeled together in the park as babies. They learned to ride tricycles at about the same time and pedaled up and down the sidewalk, often colliding with each other. They go to preschool together. Wendy and Michael have followed very similar paths. But there is a definite difference between them: their sex. How much difference does being a girl or a boy make in a child's development?

### Gender Differences—and Similarities

Not only do Wendy and Michael have different sex organs; they are also different in size, strength, appearance, physical and intellectual abilities, and personality. Which of these differences are due to the fact that Wendy is a girl and Michael is a boy, and which are simply differences between two individual human beings? As we discuss this, we need to distinguish between **sex differences,** the physical differences between males and females; and **gender differences,** the psychological or behavioral differences.

Physical differences between baby boys and girls are slight—boys are slightly larger and more muscular.

Other differences are almost nonexistent before age 3, except that boys seem to be more active. Differences do become more pronounced after that; but boys and girls, on the average, are still "more alike than they are different" (Maccoby, 1980). Just by knowing a child's sex, we cannot predict whether a particular boy or girl will be faster, stronger, smarter, more confident, or more of a leader than another child.

In their landmark review of more than 2000 studies, Maccoby and Jacklin (1974) found only a few characteristics on which boys and girls differed significantly. Three cognitive differences—girls' superior verbal ability and boys' better mathematical and spatial abilities—do not begin to show up until after age 10 or 11. Moreover, analyses have found even these differences to be very small indeed. Gender differences in verbal abilities are so small as to be almost meaningless (J. Hyde & Linn, 1988). And those in math performance are complex, but also small, and getting still smaller with time. In the general population neither sex shows better understanding of mathematical concepts; girls excel in computation (adding, subtracting, etc.); and boys show superior problem-solving ability, but not until high school (J. S. Hyde, Fennema, & Lamon, 1990).

Personality differences, too, are few. Both boys and girls, for example, become attached to their parents. The clearest gender difference, which shows up in early childhood, is that males tend to be more aggressive. Boys play more boisterously; they roughhouse more and are more apt to try to dominate other children and challenge their parents. Girls cooperate more with their parents and tend to set up rules (like taking turns) to avoid clashes with playmates (Maccoby, 1980). Boys argue and fight more often and are more apt to use force or threats of force to get their way, while girls try to defuse conflicts by persuasion rather than confrontation (P. M. Miller, Danaher, & Forbes, 1986).

Girls are more likely to be *empathic*, that is, to identify with other people's feelings (N. Eisenberg, Fabes, Schaller, & Miller, 1989; M. Hoffman, 1977). Until about age 4 or 5, boys and girls show equal interest in babies. And even after this age, boys know just as much about babies and respond as enthusiastically to adults' encouragement to take an interest in and help care for a baby (P. W. Berman, 1987; P. W. Berman & Goodman, 1984).

We need to be careful not to overemphasize differences between the sexes; those that do exist are statistically small and are valid for large groups of boys and girls but not necessarily for individuals. Some girls love rough play, and some boys hate it. Despite all this, however, both males and females *believe* that they are more different than they actually are (Matlin, 1987).

Where does that belief come from, and what are its effects?

## Attitudes toward Gender Differences

When Wendy and Michael play house, she, as the "mommy," is likely to play at cooking and taking care of the baby while Michael puts on a hat and "goes to work." When he comes home, sits at the table, and says "I'm hungry," Wendy drops what she is doing to wait on him. This scenario would be less surprising if both Wendy's and Michael's mothers did not work outside the home and if both their fathers did not do a fair amount of the housework. These children have absorbed the gender roles of their culture rather than those of their own households.

### Gender roles, gender-typing, and gender stereotypes

**Gender roles** are the behaviors, interests, attitudes, and skills that a culture considers appropriate for males and females, and expects them to show. By tradition, American women are expected to devote most of their time to being wives and mothers, while men are supposed to devote most of their time to earning money. Those roles also include expectations about personality: for example, women are expected to be compliant and nurturant while men are expected to be active and competitive.

**Gender-typing** is a child's learning of his or her gender role. Children acquire gender-typing early, through the socialization process; the brighter they are, the faster they learn it. Bright children are the first to notice the physical differences between the sexes and the expectations of their society for each sex, and to try to live up to those expectations (S. B. Greenberg & L. Peck, personal communication, 1974). Children become increasingly gender-typed between the ages of 3 and 6.

Strong gender-typing in early childhood may help children develop gender identity. Ultimately, people vary in the degree to which they take on gender roles. Perhaps children can be more flexible in their thinking about gender differences only after they know for sure that they are male or female and will always remain so.

Gender-typing frequently leads to **gender stereotypes:** exaggerated generalizations about male or female behavior. Myths about sex differences result in false assumptions that individuals will, or should, conform to gender roles: for example, that a male is bound to be aggressive and independent while a female is passive and dependent.

Anna's enjoyment of her truck shows that she is not restricted in her play by gender stereotypes. Contemporary developmentalists discourage such stereotypes, usually favoring encouraging children to pursue their own interests, even when these interests are unconventional for their sex.

Stereotyped attitudes are found in children as young as age 3. The children in one study described babies in different ways, depending on whether the baby was identified as a girl or a boy. They were more likely to call a "boy" big, and a "girl" little; a "boy" mad, a "girl" scared; a "boy" strong, a "girl" weak (Haugh, Hoffman, & Cowan, 1980).

Gender stereotypes restrict children's views of themselves and their future. They affect people in their simplest, most everyday endeavors as well as in far-reaching life decisions. Children who absorb these stereotypes may become men who will not prepare a baby's bottle or wind yarn, or women who "can't" nail boards together or bait a fish hook (Bem, 1976). Although attitudes have changed in recent years, many people still view certain activities as unmasculine or unfeminine; as

a result, they deny their natural inclinations and abilities and force themselves into ill-fitting academic, vocational, or social molds.

### Androgyny: A new view of gender

Sandra Bem (1974, 1976) maintains that the healthiest personality includes a balance of positive characteristics normally thought of as appropriate for one sex with positive characteristics considered appropriate for the other. A person having such a balance—whom Bem would describe as **androgynous**—might be assertive, dominant, and self-reliant ("masculine" traits), as well as compassionate, sympathetic, and understanding ("feminine" traits). Androgynous men and women are free to judge a particular situation on its merits and to act on the basis of what seems most effective rather than what is considered appropriate for their gender.

As we saw in discussing Bem's gender-schema theory, she believes that children can be taught to substitute other schemata for the prevailing schema in a culture. Box 7-1 lists some of her suggestions to parents for counteracting gender stereotypes and substituting androgynous ideals.

### Roots of Gender Differences

Some people insist that the root of gender differences is biological. But many psychologists besides Bem believe that the cultural environment, as interpreted to young children through parents and the media, is at least as influential. Research has not yielded an either-or answer.

### Biology

Hormones circulating before or about the time of birth seem to cause sex differences in animals. The male hormone testosterone has been linked to aggressive behavior in mice, guinea pigs, rats, and primates; and the female hormone prolactin can cause motherly behavior in virgin or male animals (Bronson & Desjardins, 1969; D. M. Levy, 1966; R. M. Rose, Gordon, & Bernstein, 1972). But because human beings are influenced far more by learning than animals are, it is risky to apply conclusions drawn from animal studies to human beings.

One line of research on humans focuses on persons who have had unusual prenatal exposure to hormones or were born with sexual abnormalities. A classic study (Ehrhardt & Money, 1967) concerned 10 girls between the ages of 3 and 14 whose mothers had taken synthetic progestins (hormones that interfere with female fertil-

BOX 7–1   THINKING CRITICALLY

## INOCULATING CHILDREN AGAINST GENDER STEREOTYPES

Today women carry briefcases as well as babies, men push strollers as well as wheelbarrows, and social institutions are trying to overcome gender stereotypes that restrict children's view of their capabilities. Preschools recruit male teachers to show children that men, too, can be nurturers. The doll corner is now the family corner, and it is stocked with tools as well as dishes. The emphasis in school, in the media, and in the family is less on what *boys* or *girls* can do than on what *children* can do.

Nevertheless, children absorb subtle or blatant gender stereotypes still present in the culture. The following suggestions are adapted from recommendations by Sandra Bem

(1983, 1985) for parents who want to "inoculate" their children against such stereotypes. As you consider these suggestions, you might also ask yourself such questions as: Is this a good idea? What benefits would accrue for the individual, the family, and society? What problems might arise from adopting Bem's suggestions?

■ *Be models of nonstereotyped behavior.* Share or alternate tasks like bathing the baby or keeping household accounts.
■ *Give children nonstereotyped gifts.* Boys can get dolls; girls can get trucks.

■ *Expose children to men and women in nontraditional occupations.* Children who know that Aunt Alice is a plumber and that Dad's friend Pete is a nurse are unlikely to think that plumbers have to be male and nurses female.
■ *Monitor young children's reading and television viewing.* Select books and programs that are not stereotyped.
■ *Emphasize anatomy and reproduction as the main distinctions between males and females.* Divert children's attention from traditional gender-typed clothing and social behavior.

---

ity) during pregnancy. Nine of the girls were born with abnormal external sex organs, but after surgery they looked normal and had normal female reproductive capability. Although raised as girls from birth, they acted like "tomboys": they liked to play with trucks and guns, and competed with boys in sports. It is unclear, however, whether these behaviors were due to prenatal hormonal exposure, parental reinforcement of "tomboy" behavior, or some combination.

Another classic study (Money, Ehrhardt, & Masica, 1968) more clearly highlights the role of environment. The subjects were 10 people aged 13 to 30 who were chromosomally male and had testes instead of ovaries but who (perhaps because their bodies were unable to utilize androgens prenatally) looked like females and had been brought up as girls. All were "typically female" in behavior and outlook. They all considered marriage and raising a family to be very important, and all had had repeated dreams and fantasies about bringing up children. Eight had played primarily with dolls and other "girls'" toys, and the seven who reported having played house in childhood had always played the mother. In this case, biology—unsupported by environmental influences—fails to account for gender-typing.

Another line of research seeks to explain cognitive differences between males and females in terms of differences in brain functioning or hormonal levels. Some studies suggest that the right and left hemispheres are more specialized in men's brains than in women's; but these differences are so small that only sophisticated statistical analyses can detect them.

A study of men with a hormonal deficiency disorder (Hier & Crowley, 1982) suggests that androgens may be responsible for normal males' superior spatial abilities. But once again, environmental influences cannot be ruled out. This gender difference does not exist in all cultures; and in a culture where it does, like ours, women (or men who do not feel fully masculine) may give up on a task that they do not deem "sex-appropriate" (Kagan, 1982).

It is possible that hormones predispose people toward certain behaviors, but the actual appearance of these behaviors is subject to environmental influences. In all these studies, the samples were very small; thus the findings are inconclusive. Furthermore, since variations among people of the same sex are larger than the average differences between the sexes, biology fails to explain large differences in behavior between the sexes.

## Culture

In Pakistan, when an Afghan boy is born, the event is celebrated with feasts and rifle shots. A girl's birth goes unnoticed. In Afghan refugee camps, where food is in short supply, women and girls must wait to eat until the men and boys have had their fill (Reeves, 1984). It is easy to see how, in such a society, personality would be strongly influenced by gender. But even in the United States, males and females are treated and valued differently.

Do societal forces encourage and accentuate biological differences, or does the culture itself create gender differences? This question is hard to answer. We do know that in all societies, some roles are considered appropriate for males and others for females. Gender roles vary from culture to culture, but in most societies men are more aggressive, competitive, and powerful than women, and this pattern is hard to change.

Yet attitudes and roles *are* changing. Today in the United States, women are moving into untraditional occupations and are gaining power in business, in government, and in the family. Egalitarian attitudes are becoming more prevalent, especially among younger and better-educated people and those with higher incomes (Deaux, 1985). And both men and women are exploring aspects of their personalities that were suppressed by the old gender stereotypes.

## Socialization

**How parents treat sons and daughters**   Even in today's more "liberated" society, parents influenced by the culture they grew up in treat sons and daughters differently. Differential treatment begins in infancy (as we saw in Chapter 5) and increases in early childhood, accentuating gender differences.

Parents tend to socialize boys more intensely than girls—to punish them more, and to praise and encourage them more, too. Parents put more pressure on boys to act "like real boys" and avoid acting "like girls" than on girls to avoid "boyish" behavior and act in "feminine" ways. Girls have had much more freedom in the clothes they wear, the games they play, and the people they play with (Maccoby & Jacklin, 1974).

Why do so many adults show more concern about boys? Even in this "enlightened" age, many parents seem to think that boys are more important and that it matters more how they turn out. It is also possible that boys demand more attention because their resistance to parental guidance is greater. Whatever the cause of this different treatment, it results in an accentuation of personality differences between males and females.

This attitude is changing, however, as adult roles in society change. For example, the preschool children (especially girls) of women who work outside the home tend to show less stereotyping (Huston, 1983).

Fathers seem particularly important to children's gender-role development. For one thing, they often care more about gender-typing than mothers do. Mothers are generally more accepting of girls' playing with trucks and boys' playing with dolls, while this kind of cross-sex play is more likely to upset men, especially in regard to their sons. Men usually accept a very active and temperamentally "difficult" son more easily than such a daughter, but they spank sons more than daughters (Biller, 1981). Also, fathers tend to be more social with, more approving of, and more affectionate toward their preschool daughters but are often more controlling and directive toward their sons, and more concerned with their sons' cognitive achievements than with their daughters' (Bronstein, 1988).

These differences in the way many men treat their children have long-range implications (Bronstein, 1988). By reserving gentleness for their daughters, they may be restricting their sons' social and emotional development. By controlling sons more, they imply that boys are expected to be aggressive and out of control, and not cooperative or empathic. And their greater concern with boys' cognitive development is a message that girls are not expected to shine intellectually.

Fathers can help boys and girls feel good about themselves in terms of gender without limiting their potential for success in a career or at nurturance. Heterosexual adults who get along well at work and in relationships are most likely to have had warm ties to fathers who were competent, strong, secure in their own masculinity, and nurturant toward their children. The son of such a father identifies with him, and his daughter will be able to carry over her good feelings about him to relationships with other males. Conversely, children of a punitive, rejecting father or a passive, ineffectual one feel less secure in their gender (Biller, 1981).

Mothers, too, contribute to gender-typing of their children, but research on children from one-parent families (which are usually headed by the mother) underscores the strength of the father's influence. Such children tend to be less stereotyped than those from two-parent families (P. A. Katz, 1987). Why should this be so? First, a single parent serves as both mother and father and thus provides a more androgynous model. Second, since in these families it is typically the father who is absent, the parent who seems to be more concerned with and more active in perpetuating gender-typing is not there to exert influence.

*Influence of television*   The typical high school graduate has watched more than 25,000 hours of television, including 356,000 commercials (Action for Children's Television, undated), and in the process has absorbed highly gender-stereotyped attitudes. Television, in fact, is more stereotyped than real life.

For example, there are about twice as many males as females on both commercial and public television in the United States and Canada, and the males are usually more powerful, dominant, and authoritative than females (Calvert & Huston, 1987). Typically, men on television have been more aggressive, more active, and more competent than women, who have been portrayed as submissive, inactive, and interested mainly in either keeping house or becoming more beautiful (Mamay & Simpson, 1981; D. M. Zuckerman & Zuckerman, 1985).

Television producers have become more sensitive to the damaging effects of gender stereotypes and have made some changes. But while women are now portrayed differently, and are more likely to be working outside the home and using their brains for activities other than housework or child care—and while men are sometimes shown caring for children or doing the marketing—a high level of gender-stereotyping still prevails (Calvert & Huston, 1987). According to social-learning theory, children who watch a great deal of television will imitate the models they see and become more gender-typed themselves, and research has borne this out.

Can the media help abolish stereotypes? The answer seems to be "Yes, but . . . ." By and large children come to the television set with preformed attitudes, and they watch and process information selectively. Boys watch more cartoons and action adventure programs than girls do, and both sexes remember sequences on television that confirm the stereotypes they already hold better than they remember nonstereotypical sequences (Calvert & Huston, 1987). However, if a mighty effort is made to present nonstereotyped situations, children's attitudes can change.

In one study, girls who saw commercials showing women as pharmacists or butchers became more interested in such nontraditional occupations (O'Bryant & Corder-Boltz, 1978). And young children who watched a series of nontraditional episodes, like one showing a father and son having fun cooking together, had less stereotyped views than children who had not seen the series (J. Johnston & Ettema, 1982). If a serious effort were made, the media could probably shape children's views of themselves and other people in terms of possibilities rather than limitations.

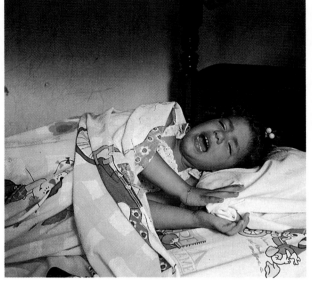

Many 6-year-olds develop fear of the dark. This and other characteristic fears of early childhood are usually short-lived.

## FEARS

When Kelly was 3 years old, she was frightened by a neighbor's large, barking dog. The next day, she refused to go out to play. When her mother asked why, she said she had a stomachache; but when dinnertime came, she cleaned her plate. The next day, Kelly again refused to go outside. When her father insisted on taking her to the store, Kelly burst into tears and clung to his arm.

Kelly had developed a fear of dogs, one of the most common fears of this most fearful age. Yet by her sixth birthday, this fear had gone away; in fact, she had to be stopped from patting strange dogs in the park.

Why do girls express more fears than boys do? It may be because parents encourage girls to be more dependent, because girls' fears are accepted and boys' fears are discouraged, or because boys do not admit having fears (Bauer, 1976; Croake, 1973; Jersild & Holmes, 1935).

### What Do Children Fear, and Why?

Temporary fears are common in 2- to 4-year-olds, many of whom are afraid of animals, especially dogs. By 6 years of age, children are more likely to be afraid of the dark. Other common fears are of thunderstorms and doctors (DuPont, 1983). Most of these fears evaporate as children grow older and lose their sense of powerlessness.

Why do children become so fearful at this age? The reasons may stem from their intense fantasy life—their inability to clearly distinguish "pretending" from reality. In one study, 75 percent of kindergartners and 50 percent of second-graders—as compared with only 5 percent of sixth-graders—expressed fear of ghosts and monsters. Older children are afraid of different things. Ten- to twelve-year-olds, who understand cause and effect, are more likely to fear bodily injury and physical danger, while 4- to 6-year-olds may fear a person who "looks ugly" (Bauer, 1976).

Underlying anxieties (like the inner conflicts discussed at the beginning of this chapter) may cause some fears. Violent television shows and movies may then provide frightening images for these anxieties.

Sometimes young children's imaginations are carried away, making them worry about being attacked by a lion or being abandoned. But often their fears come from appraisal of real dangers—like being bitten by a dog—or from actual events, as when a child who has been hit by a car becomes afraid to cross the street. Children of this age know more and have experienced more than they did before, and one thing they know is that there are many things to be afraid of.

### Preventing and Dealing with Fears

We don't know why some fears vanish and others persist. It seems, though, that adults' reactions play a part. Parents should accept fears as normal, offer reassurance, and encourage children to express their feelings without being ridiculed or punished. But children should not be allowed to avoid what they fear; avoidance does nothing to remove the cause of the fear.

Fears that linger can be treated before they become handicapping. Through conditioning, modeling, and gradual exposure to the feared object, the fear can be attacked head on, not treated as a symptom of a deeper problem (C. M. Murphy & Bootzin, 1973).

Some children seem to mask fears in aggression, which surfaces in a new way in early childhood.

### AGGRESSION

Babies do not show truly **aggressive behavior,** hostile actions intended to hurt somebody or to establish dominance. But anyone who is around children past the age of 2½ or 3 has seen enough punching, kicking, biting, and throwing to know that the age of *hostile aggression* has arrived. In the next 3 years or so, children normally shift from showing aggression with blows to showing it with words (Maccoby, 1980). Let's see how that happens—and why it sometimes doesn't happen.

This boy sees grabbing the toy he wants as the best way to get it. This kind of aggression, without intention to hurt the other child, is known as *instrumental aggression.* It surfaces mostly during social play and normally declines as children learn to ask for what they want.

### Stages of Aggression: Rise and Decline

A toddler who roughly snatches a toy away from another child is interested only in getting the toy, not in hurting or dominating the other child. This is *instrumental aggression,* or aggression used as an instrument to reach a goal.

In the early stages of aggression, children often focus single-mindedly on something they want and make threatening gestures against anyone who is keeping it from them. Between ages 2½ and 5, they commonly struggle over toys and the control of space. Aggression surfaces mostly during social play. Some aggression is normal, and the children who fight the most tend to be the most sociable and competent. The ability to show *some* aggression may be a necessary step in the social development of human beings.

As children move through early childhood from ages 2 to 5 and are better able to express themselves with words, aggression declines in frequency, initiation, and average length of episodes (Cummings, Iannotti, & Zahn-Waxler, 1989). However, individual differences that show up at age 2 tend to be fairly stable, especially among boys. Boys who hit or grab toys from other children at age 2 are still acting aggressively at age 5.

Most children become less aggressive after age 6 or 7, as empathy begins to replace egocentrism. Children are now better able to put themselves in someone else's place, can understand why someone is acting in a certain way, and can develop positive ways to deal with others.

But not all children learn to control aggression. Some become more and more destructive. Aggression may be a reaction to major problems in a child's life. It may also *cause* major problems, by making other children and adults dislike a child. Even in a normal child, aggression can sometimes get out of hand and become dangerous. Therefore, researchers have tried to find out what stimulates aggression.

## Triggers of Aggression

Although the male hormone testosterone may well underlie the tendency toward aggressive behavior and explain why males are more likely to be aggressive than females, social-learning theorists point to other contributing factors, a number of which show up in homes where parenting is ineffective (Patterson, DeBaryshe, & Ramsey, 1989). Parents of children who later become antisocial often fail to reinforce good behavior and are harsh or inconsistent or both in punishing misbehavior. They are not closely involved in their children's lives in positive ways like making sure that the children do their homework. The children tend to do poorly in school and to be rejected by their peers. Depressed, they then seek out other troubled children, who spur them on to more antisocial behavior.

Triggers of aggression that often show up in the early lives of these children include reinforcement for aggressive behavior, frustration, and imitation of aggressive models in real life or on television.

### Reinforcement

Children's clearest reward for aggression, of course, is getting what they want. But sometimes even scolding or spanking can reinforce aggressive behavior, since some children would rather get negative attention than none at all. Preschool teachers have decreased the amount of aggression shown by 3- and 4-year-old boys by ignoring aggressive behavior and reinforcing cooperative activities (P. Brown & Elliott, 1965). But it is not always safe to ignore aggression, and permitting it by not interfering with it can communicate approval.

Some parents actively encourage aggression toward other children, while discouraging it toward themselves. Their children learn not to hit their parents, but they still hit other children (Bandura, 1960).

### Frustration and imitation

Frustration—often resulting from punishment, insults, and fears—does not necessarily lead to aggression, but a frustrated child is more likely to act aggressively than a contented one (Bandura, Ross, & Ross, 1961).

Frustration and imitation can work together, as in a classic study by the social-learning theorist Albert Bandura and his colleagues in which children were exposed to one of two types of models or to no model (Bandura et al., 1961). Seventy-two 3- to 6-year-olds were divided into three groups. One by one, each child in each group went into a playroom for 10 minutes. For the children in the first group, an adult model (male for half of the children, female for the other half) would be playing quietly in a corner with toys. For the second group, the adult model would begin to assemble a construction toy, but after a minute would spend the rest of the session punching, throwing, and kicking a 5-foot-tall inflated doll. For the third group, there was no model.

After the sessions, all three groups of children were mildly frustrated, since they had seen toys that they were not allowed to play with. They then went into another playroom. The children who had seen the aggressive model were much more aggressive than those in the other groups, imitating in words and actions many of the things they had seen the model say and do. Both boys and girls were more strongly influenced by an aggressive male model than by an aggressive female model, apparently because they considered aggression more appropriate for males (gender-schema theorists would say that this was in line with the gender schema the children had learned). The children who had been with the quiet model were less aggressive than those who had not seen any model. We see, then, how adult models can influence children's behavior in more than one direction.

### Televised violence

Even if parents do not act aggressively, most children see aggressive models on television. When Anna was 3, her teacher reported that she was butting heads with her classmates. Her parents were disturbed and puzzled about this new behavior, but then they remembered that Anna had just seen a videocassette of the movie *Bambi,* which shows animals fighting in just this way. Diane and Jonathan quickly moved in to teach Anna that this might be acceptable behavior for stags in the forest, but not for children in preschool. They also stopped offering Anna the opportunity to see *Bambi.*

Three- to five-year-olds spend an average of 2 hours a day watching television (Institute for Social Research, 1985), and children's programs are much more violent than as adults' programs (Signorielli, Gross, & Morgan, 1982). Research suggests that children are influenced even more by seeing filmed violence than by seeing real people acting aggressively (Bandura, Ross, & Ross, 1963).

A body of research since the 1950s shows that children who see televised violence behave more aggressively (National Institute of Mental Health, NIMH, 1982). This is true across geographic locations and socioeconomic levels, for both boys and girls, and for normal children as well as children with emotional problems. This does not necessarily mean that televised violence *causes* aggression. It is possible that children already prone to violence become more so after seeing it onscreen. Also, they may watch more violent television. Finally, it is possible that some third factor is involved: maybe children who watch and react aggressively to televised violence are spanked more than other children.

In any case, aggressive children do watch more television than nonaggressive children, identify more strongly with aggressive characters, and are more likely to believe that aggression on television reflects real life (Eron, 1982). Aggressive acts make a more vivid impression than any punishment the "bad guy" receives (Liebert & Poulos, 1976, in Lickona, 1976). A report by the National Institute of Mental Health concludes that television encourages aggressive behavior in two ways: children imitate what they see on television, and they also absorb the values transmitted and come to accept aggression (NIMH, 1982).

Children who see television characters—both heroes and villains—getting what they want through violence and lawbreaking may fail to intervene when another child is being victimized by a bully. They are also more likely to break rules and less likely to cooperate to resolve differences.

Watching violence seems to make children more willing to hurt people. In a study of 136 boys and girls aged 5 to 9, an experimental group watched a 3½-minute segment from a popular television series, which included a chase, two fistfights, two shootings, and a knifing. A control group watched 3½ minutes of sports. Afterward, the children were asked to play a "game" that involved pushing either a "help" button (to help an unseen child win a game) or a "hurt" button (to make a handle touched by that child so hot that it would hurt). Of course, there was no such child; the only child in the experiment was the one pushing the buttons. Children who had watched the violent program were more willing to hurt the unseen child and willing to inflict more severe pain than were those who had watched the sports program (Liebert, 1972).

Some effects of televised violence seem to endure for years (D. M. Zuckerman & Zuckerman, 1985). Among 427 young adults whose viewing habits had been studied at the age of 8, the best predictor of ag-

gressiveness in 19-year-old men and women was the degree of violence in the television shows they had watched as children (Eron, 1980, 1982).

The American Psychological Association (1985) has called for a joint effort by parents and broadcasters to reduce the number of aggressive models on television. The resolution urges parents to monitor children's television watching, broadcasters to limit violence in children's programming, and researchers to study ways to lessen the effects of televised violence.

Meanwhile, television becomes more and more violent. Broadcasts of war cartoons soared from 1½ hours a week in 1982 to 48 hours a week in 1987, and the average child in the United States saw 250 episodes of such cartoons in a year. Sales of war toys jumped 700 percent during that period. In one small Canadian community that had been without television, both verbal and physical aggression increased after its introduction (T. M. Williams, 1978). And 40 studies assessing more than 4500 children in seven countries show the effects of cartoon violence and violent play: increases in fighting, kicking, choking, loss of temper, cruelty to animals, and disrespect for others, as well as decreases in sharing, imagination, and school performance (National Coalition on Television Violence, undated).

## Reducing Aggression

Parents can often nip aggressive tendencies in the bud by changing what they do early in their children's lives. Help is available from parent-training programs that instruct parents in how to reinforce good behavior, discipline consistently and appropriately, and become positively involved in their children's lives (Patterson et al., 1989).

This involvement can include monitoring their children's television watching—limiting total time and selecting appropriate programs (see Box 7-2). Television can also promote prosocial behavior.

The least aggressive children have parents who deal with misbehavior by reasoning with them, making them feel guilty, and withdrawing approval and affection. All these techniques are more likely to produce children with a strong conscience. On the other hand, children who are disciplined by spanking, threats, or withdrawal of privileges are more likely to be aggressive. (Of course, parents may also be more likely to spank aggressive children.) Parents' tendency to use the former methods with girls and the latter with boys may accentuate girls' inclination to feel guilty and boys' inclination to be aggressive (R. R. Sears, Maccoby, & Levin, 1957).

---

**BOX 7–2    PRACTICALLY SPEAKING**

## BE A CHILD'S TV GUIDE

Television is a powerful force in children's lives. American children typically watch several hours of television every day, and by the time they graduate from high school, most children have spent more time in front of the television set than in the classroom. Television viewing can heighten tendencies toward obesity, promote an inclination toward violence, and convey unrealistic messages regarding drugs, alcohol, sexuality, gender roles, and relationships (American Academy of Pediatrics, AAP, 1986b). Or it can convey positive, prosocial values.

The following suggestions for parents, teachers, baby-sitters, and caregivers (Action for Children's Television, undated; AAP, 1986b) can help make television a positive force in children's lives:

■ *Set limits.* Know how much television your children watch, and don't be afraid to reduce it. The AAP recommends that parents limit their children's viewing to 1 or 2 hours per day.

■ *Plan viewing in advance.* Help children learn to approach television like a movie rather than becoming indiscriminate "dial turners." Turn the set on for a particular program, and turn it off and discuss the program when it is over.

■ *Watch with your children.* Interpret and talk about the programs they see. Point out that much of what is shown on television is not real; discuss the differences between make-believe and real life.

■ *Be a good role model.* Because children often follow adults' ex-

ample, examine your own viewing patterns to help children form good habits early in life.

■ *Do not use television as a baby-sitter.* Offer children alternative indoor and outdoor activities like field trips, games, sports, hobbies, reading, chores, and special family activities.

■ *Resist commercials.* Help children become smart consumers by teaching them to recognize a sales pitch. Talk about foods that can cause cavities and toys that may break too soon.

■ *Complement television with new technologies.* Use a video recorder to tape worthwhile programs for convenient viewing or to show rented movies. Show educational tapes to help children learn.

---

Punishment—especially spanking—may backfire, because hitting children provides a double incentive for violence. The child not only suffers frustration, pain, and humiliation but sees aggressive behavior in an adult with whom she or he identifies. Parents who spank provide a "living example of the use of aggression at the very moment they are trying to teach the child not to be aggressive" (R. R. Sears et al., 1957, p. 266). Parents need to think about what kind of behavior they want to encourage—and how to encourage it.

## ALTRUISM: PROSOCIAL BEHAVIOR

Anna, at 3½, responded to two fellow preschoolers' complaints that they did not have enough modeling clay—her favorite toy—by giving them half of hers. Anna was showing altruistic behavior, or **prosocial behavior,** acting out of concern for another person, with no expectation of reward. Prosocial acts often entail cost, self-sacrifice, or risk on the part of the person who makes them.

### Influences on Prosocial Behavior

Why do some children reach out to comfort a crying friend or stop to help someone who has fallen while crossing a street? What makes these children generous, compassionate, and sensitive to other people's needs? From many studies dating from the 1970s, we have learned about the origins of caring behavior.

Socioeconomic status, for example, is *not* a factor: parents' income or social standing makes no difference in how a youngster will behave toward others. And in most studies, no sex differences turned up, though some research has found more generosity, helpfulness, and considerateness in girls than in boys. This may be because nurturance is generally considered a feminine trait, and so girls are encouraged more often to help others; it may also be related to the fact that parents spank girls less than boys, are more affectionate toward them, and give them more explanations of the consequences of their actions.

Age, however, does seem to be an important factor. Children as young as 18 months will show sympathy toward someone who is hurt or unhappy and may make efforts to help; but not until about age 4 do children show a significant amount of altruism. The level increases steadily until age 13, apparently in relation to children's growing empathy.

Altruistic children tend to be advanced in mental reasoning and able to take the role of others; they are also relatively active and self-confident. How do they become this way? The findings of many studies point to the home. The family is important as a model, as a source of explicit standards, and as a guide to adopting models.

### Encouraging Prosocial Behavior

One important way that parents encourage altruism is to love and respect a child, since altruistic children generally feel secure in their parents' love and affection. Preschoolers who were securely attached as infants are more likely than insecurely attached children to respond to other children's distress. They have more friends, and their teachers consider them more socially competent. Children who received empathic, nurturant, responsive care as infants develop those qualities themselves (Kestenbaum, Farber, & Sroufe, 1989; Sroufe, 1983).

Parents of prosocial children typically set an example, encourage them to empathize with others and to reflect on the implications of their actions. When Sara took candy from a store, her father did not give her an abstract lecture on honesty or tell her what a bad girl she had been. Instead, he explained how the owner of the store would be harmed because she had not paid for the candy, and then he took her back to the store to return it. When incidents like this occur, Sara's parents ask, for example, "How do you think Mr. Jones feels?" or "How would you feel if you were Mary?"

Parents of prosocial children usually hold them to high standards. The children know that they are expected to be honest and helpful. They have responsibilities in the home and are expected to meet them.

Parents also point out other models, and steer their children toward stories and television programs—like *Mister Rogers' Neighborhood*—that depict cooperation, sharing, and empathy. Many studies have shown that such programs encourage children to be more sympathetic, generous, and helpful (Mussen & Eisenberg-Berg, 1977; NIMH, 1982; D. M. Zuckerman & Zuckerman, 1985).

A recent study identified 406 non-Jewish Europeans who, during the 1930s and 1940s, had risked their lives to rescue Jews in Nazi-occupied countries, and then compared these rescuers with people who did not help

What parents themselves do and say is a major influence on whether children will be likely to help other people, strangers or those in their own families.

Jewish people. The researchers found that the rescuers' childhood homes were different from those of the control group (Oliner & Oliner, 1988). Rescuers' parents had emphasized strong ethical principles—compassion and caring for others and a sense of fairness extending to people one did not know. They put less emphasis on values like obedience, earning money, and the importance of self. The rescuers also reported closer early family relationships, especially with parents who disciplined them more by reasoning, explanations, persuasion, advice, and suggestions of how to right a wrong than by spanking. Furthermore, the parents often behaved altruistically themselves.

Obviously, parents can have an enormous impact on children's personalities. Let's look more closely at how they use that influence.

## CHILD-REARING PRACTICES

"Just as the twig is bent, the tree's inclined," wrote the eighteenth-century English poet Alexander Pope. But raising children is not so simple. Children are not saplings to be bent to their parents' will. In early childhood, as children become their own persons, their upbringing can be a baffling, complex challenge.

How are parents raising their children today? Some parents, of course, repeat the child-rearing patterns that their own parents followed. Others adopt practices that are very different from those their parents used.

### Parents' Use of Reinforcement and Punishment

Almost all parents sometimes offer rewards to get children to do something they want them to do, and use punishment to get the children to stop doing what they do *not* want them to do. Many parents are less comfortable with rewards—seeing them as bribes—than punishment, but the weight of research shows that children learn more by being reinforced for good behavior than by being punished for bad behavior.

### Reinforcement

**Behavior modification,** or behavior therapy (a form of operant, or instrumental, learning, described in Chapter 1), is a new name for the old practice of providing positive consequences when children do what parents want them to do and negative consequences when they do something the parents disapprove of. *External* reinforcements may be social ones like a smile, a hug, praise, or a special privilege. Or they may be more tangible—candy, money, toys, or gold stars. Whatever the reinforcement, the child must see it as rewarding and must get it fairly consistently after showing the desired behavior. Eventually, the behavior should provide its own *internal* reward to the child—such as a sense of pleasure and accomplishment.

### Ineffective punishment:
### "Rewarding" with punishment

"What are we going to do with that child?" Noel's mother says. "The more we punish him, the more he misbehaves!" No wonder: Noel's parents ignore him most of the time when he behaves well but scold or spank him when he acts up. In effect, they reinforce his misbehavior by paying attention when it occurs.

Most children, of course, prefer approval to disapproval. But children who get little positive attention may like disapproval more than no attention at all, and so they deliberately misbehave. Punishment thus "rewards" the very behavior it is intended to stop.

### Effective punishment:
### When does punishment work?

Most researchers stress the negative effects of punishment. But although the carrot is usually a better motivator than the stick, there are times when punishment seems necessary. For example, children have to learn very quickly not to run out into traffic and not to bash each other over the head with heavy toys. Sometimes, too, undesirable behavior may be so deep-seated that it is hard to find any good behavior to reinforce.

If punishment must be used, findings from laboratory and field research suggest the most effective ways to use it (Parke, 1977). The following criteria are important:

- *Timing.* The shorter the time between misbehavior and punishment, the more effective the punishment. When children are punished as they *begin* to engage in a forbidden act such as approaching an object they have been told to stay away from, they will go to it less often than if they are not punished until *after* they have actually touched it. It is not always possible, of course, to punish children before they misbehave; however, parents and teachers may be able to move in quickly when a child is about to *repeat* misbehavior. And they can act immediately afterward rather than postponing punishment "until your father gets home" (a practice that has, fortunately, diminished over the years).
- *Explanation.* Punishment is more effective when accompanied by a short explanation (but not a long, involved one). For example, children are less likely to play with a fragile vase if, the last time they broke one, they were told "That vase belongs to Aunt Martha" than if they were punished with no explanation.
- *Consistency.* The more consistently a child is punished, the more effective the punishment will be. When the same behavior brings punishment only some of the time, it is likely to continue longer than if unpunished all the time.
- *The person who punishes.* The better the relationship between the punishing adult and the child, the more effective the punishment. Punishment is two-edged: as it presents something negative, it withholds something positive. Therefore, the more positive the element that is being withheld (acceptance by an affectionate, nurturing adult), the more effective the punishment.

Used with care, then, punishment can be effective, at least in the short run. However, it can be harmful when it is inconsistent and is administered in a hostile way. Unwanted long-term effects may include a child's avoidance of a punitive parent, undermining the parent's ability to influence behavior. Physical punishment (aside from the risk of injury it carries) may encourage children to imitate the aggression modeled by the parent. And children who are punished often may become passive because they feel helpless to escape punishment.

Some children are punished more often than others, and not necessarily because of the seriousness of their offenses. Parents tend to spare the rod for a child who expresses remorse and tries to make up for misdeeds, whereas a child who is defiant or who ignores parents' rebukes is punished severely.

Child rearing, of course, involves far more than reinforcing and rewarding specific kinds of behaviors. Let's look at other aspects of parenting.

### Parents' Styles and Children's Competence: Baumrind's Research

Why does Nicole hit and bite the nearest person when she cannot finish a jigsaw puzzle? Why does David sit with the puzzle for an hour until he solves it? Why does Michele walk away from it after a minute's effort? In short, why are children so different in their responses to the same task? What makes them turn out the way they do?

One effort to answer these questions has related different styles of parenting to different levels of children's competence.

#### Three parenting styles

Diana Baumrind set out to discover relationships between children's social competence and parents' different styles of child rearing. Her research combined lengthy interviews, standardized testing, and home studies of 103 preschool children from 95 families. She identified children who were functioning at various levels and then sought to relate the children's adjustment to their parents' child-rearing styles. She then categorized three child-rearing styles and described typical behavior patterns of children raised according to each style (Baumrind, 1971; Baumrind & Black, 1967).

*Authoritarian parents* value control and unquestioning obedience. They try to make children conform to a set standard of conduct, and they punish them forcefully for acting contrary to that standard. They are more detached and less warm than other parents; their

children tend to be more discontented, withdrawn, and distrustful.

*Permissive parents* value self-expression and self-regulation. They make few demands, allowing children to monitor their own activities as much as possible. They consider themselves resources, not standard-bearers or models. They explain the reasons underlying the few family rules that do exist, consult with children about policy decisions, and hardly ever punish. They are noncontrolling, nondemanding, and relatively warm; their preschool children tend to be immature—the least self-controlled and the least exploratory.

*Authoritative parents* respect a child's individuality, while at the same time stressing social values. They direct their children's activities rationally, paying attention to the issues rather than to a child's fear of punishment or loss of love. While they have confidence in their ability to guide children, they respect the children's interests, opinions, and unique personalities. They are loving, consistent, demanding, and respectful of children's independent decisions, but they are firm in maintaining standards and willing to impose limited punishment. They explain the reasoning behind their stands and encourage verbal give-and-take. They combine control with encouragement. Their children apparently feel secure in knowing that they are loved and in knowing what is expected of them. As preschoolers, children of authoritative parents tend to be most self-reliant, self-controlled, self-assertive, exploratory, and content.

Recent research based on Baumrind's work also found a link between authoritative parenting and learning. A study by Pratt and his colleagues on "scaffolding," the temporary help that parents give children to do a task (see Chapter 6), found that authoritative parents were more sensitive in knowing when to shift their level of help and that their children were more successful at various tasks.

#### Authoritative child rearing

Diana Baumrind relied on correlational data. She did not find proof that these three styles of child rearing *caused* the children in her study to turn out as they did. Rather, she established relationships between each parenting style and a particular set of behaviors. Also, it is impossible to know from her data whether the children were actually raised by a particular style: it is possible, for example, that some of the well-adjusted children had been raised inconsistently, but by the time of the study, their parents had adopted the authoritative pattern.

Parenting styles influence children's personality development. Children of authoritative parents, who balance firmness with love and respect, are often the most self-reliant, self-controlled, and content.

Furthermore, Baumrind did not consider a child's influence on parents: "easy" children may stimulate parents to be authoritative while "difficult" children may drive their parents to authoritarianism. Finally, she did not look at inborn differences among children. For all these reasons, we cannot draw firm conclusions about the effects of the different styles.

But if authoritative parenting does indeed further children's development, its success may be related to the parents' reasonable expectations and realistic standards. Children from authoritarian homes are so strictly controlled, by either punishment or guilt, that often they cannot make a conscious choice about a particular behavior because they are too concerned about what their parents will do. Children from permissive homes receive so little guidance that they often become uncertain and anxious about whether they are doing the right thing. But in authoritative homes, children know when they are meeting expectations, and they are able to decide when it is worth risking their parents' displeasure or other unpleasant consequences to pursue some goal. These children are expected to perform well, to fulfill their commitments, and to participate actively in family duties as well as in family fun. They know the satisfaction of meeting responsibilities and achieving success.

Of course, no parent is authoritarian, permissive, or authoritative *all* the time. Being human, parents have different moods and react differently to various situations (Carter & Welch, 1981). And although it is easy to *know* the "right" way to act with children, it is not always easy to put it into action.

## Parents' Love and Maturity

In the long run, specific parenting practices during a child's first 5 years may be less important than how parents feel about their children and how they show their feelings. That is the conclusion of a major follow-up study (McClelland, Constantian, Regalado, & Stone, 1978) of young adults whose mothers had been interviewed about their child rearing techniques 20 years earlier (R. R. Sears et al., 1957).

The way these adults turned out seemed to bear little or no relation to how long they had been breastfed, whether they had gone to bed early or late, or a number of other factors. The most important influence—overshadowing all others—was how much their parents, especially their mothers, had loved them, enjoyed them, and shown affection for them.

The most beloved children grew up to be the most prosocially mature: most tolerant of other people, most understanding, and most likely to show active concern for others. The least mature adults had grown up in homes with adult-centered standards where they were considered a nuisance and an interference. Their parents (who may have been authoritarian) had tolerated no noise, mess, or roughhousing at home and had reacted unkindly to aggressiveness, sex play, or expressions of normal dependency.

Although the children of "easygoing, loving parents" had often behaved less acceptably when they were growing up than the children of stricter parents, this may be a necessary step toward independence from parental values (McClelland et al., 1978, p. 114).

## RELATING TO OTHER CHILDREN

Although babies are aware of other babies almost from birth, the most important people in their world are the adults who take care of them. Relationships with peers become important in early childhood. Almost every characteristic activity and personality issue of this age—such as play, gender identity, or aggressive or prosocial behavior—involves relationships with other children, either siblings or friends. But before we look at these relationships, let's look at the children who grow up without any siblings—only children.

### The Only Child

Since the 1970s, couples have had fewer babies; today, about 1 couple in 10 has an only child.

Although people often think of only children as spoiled, selfish, lonely, or maladjusted, research does not bear out this negative view. In fact, according to a statistical analysis of 115 studies comparing only children of various ages and backgrounds and children with siblings (Falbo & Polit, 1986), only children do very well. In occupational and educational achievement, intelligence, and character (or personality), the "onlies" surpassed children with siblings, especially those with many siblings or older siblings. In these three categories, as well as in adjustment and sociability, only children were like firstborns and people with only one sibling. The authors of this statistical analyis point out that only children, like firstborns and children with one sibling, have parents who can spend more time and focus more attention on them. Perhaps these children do better because their parents talk to them more, do more with them, and expect more of them.

Being an only child has implications for future development, and these implications may vary from one culture to another. Box 7-3 discusses the situation in China, which encourages one-child families.

### Brothers and Sisters

When Sally brought her third baby, Dorri, home from the hospital, both Jenny (then 3) and Nancy (5) had colds. The older sisters were so eager to hold the baby that they willingly put on hospital-type face masks. Their interest in their baby sister continued; Jenny often fed Dorri bottles of juice, and Nancy would dry and dress her after her bath. Once Dorri could toddle around, Nancy and Jenny brought her into their fantasy play, making allowances for her inability to follow their instructions or the rules of their games.

Sibling rivalry is *not* the main pattern for brothers and sisters early in life. While some rivalry exists, so do affection, interest, companionship—and influence.

Two sisters normally get along better than a sister and a brother. The older sibling usually initiates activities, and the younger one follows.

Observations of young sibling pairs (same-sex and mixed-sex) showed that siblings separated by as little as 1 year or as much as 4 years interact closely with each other in many ways (Abramovitch, Corter, & Lando, 1979; Abramovitch, Corter, Pepler, & Stanhope, 1986; Abramovitch, Pepler, & Corter, 1982). Three sets of observations—from the time younger siblings were about 1½ years old and older siblings ranged from 3 to 4½, until the younger ones were 5 and the older ones were 6½ to 8—found that, by and large, older siblings initiate more behavior, both friendly (sharing a toy, smiling, hugging, or starting a game) and unfriendly (hitting, fighting over a toy, teasing, or tattling). The younger children tend to imitate the older siblings—whether in using scissors or blowing cake crumbs out of their mouths. At the older ages, siblings are less physical and more verbal, in showing aggression (through commands, insults, threats, tattling, put-downs, bribes, and teasing) and care and affection (through compliments and comfort rather than hugs and kisses). The age difference between siblings apparently has only one effect: in closely spaced pairs, older siblings initiate more prosocial behavior. Same-sex sib-

## BOX 7–3   WINDOW ON THE WORLD

# A NATION OF ONLY CHILDREN

A group of Chinese kindergartners are learning a new skill—how to fold paper to make toys. When the toys do not come out right, some of the children try again on their own or watch their classmates and copy what they do. But other children become bored and impatient and ask someone else to do it for them, or else they give up, bursting into tears (Jiao, Ji, & Jing, 1986). The children in the second category tend to come from one-child families—a fact that worries citizens of the People's Republic of China, which in 1979 established an official policy of limiting families to one child each.

The government is intensely serious about this policy, since China's exploding population has had severe effects: not enough places in classrooms for all its children, not enough jobs for adults, not even enough food for everyone. To lower the birthrate, family-planning workers oversee factory workshops and agricultural brigades, and special birth control departments exist in every inhabited area. Furthermore, the policy goes beyond using propaganda campaigns and rewards (housing, money, child care, and school priorities) to induce voluntary compliance. There have been millions of involuntary abortions, sterilizations, and vasectomies, and people who have children without permission are fined and denied job promotions and bonuses, although recent reports indicate that

there has been some easing of controls.

As a result, the nursery schools, kindergartens, and early elementary grades of China are already filled with children who have no brothers or sisters. This situation marks a great change in Chinese society, in which newlywed couples were traditionally congratulated with the wish, "May you have a hundred sons and a thousand grandsons." No culture in human history has ever been composed entirely of only children. And now that the Chinese are seeing a real possibility of achieving this goal, some critics are asking whether they are sowing the seeds of their own destruction.

Kindergarten teachers complain that only children, raised by overindulgent parents, are spoiled brats who show an unusually large number of behavioral problems and are fussy about what they eat and wear, careless with property, selfish, and ill-tempered. In an effort to test the truth of these comments, psychologists asked urban and rural schoolchildren, aged 4 to 6 and 9 to 10, to rate their classmates on seven characteristics—independence and self-reliance, persistence, willingness to control their own behavior, tendency to become frustrated, cooperation, popularity with other children, and egocentrism. When the ratings of children from one-child families were compared with those of children with

siblings, the results were disturbing. Only children were seen as more egocentric, less persistent, less cooperative, and less well liked (Jiao et al., 1986). They were more likely to refuse to help another child or to help grudgingly, less likely to share their toys or to enjoy playing or working with other children, less modest, less helpful in group activities, and more irresponsible. It is no wonder that children liked them less than they liked children with siblings.

In a second study, however, teachers in Peking (Beijing) rated only children quite favorably, finding them gentle, shy, obedient, considerate, respectful of elders, and eager to join in collective activities. They also found them academically superior, especially in language ability. Are these children perhaps Jekyll-and-Hyde characters who are angels around adults but demons around other children? If so, they may not be model members of society, particularly a society that emphasizes individual sacrifice for the sake of collective development.

China's population policy also has wider implications of considerable concern. If it succeeds, eventually most Chinese will lack not only siblings but also aunts and uncles, nephews and nieces, and cousins. How this would affect individuals, families, and the social fabric is at present incalculable.

---

lings tend to be a bit closer and to play together more peaceably than boy-girl pairs. Siblings tend to get along better when their mother is not with them, suggesting that squabbling is often a bid for parental attention.

These researchers concluded that, despite some sibling rivalry, "prosocial and play-oriented behaviors almost always constituted a majority of the interactions" and that "it is probably a mistake to think of siblings' relationships, at least during the preschool years,

as primarily competitive or negative" (Abramovitch et al., 1986, p. 229).

Relationships between siblings set the stage for other relationships. If relationships with brothers and sisters are marked by trust and companionship, children may carry this pattern over into their dealings with playmates, classmates, and eventually friends and lovers in adulthood. If early sibling relationships are aggressive, this too may influence later social relations.

## First Friends

At 3, Sally's daughter Nancy already had a best friend. She and Janie wore a path between their backyards, they asked for each other as soon as they woke up in the morning, and neither was so happy as when she was in the company of her best friend.

Friendship develops as people develop. Although younger children may play alongside or near each other, it is only at about age 3 or so that they begin to have friends. Through friendships and more casual interactions with other children, young children learn how to get along with others. They learn the importance of *being* a friend in order to *have* a friend. They learn how to solve problems in relationships, they learn how to put themselves in another person's place, and they see models of other kinds of behavior. They learn values (including moral judgments and gender-role norms), and they get a chance to practice adult roles.

Young children define a friend as "someone you like." Because friendships are voluntary, they are more fragile than the more permanent ties with parents, siblings, and other relatives.

A study of the conceptions of friendship held by 4- to 7-year-olds confirms and adds to these findings (Furman & Bierman, 1983). The children in this study were interviewed and were asked to recognize and rate pictured activities that would make children friends. The most important features of friendships were *common activities* (doing things together), *affection* (liking and caring for each other), *support* (sharing and helping), and, to a lesser degree, *propinquity* (living nearby or going to the same school). Older children rated affection and support higher and *physical characteristics* (appearance and size) lower than younger children did.

## Behavior patterns and choice of playmates and friends

Although playing with someone and being friends are not exactly the same, the traits that make young children desirable or undesirable seem to be quite similar for both purposes. Children who have friends talk more and take turns directing and following. Children who do not have friends tend to fight with those who do, or to stand on the sidelines and watch them (Roopnarine & Field, 1984). Children like to play with peers who smile and offer a toy or a hand; they reject overtures from disruptive or aggressive children and ignore children who are shy or withdrawn (Roopnarine & Honig, 1985).

In one study, 65 kindergartners saw pictures of situations related to making and keeping friends and were asked what a child in the picture should do. Popular children's answers were more likely to promote positive relationships and to be effective. Unpopular children tended to give more aggressive responses (12 percent suggested that a child should "beat up" another child who grabs toys, compared with only 2 percent of the popular children). Unpopular children were also less resourceful; they tended to give vague strategies or look for help from an authority rather than cope with a situation themselves (S. Asher, Renshaw, Geraci, & Dor, 1979). Overall, however, the two groups were not greatly different; about two-thirds of the most common responses of popular children were also given by unpopular children.

## Parents and popularity

Not surprisingly, young children's relationships with each other are influenced by their relationships with their parents. Preschoolers in one study who had been

Young children prefer playmates or friends who smile and laugh a lot, take turns, and are not overly shy or aggressive.

---

**BOX 7–4    PRACTICALLY SPEAKING**

## HELPING YOUNG CHILDREN TO MAKE FRIENDS

Having friends helps children develop and contributes to their mental health.

Research suggests that parents and other adults can help children who have trouble finding playmates or making friends by following these recommendations and suggestions (Roopnarine & Honig, 1985):

- Use positive disciplinary techniques. Give rewards, make rules and their reasons clear, and encourage cooperation in nonpunitive ways.
- Be models of warm, nurturing, attentive behavior, and work to build children's self-esteem.
- Show prosocial behavior yourself, and praise signs of children's budding empathy and responsiveness.
- Make a special effort to find a play group for children if they do not often have an opportunity to be with other children. Social skills grow through experience.
- Encourage "loners" to play with small groups of two or three children at first, and give them ample time to get acquainted before getting involved.
- Teach "friendship skills" indirectly through puppetry, role-playing, and books about animals and children who learn to make friends.

---

securely attached as infants had more friends and were more socially competent than children who had been insecurely attached. The securely attached children were also more empathic: they responded to classmates who showed distress, whereas insecurely attached children did not (Sroufe, 1983).

Mothers of rejected or isolated children tend to lack confidence in their parenting. They seldom praise their children for good behavior, and they do not encourage independence. Their fathers often have strong ideas about how children should behave, but they pay little attention to their children, dislike being disturbed by them, and regard child rearing as women's work (Peery, Jensen, & Adams, 1984, in Roopnarine & Honig, 1985).

Parents can help their children to make friends by setting up play dates for them. When parents actively arrange their children's social lives, the children have more playmates and see them more often (Ladd & Colter, 1988). Parents who monitor preschoolers' play indirectly—by staying nearby but not getting involved in it—tend to have socially competent children. Children whose parents participate in the play activity are not so well adjusted in the classroom. It is not clear, though, which comes first. Parents' early monitoring styles may influence the way their children play with others, or parents of children who are aggressive or do not play well on their own may feel they need to maintain more of a presence.

Popular children generally have warm, positive relationships with their parents. When they need discipline, their parents reason with them rather than punish them or take away privileges (Roopnarine & Honig, 1985).

Children of authoritarian parents tend to be distrustful, withdrawn, and discontented; they are less popular than children of authoritative parents, who have learned to be both assertive and cooperative (Baumrind, 1977). See Box 7-4 for suggestions for putting findings like these into practice to help children make friends.

The connection between relationships with parents and relationships with peers seems to persist at least into the early school years. One study of first-graders suggests that children pick up from their mothers a repertoire of social behaviors that can affect their popularity (Putallaz, 1987).

How children get along with their age-mates affects one of the most important activities of early childhood—play. We'll look at play in the next section.

## PLAY

### Importance of Play

Carmen, age 4, wakes up to see her clothes laid out for her. She tries putting her overalls on backward, her shoes on the wrong feet, her socks on her hands, and her shirt inside out. At breakfast, she pretends that the pieces of cereal in her bowl are "fishies" swimming in the milk, and, spoonful by spoonful, she goes fishing. Throughout the long, busy morning, she plays. She puts on an old hat of her mother's, picks up a briefcase, and is a "mommy" going to work. Next she is a doctor, giving her doll a "shot." She runs outside to splash in puddles with a friend and then comes in for an imaginary telephone conversation.

**TABLE 7–1**
TYPES OF SOCIAL AND NONSOCIAL PLAY IN EARLY CHILDHOOD

| Category | Description |
| --- | --- |
| Unoccupied behavior | The child does not seem to be playing, but watches anything of momentary interest. |
| Onlooker behavior | The child spends most of the time watching other children play. The onlooker talks to them, asking questions or making suggestions, but does not enter into the play. The onlooker is definitely observing particular groups of children rather than anything in general that happens to be exciting. |
| Solitary independent play | The child plays alone with toys that are different from those used by nearby children and makes no effort to get close to the other children. |
| Parallel play | The child plays independently but among other children, playing with toys like those used by the other children, but not necessarily in the same way. Playing *beside* rather than *with* the others, the parallel player does not try to influence the other children's play. |
| Associative play | The child plays with other children. They talk about their play, borrow and lend toys, follow one another, and try to control who may play in the group. All the children play similarly if not identically; there is no division of labor and no organization around any goal. Each child acts as he or she wishes and is interested more in being with the other children than in the activity itself. |
| Cooperative or organized supplementary play | The child plays in a group organized for some goal—to make something, play a formal game, or dramatize a situation. One or two children control who belongs to the group and direct activities. By a division of labor, children take on different roles and supplement each other's efforts. |

*Source:* Adapted from Parten, 1932, pp. 249–251.

An adult might be tempted to smile indulgently (or enviously) at Carmen and to dismiss her activities as no more than a pleasant way to pass time. Such a judgment would be grievously in error. For play is the work of the young.

Through play, children grow. They learn how to use their muscles, they coordinate what they see with what they do, and they gain mastery over their body. They find out what the world is like and what *they* are like. They stimulate their senses by playing with water, sand, and mud. They acquire new skills and learn when to use them. And they cope with complex and conflicting emotions by reenacting real life.

## Perspectives on Play

We can look at play from different perspectives. Children have different styles of playing, and they play at different things. One kindergartner spends most of her free time playing with other children, while another likes to build block towers by himself. What can we learn about individual children by seeing how they play? To answer such questions, researchers have approached play in two broadly different ways—as a social phenomenon and as an aspect of cognition.

Considering play as a social activity, researchers evaluate children's social competence on the basis of how they play. *Social play* reflects the extent to which children interact with other children in play. *Cognitive play* shows the level of a child's cognitive development, and also enhances that development.

### Social and nonsocial play

In the 1920s, Mildred B. Parten (1932) observed forty-two 2- to 5-year-olds during free-play periods at nursery school. She identified six types of play, ranging from the most nonsocial to the most social (see Table 7-1), determined the proportion of time devoted to each type, and charted the children's activities. She found that as children get older, their play tends to become more social and cooperative.

More recent research, however, suggests different conclusions. In a similar study done 40 years later, forty-four 3- and 4-year-olds played much less sociably than the children in Parten's group (K. E. Barnes, 1971). Why was this so? The change might have reflected a changed environment: because these children watched television, they may have become more passive; because they had more elaborate toys and fewer siblings, they may have played alone more. Another possible explanation may have to do with socioeconomic status. Preschoolers from lower socioeconomic groups engage in more parallel play, while middle-class children play in more associative and cooperative ways (K. Rubin, Maioni, & Hornung, 1976).

Is solitary play less mature than group play? Parten thought so, and other observers have suggested that young children who play alone may be at risk of developing social, psychological, and educational problems. But recent research has found that much nonsocial play consists of constructive or educational activities and furthers a child's cognitive, physical, and social development.

In an analysis of children in six kindergartens, about one-third of solitary play consisted of such goal-directed activities as block building and artwork, about one-fourth was large-muscle play, about 15 percent was educational, and only about 10 percent involved just looking at the other children (N. Moore, Evertson, & Brophy, 1974). Solitary play can be a sign of independence and maturity rather than poor social adjustment.

Another study looked at nonsocial play in relation to the cognitive and social competence of 4-year-olds. It used role-taking and problem-solving tests, teachers'

ratings of social competence, and popularity with other children. Some kinds of nonsocial play turned out to be associated with a high level of competence. For example, parallel constructive play (activities like playing with blocks or working on puzzles near another child) is most common among children who are good problem solvers, are popular with other children, and are seen by teachers as socially skilled (K. Rubin, 1982).

Not all nonsocial play, then, is immature. Children need some time alone to concentrate on tasks and problems, and some simply enjoy nonsocial activities more than group activities. We need to look at what children *do* when they play, not just at whether they play alone or with someone else.

### Cognitive play

According to Piaget (1951) and Smilansky (1968), children's cognitive development in early childhood lets them progress (as shown in Table 7-2) from simple functional (repetitive) play (like rolling a ball) to constructive play (like building a block tower), pretend play (like playing doctor), and then formal games with rules (like hopscotch and marbles). These more complex forms of play, in turn, foster further cognitive development.

### Imaginative play

Kaia, at 13 months, pushes an imaginary spoon holding imaginary food into the mouth of her very real father. Joseph, at 2 years, "talks" to a doll as if it were a real person. Lee, at 3 years, wears a kitchen towel as a cape and runs around as Batman.

**TABLE 7–2**
TYPES OF COGNITIVE PLAY

| Category | Description |
| --- | --- |
| Functional play (sensorimotor play) | Any simple, repetitive muscle movement with or without objects, such as rolling a ball or pulling a pull toy. |
| Constructive play | Manipulation of objects to construct or to "create" something. |
| Dramatic play (pretend play) | Substitution of an imaginary situation to satisfy the child's personal wishes and needs. Pretending to be someone or something (doctor, nurse, Batman), beginning with fairly simple activities but going on to develop more elaborate plots. |
| Games with rules | Any activity with rules, structure, and a goal (such as winning), like tag, hopscotch, marbles. Acceptance of prearranged rules and adjustment to them. |

*Source:* Piaget, 1951; Smilansky, 1968.

This preschooler pretending to feed her "baby" is showing an important cognitive development of early childhood: the ability to use symbols to stand for people or things in the real world.

These children are engaged in **imaginative play,** play involving imaginary situations. (Imaginative play is also called *fantasy play, dramatic play,* or *pretend play.*) At one time, professionals' main interest in such play was its supposed role in helping children express their emotional concerns, but interest now focuses more on its role in cognitive and general personality development.

Imaginative play emerges during the second year of life when sensorimotor play is on the wane. It increases during the next 3 to 4 years, and then declines as children become more interested in playing games with formal rules. Piaget (1962) maintained that children's ability to pretend rests on their ability to use and remember symbols—to retain in their minds pictures of things they have seen or heard—and that its emergence marks the beginning of the preoperational stage (see Chapter 6).

About 10 to 17 percent of preschoolers' play is imaginative play, and the proportion rises to about 33 percent among kindergartners (K. Rubin et al., 1976; K. Rubin, Watson, & Jambor, 1978). The kind of play, as well as its amount, changes during these years from solitary pretending to *sociodramatic play* involving other children. Anna, who at age 3 would climb inside a box by herself and pretend to be a train conductor, will by age 6 want to have passengers on her train with whom she can enact minidramas (Iwanaga, 1973). Through pretending, children learn how to understand another person's viewpoint, develop skills in solving social problems, and become more creative.

### Influences on Play: Parents and Day Care

Parents of children who play imaginatively tend to get along well with each other, expose their children to interesting experiences, talk with them, and not spank them (Fein, 1981). Children who watch a lot of television play less imaginatively, possibly because they passively absorb images rather than generating their own.

Time in group-based day care tends to be associated with sociable play, according to researchers who compared the play of children from three centers (Schindler, Moely, & Frank, 1987). Children in a large community center and children in a small university-based center played more sociably the longer they had been in day care. This was not true of children in a small private center; they played less constructively than those at the university center. These differences may have arisen from differences in the centers. The university center and the large center had higher adult-child ratios, which may have helped the children to play with each other. They also had mixed-age groups; the private center had same-age groups. Also, they emphasized social skills; the private center stressed academic skills. The differences between these centers and the different effects they seemed to have on children underscore the need to look at every day care situation individually, rather than making sweeping statements about "effects of day care."

Children continue to play, of course, in middle childhood—the years from about age 6 to 12—which we'll examine in Chapter 8 and Chapter 9.

# SUMMARY

## PERSONALITY IN EARLY CHILDHOOD: THEORETICAL APPROACHES

■ Several types of theories attempt to explain how young children acquire gender identity—awareness that they are male or female—moral standards, and other aspects of personality. These perspectives are the psychosexual, psychosocial, social-learning, cognitive-developmental, and cognitive-social approaches.

■ According to Freud, the preschool child is in the phallic stage of psychosexual development and receives pleasure from genital stimulation. The young child's sexuality is not like that of the mature adult.

  1  Freud's concepts of the Oedipus complex in the male and the Electra complex in the female are meant to explain a child's feelings toward the parent of the other sex. Because of the conflict a child feels, he or she eventually represses sexual urges, identifies with the same-sex parent (undergoes *identification with the aggressor*), and enters latency.
  2  The superego (made up of the ego-ideal and the conscience) develops when the Oedipus or Electra complex is resolved.

■ Erikson maintains that the chief developmental crisis of early childhood is the development of a balance between initiative and guilt. The successful resolution of this conflict enables the child to undertake, plan, and carry out activities in pursuit of goals. The outcome of this stage is strongly influenced by how parents deal with their children.

■ The social-learning perspective holds that children acquire gender identity by identifying with models of the same sex and being rewarded for imitating them. Moral learning also takes place by imitation and reinforcement, according to this theory.

■ Identification is the adoption of the characteristics, beliefs, attitudes, values, and behaviors of another person or a group. It is an important personality development of early childhood.

  1  In Freudian terms, the child identifies with the same-sex parent at the resolution of the Oedipus or Electra complex.
  2  According to social-learning theory, identification occurs when the child observes and imitates one or more models.

■ The cognitive-developmental theory maintains that gender identity and moral development are related to cognitive development.

■ The gender-schema theory, a variation of cognitive-developmental theory that draws on aspects of social learning, holds that children fit their self-concept to the gender schema for their culture, a socially organized pattern of behavior for males and females. According to this theory, the gender schema of a culture or an individual can be changed.

## ASPECTS AND ISSUES OF PERSONALITY DEVELOPMENT

■ Sex differences are physical differences between males and females; gender differences are differences between the sexes that may or may not be based on biology.

■ Gender roles are the behaviors and attitudes a culture deems appropriate for males and for females. Gender-typing refers to the learning of culturally determined gender roles.

■ There are few actual behavioral differences between the sexes. After about age 10 or 11, girls do better in verbal abilities and boys, in math and spatial abilities. Boys are more aggressive than girls from early childhood, and girls are more empathic. However, these differences are quite small and usually meaningless. Boys and girls are more similar than different.

■ Despite these relatively minor gender differences, our society holds strong ideas about appropriate behaviors for the two sexes, and children learn these expectations at an early age.

■ Gender stereotypes—exaggerated generalizations that may not be true of individuals—have the potential to restrict the development of both sexes. Androgynous child rearing, which encourages the expression of both "male" and "female" characteristics, is being fostered by many individuals and social institutions.

■ Explanations for gender differences have focused on both biological and environmental factors.

■ Preschool children show many fears of both real and imaginary objects and events. Conditioning and modeling can help children overcome fears.

■ Whether children exhibit aggression or prosocial behavior is influenced by the way their parents treat them as well as by other factors, such as what they learn from the media and whether they observe aggressive or prosocial models.

■ Parents influence children's behavior partly through rewards and punishments. Rewards are generally more effective than punishments.

■ Punishments are most effective when they are immediate, consistent, accompanied by an explanation, and carried out by a person who has a good relationship with the child. Physical punishment can have damaging effects.

■ Baumrind has identified three types of child-rearing styles: authoritarian, permissive, and authoritative. Each is related to certain personality traits in children. The authoritative style has the most positive outcomes.

■ Parents' love is the most important influence on the social maturity that their children will exhibit as adults.

■ Relationships with siblings and peers appear to be important in determining the pattern of relationships later in life.

■ As siblings move through middle childhood, most of their interactions are positive. Sibling rivalry is not the dominant pattern. As they mature, their interaction is less often physical and more often verbal. Older siblings tend to be dominant and are both more aggressive and more prosocial.

■ Only children develop at least as well as children with siblings.

■ Children who are aggressive or withdrawn tend to be less popular with playmates than children who act friendly. The type of attachment they have had in infancy—as well as their parents' attitudes, disciplinary techniques, and child-rearing styles—affects the ease with which young children find playmates and friends.

■ Play is both a social and a cognitive activity. Changes in the type of play children engage in reflect their development. Through play, children exercise their physical abilities, grow cognitively, and learn to interact with other children.

## KEY TERMS

identification (page 211)
gender (211)
phallic stage (211)
Oedipus complex (211)
castration anxiety (212)
Electra complex (212)
penis envy (212)
superego (212)
initiative versus guilt (212)
gender identity (214)

gender constancy (gender conservation) (214)
gender-schema theory (215)
gender schema (215)
sex differences (216)
gender differences (216)
gender roles (217)
gender-typing (217)
gender stereotypes (217)
androgynous (218)

aggressive behavior (222)
prosocial behavior (225)
behavior modification (227)
authoritarian parents (228)
permissive parents (228)
authoritative parents (228)
social play (234)
cognitive play (234)
imaginative play (236)

## SUGGESTED READINGS

**Anthony, E. J., & Cohler, B. J. (Eds.). (1987).** *The invulnerable child.* New York: Guilford. An important sourcebook of scholarly papers on the development of competence, the interaction of personality and experience in early childhood, and the extraordinary resilience shown by many children subjected to a variety of calamities.

**Axline, V. M. (1967).** *Dibs in search of self.* New York: Ballantine. This immensely moving and readable classic is the story of the play therapy that enabled a silent, withdrawn child to become his true, intelligent, and emotionally expressive self.

**Faber, A., & Mazlish, E. (1988).** *Siblings without rivalry.* New York: Avon. This book offers dozens of practical guidelines and real-life examples for fostering healthy and cooperative sibling relationships.

**Hopson, D., & Powell-Hopson, D. (1990).** *Different and wonderful: Raising black children in a race-conscious society.* Englewood Cliffs, NJ: Prentice-Hall. On the basis of their research in this area and their experience as parents, two clinical psychologists advise on such issues as toys, choosing day care and schools, and enhancing self-esteem. This book is not just for black parents; it is a great source for anyone working with children of different races.

# THREE

# MIDDLE CHILDHOOD

During the middle years of childhood—the elementary school years, from about age 6 to about age 12—children continue to make great strides in development.

■ In **Chapter 8,** we note children's physical and intellectual progress as they continue to grow taller, heavier, and stronger and to learn new skills and concepts. By and large, however, these are years of consolidation rather than of novelty. Children become better at things they have already been doing. They can throw a ball farther and more accurately and can run faster and for a longer time. They apply their knowledge of numbers, words, and concepts more and more effectively.

■ The personality traits that children have already begun to display are etched more deeply, as we'll see in **Chapter 9.** While parents still exert an important influence, the peer group now becomes very important too. Children want to be with their friends, and they develop socially through their contacts with other youngsters.

Childhood is not, of course, a time of pure bliss. The stresses children deal with include family upheavals, difficulties in getting along with other children, demands of schoolwork, and events in the world beyond their own circle. Some children suffer emotional disturbances, partly in response to such stresses. Others seem to be energized to build healthy, fulfilling lives. To meet the challenge of these years, children develop more competence in all realms of development.

# PHYSICAL AND INTELLECTUAL DEVELOPMENT IN MIDDLE CHILDHOOD

What we must remember above all in the education of our children is that their love of life should never weaken.

NATALIA GINZBURG,
*THE LITTLE VIRTUES*, 1985

- What gains in growth and motor development do children make in middle childhood, and what health hazards do they face?
- How do schoolchildren think and remember, and what progress do they make in moral development and communicative abilities?
- How can intelligence be measured, particularly in minority and disadvantaged children?
- How can schools and parents enhance children's intellectual development?
- What are the special needs of disabled and gifted children, and how can they be met?
- What is creativity, and how can it be nurtured?

Compared with the pace of physical and intellectual development in early childhood, development between the ages of 6 and 12 may seem slow. Physical growth has slowed down considerably—except for the growth spurt toward the end of this period—and while motor abilities continue to improve, changes are less dramatic than they were earlier. But development at these ages is still highly significant. Intellectual growth is substantial, as the once-egocentric child becomes more logical. And the accumulation of day-by-day changes results in a startling difference between 6-year-olds and 12-year-olds. The former are small children, the latter almost adults.

Although these years are among the healthiest in the life span, many children today are not as healthy or as physically fit as they should be. We'll consider why this is so. We'll also look at cognitive development, which proceeds largely within the framework of school. It is hardly coincidental that the usual age in the western world for beginning formal study coincides with important changes in children's mental abilities. These changes are recognized by each of three major approaches to intellectual development: Jean Piaget described entry into the stage of concrete operations; the information-processing approach focuses on improvements in memory, communication, and problem solving; and psychometric intelligence tests are more accurate at predicting school performance. We'll examine these three approaches, along with children's moral development and their development of language. After looking at all these changes, we'll consider several aspects of schools, including how they try to meet the special needs of children with physical or mental disabilities or exceptional gifts.

## PHYSICAL DEVELOPMENT

Walk by a typical elementary school just after the last bell, and you will see a virtual eruption of children of all shapes and sizes. Tall ones, short ones, chubby ones, and thin ones dash helter-skelter through the school doors and into the freedom of the open air. Although it may not be obvious, many of these children are not as physically fit as they should be, some because they are overweight.

Follow these children on their way home from school, and you'll see some leaping up onto narrow ledges and then walking along, balancing themselves, until they jump off, trying to break distance records—but occasionally breaking bones instead. Some children will reach home (or, often, a baby-sitter's house) not to emerge for the rest of the day. They could be outdoors honing new skills in jumping, running, throwing, catching, balancing, cycling, or climbing—becoming stronger, faster, and better coordinated. Instead, many of them will stay indoors watching television or playing quietly.

School-age children are taller and thinner than they were as preschoolers. Girls retain somewhat more fatty tissue than boys, a physical characteristic that will persist through adulthood. And black children tend to be slightly taller than white children.

# GROWTH DURING MIDDLE CHILDHOOD

## GROWTH RATES

Both boys and girls gain an average of 7 pounds and 2 to 3 inches a year until the adolescent growth spurt, which begins at about age 10 for girls. Then, girls are on average taller and heavier than boys until the boys begin *their* spurt at about age 12 or 13 and overtake the girls.

Individual children vary widely, however—so widely that "if a child who was of exactly average height at his seventh birthday grew not at all for two years, he would still be just within the normal limits of height attained at age nine" (Tanner, 1973, p. 35).

Also, growth rates vary with race, national origin, and socioeconomic level. A study of 8-year-old children in different parts of the world yielded a range of about 9 inches between the average height of the shortest children (mostly from southeast Asia, Oceania, and South America) and the tallest ones (mostly from northern and central Europe, eastern Australia, and the United States) (Meredith, 1969). Although genetic differences probably account for some of this diversity, environmental influences are important. The tallest children come from parts of the world where malnutrition and infectious disease are not major problems. For similar reasons, children from affluent homes tend to be larger and more mature than children from poorer homes.

Given the wide variance in size during middle childhood, we have to be careful about assessing children's health or identifying possible abnormalities in physical growth. Especially in the United States, which is racially and ethnically diverse, we may need to develop separate growth standards for different groups.

## NUTRITION AND GROWTH

In the middle years, children usually have good appetites. And they need to eat well: their play demands energy, and their body weight will double in these years. To support constant exertion and steady growth, children need, per day, an average of 2400 calories, 34 grams of protein, and high levels of complex carbohydrates, like those in potatoes and grains. Refined carbohydrates (sweeteners) should be kept to a minimum (E. R. Williams & Caliendo, 1984).

Poor nutrition causes slowed growth. It takes energy and protein just to stay alive and more energy and protein to grow. When meals cannot support both these processes fully, growth is sacrificed to maintain the body.

Nutrition also has social implications. Children cannot play and stay alert without enough food. The effects of poor nutrition can be long-lasting. A longitudinal study in Guatemala, where malnutrition is a serious problem, found that diet from birth to age 2 is a good predictor of social behavior in middle childhood. Of 138 children, age 6 to 8, who had received dietary supplements in infancy, all had received extra calories and vitamins but only some had received proteins. The children who had not had extra proteins as infants tended to be passive, anxious, and dependent on adults, while the better-nourished children were happier, feistier, and more sociable with their peers (D. E. Barrett, Radke-Yarrow, & Klein, 1982).

Furthermore, poor nutrition may cause problems in family relationships. Mothers may respond less frequently and less sensitively to malnourished babies, who lack the energy to engage a mother's attention. The infants, in turn, become unresponsive and develop poor interpersonal skills, further reducing their mothers' and other people's inclination or desire to interact with them (B. M. Lester, 1979). If the mother is malnourished too, the cycle worsens (Rosetti-Ferreira, 1978).

Links between nutrition and cognitive development are also clear. African children in Kenya who suffered mild to moderate undernutrition scored lower than well-nourished children on a test of verbal abilities and on a matrix test that asked the child to select a pattern to fit in with a set of other patterns (Sigman, Neumann, Jansen, & Bwibo, 1989). And low-income third- to sixth-graders who took part in a school breakfast program in Massachusetts improved their scores on achievement tests (A. F. Meyers, Sampson, Weitzman, Rogers, & Kayne, 1989).

Here again, we see how closely the different domains of development—physical, personality, and cognitive—are related.

## BOX 8–1 THINKING CRITICALLY

# CHILDREN'S UNDERSTANDING OF HEALTH AND ILLNESS

Illness is frightening at any age. For children, who understand so little of what is happening, it can be especially distressing and confusing. One child who overheard the doctor refer to *edema* (an accumulation of fluid, which causes swelling) thought that her problem was "a demon." Children's understanding of their own illnesses goes through predictable developmental patterns (Brewster, 1982; Perrin & Gerrity, 1981).

At the beginning of middle childhood, children still in Piaget's preoperational stage tend to believe that illness is produced "magically" by human actions, often their own. Such magical explanations can persist for some time. One 12-year-old with leukemia, for example, said, "I know that my doctor told me that my illness is caused by too many white cells, but I still wonder if it was caused by something I did" (Brewster, 1982, p.361). It would be hard for parents or professionals who overheard this remark to keep from rushing in and saying, "There, there, of course it wasn't anything you did." But this reaction may not be helpful. Egocen-

tric explanations for illness can serve as an important defense against feelings of helplessness. If children feel that something they did made them ill, they may believe they can do something else to get better. One investigator warns, "It is never wise to break down defenses until one is sure that more desirable concepts will take their place" (Brewster, 1982, p. 362).

As children grow beyond the preoperational stage, their explanation for disease changes. They now explain all diseases in terms of germs. Hardly less magical than younger children's demons and guilt, these germs are believed to cause disease automatically. The only "prevention" is a variety of superstitious behaviors designed to ward off germs.

Children approaching adolescence may enter a third stage when they see that there can be multiple causes of disease, that contact with germs does not automatically lead to illness, and that people can do much to keep themselves healthy.

But not everyone reaches this final stage, even in adulthood, as some

recent medical developments have reminded us. The germ theory of disease is relatively new, effective methods of preventing disease are even newer, and today much of the world still knows little about germs and less about public sanitation. The current epidemic of acquired immune deficiency syndrome (AIDS) is an illustration right here in the western world. When AIDS first appeared, seemingly out of nowhere, many people saw it as a magical punishment visited on homosexuals (one of the groups at high risk). Even after researchers have identified the AIDS virus and how it is spread (through bodily fluids or sexual contact), many people still superstitiously—and wrongly—fear that any contact with the virus, with an infected person, or even with an object touched by an infected person can lead to AIDS. Thus we see that individual development occurs in a frame of social development and that when social development is stifled, the individual is limited.

## HEALTH, FITNESS, AND SAFETY

### CHILDREN'S HEALTH

Richard, aged 10, is home in bed with a cold. He sneezes, snoozes, watches television, pulls out his old books and toys, and in general, enjoys the rest from his usual routine. He is lucky. He has had no illnesses this year other than two colds, while some of his classmates have had six or seven respiratory infections. That number of respiratory infections is common during middle childhood, as germs pass freely among youngsters at school or at play (Behrman & Vaughan, 1983).

But even though children do get a lot of colds at this age, most of them are healthier than their counterparts

early in this century. The development of vaccines for many childhood illnesses has made middle childhood an extremely safe time of life. Vaccination rates are much better for children of this age than for younger ones, since proof of immunization is required for school admission. This may be one reason why the death rate in middle childhood is the lowest in the life span.

Because of their cognitive development, which we'll discuss in the next section of this chapter, children in this age group are beginning to understand that health and illness have comprehensible causes and that people can do much to promote their own health (see Box 8-1 above).

Let's look now at several aspects of health and fitness in middle childhood.

## Obesity

*Obesity*—fatness—in children has become a major health issue in the United States since the 1970s, as it has become more common among 6- to 11-year-olds. In a 6-year study of nearly 2600 mostly white and middle-class children under age 12 who were enrolled in a pre-paid health maintenance plan, about 5½ percent of 8- to 11-year-olds were diagnosed as obese (Gortmaker, Dietz, Sobol, & Wehler, 1987; Starfield et al., 1984).

What makes children fat? Research findings are most often correlational, meaning that we cannot draw cause-and-effect conclusions. However, there seems to be a strong basis for believing that overweight often results from an inherited predisposition, aggravated by behavior involving too little exercise and too much food.

Some people seem to be genetically predisposed toward obesity. Adopted adults show a positive correlation in weight with biological parents but almost none with adoptive parents (A. J. Stunkard, Foch, & Hrubec, 1986). Environment also has a strong influence: obesity is more common among lower socioeconomic groups, especially among women. Fat children are less active than other children and tend to watch more television (Dietz & Gortmaker, 1985; Kolata, 1986).

Fat children do not usually "outgrow" being fat; they tend to become fat adults (Kolata, 1986), and obesity in adulthood puts them at risk of health problems like high blood pressure, diabetes, and orthopedic problems.

Childhood obesity can be treated. Behavioral therapy, which helps children change their eating and exercise habits, is especially effective when it also involves parents (L. H. Epstein & Wing, 1987). Parents learn not to use sweet foods as rewards for good behavior, to provide a smaller variety of foods, and to stop buying particularly tempting high-calorie foods.

## Minor Medical Conditions

What health problems crop up in middle childhood? The study of mostly white middle-class children in a health maintenance plan found varied conditions, from allergies to warts (Starfield et al., 1984).

Almost all the youngsters got sick from time to time, but their ailments tended to be brief. During the 6 years of the study, almost all the children had acute (short-term) medical conditions—usually upper-respiratory infections, viruses, or eczema—but only 1 in 9 had chronic (persistent) conditions like migraine headaches or nearsightedness. Eighty percent were treated for injuries. Upper-respiratory illnesses, sore throats, strep throats, ear infections, and bed-wetting decreased with age; but acne, headaches, and transitory emotional disturbances increased as youngsters approached puberty (Starfield et al., 1984).

## Vision

Most schoolchildren have much keener vision than they had earlier in life. Children under 6 years of age tend to be farsighted because their eyes have not matured and are shaped differently from those of adults. After that age, the eyes not only are more mature but can focus better.

In a minority of children, however, vision does not develop normally. Ten percent of 6-year-olds have defective near vision, and 7 percent have defective distant vision; the latter number jumps to 17 percent by 11 years of age (U.S. Department of Health, Education, and Welfare, USDHEW, 1976).

## Dental Health

Anna's pediatrician prescribed fluoride tablets for her—recognizing that most of the teeth that must serve people for the rest of their lives appear near the onset of middle childhood.

The primary teeth begin to fall out at about age 6, to be replaced by about four permanent teeth per year for

Regular dental care is important for the growth of healthy teeth. The routine of brushing also offers a quiet time for daydreaming, as this girl seems to be doing.

the next 5 years. The first molars erupt at about age 6, followed by the second molars at about 13, and the third molars (the wisdom teeth) usually during the early twenties (Behrman & Vaughan, 1983).

About one-half of 5- to 17-year-olds in the United States have no tooth decay (U.S. Department of Health and Human Services, USDHHS, 1988). American children today have 36 percent fewer dental cavities than were reported in similar surveys at the beginning of the 1980s, when they had an average of almost five decayed or missing teeth or filled surfaces (USDHHS, 1981a, 1988). This improvement seems to be due to the widespread use of fluoride in tablets (like the ones Anna took), and also in drinking water, toothpaste, mouthwash, and foods prepared with fluoridated water—and to better dental care. Two-thirds of the decay in children's teeth is on the rough chewing surfaces; much of this can be prevented with the use of adhesive *sealants,* plastic films that harden after being painted onto teeth.

### General Fitness

Today's schoolchildren are less physically fit than children were during the mid-1960s. Their hearts and lungs are in worse shape than those of an average middle-aged jogger. In one typical midwestern working-class community, 98 percent of the 7- to 12-year-olds had at least one of the following major risk factors for developing heart disease later in life: their levels of body fat averaged 2 to 5 percent above the national average (which itself is unhealthily high), 41 percent had high levels of cholesterol, and 28 percent had higher than normal blood pressure (C. T. Kuntzleman, personal communication, 1984).

Why are these children in such poor physical shape? It may be because they are not active enough. Only half take physical education classes as often as twice a week, fewer than half stay active during cold weather, and most do not spend enough time learning such lifetime fitness skills as running, swimming, bicycling, and walking. Many watch a lot of television. Most physical activities, in and outside of school, are team and competitive sports and games, which do not promote fitness, are usually dropped once the young person is out of school, and are generally played by the most athletic youngsters, not by those who need more exercise.

### Improving Health and Fitness

Children's health and fitness *can* be improved. One important step is to bring down high blood pressure. If a child's blood pressure is above the 95th percentile for age and sex after three measurements, treatment should begin. Taking off excess weight, reducing salt intake, and increasing aerobic exercise usually help, but some children are also given drugs to avoid heart damage (American Academy of Pediatrics, AAP, Task Force on Blood Pressure Control in Children, 1987).

Sometimes, just changing everyday behavior brings about considerable improvement. One education and behavior modification program has taught about 24,000 Michigan children how to analyze foods; how to measure their blood pressure, heart rate, and body fat; and how to withstand advertising and peer pressures to smoke and to eat "junk" foods. The program also encourages children to take part in vigorous games. Results for 360 second-, fifth-, and seventh-graders who were in the program were heartening. They had become faster at running a mile; they had lowered levels of cholesterol, blood pressure and body fat; and the number without any risk factors for developing coronary disease had risen by 55 percent (Fitness Finders, 1984).

This program is in line with recommendations by pediatricians that schools provide sound physical education programs with a variety of sports for all children, with an emphasis on enjoyment rather than winning, and on activities that can be part of a lifetime fitness regimen—like tennis, bowling, running, swimming, golf, and skating (AAP Committee on Sports Medicine and Committee on School Health, 1989).

### CHILDREN'S SAFETY

Almost 22 million children are injured in the United States each year, making injury the leading cause of disability and death in children over 1 year of age (Sheps & Evans, 1987). Boys average more accidents than girls, probably because they take more physical risks (Ginsburg & Miller, 1982). Injuries increase from ages 5 to 14, possibly because children become involved in more physical activities and are supervised less (Schor, 1987).

A child's family also affects safety. A longitudinal study of 693 families who sought medical care over a 6-year period found that a small number of families accounted for a disproportionately large number of injuries. After adjustment for family size, 10 percent of the families accounted for almost 25 percent of the injuries (Schor, 1987). Only children have fewer injuries than children with siblings. Perhaps parents of more than one child are not able to be as vigilant as parents of one child, or younger children may imitate their older siblings and take more risks, or children in larger families may be more active for other reasons. Also, families with high injury rates may be undergoing stress that interferes with the ability to make the home safe or watch over children.

The most common cause of serious injury and death in young schoolchildren is being hit by a moving vehicle. Many kindergartners and first-graders walk alone to school, often crossing busy streets without traffic lights, even though they do not have the skills to do this safely. To improve safety, then, parents have to know their children's limitations as pedestrians, and schools should offer transportation to and from school (Rivara, Bergman, & Drake, 1989).

Most childhood accidents occur in (or are inflicted by) automobiles, or occur in the home; but between 10 and 20 percent take place in and around schools. Elementary school children are most likely to be injured from playground falls (Sheps & Evans, 1987). Secondary school students are most often injured in sports. Some of these injuries could probably be avoided if players were grouped by size, skill, and maturational level rather than by age (AAP Committee on Sports Medicine and Committee on School Health, 1989).

For all ages studied, children are most likely to suffer head injuries, many of which occur from bicycle accidents. In 1985 more than 500,000 visits to emergency rooms and 1300 deaths were attributed to bicycle accidents. The dangers of riding a bike can be reduced dramatically by using helmets. However, only 5 percent of child bicyclists wear safety-approved helmets (AAP Committee on Accident and Poison Prevention, 1990). Children should wear protective headgear not only for cycling but also for football, roller skating, skateboarding, horseback riding, hockey, speed sledding, and tobogganing.

## MOTOR DEVELOPMENT IN MIDDLE CHILDHOOD

Studies of 7- to 12-year-olds done more than 30 years ago, when children seem to have been more physically active, suggested that motor abilities improve with age (see the examples in Table 8-1). These studies also found sex differences: boys tended to run faster, jump higher, throw farther, and show more strength than girls (Espenschade, 1960; Gavotos, 1959). After age 13, the gap between the sexes widened; boys improved, while girls stayed the same or declined (Espenschade, 1960).

**TABLE 8–1**
MOTOR DEVELOPMENT OF BOYS AND GIRLS IN MIDDLE CHILDHOOD

| Age | Selected Behaviors |
| --- | --- |
| 6 | Girls are superior in accuracy of movement; boys are superior in forceful, less complex acts. Skipping is possible. Children can throw with proper weight shift and step. |
| 7 | Balancing on one foot without looking becomes possible. Children can walk 2-inch-wide balance beams. Children can hop and jump accurately into small squares. Children can execute accurate jumping-jack exercise. |
| 8 | Grip strength permits steady 12-pound pressure. Number of games participated in by both sexes is greatest at this age. Children can engage in alternate rhythmic hopping in a 2-2, 2-3, or 3-3 pattern. Girls can throw a small ball 40 feet. |
| 9 | Girls can jump vertically to a height of 8½ inches, and boys, 10 inches. Boys can run 16½ feet per second. Boys can throw a small ball 70 feet. |
| 10 | Children can judge and intercept pathways of small balls thrown from a distance. Girls can run 17 feet per second. |
| 11 | Standing broad jump of 5 feet is possible for boys; 6 inches less for girls. |
| 12 | Standing high jump of 3 feet is possible. |

*Source:* Adapted from Cratty, 1979, p. 222.

These enthusiastic soccer players are proving that girls are often much better athletes than they were given credit for (or given the opportunity to be) in the past. Studies show that boys and girls who take part in similar activities show similar abilities.

Today, however, it seems clear that much of the difference between the sexes' motor abilities has been due to differences in expectations and participation. Prepubescent boys and girls who take part in similar activities show similar abilities.

When third-, fourth-, and fifth-grade boys and girls who had been in excellent coeducational physical education classes for at least a year were compared on their scores on sit-ups, shuttle run, 50-yard dash, broad jump, and 600-yard walk-run, both sexes improved with age, and the girls performed about as well as the boys on most measures. Girls who were tested in the third year of the program performed even better than the boys on a number of measures (E. G. Hall & Lee, 1984).

Such findings indicate that there is no reason to separate prepubertal boys and girls for physical activities. After puberty, however, girls should not play in collision sports with boys, because their lighter, smaller frames make them too susceptible to being injured by the heavier boys (AAP Committee on Pediatric Aspects of Physical Fitness, Recreation, and Sport, 1981).

To help all children improve their motor skills, organized athletic programs should offer children the chance to try a variety of sports, should focus coaching on improving skills rather than on winning games, and should include as many youngsters as possible rather than concentrating on a few star athletes (AAP Committee on Sports Medicine and Committee on School Health, 1989).

# INTELLECTUAL DEVELOPMENT

Even today, when many children go to preschool and most go to kindergarten, the first day of "real" school is a milestone, approached with a mixture of eagerness and anxiety. "What will the teacher be like?" Julie, aged 6, wonders as she walks up the steps to the big red-brick schoolhouse, shiny new pencil case in hand. "What will we learn? Will I be able to do the work?" Julie's ability to learn and to do schoolwork will expand greatly during the next 6 years, because of her growing capacity to think conceptually, solve problems, remember, and use language—developments we'll examine in this section. But the first day of school will always be a special day, a day of promise and anticipation.

## ASPECTS OF INTELLECTUAL DEVELOPMENT IN MIDDLE CHILDHOOD

### COGNITIVE DEVELOPMENT: PIAGET'S STAGE OF CONCRETE OPERATIONS

Sometime between 5 and 7 years of age, according to Piaget, children enter the stage of **concrete operations,** when they can think logically about the here and now. They generally remain in this stage until about age 11.

## Operational Thinking

Children in Piaget's third stage are capable of *operational thinking:* they can use symbols to carry out *operations*—that is, mental activities, as opposed to the physical activities that were the basis for most of their earlier thinking. For the first time, logic becomes possible. Even though preoperational children can make mental representations of objects and events that are not immediately present, their learning is still closely tied to physical experience. Concrete operational children are much better than preoperational children at classifying, working with numbers, dealing with concepts of time and space, and distinguishing reality from fantasy.

Since they are much less egocentric by now, children in the stage of concrete operations can *decenter*—they can take all aspects of a situation into account rather than focusing on only one aspect, as they did in the preoperational stage. They realize that most physical operations are reversible. Their increased ability to understand other people's viewpoints lets them communicate more effectively and be more flexible in their moral thinking.

But while school-age children think more logically than younger children, their thinking is still anchored in the here and now. According to Piaget, not until the stage of formal operations, which usually comes with adolescence (see Chapter 10), will young people be able to think abstractly, test hypotheses, and understand probabilities.

## Conservation

### What is conservation?

One important ability that develops during the stage of concrete operations is conservation. *Conservation* is the ability to recognize that two equal quantities of matter remain equal—in substance, weight, or volume—so long as nothing is added or taken away.

In a typical conservation task, Stacy is shown two equal balls of clay. She agrees that they are equal. She is said to conserve *substance* if she recognizes that even after one of the balls has been rolled into the shape of a worm, the two lumps of clay still have an equal amount of matter. In *weight* conservation, she recognizes that the ball and the worm weigh the same. And in conservation of *volume,* she realizes that the ball and the worm displace equal amounts of liquid when they are placed in glasses of water.

Children develop different types of conservation at different times. At age 6 or 7, they typically are able to conserve substance; at 9 or 10, weight; and at 11 or 12, volume. The underlying principle is identical for all three kinds of conservation, but children are unable to transfer what they have learned about one type of conservation to a different type. *Horizontal décalage* is the term Piaget used for this inability.

Thus, we see how concrete a child's reasoning still is. It is tied so closely to particular situations that children cannot easily apply the same basic mental operation to a different situation.

### How is conservation developed?

Children typically go through three stages in mastering conservation. Let's see how this works for conservation of substance.

In the *first* stage, preoperational children fail to conserve. They center or focus on one aspect of the situation (for example, that the ball of clay becomes longer when it is rolled into a "worm") and do not notice that the worm is also narrower than the ball was. Evidently, they are fooled by appearances and decide that the worm contains more clay. Because preoperational children do not understand the concept of reversibility, they do not recognize that they could restore the original shape (and show that nothing has been added) by rolling the worm back into a ball.

The *second* stage is transitional. Children go back and forth, sometimes conserving and sometimes not. They may notice more than one aspect of a situation—such as height, width, length, and thickness—but may fail to recognize how these dimensions are related. These children may answer correctly when they see a short worm but fail to conserve if the worm is very long and thin.

In the *third* and final stage, children conserve and give logical reasons for their answers. These reasons may refer to *reversibility* ("If the clay worm were shaped into a ball, it would be the same as the other ball"); *identity* ("It's the same clay; you haven't added any or taken any away"); or *compensation* ("The ball is shorter than the worm, but the worm is thinner than the ball, so they both have the same amount of clay"). Thus concrete operational children show a qualitative cognitive advance over preoperational children. Their thinking is reversible, they decenter, and they are aware that transformations are only perceptual changes.

Piaget stressed that children develop the ability to conserve when they are neurologically mature enough. He believed that conservation is only minimally affected by experience. However, factors other than maturation do affect conservation. Children who learn conservation skills earliest have high grades, high IQs, high verbal ability, and nondominating mothers (Almy, Chittenden, & Miller, 1966; Goldschmid & Bentler, 1968). Black children from higher socioeconomic levels do better than black children of lower socioeconomic levels on conservation tasks (as well as on other Piagetian operations) (Bardouille-Crema, Black, & Feldhusen, 1986). Also, children from different countries—Switzerland, the United States, Great Britain, and other nations—achieve conservation at different average ages. Therefore culture, and not maturation alone, apparently plays a role.

## MORAL DEVELOPMENT: THREE THEORIES

The most influential explanation of moral development today is that moral values develop in a rational process coinciding with cognitive growth. Jean Piaget and Lawrence Kohlberg, two of the most influential modern theorists on the development of moral reasoning, maintained that children cannot make sound moral judgments until they shed egocentric thinking and achieve a certain level of cognitive maturity. Selman holds that moral development is closely linked to "role-taking" ability. Let's examine their theories.

### Piaget and Moral Stages

According to Piaget, children's conception of morality develops in two major stages (summarized in Table 8-2), which coincide approximately with the preoperational and operational stages. People go through these moral stages at varying times, but the sequence is always the same.

The first stage, **morality of constraint** (also called *heteronomous morality*), is characterized by rigid, simplistic judgments. Young children see everything in black and white, not gray. Because they are egocentric, they cannot conceive of more than one way of looking at a moral question. They believe that rules are unalterable, that behavior is either right or wrong, and that any offense—no matter how minor—deserves severe punishment. (Of course, children often disobey rules they insist upon for others.)

The second stage, **morality of cooperation** (or *autonomous morality*), is characterized by moral flexibility. As children mature and interact more with other children and with adults, they think less egocentrically. They have ever-increasing contact with a wide range of viewpoints, many of which contradict what they have learned at home. Children conclude that there is not one unchangeable, absolute moral standard, but that rules are made by people and can be changed by peo-

ple, including themselves. They look for the intent behind the act, and they believe that punishment should fit the "crime." They are on the way to formulating their own moral codes.

To illustrate one aspect of this change, Piaget (1932) told this story:

> Once upon a time there were two little boys, Augustus and Julian. Augustus noticed one day that his father's inkpot was empty, and he decided to help his father by filling it. But in opening the bottle, he spilled the ink and made a large stain on the tablecloth. Julian played with his father's inkpot and made a small stain on the tablecloth. Piaget then asked, "Which boy is naughtier and why?"

A child in the stage of constraint is likely to consider Augustus the greater offender, because he made the larger stain. But an older child will probably recognize that Augustus meant well, whereas the smaller stain Julian made was the result of doing something he should not have been doing. Immature moral judgments, being egocentric, center on one dimension: the magnitude of the offense. Mature judgments take intention into account.*

### Selman and Role-Taking

Questions like the one about Augustus and Julian involve **role-taking:** putting oneself into another person's position and imagining how that person thinks and feels. Selman (1973) describes the development of role-taking in five stages (0 to 4), which are summarized in Table 8-3.

At *stage 0* (about age 4 to age 6), children think and judge egocentrically, and so they cannot assume other people's roles or points of view. Suppose that we tell Moira, who is 5 years old, a story about a little girl who has promised her father not to climb trees but then sees a kitten trapped on a high branch. At this stage, Moira sees no problem in this situation. Since she likes kittens herself, she assumes that her father or anyone else will automatically favor climbing the tree to save the kitten.

---

*The issue of intention versus consequences is far from clear-cut even among adults, as we can see in our criminal codes. Penalties are more severe for murder than for *attempted* murder, even though both may involve wanting to kill. And a drunken driver who has injured someone is usually punished more harshly than one who has not, even though neither driver intended to hurt anyone. Consequences matter so much to most people that society has institutionalized its responses on the basis of what actually happens.

**TABLE 8–2**
PIAGET'S TWO STAGES OF MORAL DEVELOPMENT

| Aspect of Morality | Morality of Constraint | Morality of Cooperation |
| --- | --- | --- |
| Point of view | Child views an act as either totally right or totally wrong and thinks everyone sees it the same way. Children cannot put themselves in place of others. | Children can put themselves in place of others. They are not absolutist in judgments but see that more than one point of view is possible. |
| Intentionality | Child judges acts in terms of actual physical consequences, not the motivation behind them. | Child judges acts by intentions, not consequences. |
| Rules | Child obeys rules because they are sacred and unalterable. | Child recognizes that rules were made by people and can be changed by people. Children consider themselves just as capable of changing rules as anyone else. |
| Respect for authority | Unilateral respect leads to feeling of obligation to conform to adult standards and obey adult rules. | Mutual respect for authority and peers allows children to value their own opinions and abilities and to judge other people realistically. |
| Punishment | Child favors severe punishment. Child feels that punishment itself defines the wrongness of an act; an act is bad if it will elicit punishment. | Child favors milder punishment that compensates the victim and helps the culprit recognize why an act was wrong, thus leading to reform. |
| "Immanent justice" | Child confuses moral law with physical law and believes that any physical accident or misfortune that occurs after a misdeed is a punishment willed by God or some other supernatural force. | Child does not confuse natural misfortune with punishment. |

*Source:* Adapted partly from M. Hoffman, 1970; Kohlberg, in M. Hoffman & Hoffman, 1964.

**TABLE 8–3**
STAGES OF ROLE-TAKING

| Stage | Approximate Ages | Development |
| --- | --- | --- |
| 0 | 4–6 | Child thinks that his or her own point of view is the only one possible. |
| 1 | 6–8 | Child realizes that others may interpret a situation in a way different from his or her own interpretation. |
| 2 | 8–10 | Child has reciprocal awareness, realizing that others have a different point of view and that others are aware that he or she has a particular point of view. Child understands the importance of letting others know that their requests have not been ignored or forgotten. |
| 3 | 10–12 | Child can imagine a third person's perspective, taking into account several |
| 4 | Adolescence | Person realizes that communication and mutual role-taking do not always resolve disputes over rival values. |

*Source:* Selman, 1973.

At *stage 1,* from about age 6 to age 8, children realize that other people may interpret a situation differently. Now Moira says, "If the father doesn't know why she climbed the tree, he will be angry. But if he knows why she did it, he will be glad." Moira now realizes the importance of intention.

Reciprocal awareness marks *stage 2,* from 8 to 10 years of age. Now, not only can Moira put herself into someone else's place (as she could in stage 1), but she knows that someone else can imagine *her* thoughts and feelings. Thus, she reasons, the father would realize that the girl believed that he would approve her breaking the promise under the circumstances, and so he would think that it was all right. But if he thought that she did not consider what his reaction might be, he would be angry.

In *stage 3,* from about age 10 to age 12, a child can step outside a relationship and view it from a third point of view—for example, that of an objective outsider like a judge.

*Stage 4* arrives, usually during adolescence, when a person realizes that mutual role-taking does not always resolve disputes. There might be rival values that simply cannot be communicated away.

Selman's analysis of the development of role-taking was inspired by the concepts of Piaget and Kohlberg—the idea that moral development accompanies intellectual growth.

## Kohlberg and Moral Reasoning

How would *you* respond to this moral dilemma? A woman is near death from cancer. A druggist has discovered a drug that doctors believe might save her. The druggist is charging $2000 for a small dose—10 times what it costs him to make the drug. The sick woman's husband, Heinz, borrows from everyone he knows but can scrape together only $1000. He begs the druggist to sell him the drug for less or let him pay later. The druggist refuses, saying, "I discovered the drug, and I'm going to make money from it." Heinz, desperate, breaks into the man's store and steals the drug. Should Heinz have done that? Why, or why not? (Kohlberg, 1969).

### Kohlberg's moral dilemmas

"Heinz's" problem is the most famous example of Kohlberg's approach. For some 20 years, he studied a group of 75 boys who were from 10 to 16 years old when he began. Kohlberg told them stories posing hypothetical moral problems about unfamiliar people—dilemmas like Heinz's—and he asked how they would solve them. At the center of each dilemma was the concept of justice.

Then Kohlberg and his colleagues asked the boys questions to find out how they came to their decisions. He was less interested in answers than in the reasoning that led to them; thus two boys who gave opposite answers to a dilemma could both be at the same moral level if their reasoning was based on similar factors.

### Kohlberg's levels of moral reasoning

From the boys' responses, Kohlberg concluded that levels of moral reasoning are related to cognitive levels. The reasoning behind the boys' answers convinced Kohlberg that many people arrive at moral judgments independently rather than merely "internalizing" the standards of parents, teachers, or peers. On the basis of the different thought processes shown by the answers, Kohlberg described three levels of moral reasoning:

- *Level I*—**Preconventional morality** (ages 4 to 10). Children, under external controls, obey rules to get rewards or avoid punishment.
- *Level II*—**Conventional morality** (ages 10 to 13). Children have internalized the standards of authority figures. They obey rules to please others or to maintain order.
- *Level III*—**Postconventional morality** (age 13 or later, if ever). Morality is fully internal. People now recognize conflicts between moral standards and choose between them.

Each of the three levels is divided into two stages. Table 8-4 gives detailed descriptions of the six stages with illustrative answers to Heinz's dilemma.

Kohlberg's lower stages are similar to Piaget's, but his advanced stages go farther—into adulthood. Selman's stages correspond to Kohlberg's. For example, the more advanced a person is in role-taking, the more complicated Heinz's dilemma becomes. A child in Selman's stage 3 of role-taking says that if Heinz were caught, a judge would listen to his explanation, see the validity of his argument, and let him go. But in Selman's stage 4, the child realizes that no matter how good the explanation seems to Heinz, the judge has sworn to uphold the law and will not excuse the theft.

### Evaluating Kohlberg's theory

Kohlberg's theory has generated considerable research. He and his colleagues found that the American boys they followed for 20 years progressed through Kohlberg's stages in sequence and none skipped a stage. Moral judgments correlated positively with the boys' age, education, IQ, and socioeconomic status (Colby, Kohlberg, Gibbs, & Lieberman, 1983).

**TABLE 8–4**
KOHLBERG'S SIX STAGES OF MORAL REASONING

| Levels | Stages of Reasoning | Typical Answers to Heinz's Dilemma |
|---|---|---|
| **Level 1: Preconventional Morality (ages 4 to 10)** Emphasis in this level is on external control. The standards are those of others, and they are observed either to avoid punishment or to reap rewards. | **Stage 1** *Orientation to punishment and obedience.* ''What will happen to me?'' Children obey the rules of others to avoid punishment. They ignore the motives of an act and focus on its physical form (such as the size of a lie) or its consequences (for example, the amount of physical damage). | *Pro:* ''He should steal the drug. It isn't really bad to take it. It isn't as if he hadn't asked to pay for it first. The drug he'd take is worth only $200: he's not really taking a $2000 drug.'' *Con:* ''He shouldn't steal the drug. It's a big crime. He didn't get permission; he used force and broke and entered. He did a lot of damage, stealing a very expensive drug and breaking up the store, too.'' |
| | **Stage 2** *Instrumental purpose and exchange.* ''You scratch my back, and I'll scratch yours.'' Children conform to rules out of self-interest and consideration for what others can do for them in return. They look at an act in terms of the human needs it meets and differentiate this value from the act's physical form and consequences. | *Pro:* ''It's all right to steal the drug, because his wife needs it and he wants her to live. It isn't that he wants to steal, but that's what he has to do to get the drug to save her.'' *Con:* ''He shouldn't steal it. The druggist isn't wrong or bad; he just wants to make a profit. That's what you're in business for—to make money.'' |
| **Level II: Conventional Morality (ages 10 to 13)** Children now want to please other people. They still observe the standards of others, but they have internalized these standards to some extent. Now they want to be considered ''good'' by those persons whose opinions are important to them. They are now able to take the roles of authority figures well enough to decide whether an action is good by their standards. | **Stage 3** *Maintaining mutual relations, approval of others, the golden rule.* ''Am I a good boy or girl?'' Children want to please and help others, can judge the intentions of others, and develop their own ideas of what a good person is. They evaluate an act according to the motive behind it or the person performing it, and they take circumstances into account. | *Pro:* ''He should steal the drug. He is only doing something that is natural for a good husband to do. You can't blame him for doing something out of love for his wife. You'd blame him if he didn't love his wife enough to save her.'' *Con:* ''He shouldn't steal. If his wife dies, he can't be blamed. It isn't because he's heartless or that he doesn't love her enough to do everything that he legally can. The druggist is the selfish or heartless one.'' |
| | **Stage 4** *Social system and conscience.* ''What if everybody did it?'' People are concerned with doing their duty, showing respect for higher authority, and maintaining the social order. They consider an act always wrong, regardless of motive or circumstances, if it violates a rule and harms others. | *Pro:* ''You should steal it. If you did nothing you'd be letting your wife die. It's your responsibility if she dies. You have to take it with the idea of paying the druggist.'' *Con:* ''It is a natural thing for Heinz to want to save his wife, but it's still always wrong to steal. He still knows that he's stealing and taking a valuable drug from the man who made it.'' |

*(Continued)*

**TABLE 8–4**
(CONTINUED)

| Levels | Stages of Reasoning | Typical Answers to Heinz's Dilemma |
|---|---|---|
| **Level III: Postconventional Morality (age 13, or not until young adulthood, or never)** This level marks the attainment of true morality. For the first time, the person acknowledges the possibility of conflict between two socially accepted standards and tries to decide between them. The control of conduct is now internal, both in the standards observed and in the reasoning about right and wrong. Stages 5 and 6 may be alternative methods of the highest level of moral reasoning. | **Stage 5** *Morality of contract, of individual rights, and of democratically accepted law.* People think in rational terms, valuing the will of the majority and the welfare of society. They generally see these values best supported by adherence to the law. While they recognize that there are times when human need and the law conflict, they believe that it is better for society in the long run if they obey the law. | *Pro:* "The law wasn't set up for these circumstances. Taking the drug in this situation isn't really right, but it's justified." *Con:* "You can't completely blame someone for stealing, but extreme circumstances don't really justify taking the law into your own hands. You can't have people stealing whenever they are desperate. The end may be good, but the ends don't justify the means." |
| | **Stage 6** *Morality of universal ethical principles.* People do what they as individuals think right, regardless of legal restrictions or the opinions of others. They act in accordance with internalized standards, knowing that they would condemn themselves if they did not. | *Pro:* "This is a situation that forces him to choose between stealing and letting his wife die. In a situation where the choice must be made, it is morally right to steal. He has to act in terms of the principle of preserving and respecting life." *Con:* "Heinz is faced with the decision of whether to consider the other people who need the drug just as badly as his wife. Heinz ought to act not according to his particular feelings toward his wife, but considering the value of all the lives involved." |

*Source:* Adapted from Kohlberg, 1969, 1976, in Goslin, 1969.

Cross-cultural studies confirm this sequence—up to a point. Older subjects from countries other than the United States do tend to score at higher stages than younger people, but people from nonwestern cultures rarely score above stage 4 (Edwards, 1977; Nisan & Kohlberg, 1982; Snarey, 1985). It is possible that these cultures do not foster higher development—but it also seems that Kohlberg's definition of morality as a system of justice is not as appropriate for all societies. His scheme may miss higher levels of reasoning in some cultural groups (Snarey, 1985). (See Box 12-2, about Chinese conceptions of morality, in Chapter 12.)

Furthermore, critics have questioned whether Kohl-berg's definition of morality applies to females, on the ground that his theory stresses "masculine" values (justice and fairness) rather than "feminine" values (caring for others). In Chapter 12, we will examine a compelling alternative theory proposed by Carol Gilligan (1982).

Others challenge Kohlberg's belief that children are "moral philosophers" who work out their moral systems by independent discovery. On the contrary, studies show that moral judgments are strongly influenced by education—as by simply telling children the "right" answers to moral reasoning tasks (Carroll & Rest, 1982; Lickona, 1973).

Another problem with Kohlberg's system lies in the time-consuming testing procedures. The standard tasks (like the story of Heinz) need to be presented to each subject individually and then scored by trained judges. One alternative is the Defining Issues Test (DIT), which can be given quickly to a group and scored objectively (Rest, 1975). The DIT asks 12 questions about each of 6 moral dilemmas; its results correlate moderately well with scores on Kohlberg's traditional tasks.

Still another issue is the relationship between moral reasoning and action. People at postconventional levels of thought do not necessarily act more morally than those at lower levels (Kupfersmid & Wonderly, 1980). This finding is not surprising in view of research on children's cheating, which found that almost all children who cheat are just as likely as noncheaters to *say* that cheating is wrong (Hartshorne & May, 1928–1930).

While Kohlberg's stages do, then, seem to apply to American males, they are less applicable to women and to nonwesterners, and there are questions about the testing methods and about the link between judgment and behavior.

At one point Kohlberg himself questioned his sixth stage, citing the difficulty of finding people at such a high level of moral development (Muuss, 1988). Still later, however, he proposed a seventh stage that was more religious in orientation (Kohlberg, 1981). Kohlberg's rethinking of his concepts illustrates the dynamic nature of theories—that they can respond to new research findings or new insights.

Kohlberg has had a major impact. His theory has enriched our thinking about how morality develops, has supported an association between cognitive maturity and moral maturity, and has stimulated both research and the elaboration of theories of moral development.

## DEVELOPMENT OF MEMORY: INFORMATION PROCESSING

The information-processing approach to cognitive development pays particular attention to memory. As cognitive development advances, so in most cases does memory. The ability to remember thus improves greatly by middle childhood. This happens in part because children's memory capacity—the amount of information they can remember—increases, and in part because they learn to use a variety of *strategies,* or deliberate plans, to help them remember (see Chapter 6). An important development is metamemory, an understanding of how one's own memory processes work.

## How Memory Works: Encoding, Storing, and Retrieving

According to information-processing theory, memory is like a filing system. It operates through three basic steps: encoding, storage, and retrieval. After perceiving something, we need to decide where to file it. Thus the first step is to *encode,* or classify it—for example, under "people I know" or "places I've been." Second, we *store* the material so that it stays in memory. And third, we need to be able to *retrieve* information, or get it out of storage. Forgetting can occur because of a problem with any of these three steps.

Immediate memory increases rapidly in middle childhood. We can see this by asking children to recall a series of digits in the reverse of the order in which they heard them (to recite "8-3-7-5-1-6" if they have heard "6-1-5-7-3-8"). At ages 5 to 6, children can typically remember only two digits; by adolescence they can remember six. Younger children's relatively poor immediate memory may help to explain why they have trouble solving certain kinds of problems (such as conservation). They may not be able to hold all the relevant pieces of information in memory (Siegler & Richards, 1982). They may, for example, forget that two differently shaped balls of clay were equal in the first place, and so by the time they are asked about the ball and the "worm," they can judge only on present appearance.

## Mnemonic Devices: Strategies for Remembering

Older children can usually remember a list of numbers better than younger children can, partly because they have discovered that they can take deliberate actions to help them remember. Devices to aid memory are called **mnemonic strategies.** As children get older, they develop better strategies and tailor them to meet the need to remember specific things. Mnemonic techniques need not be discovered haphazardly. Children can be taught to use them earlier than they would spontaneously. Some of the most common strategies are rehearsal, organization, elaboration, and external aids.

### Rehearsal

When you look up a telephone number, you may repeat it over and over in your mind on your way from the directory to the phone, as actors rehearse their lines. **Rehearsal** (conscious repetition) is a commonly used mnemonic strategy.

Children generally do not begin using rehearsal spontaneously until after age 6. In one study (Flavell, Beach, & Chinsky, 1966), first-graders who had been

Contestants in a spelling bee can make good use of mnemonic strategies—devices to aid memory. This boy may be trying to remember by putting a word into a mental category with other words that contain similar elements.

told that they would be asked to recall a sequence of pictures sat and waited until they were asked for the information. Second- and fifth-graders, on the other hand, moved their lips and muttered, suggesting that they were rehearsing the material. Not surprisingly, the older children remembered the material better than the younger ones. When the experimenters asked first-graders to name the pictures out loud when they first saw them (a form of rehearsal), the children recalled the order better. Young children who were taught to rehearse applied the technique to the immediate situation but did not apply it to new situations (Keeney, Canizzo, & Flavell, 1967).

More recent research, however, shows that some children between 3 and 6 years old do use rehearsal. And although 6-year-olds are more likely than 3-year-olds to rehearse, those 3-year-olds who do rehearse can remember a grocery list just as well as 6-year-olds (Paris & Weissberg-Benchell, in Chance & Fischman, 1987).

Children older than 6 learn and use more sophisticated mnemonic techniques: organization, elaboration, and external aids.

### Organization

It is easier to remember material if we mentally organize it into categories. Adults generally do this automatically. Children younger than 10 or 11 do *not* normally use **organization** spontaneously; but they can be taught to do it, or they may pick it up by imitating others (Chance & Fischman, 1987). If they see randomly arranged pictures of, say, animals, furniture, and clothing, they do not mentally sort the items into categories. If shown how to organize, they recall the pictures as well as older children do; but they do not generalize the learning to other situations.

### Elaboration

To help ourselves remember items, we can link them together in an imagined scene or story—a strategy called **elaboration.** To remember to buy lemons, ketchup, and napkins, for example, we might imagine a ketchup bottle balanced on a lemon, with napkins handy to wipe up spilled ketchup. Older children are more likely than younger ones to use elaboration spontaneously, and they remember better when they make up the elaborations themselves. Younger children remember better when someone else makes up the elaborations for them (Paris & Lindauer, 1976; Reese, 1977).

### External aids

The mnemonic strategies used most commonly by both children and adults involve prompting by something outside the person. You write down a telephone number, make a list, tie a string around your finger, set a timer, or ask someone to remind you. Even kindergartners recognize the value of such **external aids,** and as children mature, they use them more (Kreutzer, Leonard, & Flavell, 1975).

## Metamemory:
## Understanding the Processes of Memory

Older children are more likely to use mnemonic strategies than younger children, partly because older children are more conscious of how memory works. **Metamemory**—knowledge of the processes of memory—develops in middle childhood.

From kindergarten through fifth grade, children advance steadily in understanding memory (Kreutzer et al., 1975). Kindergartners and first-graders know that people remember better if they study longer, that people forget things with time, that relearning something is easier than learning it for the first time, and that external aids can help them remember. By third grade, children know that some people remember more than others and that some things are easier to remember than others.

## DEVELOPMENT OF LANGUAGE: COMMUNICATION

Language, too, develops quickly in middle childhood. Children can understand and interpret communications better, and they are better able to make themselves understood.

### Grammar: The Structure of Language

Suppose that you are looking at a snow-covered driveway and you ask someone how you are going to get the family car out of the garage. You might be told either (1) "Ken promised Barbie to shovel the driveway" or (2) "Ken told Barbie to shovel the driveway." Depending on which answer you received, you would know whether Ken or Barbie would be getting to work. But many children under 5 or 6 years of age do not understand the structural difference between these two sentences and think that *both* mean that Barbie is to do the shoveling (C. S. Chomsky, 1969). Their confusion is understandable, since almost all English verbs that might replace *told* in the second sentence (such as *ordered, wanted,* and *expected*) would put the shovel in Barbie's hand.

Most 6-year-olds have not yet learned how to deal with grammatical constructions in which a word is used as *promise* is used in the first sentence, even though they know what a promise is and are able to use and understand the word correctly in other sentences. But by age 8, most children can interpret the first sentence correctly.

Even though six-year-olds speak on a rather sophisticated level, using complex grammar and several thousand words, they still have a way to go before they master the niceties of syntax—the way in which words are organized in phrases and sentences. During the

These girls sharing a secret demonstrate growing sophistication in the use of language to communicate. By the early school years, most children use complex grammar and have vocabularies of several thousand words. But because they still do not fully understand the processes of communication, they sometimes misinterpret what they hear.

early school years, they rarely use the passive voice, verbs that include the form *have,* or conditional ("if . . . then") sentences.

Children develop an increasingly complex understanding of syntax up to and possibly after age 9 (C. S. Chomsky, 1969). When testing forty 5- to 10-year-olds on their understanding of syntactic structures, Chomsky found considerable variation in the ages of children who understood them and those who did not (see Table 8-5 below).

**TABLE 8–5**
ACQUISITION OF COMPLEX SYNTACTIC STRUCTURES

| Structure | Difficult Concept | Age of Acquisition |
|---|---|---|
| John is easy to see. | Who is doing the seeing? | 5.6 to 9 years.* |
| John promised Bill to go. | Who is going? | 5.6 to 9 years.* |
| John asked Bill what to do. | Who is doing it? | Some 10-year-olds have still not learned this. |
| He knew that John was going to win the race. | Does the "he" refer to John? | 5.6 years. |

*All children aged 9 and over know this.
*Source:* C. S. Chomsky, 1969.

## Metacommunication: Understanding the Processes of Communication

When Leroy, aged 6, received a fluoride treatment from his dentist, he was told by the hygienist not to swallow anything for half an hour. Soon after leaving the examining room, Leroy started to drool and to look very upset. He was greatly relieved when the dentist saw his concern and reassured him that he *could* swallow his saliva.

Despite Leroy's sophisticated linguistic ability, he was still having problems with communication, as do many children of his age. Of course, adults, too, often misinterpret what other people say. But children's failures in interpreting messages often stem from difficulties in **metacommunication,** that is, in their knowledge of the processes of communication. This knowledge grows throughout middle childhood.

To study children's ability to transmit and understand spoken information, researchers have designed a number of ingenious experiments. In one (Flavell, Speer, Green, & August, 1981), kindergartners and second-graders were asked to construct block buildings exactly like those built by another child and to do this on the basis of the first child's audiotaped instructions—without seeing the buildings themselves. The instructions were often incomplete, ambiguous, or contradictory. The "builders" were then asked whether they thought that their buildings looked like the ones they were supposed to be copies of and whether they thought that the instructions were good or bad.

The older children monitored their understanding better. When instructions were inadequate, they noticed more and paused or looked puzzled. They were more likely to know when they did not understand something and to see the implications of unclear communication—that their buildings might not look exactly like the ones they were copying because the instructions were not good enough. Younger children sometimes knew that the instructions were unclear, but they did not realize that this meant that they could not do their job well. And even the older children (who, after all, were only 8 years old or so) lacked complete awareness of the communication process (Flavell et al., 1981).

Findings like these have important implications. Young children do not understand all of what they see, hear, or read, but often they do not know that they do not understand. They may be so used to not understanding things in the world around them that this does not seem unusual. Adults therefore need to be aware that children's understanding cannot be taken for granted. For the sake of children's safety, well-being, and academic progress, we have to find out ways to determine whether children do, in fact, know what we want them to know.

Among other things, children's ability to understand and follow instructions makes a big difference in how accurately we can measure their intelligence—a topic we'll consider next.

## DEVELOPMENT OF INTELLIGENCE: PSYCHOMETRICS

### IQ Tests

Bart's third-grade teacher told the boy's parents, "Bart is underachieving—he's not working up to his ability." It is likely that what she meant by Bart's *ability* was his score on an IQ test. When she meant by *underachieving* could have been either his classwork or his scores on group achievement tests, which measure how much children know in various subject areas, like mathematics, history, and so forth. Achievement tests assess children's progress and let the school know how effectively it is teaching. They are different from the group intelligence tests that students in many schools receive every few years, which supposedly measure children's basic *aptitude,* or general intelligence.

Because individual tests are more precise, youngsters are sometimes tested individually either for admission to a selective program or to uncover specific problems or strengths that the school should address.

The most widely used *individual* test for schoolchildren is the **Wechsler Intelligence Scale for Children (WISC-R).** This test measures verbal and performance abilities, yielding separate scores for each, as well as a total score. Separating the subtest scores makes the diagnosis of specific deficits easier. For example, if a child does much better on the verbal tests (by, say, understanding a written passage and knowing vocabulary words) than on the performance tests (as in mastering mazes and copying a block design), this may signal problems with perceptual or motor development. If the child does much better on the performance tests, there may be a problem with language development.

A popular *group* test is the **Otis-Lennon School Ability Test,** which covers children from kindergarten to twelfth grade. Paper-and-pencil tests like this are usually given to children in small groups. They are asked to classify items, to show an understanding of verbal and numerical concepts, to display general information, and to follow directions (see Figure 8-1 on the opposite page).

Part I.    *Classification*:  Mark the picture that does not belong with the other three, the one that is different.

(Pictorial)

(Geometric)

Part II.    *Verbal conceptualization*:  Mark the picture that shows a flame.

*Quantitative reasoning*:  Mark the picture that shows the same number of dots as there are parts in the circle.

*General information*:  Mark the picture of the thing we talk into.

*Following directions*:  Mark the picture that shows a glass inside a square with a cross on top.

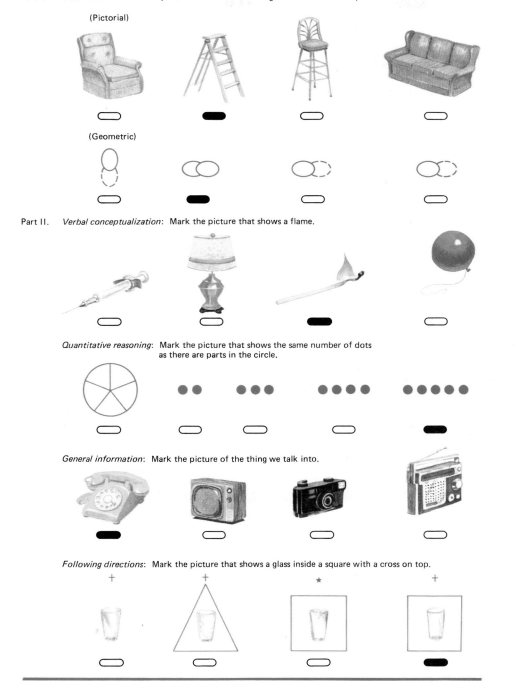

FIGURE 8-1
Items illustrative of the Otis-Lennon School Ability Test (Primary I and Primary II levels), a paper-and-pencil test administered to groups of children. (*Source:* Psychological Corporation. See Otis & Lennon, 1967.)

## Norms, Reliability, and Validity

There are pros and cons to using the familiar IQ tests. On the positive side, they have been standardized, and so we have extensive information about norms (standards of performance), reliability (consistency of results), and validity (whether the tests measure what they claim to measure).

*Norms* are established by giving a test to a representative group of test-takers; their average performance becomes the standard against which later test-takers' performance is measured (see Chapter 4).

*Reliability* can be determined by giving the same person the same test more than once, or (to eliminate variables like differences in testing conditions and the tendency to do better the second time) by comparing a person's score on half the answers with his or her score on the other half.

*Validity* depends on how well the results correlate with other measures or predict outcomes. IQ scores are good predictors of achievement in school, especially for highly verbal children, and they can often identify youngsters who are especially bright or who need special help. On the other hand, we have already pointed out the poor predictive abilities of psychometric intelligence tests for infants and the likelihood that motor-oriented tests underestimate the abilities of disabled children. Below, we'll see how intelligence tests may underestimate the intellectual abilities of minority-group members. (And in Chapters 12, 14, and 16, we'll discuss the inadequacies of standardized IQ testing for adults, and particularly how it has contributed to an underestimation of intellectual ability in late life.) Problems with validity reflect a fundamental criticism of IQ tests: that they overlook some important aspects of intelligence and measure others imperfectly.

## A Critique of IQ Tests

As a schoolboy, Robert Sternberg did not do well on intelligence tests. Neither did many other people who later turned out to have brilliant minds. Sternberg—now a professor of psychology at Yale University—is among many who believe that intelligence is more than what IQ tests measure (Sternberg, 1985b, 1987).

He and other critics point out that rather than assessing skills directly, psychometric tests infer them from children's knowledge, and that this leads to problems of cultural bias. Starting in middle childhood, the tests are fairly dependable predictors of academic performance; but these critics say that the tests miss other aspects of intelligence which may be at least as important, especially outside of school. Sternberg's *triarchic*, or three-part, theory of intelligence (discussed in detail in Chapter 12) suggests at least three important aspects of intelligence that psychometric tests tend to overlook. First, IQ tests fail to measure creative insight. Second, they ignore the practical side of intelligence. Finally, because IQ tests are timed, they wrongly equate intelligence with speed.

Another major problem with intelligence tests is that although they are meant to measure inborn aptitude rather than what a child has learned, the scores turn out to be more closely related to the amount of schooling a child has had than to the child's age (Cahan & Cohen, 1989). Therefore, it is impossible to separate "intelligence" from scholastic achievement. Schooling has the greatest impact on verbal abilities, but it also affects performance on number and figure tasks.

## Race, Culture, and IQ Tests

The failings of IQ tests become especially serious when the tests are misused to classify children (or adults) and to limit expectations and opportunities on the basis of test scores (Sternberg, 1987). The importance and sensitivity of this issue are most evident when we consider racial differences and cultural differences in test results.

### Intelligence testing of African American children

African Americans tend to score about 15 points lower on IQ tests than white Americans (E. B. Brody & Brody, 1976). There is considerable overlap: some black people score higher than most white people. Still, the difference exists, and what it means is highly controversial. There are two basic ways of interpreting it. Most modern educators maintain that it reflects typical differences in environments between the two groups—in education, living conditions, and other circumstances that affect self-esteem and motivation as well as academic performance itself (Kamin, 1974). The other view is that disparities in IQ reflect hereditary (genetic) differences and therefore that black people are innately inferior intellectually (Jensen, 1969). This latter view overlooks much evidence showing the importance of the environment. Let us see why the first position seems more solidly based.

For one thing, differences favoring white children do not appear until about age 2 or 3 (Golden, Birns, & Bridger, 1973). Some research suggests, in fact, that black babies are precocious on infant intelligence tests, especially in motor abilities (Bayley, 1965; Geber, 1962; Geber & Dean, 1957). The difference that shows up later may reflect the switch from predominantly motor tests to verbal tests. Verbal ability is highly influenced by environmental factors.

We also see the importance of the environment when we compare people from different socioeconomic levels. The same pattern that holds between white American and African American test-takers (an average difference of 15 points) also holds for American middle-class and deprived rural and mountain children, and for English middle-class and low-income canal-boat and Gypsy children (Pettigrew, 1964). Furthermore, black children who live in northern cities score higher than those in the rural south (Baughman, 1971), and middle-class black children score better than poor black children (Loehlin, Lindzey, & Spuhler, 1975). The relationship between schooling and test scores (Cahan & Cohen, 1989) may point to differences in the quantity and quality of school experiences between African American and white American children.

Another argument is that the apparent differences between black people's and white people's average intelligence reflect culture-related defects in the construction of the tests. We examine that problem next.

### Cultural bias

In 1986, a 15-year lawsuit ended with the upholding of a federal court order that because IQ tests are "culturally biased," California schools may not use them to place black students in special classes. The court had found that a disproportionate number of black youngsters were being wrongly consigned to classes for the mentally retarded.

This controversial decision was unprecedented; but as far back as 1920, researchers had recognized the difficulty of devising tests to measure intelligence in different cultural groups. Since then, test developers have tried in vain to devise tests that can measure innate intelligence without introducing *cultural bias*—the tendency to include test elements or procedures that are more familiar, significant, or comfortable for members of certain cultures. Language, of course, is one factor. Another is the nature of the test questions themselves, which—because they do not adequately separate what children have already learned from their ability to acquire new knowledge—favor children from advantaged backgrounds (Sternberg, 1985b).

Finally, according to Miller-Jones (1989), test developers' decisions about which answers to accept sometimes seem arbitrary. For example, a 4- to 6-year-old taking the 1973 edition of the Stanford-Binet Intelligence Scale is asked, "What is a house made of?" The answer "A house is made of walls" would be considered incorrect; a "correct" answer must give materials—like wood, bricks, or stone. Miller-Jones concludes, "The accepted responses do not incorporate all reasonably intelligent responses to the question" (p. 361).

***"Culture-free" and "culture-fair" tests*** Some tests do not require language. Testers use gestures, pantomime, and demonstrations for tasks like tracing mazes, finding absurdities in pictures, putting the right shapes in the right holes, and completing pictures. But it has not been possible to eliminate all cultural content from these tests. For example, in a test asking for absurdities in a picture, a culture's artistic conventions may affect the way people view the picture. A group of Asian immigrant children in Israel, when asked to provide the missing detail for a picture of a face with no mouth, said that the *body* was missing. They were not used to considering a drawing of a head as a complete picture and "regarded the absence of a body as more important than the omission of a mere detail like the mouth" (Anastasi, 1988, p. 360).

Recognizing the impossibility of designing a ***culture-free*** test—one with no culture-linked content—test developers have tried to produce ***culture-fair*** tests that deal with experiences common to various cultures. But these tests are not really culture-fair. For one thing, they almost invariably call for skills that are more familiar to some groups than to others (Anastasi, 1988; Sternberg, 1985a).

Furthermore, it is almost impossible to screen for culturally determined values and attitudes. Different cultures define intelligent behavior differently. The ability to sort names of living things according to their biological classifications (for example, to put *bird* and *fish* under *animal*) is considered intelligent in western society. But among the Kpelle tribe of Liberia, it is considered more intelligent to sort things according to what they do (see Box 1-1 in Chapter 1); for example, a Kpelle might put *animal* with *eat*. In the United States, parents at lower socioeconomic levels tend to value rote memory, while middle- and upper-class parents are more apt to encourage their children to reason (Sternberg, 1985b; Sternberg, 1986; Sternberg, in Quinby, 1985). (See Box 8-2 on page 262 for a discussion of cultural factors affecting measurement of intelligence in Asian and American children.)

Nowhere are the effects of heredity and environment more closely interwoven than in the measurement of whatever it is that we mean by *intelligence*. To separate inborn potential from the impact of life experience is a goal that, for the most part, has eluded test designers.

## BOX 8–2    WINDOW ON THE WORLD

# HOW CAN ASIAN CHILDREN ACHIEVE SO MUCH?

Of the 14 New York City finalists in the 1988 national Westinghouse science awards competition, 11 were Asian (Graubard, 1988). In the San Diego area, Asian high school students have higher grade-point averages than other students; Asian students take more advanced high school courses and graduate with more credits than their peers (Brand, 1987). How are young Asian Americans able to make such a strong showing? Researchers have come up with some answers.

### GENERAL COGNITIVE ABILITY

In a cross-cultural study of American, Japanese, and Chinese children, an international research team assessed cognitive abilities on the basis of common experiences (H. W. Stevenson et al., 1985). Test items in all three languages included verbal tasks (repeating lists of words and numbers, following spoken directions, answering questions about stories and everyday facts, and defining words) and nonverbal tasks (learning a code, completing a square, matching shapes, and recalling rhythms). Urban first- and fifth-graders in all three countries also took reading and math tests.

Apparently, Asian students do not start out with any overall cognitive superiority. In fact, American first-graders outperformed the others on many tasks, possibly because they were more used to answering adults' questions and had had more cultural experiences like going to museums, zoos, and movies. In another study, American children did better at ages 4 to 6 at counting and judging when something is more or less than something else, but by age 7 or 8, Korean children had surpassed them (Song & Ginsburg, 1987).

Children from Asian families often do better in school than other American youngsters. The reasons seem to be cultural, not genetic.

The Japanese and Chinese children performed better on math tests, and the Chinese children did best in reading; but by the fifth grade, children in all three cultures performed similarly, overall, on tests of cognition. The superior performance of Asian children, then, seems to be related to cultural and educational differences.

For example, the Japanese celebrate more when children enter first grade (the children receive expensive school-related gifts) than when they graduate from high school. Japanese and Korean parents spend a great deal of time helping children with schoolwork, and Japanese children who fall behind receive private tutoring or go to *jukus*, private remedial and enrichment schools (McKinney, 1987; Song & Ginsburg, 1987).

Academic and classroom practices differ, too (Stigler, Lee, & Stevenson, 1987; Song & Ginsburg,

1987). Asian teachers spend more than three-fourths of their time teaching the entire class; American teachers spend less than half of their time with the whole class, focusing more on small groups. American children spend more time working alone (often at problems they do not understand) or in small groups (with other children who do not understand the work), rather than listening to the teacher teach. The American approach offers more individual attention, but each child ends up with less total instruction.

Classroom behavior also plays a part. American children are out of their seats and engaged in irrelevant activities 5 times more often than Chinese and Japanese children; and Asian children are more obedient.

Furthermore, Chinese and Japanese children spend more time on homework, get more help from parents, and like doing it more than

**BOX 8–2    (CONTINUED)**

American children (Chen & Stevenson, 1989).

Finally, Asian children spend more time in school each year, more time in class each day, and more time being taught mathematics. The curriculum is centrally set rather than left up to individual teachers, and Asian teachers (who are generally not as well educated as American teachers) are more knowledgeable in their subject matter.

What happens to students when they leave school? Although 90 percent of Japanese students graduate from high school, compared with about 75 percent in the United States, only 29 percent go to college, compared with 58 percent in the United States (Simons, 1987). And what are these people like as adults? Many Japanese parents, students, and lawyers argue that regimentation stifles individuality, and are raising legal

challenges to many long-established practices (Chira, 1988). Ultimately, in designing an educational system, a society's leaders have to ask what kinds of citizens they want to produce, since culture shapes attitudes and encourages some kinds of behaviors rather than others. It is apparently culture rather than inborn ability that has helped Asian students to achieve so much in school.

---

*The test situation*    Cultural attitudes may bias the testing situation as well as the test itself. Such factors as rapport with the test-giver, interest in the tasks, motivation to excel, and modes of problem solving may be culturally influenced (Anastasi, 1988). A child in a society that stresses slow, deliberate, painstaking work is handicapped in a timed test. A child from a culture that stresses sociability and cooperation is handicapped in taking a test alone. And a child who is not accustomed to being asked questions by an adult who knows the answers is dealing with a new situation when being tested individually (Miller-Jones, 1989).

Research with hundreds of children in four American cities has shown that African American and Hispanic students, as well as students who are disabled and students from low socioeconomic backgrounds, often do better in familiar settings (like their own classrooms) with examiners they know (like their own teachers) than in strange rooms with unfamiliar examiners. These children also do better when they are tested more than once with standardized tests based on the curricula they have been studying (D. Fuchs & L. S. Fuchs, 1986; L. S. Fuchs & D. Fuchs, 1986).

The function of intelligence tests is not just to measure intelligence but to find out how to improve it. Since recent research has shown close ties between schooling and intelligence test scores, it makes sense to improve school for all children, and most especially for those from minority groups, who have traditionally scored lower on such tests than children in the majority culture. Let's now look briefly at the impact of school in these middle years.

## CHILDREN IN SCHOOL

Whether children love school or hate it, they spend many of their waking hours there. Because school is central in children's lives, it affects and is affected by every aspect of their development. However, child-care professionals and educators often disagree on how school can best enhance children's development.

### EDUCATIONAL TRENDS

Conflicting views, along with historical events, have brought great swings in educational theory and practice during this century. The traditional curriculum, centered on the "three R's" (reading, 'riting, and 'rithmetic), gave way first to "child-centered" methods that focused on children's interests and then, during the late 1950s, to an emphasis on science and mathematics in order to overcome a Soviet lead in the space race. Rigorous studies were then replaced during the turbulent 1960s by student-directed learning in "open classrooms," where children engaged in varied activities and teachers served as "facilitators." High school students took more electives and student-initiated courses. Then, in the mid-1970s, a decline in high school students' scores on the Scholastic Aptitude Test (SAT) sent schools back to the "basics" (Ravitch, 1983).

It turned out, however, that while children were becoming better grounded in basic skills, they were not learning to think (National Assessment of Educational Progress, NAEP, 1981, 1985). Thus, a "fourth R"—reasoning—has now been added. Since research shows that aspects of performance on intelligence tests and

BOX 8–3   PRACTICALLY SPEAKING

# TEACHING CHILDREN TO THINK

Teachers complain that it is easier to teach children bald facts to feed back on tests than it is to teach them how to think for themselves. *Can* children be taught to think? Research says "yes."

Thinking arises at least partly from experience. Therefore, for children to learn how to think—which includes how to evaluate a situation, how to focus on the most important aspects, how to decide what to do, and how to go about doing it—they need experiences. The following suggestions for ways by which parents and teachers can provide such experiences come from findings in cognitive studies (Marzano & Hutchins, 1987; Maxwell, 1987):

■ Teach thinking skills in connection with everyday activities at home or at school. This can begin very early. Asking toddlers open-ended questions (beginning with *what, why,* and *how*) while reading to them encourages them to improve their verbal skills; it also helps them learn to think. The same kind of approach helps older children.

■ Ask children to "match" information, to compare new data with what they already know. This helps them learn to identify links among words or concepts (what two items have in common or how they differ). Schoolchildren can, say, categorize a country as European or African, democratic or totalitarian. Categorization can help them remember facts better, too, as we point out in our discussion of memory.

■ Demonstrate "critical thinking," the ability to evaluate information. Teach children to ask four questions about anything they hear or read: (1) Is it unusual? (2) Is it common knowledge ("the sky is sometimes blue")? (3) If not, what is the evidence? (4) If there is evidence, is it reliable? If not, they should learn not to accept the statement.

■ Show children how to approach a problem: (1) They need to identify what they know, what they do not know, and what has to be done. They can then (2) design a plan to solve it, (3) carry out the plan, and (4) evaluate the plan (decide whether it worked).

■ Use "guided imagery" (imagining an event or experience). Sensory images help us store information in long-term memory, and the more senses are involved, the better. Thus children studying the Sahara Desert might be asked to "see" it, "touch" the sand, "hear" the wind, and "feel" hot and thirsty. This approach uses elaboration, a memory strategy discussed in this chapter.

■ Teach children to go beyond what they have learned. Children studying the American Revolution might be asked, "How did the soldiers feel at Valley Forge? What were they wearing? Imagine that you were there, and write a letter to your family."

■ Inspire invention. Ask children to create new information or products, like a household gadget to help in some regular chore.

■ Suggest creative projects, like writing a poem or drawing a picture. Encourage children to produce a first version—and then to polish or revise it.

■ Give children basic tools by teaching them how and when to use procedures, like reading a map, doing arithmetic, and using a microscope.

■ Encourage children to set goals within a time frame and to write down the goals so that they can check their progress.

■ Help children learn how to find the most important points in what they read, see, or hear.

■ Encourage children to write, since the process of putting thoughts down on paper forces the writer to organize them. Projects that children can enjoy, as well as learn from, include keeping a journal, presenting an argument to one's parents (for an allowance increase or a special purchase or privilege), or writing a letter to a business or famous person.

specific skills (like critical thinking) can be improved by training, schools have adopted a variety of programs to teach thinking skills (see Box 8-3).

What do all these changes mean for children? They illustrate, for one thing, the underlying American faith that our future depends on the way our children turn out, and that an important way to affect children's development is through education.

## TEACHERS' CHARACTERISTICS AND EXPECTATIONS

If you're lucky, you may have had a special teacher who had a major influence on you—who inspired a love of knowledge and spurred you to work and to learn.

One study showed the power of a teacher's influence by linking the success of a number of people who had grown up in a poor city neighborhood with a very special first-grade teacher. Many more of "Miss A's" former pupils than other disadvantaged youngsters showed increases in IQ over the years. Alumni of Miss A's classroom also scored higher on measures of work status, type of housing, and personal appearance than other graduates of the same school (Pederson, Faucher, & Eaton, 1978). What did Miss A do? She showed her confidence in children's ability, gave extra time to those who needed it, was affectionate and generous, and remembered pupils by name, even 20 years later.

Miss A's belief in her pupils undoubtedly had much to do with how well they did. According to the principle of the ***self-fulfilling prophecy,*** students live up to or down to the expectations that other people have for them. In the famous "Oak School" experiment, teachers were told at the beginning of the term that some students had shown unusual potential for intellectual growth. Actually, the children named as potential "bloomers" had been chosen at random. Yet several months later, many of them—especially first- and second-graders—showed unusual gains in IQ. The teachers did not spend more time with these children than with the others, nor did they treat them differently in any obvious ways. Subtler influences may have been at work—possibly the teachers' tone of voice, facial expressions, touch, and posture (R. Rosenthal & Jacobson, 1968).

Although this research has been criticized for methodological shortcomings, work by many other researchers using a variety of methods has confirmed the basic principle—that teachers' expectations "can and do function as self-fulfilling prophecies, although not always or automatically" (Brophy & Good, 1974, p. 32). This principle has important implications for minority-group and poor children. Since many middle-class teachers may be convinced (often subconsciously) that such students have intellectual limitations, they may somehow convey their limited expectations to the children, thus getting from them the little that they expect.

An exceptional teacher's influence can extend far into the future, and an interest she or he inspires may shape a child's entire life.

## PARENTS' INFLUENCE

Teachers are not, of course, the only adults who make an important difference in how well children do in school. The direct or indirect involvement of parents improves children's grades and their scores on IQ and achievement tests, as well as their behavior and attitude toward school. It also results in better schools (A. Henderson, 1987).

A report of the U.S. Department of Education (1986b) indicates that parents of achieving children do the following:

■ They read, talk to, and listen to children. They tell their children stories, play games, share hobbies, and discuss news, television programs, and current events.
■ They provide a place to study and to keep books and supplies.
■ They set and insist on times for meals, sleep, and homework, making sure that children meet school deadlines.
■ They monitor how much television their children watch, and they monitor what their children do after school.
■ They show interest in children's lives at school, partly by talking about school events and about problems and successes.

## EDUCATION FOR SPECIAL NEEDS

### Children with Disabilities

Education for children with disabilities has come a long way since the beginning of this century, when the family of Helen Keller had to travel to distant cities to find help for their deaf and blind daughter, who later became a famous author and lecturer. Let us look at three of the most common educational disabilities—and then at how children with them are educated.

### *Mental retardation*

Most retarded children can benefit from schooling, at least up to sixth-grade level. *Mental retardation* is defined as below-average intellectual functioning, a deficiency in adaptive behavior appropriate to current age, and the appearance of such characteristics before age 18 (*Diagnostic and Statistical Manual of Mental Disorders*, 3d ed., rev., DSM-III-R, 1987). Low-level intellectual functioning (defined as a score of 75 or below on IQ tests) is important in determining retardation. But so is the person's behavior in everyday life—skills of communication, sociability, and daily living. A supportive and stimulating early environment and a continued level of guidance and help bring about a promising outcome for many of these children, including many born with Down syndrome (see Chapter 2).

**TABLE 8–6**
LEVELS OF MENTAL RETARDATION

| Level | Description |
|---|---|
| Mildly retarded | About 85 percent of the retarded population. Mildly retarded people can acquire skills up to about the sixth-grade level, hold low-level paid jobs in adulthood, and live in the community. Although they can usually function on their own, they may need guidance and help at times of unusual stress. |
| Moderately retarded | About 10 percent of the retarded population. Moderately retarded people can learn academic subjects to the second-grade level, can learn occupational and social skills, and in adulthood may work in sheltered workshops or in regular jobs with close supervision. They can do a fair amount for themselves, but usually live in supervised group homes. |
| Severely retarded | About 3 to 4 percent of the retarded population. Severely retarded people may learn to talk during the school years, can be trained in personal hygiene, and can sometimes learn to recognize such "survival" words as *men, women,* and *stop.* They typically live in group homes or with their families. |
| Profoundly retarded | About 1 to 2 percent of the retarded population. Profoundly retarded people have minimal sensorimotor functioning, but may respond to some training in getting around, in self-care, and in communicating, especially if they have a one-to-one relationship with a caregiver. They live in group homes, in intermediate-care facilities, with their families, or in institutions. |

The mentally retarded account for about 1 percent of the population; about 1.5 males are affected for every female. The retarded are generally classified by four categories, based on severity—mildly, moderately, severely, and profoundly retarded (see Table 8-6).

In 30 to 40 percent of cases, the cause of retardation is unknown. Known causes include problems in embryonic development (30 percent), environmental influences and mental disorders (15 to 20 percent), problems with pregnancy and childbirth (10 percent), hereditary factors (5 percent), and physical disorders acquired in childhood (5 percent) (DSM-III-R, 1987).

### Learning disabilities

Nelson Rockefeller, who was a governor of New York and a vice president of the United States, had so much trouble reading that he ad-libbed his speeches instead of using a script. Thomas Edison never learned how to spell or write grammatically. General George Patton read poorly and got through West Point by memorizing entire lectures (Schulman, 1986). All these people suffered from *dyslexia*—a developmental reading disorder in which reading achievement is at least 2 years below the expected level.

Dyslexic children—some 3 to 6 percent of the school population—often confuse up and down and left and right; they may read *saw* for *was* and have trouble with arithmetic as well as reading. Dyslexia affects males and females equally, is more common in children from large families and in lower socioeconomic levels, and seems to have a hereditary component (Council on Scientific Affairs of the American Medical Association, 1989; DeFries, Fulker, & LaBuda, 1987; S. E. Shaywitz, Shaywitz, Fletcher, & Escobar, 1990). The reading problem is part of a generalized language impairment ("Dyslexia," 1989). Dyslexic children are late in starting to talk, suffer subtle deficits in both spoken and written language, and have limited memory for verbal materials. If diagnosed before third grade, the child's prognosis is better.

Dyslexia is only one of a number of *learning disabilities (LDs)*—disorders that interfere with a specific aspect of school achievement. An estimated 5 to 10 percent of the population are affected (Interagency Committee on Learning Disabilities, 1987). Since success in school is important for self-esteem, learning disabilities can have devastating effects on the psyche as well as on the report card.

Children with learning disabilities typically have average or higher general intelligence and normal vision and hearing (Feagans, 1983). But they have trouble processing what comes through their senses. As one child said, "I know it in my head, but I can't get it into my hand."

Many different disorders affect one or more aspects of learning, including reading, processing spoken words, small-motor or large-motor coordination, and speech. The cause of most of these disabilities is unknown. They may be related to behavioral problems; "LD children" tend to be less task-oriented, more easily distracted, and less able to concentrate than other children. There may be a failure of cognitive processing; these children are less organized as learners and are less likely to use memory strategies (Feagans, 1983). Or the cause may be physiological; some differences have been found in the brains of people with learning disabilities (Blakeslee, 1984). Learning disabilities often run in families, and research suggests that genetic transmission of chromosomal abnormalities may play a role (DeFries et al., 1987; M. D. Levine, 1987). But it is also possible that many children classified as learning-disabled are simply youngsters whom schools have failed to teach and control effectively (McGuinness, 1986).

Children at highest risk of learning disabilities are those who were very low-birthweight infants, who suffered birth trauma or malnutrition, who have a "difficult" temperament, or who come from poor, chaotic families. Those who do best are those whose problems were discovered and responded to early (M. D. Levine, 1987). Among the most successful aids are behavioral modification techniques to help concentration, techniques for improving basic skills and using cognitive strategies, help in organizing life outside school as well as in it, and encouragement of progress in both academic and nonacademic areas.

Children do not outgrow learning disabilities; some 5 to 10 million adults suffer from them (Schulman, 1986). But if children take tests to establish their strengths and weaknesses, if they learn skills to help them use their strengths to compensate for their weaknesses, and if they get psychological help for such problems as poor self-esteem (often caused by school problems), they can often lead satisfying, productive lives. Some go on to college and professional careers and, while never cured of their disabilities, learn how to cope with them.

A behavior disorder that often accompanies learning disorders is hyperactivity, which we'll consider next.

### Hyperactivity

The story is all too familiar to many parents and teachers. Johnny cannot sit still, cannot finish even a simple task, cannot keep a friend, and is always in trouble. His teacher says, "I can't do a thing with him." His family doctor says, "Don't worry; he'll grow out of it." And his next-door neighbor says, "He's just a spoiled brat."

The syndrome that Johnny is probably suffering from, formally known as **attention deficit hyperactivity disorder (ADHD),** is marked by inattention, impulsivity, low tolerance of frustration, temper tantrums, and a great deal of activity at the wrong time and in the wrong place, like the classroom. These traits appear to some degree in all children; but in about 3 percent of school-age children (6 to 9 times more boys than girls), they are so pervasive that they interfere with the child's functioning in school and daily life. These children are considered hyperactive. Hyperactivity shows up before age 4 in about half the cases, but it is often not recognized until the child starts school (DSM-III-R, 1987).

Hyperactivity is probably caused by a combination of genetic, neurological, biochemical, and environmental factors (Weiss, 1990). One team of researchers found that the brains of adults who had been hyperactive as children were different from those of other adults in the way they metabolized glucose, a sugar. These differences were especially notable in the areas associated with regulation of attention and motor activity (Zametkin et al., 1990). This suggests that the disorder has a specific neurological aspect. However, there are so many possible causes of hyperactivity that it is difficult to determine the origin of any one case. It often runs in families, and data suggest that it may be at least partly inherited (DSM-III-R, 1987).

Whatever the cause, parents and teachers can help hyperactive children do better at home and in school. First, they have to understand and accept the child's basic temperament. Then they can teach the child how to break up work into small, manageable segments; they can incorporate physical activity into the daily classroom schedule; and they can offer alternative ways for children to show what they have learned, such as individual conferences or tape-recorded reports, instead of written reports (M. A. Stewart & Olds, 1973).

ADHD is sometimes treated with drugs, most often stimulants, prescribed to help children focus on the task at hand and reduce problem behaviors. In the short run, the drugs often help, but at the end of a few years, drug-treated children do not do any better than untreated ones on academic achievement tests (McDaniel, 1986). Furthermore, not all hyperactive children are helped by drugs, and we do not know the long-range effects of giving drugs to what many believe to be basically normal children. Although the recent findings on brain abnormalities seem to support the use of stimulants, it still seems best to consider drugs only after trying other approaches, and then to use them only in combination with behavior modification programs that teach social skills and control of impulsive behavior

(AAP Committee on Children with Disabilities and Committee on Drugs, 1987; McDaniel, 1986; M. A. Stewart and Olds, 1973).

One treatment that has received much attention is a diet free of artificial food colorings and flavorings. However, an additive-free diet seems to help only a small number of hyperactive children, and the National Institutes of Health do not recommend it in all cases (Hadley, 1984). Recent research suggests that these children may benefit from eating protein-rich breakfasts, but such findings are only preliminary (Conners, 1988).

About half of the children diagnosed as hyperactive grow up to function normally as adults (Mannuzza, Klein, Bonagura, Konig, & Shenker, 1988). Many, however, have higher rates of job changes, marital disruption, traffic accidents, and brushes with the law (B. Henker & Whalen, 1989). The long-range problems that occur are most likely to revolve around getting along with other people, drug abuse, and conduct disorders. On the bright side, although hyperactive people generally continue to be restless and impulsive, they also tend to have such positive personality traits as spontaneity, zest, and energy.

### Educating children with disabilities

In 1975, Congress passed the Education for All Handicapped Children Act (Public Law 94.142), which ensures an appropriate public education for all disabled children. This law provides for an evaluation of each child's needs and the design of an appropriate program, for the involvement of parents in the decision about their children's education, and for the allocation of necessary funds. Eight out of ten children in the program are mentally retarded, learning-disabled, or speech-impaired.

This law recommends **mainstreaming,** the integration of disabled and nondisabled students, as much as possible. Under mainstreaming, disabled children are in regular classes with nondisabled youngsters for all or part of the day, instead of being segregated in special classes. Thus, disabled people learn to get along in a society where most people do not share their impediments, and nondisabled people get to know and understand the disabled. However, critics of this policy maintain that disabled children can be taught better and more humanely by specially trained teachers in small classes.

Retarded children do about the same academically in mainstreamed classes as in special classes (Gruen, Korte, & Baum, 1974). However, the other children in regular classes do not accept them socially; mainstreaming does not diminish the stigma of being retarded (Taylor, Asher, & Williams, 1987).

Mainstreaming in schools gives disabled and nondisabled children an opportunity to learn how to get along with and understand each other.

Mainstreaming requires innovative teaching techniques that meet the needs of all students. Not all teachers can rise to the challenge, but many have effectively taught classes of both disabled and nondisabled students, drawing on teachers' aides, individual tutors, and computers (D. Thomas, 1985). The best solution seems to be a combination of mainstreaming and special classes. A retarded child, for example, might be able to take physical education in a regular class, while receiving academic instruction in a class with slow learners. Or a child with cerebral palsy might be in a regular academic class but receive special physical training while classmates go to gym.

### Gifted, Talented, and Creative Children

At age 12, Balamurati Krishna Ambati, who was born in India, was a third-year premedical student at New York University. He had mastered calculus at age 4, had scored 750 on the math SAT at age 10, and hoped to be a doctor before age 18 (Stanley, 1990). His path has not been easy: although his parents encouraged his achievements from the beginning, his teachers urged him to slow down and his peers have not always understood his drive to excel.

Giftedness can be a mixed blessing. Many promising children—more than half, by one report—achieve below their tested potential (National Commission on Excellence in Education, 1983). Why is this so? One reason is that schools often do not meet their needs for intellectual stimulation.

About 2.5 million children—some 3 to 5 percent of the school population—are estimated to be gifted, but fewer than 1 million get special attention. The number of mentally retarded children in the population is about the same, but more funds are spent on their education (Horowitz & O'Brien, 1986).

### Defining and identifying giftedness

Like intelligence, giftedness is hard to define. The traditional definition, which is the one most often used to select children for special programs, is narrow—an IQ score of 130 or higher (Horowitz & O'Brien, 1986). This definition does not identify creative children (whose unusual answers often lower their test scores), gifted children from minority groups (whose abilities may not be well developed, though the potential is there), or children with aptitudes in specific areas.

We favor a broader definition of **giftedness,** including—but not limited to—one or more of the following: superior general intellect, superiority in a single domain (like mathematics or science), talent in the arts (like painting, writing, or acting), leadership, or creative thinking (looking at problems in a new way).

Two new ways of looking at giftedness stem from new theories of intelligence. According to Sternberg (1985b; J. E. Davidson & Sternberg, 1984), gifted children process information efficiently, especially on novel tasks requiring insight. And according to Gardner's theory of multiple intelligences (Gardner, 1983), people can be gifted in one or more of at least seven separate and relatively independent intelligences. Some of these intelligences—musical, bodily kinesthetic (moving precisely as in dance), interpersonal (understanding others), and intrapersonal (knowing oneself)—are not tapped by traditional intelligence tests. The others are linguistic (reading and writing), logical-mathematical (using numbers and solving logical problems), and spatial (finding one's way around an environment).

The use of IQ tests to identify gifted children goes back to Lewis M. Terman, the professor who brought the Binet test to the United States. Terman, in the 1920s, began a major longitudinal study of more than 1500 California children with IQs of 135 or more. Researchers who have followed the progress of Terman's subjects up to the present found that their intellectual, scholastic, and vocational superiority has held up over 60 years. They were 10 times more likely than an unselected group to have graduated from college and 3 times more likely to have been elected to honorary societies like Phi Beta Kappa. By midlife, they were highly represented in listings such as *Who's Who in America*. Almost 90 percent of the men were professional or semiprofessional or were in high echelons of business (Terman & Oden, 1959).

Thus IQ tests (even in their early days) correctly identified some children of unusual promise. Yet Terman's bright group never produced a great musician, an exceptional painter, or a Nobel prize winner—evidence that IQ does not predict creative achievement. Indeed, other classic studies found that the most academically able children are not necessarily the most creative thinkers—innovators who solve problems in original ways or find problems that others overlook (Getzels, 1964, 1984; Getzels & Jackson, 1962). And the most creative children, whose minds take twists that teachers do not expect, may not do especially well in school (Renzulli & McGreevy, 1984).

One line of research has tried to identify creative children by analyzing how they think. Guilford (1959) distinguished between two kinds of thought: **convergent thinking,** which seeks a single "right" answer (usually the traditional one); and **divergent thinking,** which comes up with fresh, unusual possibilities.

Special tests have been devised to find divergent thinkers. The Torrance Tests of Creative Thinking, for example, ask children to find ways of improving a toy, to list unusual uses for common objects, to draw pictures starting with a few given lines, and to write down what various sounds bring to mind. One problem with these tests is that the score depends partly on speed, which is not a hallmark of creativity. Furthermore, although the tests are fairly reliable (they yield consistent results), there is little evidence that they are valid—that children who do well on them are creative in real life (Anastasi, 1988; Mansfield & Busse, 1981). Much more research needs to be done before we can identify youngsters who will be creative adults (see Chapter 14).

Would Wolfgang Amadeus Mozart have composed some of the world's most beautiful music if his gifts had not been recognized, nurtured—and exploited—at an early age? His father, a fine musician and composer himself, taught Wolfgang, shown here with his sister, and encouraged him to perform.

### Educating and nurturing gifted children

When Terman's study began, the popular image of a bright child was a puny, pasty-faced bookworm. Terman debunked that stereotype. The children in his sample tended to be taller, healthier, and better coordinated than average, as well as better adjusted and more popular with other children (Wallach & Kogan, 1965). Other studies, however, have found that gifted underachievers and extremely gifted children—those with IQs of 180 or more—do tend to have social and emotional problems; possibly these problems are caused in part by unchallenging school experiences (Janos & Robinson, 1985).

Three elements essential to the flowering of gifts and talents seem to be inborn ability, a drive to excel, and encouragement by adults (B. S. Bloom, 1985;

Gardner, 1979; P. Sears, 1977; P. Sears & Barbee, 1978). Nurturing appears to be especially crucial (Horowitz & O'Brien, 1986). Children identified as gifted are likely to have well-educated, well-to-do, emotionally supportive, happily married parents who spend time with them, answer their questions, and encourage their curiosity (Janos & Robinson, 1985).

Parents of creative children tend to be special themselves, according to a review of 61 studies. They usually have occupations they consider meaningful or pursue intellectual or artistic hobbies. They are uninhibited and unconventional and do not worry about what "the Joneses" think. They expect their children to do well, and they give them both freedom and responsibility. These parents are not rigidly controlling; they let their children be themselves (B. Miller & Gerard, 1979). However, another report of studies on the rearing of future scientists found a less clear-cut relationship between creativity and parental control (Mansfield & Busse, 1981).

Creativity often fades after children enter school, where they are rewarded for doing what adults want them to do. Those who remain creative tend to be the rebellious ones who annoy teachers with questions like "What would birds look like if they couldn't fly?" or are lost in imagination when they should be doing homework. When teachers accept unconventional questions, praise original ideas, and refrain from grading everything children do, schoolchildren are more creative and better behaved (Torrance, in Chance & Fischman, 1987).

What kind of education is best for gifted and talented students? One successful approach involves coaching by *mentors*—experts in the child's field of talent or interest (B. S. Bloom, 1985). Another approach involves special schools or classes for the artistically talented or intellectually gifted.

Most programs concentrate on enrichment (broadening and deepening studies through special activities like field trips and research projects) or acceleration (rapid movement through the curriculum), as exemplified by the "Talent Search" for mathematically and verbally precocious youth begun at Johns Hopkins University (Horowitz & O'Brien, 1986). A comprehensive national study concluded that a wide range of "able learners"—perhaps 25 percent of all students—should be served through a combination of enrichment and acceleration, geared to their individual needs (Cox, Daniel, & Boston, 1985).

There is no firm line between being gifted and not being gifted. What we learn about fostering intelligence, creativity, and talent for the small, special population of the gifted and talented can help all children make the most of their potential.

## SUMMARY

### GROWTH DURING MIDDLE CHILDHOOD

■ Physical development is less rapid in middle childhood than in the earlier years. Boys are slightly larger than girls at the beginning of this period, but girls undergo the growth spurt of adolescence at an earlier age and thus tend to be larger than boys at the end of the period. Wide differences in height and weight exist between individuals and between groups.

■ Proper nutrition is essential for normal growth and health. Malnutrition can impair activity and sociability.

### HEALTH, FITNESS, AND SAFETY

■ Obesity among children is increasingly common.

■ Respiratory infections and other common health problems of middle childhood tend to be of short duration rather than persistent and tend to run in clusters.

■ Vision becomes keener in middle childhood, but up to 17 percent of children have defective distance vision by the age of 11.

■ Although about one-half of American children aged 5 to 17 have no tooth decay, there are some dental problems in this group.

■ Children today are less healthy and less fit than children in the mid-1960s. This disturbing trend seems to be occurring because children are less physically active today.

■ Accidents are the leading cause of death in children over age 1. Most childhood accidents occur in or from automobiles, or in the home.

### MOTOR DEVELOPMENT IN MIDDLE CHILDHOOD

■ Because of improved motor development, boys and girls in middle childhood can engage in a wider range of motor activities than preschoolers.

■ Studies conducted several decades ago suggested that boys excel in motor skills, but more recent research indicates that boys and girls have similar motor abilities.

## ASPECTS OF INTELLECTUAL DEVELOPMENT IN MIDDLE CHILDHOOD

■ The child from age 7 to age 11 is in the Piagetian stage of concrete operations and can use symbols (mental representations) to carry out operations (mental activities).

■ Children at this stage are less egocentric than before and are more proficient at tasks requiring logical reasoning, such as conservation. However, their reasoning is largely limited to the here and now.

■ According to Piaget, Kohlberg, and Selman, moral development coincides with cognitive development. Moral development is influenced by a child's maturational level, social role-taking skills, and interactions with adults and other children.

1 According to Piaget, moral development occurs in two stages. The first, morality of constraint, is characterized by moral rigidity. The second, morality of cooperation, is characterized by moral flexibility.
2 Selman has proposed a theory which links moral development to role-taking.
3 Kohlberg, who defines morality as a sense of justice, extended Piaget's view to include six stages of moral reasoning organized on three levels: preconventional morality, conventional morality, and postconventional morality.

■ Memory improves greatly during middle childhood because children's capacity increases rapidly and because they become more adept at using memory strategies such as rehearsal, organization, elaboration, and external aids. Metamemory (the understanding of how memory works) also improves.

■ Children's understanding of increasingly complex syntax develops up to and perhaps even after age 9. Although the ability to communicate improves, even older children may not have a complete awareness of the processes of communication.

■ The intelligence of school-age children is assessed by group tests (such as the Otis-Lennon School Ability Test) and individual tests (such as the WISC-R).

■ Critics claim that psychometric intelligence tests overlook practical intelligence and creative insight and falsely equate mental efficiency with speed. New methods are being devised to test and train intelligence.

■ African Americans tend to score lower on intelligence tests than white Americans. Numerous findings indicate that the difference in scores is more likely to reflect environmental than innate racial differences.

■ Developers of intelligence tests have attempted to devise "culture-fair" tests, tests that focus on experiences common across cultures. None of the attempts has been completely successful.

## CHILDREN IN SCHOOL

■ Teachers influence children's success in school and thus their self-esteem. Self-fulfilling prophecies often limit the achievement of poor and minority children.

■ Parents' involvement enhances children's learning.

■ Under the law in the United States, every handicapped child is entitled to an appropriate education at public expense, and parents must be consulted in planning the child's program. Children must be mainstreamed, or placed in regular classes, as much as possible.

■ Mental retardation is defined as below-average intellectual functioning, a deficiency in age-appropriate adaptive behavior, and the appearance of these characteristics before age 18. Most retarded people can benefit from schooling at least up to sixth grade.

■ Learning disabilities interfere with learning to read and other school tasks. The causes of these disabilities are unclear. Many learning-disabled children can lead productive lives if they get individual attention early.

■ An IQ of 130 is the most common standard for identifying gifted children for special programs, but this measure misses some children.

■ Creativity is sometimes identified as divergent (rather than convergent) thinking. The validity of tests for creativity is questionable.

■ Although Terman's study found that gifted children tend to be unusually successful adults, some gifted children do not live up to their apparent potential, possibly because schools do not meet their needs.

■ The development of gifts, talents, and creativity depends greatly on nurturance. The child's drive to excel is another crucial factor. Most special school programs for the gifted stress enrichment or acceleration. Each of these methods meets the needs of some students.

## KEY TERMS

concrete operations (page 248)
operational thinking (249)
decenter (249)
conservation (249)
horizontal décalage (249)
morality of constraint (250)
morality of cooperation (250)
role-taking (250)
preconventional morality (252)
conventional morality (252)
postconventional morality (252)

mnemonic strategies (255)
rehearsal (255)
organization (256)
elaboration (256)
external aids (256)
metamemory (256)
metacommunication (258)
Wechsler Intelligence Scale for
   Children (WISC-R) (258)
Otis-Lennon School Ability Test (258)
culture-free (261)

culture-fair (261)
self-fulfilling prophecy (265)
dyslexia (267)
learning disabilities (LDs) (267)
attention deficit hyperactivity disorder
   (ADHD) (268)
mainstreaming (268)
giftedness (269)
convergent thinking (270)
divergent thinking (270)

## SUGGESTED READINGS

**Coles, R. (1986).** *The moral life of children.* Boston: Atlantic Monthly. Coles, a prominent child psychiatrist, offers his rebuttal to Kohlberg's theory that moral development rests on cognitive development and that schoolchildren are too young to live moral lives. The book contains many moving quotations from children discussing morality in their own experience.

**Gardner, H. (1989).** *To open minds: Chinese clues to the dilemma of contemporary education.* New York: Basic Books. This thoughtful and readable book by a leading cognitive psychologist draws on his extensive research on creativity at Harvard University and his observations of children in modern Chinese classrooms. He discusses both the progressive and the traditional approaches to education, using many lively anecdotes to make his points.

**Healy, J. M. (1990).** *Endangered minds: Why our children don't think.* New York: Simon & Schuster. In this thought-provoking book a noted educator examines the reasons children today are less able to concentrate and less able to absorb information than previous genera-

tions. Healy's theory is that forces in today's society (such as the electronic media, unstable family patterns, environmental hazards) are changing the way children think and may even be changing the brain's physical structure.

**Kidder, T. (1990).** *Among schoolchildren.* New York: Avon. The author spent an entire school year observing a fifth-grade class in Holyoke, Massachusetts, and this is the story of that teacher and her students. It is a remarkable depiction of the demands on a teacher and portrays with compassion the triumphs and failures of her students.

**Radford, J. (1990).** *Child prodigies and exceptional early achievers.* New York: Free Press/Macmillan. This exploration of the lives of gifted children charts the impact of environmental and genetic influences in their lives. Telling the stories of dozens of early achieving children, the author, a psychology professor, stresses the importance of stimulating environments and of inspiring mentors, and discusses the problems such children can encounter.

## CHAPTER 9

# PERSONALITY AND SOCIAL DEVELOPMENT IN MIDDLE CHILDHOOD

The healthy human child will keep
Away from home, except to sleep.
Were it not for the common cold
Our young we never would behold.

OGDEN NASH,
*YOU CAN'T GET THERE FROM HERE*, 1956

- How does the self-concept develop, and how does it affect children's behavior?
- What do schoolchildren do with their time, and how does a schoolchild's daily life today differ from the daily life of children in previous generations?
- How does the peer group influence children, and why do some children make friends more easily than others?

- What changes occur in family relationships in middle childhood, and how are children affected by parents' employment, by parents' divorce, and by living in a single-parent family?
- What are some emotional disturbances of childhood, and how are they treated?
- How do school-age children handle stress?

At age 9, Laurie became a "published author" when her fourth-grade class put together a collection of its verse. Laurie's poem told how her mother cared for her when she was sick or hurt her knee or got a D or had a nightmare. Gareth's poem extolled the pleasure of popping corn; Jeff's cheerfully ticked off his parents' complaints about his table manners; and Shani's recalled how she had cried when her father and mother made her return her pet frog to the pond. Uri's confessed to an occasional urge to hit his pesty little brother, and Dina's revealed the "funny feeling" she got in her stomach right before a test.

The lives of school-age children are rich and varied, and their feelings about their broadening experiences are mixed. In this chapter, we trace the social and personality growth that goes along with the cognitive changes of middle childhood.

The self-concept, of course, develops continuously from infancy onward, as we'll see in this chapter. We examine it at this point because it is particularly important for personality and social development during the years of middle childhood. From about age 6 to the onset of puberty at about age 12, youngsters develop more realistic concepts of themselves and of what they need to survive and succeed in their culture. They become more independent of their parents and more involved with other people, particularly other children. Through interaction with their peers, they make discoveries about their own attitudes, values, and skills. But the family remains a vital influence. Children have been profoundly affected by new patterns of family life, as well as by other societal changes.

Although most children are healthy, both physically and emotionally, some succumb to emotional disorders of one kind or another, sometimes in response to stress, sometimes because of biological malfunction. Other, more resilient children face childhood stresses and emerge from them healthier and stronger.

## THE SELF-CONCEPT

### COMPONENTS OF THE SELF-CONCEPT

"'Who in the world am I?' Ah, *that's* the great puzzle," said Alice in Wonderland, after her size had abruptly changed—again. Solving Alice's "puzzle" entails a lifelong process of getting to know our developing selves.

We may (like the psychologist William James) think of the self as having two sides: the "me" that is the object of our thoughts about ourselves and the "I" that does the thinking. The *self-concept* is our sense of self. The *content* of our self-concept is our knowledge of what we have been and done; its *function* is to guide us in deciding what to be and do in the future. Our self-concept, then, helps us to understand ourselves and also to control or regulate our behavior (Markus & Nurius, 1984). How do children develop these complementary aspects of the self-concept?

### Self-Recognition and Self-Definition

The sense of self grows slowly. It begins with *self-awareness:* the gradual realization (beginning in infancy) that we are beings separate from other people and things, with the ability to reflect on ourselves and our actions. Self-awareness crystallizes in the first moment of *self-recognition,* around 18 months of age, when toddlers recognize themselves in a mirror.

The next step is **self-definition:** identifying the inner and outer characteristics we consider significant in describing ourselves. At about age 3, children think of themselves mostly in terms of externals—what they look like, where they live, what they do. (Some people never progress beyond this level, defining themselves even as adults by the image in the mirror, the work they do, and the neighborhood they live in.) Not until about age 6 or 7 do children begin to define themselves in psychological terms.

With self-definition, children develop a concept of who they are (the **real self**) and also of who they would like to be (the **ideal self**). By the time they achieve this growth in self-understanding, young children have made significant progress from parental control toward increasing self-regulation.

The ideal self incorporates many of the "shoulds" and "oughts" children have learned and helps them control their impulses for the sake of being considered "good." A large gap between a child's real self and ideal self is usually a sign of maturity and social adjustment (Maccoby, 1980). Children who set high standards for themselves seem aware of the difference between what they are and what they would like to be, and working toward the goal of the ideal self helps children mature.

### Self-Regulation

The sense of self might seem the most personal thing in the world. But most theoreticians and researchers see the self-concept as a *social* phenomenon, "the meeting ground of the individual and society" (Markus & Nurius, 1984, p. 147). Middle childhood seems to be the appointed time for that meeting. Children peer into the looking glass of their society and blend the image that they see reflected there with the picture they already have of themselves.

Children are now able to do more than they could earlier. They also have more responsibilities: homework, chores, rules at home and at school, and perhaps some care of younger brothers or sisters. Children begin to regulate their behavior not only to get what they need and want (as they did earlier) but also to meet other people's needs and wants.

As children internalize society's behavioral standards and values, they coordinate personal and social demands. Now they voluntarily do things (like homework and sharing) that at an earlier age they would not have done without prodding.

As they strive to become functioning members of society, children must complete several important tasks in the development of the self-concept (Markus & Nurius, 1984).

This newspaper deliverer is accomplishing several important tasks of middle childhood related to the self-concept. By taking on responsibilities to match her growing capabilities, she learns about how her society works, her role in it, and what doing a job well means.

They must (among other things):

- *Expand their self-understanding*—to reflect other people's perceptions, needs, and expectations. They have to learn what it means to be a friend or a teammate.
- *Learn more about how society works*—about complex relationships, roles, and rules. A child comes to realize, for example, that his or her own mother had a mother, and that the same person can be nice at one moment and mean at another.
- *Develop behavioral standards*—standards that are both personally satisfying and accepted in society. This is sometimes hard, since children belong to *two* societies—that of the peer group and that of adults—which sometimes have conflicting standards.
- *Manage their own behavior.* As children take responsibility for their own actions, they must *believe* that they can behave according to both personal and social standards, and they must develop the skills and strategies to *do* it.

## Self-Esteem

As Erikson (1950), among others, points out, middle childhood is an important time for the development of **self-esteem**: a positive self-image or self-evaluation. Children compare their real selves and their ideal selves, and judge themselves by how well they measure up to the social standards and expectations they have taken into their self-concept and by how well they perform.

Children's opinions of themselves have tremendous impact on their personality development. Indeed, a favorable self-image may be the key to success and happiness throughout life. Let's look at two typical examples.

Paul likes himself. He is confident of his abilities and approaches life with an open attitude that unlocks many doors. He takes criticism well, and when he feels strongly about something, he is willing to risk making other people angry. He challenges parents, teachers, and others in authority. He feels that he can cope with obstacles; he is not burdened by self-doubt. He solves problems in original, innovative ways. Because he believes that he *can* succeed in the goals he sets for himself, he generally *does* succeed. His success renews his self-respect and makes it easy for him to respect and love others. They, in turn, admire, respect, and enjoy him.

Peter does not feel good about himself. He is hampered wherever he turns. Convinced that he cannot succeed, he does not try hard. His lack of effort almost always ensures continued failure, resulting in a downward spiral of still less confidence and still less success. He often worries whether he is doing the right thing. He breaks things and hurts people's feelings, even though he tries so hard to please others that he often strikes people as "wimpy." He is plagued by one unexplained pain after another. Because of his self-doubts, he is not much fun to be with, and so he has trouble making and keeping friends—which, of course, drives his opinion of himself even lower.

These two portraits are composites drawn from an important study of self-esteem in children. Coopersmith (1967) administered a questionnaire to hundreds of fifth- and sixth-graders, both male and female. The boys and girls in this initial sample did not differ, on the average; but for intensive interviewing and observation, Coopersmith chose 85 boys and no girls, to eliminate gender as a possible factor. Although the final sample was limited to middle-class white boys within a 2-year age span, the findings may apply more widely.

A child's sense of competence—whether it derives from winning an athletic competition or from making the honor roll—contributes mightily to his or her self-esteem. A positive self-image can strongly influence a child's future success and happiness.

Coopersmith concluded that people base their self-image on four criteria: (1) *significance* (the extent to which they feel loved and approved of by people important to them), (2) *competence* (in performing tasks they consider important), (3) *virtue* (attainment of moral and ethical standards), and (4) *power* (the extent to which they influence their own lives and the lives of others). Although people may draw favorable pictures of themselves if they rate high on some of these dimensions and low on others, they are more likely to rate themselves high if they rate high on all four criteria.

Not surprisingly, the boys in the study who had high self-esteem were more popular and did better in school than those with low self-esteem, who were more likely to be loners, bed-wetters, or poor students. No relationship showed up between self-esteem and height, weight, or physical attractiveness; and there was only a slight relationship between self-esteem and socioeconomic status. But family influences made a difference. Firstborn or only children, especially those with warm parents and dominant mothers, were likely to have high self-esteem.

The parents of the boys with good self-images tended to have an authoritative parenting style (see Chapter 7). They loved and accepted their sons and made strong demands for academic performance and good behavior. They showed respect and allowed individual expression. They defined and enforced limits, relying more on reinforcements than on punishment. Furthermore, they themselves had high self-esteem and led active, rewarding lives.

Parents who are both democratic and strict help their children in several ways, Coopersmith believes. By setting clear, consistent rules, they let children know what behavior is expected of them. Knowing what to expect helps children gain internal control; as they function within rule systems, they learn to consider the demands of the outside world. And children of demanding parents know that their parents believe in their ability to meet demands—and care enough to insist that they do.

It makes sense that parents' treatment of their children affects the children's feelings about themselves, and yet there is another way to look at the relationship between parenting and children's self-esteem. Children with high self-esteem may have characteristics that encourage their parents to be loving, firm, and democratic. Children who are self-confident, cooperative, and competent are easy to bring up. Thus we see again the bidirectionality of influence between parents and children—how they continually influence each other (Maccoby, 1980).

## THEORETICAL PERSPECTIVES ON THE SELF-CONCEPT

Each of the major theoretical perspectives discussed in this book offers some explanation for the continuous development of the self-concept.

### Psychosexual Theory: Freud's Latency Period

Freud—whose central concern was the development of the self—called middle childhood the *latency period,* a period of relative sexual calm between the turbulence of early childhood and the storminess of adolescence. By this time, according to Freud, youngsters have resolved the Oedipal conflict, adopted gender roles, and developed the superego, which keeps the id in check. Freed from the dominance of the id, children become socialized rapidly, develop skills, and learn about themselves and society.

However, Freud's idea that this is a time of asexuality, or lack of interest in sex, has been largely discredited. Instead, many contemporary researchers believe that children in middle childhood hide their sexual interest because they have learned that adults disapprove of it, but that they still engage in sex play, masturbate, and ask questions about sex (Calderone & Johnson, 1981).

### Psychosocial Theory: Erikson's Crisis 4—Industry versus Inferiority

Erikson, too, sees middle childhood as a time of relative emotional calm, when children can attend to their schooling and learn the skills their culture requires. According to Erikson, the characteristic crisis of this period is *industry versus inferiority.* The issue to be resolved has to do with a child's capacity for productive work, though the nature of productive work varies from culture to culture. For example, an Arapesh boy in New Guinea learns to make bows and arrows and to lay traps for rats; an Arapesh girl learns to weed, plant, and harvest; an Alaskan Inuit learns to hunt and fish. Children in industrialized countries learn to count, read, and use computers.

Middle childhood is a time for learning the skills that one's culture considers important. In Tanzania, a Masai boy learns to herd cattle. In the United States, children learn to count, read, and use computers.

These efforts at mastery help children form a positive self-concept. The "virtue" that develops with successful resolution of this crisis is *competence,* a view of the self as able to master and complete tasks—as productive and industrious. As children compare their own abilities with those of their peers, they build a sense of who they are. If they feel inadequate by comparison, Erikson believes, they may regress to an earlier level of development in which they lack the sense of initiative needed to pursue a goal or the sense of competence gained from attaining it. If, on the other hand, they become *too* industrious, they may neglect relationships with other people and become "workaholics."

### Social-Learning Theory

Social-learning theorists note that school-age children's keen self-awareness and observation make them more receptive to the influence of people they admire or people who are perceived as powerful and rewarding. Whereas the young child responds mostly to material reinforcers, in middle childhood the approval or disapproval of parents, teachers, and peers becomes a powerful shaper of self-concept and behavior.

### Cognitive-Developmental Theory

Because school-age children are less egocentric than younger children (according to Piaget), they can see themselves better from other people's viewpoints and are more sensitive to what others think of them. Their increasing ability to decenter enables them to take more than one view of the self ("Today I'm being bad, but yesterday I was good"). This change allows greater complexity in moral reasoning and lets them consider social as well as personal needs.

### Information-Processing Approach

The information-processing approach views the self-concept as a **self-schema,** a set of "knowledge structures" which organizes and guides the processing of information about the self (Markus & Nurius, 1984, p. 158). Children build, test, and modify their self-schemata (hypotheses about themselves) on the basis of their social experiences. Self-schemata help children use the results of their past behavior to make quick judgments for acting in the present and to define the possible self of the future. Strong and lasting self-schemata ("I am popular," "I am a good student," "I am a fast runner") take shape during middle childhood as the many physical, intellectual, and social skills that children develop let them see themselves as valuable members of society (Markus, 1980).

## ASPECTS OF PERSONALITY DEVELOPMENT IN MIDDLE CHILDHOOD

### EVERYDAY LIFE

"You're it!" "No, *you're* it!" For thousands of years, impromptu games of tag, catch, jacks, marbles, and "let's pretend" have served the time-honored mandate of childhood: to learn through play. Such games give children physical contact, self-confidence, and practice in using their imagination and getting along with others. Play offers socially acceptable ways for children to compete, to blow off energy, and to act aggressively.

Today, however, new social patterns are replacing traditional ones, as technology changes the tools and habits of leisure. Television has seduced many children away from active playing. Computer games demand few social skills. Children engage in more organized sports, which replace children's rules with adult rules, and in which adult referees settle disputes so that children do not learn to resolve matters among themselves.

In other ways, too, the society of childhood mirrors changes in the larger society. Children of today's changing families act, think, and live differently from children in previous cohorts. Many children live with only one parent. Some are in day care after school; others care for themselves and for younger brothers or sisters. Some children have a great deal of unsupervised time on their hands; others have heavily organized schedules of activities.

In another time or place, these boys might have been out kicking a ball instead of playing Nintendo. As technology changes the tools and habits of leisure, children's play is becoming less active and often calls for fewer social skills.

**TABLE 9–1**
HOW SCHOOL-AGE CHILDREN SPEND THEIR TIME: CHILDREN'S TOP 10 ACTIVITIES
(AVERAGE HOURS AND MINUTES PER DAY)

| Activity | Weekdays | | Weekends | |
|---|---|---|---|---|
| | Ages 6–8 | Ages 9–11 | Ages 6–8 | Ages 9–11 |
| Sleeping | 9:55 | 9:09 | 10:41 | 9:56 |
| School | 4:52 | 5:15 | — | — |
| Television | 1:39 | 2:26 | 2:16 | 3:05 |
| Playing | 1:51 | 1:05 | 3:00 | 1:32 |
| Eating | 1:21 | 1:13 | 1:20 | 1:18 |
| Personal care | 0:49 | 0:40 | 0:45 | 0:44 |
| Household work | 0:15 | 0:18 | 0:27 | 0:51 |
| Sports | 0:24 | 0:21 | 0:30 | 0:42 |
| Religious observance | 0:09 | 0:09 | 0:56 | 0:53 |
| Visiting | 0:15 | 0:10 | 0:08 | 0:13 |

*Source:* Adapted from Institute for Social Research, 1985.

### How Do Children Spend Their Time?

American children spend about two-thirds of their time on essentials—sleeping, eating, school, personal care, housework, and religious observance—leaving about 55 hours a week of leisure time (Institute for Social Research, 1985; see Table 9-1).

The two main things that children *choose* to do are playing (alone or with other children) and watching television. These two activities take up anywhere from 50 to 70 percent of their free time. Children aged 6 to 8 spend more time playing; by 9 years of age, the balance shifts in favor of television, which consumes an average of 2½ to 4 hours a day (W. A. Collins, 1984; Institute for Social Research, 1985).

Children watch television more in middle childhood than during any other period of childhood, and 11- and 12-year-old boys watch the most, particularly action and adventure shows. Disadvantaged children are 3 times as likely as other children to be heavy viewers (W. A. Collins, 1984; Institute for Social Research, 1985; Medrich, Roizen, Rubin, & Buckley, 1982). Children who read for pleasure every day are, not surprisingly, likely to be less frequent viewers. But even children who read almost every day at age 9 are less likely to do so by age 13 (National Assessment of Educational Progress, 1982).

School-age youngsters spend many hours on sports, clubs, religious groups, scouting, camps, private lessons, and other organized activities (W. A. Collins, 1984). Participation in athletics and other activities is strongly influenced by the ethnic and social group. For example, black boys are more likely to be involved in team games; white boys, in individual sports like swimming and tennis (Medrich et al., 1982).

### With Whom Do Children Spend Their Time?

When Sally's eldest daughter, Nancy, was 10 years old, her parents drove 300 miles to visit her at summer camp. She waved to them, called out "Hi," and then went back to playing softball. They had just received the first of many lessons (from all three of their children) about the powerful draw of the peer group.

School-age children spend relatively little time with their parents (Medrich et al., 1982); the peer group becomes central. Just counting minutes and hours, however, can be deceptive. Relationships with parents continue to be the most important ones in children's lives.

Different relationships serve different purposes for children, as a questionnaire study of 199 mostly middle-class fifth- and sixth-graders showed (Furman & Buhrmester, 1985). In rating the important relationships in their lives, the children named their parents as most important. They looked to them for affection; guidance; lasting, dependable bonds; and affirmation of competence or value as a person. They rated mothers higher than fathers as companions, and they were generally more satisfied with their relationships with their mothers than those with their fathers. After parents, the most important people were grandparents, who were often warm and supportive, offering affection and enhancement of worth. Although the children looked for and got guidance from teachers, too, they were least satisfied with relationships with teachers.

Children turned most often to friends for companionship, and to friends and mothers for intimacy. Although they also looked to siblings (especially those of the same sex and close in age) for companionship and intimacy and to older siblings for guidance, sibling relationships generally involved the most conflict.

Some gender differences emerged. Girls were closer to their mothers than to their fathers; for boys, there was no difference. Also, girls relied on best friends more than boys did, and their friendships were more intimate, affectionate, and worth-enhancing. Since these three qualities seem to be more characteristic of older children's friendships, school-age girls' closest friendships may be more mature than those of boys.

Now let's look more closely at this diverse and nurturing social world to see the importance of the peer group and the family.

## THE CHILD IN THE PEER GROUP

Babies are aware of one another, and preschoolers begin to make friends, but not until middle childhood does the peer group come into its own.

### Functions and Influence of the Peer Group

In our highly mobile, age-segregated society, the peer group is a particularly strong influence, for both good and ill.

The peer group is an important arena for developing the self-concept and building self-esteem. It helps children form an opinion of themselves by seeing themselves as others see them. It gives them a basis of comparison—a gauge of their own abilities and skills. Only within a large group of their peers can children get a sense of how smart, how athletic, and how personable they are.

The peer group helps children choose values to live by. Testing their opinions, feelings, and attitudes against those of other children helps them sift through the parental values they previously accepted unquestioningly and decide which to keep and which to discard.

The peer group offers emotional security. Sometimes another child can provide comfort that an adult cannot. It is reassuring to find out that a friend also harbors "wicked" thoughts that would offend an adult, and it can be emotionally healthy to enact forbidden fantasies in dramatic play with another child.

Interacting with other children also seems to help children in cognitive ways. One study compared children working on computer tasks alone with children working in pairs. Although those who worked with a partner seemed to concentrate less on the task and more on the social interaction, the paired children enjoyed the sessions more and learned more from them (Perlmutter, Behrend, Kuo, & Muller, 1989).

Finally, the peer group helps children learn how to get along in society. They learn how and when to adjust their needs and desires to those of others—when to yield and when to stand firm.

On the positive side, then, the peer group offers a counterweight to parents' influence, opens new perspectives, and frees children to make independent judgments.

On the negative side, however, the peer group may impose values on the emerging individual, and children (especially those who have low status in the group) may be too weak to resist. In some countries—such as Israel, the Soviet Union, and China—as well as in some behavior modification programs in the United States, the peer group is used deliberately to mold behavior. During middle childhood, children are especially susceptible to pressure to conform (Costanzo & Shaw, 1966).

Peer influence is strongest when issues are ambiguous. Since we live in a world with many ambiguous issues that require careful judgment, the consequences of peer-group influences can be severe. And although peer groups do many constructive things together—playing games, scouting, and the like—it is usually in the company of friends that children also begin to smoke and drink, sneak into the movies, and perform other antisocial acts. Sixth-graders who are rated more "peer-oriented" report more antisocial behavior than "parent-oriented" children (J. C. Condry, Siman, & Bronfenbrenner, 1968). On the other hand, youngsters who are headed for more serious trouble with the law tend *not* to get along with their peers. These children are often immature, and they lack social skills (Hartup, 1989).

For children—as for adults—some degree of conformity to group standards is a healthy mechanism of adaptation. Conformity is unhealthy only when it becomes destructive or causes people to act against their better judgment.

### Makeup of the Peer Group

Peer groups form naturally among children who live in the same neighborhood or go to school together (Hartup, 1984). Children who play together are usually within a year or two of the same age, though an occasional neighborhood play group will form that includes small children along with older ones. Too wide an age

Members of a neighborhood peer group are usually of the same age, sex, race, and socioeconomic status, and they enjoy doing things together. While the peer group helps children build their self-concept and become independent from parents, it also exerts pressure to conform to group standards of dress, hair style, and behavior.

range brings problems with differences in size, interests, and levels of ability.

In the elementary school years, peer groups are usually all girls or boys, partly because children of the same sex have common interests, and girls are generally more mature than boys. These same-sex groupings offer "classrooms" for learning "gender-appropriate" behaviors.

Members of a peer group are usually of the same race and of the same or similar socioeconomic status, especially in segregated neighborhoods. Racial segregation in peer groups (as in adult society) often results from **prejudice**—negative attitudes toward certain groups, which can corrode the self-esteem of members of these groups. Studies conducted from the 1960s to the mid-1970s found bias against blacks among both white and black children in northern and southern American cities, from preschool through the early school years (Morland, 1966; J. Williams, Best, & Boswell, 1975).

Court-ordered school integration, which began in the mid-1950s, has brought more acceptance of racial differences, even though children still tend to choose friends of the same race. One study of midwestern third- and sixth-graders who had been in integrated classrooms since kindergarten found that although the youngsters (particularly the older African American children) preferred members of their own race, they rated classmates of the other race quite positively (Singleton & Asher, 1979).

Some schools have worked to reduce prejudice by recruiting and training more minority-group teachers and by emphasizing the cultural contributions of minorities. The most effective programs, however, are those that get children from different racial groups to work together. Like sports teams, interracial learning groups provide a common goal—and result in positive feelings between children of different races (Gaertner, Mann, Murrell, & Dovidio, 1989).

### Friendship

Jordan met his best friend at school; their favorite activity is playing ball together. Melissa and her best friend eat lunch together, play together at recess, walk home together, and then talk on the phone to each other.

Children may spend much of their free time in groups, but only as individuals do they form friendships. Children's ideas about friendship change enormously during the elementary school years. Now a friend is someone a child feels comfortable with, likes to do things with, and can share feelings and secrets with. Friendships make children more sensitive and loving, more able to give and receive respect. Children cannot be true friends or have true friends until they achieve the cognitive maturity to consider other people's viewpoints and needs, as well as their own.

Robert Selman has traced changing forms of friendship through five overlapping stages, on the basis of interviews with more than 250 people between the ages of 3 and 45 (Selman & Selman, 1979; see Table 9-2 on page 284). Most school-age children are in either stage 2 (fair-weather relationships based on reciprocal self-interest) or stage 3 (intimate, mutual relationships). In general, girls value *depth* of relationships, while boys value *number* of relationships (Furman, 1982). Middle-childhood friends are typically of the same sex and have common interests (Hartup, 1989).

Having a true friend is a milestone in development. Mutual affection enables children to express intimacy, to bask in a sense of self-worth, and to learn what being human is all about (Furman, 1982; H. S. Sullivan, 1953).

**TABLE 9–2**
STAGES OF FRIENDSHIP

| Stage | Ages* | Characteristics |
|---|---|---|
| **0** Momentary playmateship (undifferentiated) | 3–7 | Children are egocentric—they think only about what they want from a relationship. Children define friends by how close they live. ("She's my friend—she lives on my street.")<br><br>Children value friends for material or physical attributes. ("He's my friend—he's got a giant Superman doll and a real swing set.") |
| **1** One-way assistance (unilateral) | 4–9 | Children define a good friend as someone who does what they want the friend to do. ("He's my friend—he lets me borrow his eraser," or, "She's not my friend anymore—she wouldn't go skating with me.") |
| **2** Two-way, fair-weather cooperation (reciprocal) | 6–12 | Friendship involves give-and-take but still serves separate self-interests rather than common interests. ("We're friends—we do things for each other," or, "A friend is someone who plays with you when you don't have anybody else to play with.") |
| **3** Intimate, shared relationships (mutual) | 9–15 | Children view friendship as an ongoing, systematic, committed relationship involving more than doing things for each other.<br><br>Children become possessive of their friends, demanding exclusivity. ("It takes a long time to make a close friend, and so you feel bad if she gets to be friends with someone else.")<br><br>Girls develop one or two close friendships; boys have more, but less intimate, friends. |
| **4** Autonomous interdependence (interdependent) | 12 on | Children respect friends' needs for both dependency and autonomy. ("A good friendship is a real commitment, a risk you have to take. You have to be able to support and trust and give, but you have to be able to let go, too.") |

*Ages of the various stages may overlap.
*Source:* Selman & Selman, 1979.

## Popularity

We all want other people to like us. What our peers think of us matters terribly, affecting our present happiness and often echoing through the years to affect later success and well-being.

Why are some children sought out while others are ignored or rebuffed? Why do some children have many friends while others have none? What are popular and unpopular children like? What can be done to help children who are neglected or rejected by their peers? Let's look at these issues.

### The popular child

Popular children share a number of characteristics. Typically, they are cooperative and help other children

(Coie & Kupersmidt, 1983; K. H. Rubin, Daniels-Beirness, & Hayvren, 1982). They have a good sense of humor (Masten, 1986) and are physically attractive (R. Lerner & Lerner, 1977). They are healthy and vigorous, poised, capable of initiative, adaptable, dependable, affectionate, and considerate; and they are original thinkers (Bonney, 1946). They think well of themselves, radiating self-confidence without being overbearing or seeming conceited (Reese, 1961).

Popular children show mature dependence: they ask for help when they need it and for approval when they think that they deserve it, but they do not cling or make infantile plays for affection (Hartup, 1970). They are not goodie-goodies, but they make other people feel good about being with them (M. Feinberg, Smith, & Schmidt, 1958; Tuddenham, 1951).

### The unpopular child

One of childhood's saddest figures is the child who is chosen last for every team, is on the fringes of every group, walks home alone after school, is not invited to birthday parties, and sobs in despair, "Nobody wants to play with me."

**Why are some children unpopular?**   Children can be unpopular for many reasons; some of the causes are within their power to change, but others are not. Unpopular youngsters may walk around with a chip on their shoulder, expressing unprovoked aggression and hostility (Dodge, 1983). Or they may be withdrawn (K. H. Rubin et al., 1982). Or they may act silly and infantile, showing off in immature ways; or be anxious and uncertain, so pathetic in their lack of confidence that they repel other children, who find them no fun to be with. Very fat or unattractive children, children who act strange in any way, and retarded or slow-learning youngsters also tend to be outcasts.

A major problem may be a child's expectation of not being liked. Two groups of unpopular children— third-grade boys and fourth- and fifth-grade girls—took part in an experiment. Some were told that other children whom they had met only once before really liked them and looked forward to seeing them again, and then they were brought back together with these other children. The children who got this positive "feedback" were liked better by their new acquaintances than children in a control group who had received no such message. Furthermore, when the children were rated on their behavior by independent observers, the girls who got positive messages behaved in more socially competent ways (Rabiner & Coie, 1989). Apparently, some unpopular children, expecting not to be liked, do not exert themselves with others.

**How can unpopular children be helped?**   Popularity in childhood is not a frivolous issue. Aside from the sadness, sense of rejection, and poor self-esteem that unpopular children feel, they are also deprived of a basic developmental experience: the positive interaction with other youngsters that helps them to grow as individuals.

Unpopularity during the preschool years is not necessarily cause for concern, but by middle childhood peer relationships are strong predictors of later adjustment. Children who have trouble getting along with their peers are more likely to have psychological problems, to drop out of school, and to become delinquent (Hartup, 1989; M. E. Lamb, 1978; Parker & Asher, 1987).

Antisocial behavior often shows up first in the family. The parents of aggressive children are often either coercive or inept in dealing with them. Then, the children are so impulsive, mean, and disruptive that other children dislike them. As a result, they tend to seek out friends who are just as antisocial as they are (Hartup, 1989). (It is not clear, though, whether unpopularity during middle childhood *causes* later disturbances or *reflects* developmental problems that show up in more serious form later on.)

Since relationships with other children are vital to a child's happiness and healthy emotional development, adults sometimes try to help unpopular children make friends. Children who are simply *neglected* or overlooked by their classmates or other peers may do better in a different class or a new school, or if they join a new club or go to a new camp. But children who are actively *rejected* by their peers—and it is rejected children who are most at risk of developing emotional and behavioral difficulties in later life—usually cannot be rescued simply by being moved into a new group or situation. They need to learn how to make other children like them.

In one study, fifth- and sixth-graders received training in social skills. They learned how to carry on a conversation: how to share information about themselves, how to show interest in others by asking questions about them, and how to give help, suggestions, invitations, and advice. When they had a chance to practice their new conversational skills in a group project with other children, they became better liked by the others and interacted more with them (Bierman & Furman, 1984).

The children who received the training showed more general and lasting improvement over a 6-week period (according to measures of conversational skills, rates of interaction, peer acceptance, and self-perception) than those who received no training, those who received the training but then did not participate in the peer-group project, and those who took part in the group project but were not taught any skills.

We see, then, that children not only need social skills but also need to be in situations where they can use these skills and where other children can see the changes that have taken place in them. Otherwise, other children may hold on to their former opinions about these youngsters and may not give them a chance to show their new skills.

Furthermore, since it seems that children who expect to be liked actually are better liked (Rabiner & Coie, 1989), some kind of positive expectation should be built into programs that are developed to increase children's popularity.

## THE CHILD IN THE FAMILY

School-age children spend more time away from home than they did when they were younger. School, friends, games, and movies all draw them away from the house and keep them apart from the family. Yet home is still the most important part of their world, and the people who live there are the most important to them (Furman & Buhrmester, 1985). Let's see how relationships with parents and siblings develop during middle childhood and how societal change is affecting family life.

### Parent-Child Relationships

Not surprisingly, outside obligations and interests increase at a time when children are more self-sufficient and need less physical care and supervision than before. One study found that parents spend less than half as much time caring for 5- to 12-year-olds—teaching them, reading and talking to them, and playing with them—as they spend caring for preschoolers (C. R. Hill & Stafford, 1980). Still, the job of parenting is far from over.

### *Issues between parents and children*

As children's lives change, the issues that arise between them and their parents change, too (Maccoby, 1984). One important new area of concern is school. Parents worry about how a child is doing with schoolwork and wonder how involved they should become. They may have to deal with a child who complains about his or her teacher, pretends to be sick to avoid going to school, or cuts school.

Parents usually want to know where their children are and whom they are with when they are not in school. Some parents even tell children whom they may and may not play with. Parents and children often disagree over what household chores children should do, whether they should be paid for doing them, and how much allowance they should get. (Of course, many of these issues do not even come up in some societies, where children over the age of 6 must work to help the family survive.)

The profound changes of middle childhood in children's lives and in the kinds of issues that arise between them and their parents bring changes in the ways parents handle discipline and control. Yet, as we'll see, most parents do *not* change their basic approach to their job as their children mature.

### *Discipline*

When Jared was 18 months old and reached for the shaving cream, his father would try to distract him with a toy and, failing that, would picked him up and move

Parents who enjoy being with their children, like this mother giving a lesson in making tortillas, are likely to raise children who feel good about themselves—and about their parents.

him to another room. When Jared, at age 4, made loud noises while his mother was trying to listen to a record, she first tried to ignore him and then sent him to his room.

Every parent struggles with the constant decisions involved in bringing up human beings who will think well of themselves, fulfill their potential, and become happy, productive people. This struggle is what ***discipline*** is all about. Many people think of *discipline* as a synonym for *punishment*, but the word is from the Latin for "knowledge" or "instruction" and is principally defined this way in dictionaries. Parents differ in the way they try to teach their children character, self-control, and moral behavior. And most parents go about it differently with school-age and younger children (Maccoby, 1984; G. C. Roberts, Block, & Block, 1984).

For example, Jared's parents rely more on praise for what he does right than on punishment for what he does wrong. When they do feel that punishment is called for, they usually deprive him of some privilege, like watching a favorite television show. They reason with him, appealing to his self-esteem ("What happened to the helpful boy who was here yesterday?"), sense of humor ("If you go one more day without a bath, we won't have to look to know when you're coming!"), sense of guilt ("A big, strong boy like you shouldn't sit on the bus and let an old person stand"), or appreciation ("Aren't you glad that you have a father who cares enough to remind you to wear boots so that you won't catch a cold?"). Above all, Jared's parents let him know that he is responsible for the consequences of his behavior ("No wonder you missed the school bus today—you stayed up too late last night reading in bed! Now you'll have to walk to school").

This evolution is typical as children gain cognitive awareness. Rather than knuckling under to sheer power, children are now more likely to defer to parents' wishes because they recognize that their parents are fair, that they contribute to the whole family's well-being, and that they often "know better" because of their wider experience. On the other hand, parents often defer to their children's growing judgment and take a strong stand only on the most important issues. For example, parents of schoolchildren less often impose their own taste in clothing, recognizing that children use clothing to express personality and assert independence (Schiro, 1988).

Yet a parent's child-rearing philosophy seems to remain fairly consistent over time, especially with regard to control, enjoyment, and emotional investment. In one longitudinal study, parents of 3-year-old boys and girls from a wide range of backgrounds filled out long questionnaires, and then answered the same questions again when their children were 12 years old. The questions related to independence, control, suppression of aggression and sex, emphasis on health and achievement, expression of feelings, protectiveness, supervision, rational guidance, and punishment. Over the 9-year period, the parents' basic values and approach to child rearing seemed to remain constant, emphasizing rational guidance and praise. Shifts that did occur were appropriate to children's development (G. C. Roberts et al., 1984).

### Control and coregulation

Control of a child's behavior gradually shifts from the parents to the child. The process begins during the second year of life; then, a child's gradual acquisition of self-control and self-regulation steadily reduces the need for constant parental scrutiny. But not until adolescence or even later do most young people make their own decisions about how late they should stay out, with whom they should associate, and how they should spend their money.

Middle childhood is a transitional stage of *coregulation*, in which parent and child share power; "parents continue to exercise general supervisory control, while children begin to exercise moment-to-moment self-regulation" (Maccoby, 1984, p. 191). Coregulation reflects the child's developing self-concept. As children of this age begin to coordinate their own wishes with societal demands, they are more likely to anticipate how their parents or other people will react to what they do, or to accept a reminder from their parents that others will think better of them if they behave differently.

Coregulation is a cooperative process; it succeeds only when parents and children communicate clearly. If children do not tell their parents where they are, what they are doing, and what problems they are facing, or if parents are preoccupied with their own activities and fail to take an interest in those of their children, the parents will not be able to judge when to step in.

To make this transitional phase work, parents need to influence their children when they are with them and monitor them when they are not, by phone or babysitter. They also need to teach children to monitor their *own* behavior—to adopt acceptable standards, avoid undue risks, and recognize when they need their parents' support or guidance (Maccoby, 1984).

### Parents' Work: How It Affects Their Children

Since so much of adults' time, effort, and ego involvement goes into their occupations, a number of researchers have explored how these occupations affect the family—especially now, when adults' roles are in transition. Let's look at some of the ways parents' work affects children.*

### *Mothers' work*

Most of the research on the way women's work affects their children has focused not on the kind of work they do or its demands on them, but on whether they work at all for pay. And much of this research refers to a time when the working mother was the exception rather than the rule, as she is today, when almost 7 out of 10 married women with children under 18 and 8 out of 10 single mothers are in the work force (see Table 9-3 on page 288). With more than half of all new mothers going to work soon after giving birth, many children have never known a time when their mothers were *not* working.

---

*This section about the impact of parents' work on their children is indebted to Lois Wladis Hoffman (1984, 1989), who conceptualized and researched many of these issues. Statements not otherwise referenced in this discussion rely on her analysis.

**TABLE 9–3**

PERCENTAGE OF MOTHERS IN TWO-PARENT FAMILIES IN LABOR FORCE, 1975–1986

|  | 1975 | 1980 | 1986 |
|---|---|---|---|
| With youngest child under 6 | 42 | 52 | 59 |
| With youngest child 6–17 | 52 | 62 | 69 |
| Total with children under 18 | 45 | 54 | 61 |

*Note:* Percentages are rounded to nearest whole number.
*Source:* Matthews & Rodin, 1989.

How does a mother's employment affect her children? That depends on many variables. Is she married or single? Does she work full time or part time? How does she feel about her work? Does the family need the money? How are the children cared for? Fifty years of research do not show any overall ill effect of working. Rather, many contemporary researchers emphasize the positive effects of a mother's employment on her entire family.

***The mother's psychological state***   Despite the guilt many working mothers feel over being away from their children, employed women often feel more competent, more economically secure, and more in charge

This mother, talking to her daughter as she gets ready to leave for work, is typical of the majority of today's mothers, who have jobs outside the home. How a mother's employment affects her children depends on many variables.

of their lives. Thus, their self-esteem tends to be higher than that of homemakers, whose work is generally undervalued in our society. By and large, the more satisfied a woman is with her life, the more effective she is as a parent. This effect cuts across socioeconomic levels, but may be especially significant at lower income levels, especially for single mothers who have had little education.

***Interactions in working-mother families***   The husband of a working mother can spend more time with his children, since he is less likely to hold a second job. In working-mother families, the division of labor between the parents is somewhat less traditional. Even though the typical working mother still has more responsibility for housework and child care, her husband tends to be more involved than men in homemaker-mother families. He is most involved when the mother works full time, when they have more than one child, when the children are quite young, and when she earns close to what he does (L. Hoffman, 1986). The involved father shows his children a nurturing side—expresses love, tries to help them with their worries and problems, makes them feel better when they are upset, and gives them continuing care and attention (Carlson, 1984). Thus his children see a side of the personality that has traditionally been less visible in men.

***Working mothers and children's values***   Daughters of working women and sons of involved fathers have fewer stereotypes about gender roles than children in "traditional" families (Carlson, 1984). This effect seems to depend more on the mother's attitude toward the father's participation in home duties than on how much he actually does (G. K. Baruch & Barnett, 1986).

***Children's reactions to mothers' work***   School-age children of employed mothers seem to have two advantages over children of homemakers. They tend to live in more structured homes, with clear-cut rules giving them more household responsibilities; and they are encouraged to be more independent. Encouragement of independence seems to be especially good for girls, helping them to become more competent, to achieve more in school, and to have higher self-esteem; but it may put pressure on some boys (Bronfenbrenner & Crouter, 1982).

Findings for boys are less clear-cut and more varied by social class. For example, boys in both single-parent and two-parent lower-income families seem to benefit when their mothers work; these boys achieve more in school. They are probably benefiting from the family's

# WHEN SCHOOL-AGE CHILDREN CARE FOR THEMSELVES

When Ben, 11, comes home from school, he unlocks the front door, throws down his books, and feeds his cat before sitting down for his own snack. Then he calls his father to check in and tell him whether he will be staying home, going outside to play, or going to a friend's home. Depending on what needs to be done, he may fold clean laundry, set the table, or start dinner. If he wants to watch a special television show at night, he will do his homework in the afternoon.

Ben is among some 2 million **self-care children,** who regularly care for themselves at home without adult supervision because both parents or a single custodial parent works outside the home (Cole & Rodman, 1987). Although most self-care takes place after school, some children spend time alone in the morning or evening, too. Most are alone for no more than 2 hours a day (Cain & Hofferth, 1989).

The term *latchkey child* has a negative connotation—a stereotype of a lonely, neglected child—and although the past few years have seen some balancing of this image, there is still very little solid information about the impact of self-care on child development. Research is contradictory. Some studies report no differences between supervised and self-care children on such criteria as self-esteem and school and social adjustment, and others show such disadvantages for self-care children as high levels of fear and school problems (Cole & Rodman, 1987; Rodman & Cole, 1987). Research has dispelled one misconception—that most of these children are from poor, single-parent families in high-risk inner-city settings. Most self-care children are, in fact, from well-educated, middle- to upper-class families in suburban or rural areas (Cain & Hofferth, 1989). For these families, self-care seems to be a choice rather than a necessity.

How can parents tell when a child is ready for self-care, and how can they make the situation as comfortable as possible for the child? The following guidelines can help answer these questions (Cole & Rodman, 1987; Olds, 1989).

*Before children take care of themselves, they should be able to:*

■ Control their bodies well enough to keep from injuring themselves.
■ Keep track of keys and handle doors well enough to avoid locking themselves in or out.
■ Safely operate necessary household equipment.
■ Stay alone without being too afraid or lonely.
■ Be flexible and resourceful enough to handle the unexpected.

■ Be responsible enough to follow important rules.
■ Understand and remember spoken and written instructions.
■ Read and write well enough to take telephone messages and use a pay phone in an emergency.
■ Know what to say and do about visitors and callers (not tell people they do not know that they are alone, and not open the door to anyone but family and close friends).
■ Know how to get help in an emergency (how to call police and fire fighters, which friends and neighbors to call, and what other resources to call on).

*Parents and guardians can help by:*

■ Staying in touch by phone (preferably by setting up a regular time for check-in calls).
■ Telling children what to do and how to reach a responsible adult in an emergency.
■ Setting up a structure for self-care time.
■ Instituting safety procedures.
*Alone at Home: Self-Care for Children of Working Parents,* by H. Swan and V. Huston (Prentice-Hall, 1985) is a training manual for 9- to 14-year-olds, giving useful guidance for mastering difficult situations.

higher income. Sons of middle-class working mothers, however, have done less well in school than have the sons of homemakers (Heyns & Catsambis, 1986). However, the data for this study were collected in the 1960s and 1970s, when opportunities for women and options for child care were not as broad as they are today. As society adjusts to the fact that now the *typical* mother is a working mother, there should be fewer negative effects on boys.

Children do complain that they have too little time with their working mothers (General Mills, 1977). And many mothers are concerned about the difficulties of finding competent day care and after-school care for younger children and of supervising older ones, especially when the children care for themselves part of the day (see Box 9-1). Time-related problems are not, of course, as severe for women who work part time or have flexible hours.

The dual-income family does not follow one single pattern. Probably the most influential factor is the parents' attitudes. "Where the pattern itself produces difficulties, they seem often to stem mainly from the slow pace with which society has adapted to this new family form" (L. W. Hoffman, 1989, p. 290). When good child care is more available and affordable, when men assume a larger role in the home, and when employers support workers' family roles, the benefits will be felt in millions of American families.

### Fathers' work

Most of the research on how men's work affects their families has focused on the nature of the work itself. Some of the findings regarding men can also apply to women.

When work does not fully satisfy a man's (or a woman's) psychological needs, children may benefit. A man whose work is not exciting may throw himself enthusiastically into family life and, through his children, gain a sense of accomplishment, fun, intellectual stimulation, moral values, and self-esteem. But children may also suffer if a man takes out his frustration at having little autonomy at work by being hostile and severe with his children (McKinley, 1964), or if a man's work is so fulfilling that he does not invest much of himself in his family (Veroff, Douvan, & Kulka, 1981). The dominant mood of a man's work may also go home with him—whether it is a feeling of satisfaction or the kind of tension that, for example, often follows police officers home (Nordlicht, 1979).

How does a father's work schedule affect his children? There seems to be little if any relationship between the number of hours a father works and how much interest he takes in his children (Clark & Gecas, 1977).

When a father loses his job and becomes irritable and pessimistic, he is likely to nurture his children less and punish them more. The children may react to this treatment with emotional or behavior problems and reduced aspirations (McLoyd, 1989). Not all unemployed fathers react this way, however; a man's reactions are tempered by his wife's relationship with him and his children—and by the children's personalities and temperaments. Some fathers find something positive in being out of work—the chance to spend more time with their children. In general, though, a father's not having a job is considered to have damaging effects on his children, while a mother's having one has been thought disruptive for her family (Bronfenbrenner & Crouter, 1982).

We see, then, that the work lives of both mothers and fathers affect their children in many different ways. But—as we note so often in this book—a single influence (like parents' employment) always has to be considered in context with other aspects of a child's world.

## Children of Divorce

Children suffer when their parents split up. The children, as much as or more than the parents, may feel pain, confusion, anger, hate, bitter disappointment, a sense of failure, and self-doubt. For many, this family disruption is the central event of childhood, with ramifications that follow them into adult life.

More than 1 million children under the age of 18 are involved in divorces each year. About half of the children born in the late 1970s and early 1980s will experience their parents' divorce and then spend an average of 5 years in a single-parent home before the custodial parent remarries (P. C. Glick & Lin, 1986b; Wegman, 1986).

No matter how unhappy a marriage has been, its breakup usually comes as a shock to the children. The children of divorcing parents often feel afraid of the future, guilty about their own (usually imaginary) role in causing the divorce, hurt at the rejection they feel from the parent who moves out, and angry at both parents. They may become depressed, hostile, disruptive, irritable, lonely, sad, accident-prone, or even suicidal; they may suffer from fatigue, insomnia, skin disorders, loss of appetite, or inability to concentrate; and they may lose interest in schoolwork and in social life. Children of different ages react to divorce in different ways.

### Children's adjustment to divorce

*"Tasks" of adjustment*  The children of divorcing parents face special challenges and burdens in addition to the usual issues of emotional development. In a longitudinal study of 60 divorcing families in California whose children ranged in age from 3 to 18 at the time of the separation, six special "tasks" emerged as crucial to the children's adjustment (Wallerstein, 1983; Wallerstein & Kelly, 1980):

1 *Acknowledging the reality of the marital rupture.* Small children often do not understand what happened, and many older children initially deny the separation. Others either are overwhelmed by fears of total abandonment or retreat into fantasies of reconciliation. Most children face the facts by the end of the first year of separation.

**2** *Disengaging from parental conflict and distress and resuming customary pursuits.* At first, children are often so worried that they cannot play, do school work, or take part in other usual activities. They need to put some distance between themselves and their distraught parents and go on with living their own lives. Most children do this by the end of the first 1 to 1½ years after the separation.

**3** *Resolving loss.* Absorbing all the losses caused by divorce may be the single most difficult task. Children need to adjust to loss of the parent they are not living with, to loss of the security of feeling loved and cared for by both parents, to loss of their familiar daily routines and family traditions, and often to loss of a whole way of life. Some children take years to deal with these losses, and some never do, carrying a sense of being rejected, unworthy, and unlovable into adulthood.

**4** *Resolving anger and self-blame.* "Children . . . do not believe in no-fault divorce. They may blame themselves" (Wallerstein, 1983, p. 239). Children realize that divorce, unlike death, is voluntary, and they often stay angry for years at the parent (or parents) who could do such a terrible thing to them. When and if they do forgive their parents and themselves, they feel more powerful and more in control of their lives.

**5** *Accepting the permanence of the divorce.* Many children hold on for years to the fantasy that their parents will be reunited, even after both have remarried. Many youngsters accept the permanence of the situation only after they achieve psychological separation from their parents in adolescence or early adulthood.

**6** *Achieving realistic hope regarding relationships.* Many youngsters who have adjusted well in other ways come through a divorce feeling afraid to take a chance on intimate relationships themselves, for fear that they will fail as their parents did. They may become cynical, depressed, or simply doubtful of the possibility of finding lasting love.

Many children do, of course, succeed at all these tasks and come through the painful experience of divorce with a basically intact ego. The ability to do this seems to be related partly to a child's own resilience (see the discussion of resilience later in this chapter, page 301). It also seems to be related partly to the way parents handle issues entailed by the separation (see Box 9-2 on page 292) and the challenge of raising children alone.

**Influences on children's adjustment to divorce**
Children—especially boys—who live with their divorced mothers have more social, academic, and behavioral problems than children in intact homes (J. B. Kelly, 1987). However, a number of factors, like the following, seem to influence how well children adjust to divorce.

*Parenting styles and parents' satisfaction.* Children of divorced authoritative parents usually show fewer behavior problems (Hetherington, 1986), do better in school, and have fewer problems getting along with other children (Guidubaldi & Perry, 1985) than children of authoritarian or permissive parents (see Chapter 7 for descriptions of these parenting styles). These effects are especially significant for boys.

In a study of families in which the parents had divorced 6 years earlier, Hetherington (1986) found that custodial mothers who did not remarry had more emotional problems and were less satisfied with their lives than remarried or nondivorced mothers. The unmarried mothers were still in intense, ambivalent, conflicted relationships with their sons, who tended to show behavior problems and spend less time at home with adults. However, the mothers had good relationships with their daughters, who tended to be fairly well adjusted.

Children whose parents are able to control their anger, cooperate in parenting, and not expose the children to quarreling have fewer emotional and social problems (Hetherington, Stanley-Hagen, & Anderson, 1989).

*Remarriage of the mother.* It generally takes 2 to 3 years for children to adjust to a single-parent household; when a mother remarries, they have to adjust again; and sometimes they have to adjust to the breakup of this new marriage (Hetherington et al., 1989). Remarried mothers tend to be happier, better adjusted, and more satisfied with life, and their sons do better with a stepfather. However, their daughters often have more problems than the daughters of divorced women who have not remarried or of nondivorced mothers. Typically, however, these girls do adjust eventually (Hetherington, 1986).

*Relationship with the father.* Among 16- to 18-year-old boys whose parents had divorced 10 years earlier, the boys' relationships with their fathers were important to the boys' adjustment. The sons of erratic and rejecting fathers felt hurt, trapped, and humiliated; and they often reacted with anger against their mothers (Wallerstein, 1987).

## BOX 9–2    PRACTICALLY SPEAKING

# HELPING CHILDREN ADJUST TO DIVORCE

Parents can help their children in making the difficult adjustment to divorce. The following guidelines are based on the advice of experts on family relations:

■ *All the children should be told at the same time about the divorce, in language suited to their age.* Some 80 percent of preschoolers are given no explanation because their parents think they are too young to understand (Wallerstein & Kelly, 1980). Even very young children know, however, that a change is taking place, and they need to be told often, in various ways, what is happening. Both parents should be present, to let the children see that both are still involved in their lives and will continue to be available to them.

■ *Children should be told only as much as they need to know.* It may be tempting for parents to talk about what they see as causes for the divorce—an affair, alcoholism, gambling, sexual incompatibility. Yet this talk may confuse and wound children far more than it helps them. It puts a heavy burden on them to judge the parent "in the wrong." At a time when they need as much emotional support as possible, they may lose faith in at least one parent, and perhaps both.

■ *Children need to know that they have not caused the divorce.* Young children are egocentric. They tend to see the whole world as revolving around themselves, to assume that something they did or thought drove their parents to divorce, and to become tortured by guilt.

■ *Parents must emphasize the finality of their decision.* The fantasy of a reunion is almost universal. As long as children dream of reunion, they cannot accept reality. Once they give up believing that they can reunite their parents, they can pay attention to lessening the pain of the rupture.

■ *Arrangements for the children's care should be carefully explained.* Although children may not talk about their fear of abandonment, they need reassurance that they will continue to be cared for. Parents should explain custody arrangements in detail and should emphasize (if it is true) that they will continue to consult each other on important issues concerning the children.

■ *Children should be reassured of both parents' continuing love.* They need to know that there is no such thing as divorce between parent and child and that the non-custodial parent will continue to love and care for them.

■ *Children should be encouraged to express fear, sadness, and anger.* When they can show these emotions openly, they can begin to understand and deal with them. Parents can admit their own sadness, anger, and confusion, and can seek out a discussion group for children of divorced parents.

■ *Limits should be set on children's behavior.* The parents should maintain firm, friendly discipline. Children need to know that someone stronger loves them enough to stop them from losing control.

■ *Parents should enlist the help of other adults.* A person from outside the immediate family—such as a teacher, scout leader, relative, or friend—can show a caring concern that helps a child through the crisis.

■ *Battling parents should declare a truce when they are with the children.* Divorced parents do not have to be friends, but they help their children by cooperating on child-rearing issues.

■ *Children should not be used as weapons.* Children suffer when they are forced to transmit angry messages or relay information, when they are drawn into arguments over money, when they are asked to choose sides, or when family visits turn into battles. Parents who use children this way are sacrificing a child's welfare for their own immediate satisfaction.

■ *Parents must recognize the conflict between their needs and their children's needs.* Parents need to spend time with other adults, but children need their parents' company. Adults have to be sensitive to this problem and work out solutions that will meet the needs of both generations.

■ *Children's lives should be changed as little as possible.* Any change is stressful; the fewer minor adjustments children have to make, the more energy they have to cope with the major one. If possible, the parent who has custody should postpone taking a job for the first time or moving into a new house. If changes must be made, parents should realize that children need extra understanding.

■ *Parents should use whatever resources they can find for themselves and their children.* These include helpful books, discussion groups, and community programs.

*Accessibility of both parents.* The best custody arrangement usually seems to be with the parent of the same sex. Predictable and frequent contact with the other parent is important, too, and the typical practice of limited visitation for fathers deprives children. Children who have reliable, frequent contact with the noncustodial parent (usually the father) are usually better adjusted; this is especially true for boys (J. B. Kelly, 1987). However, joint custody—shared custody by both parents—does not seem to improve a child's situation in an amicable divorce and may worsen it in a bitter divorce (Kline, Tschann, Johnston, & Wallerstein, 1989).

Adolescents who do not get along with their mothers and are able to make their homes with their fathers often have adjustment problems at the time of the divorce, but they show psychological growth in the long run. When the parent a young person turns to is responsive, this parent can protect and help the child; but when this is not the case, "bitter, even tragic disappointment" often results (Wallerstein, 1987, p. 211).

### Long-term effects of divorce on children

Longitudinal studies that have followed up children of divorcing parents have found that many children adjust well, but that others are still troubled at least 10 years later.

Among thirty-eight 16- to 18-year-olds whose parents had divorced 10 years earlier, three-quarters of the girls and about half of the boys were doing fairly well (Wallerstein, 1987). Most were in school full time, working part time, law-abiding, and living at home (3 out of 4 with their mothers; those living with their fathers had moved during adolescence). The girls were getting along well with their mothers and were likely to be dating and involved in sexual relationships, while the boys were far more likely to be lonely, to be emotionally constricted, and to hold back in relationships with girls.

The divorce had left its mark on most of these young people. Burdened by sadness, neediness, and a sense of their own powerlessness, they missed their fathers (whom they tended to idealize), were anxious about their own love relationships and chances for successful marriage, and were afraid of being betrayed, hurt, and abandoned (Wallerstein, 1987).

While divorce is a wrenching experience for everyone in the family, the resilience of the human spirit allows many children to come through the painful times with an increased sensitivity and compassion that serve them well in their own adult lives.

## The One-Parent Family

### Current trends

An important consequence of a high divorce rate is the large number of children being raised by single parents. One-parent families may be created by a parent's death or a mother's never marrying, but they most commonly result from divorce, separation, or desertion. Nearly 1 in 4 American children (almost 15 million) live in homes with only one parent. This includes 18 percent of white children, 30 percent of Hispanic children, and 53 percent of African American children (U.S. Bureau of the Census, 1988). The number of single-parent families almost tripled between 1960 and 1986, but the rate of increase has slowed.

In 90 percent of divorced and separated couples the mother is the custodial parent, but the number of fathers caring for children increased during the 1970s and 1980s (U.S. Bureau of the Census, 1985). Children who live with their fathers tend to be of school age or older and are more often boys (Hanson, 1988). The fathers are generally better educated, are better paid, and have more prestigious occupations than the average father; most in the general community are white, but many in the military are nonwhite (Hanson, 1988).

Most of these men rely on child-care resources in the community (preschools and day care centers, after-school care, self-care, and friends and family) more than on hired housekeepers; and they generally bemoan the lack of high-quality, low-cost child-care services. In one study, the single fathers who did best had been actively involved in child care and household tasks before the divorce, sought extra counseling and education after the divorce, and purposefully worked toward a good relationship with their children. Most of them were happy with their decision and felt that they were the better choice for custodial parent (Hanson, 1988).

### Stresses on children

Children growing up with one parent do not have two adults who can share child-rearing responsibilities, take children to activities, serve as gender role models, and model the interplay of personalities. What is more, the average income of families headed by women is less than half that of families with two parents (U.S. Bureau of the Census, 1984), and this has negative effects on children's health, well-being, and school achievement.

The strains of divorce also affect parenting. For several years following a separation, the single parent may be preoccupied with personal concerns and be less attentive and responsive to the child. Housekeeping and normal routines like bedtime and bath time may be neglected (Hetherington, Cox, & Cox, 1975). These effects often wear off in time, especially if the custodial parent forms a new relationship. But school-age children may continue to feel torn between two hostile parents and to reject a stepparent.

### Effects on schooling

One study of 18,000 elementary school and high school students in 14 states found that students from one-parent homes achieved less in school, liked school less, had more problems with peers, and were more likely to need disciplinary action than those with two parents. However, a follow-up analysis and interviews with parents showed once again that family income is critical. Lower income affected achievement more strongly than the number of parents at home—an important finding, since one-parent households tend to have lower incomes (Zakariya, 1982). What looks like a "single-parent" effect may often be a "low-income" effect. Other factors that influence achievement are parents' expectations and the number of books in the home (Milne, Myers, Rosenthal, & Ginsburg, 1986).

Teachers can help these children. A Maryland study found that when elementary school teachers made systematic efforts to get parents to help their children at home, single parents helped as much and as effectively as married ones (J. L. Epstein, 1984). Schools have begun to look at other ways to cooperate with single parents, most of whom are working mothers. They offer evening, breakfast, or weekend meetings, conferences, and programs; baby-sitters for younger children during school events; late-afternoon transportation for students after sports or band practice; and send notices and report cards to the noncustodial parent.

### Long-term effects

Do youngsters with only one parent get into more trouble than those with two parents? Some studies say that they do, and that they may also be at greater risk, later in life, of marital and parenting problems themselves (Rutter, 1979a). Children benefit from rich family relationships—and as children grow older and more independent, single parents need more help in guiding them.

Yet the one-parent home is not necessarily pathological, and the two-parent family is not always healthy. In general, children grow up better adjusted when they have a good relationship with one parent than when they grow up in a two-parent home filled with discord and discontent (Rutter, 1983); and an inaccessible, rejecting, or hostile parent is worse than an absent one (Hetherington, 1980).

### Stepfamilies

The word *stepparent* conjures up vivid storybook images of wicked and cruel interlopers. Such images often sabotage the efforts of the kindest stepparents to form close, warm relationships with their spouses' children. Yet many make the effort, and many succeed. With today's high rate of divorce and remarriage, families made up of "yours, mine, and ours" are common.

The stepfamily—also called the *blended* or *reconstituted* family—is different from the "natural" family. It has a larger supporting cast, with all the relatives from four adults (the married pair, plus both former spouses). And it has many stresses to deal with. Because of losses resulting from death or divorce, both children and adults may be afraid to trust or to love. A child's loyalties to an absent or dead parent may interfere with forming ties to a stepparent, especially when the child goes back and forth between two households. Disparities in life cycles often arise, as when a father of adolescents marries a childless woman (E. Visher & Visher, 1983).

The most common stepfamily consists of a mother, her children, and a stepfather. One study (Santrock, Sitterle, & Warshak, 1988) found that these remarried mothers were just as involved, nurturant, and available to their children—though many were working—as mothers in intact marriages. These women's greater satisfaction with life seems to carry over to their relationships with their children.

Most of the children were doing well and had good feelings about their stepfathers, who had been in the role an average of 3 years. These men were somewhat involved with the children's care but were relatively distant from them. Their detachment seemed to be deliberate, prompted by what they saw as the children's needs. Nearly one-fourth of the men said that they had tried to assume a parental role too fast and that this had caused problems in their relationships with the children. Other research has found that a man has the best chance of being accepted by his stepson if he makes friends with the boy first, supports the mother's parenting, and later moves into an authoritative role (Hetherington, 1986). This does not work so well with a girl, who is less likely to accept a stepfather as a parent. Boys benefit from having a stepfather, while stepdaughters seem to have more behavioral problems than daughters of nondivorced women or of women who have not remarried (J. B. Kelly, 1987).

A comparison group of stepmothers were much more involved, taking their stepchildren to and from school and other activities, providing emotional support and comfort, and disciplining them (Santrock et al., 1988). Still, for most stepchildren their most enduring

This "blended" family consists of a couple and three sets of children: a teenager from the husband's first marriage, two children from the wife's first marriage, and a toddler from the present marriage. Life is more complex in such families, but studies show that most of the children in them adjust and thrive.

ties are with their biological custodial parents, and "the positive nature of the relationship between the remarried parent and the child [is] a key ingredient in helping the child through the disruption and disequilibrium, as the family [moves] from the status of intact to divorced to becoming a stepfamily" (Santrock et al., 1988, p. 161).

## Sibling Relationships

"I fight more with my little brother than I do with my friends," reports Monica. "But when I fight with Billy, we always make up." The tie between Monica and Billy is deeper and more lasting than ordinary friendships, which may founder on a quarrel or just fade away. It is also ambivalent, marked by special affection as well as by intense competition and resentment.

Siblings influence each other *directly,* through interaction, and *indirectly,* through their impact on each other's relationship with the parents. A major direct influence is the way siblings help one another develop a self-concept. When Monica sees that she and her brother are different despite all their shared bonds, she forms a stronger sense of herself as an individual.

Sibling relations are also a laboratory for learning how to resolve conflicts. The ties of blood and physical closeness impel siblings to make up after quarrels, since they know they will see each other every day. They learn that expressing anger does not end a relationship. Younger siblings become quite skillful at sensing other people's needs, negotiating for what they want, and compromising. While firstborns like Monica tend to be bossy and more likely to attack, interfere with, ignore, or bribe their siblings, later-borns like Billy plead, reason, and cajole (Cicirelli, 1976a).

Monica and Billy's relationship is helped by the fact that she is a girl and he is a boy. Children are more apt to squabble with same-sex siblings; two brothers quarrel more than any other combination (Cicirelli, 1976a).

Siblings learn how to deal with dependence in relationships by being dependent on each other. Although children in American society take care of younger brothers and sisters less than is common in many other countries, a good deal of caretaking does take place. Older children often mind younger ones when parents are at work; they also help younger siblings with home-

Relationships with siblings are important during middle childhood. Older sisters talk and explain more to their younger siblings than older brothers do.

work. This help is most likely to be effective (and accepted) when it comes from a sibling—especially a sister—who is at least 4 years older. Girls explain more to younger siblings than boys do, and when girls want younger siblings to do something, they are more apt to reason with them or to make them feel obligated; older brothers tend to attack (Cicirelli, 1976a, 1976b). Gender differences also affect the way parents divide their time among their children. Mothers tend to talk more, explain more, and give more feedback to children with older brothers than to children with older sisters, maybe because of girls' greater effectiveness with younger siblings (Cicirelli, 1976a).

## CHILDHOOD EMOTIONAL DISTURBANCES

One child's fear of the dark keeps him from going to summer camp, another's anxiety requires large doses of reassurance before such routine events as exams and doctor's visits, and a third's constant temper tantrums antagonize the most important adults in her life.

These children are typical of as many as 20 to 25 percent of school-age children whose lives are impaired by psychiatric problems. Only about 1 in 5 of these troubled children receive help. This disturbing finding emerges from several recent surveys of children's mental health. One study in Pittsburgh found that 22 percent of 789 seven- to eleven-year-olds visiting their pediatricians had had a psychiatric problem during the previous year (Costello et al., 1988). Other studies have found a lower percentage of troubled children—from 5 to 15 percent—but this lower figure still represents some 3 to 9 million children (Knitzer, 1984; U.S. Department of Health and Human Services, USDHHS, 1980).

Boys, African American children, and children from poor families are at especially high risk, as are those who have recently experienced a stressful life event, who have repeated a grade in school, or whose parents are having difficulties or have a psychiatric problem (Costello et al., 1988). Some problems seem to be associated with a particular phase of a child's life and will go away on their own, but others need to be treated to prevent problems in the future.

## TYPES OF EMOTIONAL PROBLEMS

We have discussed sleep problems (Chapter 6) and hyperactivity (Chapter 8); now we'll look at some other childhood problems—acting-out behavior, anxiety disorders, and depression.

### Acting-Out Behavior

Children's emotional troubles often surface in their behavior: they show by what they do that they need help. They fight, they lie, they steal, they destroy property, and they break rules. These are common forms of *acting-out behavior:* misbehavior that is an outward expression of emotional turmoil.

Of course, almost all children make up fanciful stories as a form of make-believe or lie occasionally to avoid punishment. But when children past the age of 6 or 7 continue to tell tall tales, they are often signaling a sense of insecurity. They may need to make up glamorous stories to secure the attention and esteem of others; or obvious or habitual lying may be a way to show hostility toward their parents (Chapman, 1974).

Occasional minor stealing, too, is common. Although it needs to be dealt with, it is not necessarily a sign that anything is seriously wrong. But when children repeatedly steal from their parents or steal so openly from others that they are easily caught, they are—again—often showing hostility toward their parents and their parents' standards. In some cases, the stolen items seem to symbolize parents' love, power, or authority, of which the child feels deprived.

Any chronic antisocial behavior should be regarded as a possible symptom of deep-seated emotional upset. In Chapter 11, we'll discuss some extreme forms of misbehavior, those that get adolescents into trouble with the law.

### Anxiety Disorders

Various anxiety disorders begin in childhood. Here, we'll consider separation anxiety disorder and school phobia.

#### Separation anxiety disorder

Jessica wakes up complaining of nausea. Yesterday morning it was a headache, the day before that it was a stomachache, and last week she vomited three mornings in a row. Yet as soon as her mother says she can stay home from day camp, her symptoms disappear, and she spends the rest of the day happily playing in her room. Jessica is suffering from *separation anxiety disorder,* a condition involving excessive anxiety for at least 2 weeks, concerning separation from people to whom the child is attached. This condition is very different from the normal separation anxiety children show in the first year or two of life (see Chapter 5).

A child like Jessica may refuse to visit or sleep at friends' homes, go on errands, or attend camp or school; may "cling" to and shadow a parent around the house; and may complain of stomachaches, headaches, nausea, and vomiting before or during a separation. The condition affects boys and girls equally and may begin in early childhood and persist through the college years. Affected children tend to come from close-knit, caring families and to develop the anxiety after a life stress like the death of a pet, an illness, or a move to a new neighborhood.

### School phobia

*School phobia*—unrealistic fear that keeps children away from school—may be a form of separation anxiety disorder. It seems to have more to do with a fear of leaving the mother than a fear of school itself. Virtually no research has been done on the school situation of school-phobic youngsters, and so we know very little about their perceptions of school or how they get along there. If there *is* a problem at school—a sarcastic teacher, a bully in the schoolyard, or overly difficult work—the child's fears may be realistic; the environment, not the child, may need changing.

What *do* we know about school-phobic children? First, they are not truants; their parents usually know when they are absent. They tend to have average or higher than average intelligence and to be average or good students. Their ages are evenly distributed from 5 to 15, and they are equally likely to be boys or girls. Although they come from a variety of backgrounds, their parents tend to be professionals. Their parents are also more likely than a control group to be depressed, to suffer from anxiety disorders themselves, and to report disturbed family functioning (Bernstein & Garfinkel, 1988).

The most important element in the treatment of a school-phobic child is an early—but gradual—return to school. Usually children go back to school without too much difficulty once treatment is begun. The few studies that have followed up school-phobic children in later years are unclear, though, in determining how well treatment helped their overall adjustment (D. Gordon & Young, 1976).

### Childhood Depression

"Nobody likes me" is a common complaint in middle childhood, when children tend to be popularity-conscious. But when these words were addressed to a school principal by an 8-year-old boy in Florida whose classmates had accused him of stealing from the teacher's purse, it was a danger signal. The boy vowed that he would never return to school—and he never did. Two days later, he hanged himself by a belt from the top rail of his bunk bed ("Doctors rule out," 1984).

Everyone feels "blue" at times, but a child's chronic depression can be a danger signal and should be taken seriously, especially when it represents a marked change from the child's usual behavior.

Fortunately, depressed children rarely go to such lengths, though suicide among young people is on the increase (see Chapter 18). How can we tell the difference between a harmless period of the "blues" (which we all experience at times) and a major *affective disorder*—that is, a disorder of mood? The basic symptoms of an affective disorder are similar from childhood through adulthood, but some features are age-specific (Diagnostic and Statistical Manual of Mental Disorders, 3d ed., rev., DSM III-R, 1987).

Friendlessness is only one sign of *childhood depression.* This disorder also involves an inability to have fun, to concentrate, and to show normal emotional reactions. Depressed children are often tired, extremely active, or inactive. They walk very little, cry a great deal, have trouble concentrating, sleep too much or too little, lose their appetite, start doing poorly in school, look unhappy, complain of physical ailments, feel overwhelmingly guilty, suffer severe separation anxiety (as in school phobia), or think often about death or suicide (Malmquist, 1983; Poznanski 1982). Any four or five of these symptoms may support a diagnosis of depression, especially when they represent a marked change from the child's usual pattern. Parents do not always recognize "minor" problems like sleep disturbances, loss of appetite, and irritability as signs of depression, but children themselves can often describe how they feel.

No one is sure of the cause of depression in either children or adults. There is some evidence for a biochemical predisposition, which may be triggered by specific experiences. The parents of depressed children are more likely to be depressed themselves, suggesting a possible genetic factor, a reflection of general stress in these families, or a result of poor parenting practices by disturbed parents (Weissman et al., 1987). Depressed school-age children are likely to lack social and academic competence, but it is not clear whether incompetence causes depression or vice versa (Blechman, McEnroe, Carella, & Audette, 1986).

Moderate to severe depression is fairly easy to spot, but milder forms are harder to diagnose. The presence of any of the above symptoms should, therefore, be followed closely; if they persist, the child should get psychological help.

## TREATMENT FOR EMOTIONAL PROBLEMS

The choice of a specific kind of treatment for a particular disorder depends on many factors: the nature of the problem, the child's personality, the family's willingness to participate, the availability of treatment in the community, the family's financial resources, and, often, the orientation of the professional first consulted.

### Therapies

Psychological treatment can take several forms. In *individual psychotherapy* a therapist sees a child one on one, to help the child gain insights into his or her personality and relationships, and interpret feelings and behavior. This may be helpful at a time of great stress in the child's life, like the death of a parent, even when a child has not shown any signs of disturbance. The therapist shows acceptance of the child's feelings—and the child's right to them. Child psychotherapy is usually much more effective when combined with counseling for the parents.

Sometimes the parents come with the child, as in *family therapy*. The family therapist sees the whole family together, observes the way members act with one another, and points out their patterns of functioning—both growth-producing patterns and inhibiting or destructive patterns. Sometimes the child whose problem

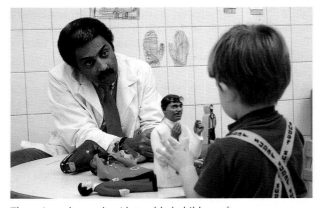

Therapists who work with troubled children often encourage them to express themselves through play, which helps bring out their emotions.

brings the family into therapy is, ironically, the healthiest member, responding to a troubled family situation. Through therapy, parents are often able to confront their own differences and begin to resolve them—the first step toward solving the children's problems as well.

*Behavior therapy,* or *behavior modification,* uses principles of learning theory to alter behavior—to eliminate undesirable behaviors like temper tantrums or to develop desirable ones like doing homework. A behavior therapist does not look for underlying reasons for behavior and typically does not try to offer a child insight into his or her situation, but aims simply to change the behavior. The therapist may use operant conditioning to encourage a behavior like putting dirty clothes into the hamper. Every time the child does it, she or he gets a reward, like words of praise, some kind of treat, or a token that can be exchanged for toys.

During the 1980s, an increase occurred in the use of *drug therapy* to treat childhood emotional problems (Tuma, 1989). Now, antidepressants are commonly prescribed for bed-wetters, stimulants for hyperactive children, and antipsychotics for children with severe psychological problems.

### Effectiveness of Therapy

Overall, psychological therapy generally helps (R. J. Casey & Berman, 1985). In a review of 75 studies, the children who received treatment scored better than children with similar problems who did not receive it, on a variety of measures (including self-concept, adjustment, personality, social skills, achievement in school, cognitive functioning, and resolution of fears and anxieties).

Treatment for specific problems (like impulsiveness or hyperactivity) brings more improvement than therapy aimed at better social adjustment. No one form of therapy (play or nonplay, individual or group, "child-only" or treatment of child and parents) seems superior to another overall, but some kinds of treatment are better for certain problems (Tuma, 1989). Behavior therapy is especially effective for phobias, bed-wetting, and problems with general self-control.

Drugs help in the treatment of some childhood emotional disturbances, but their use should not eliminate psychotherapy. Drugs are usually most effective combined with other treatments. But giving pills in order to change children's behavior is a radical step. Many medicines have undesirable side effects; and in some cases the drugs relieve only behavioral symptoms and do not get at underlying causes. Thus many therapists use drugs only as a last resort.

While parents, therapists, and researchers often see definite gains in children who receive therapy, teachers and peers tend not to notice much improvement. First impressions are hard to overcome. It often helps when parents point out a child's improvement to the teacher and help the child make new friends who do not know what she or he was like before treatment.

## STRESS AND RESILIENCE

### SOURCES OF STRESS: LIFE EVENTS, FEARS, AND THE "HURRIED CHILD"

Stressful events are part of every childhood. Illness, the birth of a sibling, sibling rivalry, frustration, and temporary absences of parents are common sources of stress. In addition, the divorce or death of parents, hospitalization, and the day-in, day-out grind of poverty affect the lives of many children. Other children live through homelessness, wars, and earthquakes. Violent events like kidnappings and attacks by playground snipers make children realize that their world is not as safe as they had thought and that their parents cannot always protect them. Such realizations affect children in the short and possibly the long run (Garmezy, 1983; Pynoos et al., 1987). Children's fears reflect their awareness of many modern stresses, as we see in Box 9-3 below.

Sometimes, as in physical or psychological abuse, the parents themselves are a source of difficulty (see Box 9-4 on page 300). In other cases, society imposes pressures, like forcing children to grow up too soon. Some children, however, are able to overcome enor-

## BOX 9–3   WINDOW ON THE WORLD

# WHAT CHILDREN ARE AFRAID OF

Over the past several years, adults have become increasingly concerned about the number of possible dangers facing children and have become concerned over children's worries about personal or global catastrophes like homelessness, AIDS, drug abuse, criminal attack, or nuclear war. These dangers do arouse anxiety in children, but many childhood fears are much more intrinsic to youngsters' daily lives. According to recent research in six countries—Australia, Canada, Egypt, Japan, the Philippines, and the United States—children around the world are remarkably alike in the things they are afraid of (Yamamoto, Soliman, Parsons, & Davies, 1987).

When third- through ninth-grade children were asked to rank a list of 20 events in order of how upsetting each one would be, the primary fear among children in each country was the same: the fear of losing a parent. Close in importance to this, however, are events that would embarrass children—being kept back in school, wetting their pants in public, or being sent to the principal. The children of every country ranked the birth of a new sibling least upsetting of all (perhaps showing that at this age children's lives are so busy outside the home that they are less affected by a new arrival, or that at an average age of about 9, few were dealing with a new baby at home). Boys and girls

rated events about the same; by and large, so did children of different ages.

For most children, school is a specially fertile breeding ground for insecurity—partly because it is so important in their lives and partly because so many belittling practices (like ridiculing children in class or accusing them of lying) flourish there. Adults can do a great deal to stem these fears by respecting children, by encouraging them to talk about their worries, and by not expecting fears to disappear on their own.

Most childhood fears are normal, and overcoming them helps children to grow, achieve identity, and master their world.

# PSYCHOLOGICAL MALTREATMENT

"Why are you so stupid?" "I wish you had never been born!" "Some athlete you are!" "Can't you do anything right?" "Don't bother me! Do you think I have nothing better to do than pay attention to you?" How do children feel when remarks like these are addressed to them?

The pain of physical abuse may heal quickly, but its psychological scars may never go away. The same is true when children's minds rather than their bodies are battered. Physicians, legislators, and mental health professionals are becoming increasingly concerned about *psychological maltreatment,* which has been broadly defined as action (or a failure to act) that damages children's behavioral, cognitive, emotional, or physical functioning (Hart & Brassard, 1987). Abusing parents may reject, terrorize, isolate, exploit, degrade, ridicule, insult, and corrupt children and be emotionally unresponsive to them (Hart & Brassard, 1987; M. S. Rosenberg, 1987). As a result, children may never reach their full potential as adults (E. G. Garrison, 1987).

The impact of psychological maltreatment is unpredictable; many maltreated children grow up to lead

healthy, productive lives (Hart & Brassard, 1987; M. S. Rosenberg, 1987). These children are called "resilient" (we talk about them in this chapter). Many others, however, suffer for years as the result of childhood abuse, either physical or psychological.

Psychological maltreatment is part of the more than 2 million cases of child abuse and neglect. It often occurs without physical abuse and is inflicted by adults who would be horrified to hear themselves called "abusers." It has been linked to children's lying, stealing, low self-esteem, emotional maladjustment, dependency, underachievement, depression, failure to thrive, aggression, homicide, and suicide, as well as to psychological distress in later life, and it may also play a part in learning disorders (Hart & Brassard, 1987).

Psychological maltreatment occurs both in families and in such institutions as schools, hospitals, day care centers, and juvenile justice programs. School has come a long way since "reading, 'riting, and 'rithmetic" were "taught to the tune of a hickory stick" and with a dunce cap as a "reward," but some schools still try to instill discipline through fear,

intimidation, and degradation (Hart & Brassard, 1987).

Institutional maltreatment is easier to stop than maltreatment by parents. In most states, children may be taken from abusive parents; but the courts are often reluctant to take this step except in extreme cases, especially when it is unclear that institutional care will be better (Melton & Davidson, 1987).

Since a favorable self-image is so important to a good life, treatment from important adults that robs a child of self-esteem can have far-reaching consequences both on individual lives and on society. Much antisocial behavior seems to have its roots in early maltreatment.

The best time to prevent such maltreatment is before birth. How, though, can social service agencies identify high-risk parents? How can more adults learn about child development and become more sensitive to the needs of babies and older children? And how can psychologically abusive parents become sensitive to the harm they are inflicting on their children? To eliminate psychological maltreatment, our society has to question its values and clearly make the needs of children a high priority.

mous stress in their lives, and we'll take a look at what helps them do this.

Children today have a special set of pressures to cope with. Because families move around more than they used to, children are more likely to change schools and friends and less likely to know many adults well. They know more about technology, sex, and violence than children of previous generations, and because of single-parent homes and parents' work schedules, they are likely to shoulder adult responsibilities.

The child psychologist David Elkind has called to-

day's child the "hurried child" (1981, 1987b). He believes that the pressures of life today are making children grow up too soon and are making their shortened childhood too stressful. Today's children are pressured to succeed in school, to compete in sports, and to meet their parents' emotional needs. On television and in real life, children are exposed to many adult problems before they have mastered the problems of childhood. Yet children are not small adults. They feel and think like children, and they need these years of childhood for healthy development.

## COPING WITH STRESS: THE RESILIENT CHILD

Children's reactions to stressful events may depend on such factors as the event itself (children respond differently to a parent's death than to divorce), the child's age (preschoolers and adolescents react differently), and the child's sex (boys are often more vulnerable than girls) (Rutter, 1984). Yet if two children of the same age and sex are exposed to the same stressful experience, one may crumble while the other copes well. Why?

Resilient children are those who bounce back from circumstances that would blight the emotional development of most children. These are children of the ghetto who go on to distinguish themselves in the professions. These are neglected or abused children who go on to form intimate relationships, be good parents to their own children, and lead fulfilling lives. What is special about them?

Several studies have identified "protective factors" that may operate to reduce the effects of such stressors as kidnapping or poor parenting (Anthony & Koupernik, 1974; Garmezy, 1983; Rutter, 1984). Several of these factors may also protect children who have been psychologically abused (M. S. Rosenberg, 1987).

Factors like the following seem to contribute to children's resilience:

■ *The child's personality.* Resilient children tend to be adaptable enough to cope with changing circumstances, and to be positive thinkers who are friendly, sensitive to other people, and independent. They feel competent and have high self-esteem. Intelligence, too, may be a factor; good students seem to cope better (Rutter, 1984).

■ *The child's family.* Resilient children are likely to have good relationships with parents who are emotionally supportive to them and to each other, or, failing that, to have a close relationship with at least one parent. If they lack even this, they are likely to be close to at least one other adult who expresses interest in them and obviously cares for them, and whom they trust.

■ *Learning experiences.* Resilient children are likely to have had experience solving social problems. They have seen parents, older siblings, or others deal with frustration and make the best of a bad situation. They have faced challenges themselves, have worked out solutions, and have learned that they can exert some control over their lives.

■ *Reduced risk.* Children who have been exposed to only one of a number of factors strongly related to psychiatric disorders (such as discord between the parents, low social status, overcrowding at home, a disturbed mother, a criminal father, and experience in foster care or institutions) are often able to overcome the stress; but when two or more of these factors are present, the children's risk of developing an emotional disturbance goes up fourfold or more (Rutter, in Pines, 1979). When children are not besieged on all sides, they can often cope with adverse circumstances.

■ *Compensating experiences.* A supportive school environment and successful experiences—for example, in sports, in music, or with other children—can help make up for a dismal home life, and in adulthood a good marriage can compensate for poor relationships earlier in life.

All this research does not, or course, mean that what happens in a child's life does not matter. In general, children with unfavorable backgrounds have more problems in adjustment than those with favorable backgrounds. The heartening promise of these findings, however, lies in the recognition that what happens in childhood does not necessarily determine the outcome of a person's life.

## SUMMARY

### THE SELF-CONCEPT

■ The self-concept is the sense of self. It helps people understand themselves and regulate their behavior. The self-concept develops greatly during middle childhood.

■ Self-esteem, or a positive self-image, is an important development of middle childhood.

1 Four factors that may influence self-esteem are a sense of significance, competence, virtue, and power.

2 Parents of children with high self-esteem tend to have authoritative parenting styles.

■ A number of theories give insights into the development of self-concept during middle childhood.

1  Freud saw middle childhood as a period of latency, or relative sexual calm. The development of the superego keeps the id under control, allowing the ego to deal with the outside world and resulting in rapid socialization and skill development.
2  Erikson's fourth crisis, which takes place in middle childhood, is industry versus inferiority; the "virtue" that should come out of it is *competence*.
3  Social-learning theorists point to the influence of parents, teachers, and peers as models who become powerful shapers of self-concept.
4  Piaget's cognitive-developmental approach holds that the decline of egocentrism and the ability to decenter make children more sensitive to what others think of them and also more able to see themselves from different viewpoints.
5  According to the information-processing approach, children build, test, and modify self-schemata (hypotheses or knowledge structures about themselves) on the basis of experience. Many lasting self-schemata develop during middle childhood.

## ASPECTS OF PERSONALITY DEVELOPMENT IN MIDDLE CHILDHOOD

■ Schoolchildren spend more of their leisure time watching television and less time playing today than in the past. As children move through elementary school, they read less for pleasure. Many children are involved in sports and other organized activities.

■ The society of childhood mirrors changes in adult society. Many children today are from more mobile families and thus have weaker social bonds than children in previous generations, and so the peer group sometimes tends to substitute for kinship bonds.

■ The peer group is an important arena for the building of self-concept and self-esteem.

■ School-age youngsters are most susceptible to pressure to conform, which may encourage anti-social behavior in children who are too weak to resist.

■ Most children select peers who are like them in age, sex, race, and socioeconomic status. Racial prejudice among schoolchildren appears to be diminishing as a result of school integration.

■ The basis of friendship changes in middle childhood. Children choose friends they feel comfortable with and see friendship as involving give-and-take.

■ Popularity influences self-esteem. Children who are not only ignored by their peers but rejected by them are at risk of emotional and behavioral problems. They need to learn social skills.

■ Although school-age children spend less time with their parents than with their peers, relationships with parents continue to be most important. Other important relationships are with grandparents, siblings, friends, and teachers. Different relationships serve different purposes for children.

■ New issues related to school and the use of leisure time arise during this period.

1  Although school-age children require less direct care and supervision than younger children, it is still important for parents to monitor their children's activities.
2  Although disciplinary methods evolve with children's cognitive development, there appears to be an underlying consistency in parents' child-rearing attitudes. There are some differences among social classes in parents' interactions with school-age children.
3  Coregulation is an intermediate stage in the transfer of control from parent to child, in which children make more of their own day-to-day decisions under their parents' general supervision.

■ Children today are growing up in a variety of family situations besides the traditional nuclear family. These include families in which mothers work outside the home (now a majority of families), families with divorced parents, and one-parent families. In any of these, an atmosphere of love, support, and respect for family members will provide an excellent prognosis for healthy development.

1  Age affects children's reactions to both mothers' employment and divorce. Whether children make a successful adjustment to either situation depends largely on the way the parents handle it.
2  Children of employed mothers (particularly girls) may benefit from their mothers' enhanced self-esteem, from added family income, and from less stereotyped gender attitudes. However, sons may show some negative effects, and self-care children may be at greater risk if they are not mature enough to care for themselves.
3  Children living with only one parent are under special stress and are at risk of lower achievement in school and other problems. These children do better in school when their parents are involved with the children's schooling.

■ Siblings exert a powerful influence on each other either directly (through their interactions) or indirectly (through their impact on each other's relationship with their parents).

## CHILDHOOD EMOTIONAL DISTURBANCES

■ Some 3 to 9 million children suffer from a variety of emotional disorders including acting-out behavior, anxiety disorders, and childhood depression.

■ Studies show that psychological therapy is generally effective. However, only 1 in 5 troubled children gets help.

## STRESS AND RESILIENCE

■ Normal childhood stesses take many forms and can affect the healthy emotional development of children. Unusual stesses, such as natural disasters and wars, also affect many children.

■ Psychological maltreatment of children appears to be widespread among both families and institutions. It results in damage to children's behavioral, cognitive, emotional, or physical functioning and may prevent them from fulfilling their potential.

■ As a result of advanced technology, family responsibilities, and pressure to grow up too soon, many children today are experiencing a shortened and stressful childhood.

■ Psychologists have studied factors that enable some children to withstand stress better than others. Resilient children are those who are able to ''bounce back'' from unfortunate circumstances.

## KEY TERMS

self-concept (page 276)
self-awareness (276)
self-recognition (276)
self-definition (277)
real self (277)
ideal self (277)
self-esteem (278)

industry versus inferiority (279)
self-schema (280)
prejudice (283)
discipline (286)
coregulation (287)
self-care children (289)

acting-out behavior (296)
separation anxiety disorder (296)
school phobia (297)
affective disorder (297)
childhood depression (297)
psychological maltreatment (300)

## SUGGESTED READINGS

**Coles, R. (1990).** *The spiritual life of children.* Boston: Houghton Mifflin. The author, a child psychiatrist, interviewed hundreds of children of many faiths about their religious beliefs. In this book he reports their opinions on heaven, hell, God's wishes for humankind, and their doubts.

**Elkind, D. (1988).** *The hurried child* (rev. ed.) New York: Addison-Wesley. This book, by a well-known psychologist, examines how parents can raise healthy children who enjoy childhood, despite a social trend toward pressure to grow up fast.

**Lansky, V. (1989).** *Vicky Lansky's divorce book for parents: Helping your children cope with divorce and its* aftermath. New York: New American Library. Based on the author's own experiences as well as those of other families, this practical guide for divorcing parents deals with issues chronologically, from the decision to separate to long-term adjustment.

**Simon, S. B., & Olds, S. W. 1991.** *Helping your child find values to live by.* Hadley, MA: Values Press. A self-help manual for parents for establishing moral values and emotional self-awareness in children. The authors explain why values themselves cannot be taught but how parents can teach children a process for arriving at their own values.

## PART FOUR

# ADOLESCENCE

In adolescence, young people's appearance changes as a result of the hormonal events of puberty. Their thinking changes as they develop the ability to deal with abstractions. Their feelings change about almost everything. All areas of development converge as adolescents confront their major task, establishing an adult identity.

■ In **Chapter 10,** we examine the dramatic physical and intellectual development that occurs from about age 12 till about age 20. We see the impact of early and late maturation, we look at health problems that affect adolescents, and we see how their advances in intellectual competence help them consider abstract ideas, moral issues, and career choices. Finally, we look at the roles of school and work in teenagers' lives.

■ In **Chapter 11,** we see how adolescents incorporate their new appearance, their puzzling physical yearnings, and their new intellectual abilities into their sense of self. We examine the major task of adolescence—the achievement of identity, including sexual identity. We look at the relationships adolescents have with their parents and their peers, and we see how the peer group serves as the testing ground for teenagers' ideas about life and about themselves. We look at some problems that arise during the teenage years, as well as some of the strengths of adolescents.

## CHAPTER 10

# PHYSICAL AND INTELLECTUAL DEVELOPMENT IN ADOLESCENCE

I think what is happening to me is so wonderful, and not only what can be seen on my body, but all that is taking place inside.

ANNE FRANK,
*THE DIARY OF A YOUNG GIRL*, 1952
(ENTRY WRITTEN JANUARY 5, 1944)

- What physical changes do adolescents experience, and how do these changes affect them psychologically?
- How prevalent are eating disorders, drug abuse, and sexually transmitted diseases in adolescence, and what can be done about them?

- How does cognitive development affect the way adolescents solve problems and make moral judgments and life decisions?
- What factors affect the value of secondary schooling, and why do some adolescents drop out of school?
- What factors influence young people's vocational choices?

Apache Indians in the southwestern United States mark a girl's sexual maturation with a traditional ritual: after she menstruates for the first time, her elders chant from sunrise to sunset for 4 days (see Box 10-1). Jewish people welcome 13-year-old boys and girls into the adult community with bar mitzvah and bas mitzvah celebrations.

Such coming-of-age rites are common in many traditional societies in which the attainment of sexual maturity is considered the beginning of adulthood. Rites of passage may include religious blessings; separation from the family; severe tests of strength and endurance; mutilation, like circumcision of both boys and girls, piercing of ears, filing of teeth, or elaborate tattooing; and acts of magic.

In modern industrial societies, no single initiation rite marks the passage from childhood to adulthood, and the sexual aspects of coming-of-age are often only whispered about. Instead, we recognize a lengthy transitional stage known as *adolescence.*

*Adolescence* is a developmental transition between childhood and adulthood. It is generally considered to begin at about age 12 or 13 and to end in the late teens or early twenties. However, its physical basis has actually begun long before, and its psychological ramifications may continue long after. In this chapter we look at the dramatic physical changes of this stage and at how they affect and are affected by psychological changes. Then we see how adolescents develop intellectually as they become able to think abstractly, even though they retain traces of egocentric thought. Their thinking processes affect not only their moral reasoning but also their education and career goals, as we'll see in this chapter. We'll delve more deeply into the adolescent quest for identity in Chapter 11.

## ADOLESCENCE: A DEVELOPMENTAL TRANSITION

Adolescence is generally considered as beginning at *puberty,* the process that leads to sexual maturity, when a person is able to reproduce.* Although the physical changes of this time of life are dramatic, they do not burst full-blown at the end of childhood. Instead, puberty is part of a long and complex process that began even before birth. The biological changes that signal the end of childhood produce rapid growth in height and weight (a rate of growth second only to that of infancy), changes in body proportions and form, and the attainment of sexual maturity. But adolescence is also a social and emotional process. It has been said that "adolescence begins in biology and ends in culture" (Conger & Peterson, 1984, p. 92).

Before the twentieth century, children entered the adult world when their bodies were mature or when they began a vocational apprenticeship. Now, however, the entry into adulthood is not so clear-cut. Puberty occurs earlier than it used to (see our discussion of the *secular trend* later in this chapter). And because of the longer period of education required by our complex society, adulthood takes longer to arrive.

Americans consider themselves adult at various ages, depending on which marker they use. They may draw on a variety of legal definitions. James may consider himself an adult at 17 when he can enlist in the army, Madeline at age 18 when she can marry without

---

*Some people use the term *puberty* to mean the end point of sexual maturation and refer to the process as *pubescence,* but our usage conforms to that of most psychologists today.

## BOX 10–1   WINDOW ON THE WORLD

# AN APACHE GIRL COMES OF AGE

Among the Apache Indians of the American southwest, a girl's entrance into puberty is celebrated by a 4-day ceremony of chanting from sunrise to sunset, which reenacts the tribe's version of how the world was created (Heard Museum of Anthropology and Primitive Art, 1987).

According to Apache lore, the first woman on earth was a deity called Changing Woman, the mother of twins who cleansed the world of evil so that human beings could live well. During the puberty rite (also called "gifts of Changing Woman"), the deity's spirit is believed to enter the girl to prepare her for her role as a mother and life giver. Among the gifts that Changing Woman is believed to bestow upon her are strength, an even temperament, prosperity, and a long life.

As male members of the tribe gather around, chanting, the girl approaches a ceremonial blanket laid out on the ground, on which a buckskin has been placed. She wears an abalone shell on her forehead and carries a staff to represent longevity and a cane that she will need when she is old. The buckskin on which she stands symbolizes the hope that she will always have plenty of meat and not go hungry.

The girl kneels before the sun and is massaged to "mold" her body into

The Apache Indians of the American southwest celebrate a girl's entrance into puberty with a 4-day ritual that includes special clothing, a symbolic blanket, and singing from sunrise to sunset. In modern industrial societies, there is no single comparable initiation rite.

adult form and to give her strength. In the past, the girl danced throughout the night, but more recently a surrogate—usually a godmother or best friend—has been allowed to take over for her. On the last day of the ceremony, the girl is blessed with pollen, symbolizing her newfound reproductive powers.

In many traditional cultures, ceremonies like this one recognize the importance and value of the physical changes that prepare a young person for an adult role in the society.

her parents' permission; others may go by the age when they can be held legally responsible for contracts (18 to 21, depending on the state). Or people may consider themselves to have achieved sociological adulthood when they are self-supporting or have chosen a career, or married, or founded a family. Intellectual maturity is generally considered to coincide with the capacity for abstract thought. Emotional maturity depends on such achievements as discovery of identity, independence from parents, development of a system of values, and ability to form mature relationships of friendship and love (see Chapter 11). Some people, of course, never leave adolescence emotionally or socially, no matter what their chronological age.

# PHYSICAL DEVELOPMENT

## MATURATION IN ADOLESCENCE

Adolescents' maturation involves not only physical changes but also the psychological effects of these changes. Let's explore both aspects.

### PHYSICAL CHANGES

The biological changes that signal the end of childhood include the adolescent growth spurt, the beginning of menstruation for girls, the presence of sperm in the urine of males, the maturation of organs involved in reproduction, and the development of secondary sex characteristics. When do most young people in the United States experience these changes?

### Puberty and the Secular Trend

Any eighth- or ninth-grade class picture presents startling contrasts. Flat-chested little girls stand next to full-bosomed, full-grown young women. Skinny little boys are seen next to broad-shouldered, mustached young men. This variance is normal. There is about a 6- to 7-year range for puberty in both boys and girls.

During puberty, the reproductive functions mature, the sex organs (see Table 10-1) enlarge, and the secondary sex characteristics appear (see Table 10-2). The process takes about 4 years and begins about 2 years earlier for girls than for boys. Girls, on the average, begin to show pubertal change at 9 or 10 years of age, achieving sexual maturation by 13 or 14. Normal girls, however, may show the first signs as early as age 7 or as late as 14 (becoming sexually mature at ages 9 to 16). The average age for boys' entry into puberty is 12, with sexual maturity coming at age 14. But normal boys may begin to show changes from ages 9 to 16 (achieving maturity from ages 11 to 18) (Chumlea, 1982). As we'll see, maturing early or late often has social and psychological consequences.

The physical changes of adolescence unfold in a sequence that is much more consistent than their actual timing, though even this order varies somewhat from one person to another. The usual sequences are shown in Table 10-3. Some people move through puberty very quickly, while for others the process takes much longer. One girl, for example, may be developing breasts and body hair at about the same rate; but the body hair of another may grow so much faster than her

**TABLE 10-1**
PRIMARY SEX CHARACTERISTICS: SEX ORGANS

| Female | Male |
| --- | --- |
| Ovaries | Testes |
| Fallopian tubes | Penis |
| Uterus | Scrotum |
| Vagina | Seminal vesicles |
| | Prostate gland |

**TABLE 10-2**
SECONDARY SEX CHARACTERISTICS

| Girls | Boys |
| --- | --- |
| Breasts | Pubic hair |
| Pubic hair | Axillary (underarm) hair |
| Axillary (underarm) hair | Facial hair |
| Increased width and depth of pelvis | Changes in voice |
| Changes in voice | Changes in skin |
| Changes in skin | Broadening of shoulders |

breasts that her adult hair pattern appears a year or so before her breasts develop. The same kinds of variations occur among boys (Tobin-Richards, Boxer, Kavrell, & Petersen, 1984).

Puberty occurs in response to changes in the body's hormone system, which are triggered by some physiological signal, possibly related to a critical weight level. Whatever the signal is, its response in a girl is for her ovaries to sharply step up their production of the female hormone estrogen; and in a boy, for his testes to increase the manufacture of androgens, particularly testosterone. Both boys and girls have both types of hormones, but girls have higher levels of estrogen and boys have higher levels of androgens (Tobin-Richards et al., 1984). As early as age 7 the levels of these sex hormones begin to rise, setting the events of puberty in motion. Estrogen stimulates growth of the female genitals and development of the breasts; androgens stimulate the growth of the male genitals and body hair.

Hormones are also closely associated with emotions, specifically with aggression in boys and with both aggression and depression in girls (Brooks-Gunn, 1988). Some researchers attribute the increased emotionality and moodiness of early adolescence to hor-

**TABLE 10–3**
USUAL SEQUENCE OF PHYSIOLOGICAL CHANGES IN ADOLESCENCE

| Girls' Characteristics | Age of First Appearance |
|---|---|
| Growth of breasts | 8–13 |
| Growth of pubic hair | 8–14 |
| Body growth | 9.5–14.5 (average peak, 12) |
| Menarche | 10–16.5 (average, 12.5) |
| Underarm hair | About 2 years after pubic hair |
| Increased output of oil- and sweat-producing glands (which may lead to acne) | About the same time as underarm hair |

| Boys' Characteristics | Age of First Appearance |
|---|---|
| Growth of testes, scrotal sac | 10–13.5 |
| Growth of pubic hair | 10–15 |
| Body growth | 10.5–16 (average peak, 14) |
| Growth of penis, prostate gland, seminal vesicles | 11–14.5 (average, 12.5) |
| Change in voice | About the same time as growth of penis |
| First ejaculation of semen | About 1 year after beginning of growth of penis |
| Facial and underarm hair | About 2 years after appearance of pubic hair |
| Increased output of oil- and sweat-producing glands (which may lead to acne) | About the same time as underarm hair |

mones, but we need to remember that social influences combine with hormonal ones and sometimes predominate. For example, even though there is a well-established relationship between the production of the hormone testosterone and sexuality, adolescents begin sexual activity more in accord with what their friends do than with what their glands secrete (Brooks-Gunn, 1988).

On the basis of historical sources, developmentalists have inferred the existence of a **secular trend** *—a lowering of the age when puberty begins and young people reach adult height and sexual maturity. This trend, which also involves increases in adult height and weight, began about 100 years ago and has occurred in the United States, western Europe, and Japan, but not in some other countries (Chumlea, 1982).

The most obvious explanation for this secular trend seems to be a higher standard of living. Children who are healthier, better nourished, and better cared for mature earlier and grow bigger. This explanation is supported by evidence: the age of sexual maturity is

later in less developed countries than in more industrialized countries. In New Guinea, for example, girls do not begin to menstruate until sometime between age 15.4 and age 18.4, compared with an average age of 12.5 years in the United States (Eveleth & Tanner, 1976).

The secular trend appears to have ended, at least in the United States, probably as a reflection of higher living standards in most segments of our population (Schmeck, 1976). The leveling of the trend suggests that the age of sexual maturity has now reached some genetically determined limit and that better nutrition is unlikely to lower the age any further.

### The Adolescent Growth Spurt

An early sign of maturation is the **adolescent growth spurt,** a dramatic increase in height and weight. It generally begins to appear in girls between ages 9½ and 14½ (usually at about age 10) and in boys between ages 10½ and 16 (usually at about age 12 or 13). It typically lasts about 2 years. Soon after the spurt ends, the young person reaches sexual maturity. Most girls reach their adult height by age 14 or 15, and most boys by age 18 (Elkind, 1984).

---

*A secular trend is a trend that can be seen only by observing several generations.

As these young dancers demonstrate, during the years from 11 to 13, girls are on the average taller, heavier, and stronger than boys, who achieve their adolescent growth spurt later than girls do. If our society did not have such a rigid idea that males must be taller than females, this temporary state would be less embarrassing for the boys.

Before the growth spurt, boys are typically only about 2 percent taller than girls. Since girls' growth spurt usually occurs earlier than that of boys, there is a period of several years when girls are taller, heavier, and stronger. After the growth spurt, boys are larger again, now by about 8 percent. The growth spurt in boys is more intense, and its later appearance allows for an extra period of growth, since growth goes on at a faster rate before puberty.

Boys and girls grow differently during adolescence. A boy becomes larger overall, his shoulders are wider, his legs are longer relative to his trunk, and his forearms are longer relative to both his upper arms and his height. A girl's pelvis widens during adolescence to make childbearing easier, and layers of fat are laid down just under the skin, giving her a more rounded appearance.

In both sexes, the adolescent growth spurt affects practically all skeletal and muscular dimensions. The changes, which are greater in boys than in girls, follow their own timetables, so that parts of the body may be out of proportion for a while. The result is the familiar teenage awkwardness or gawkiness that accompanies unbalanced, accelerated growth.

## Primary Sex Characteristics

The **primary sex characteristics** are the organs necessary for reproduction. In the female, the sex organs are the ovaries, uterus, and vagina; in the male, the testes, prostate gland, penis, and seminal vesicles (see Figure 2-1 on page 42 and Table 10-1). The gradual enlargement of these body parts occurs during puberty, leading to sexual maturation.

The principal sign of sexual maturity in girls is menstruation. In boys, the principal sign is the presence of sperm in the urine (a boy is fertile as soon as sperm are present). Both the onset of menstruation and the first appearance of sperm in the urine are highly variable. There has been very little research on the development of male reproductive capability, but one longitudinal study found that only 2 percent of 11- to 12-year-old boys showed sperm in the urine compared with 24 percent of 15-year-olds (Richardson & Short, 1978).

Another sign of puberty in a boy is the occurrence of an ejaculation of semen while he is asleep, known as a *nocturnal emission* (and commonly referred to as a *wet dream*). Most adolescent boys, whether or not they are having sexual intercourse or masturbating on a fairly regular basis, have these emissions, which are perfectly normal and may or may not occur in connection with an erotic dream.

## Secondary Sex Characteristics

The **secondary sex characteristics** are physiological signs of sexual maturation that do not directly involve the sex organs. They include the breasts of females and the broad shoulders of males. Other secondary sex characteristics involve changes in the voice, skin texture, and body hair. The timing of these signs is variable, but the sequence is fairly consistent (see Table 10-2).

The first sign of puberty for girls is usually the budding of the breasts. The nipples enlarge and protrude; the areolae, the pigmented areas surrounding the nipples, enlarge; and the breasts assume first a conical and then a rounded shape. The breasts are usually fully developed before menstruation begins. Much to their distress, some adolescent boys experience temporary breast enlargement; this is normal and may last from 12 to 18 months.

Various forms of hair growth, including pubic hair and axillary (armpit) hair, also signal maturation. Boys usually welcome the appearance of hair on face and chest, but girls tend to be dismayed if the slightest amount of hair appears on their faces and around their nipples, though this is normal.

The skin of adolescent boys and girls becomes coarser and oilier, and the increased activity of the sebaceous glands causes outbreaks of pimples and blackheads. Acne is more common in boys than in girls and seems to be related to increased amounts of the male hormone testosterone. The voices of both boys and girls deepen, partly in response to growth of the larynx and partly—especially in boys—in response to the production of male hormones.

These young ballerinas show the budding breasts that are usually the first sign of puberty for girls. Other secondary sex characteristics will soon follow.

## Menarche

The most dramatic sign of a girl's sexual maturity is *menarche*—the first menstruation, or monthly shedding of tissue from the lining of the womb. Menarche occurs fairly late in the sequence of female development (see Table 10-3). On the average, a girl in the United States first menstruates at the age of 12½, about 2 years after her breasts have begun to develop and her uterus has begun to grow, and after her growth spurt has slowed down.

Although in many cultures menarche is taken as the sign that a girl has become a woman, the early menstrual periods usually do not include ovulation, and many girls are unable to conceive for 12 to 18 months after menarche. Since ovulation and conception do sometimes occur in these early months, however, girls who have begun to menstruate should assume that if they have sexual intercourse, they can become pregnant.

Adolescent boys usually welcome the need to shave, since facial hair is one of the secondary sex characteristics that signal sexual maturation.

What effect does strenuous exercise have on the menstrual cycle? Most female athletes do not experience menstrual irregularity; but those who do usually become regular when they stop training and can then go on to have normal childbearing experiences (Bullen et al., 1985; Shangold, 1978).

## PSYCHOLOGICAL IMPACT OF PHYSICAL CHANGES

The physical changes of adolescence have many psychological ramifications. Let's look at some of them.

### Effects of Early and Late Maturation

One of the great paradoxes of adolescence is the conflict between a young person's yearning to find an individual identity—to assert a unique self—and an overwhelming desire to be exactly like his or her friends. Anything that obviously sets an adolescent apart from the crowd can be unsettling, and youngsters are often disturbed if they mature sexually either much earlier or much later than their friends. Though neither late maturing nor early maturing is necessarily an advantage or a drawback, the timing of maturation can have significant psychological effects.

## Early and late maturation in boys

Some research has found early-maturing boys to be more poised, relaxed, good-natured, popular with peers, and likely to be leaders—and less affected and impulsive than late maturers. Other studies have found them to be more worried about being liked, more cautious, and more bound by rules and routines.

Late maturers have been variously found to feel more inadequate, rejected, and dominated; to be more dependent, aggressive, and insecure; to rebel more against their parents; and to think less of themselves (Mussen & Jones, 1957; Peskin, 1967, 1973; Siegel, 1982). While some studies have shown that early maturers retain a head start in intellectual performance into late adolescence and adulthood (Gross & Duke, 1980; Tanner, 1978), many differences seem to disappear by adulthood (M. C. Jones, 1957).

There are pluses and minuses in both situations. Boys like to mature early, and those who do seem to be at an advantage. They reap the benefits to self-esteem of having the edge in sports and dating. Since they are more muscular, they are stronger and better in sports and they have a more favorable body image (Blyth et al., 1981). They also enjoy the benefit of being at the same maturity level as girls of their own age.

But an early maturer is likely to be given more responsibility by adults than a late maturer and sometimes has trouble living up to others' expectations that he should act as mature as he looks. Furthermore, he may have too little time to prepare for the changes of adolescence. Late maturers may feel and act more childish; but they may benefit from the longer period of childhood, when they do not have to deal with the new and different demands of adolescence, and they may become more flexible as they adapt to the problems of being smaller and more childish-looking than their peers (N. Livson & Peskin, 1980).

## Early and late maturation in girls

Advantages and disadvantages of early and late maturation are less clear-cut for girls than for boys. Girls tend not to like to mature early; they are generally happier when they mature neither earlier nor later than their peers. Early-maturing girls tend to be less sociable, expressive, and poised; more introverted and shy; and more negative about menarche (M. C. Jones, 1958; N. Livson & Peskin, 1980; Ruble & Brooks-Gunn, 1982). They are apt to have a poor body image and lower self-esteem than later-maturing girls (Simmons, Blyth, Van Cleave, & Bush, 1979).

One reason why an early-maturing girl may feel less attractive (Crockett & Petersen, 1987) is that her new curviness clashes with cultural standards equating beauty with thinness. She may also be reacting to other people's concerns about her sexuality. Parents and teachers, for example, may assume that girls with physically mature bodies *are* sexually active because they look as if they *could* be. Therefore, adults may treat an early-maturing girl more strictly and more disapprovingly than they treat less-developed girls. Other adolescents may also stereotype her, putting pressures on her that she is ill-equipped to handle.

A girl who is bigger than many of the boys she knows and more bosomy than other girls will often feel uncomfortably conspicuous; but working through these problems may give her valuable experience in dealing with problems later in life. Some researchers have, in fact, found that early-maturing girls make better adjustments in adulthood (M. C. Jones & Mussen, 1958; N. Livson & Peskin, 1980).

Effects of early or late maturation are most likely to be negative when adolescents are very different from their peers—either by being much more or much less developed—and when they do not see the changes as advantageous (Simmons, Blyth, & McKinney, 1983).

It is hard to generalize about the psychological effects of timing of puberty, because they depend—at least in part—on how the adolescent and the people in his or her world interpret this event. Adults need to be sensitive to the potential impact of these changes so that they can help young people experience these years as positively as possible.

## Reactions to Menarche and Menstruation

Menarche is more than a physical event; it is "a concrete symbol of a shift from girl to woman" (Ruble & Brooks-Gunn, 1982, p. 1557). Girls who have begun to menstruate seem more conscious of their femaleness than girls of the same age who have not yet reached menarche. They are more interested in boy-girl relations and in adorning their bodies, and when they draw female figures, they show more explicit breasts. They also seem more mature in certain personality characteristics (Grief & Ulman, 1982).

Unfortunately, in the past, the negative side of menarche—the sometimes unexpected discomfort and embarrassment that may accompany it—has been emphasized. Cultural taboos have reinforced negative attitudes and have prevented the development of rituals to welcome young girls to womanhood (Grief & Ulman, 1982). One team of researchers concluded that our culture treats menarche not as a rite of passage (as in Box 10-1) but as a hygienic crisis, arousing girls' anxieties about staying clean and sweet-smelling but not instilling pride in their womanliness (Whisnant & Zegans, 1975).

Today, although many girls have mixed feelings about menarche and menstruation, most take these events in stride. The better prepared a girl is for menarche, the more positive her feelings and the less her distress (Koff, Rierdan, & Sheingold, 1982; Ruble & Brooks-Gunn, 1982). Unfortunately, though, some girls are uninformed or, worse yet, misinformed; as a result, they have unhappy memories of first menstruation (Rierdan, Koff, & Flaherty, 1986). Those whose menarche comes early are most likely to find it disruptive (Ruble & Brooks-Gunn, 1982)—possibly because they are less prepared or because they simply feel out of step with their friends.

How can menstruation be a more positive experience? Young girls need good information, not too technical and not too impersonal. They need to be told about the body parts and processes and what they can expect. They need to realize that menstruation is a special, universal female experience, different from injury or disease.

Parents should bring up the subject as soon as a girl's breasts and pubic hair begin to develop. They should reassure her that menstruation is normal and that she will be able to continue with all her usual activities, like sports, swimming, and bathing. They should encourage her to ask questions, and all family members, including fathers and brothers, should maintain an open, matter-of-fact attitude. Celebrating menarche with a family ritual can underline the positive meaning of this event in a girl's life.

### Feelings about Physical Appearance

Most young teenagers are more concerned about their looks than about any other aspect of themselves, and many do not like what they see in the mirror (Siegel, 1982). Boys want to be tall, broad-shouldered, and athletic; girls want to be pretty, slim but shapely, with nice hair and skin (Tobin-Richards, Boxer, & Petersen, 1983). Anything that makes boys think that they look feminine or girls think that they look masculine makes them miserable. Teenagers of both sexes worry about their weight, their complexion, and their facial features.

Girls tend to be unhappier about their looks than boys of the same age, no doubt because our culture places greater emphasis on women's physical attributes. When adolescents are asked what they like least about their bodies, boys often say "nothing," while girls complain mostly about their legs and hips (Tobin-Richards et al., 1983).

Adolescent girls are more prone to depression than

Most teenagers are more concerned about their physical appearance than about any other aspect of themselves, and many are dissatisfied with what they see in the mirror—especially if they are maturing much sooner or later than most of their friends.

boys, mainly because of worries about their appearance. They feel "ugly"; consider themselves too fat, too short, or too tall; or hate their hair or their complexion. Before puberty, rates for depression are the same in boys and girls; but at about age 12 girls start to have higher rates, and by age 14 girls' rates are twice as high as boys' (Lewinsohn, in Goleman, 1990b; Rierdan, Koff, & Stubbs, 1988, 1989).

Adults often dismiss adolescents' preoccupation with their looks. But in a society in which personality is often judged by appearance (Dion, Berscheid, & Walster, 1972), self-image can have long-lasting effects on young people's feelings about themselves. Adults who thought they were attractive during their teenage years have higher self-esteem and are happier than those who did not. Not until the mid-forties do the differences in self-esteem and happiness disappear (Berscheid, Walster, & Bohrnstedt, 1973).

# HEALTH CONCERNS OF ADOLESCENCE

Illness is rare among adolescents, who have low rates of disability and chronic disease. The health problems they do have are often preventable, stemming as they do from personality, poverty, and lifestyle factors. Adolescents' increasing tendency to take risks is reflected in their high rates of death from accidents, homicide, and suicide. Teenagers' concerns about their health tend to revolve around stress and nervousness (R. Blum, 1987). But adults' concerns about teenagers' health focus on their high rates of sexually transmitted diseases, drug abuse, and pregnancy (Millstein, 1989).

In Chapter 11 we examine teenage pregnancy, and in Chapter 18 we discuss the growing rates of suicide among adolescents. In this chapter we deal with such major health problems as eating disorders, drug abuse, and sexually transmitted diseases.

The health status of adolescents is expected to get worse over the next few decades, largely because more young people will be living in poverty, a distinctly unhealthy condition. Adolescents from poor families are 3 times more likely than adolescents from families above the poverty line to be in poor health or only fair health, and 47 percent more likely to suffer from disabling chronic illnesses (Newacheck, 1989). These teenagers need access to medical care; research indicates that they will use it. In one study, teenagers with Medicaid coverage went to doctors at rates similar to teenagers from more affluent families; those without such coverage sought less care (Newacheck, 1989).

## NUTRITION AND EATING DISORDERS

### Nutritional Needs

The adolescent growth spurt is accompanied by an eating spurt, especially among boys. Since boys grow more during adolescence, they need more calories than girls. On the average, a girl needs about 2200 calories per day, and a boy needs about 2800. Protein is important to sustain growth, and teenagers should avoid eating large amounts of "junk foods" like french fries, soft drinks, ice cream, fatty meats, and snack chips and dips.

The most common mineral deficiencies of adolescents are of calcium, iron, and zinc. The need for calcium, which supports bone growth, is best met by drinking enough milk. Girls are especially prone to calcium deficiency, a problem that may haunt them later in the form of osteoporosis (thinning of the bones), which afflicts 1 in 4 postmenopausal women (see Chapter 14). Teenagers need a steady source of iron-rich foods like iron-fortified breads, dried fruits, and leafy green vege-

tables. Iron-deficiency anemia is common among American adolescents, because their diet tends to be iron-poor. Foods containing zinc—like meats, eggs, seafood, and whole-grain cereal products—are also important, since even a mild zinc deficiency can delay sexual maturity (E. R. Williams & Caliendo, 1984).

Many adolescents put on weight, and some—especially girls—react by embarking on a lifelong struggle to reduce for the sake of health and beauty. Some are fighting real obesity. But in recent years, two eating problems—*anorexia* and *bulimia*—have become increasingly common. Both reflect our society's stringent standards of female beauty, exalting slenderness above all else, and individual pathologies of people who try to meet those standards through bizarre eating patterns.

### Obesity

*Obesity,* overweight involving a skinfold measurement in the 85th percentile, is the most common eating disorder in the United States, affecting some 15 percent of adolescents. Obese teenagers tend to become obese adults, subject to a variety of health risks (Maloney & Klykylo, 1983). Even in adolescence, obesity is a health problem, associated with degenerative disorders of the circulatory system and an increased likelihood of heart disease and other health problems.

It is worrisome, therefore, that obesity has been on the rise among adolescents—there has been a 39 percent increase in prevalence between 1963 and 1980, along with a 64 percent increase in superobesity (skinfold measurement in the 95th percentile) (Gortmaker, Dietz, Sobol, & Wehler, 1987). (See Figure 10-1.)

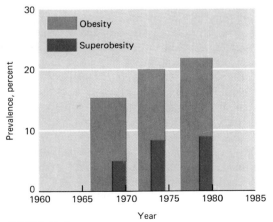

**FIGURE 10-1**
Estimated trends in obesity and superobesity in adolescents 12 to 17 years old in the United States. Even at these early ages, obesity is associated with a number of health problems. (*Source*: Adapted from Gortmaker, Dietz, Sobol, & Wehler, 1987.)

Obesity results when people consume more calories than they expend. Obese adolescents—and adults—are widely regarded as having too little "willpower," but this is an oversimplification. Risk factors having nothing to do with willpower seem to make some people likely to become overweight. These factors include genetic regulation of metabolism (obesity often runs in families, as we noted in Chapter 2); developmental history (inability to recognize body clues about hunger and when it should be satisfied, or the development of an abnormally large number of fat cells during childhood); rates of physical activity; emotional stress; and brain damage.

No matter what the cause, however, obese people can lose weight. Programs using behavior modification to help adolescents make changes in diet and exercise have had some success in taking off pounds.

Sometimes, however, a determination *not* to become obese can result in even graver problems than obesity itself.

### Anorexia Nervosa and Bulimia Nervosa

#### *Anorexia*

Someone suggests to Susie, 14, that she could stand to lose a few pounds. She loses them—and then continues to diet obsessively, refusing to eat, until she has lost at least 15 to 25 percent of her original body weight. Meanwhile, Susie stops menstruating, thick soft hair spreads over her body, and she becomes intensely overactive.

This is a typical scenario for ***anorexia nervosa,*** or self-starvation, an eating disorder seen mostly in young white women (*Diagnostic and Statistical Manual of Mental Disorders,* 3d ed., rev., DSM-III-R, 1987). The disorder may affect people of both sexes from age 8 to the thirties or even older; but it is most likely to occur in a bright, well-behaved, appealing female between puberty and the early twenties, from a stable, well-educated, well-off family. It is estimated to affect from 0.5 to 1 percent of 12- to 18-year-old girls; only about 6 percent of patients are adolescent boys (DSM-III-R, 1987), although the number of males affected is increasing. From 2 to 8 percent of people with anorexia eventually die of starvation (D. B. Herzog, Keller, & Lavori, 1988).

Typically, Susie is preoccupied with food—cooking it, talking about it, and urging others to eat—but she eats very little herself. She has a distorted view of herself: she literally cannot see how shockingly thin she is. She is a good student, described by her parents as a "model" child; but she is also withdrawn, depressed, and obsessed with repetitive, perfectionist behavior.

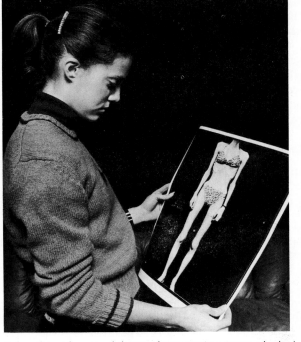

Before this girl received therapy for anorexia nervosa, she had a grossly distorted body image. When she looked like the girl in the picture she is holding, she could not see how shockingly thin she was.

The cause of anorexia is unknown. Many observers consider it a reaction to extreme societal pressure to be slender—a response to a standard of attractiveness in the media that is thinner for women than for men and the thinnest it has been since the 1920s, the time of the last epidemic of similar eating disorders (Silverstein, Perdue, Peterson, et al., 1986; Silverstein, Peterson, & Perdue, 1986).

Others see it as a psychological disturbance related to a fear of growing up, a fear of sexuality, or an extremely malfunctioning family. These girls' families often seem harmonious on the surface, but are actually overdependent and too involved in each other's lives and have difficulty dealing with conflict (Dove, undated). Some people with anorexia seem to feel that controlling their weight is the only way to control any part of their lives.

Depressive symptoms are often a part of the disorder. A Canadian study that followed anorexic patients (some of whom also had bulimia, which we discuss below) between 5 and 14 years after treatment found that they were likely to suffer from depression or anxiety disorders later in life (Toner, Garfinkel, & Garner, 1986).

Still others suggest that anorexia may be a physical disorder caused by a deficiency of a crucial chemical in the brain or by a disturbance of the hypothalamus. The syndrome is probably due to a combination of factors.

Early warning signs of anorexia include a dieter's lowering weight goals after reaching an initial desired weight, determined dieting in isolation, dissatisfaction even after losing weight, and interruption of regular menstruation. As soon as symptoms like these appear, treatment should be sought.

### Bulimia

An eating disorder closely related to anorexia also affects mostly adolescent girls and young women. In **bulimia nervosa,** a person regularly (at least twice a week) goes on huge eating binges (consuming up to 5000 calories in a single sitting, nearly always in secret) and then purges by self-induced vomiting, strict dieting or fasting, vigorous exercise, or use of laxatives or diuretics (DSM-III-R, 1987). People with bulimia are obsessed with their weight and body shape. They do not become abnormally thin, but they become overwhelmed with shame, self-contempt, and depression over their abnormal eating habits. They also suffer extensive tooth decay (caused by repeated vomiting of stomach acid), gastric irritation, skin problems, and loss of hair. There is some overlap between anorexia and bulimia; some victims of anorexia have bulimic episodes, and some people with bulimia lose weight. But the two are separate disorders.

The cause of bulimia is also unknown. The two major theories are that it stems from an electrophysiologic disturbance in the brain (as evidenced by a high number of abnormalities in brain-wave tracings of bulimic patients) and that it results from a depressive disorder (McDaniel, 1986). Another theory provides a psychoanalytic explanation for bulimia: that these people try to meet with food their hunger for the love and attention that they did not receive from their parents. There is some basis for this explanation: bulimic patients in one study reported that they felt abused, neglected, and deprived of nurturing from their parents (Humphrey, 1986).

### Treatment for anorexia and bulimia

The immediate goal of treatment for anorexia is to get patients to eat, to gain weight—and to live. They are likely to be admitted to a hospital, where they may be given 24-hour nursing, drugs to encourage eating and inhibit vomiting, and behavior therapy, which rewards eating by granting such privileges as getting out of bed and leaving the room. People with bulimia also need medical treatment to stabilize their health.

Both anorexia and bulimia are also treated by other therapies, which help patients gain insight into their feelings. Since both anorexic and bulimic patients are at risk of depression, and bulimics are at risk of suicide, the discovery that antidepressant drugs can help is heartening (Hudson, Pope, & Jonas, 1983; McDaniel, 1986; Pope, Hudson, Jonas, & Yurgelun-Todd, 1983).

Treatment is generally more effective for patients whose illness began before age 18 and lasted less than 3 years before treatment (Russell, Szmukler, Dare, & Eisler, 1987). Patients with anorexia seem to need long-term support even after they have stopped starving themselves. Some 27 months after completion of treatment, most of the 63 females in one study had continued to gain weight, had resumed menstruating, and were functioning in school or at work. Still, they continued to have problems with body image. Even though they averaged 8 percent below ideal weight, most thought of themselves as being overweight and as having excessive appetites, and many felt depressed and lonely (Nussbaum, Shenker, Baird, & Saravay, 1985).

## USE AND ABUSE OF DRUGS

### Current Trends

Throughout recorded history, people have used drugs to relieve physical ills as well as to alleviate unhappiness and to give their lives a lift. Why, then, is the use of drugs so troubling today? Major causes for concern include the early age at which many people begin to abuse drugs and the prevalence of drug abuse among adolescents, many of whom begin taking drugs mainly out of curiosity or because of peer pressure.

Use of drugs among adolescents is less prevalent than it was at its peak during the 1960s. Surveys of high school students around the United States show an almost continuous decline in use of most drugs from 1979 to 1989 (University of Michigan News and Information Services, 1990). Although these surveys probably underestimate drug use—since they do not reach high school dropouts, who are thought to have higher rates—they do show a steady decline among students and recent graduates.

Still, many young people are using such drugs as alcohol, nicotine, marijuana, LSD, amphetamines, barbiturates, heroin, and cocaine; and many begin to use them in elementary school. The National Adolescent Student Health Survey (National Institute on Drug Abuse, NIDA, 1988) found that 77 percent of eighth-graders had tried alcohol, 51 percent had smoked tobacco, 21 percent had tried inhalants, and 15 percent

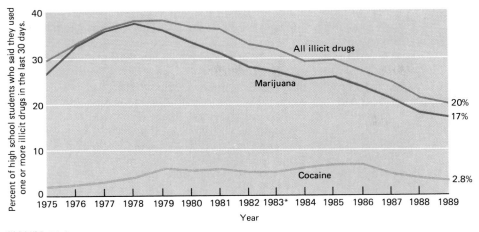

**FIGURE 10-2**
Adolescents' use of most drugs has declined since its peak during the 1960s, according to surveys of high school students. The figures are based on a confidential survey of high school students by the Institute of Social Research, University of Michigan; 16,700 responded in 1989. (Note: In 1983, nonprescription stimulants were excluded.) (*Sources*: University of Michigan News and Information Service, 1990; *New York Times*).

had used marijuana. Substantial numbers of these students had first used drugs by sixth grade. In a survey in 1989 of almost 17,000 high school seniors (University of Michigan News and Information Services, 1990), 1 in 5 students admitted using illicit drugs at least once in the previous month, and more than half said that they had tried an illicit drug at some time. (Both figures, however, were lower than in 1988.)

Use of cocaine in the previous 30 days continued the decline begun in 1987; it was down to 2.8 percent in 1989 (compared with 6.2 percent in 1986; see Figure 10-2). Use of "crack," a smokable form of cocaine, however, did *not* decline during the previous year: 3.1 percent of high school seniors had used it in the past year in 1989, the same proportion as in 1988. Use of crack in the previous 30 days was 1.4 percent in 1989.

While adolescent drug users extol drugs, their effects are harmful in adolescence and beyond. In one longitudinal study, more than 1000 high school sophomores and juniors were interviewed again at age 24 or 25. Those who had begun using a certain drug in their teens tended to continue to use it (Kandel, Davies, Karus, & Yamaguchi, 1986). Users of illicit drugs, including marijuana, were in poorer health than nonusers, had more unstable job and marital histories, and were more likely to have been delinquent. Cigarette smokers tended to be depressed and to have lung problems and breathing problems.

Alcohol, marijuana, and tobacco are the three drugs most popular with adolescents.

## Alcohol

Many of the same people who worry about the illegal use of marijuana by young people are brought up short when reminded that alcohol, too, is a potent, mind-altering drug, that it is illegal for most high school students and many college students (even though it is usually easy to get)—and that it is a much more serious problem nationwide. High school students seem to be drinking less than they used to, but college students and young adults have shown much slighter decreases. Although nearly all high school seniors in the 1989 University of Michigan survey reported drinking alcoholic beverages in the previous year, the percentage who had had a drink during the previous month dropped to 60 percent from the peak rate of 72 percent in 1980. Fewer students reported drinking heavily, too: 33 percent said that they had had five or more drinks in a row during the previous 2 weeks, down from a high of 41 percent in 1983.

Boys are more than twice as likely as girls to drink every day or to drink a large amount in one sitting, and young people who do not plan to go to college drink more than those who are college-bound. Most young people have their first drink before they get to high school (L. D. Johnston, O'Malley, & Bachman, 1988).

Most teenagers start to drink because it seems a grown-up thing to do, and they continue to do so for the same reasons adults do—to add a pleasant glow to social situations, to reduce anxiety, and to escape from

To prevent deaths among young Americans caused by alcohol-related motor vehicle accidents, educational campaigns now stress the importance of naming a "designated driver," one person in a group who will take the wheel and will agree not to drink on a specific night.

problems. Although the average teenager drinks moderately and has no problems with alcohol, some young people, like some adults, cannot handle this drug. In a survey sponsored by the National Institute on Alcohol Abuse and Alcoholism (NIAAA), more than 3 out of 10 young people were classified as "problem drinkers." These youngsters had been drunk at least four times in the previous year or had gotten into trouble through drinking at least twice in the previous year (Rachal et al., 1980). The dangers of driving after drinking are well known: the leading cause of death among 15- to 24-year-olds is alcohol-related vehicle accidents (American Academy of Pediatrics, AAP, Committee on Adolescence, 1987).

### Marijuana

Marijuana has been used all over the world for centuries, but only since the 1960s has it become popular among the American middle class. Despite a decline in use since 1979 (from 37 percent to 17 percent of teenagers who smoked it during the past 30 days, according to the University of Michigan survey), it is still by far the most widely used illicit drug in this country.

Adolescents start to smoke marijuana for many of the same reasons they begin to drink alcohol. They are curious, they want to do what their friends do, and they want to hurtle into adulthood. Another appeal of marijuana was its value as a symbol of rebellion against parents' values, but this attraction may be slipping, since today's teenagers are much more likely to have parents who smoked (or smoke) marijuana themselves.

Heavy use of marijuana can lead to heart and lung trouble, contribute to traffic accidents, and impede

memory and learning. It may also lessen motivation, interfere with schoolwork, and cause family problems.

Among 49 boys in one study (average age about 16), those who drank alcoholic beverages and also smoked marijuana more than twice a week were more likely than those who did not smoke marijuana to have poor eating habits and such health problems as respiratory infections and general fatigue (Farrow, Rees, & Worthington-Roberts, 1987).

### Tobacco

Sneaking a cigarette behind the barn was once a humorous staple of adolescent lore. But adults' amused indulgence toward young people's use of tobacco has turned to concern, with new awareness of health hazards. The publication in 1964 of the U.S. Surgeon General's report clearly linked smoking to lung cancer, heart disease, emphysema, and several other illnesses.

Many adolescents got the message. Teenagers express concern about the effects of smoking on health, and smokers feel the disapproval of their peers. Still, 29 percent of high school seniors smoke regularly, a rate that has not changed in the past decade (L. D. Johnston, Bachman, & O'Malley, in University of Michigan News and Information Services, 1990).

Today, more adolescent girls than boys smoke, reversing the former male-female ratio. As a result, one type of equality women have achieved is a death rate from lung cancer almost equal to that of men, although about 2½ times as many men develop the disease (American Cancer Society, 1985).

Smokers usually take their first puff between 10 and 12 years of age; they continue to smoke even though they do not enjoy it at first, and they become physically dependent on nicotine at about age 15. Young people are more likely to smoke if their friends and family do (McAlister, Perry, & Maccoby, 1979; National Institute of Child Health and Human Development, 1978). Since peer pressure has been effective in inducing people to smoke, its influence in the other direction may be the best preventive mechanism (L. D. Johnston, Bachman, & O'Malley, 1982; McAlister et al., 1979).

## SEXUALLY TRANSMITTED DISEASES (STDs)

### What Are STDs?

**Sexually transmitted diseases (STDs),** also referred to as *venereal diseases,* are diseases spread by sexual contact. Rates of STDs have soared for all ages since the 1960s, with particularly severe effects on adolescents. Of the 8 to 12 million cases of STDs each year

BOX 10–2   PRACTICALLY SPEAKING

# PROTECTING AGAINST SEXUALLY TRANSMITTED DISEASES

How can people who are sexually active protect themselves against sexually transmitted diseases (STDs)? The following guidelines (adapted from American Foundation for the Prevention of Venereal Disease, AFPVD, 1986; and Upjohn Company, 1984) minimize the possibility of acquiring an STD and maximize the chances of getting good treatment if one is acquired.

■ Have regular medical checkups. All sexually active persons should request tests specifically aimed at diagnosing STDs.
■ Know your partner. The more discriminating you are, the less likely you are to be exposed to STDs. Partners with whom you develop a relationship are more likely than partners you do not know well to inform you of any medical problems they have.
■ Avoid having sexual intercourse with many partners, promiscuous persons, and drug abusers.
■ Avoid sexual activity involving exchange of bodily fluids. Use a latex condom during intercourse.

■ Avoid anal intercourse.
■ Use a contraceptive foam, cream, or jelly; it will kill many germs and help to prevent certain STDs.
■ Learn the symptoms of STDs: vaginal or penile discharge; inflammation, itching, or pain in the genital or anal area; burning during urination; pain during intercourse; genital, body, or mouth sores, blisters, bumps, or rashes; pain in the lower abdomen or in the testicles; discharge from or itching of eyes; and fever or swollen glands.
■ Inspect your partner for any visible symptoms.
■ If you develop any symptoms yourself, get immediate medical attention.
■ Just before and just after sexual contact, wash genital and rectal areas with soap and water; males should urinate after washing.
■ Do not have any sexual contact if you suspect that you or your partner may be infected. Abstinence is the most reliable preventive measure.

■ Avoid exposing any cut or break in the skin to anyone else's blood (including menstrual blood), body fluids, or secretions.
■ Practice good hygiene routinely: frequent, thorough hand washing and daily fingernail brushing.
■ Make sure needles used for ear piercing, tattooing, acupuncture, or any kind of injection are either sterile or disposable. Never share a needle.
■ If you contract any STD, notify all recent sexual partners immediately so that they can obtain treatment and avoid passing the infection back to you, or on to someone else. Inform your doctor or dentist of your condition so that precautions can be taken to prevent transmission. Do not donate blood, plasma, sperm, body organs, or other body tissue.

For more information, contact American Foundation for the Prevention of Venereal Disease, AFPVD, 799 Broadway, Suite 638, New York, NY 10003.

in the United States, 3 out of 4 occur among 15- to 24-year-olds (U.S. Department of Health and Human Services, USDHHS, 1980).

The most prevalent STD is chlamydia, which causes infections of the urinary tract, the rectum, and cervix and can lead, in women, to pelvic inflammatory disease (PID), a serious abdominal infection. Other STDs, in order of incidence, are gonorrhea, genital (venereal) warts, herpes simplex, syphilis, and acquired immune deficiency syndrome (AIDS).

Genital herpes simplex is a chronic, recurring, often painful disease caused by a virus (a different strain of which also causes cold sores on the face). Although no hard figures on its incidence are available, it is highly contagious, with about 500,000 new cases reported every year (Goldsmith, 1989). The condition can be fatal to the newborn infant of a mother who has an outbreak of genital herpes at the time of delivery, and to a person with a deficiency of the immune system. It has been associated with increased incidence of cervical cancer. There is no cure, but the antiviral drug acyclovir can prevent active outbreaks.

AIDS is a failure of the body's immune system that leaves affected persons vulnerable to a variety of fatal diseases. The virus that causes it is transmitted through bodily fluids (mainly blood and semen) and stays in the body for life, even though the person carrying it may not show any signs of illness. Symptoms may not appear until from 6 months to 7 or more years after initial infection. Most victims in this country are drug abusers who share contaminated hypodermic needles, homosexual and bisexual men, people who have re-

**TABLE 10–4**
THE MOST COMMON SEXUALLY TRANSMITTED DISEASES

| Disease | New Cases Annually | Cases (%) Male/Female | Cause | Symptoms: Male | Symptoms: Female | Treatment | Consequences If Untreated |
|---|---|---|---|---|---|---|---|
| Chlamydia | 4 million | 60/40 | Bacterial infection | Pain during urination, discharge from penis. | Vaginal discharge, abdominal discomfort.† | Tetracycline or erythromycin. | Can cause pelvic inflammatory disease or eventual sterility. |
| Gonorrhea | 1–2 million | 60/40 | Bacterial infection | Discharge from penis, pain during urination.* | Discomfort when urinating, vaginal discharge, abnormal menses.† | Penicillin or other antibiotics. | Can cause pelvic inflammatory disease or eventual sterility; can also cause arthritis, dermatitis, and meningitis. |
| Genital warts | 750,000 | 40/60 | Viral infection | Painless growths that usually appear on penis, but may also appear on urethra or in rectal area.* | Small, painless growths on genitalia and anus; may also occur inside the vagina without external symptoms.* | Removal of warts. | May be associated with cervical cancer; in pregnancy, warts enlarge and may obstruct birth canal. |
| Herpes | 500,000 | 40/60 | Viral infection | Painful blisters anywhere on the genitalia, usually on the penis.* | Painful blisters on the genitalia, sometimes with fever and aching muscles; women with sores on cervix may be unaware of outbreaks.* | No known cure, but controlled with antiviral drug acyclovir. | Possible increased risk of cervical cancer. |

ceived transfusions of infected blood or blood products, and infants who have been infected in the womb or during birth.

Some 1.5 million Americans are estimated to be carriers; one-third of them may develop AIDS or a related condition (Blue Cross and Blue Shield Association, BCBSA, 1988). The disease has continued to spread since the early 1980s, when it first exploded as a public health concern. Education has reduced its spread in the homosexual community, blood screening has reduced the risk of contraction by transfusion, and current efforts focus on halting it among drug users. As of now, it is incurable.

Box 10-2 (page 321) lists steps that adolescents and adults can take to protect themselves from STDs. Table 10-4 (above) summarizes the most common STDs and their incidence, causes, most frequent symptoms, treatment, and consequences.

**TABLE 10–4**
(CONTINUED)

| Disease | New Cases Annually | Cases (%) Male/Female | Cause | Symptoms: Male | Symptoms: Female | Treatment | Consequences If Untreated |
|---|---|---|---|---|---|---|---|
| Syphilis | 100,000 | 70/30 | Bacterial infection | In first stage, reddish-brown sores on the mouth or genitalia or both, which may disappear, though the bacteria remain; in the second, more infectious stage, a widespread skin rash.* | Same as in men. | Penicillin or other antibiotics. | Paralysis, convulsions, brain damage, and sometimes death. |
| AIDS (acquired immune deficiency syndrome) | 80,000 (projected in 1992) | 93/7 | Viral infection | Extreme fatigue, fever, swollen lymph nodes, weight loss, diarrhea, night sweats, susceptibility to other diseases.* | Same as in men. | No known cure, but experimental drug AZT may extend life. | Death, usually due to other diseases, such as cancer. |

*May be asymptomatic.
†Often asymptomatic.
*Sources:* Adapted from Centers for Disease Control, 1986; Goldsmith, 1989; Morbidity and Mortality Weekly Report, MMWR, 1987.

## STDs and Adolescents

The reasons for the high rates of sexually transmitted diseases among young people are many: increased sexual activity, especially among teenage girls; use of oral contraceptives, which do not protect against STDs, instead of condoms, which often do; the complacent assumption that STDs can be cured easily; adolescents' belief that they and their sexual partners are immune to the diseases that affect *other* people; and young people's willingness to take risks because they want to have sexual intercourse more than they fear contracting a disease.

Young girls may be even more susceptible than mature women to STD-caused infections of the upper genital tract, which can lead to serious, even dangerous, complications. Teenagers are more likely than adults to put off getting medical care (often because they are worried that their parents will find out), they are less likely to follow through with treatment, they are often ashamed and embarrassed to alert their sexual partners when they contract an STD, and STDs are more likely to be misdiagnosed in teenagers than in adults (Centers for Disease Control, 1983). Most educational campaigns aimed at eradicating STDs focus on early diagnosis and treatment. Not until at least equal prominence is given to prevention and to the moral obligation to avoid passing them on will headway be made in stopping this epidemic.

# INTELLECTUAL DEVELOPMENT

The major element that puts adolescent thinking on a higher level than the thought processes of childhood is the concept "What if . . . ?" Adolescents can think in terms of what *might* be true, rather than just in terms of what they see in a concrete situation. Since they can imagine an infinite variety of possibilities, they are capable of hypothetical reasoning. They are able to think in broader terms about moral issues and about plans for their own future.

## ASPECTS OF INTELLECTUAL DEVELOPMENT IN ADOLESCENCE

### COGNITIVE DEVELOPMENT: PIAGET'S STAGE OF FORMAL OPERATIONS

The dominant explanation for the changes in the way teenagers think has been that of Jean Piaget, who saw them entering the highest level of cognitive development people are capable of. Piaget called this level, which is marked by the capacity for abstract thought, *formal operations.*

### Cognitive Maturity: The Nature of Formal Operations

The attainment of formal operations gives adolescents a new way to *manipulate*—or operate on—information. They are no longer limited to thinking about the concrete here and now, as they were in the previous cognitive stage, concrete operations. Now, they can deal with abstractions, test hypotheses, and see infinite possibilities.

This advance opens many new doors. It enables teenagers to analyze political and philosophical doctrines, and sometimes to construct their own elaborate theories, with an eye to reforming society. It even enables them to recognize the fact that in some situations there are no definite answers.

The ability to think abstractly has emotional ramifications, too. "Whereas earlier the adolescent could love his mother or hate a peer, now he can love freedom or hate exploitation. The adolescent has developed a new mode of life: the possible and the ideal captivate both mind and feeling" (Ginsburg & Opper, 1979, p. 201).

Much of childhood appears to be a struggle to come to grips with the world as it is. Now young people become aware of the world as it could be.

We can glimpse the nature of formal operations in different reactions to a story told by Peel (1967):

> Only brave pilots are allowed to fly over high mountains. A fighter pilot flying over the Alps collided with an aerial cable-way, and cut a main cable causing some cars to fall to the glacier below. Several people were killed.

A child still at the concrete operations level said, "I think that the pilot was not very good at flying. He would have been better off if he went on fighting." Only one answer springs to the child's mind—that the pilot was inept and not doing his real job, fighting.

By contrast, an adolescent who had reached the level of *formal operations* found a variety of possible explanations for what happened: "He was either not informed of the mountain railway on his route, or he was flying too low; also, his flying compass may have been affected by something before or after takeoff, thus setting him off course and causing the collision with the cable" (Peel, 1967). We see in the adolescent a new flexibility and complexity of thinking.

### Tracing Cognitive Development: The Pendulum Problem

Cognitive development can be traced from stage to stage by following the progress of a typical child in dealing with a classical Piagetian problem in formal reasoning, the pendulum problem. The child, Adam, is shown the pendulum—an object hanging from a string. He is then shown how he can change the length of the string, the weight of the object, the height from which the object is released, and the amount of force he can use to push the object. Then he is asked to figure out which factor or combination of factors determines how fast the pendulum swings.

When Adam first sees the pendulum, he is not yet 7 years old and is in the preoperational stage. At this age he is unable to formulate a plan for attacking the problem, but instead tries one thing after another in a hit-or-miss manner. First he puts a light weight on a long pendulum and pushes it, then he tries swinging a heavy weight on a short pendulum, and then he removes the weight entirely. His method is random, and he cannot understand or report what has actually happened. He is convinced that his pushes make the pendulum go faster, and even though this is not so, he reports it as observed fact.

Adam next encounters the pendulum at age 11, when he is in the stage of concrete operations. This time, he looks at some possible solutions, and he even hits upon a partially correct answer. But he fails to try

What determines how fast the pendulum swings: The length of the string? The weight of the object suspended from it? The height from which the object is released? The amount of force used to push the object? According to Piaget, an adolescent who has achieved the stage of formal operations can form a hypothesis and figure out a logical way to test it. Research suggests, however, that as many as half of teenagers and more than one-third of adults cannot solve this problem.

out every possible solution systematically. He varies the length of the string and the weight of the object, and he thinks that both length and weight affect the speed of the swing. But because he varied both factors at the same time, he cannot tell which one is critical or whether both are.

Not until Adam is confronted with the pendulum again when he is 15 years old does he go at the problem systematically. He now realizes that any one of the four factors, or some combination of them, might affect the speed of the swing. He carefully designs an experiment to test all the possible hypotheses by varying one factor at a time while holding the others constant. By doing this, he is able to determine that only one factor—the length of the string—determines how fast the pendulum swings.*

---

*This description of age-related differences in the approach to the pendulum problem has been adapted from Ginsburg & Opper (1979).

Adam's last solution to the pendulum problem shows that he has arrived at the stage of formal operations, a cognitive level usually attained at about age 12. Adam can now think in terms of what might be true and not just in terms of what he sees in a concrete situation. Since he can imagine a variety of possibilities, he is, for the first time, capable of *hypothetical-deductive* reasoning. Once he develops a hypothesis, he can construct a scientific experiment to test it. He considers all the possible relationships that might exist and goes through them one by one, to eliminate the false and arrive at the true.

This systematic reasoning process operates for all kinds of problems, from the simple mechanics of day-to-day living to the construction of elaborate political and philosophical theories. Adam, for example, can bring to bear what he has learned in the past to fix the family car or to plan for his future career. However, it is obvious that people who are capable of systematic formal thought do not always use it, even when a situation calls for it.

## What Brings Cognitive Maturity About?

Inner and outer changes in adolescents' lives combine to bring about cognitive maturation, according to Piaget. The brain has matured and the social environment is widening, offering more opportunities for experimentation.

Interaction between the two kinds of changes is essential: even if young people are sufficiently developed neurologically to reach the stage of formal reasoning, they may never attain it if they have not been encouraged culturally and educationally. By the same token, children who are *guided* toward rational thinking may reach the stage of formal operations earlier than they would if they were left to discover the necessary processes on their own.

One-third to one-half of American adults never seem to attain the stage of formal operations at all (Kohlberg & Gilligan, 1971). In a cross-sectional study, 265 people were asked to solve the pendulum problem. Among 10- to 15-year-olds, 45 percent were successful; among 16- to 20-year-olds, 53 percent; among 21- to 30-year-olds, 65 percent; and among 45- to 50-year-olds, 57 percent.

This suggests that even by late adolescence or adulthood not everyone is capable of abstract thought, at least as measured by responses to the pendulum problem. Other research (Papalia, 1972) suggests that about half of teenagers fail to conserve volume, another measure of formal operations.

## Assessing Piaget's Theory

What do *knowing* and *thinking* mean? How do we establish the "highest reaches" of cognitive development? Measuring these things by a person's ability to solve problems (like the pendulum problem) or to conserve volume defines cognition in terms of mathematical and scientific thinking. This is a narrow perspective, which "conveys a view of the individual as living in a timeless world of abstract rules" (Gilligan, 1987, p. 67).

The Piagetian approach minimizes the importance of other aspects of intelligence, such as the ability to handle "real-life" problems and the wisdom that helps people cope with an often ambiguous world. Nor does it foster the learning of "nonscientific" subjects like history, languages, writing, and the arts. In fact, as more psychologists have defined cognition in Piagetian terms, more educators have emphasized scientific subjects and have seen a drop in interest in the humanities. Piaget's definition of cognitive maturity is important, but formal reasoning is not the only—or even the most prominent—aspect of mature thinking. (We will consider other aspects of mature thought further in later chapters.)

## ADOLESCENT EGOCENTRISM

Those totally egocentric beings whose interest extended not much farther than the nipple have developed, by adolescence, into people who can solve complex problems, analyze moral dilemmas, and envision ideal societies. Yet in some ways, adolescents' thought often remains immature. They tend to be extremely critical (especially of authority figures), argumentative, self-conscious, self-centered, indecisive, and apparently hypocritical—characteristics that still reflect some egocentrism.

The psychologist David Elkind (1984) has described several typical adolescent behaviors that indicate egocentric thinking; let's consider them one by one.

### Finding Fault with Authority Figures

In adolescence, young people have a new ability to imagine an ideal world. They realize that the people they once nearly worshiped fall far short of their ideal, and they feel compelled to say so—often. Parents who do not take this criticism personally but rather look at it as a necessary stage in teenagers' cognitive and social development will be able to answer such comments matter-of-factly (and with a touch of humor), indicating that nothing—and nobody (not even a teenager!)—is perfect.

Even when a parent's viewpoint is valid, an adolescent's egocentrism often leads to argumentativeness. Those people who once seemed so perfect—the teenager's parents—are now objects of criticism.

### Argumentativeness

Adolescents want to practice their new ability to see the many nuances in an issue. If adults encourage and take part in arguments about principles while carefully avoiding discussion of personality, they can help young people stretch their reasoning ability without getting embroiled in family feuding.

### Self-Consciousness

Hearing his parents whispering, Dale "knows" that they are talking about him; and when Mesha passes some boys laughing raucously, she "knows" that they are ridiculing her. The extreme self-consciousness of young adolescents can be explained by the concept of the ***imaginary audience:*** an observer who exists only in their own minds and who is as concerned with their thoughts and behaviors as they are themselves.

Adolescents can put themselves into the mind of someone else—they can think about someone else's thinking. Since they have trouble distinguishing what is interesting to them from what is interesting to someone else, however, they assume that everyone else is thinking about the same thing they are thinking about—themselves.

The imaginary audience stays with us to a certain degree in adulthood. Who among us, for example, has not agonized over what to wear to an event—thinking that others present will actually care what clothes we have on—and then realized that most people were so busy thinking about the impression *they* were making that they hardly noticed our carefully chosen outfit at all! Because this kind of self-consciousness is especially agonizing in adolescence, however, Elkind emphasizes the importance of adults' avoiding any public criticism or ridicule of young teenagers.

### Self-Centeredness

Elkind uses the term **personal fable** for the conviction that we are special, that our experience is unique, and that we are not subject to the natural rules that govern the rest of the world. This egocentric belief accounts for a great deal of self-destructive behavior by young teenagers who think that they are magically protected from harm. Amanda thinks that *she* cannot get pregnant; Tony thinks that *he* cannot get killed on the highway; teenagers who experiment with drugs think that *they* cannot get hooked. "These things happen only to other people, not to me" is the unconscious assumption that helps explain much of adolescents' risk taking. Young people have to maintain a sense of being special while realizing that they are not exempt from the natural order of things.

### Indecisiveness

Teenagers have trouble making up their minds about even the simplest things because they are suddenly aware of the multiplicity of choices in virtually every aspect of life.

### Apparent Hypocrisy

Young adolescents often do not recognize the difference between expressing an ideal and working toward it. Thus Will marches against pollution while littering along the way, and Beth becomes aggressive while protesting for peace. Part of growing up involves the realization that "thinking does *not* make it so," that values have to be acted upon to bring about change.

The more adolescents talk about their personal theories and listen to those of other people, the sooner they arrive at a mature level of thinking (Looft, 1971). As their thought processes mature, they are better able to think about their own identities, to form adult relationships, and to determine how and where they fit into society.

## MORAL DEVELOPMENT: KOHLBERG'S LEVELS OF MORALITY

Obviously, a person cannot have a moral code based on ideals before developing a mind that is capable of imagining ideals. In Kohlberg's theory (introduced in Chapter 8), moral reasoning is a function of cognitive development. Moral development generally continues in adolescence, as the ability to think abstractly lets young people understand universal moral principles. Of course, advanced cognition does not *guarantee* advanced morality (intelligence and evil are too often linked), but—according to Kohlberg—it must *exist* for moral development to take place.

Adolescents apply moral reasoning to many kinds of problems, from lofty social issues to personal choices. Just as not all adolescents are at Piaget's stage of formal operations, not all of them are on the same rung of Kohlberg's moral ladder (see Table 8-4 in Chapter 8). In Kohlberg's view, it is the reasoning underlying the conclusion a person reaches in response to a moral problem (like "Heinz's dilemma"), not the conclusion itself, that indicates the person's stage of moral development. Adolescents may be found at each of Kohlberg's three levels.

### Level I: Preconventional Morality

Some delinquent adolescents (as well as some nondelinquents and some adults) are still at Kohlberg's level I. They think in terms of fear of punishment or in terms of the magnitude of an act (stage 1), or they think in terms of self-interest (stage 2)—concerns that are more characteristic of childhood thought. Preconventional adolescents might justify copying someone's answers on a test by saying that they were cheating "only a little bit" or that they needed a good grade to get into college; or they might refrain from cheating for fear of getting caught.

### Level II: Conventional Morality

Most adolescents—like most adults—are at Kohlberg's level II. They conform to social conventions, are motivated to support the status quo, and think in terms of doing the right thing in order to please others (stage 3) or to obey the law (stage 4). One person at this level might be tempted to "share" test answers to help a friend, while another at the same level would refuse because it is against the rules. Or we might imagine one teenager at level II smoking marijuana to follow the crowd, while another—also at at level II—refrains because it is against the law.

### Level III: Postconventional Morality

Even though many adolescents are capable of abstract thought, not until young adulthood are they likely to move into Kohlberg's level III, in which they develop their own moral principles (as we'll see in Chapter 12). Before people can reach this level of autonomous moral thought, they must recognize the fact that moral standards are relative. That is, they must come to understand that every society evolves its own definition of right and wrong and that the values of one culture may seem shocking to another culture. Many young people discover such cultural differences when they enter college, which explains why college students are most likely to score at the postconventional level on Kohlberg's tasks.

This stress on typical influences of the college experience also explains why Kohlberg's theory has been criticized as elitist. Another objection is its apparent advocacy of relativistic standards. Some critics maintain that the theory leads to moral chaos by implicitly encouraging individuals to develop their own systems of moral behavior rather than conform to an overall standard.

Research suggests that it is possible to help young people move to higher levels of moral reasoning. The most effective way to do this seems to be to give adolescents ample opportunities to talk about, interpret, and enact moral dilemmas, and to expose them to people at a level of moral thinking slightly higher than their own present level. Many young people think differently about moral issues when they meet people whose values, culture, and ethnic backgrounds are different from their own. This is a major argument for diversity in the school experience.

## HIGH SCHOOL

### HIGH SCHOOL TODAY

High school is the central organizing experience in most adolescents' lives. It offers opportunities to learn new information, master new skills, and sharpen old ones; to preview career choices; to take part in sports; and to get together with friends. It widens young people's intellectual and social horizons as it combines encounters with peers and with a variety of adults. It also provides an important life transition as young people move from the security of the simpler world of childhood to a large-scale organizational environment (see Box 10-3 on the opposite page).

The social, vocational, and athletic functions of high school are important, but the primary focus of high school continues to be on basic academic subjects. During the past two decades standardized test scores fell, most dramatically in vocabulary and reading. One analysis attributed this decline to "a decreased academic emphasis on the educational process" (Rock, Ekstrom, Goertz, Hilton, & Pollack, 1985). However, another reason seems to be that a broader base of students now go to high school. The National Commission on Excellence in Education (1983) found that the average high school or college *graduate* today is not as well educated as the average graduate of previous generations, when fewer people finished high school or college. However, the average *citizen* today is better educated than the average citizen of the past.

In response to concern over falling academic performance, the 1980s and 1990s have seen a greater emphasis on basic academic subjects. More students are studying foreign languages (Maeroff, 1984), but some observers still believe that American high school students do not study as much science and mathematics as they should (National Center for Education Statistics, NCES, 1984).

What makes a high school good? Research has pointed to such factors as an active, energetic principal; an orderly, unoppressive atmosphere; teachers who take part in making decisions; a principal and teachers whose expectations for students are high; an emphasis on academics (as opposed to athletics and other extracurricular activities); and frequent monitoring of students' performance (Linney & Seidman, 1989).

Today, more than three-fourths of Americans who are 25 years old and older (76.5 percent) have graduated from high school; some finished high school at the usual age, and others earned their diplomas later. Nearly 1 in 5 Americans over 25 (19.9 percent) have completed 4 years of college, setting a new record (U.S. Bureau of the Census, 1988). This increase stems from many causes—a general widening of educational opportunities, encouragement of minority-group students, and financial aid programs for students from low-income families.

### HOME INFLUENCES ON ACHIEVEMENT IN HIGH SCHOOL

Even though adolescents are more independent than elementary school children and are less likely to look to their parents for direct help with schoolwork, more subtle home influences still affect how well they do in school.

---

## THE TRANSITION TO JUNIOR HIGH OR HIGH SCHOOL

At the end of sixth grade, most American children leave the familiar surroundings of a small elementary school to enter a junior high school with many more students and a more impersonal setting in which teachers, classrooms, and classmates change constantly throughout the day. In 3 more years they move again, to an even larger high school. This typical sequence is known as the *6-3-3 pattern*. A few children follow a different pattern—the *8-4 pattern*—staying in elementary school through eighth grade and then going directly to high school.

The second pattern may well be better, since a number of stresses are associated with the more typical sequence. One 5-year longitudinal study followed 594 white students in the Milwaukee public schools from sixth through tenth grades, comparing students in the 6-3-3 pattern with those in the 8-4 pattern (Blyth, Simmons, & Carlton-Ford, 1983). Researchers looked at students' self-esteem, social adjustment (based on extracurricular activity), academic progress (by grade-point average—GPA—and performance on achievement tests), and perception of the "anonymity" of their schools (how much they felt other people knew them).

Students who went to junior high school in seventh grade had more problems than those who did not leave elementary school until ninth grade. Girls were especially vulnerable. Both boys and girls in the 6-3-3 pattern had a decrease in grade-point averages, took less part in extracurricular activities, and saw their schools as more anonymous. Furthermore, the girls' self-esteem dropped, an effect that persisted into tenth grade.

Why do girls have more problems? One clue emerges from a study that found that the more life changes are taking place in a student's life, the more likely both GPA and extracurricular participation are to decrease for both sexes and the more likely girls' self-esteem is to drop (Simmons, Burgeson, Carlton-Ford, & Blyth, 1987).

Girls usually enter puberty sooner than boys and begin to date earlier, making it more likely that they will experience "life-change overload." Furthermore, there is more emphasis on girls' looks and popularity, and they may miss the security of being with old friends. Other research, too, has shown that girls react more negatively than boys to stress in adolescence, unlike childhood, when males are more vulnerable.

Total comfort and complete stability, of course, are not only impossible to achieve at any age but also undesirable. Throughout life, we grow and develop as we learn to cope with challenges. We do this best, however, if we can deal with one change at a time. How, then, can teachers, parents, and other adults offer a sense of security and nurturance to young adolescents making a major transition, like that to a new school setting?

---

### Parents' Interest

A survey of more than 30,000 high school seniors in more than 1000 schools (NCES, 1985) showed that the students with the best grades tend to be those whose parents are most involved in their children's lives (see Table 10-5 on page 330). This is particularly true of fathers, whose involvement is more variable than that of mothers: the less involved a father is, the worse his children fare, in general. In this survey, 85 percent of the A students but only 64 percent of the D students had fathers who kept close track of their progress in school.

These correlational findings do not prove that parents' involvement improves students' grades. If there is a cause-and-effect relationship, it may, in fact, work the other way: that is, children who do well in school may spur their parents' interest in their activities. But it seems more likely that parents' involvement and concern stimulate their children to do better in school.

The parents of students who do the best are interested in more than homework and grades. They make time to talk to their children, to know what their children are doing, and to be available. They go to PTA meetings. They take the children seriously both in and out of school, and the children reward that interest. Three-fourths of the youngsters with top grades in the NCES (1985) study had parents who talked with them almost every day, compared with only 45 percent of the D students.

**TABLE 10–5**
PARENTS' INVOLVEMENT AND HIGH SCHOOL STUDENTS' GRADES

| Survey Item | Self-Reported Grades | | | |
| --- | --- | --- | --- | --- |
| | Mostly A's | Mostly B's | Mostly C's | Mostly D's |
| Mother keeps close track of how well child does in school. | 92% | 89% | 84% | 80% |
| Father keeps close track of how well child does in school. | 85% | 79% | 69% | 64% |
| Parents almost always know child's whereabouts. | 88% | 81% | 72% | 61% |
| Child talks with mother or father almost every day. | 75% | 67% | 59% | 45% |
| Parents attend PTA meetings at least once in a while. | 25% | 22% | 20% | 15% |
| Child lives in household with both parents. | 80% | 71% | 64% | 60% |

*Note:* This table, based on a survey of more than 30,000 high school seniors, shows the percentage of students with various grade averages who gave positive answers to each survey item. In each instance, the higher the grades were, the more likely the parents were to be involved with the child.
*Source:* National Center for Education Statistics, NCES, 1985.

## Parenting Styles

In high school, as in preschool, children who are raised by authoritative parents (see Chapter 7) show more competence. More than 7000 high school students in the San Francisco Bay area filled out questionnaires showing how they perceived their parents' attitudes and behaviors (Dornbusch, Ritter, Leiderman, Roberts, & Fraleigh, 1987), and the researchers compared their grades with their descriptions of their parents. The survey identified three styles of parenting, as follows:

1 *Authoritative parents* tell adolescents to look at both sides of issues, admit that children sometimes know more than parents, talk about politics, and welcome teenagers' participation in family decisions. Students receive praise and freedom if they get good grades; poor grades bring encouragement to try harder, offers of help, and loss of freedom.
2 *Authoritarian parents* tell adolescents not to argue with or question adults, and tell them they will "know better when they are grown up." Good grades bring admonitions to do even better, and poor grades upset parents, who then punish by reducing allowances or "grounding."

3 *Permissive parents* do not care about grades, make no rules about watching television, do not attend school programs, and neither help with nor check their children's homework. (The term *permissive* can apply to parents who are neglectful and uncaring, or to those who are caring and concerned but believe that children should be responsible for their own lives.)

A strong relationship showed up between authoritative parenting and high achievement in school. Students who got low grades were more likely to have authoritarian or permissive parents or parents who waffled between styles. Inconsistency was associated with the lowest grades, possibly because children who do not know what to expect from their parents become anxious and less able to concentrate on their work. These relationships were stronger in white families than in Hispanic, African American, or Asian families, all of which tended to be more authoritarian. The study does not explain the success of Asian students in American schools. It does, though, suggest a possible reason for the lower school achievement of the children of single parents, who tend to be more permissive. The style of parenting seems to make the difference, not the single-parent status itself.

## Socioeconomic Status

So many educators consider socioeconomic status so important to school achievement that the association between the two is often taken for granted. However, a statistical analysis of 101 studies (K. R. White, 1982) found that socioeconomic status (traditionally defined by income, occupation, and education) is only weakly correlated with academic achievement. The correlation decreases as students get older, partly because schools provide enriching experiences and partly because many students have dropped out—and dropping out is more common among both low achievers and students from low-income homes.

The major influence on achievement is a student's home atmosphere—how much reading matter is available, how the parents feel about education, what they want for their children, what they do for and with their children, how and how much they talk to their children, and how stable the family is. Both rich and poor families are able to create a home atmosphere that fosters learning. "Even though family background does have a strong relationship to achievement, it may be *how* parents rear their children . . . and not the parents' occupation, income, or education that really makes the difference" (K. R. White, 1982, p. 471).

## DROPPING OUT OF HIGH SCHOOL

Students who leave school before receiving a diploma make a crucial decision that reduces their opportunities in the future. Dropping out of high school does not guarantee poverty, but dropouts do have to scramble harder to start a career—if they ever have one. Many employers require a high school diploma, and many jobs require skills that are based on a solid education.

### Who Drops Out?

More than half a million students (about 15 percent) who were sophomores in 1980 left high school before graduation and had not returned by 1982 (NCES, 1987). The national high school graduation rate declined from 71.7 percent in 1987 to 71.1 percent in 1988, and test scores dropped as well ("Students Learning," 1990). Almost one-half of the dropouts left in the eleventh grade, almost one-third in the senior year, and about one-fourth in the tenth grade. Boys are more likely to drop out than girls.

Asian American students have the lowest dropout rate (4.8 percent), followed by (in increasing order) white students (12.2 percent), African American students (16.8 percent), Hispanic students (18.7 percent),

and Native American students (22.7 percent). When socioeconomic status is held constant, however, the large difference among white, African American, and Hispanic young people narrows or even vanishes. In fact, at equal socioeconomic levels, black students' attainment is higher than white students' (NCES, 1987). Thus while socioeconomic status does not seem to affect performance while students are actually in school, it does make a difference in whether they stay there long enough to graduate.

### Why Do They Drop Out?

The reasons dropouts give for their decision are not surprising, although they do not tell the whole story. When asked 2 years later why they had dropped out, one group of males mentioned poor grades (36 percent), not liking school (25 percent), being expelled or suspended (13 percent), or having to support a family (26 percent). Girls attributed dropping out to marriage or plans to marry (31 percent), feeling that "school is not for me" (31 percent), poor grades (30 percent), pregnancy (23 percent), and a job (11 percent) (NCES, 1983.)*

It is hard to pin down the reasons for dropping out. More than half of the girls said that they left because of pregnancy or marriage—but they may have become pregnant or gotten married because they were not doing well or were not interested in school. The boys' explanations tell us just as little. Some researchers have attributed dropping out to lack of motivation and low self-esteem, minimal parental encouragement of education, teachers' low expectations for students, and disciplinary problems at home and at school (Rule, 1981).

The students who are most likely to drop out of school tend to share some characteristics. Those whose parents are poorly educated and in low-level jobs and who are in large single-parent families are 3 to 5 times more likely to drop out than children in more privileged circumstances (NCES, 1987). Other factors associated with dropping out include having repeated a grade in elementary school, working more than 15 hours a week while in high school, being married, having a child, and such signs of antisocial behavior as suspension, probation, or trouble with the law (NCES, 1987).

---

*The figures total more than 100 percent because some respondents gave more than one reason for dropping out.

## What Happens to Dropouts?

Dropouts have trouble getting jobs; the work they do get is in low-level, poor-paying occupations; and they are more likely to lose their jobs. In one national study, 27 percent of male high school dropouts and 31 percent of female high school dropouts were looking for work; 32 percent of the women were not looking for work because they were full-time homemakers. Of those who were working, only about 14 percent of the men and 3 percent of the women had jobs that required technical skills. Typical jobs were waiting on tables, manual labor, factory work, clerking in stores, baby-sitting, clerical work, and farm work. More than half the dropouts regretted leaving school very soon after they had done so, and only a small percentage were taking part in educational programs (NCES, 1987).

## How Can Dropping Out Be Prevented?

Society suffers, too, when many young people do not finish school. Dropouts are more likely to end up on welfare, to be unemployed, and to become involved with drugs, crime, and delinquency. In addition, the loss of taxable income burdens the public treasury (NCES, 1987). Both public and private organizations have developed a variety of programs aimed at encouraging young people to stay in school.

One successful federally funded program, Upward Bound, was established in 1964 and by 1988 had seen 80 percent of its graduates go on to 4-year colleges. Students from low-income families whose parents and siblings did not go to college are selected on the basis of school records, teachers' recommendations, a personal interview, and an assessment of applicants' and parents' commitment to the program. The program stresses high expectations; has a rigorous curriculum; and offers tutoring, peer counseling, and counseling on drug abuse, self-esteem, study skills, preparing for the Scholastic Aptitude Tests (SATs), applying to colleges, and planning careers (Wells, 1988).

Programs like Upward Bound show that it is possible to prevent dropping out. With commitment by government, educators, and parents, millions of young people can be helped to have a brighter future.

# DEVELOPING A CAREER

"Is there life after high school? Where will this education lead to? What kind of work will I do? Do I need still more education?" These are the questions that adolescents ask themselves with more urgency as their high school years come to an end.

## STAGES IN VOCATIONAL PLANNING

At age 6, Sally's daughter Nancy wanted to be a ballerina. Then a ninth-grade honors biology class awakened her interest in science. In high school, she considered studying anthropology or sociology (not knowing exactly what either field was); and later, in college, she ended up majoring in environmental studies. An internship at a natural history museum (as part of her college requirements) inspired her to study for a doctorate in biology; and after she had earned her Ph.D., she became the curator of natural sciences at a different museum.

Nancy's progression of goals was typical, following three classic stages in career planning: (1) the fantasy period, (2) the tentative period, and (3) the realistic period (Ginzberg et al., 1951). During the *fantasy* period, in the elementary school years, children's career choices are active and exciting rather than realistic, and their decisions are emotional rather than practical. The *tentative* period, which comes at puberty, ushers in a somewhat more realistic effort by youngsters to match interests with abilities and values. By the end of high school, students enter the *realistic* period and can plan for the appropriate education to meet their career requirements.

Many young people, however, are still not realistic in late adolescence. In one study, for instance, more than 6000 high school seniors in Texas were asked to name their top three career choices and to report on their interests and their educational plans. At a time when they had to make crucial choices about education and work, these students showed very limited knowledge about occupations. Not surprisingly, they tended to know more about their first career choice and increasingly less about the next two choices. But even of those who felt that they had a good understanding of their first career choice, only about half were planning to get the right amount of education. Some seemed bent on schooling that would leave them overeducated for their chosen careers, and others were not planning for enough training. Furthermore, most of the students did not seem to be making a good match between their career choices and their own interests (Grotevant & Durrett, 1980).

## INFLUENCES ON VOCATIONAL PLANNING

How do adolescents make career choices? Many factors enter in, including individual ability and personality; education; socioeconomic, racial, or ethnic background; societal values; and the accidents of particular life experiences.

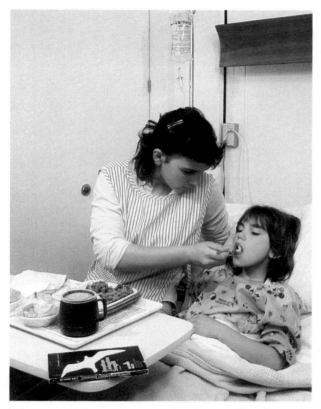

Volunteer work is one way to preview the rewards and frustrations of a particular career. If this teenage "candy-striper" finds hospital work rewarding, she may pursue a career as a doctor or a nurse.

## Part-Time Work

Many adults would give a quick, unqualified "yes" to the question "Does work help adolescents develop?" The traditional American ethic contends that paid work teaches young people to handle money responsibly, helps them develop good work habits, and guides them in choosing a career.

Research has found, however, that teenagers who work are no more independent in making financial decisions than their classmates who do not hold jobs (Greenberger & Steinberg, 1986). Furthermore, most students who work part time during high school do not learn skills that will be useful later in life (Hamilton & Crouter, 1980), and they are not likely to earn any more money afterward than they would if they had not held jobs during high school (Greenberger & Steinberg, 1986).

Moreover, work seems to undermine performance in school, especially for teenagers who work more than 15 or 20 hours per week. Grades, involvement in school, and attendance decline. In fact, working more than 15 hours a week is related to dropping out of school (NCES, 1987). Thus, the experience gained by working is offset by the reduced school experience.

And there are other hidden costs. Some teenagers spend their earnings on alcohol or drugs, develop cynical attitudes toward work, and cheat or steal from their employers. Teenagers who work tend to spend less time with their families and to feel less close to them. Furthermore, they have little contact with adults on the job, and they are usually placed in gender-stereotyped jobs (Greenberger & Steinberg, 1986).

Some of the undesirable tendencies may be caused not by working itself but by the factors that motivate some teenagers to take jobs. Some teenagers may want to work because they are uninterested in school, are alienated from their families, and want money to buy drugs and liquor. Working does not help such young people manage their lives better.

Some teenagers, of course, do learn from work how to manage both money and time, how to find a job, and how to get along with a variety of people. Some discover how demanding and difficult the world of work is and how unprepared they are for it—and are therefore motivated to continue their education. In general, though, work experience during school is not as valuable as a solid academic foundation

Two influences on vocational planning that *are* important are parents and gender. Let's consider each of these.

## Parents

Parents' encouragement and financial support influence their children's aspirations and achievement. If parents do not encourage children to pursue higher education and do not help them financially, it is much harder for the children.

Parental encouragement is a better predictor of high ambition than social class. When 2622 sixth-, eighth-, tenth-, and twelfth-grade students—black and white, from all social strata—were asked to describe their own expectations for their education and their fathers' and mothers' expectations for them, more than half the students agreed with the perceived goals of each parent. A greater level of agreement existed between students and their mothers than between students and their fathers, probably because women have traditionally spent more time with children (T. E. Smith, 1981).

What about the parents' own careers? How weighty is their influence? Historically, men's occupations have influenced their sons' career choices, but not their daughters' (Conger & Petersen, 1984). Werts (1966, 1968) found that 43.6 percent of doctors' sons chose to enter medicine and that 27.7 percent of attorneys' sons chose to enter the law; a similar influence was shown by sons of physical and social scientists. Newer research shows that college-educated daughters of working mothers have higher career aspirations and achieve more in their careers than daughters of homemakers (L. Hoffman, 1979).

## Gender

A woman who entered engineering school at Ohio State University in 1945 was one of only six females in her class. Some 35 years later, women made up about 30 percent of the entering class (R. D. Feldman, 1982). Similar increases have been seen in medicine, law, and other former bastions of male prominence.

Although gender-typing in occupational choice has broken down to a great extent, it is still a factor. Some counselors still steer young people into gender-typed careers on the basis of females' supposed superiority in verbal abilities and males' supposed superiority in mathematics (Matlin, 1987).

However, there is little or no difference between boys and girls in either mathematical or verbal ability (J. S. Hyde, Fennema, & Lamon, 1990; J. Hyde & Linn, 1988). Recent analysis has found gender differences in verbal abilities so small as to be almost meaningless (J. Hyde & Linn, 1988). And research also refutes the common idea that males have more mathematical ability overall than females. As we pointed out in Chapter 7, females actually excel at computation, neither sex shows better understanding of mathematical concepts, and males' advantage in problem solving does not show up until high school. Furthermore, gender differences have decreased in recent years (J. S. Hyde et al., 1990).

Significant gender differences that favored mathematically gifted seventh- and eighth-grade students who took the mathematics portion of the Scholastic Aptitude Test (SAT) have received a great deal of notice (Benbow & Stanley, 1980, 1983). But these findings seem to apply only to gifted students, not the general population; and some researchers believe that the findings may reflect differences in socialization, attitudes, and experience with mathematics, or that differences in mathematical ability may be related to the spatial nature of many mathematical problems (Matlin, 1987). Another explanation for gender differences in high school is that more boys than girls drop out of school, thereby removing many low-scoring boys from high school samples. Furthermore, more girls than boys take the SAT, and the girls tend to be drawn from a wider socioeconomic background.

The fact that high school girls begin to perform more poorly than boys at mathematical problem solving tasks is troublesome, however. Such problem solving is critical for success in many occupations, and people with less developed mathematical skills are not likely to choose careers in such fields as engineering, chemistry, or physics. Furthermore, girls' lower scores on the mathematics portions of the SAT are a serious disadvantage in applying to college. The tests themselves need to be examined, not only for evidence of gender bias but also to determine whether they require skills that are not being taught well enough in high school (J. S. Hyde et al., 1990). However, the gender disparity in mathematics is not likely to diminish until educators consider remedial math teaching (which would probably help more girls) just as important as remedial reading programs (which reach higher proportions of boys).

Finally, it should be noted that studies published before 1973 showed larger gender differences than more recent research. The differences may have declined as a result of increased flexibility in gender roles. Or perhaps researchers are more likely now than they used to be to publish when they have found *no* significant gender differences. In any case, the small differences that still do show up have no real psychological or educational implications. There is no basis for steering boys and girls toward different careers. It does not matter whether most boys are better at mathematics or most girls are better at writing—it is how well a particular person solves mathematical problems or writes that will affect the individual's chances of success in a chosen field.

The choice of a career is closely tied in with a central personality issue during adolescence: the continuing effort to define the self, to discover and mold an identity. The question "Who shall I be?" is very close to "What shall I do?" If we choose a career that we feel is worth doing and one we can do well, we feel good about ourselves. On the contrary, if we feel that it wouldn't matter to anyone whether we did our work or not, or if we feel that we're not very good at it, the core of our emotional well-being can be threatened.

How adolescents' sense of identity develops will be discussed in Chapter 11, along with other personality issues.

## SUMMARY

### ADOLESCENCE: A DEVELOPMENTAL TRANSITION

■ Adolescence is a developmental transition between childhood and adulthood. It begins with puberty, a process that leads to sexual maturity, when a person is able to reproduce.

■ The end of adolescence is not clear-cut in western societies, since no single sign indicates that adulthood has been reached. In some nonwestern cultures, adulthood is regarded as beginning at puberty and is signified by puberty rites, which take a variety of forms.

### MATURATION IN ADOLESCENCE

■ A *secular trend* is a trend that can be observed over several generations. A secular trend toward earlier attainment of adult height and sexual maturity began about 100 years ago, probably because of improvements in living standards; it seems to have ended in the United States.

■ Dramatic physiological changes mark adolescence.

  1 Both sexes undergo an adolescent growth spurt: sharp growth in height, weight, and muscular and skeletal development.
  2 Primary sex characteristics are the characteristics directly related to reproduction, namely, the female and male reproductive organs. These enlarge and mature during puberty.
  3 The secondary sex characteristics include the breasts in females, the broadened shoulders in males, and the adult voices, skin, and growth of body hair characteristic of men and women.
  4 Menarche in females occurs at an average age of 12½ in the United States. Males experience sperm in their urine and nocturnal emissions.

■ An adolescent's rapid body changes and physical appearance affect self-concept and personality. The effect of early or late maturing is particularly pronounced during adolescence but generally disappears in adulthood.

■ Girls adjust better to menarche if they are prepared for it with accurate information.

### HEALTH CONCERNS IN ADOLESCENCE

■ Adolescents have low rates of disability and chronic disease. Their tendency to take risks is reflected in their high death rates from accidents, homicide, and suicide. Health problems such as obesity, anorexia nervosa, bulimia nervosa, drug abuse, and sexually transmitted diseases affect a sizable number of adolescents.

### ASPECTS OF INTELLECTUAL DEVELOPMENT IN ADOLESCENCE

■ Many adolescents attain Piaget's stage of formal operations, which is characterized by the ability to think abstactly.

  1 People in the stage of formal operations can engage in hypothetical-deductive reasoning. They can think in terms of possibilities, deal flexibly with problems, and test hypotheses.
  2 Since experience plays a more important part in the attainment of this cognitive stage than in that of previous Piagetian stages, not all people become capable of formal operations.

■ Although the adolescent is not egocentric in the sense that a younger child is, adolescents show egocentric tendencies. These include finding fault with authority figures, argumentativeness, self-consciousness, self-centeredness, indecisisiveness, and apparent hypocrisy.

■ Most adolescents are at Kohlberg's conventional level (stages 3 and 4) of moral development. However, some young people in adolescence are at the preconventional stage and some are at the postconventional stage.

### HIGH SCHOOL

■ With the achievement of virtually universal secondary education in the United States, high school is the central organizing exprience—intellectually and otherwise—in the lives of most adolescents.

■ Home atmosphere, parents' involvement, and family relationships appear to make a greater difference than socioeconomic status in how well adolescents do in school.

■ Although most adolescents graduate from high school, over half a million students who were sophomores in 1980 dropped out before graduating. It is hard to pin down the precise reason for dropping out. Programs are being developed to prevent it.

### DEVELOPING A CAREER

■ The search for identity is closely linked to vocational choice. Vocational choice is linked to a number of factors including whether or not the adolescent works part time. Part-time work appears to have little educational, social, or occupational benefit.

■ Parental attitudes and gender also influence educational and vocational aspirations and choices.

## KEY TERMS

adolescence (page 308)
puberty (308)
secular trend (311)
adolescent growth spurt (311)
primary sex characteristics (312)

secondary sex characteristics (312)
menarche (313)
obesity (316)
anorexia nervosa (317)
bulimia nervosa (318)

sexually transmitted diseases (STDs) (320)
formal operations (324)
imaginary audience (326)
personal fable (327)

## SUGGESTED READINGS

**Byrne, K. (1987).** *A parent's guide to anorexia and bulimia.* New York: Holt. In this sensible and reassuring book, the author, herself the mother of a recovering anorexic, discusses how to identify eating disorders, when to seek professional help, and what to expect from these professionals. She also offers suggestions on how to communicate with the eating-disordered member of the family.

**Elkind, D. (1984).** *All grown up and no place to go.* Reading, MA: Addison-Wesley. A thought-provoking book about the difficulties today of being a teenager and raising teenagers. Elkind argues that teenagers are unprepared for the adult challenges they are asked to face, and so they exhibit many problem behaviors. The chapter relating formal operational thinking abilities to behaviors such as self-centeredness, self-consciousness, and argumentativeness is outstanding.

**Freedman, S. G. (1990).** *Small victories: The real world of a teacher, her students, and their high school.* New York: Harper & Row. This account of a year in the life of a New York City teacher shows what an imaginative, dedicated person can bring to the lives of immigrant students and others who live and go to high school in a rundown inner-city neighborhood. The book also includes portraits of other faculty members as well as students. It leaves the reader with the sense that good teaching is a vocation, not a job.

**Greenberger, E., & Steinberg, L. (1986).** *When teenagers work.* New York: Basic Books. An absorbing and controversial analysis of research on the impact that working has on teenagers. The authors conclude that working during the teens entails a number of hidden costs that affect development negatively.

- How do different theories explain the development of personality in adolescence?
- How do adolescents search for their identity?
- How inevitable is "adolescent rebellion," and how are adolescents' attitudes and behavior influenced by parents and peers?
- What sexual practices and attitudes are current among adolescents?
- What are the causes and consequences of teenage pregnancy and juvenile delinquency?
- What are these years like for most adolescents?

A central question in the drama of adolescence is "Who am I?" The theme of these years—and a major theme for years to come—is the search for identity: what makes each person an individual unlike any other who has ever lived or will ever live. The question "Who am I?" begins to form in infancy, when babies first discover that they are separate from their mothers. Children begin to find answers as they learn the boundaries of self, shed much of their egocentric thinking, and size up their skills and values in the mirror of the peer group.

The question of selfhood crests in adolescence, when physical, cognitive, and social and emotional development also reach a peak. At the age of 15, for example, Meredith has the body of a woman. Now capable of adult sexual behavior and of advanced problem solving, she knows that she will soon be responsible for her own life. How will she choose to live it? What kind of work will she do? What decisions will she make about sexual relationships and other ties? What beliefs and values will she live by?

These choices are not easy, and they are often accompanied by emotional turmoil. Underlying teenagers' alternating high and low spirits are two major preoccupations—identity and intimacy. These years are not easy for parents, either. Adolescents who are trying their wings are often as erratic and unpredictable as birds taking their first flights from the nest. Chafing at the ties that bind them to an older generation, they often see mothers and fathers as inhibiting more than helpful. Yet while teenagers look to their peers as companions in the struggle for independence, they still turn to their parents for important guidance and emotional support.

In this chapter, we first examine some fundamental issues of personality development in adolescence from the perspectives of theory and research. We discuss relationships with peers and parents and how adolescents come to terms with their sexuality. Then we turn to two serious problems, teenage pregnancy and juvenile delinquency. Finally, we look at positive aspects of adolescence—what adolescence is like for most normal young people.

"Who am I?" is the major question of adolescence, as young people search for identity and ponder their life choices.

# UNDERSTANDING PERSONALITY DEVELOPMENT

## THEORETICAL PERSPECTIVES

What accounts for the emotional ups and downs of adolescence? Why do teenagers often come into conflict with adults? How do young people emerge from this period as unique, mature personalities? There are several important theories about the nature of adolescence.

### G. Stanley Hall: "Storm and Stress"

Hall, the first psychologist to formulate a theory of adolescence, proposed that the major physical changes that take place at this time cause major psychological changes (G. S. Hall, 1904/1916). He believed that young people's efforts to adjust to their changing bodies ushered in a period of *storm and stress.* Hall saw adolescence as a period of intense, fluctuating emotions, from which young people may emerge morally stronger. Although this view of adolescence as an invariably stormy period of life was widely accepted for many years, the dominant opinion today is that storm and stress are not inevitable for most adolescents.

### Margaret Mead: The Cultural Factor

Margaret Mead, an anthropologist who studied adolescence in the South Pacific islands of Samoa (1928) and New Guinea (1935), emphasized the importance of cultural factors in the transitions of adolescence. In Samoa, for example, Mead observed no "storm and stress" but rather a serene, gradual transition from childhood to adulthood and an easy acceptance of adult roles. She concluded that adolescence is relatively stress-free in a society that lets children see adults' sexual activity, watch babies being born, engage in sex play, regard death as natural, do important work, show assertive and even dominant behavior, and know precisely what they will be expected to do as adults.

Mead has been criticized by D. Freeman (1983), who claimed that adolescence in Samoa is indeed tumultuous and stressful. But others have defended Mead's work (L. D. Holmes, 1987). In any case, the controversy, coming nearly 60 years after Mead's fieldwork—which was done in 1925—has had little impact. Today, storm and stress are no longer considered inevitable even for adolescents in the United States, as we shall see.

Margaret Mead, shown here when she was studying adolescence in Samoa, believed that young girls felt comfortable confiding in her because she was only in her early twenties herself, not much older than her subjects. She concluded from her research that when a culture provides a serene and gradual transition from childhood to adulthood, as Samoa does, there is no storm and stress, but an easy acceptance of the adult role.

### Sigmund Freud: The Genital Stage

Sigmund Freud, like Hall, saw conflict as a result of the physical changes of adolescence. In Freud's view, this conflict is preparatory to the *genital stage* of mature adult sexuality. The physiological changes of puberty reawaken the *libido,* the basic energy source that fuels the sex drive. The sexual urges of the earlier phallic stage—urges that "went underground" during the latency period of middle childhood—resurface. But now these urges are directed into socially approved channels—heterosexual relations with partners outside the family.

To achieve mature sexuality, adolescents must overcome their unresolved sexual feelings toward the mother or father. Through the defense mechanism of **reaction formation**—expressing the opposite of what one really feels—adolescents replace sexual longing with hostility. Thus, Freud also saw storm and stress as inevitable in adolescence, part of a phenomenon known as *adolescent rebellion.*

In freeing themselves from sexual dependency upon the parent of the other sex, Freud said, young adolescents typically go through a "homosexual" stage, which may take the form of excessive admiration of an adult of the same sex or a close friendship with a young person of the same sex. Such a relationship is a forerunner of mature relationships with persons of the other sex.

Another transition of adolescence, according to Freud, is a change in sexuality, from a desire only for pleasure to a mature drive with reproduction as a goal. The urge to masturbate becomes stronger in early adolescence, preparing the young person for eventual sexual release with a partner; after that is achieved, the need for masturbation diminishes. Girls (according to Freud) need to switch from the immature clitoral orgasm (obtained from masturbation) to the mature vaginal orgasm (achieved in sexual intercourse) (S. Freud, 1925/1959, 1953).

Research has challenged several aspects of Freud's theory. For example, masturbation does *not* decline with age and sexual experience. Older adolescents (16 to 19 years old) and nonvirgins are actually more likely to masturbate than 13- to 15-year-olds and virgins (R. C. Sorensen, 1973). Furthermore, the clitoral orgasm characterizes the sexual response of many normal, well-adjusted adult women (Masters & Johnson, 1966).

## Anna Freud:
### Ego Defenses of Adolescence

Anna Freud (1946), Sigmund Freud's daughter, who also became a psychoanalyst, considered the adolescent years more important for the formation of personality than her father, who emphasized the impact of early experience. She believed that the libido, which quieted during the latency years, reawakens in adolescence and threatens to upset the delicate balance of ego and id. The resultant anxiety calls forth such ego defense mechanisms as intellectualization and asceticism.

**Intellectualization**—translating sexual impulses into abstract thought—may be seen in adolescents' fondness of all-night debates about religion, politics, and the meaning of life. Although other investigators relate these conversations to adolescents' search for identity or to their increased ability to deal with abstract thought, Anna Freud considered them a defense. She

Anna Freud believed that the glandular changes which produce physiological changes in adolescence also affect psychological functioning, and result in the use of defense mechanisms, such as intellectualization and asceticism.

believed that young people are not trying to solve real problems but are manipulating words and ideas to respond to instinctual needs of their changing bodies.

She also saw **asceticism**—self-denial—as a defense mechanism. Because adolescents are afraid of losing control of their impulses, some may overcontrol themselves by renouncing simple pleasures, like favorite foods or attractive clothing. Later in life, Anna Freud said, as people gain confidence in their ability to control dangerous impulses, they tend to relax and to be less strict with themselves.

## Erik Erikson:
### Crisis 5—Identity versus Identity Confusion

Erikson's fifth crisis reflects his own youth. After completing his education, Erikson wandered around Europe, unsure of what career to follow. He tried painting and wood carving, and then accepted an offer to teach art at a private school in Vienna for children whose parents were undergoing analysis at Freud's Psychoanalytic Institute. The association with Freud led to Erikson's decision to become a psychoanalyst.

Erikson (1968) believed that the chief task of adolescence is to resolve the conflict of ***identity versus identity confusion***—to become a unique adult with an important role in life. To form a person's identity, the ego organizes abilities, needs, and desires and helps adapt them to the demands of society.

The search for identity is lifelong—it comes into focus during adolescence (which Erikson saw as lasting till the mid-twenties, as it did for him) and may recur from time to time during adulthood. This effort to make sense of the self and the world is a healthy, vital process that contributes to the ego strength of the adult. The conflicts involved spur growth and development.

One of the most significant aspects of the search for identity is deciding on a career. In the previous stage—characterized by the conflict of industry versus inferiority—children acquire the skills needed in their culture. As adolescents, they need to find ways to use these skills. Physical growth and new genital maturity alert young people to their impending adulthood, and they begin to wonder about their roles in adult society.

Erikson sees the prime danger of this stage as identity (or role) confusion, which can express itself in a young person's taking an excessively long time (until after age 30) to reach adulthood. However, a certain amount of identity confusion is normal and accounts for the chaotic, volatile nature of much adolescent behavior, as well as self-consciousness about appearance.

Cliquishness and intolerance of differences—both hallmarks of the adolescent social scene—are defenses against identity confusion, Erikson says. Adolescents may also show confusion by regressing into childishness to avoid resolving conflicts or by committing themselves impulsively to poorly thought-out courses of action. However, Erikson sees ideological commitment as a valuable growth mechanism. During the *psychosocial moratorium*—a "time out" period provided by adolescence and youth—many people search for commitments to which they can be faithful (Erikson, 1950). This searching helps to explain many adolescents' susceptibility to fads, cults, and gang loyalties. The extent to which young people can be true to ideological and personal commitments determines their ability to resolve the crisis of identity versus identity confusion.

The fundamental "virtue" that arises from this crisis is the *virtue of fidelity*—sustained loyalty, faith, or a sense of belonging to friends and companions, to a loved one, or to a set of values, an ideology, a religion, a movement, or an ethnic group. Self-identification emerges when young people choose the values and people they will be loyal to, rather than simply accepting those of their parents. Fidelity represents a higher level of the virtue of trust (which was developed in infancy): fidelity is not only the capacity to trust others and oneself but also the capacity to be trustworthy. Also, adolescents transfer trust from parents to other people, including mentors and loved ones.

Love is another avenue toward identity, according to Erikson. By becoming intimate with another person and sharing thoughts and feelings, the adolescent offers up his or her own tentative identity, sees it reflected in the loved one, and is better able to clarify the self.

Adolescent intimacies differ from true intimacy, which involves commitment, sacrifice, and compromise. Erikson believed that males cannot achieve intimacy until they have achieved a stable identity (see Chapter 13 for a discussion of intimacy in young adulthood). Females, he thought, achieve intimacy before identity: an adolescent girl puts her identity aside as she prepares to define herself by the man she will marry. Erikson's scheme, then, like Freud's, takes male development as the norm. This orientation has led to important criticisms of Erikson's theory.

## RESEARCH ON IDENTITY

Kate, Mark, Nick, and Andrea are all about to graduate from high school. Kate has weighed her interests and talents and has settled on a career—music therapy. After carefully researching colleges, she has applied to three that offer good programs. Mark also knows exactly what he is going to do: his parents have always assumed that he will go into the family business, and he has never given much thought to doing anything else. Nick has no idea of what he wants to do, but he is not worried. He figures that he will go to college, have a good time, and see what happens. Andrea has not yet made a decision about her life goals and is agonizing over them. She thinks that she may be interested in something having to do with science, but she is torn between a premedical program and engineering school.

All four young people are involved in identity formation, but the process—like the result—is different for each. What accounts for the differences?

### Identity States

James E. Marcia defines identity as "an internal, self-constructed, dynamic organization of drives, abilities, beliefs, and individual history" (1980, p. 159). In research based on Erikson's theory, Marcia identified four *identity states,* or *statuses,* which he correlates with other aspects of personality, like anxiety, self-esteem, moral reasoning, and patterns of social behavior. These states are not "stages" in the search for identity, since they do not form a progression; but neither are they necessarily permanent—identity status may change as a person continues to develop (Marcia, 1979).

**TABLE 11–1**
CRITERIA FOR IDENTITY STATUSES

| Identity Status | Position on Occupation and Ideology | |
|---|---|---|
| | Crisis (Period of Considering Alternatives) | Commitment (Adherence to a Path of Action) |
| Identity achievement | Present | Present |
| Foreclosure | Absent | Present |
| Identity diffusion | Present or absent | Absent |
| Moratorium | In crisis | Present but vague |

*Source:* Adapted from Marcia, 1980.

Marcia's four identity states (see Table 11-1) are determined by the presence or absence of the two elements which, according to Erikson, are crucial in forming identity: crisis and commitment. **Crisis** is defined as a period of conscious decision making, and **commitment** as personal investment in an occupation or a system of beliefs (an ideology).

To evaluate a person's identity status, Marcia (1966) developed a semistructured 30-minute interview (see Table 11-2 for sample questions and answers). On the basis of their answers, people are classified in one of the following four categories:

1  *Identity achievement (crisis leading to commitment).* People in **identity achievement** (like Kate) have spent a great deal of time actively thinking about the important issues in their lives (that is, they have gone through the crisis period), they have made crucial choices, and they now express strong commitment to those choices. "Identity achievers" are characterized by *flexible strength:* they tend to be thoughtful, but not so introspective that they cannot do anything. They have a sense of humor, have high self-esteem, function well under stress, are autonomous, are capable of intimate relationships, and are open to new ideas while maintaining their own standards.

2  *Foreclosure (commitment without crisis).* People in **foreclosure** (like Mark) have made commitments, but instead of considering alternative choices (going through a crisis), they have accepted other people's plans for their lives. A woman becomes a devoutly religious homemaker because her mother was one, or a man becomes a farmer and a Republican like his

**TABLE 11–2**
IDENTITY-STATUS INTERVIEW

| Sample Questions | Typical Answers for the Four Statuses |
|---|---|
| *About occupational commitment:* "How willing do you think you'd be to give up going into ____ if something better came along?" | *Identity achievement.* "Well, I might, but I doubt it. I can't see what 'something better' would be for me." <br> *Foreclosure.* "Not very willing. It's what I've always wanted to do. The folks are happy with it and so am I." <br> *Identity diffusion.* "Oh sure. If something better came along, I'd change just like that." <br> *Moratorium.* "I guess that if I knew for sure, I could answer that better. It would have to be something in the general area—something related. . . ." |
| *About ideological commitment:* "Have you ever had any doubts about your religious beliefs?" | *Identity achievement.* "Yes, I even started wondering whether there is a god. I've pretty much resolved that now, though. The way it seems to me is . . ." <br> *Foreclosure.* "No, not really; our family is pretty much in agreement on these things." <br> *Identity diffusion.* "Oh, I don't know. I guess so. Everyone goes through some sort of stage like that. But it really doesn't bother me much. I figure that one religion is about as good as another!" <br> *Moratorium.* "Yes, I guess I'm going through that now. I just don't see how there can be a god and still so much evil in the world or . . ." |

*Source:* Adapted from Marcia, 1966.

father. "Foreclosers" are characterized by *rigid strength:* they tend to be happy and self-assured, sometimes smug and self-satisfied, and to have a strong sense of family ties. They believe in law and order, like to follow a strong leader, and become dogmatic when their ideas are threatened.

**3** *Identity diffusion (no commitment).* People in **identity diffusion** (like Nick) may or may not have gone through a period of considering alternatives (crisis), but in any case they have made no commitments. They may be seemingly carefree people who have actively avoided commitment or aimless floaters. Drifting and centerless, they tend to be superficial or unhappy and often lonely because they have no truly intimate relationships.

**4** *Moratorium (in crisis).* People in **moratorium** (like Andrea) are in a stage of ambivalent struggle. Currently in the process of making decisions, they seem to be heading for commitment and will probably achieve identity. They tend to be lively, talkative, and in conflict. They are close to the other-sex parent and are competitive and anxious. They want intimacy and understand what it involves but do not necessarily have intimate relationships.

### Gender Differences in Identity Formation

Freud's statement "Biology is destiny" has become infamous. Today, psychologists emphasize the role of socialization, rather than biology, in forming identity. Whatever the reasons, however, there are differences between the sexes in the struggle to define identity. Although early theorists like Freud and Erikson saw different paths toward identity development in males and females, only in recent years have researchers paid much attention to the female quest for identity.

Carol Gilligan (1982) has studied women in several contexts and has concluded that women define themselves less in terms of achieving a separate identity and more in terms of relationships with other people. They judge themselves on their responsibilities and on their ability to care for others as well as for themselves. They achieve identity less through competition and more through cooperation.

Marcia (1979) modified his original interviews to explore issues of female identity. He added questions about attitudes toward premarital intercourse, women's roles, and lifestyles. The results were surprising. Whereas the men in moratorium most closely resembled those who had achieved identity, the women who seemed closest to achieving identity were those in foreclosure. Marcia points out that society pressures women to transmit social values to the next generation.

The psychologist Carol Gilligan has studied females' identity formation in adolescence and adulthood and concluded that girls and women achieve identity differently from boys and men. The female route is less through competition and more through cooperation.

Because of this, *stability* of identity is important for women. Thus, it is just as adaptive for them to achieve identity early in life without much effort on their own part as to struggle to forge their own identity. Marcia also maintains that women do not wait to develop the capacity for intimacy after they have achieved identity, as in Erikson's male-based pattern; for women, identity and intimacy develop together. These conclusions support other research indicating that intimacy is more important for girls than for boys, even in grade-school friendships (Blyth & Foster-Clark, 1987; Bukowski & Kramer, 1986).

## ASPECTS OF PERSONALITY DEVELOPMENT IN ADOLESCENCE

An essential aspect of the search for identity is the need to become independent of parents. An important path for this part of the search leads to the peer group. In this section we'll examine adolescents' relationships with parents and peers before looking at the development of sexual identity, which is related to both.

The storm and stress often associated with the teen-age years in the United States and other western cultures have been called **adolescent rebellion**—rebellion that may encompass not only conflict within the family but a general alienation from adult society and hostility toward its values. Yet studies of adolescents typically find that fewer than 1 out of 5 fit this "classical" pattern of tumult (Offer, Ostrov, & Howard, 1989).

Age does become a powerful bonding agent in adolescence—more powerful than race, religion, community, or sex. American teenagers spend much of their free time with people of their own age, with whom they feel comfortable and can identify. They have their best times with their friends, with whom they feel free, open, involved, excited, and motivated. These are the people they most want to be with. Young people are caught up in "generational chauvinism": they tend to believe that most other adolescents share their personal values and that most older people do not (Csikszentmihalyi & Larson, 1984; R. C. Sorensen, 1973).

Nevertheless, adolescents' rejection of parental values is often partial, temporary, or superficial. Teenagers' values tend to remain closer to those of their parents than many people realize, and "adolescent rebellion" often amounts to little more than a series of minor skirmishes.

## RELATIONSHIPS WITH PARENTS

### How Adolescents and Their Parents Conflict

The myth is that parents and teenagers do not like each other and do not get along with each other. The fact is that most adolescents feel close to and positive about their parents, have similar values on major issues, and seek their parents' approval ( J. P. Hill, 1987; Offer et al., 1989).

But this does not, of course, mean that teenagers and their parents live in a calm, stress-free relationship. Let's look at some aspects of the conflicts between them.

### *The roots of conflict*

Young people feel a constant tension between needing to break away from their parents and realizing how dependent they really are on them. They have to give up the identity of "the Smiths' little boy" or "the Millers' little girl" and establish their own private identity, while at the same time keeping parental and family ties (Siegel, 1982).

Most adolescents feel close to and positive about their parents, have similar values on major issues, and value their parents' approval. Also, parent and teenager often enjoy being in each other's company.

Adolescents' ambivalent feelings are often matched by their parents' own ambivalence. Torn between wanting their children to be independent and wanting to keep them dependent, parents often find it hard to let go. As a result, parents may give teenagers "double messages"—that is, the parents will say one thing but will actually communicate just the opposite by their actions.

Conflict is more likely to surface between adolescents and their mothers than adolescents and their fathers (Steinberg, 1981, 1987). This may be partly because mothers have been more closely involved with their children and may find it harder to give up their involvement. It may also be because fathers sometimes tend to withdraw from their teenage children—from their developing daughters, out of discomfort with the sexual stirrings they may feel toward them; and from their sons, who may now be bigger than both parents and more aggressive.

Still, the emotions attending this transitional time do not necessarily lead to a break with either parental or societal values. In fact, a number of studies of American teenagers have found little turmoil (Brooks-Gunn, 1988; Offer et al., 1989). For one thing, although teenagers report slightly more negative moods than younger children, they do not report the wide swings in emotional states that are often considered inevitable in adolescence (Larson & Lampman-Petraitis, 1989). Research is fairly consistent in reporting significant conflict only in 15 to 25 percent of all families, and these are often families that had problems *before* the children approached adolescence (W. A. Collins, 1990; J. P. Hill, 1987; Offer et al., 1989).

In his classic studies of midwestern boys, Daniel Offer (1969) found a high level of bickering over relatively unimportant issues by 12- and 14-year-olds and their parents, but he found little "turmoil" or "chaos." A follow-up study of the same boys 8 years later (Offer & Offer, 1974) found most of them happy, reasonably well-adjusted, with a realistic self-image. Less than one-fifth had experienced a tumultuous adolescence. Similar results held true for wider groups of adolescents, as we'll see later in this chapter (Offer et al., 1989).

### The nature of conflict

By and large, parents and teenagers do not clash over economic, religious, social, or political values. Most arguments are about mundane matters like schoolwork, chores, friends, dating, curfews, and personal appearance (see Table 11-3 for sources of conflict, which have been very similar over the years). Later in adolescence, conflict is more likely to revolve around dating and alcohol (Carlton-Ford & Collins, 1988).

Most disagreements are resolved with less trouble than popular mythology suggests. Quarrels may reflect some deep quest for independence (as is often speculated), or they may be just a continuation of parents' efforts to teach children to conform to social rules. "This [socializing] task inescapably produces a certain amount of tension. . . . At this point it is simply not clear whether parent-adolescent conflict has a 'deeper meaning' than this" (Montemayor, 1983, p. 91).

Discord generally increases during early adolescence, stabilizes during middle adolescence, and then decreases after the young person is about 18 years of age. The increased conflict in early adolescence may be related more to puberty than to chronological age, and some intriguing new research suggests that it may even be bidirectional (Steinberg, 1988).

**TABLE 11–3**
THREE MOST COMMON CAUSES OF ARGUMENTS WITH PARENTS ACCORDING TO ADOLESCENTS (SELECTED STUDIES, 1929–1982)

| Study | Sample | Causes of Arguments |
|---|---|---|
| Lynd & Lynd (1929) | 348 males, 382 females: grades 10–12 | 1 The time I get in at night. 2 Number of times I go out during school nights. 3 Grades at school. |
| Punke (1943) | 989 males, 1721 females: high school students | 1 Social life and friends. 2 Work and spending money. 3 Clothes. |
| Remmers (1957) | 15,000 males and females: high school students | 1 I'm afraid to tell parents when I've done wrong. 2 Parents are too strict about my going out at night. 3 Parents are too strict about the family car. |
| Johnstone (1975) | 1261 males and females: ages 13–20 | 1 Studying. 2 Use of spare time. 3 School. |
| D. A. Rosenthal (1982) | 630 males and females: ages 13–16 | 1 Drinking or smoking. 2 Time and frequency of going out. 3 Doing jobs around the house. |

*Source:* Condensed from Montemayor, 1983.

Communication between parents and adolescents may flow more naturally when they are engaged in a shared pursuit. Grinding corn in the traditional manner strengthens the bond between this Navajo mother and daughter.

In a study relating the timing of puberty to parent-child relationships, Steinberg (1988) found that as young people develop physically, they bicker and squabble more with their parents. Furthermore, girls who argue more with their mothers mature faster physically than girls who have calmer relationships. What might account for this relationship? It is possible that a very close mother-daughter tie at a time when a girl is striving for independence might be stressful, and that stress might in turn affect the hormonal secretions that govern puberty.

For most teenagers, then, the "storm and stress" concept is exaggerated. Conflict is part of every relationship, and since the transitions of adolescence challenge the established interaction between parent and child, it is not surprising that some contention arises. Usually, however, parents and children resolve their disagreements to their mutual satisfaction, and parents continue to exercise considerable influence on teenagers' basic values. When family conflicts are severe and cannot be resolved easily, however, adolescents are at risk of serious problems. Intervention and counseling can often help such families (Offer et al., 1989).

## What Adolescents Need from Their Parents

Many of the arguments between teenagers and their parents are about "how much" and "how soon": how much freedom teenagers should have to schedule their own activities, or how soon they can take the family car. Parents of adolescents have to be more flexible in their thinking—and more egalitarian with their children than they were when the children were younger. They need to walk a fine line between granting their children a gradually increasing level of independence and protecting them from immature lapses in judgment.

If separation or emotional independence from the family or other important adults comes too early, it can spell trouble for a teenager. This trouble can take the form of alienation, susceptibility to negative peer influences, and unhealthy behavior like drug abuse or premature sexual activity (Steinberg, 1987; Steinberg & Silverberg, 1986). Still, parents should not try to keep their children from taking *any* risks. Positive exploration that involves trying a new activity, making new friends, learning a difficult skill, taking on a new challenge, or resisting peer pressure (thus taking the risk of alienating old friends) poses challenges that help people grow (Damon, 1984).

The kind of parenting that seems to provide the right balance is, again, authoritative parenting. This offers warmth and acceptance; assertiveness with regard to rules, norms, and values; and willingness to listen, explain, and negotiate (J. P. Hill, 1987). One reason it works so well with teenagers is that it takes their cognitive growth into account. By explaining the reasons behind a stance, parents acknowledge that adolescents can often evaluate situations on a very sophisticated level (Baumrind, 1968).

We have already seen how important parents are to their children's performance in school. This remains true for adolescents. The stronger the parents' interest in teenagers' lives, the more likely the teenagers are to get high marks in school.

## How Adolescents Are Affected by Their Parents' Life Situation

### Parents' employment

Most of the research about the impact of parents' work patterns on adolescents has involved mothers' employment, and the findings have been somewhat inconsistent.

In one study, for example, 7 out of 10 teenagers said that their mothers' working had either a positive effect or no effect on them (General Mills, Inc., 1981). This is understandable. Teenagers want to be independent—to make their own decisions. Mothers who are at home are more likely to continue to direct their adolescents' activities, and a mother will often feel personally rebuffed if her well-meaning advice or questions are rejected. Another study concluded that adolescent children of working mothers tend to be better adjusted socially, feel better about themselves, have more of a sense of belonging, and get along better with families and with school friends than other teenagers (D. Gold & Andres, 1978a).

On the negative side, however, teenage children of working mothers tend to spend less time on homework and reading and more time watching television (Milne, Myers, Rosenthal, & Ginsburg, 1986). With less supervision, they may also be more subject to peer pressure leading to behavior problems.

In the 1950s, 1960s, and 1970s, when most mothers who could afford to stay home did so, some research found certain differences between children of employed mothers and children of at-home mothers. For example, the adolescent sons of working women held less stereotyped views of the female role; their daughters had higher and less gender-stereotyped career aspirations, were more outgoing, scored higher on several academic measures, and seemed better adjusted on various social and personality measures (L. Hoffman,

1979). More recent analysis, however, suggests that a mother's work status is just one of many factors that shape children's attitudes toward women's roles (Galambos, Petersen, & Lenerz, 1988). Since we seem to be coming to the end of a historical period in which mothers' work outside the home was not the norm, maternal employment may be considered a history-graded influence on sex typing (see Chapter 1).

Today, maternal employment in itself does not seem to affect teenagers much for either good or ill. Rather, whatever effect it has is filtered through other factors, like the warmth of a relationship or a mother's satisfaction with her role. Teenage sons of working mothers are likely to have more flexible attitudes toward gender roles when they have warm relationships with their mothers, and teenage daughters have egalitarian attitudes toward gender roles when their mothers are happy with their own roles (Galambos et al., 1988).

### "Self-care" adolescents

At 13, Theo is too old for day care or a baby-sitter, and like many other young people, he is responsible for himself for at least part of the day. Lack of supervision does not in itself make preteens and young teenagers especially vulnerable to peer pressure. But differences do show up, depending on the kind of self-care, parents' involvement with self-care, and parenting styles.

Steinberg (1986) gave questionnaires to 865 ten- to fifteen-year-olds in Madison, Wisconsin, asking them what they would do about hypothetical antisocial situations (like stealing, vandalism, and cheating on a test) if a "best friend" suggested one course while they themselves really thought they should do something else. Some of Steinberg's respondents, like Theo, stayed home alone after school; they were in telephone contact with their parents, followed an agreed-upon schedule of homework and chores, and were in a familiar environment that reminded them of family values. These young people were no more influenced by their friends than were youngsters who were at home with adults or older siblings. But the further removed his respondents were from even the possibility of adult supervision, the more they were affected by peers. Thus, those who spent time unsupervised at a friend's house were more influenced by peers than those who stayed home alone, and those who just "hung out" with a group were the most easily swayed. Yet even in this last category, youngsters whose parents knew where they were turned out to be only slightly more susceptible to peer influence than those who were actually with adults. Furthermore, young people whose parents were authoritative found it easier to resist peer pressure, apparently because they had taken their parents' standards as their own.

This study emphasizes the importance of considering differences among "self-care" adolescents. However, we need more research before we can draw general conclusions. For one thing, since most of Steinberg's subjects were suburban, his findings might not apply to rural or urban teenagers. For another, it is not clear whether being supervised by adults helps adolescents resist peer pressure or whether being more peer-oriented leads adolescents to resist adult supervision. Finally, these subjects were responding to hypothetical situations; their responses may have been very different from their behavior in real life. But another study of young people from the same schools did find that their responses to hypothetical situations were related to reports of actual misconduct (B. B. Brown, Clasen, & Eicher, 1986); this approach may thus hold the promise of predicting behavior.

One theme comes through loud and clear from all these studies of parents' influence—and it has gathered force from early childhood on. That theme is the importance of continued supervision by parents even after children reach an age when they are spending much of their time on their own.

## RELATIONSHIPS WITH PEERS

An important source of support during the complex transition of adolescence—and a source of pressure for behavior that their parents may deplore—is young people's growing involvement with their peers.

Adolescents going through rapid physical changes take comfort from being with others who are going through similar changes. Young people questioning adult standards and the need for parental guidance find it reassuring to turn for advice to friends who can understand and symphathize because they are in the same position themselves. Teenagers "trying on" new values can test their ideas with their peers with less fear of being ridiculed or "shot down" than they might have with parents or other adults. The peer group is a source of affection, sympathy, and understanding; a place for experimentation; and a supportive setting for achieving autonomy and independence from parents (Coleman, 1980; Newman, 1982). It is no wonder, then, that adolescents like to spend time with their peers.

### How Adolescents Spend Their Time —and with Whom

What do teenagers do on a typical day? With whom do they do it? Where do they do it? And how do they feel about what they are doing?

Adolescents, like these students in a high school cafeteria, spend more than half their waking hours with other teenagers and only about 5 percent of their time with a parent. Before young people become truly independent, they go from being dependent on parents to being dependent on peers.

For 1 week, 75 high school students in a suburb of Chicago carried beepers that rang at random times once every 2 hours during the day. The students were asked to report what they were doing when the beeper sounded—and where, and with whom. The average student received and responded to 69 percent of the beeper signals, yielding a total of 4489 self-reports, from which researchers described what it is like to be a teenager today (Csikszentmihalyi & Larson, 1984).

The results (see Figures 11-1 and 11-2 on the opposite page, and 11-3 on page 352) showed the importance of the peer group. These students spent more than half their waking hours with other teenagers— friends (29 percent of the time) and classmates (23 percent)—and only about 5 percent of their time with one or both parents. They were happiest with friends; being with the family ranked second; next came being alone; and last, being with classmates. Teenagers have more fun with friends—joking, gossiping, and "goofing around"—than they do at home, where activities tend to be more serious and more humdrum.

These adolescents reported that they felt good most (71 percent) of the time. They tended to be happiest when doing something active, productive, and challenging, like playing football or the piano, dancing, or trading jokes—something involving roles to be learned and something that gave them feedback on their competence. They were happier doing schoolwork or paid work than watching television, reading, thinking, or resting. They also liked to relax away from adult supervision—getting together informally with friends in a park or some other public place, at a friend's house, or at a student center.

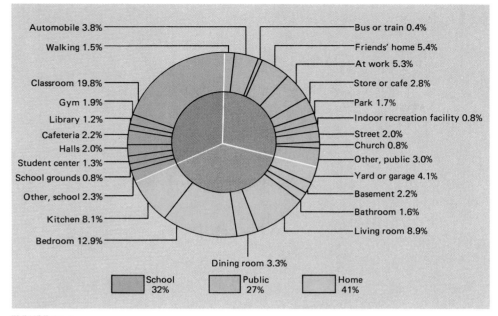

**FIGURE 11-1**
Where adolescents spend their time: percentage of self-reports in each location by 2734 high school students. Here and in Figures 11-2 and 11-3, 1 percentage point is equivalent to about 1 hour per week spent in the given location or activity. (*Source*: Csikszentmihalyi & Larson, 1984, p. 59.)

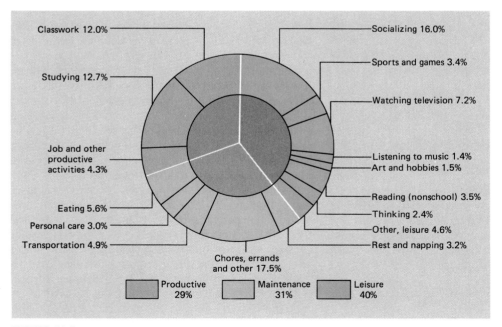

**FIGURE 11-2**
What adolescents spend their time doing. (*Source*: Csikszentmihalyi & Larson, 1984, p. 63.)

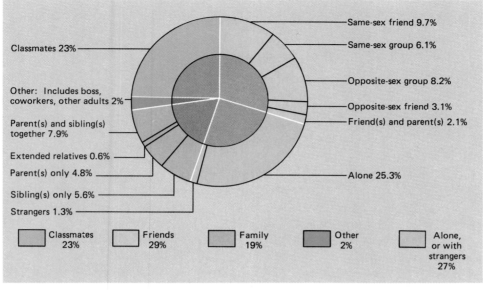

Same-sex friend 9.7%

Same-sex group 6.1%

Opposite-sex group 8.2%

Opposite-sex friend 3.1%

Friend(s) and parent(s) 2.1%

Alone 25.3%

Classmates 23%

Other: Includes boss, coworkers, other adults 2%

Parent(s) and sibling(s) together 7.9%

Extended relatives 0.6%

Parent(s) only 4.8%

Sibling(s) only 5.6%

Strangers 1.3%

| Classmates 23% | Friends 29% | Family 19% | Other 2% | Alone, or with strangers 27% |

**FIGURE 11-3**
With whom adolescents spend their time. (*Source*: Csikszentmihalyi & Larson, 1984, p. 71.)

The community an adolescent lives in has a major impact on whether she or he will pay more attention to adults or to other young people. The findings from a study of several hundred teenagers in several communities in New York state—a rural area, a poor inner-city neighborhood with many minority-group residents, and an upper-middle-class suburb—tell us that we cannot draw sweeping conclusions about teenagers as if they were all alike (Ianni, 1983). Unfortunately, there is very little good research on African American, Hispanic, Native American, and Asian American adolescents, or on teenage children of single-parent, dual-income, and remarried families (J. P. Hill, 1987).

The importance of such research can be seen in the findings from this New York study. Urban teenagers faced with conflicting standards of family, school, and social agencies were apt to reject all these values and create their own, often among peers. Suburban and rural teenagers, however, were more likely to have values very close to those held by the important adults in their lives—they might question adults' values, but they wanted consistent rules and standards that they could evaluate (Ianni, 1983).

**Friendships in Adolescence**

"What *do* you talk about for so long?" Sally's mother used to ask her when she had been on the phone for an hour with the best friend she had seen no more than 2 hours before. Sally was not surprised, then, to see the

same pattern emerge when her own daughters entered their teens. The intensity of friendships is greater in adolescence than at any other time in the life span (Berndt & Perry, 1990).

There is some continuity from middle childhood into adolescence: both age groups see mutual help, mutual interaction, and mutual liking as the core of friendship. And for both, friendships seem to last about as long and to involve about the same level of conflict.

But there are also differences. In early adolescence, friends are more intimate and supportive than they are at earlier ages, adolescents regard loyalty as more critical to a friendship, and adolescents compete less and share more with their friends than younger children do (Berndt & Perry, 1990). These features of friendship continue into adulthood. Their appearance, therefore, marks a transition to adultlike relationships.

Such changes are due partly to cognitive development. Adolescents are better able than younger children to express their thoughts and feelings and share them with friends; they are also better able to consider another person's point of view, and so they can better understand their friends' thoughts and feelings.

Gender affects friendships, too. Emotional support and sharing of confidences are particularly vital to female friendships throughout life (Blyth & Foster-Clark, 1987; Bukowski & Kramer, 1986). Boys and men tend to count more people as friends than girls and women do, but male friendships are rarely as close as female friendships.

Friendships are likely to be closer and more intense in adolescence than at any other time in the life span. Adolescents have the most fun when they are doing something with their friends, with whom they feel free, open, involved, excited, and motivated.

However, girls who seek from a "best friend" the intimacy they lack at home are likely to be disappointed. In a survey of 134 sixteen- to eighteen-year-old girls, those who had the closest friendships also had affectionate ties with their mothers, saw their mothers as nonauthoritarian, and wanted to be like their mothers (M. Gold & Yanof, 1985). Their close relationships with their mothers may well have helped these girls to develop enough trust and autonomy to be ready for intimacy with other people.

Such differences illustrate some of the other factors that influence people's ability to make and keep friends. Adolescents who have close friends are high in self-esteem, consider themselves competent, and do well in school; those whose friendships involve a high degree of conflict score lower on all these measures (Berndt & Perry, 1990).

Adolescents tend to choose friends who are already like them; then, friends influence each other to become even more alike (Berndt, 1982; Berndt & Perry, 1990). Friends tend to have similar status within the larger peer group (Berndt & Perry, 1990). Similarity is more important to friendship in adolescence than later in life, probably because teenagers are struggling to differentiate themselves from their parents and, as a result, need support from people who are like them (Weiss & Lowenthal, 1975).

This need for support also shows in the way adolescents often imitate each other's behavior and are influenced by peer pressure. As a result, adolescents sometimes find themselves in a tug-of-war between parents and peers.

## Peer Pressure versus Parents' Influence

If the other girls in her group wear ripped jeans and unlaced running shoes, Heather will not come to school in a plaid skirt and penny loafers. If her crowd gathers at a drive-in restaurant at night, Heather will not—at least by choice—spend her evenings in the library. Her friends influence not only her clothes and hairdos but also her social activities, sexual behavior, and use or nonuse of drugs. Members of the adolescent peer group are constantly influencing and being influenced by each other. Even the most outspoken "nonconformists" usually follow the customs of their chosen group.

An important part of many teenagers' lives is the music they listen to, binding them to their peers and separating them from their parents. (The sexual rhythms and lyrics in rock music are a basis for many parent-child conflicts.) For a look at the role of rock music in adolescents' lives, see Box 11-1 (page 354).

Still, "peer power" is not everything. Most teenagers have positive ties with their parents (J. P. Hill, 1987) and maintain two reference groups—parents and peers. Peers tend to have more to say about everyday social issues; parents have more influence about deeper concerns: what to do about a moral dilemma, what job to take, and what education to pursue (Brittain, 1963; Emmerick, 1978).

Also, as adolescents become surer of themselves, they become more autonomous; they are more likely to make up their own minds and to stick with their decisions in the face of disagreement from either parents or peers (Newman, 1982).

BOX 11–1   THINKING CRITICALLY

# THE ROLE OF ROCK MUSIC IN ADOLESCENTS' LIVES

A parent's appeal to "turn down that volume!" is heard almost daily in most homes where teenagers live. Between the seventh and twelfth grades, the average teenager listens to 10,500 hours of rock music—only slightly less than the total number of hours spent in the classroom from kindergarten through high school (S. Davis, 1985).

To parents, the volume of rock music is often its least objectionable aspect—and volume also seems to be its least important appeal for teenagers (E. F. Brown & Hendee, 1989). Music can be an important symbol, and rock music stands for many things in teenagers' lives. It stands for control: teenagers choose their own music, often listen to it in private (with earphones or in their own rooms), and are rarely impeded by censorship or parental disapproval. It is a badge of identity: the music that teenagers listen to locates them within a particular subgroup; it helps them choose friends, find something to talk about, and be with other adolescents. It represents independence from parents: the fact that parents are distinctly not enamored of the rhythms, sounds, and themes of rock is a big part of its allure. It provides information: rock lyrics describe sexuality, alternative lifestyles, and other topics that are often taboo. And it provides an organizing theme to adolescent's lives: devotees of some kinds of music dress in certain ways or embrace certain political causes.

Many adults deplore the powerful presence of rock music in teenagers' lives. They point to an association between poor achievement in school and frequent listening as proof that

An important part of many teenagers' lives is the music they listen to, binding them to their peers and separating them from their parents. Music is an important symbol, and rock music stands for many things in teenagers' lives.

the music interferes with learning. They point to a growing emphasis on sex, violence, and suicide in rock lyrics as an unhealthy influence. They are especially alarmed by the lyrics of "heavy metal" rock, glorifying racial hatred, abuse, degradation of women, sexual deviance, and occasionally even satanism. These concerns have led to a recent decision by record producers to label some albums, "Explicit Lyrics—Parental Advisory."

Defenders of rock say that it is a "safety valve" for teenagers' feelings of alienation. Some counter the charge that it interferes with school by citing research which indicates that problems at school usually come *before* heavy involvement with rock music. Others cite reports that students often do not interpret the lyrics the way adults do: about half of a

group of college students interpreted Bruce Springsteen's song "Born in the U.S.A." as patriotic, whereas adults see it as a cry of alienation (Greenfield et al., 1987).

What, then, is the role of this music? If, as some observers believe, it is a symbol of alienation from adult society and an unhealthy influence, what should be done? Should parents monitor the music their children buy and listen to? Should record stores refuse to sell objectionable items? Should recordings be legally censored? Should warning labels be more detailed than they are now—or should they be removed altogether? Should music (like books) be treated as speech and protected under the First Amendment of the Bill of Rights, so that we rely on education, free discussion, and the vote of the marketplace to regulate it?

## ACHIEVING SEXUAL IDENTITY

Let's now see how adolescents achieve sexual identity and examine how they deal with their parents concerning this exciting yet troubling new aspect of their lives.

A profound change in an adolescent's life is the movement from close friendships only with people of the same sex to friendships and romantic attachments with members of the other sex. Seeing oneself as a sexual being, coming to terms with one's sexual stirrings, and developing an intimate romantic relationship— all these are important aspects of achieving sexual identity.

Adolescents' self-images and relationships with peers and parents are bound up with sexuality. Sexual activity—casual kissing, necking and petting, and genital contact—fulfills a number of adolescents' important needs, only one of which is physical pleasure. Teenagers become sexually active to enhance intimacy, to seek new experience, to prove their maturity, to keep up with their peers, to find relief from pressures, and to investigate the mysteries of love.

### Studying Adolescents' Sexuality

It is extremely difficult to do research on sexuality. Virtually every study about sex—from Kinsey's surveys in the 1940s to those being done now—has been criticized for inaccuracy on the basis that people who answer questions about sex tend to be sexually active and liberal in their attitude toward sex, and therefore are not a representative sample of the population. Also, there is no way to corroborate what people say: some may lie to conceal their sexual activities while others may exaggerate. When young people are being asked about behaviors that are often "regarded as inappropriate and immoral, if not illegal and sinful" (Dreyer, 1982, p. 564), the problems multiply. Then, too, parental consent is often needed for the participation of minors, and parents who grant permission may not be typical.

Still, surveys have merit: even if we cannot generalize findings to the population as a whole, within the groups that take part we can see trends over time, which reveal changes in sexual mores. We need to remember, however, that attitudes may be changing more than behavior. Although teenagers today *seem* to be more sexually active than teenagers of a generation or two ago, it is possible that they are not acting much differently but are more willing to talk about their sexual activities.

### Sexual Attitudes and Behavior

#### *Masturbation*

*Masturbation,* or sexual self-stimulation, is the first sexual experience for most young people and is almost universal. Yet, because most adults in our society are more anxious about discussing masturbation than any other aspect of sexuality (E. J. Roberts, Kline, & Gagnon, 1978), there has been very little research on it.

The research we do have shows an increase since the early 1960s in the number of adolescents who say that they masturbate (Dreyer, 1982). In the early 1970s, 50 percent of boys and 30 percent of girls under 15 years of age said that they masturbated; in the late 1970s, 70 percent of boys and 45 percent of girls under the age of 15 admitted to it. Apparently, a significant change did take place, even though we do not know whether boys and girls actually did masturbate more or whether they were simply more willing to say they did.

Still, teenagers continue to regard masturbation as shameful; fewer than one-third questioned by Coles and Stokes (1985) said that they felt no guilt about it. This suggests that attitudes toward masturbation have changed more radically among sex educators than among teenagers. Educators today stress that masturbation is normal and healthy, that it cannot cause physical harm, that it helps people learn how to give and receive sexual pleasure, and that it provides a way to gratify sexual desire without entering into a relationship for which a person is not emotionally ready.

#### *Sexual orientation*

It is in adolescence that a person's *sexual orientation* is usually expressed: whether that person will consistently be sexually and affectionally interested in members of the other sex *(heterosexual)* or in persons of the same sex *(homosexual).*

***What determines sexual orientation?*** Many researchers have sought to find out why people become heterosexual or homosexual. Much of their work has been spurred by efforts to explain the less common pattern, homosexuality; and a number of hypotheses have been advanced to account for it.

The oldest theory is that homosexuality represents a kind of mental illness. But in a classic study, Hooker (1957) could find no evidence to support this contention. Her conclusions and those of other researchers (along with political lobbying and changes in public attitudes) eventually led the American Psychiatric Association to stop classifying homosexuality as a "mental disorder." The latest edition of the *Diagnostic and Statistical Manual of Mental Disorders* classifies as a disorder only "persistent and marked distress about one's sexual orientation" (DSM-III-R, 1987, p. 296).

Other theories include a genetic factor, a hormonal imbalance, a family with a dominating mother and a weak father (thought by some to cause male homosexuality), and chance learning (developing a preference for one's own sex after having been seduced by a homosexual). So far, no scientific support has been found for family constellation or chance learning as a cause, and there is only tentative evidence for the genetic and hormonal theories.

Another theory (Ellis & Ames, 1987) is that sexual orientation is determined by a complex prenatal process involving both hormonal and neurological factors. If levels of sex hormones are in the typical female range between the second and fifth months of gestation, the person will be attracted to males after puberty; if these levels are in the male range, the person will be attracted to females. According to this theory, social and environmental influences would have to be very strong to overcome the originally programmed predisposition toward heterosexuality or homosexuality.

The prevailing view today is that there are a number of different reasons why a person becomes heterosexual or homosexual, and that interaction among various hormonal and environmental events is crucial.

***Homosexuality***   Many young people have one or more homosexual experiences as they are growing up, usually before age 15 (Dreyer, 1982). Isolated experiences do not, however, determine eventual sexual orientation, and few go on to make this a regular pattern. Only about 3 percent of adolescent boys and 2 percent of girls have ongoing homosexual relationships, even though about 15 percent of boys and 10 percent of girls have had a homosexual contact during adolescence (Chilman, 1980).

Despite the fact that homosexuality is more visible today than it used to be, with more people openly declaring their preference for people of the same sex, research suggests that homosexual behavior has been stable or has declined during the past 30 years (Chilman, 1980). Its incidence seems to be similar in a number of cultures (J. S. Hyde, 1986).

### Attitudes, behavior, and the "sexual evolution"

The early 1920s through the late 1970s witnessed a sexual *evolution* (rather than a *revolution*), both in what people do sexually and in how they feel about their sexual behavior. There has been a steady trend toward acceptance of more sexual activity in more situations.

Over the past 50 years attitudes toward sexuality have changed, to include approval of premarital sex in a loving relationship and a decline in the double standard by which males are freer sexually than females. Most teenagers are not promiscuous; sexual activity usually occurs within a monogamous relationship.

One major change has been the approval of premarital sex in a loving relationship. Another is a decline in, although not an end to, the *double standard*—the code that gives males more sexual freedom than females. The sexual evolution may now have reached a plateau or may even be reversing itself; but meanwhile, like the rest of the population, today's teenagers are more sexually active and liberal than the generation before them. This is especially true of girls.

In 1969, most studies showed that fewer than half of college students approved of sex before marriage (Mussen, Conger, & Kagan, 1969); by 1979, 90 percent of college men and 83 percent of college women approved (Mahoney, 1983). Between 1925 and 1965, about 10 percent of girls in their last year of high school were no longer virgins. By 1973, nonvirgins accounted for 35 percent; by 1979, more than 80 percent of 17-year-old white girls had had sexual intercourse. The incidence among black teenagers was higher, but by a smaller margin than in years past (Zelnik & Shah, 1983). A girl is likely to have her first sexual relations with a steady boyfriend; a boy is likely to have his with someone he knows casually (Dreyer, 1982; Zelnik, Kantner, & Ford, 1981; Zelnik & Shah, 1983).

There is often a discrepancy between what people of any age *say* about sex and what they *do*. Most teenagers apparently become sexually active earlier than they say they should. In one poll (Louis Harris & Associates, 1986), teenagers gave a median age of 18 as the "right age" to start having intercourse, even though most of the 17-year-olds and nearly half of the 16-year-olds were no longer virgins. In another study, of 3500 junior high and high school students, 83 percent of nonvirgins gave a "best age for first intercourse" higher than the age at which they had experienced it themselves, and 88 percent of young mothers gave a higher "best age for first birth."

Many adolescents, then, hold "values and attitudes consistent with responsible sexual conduct, but not all of them are able to translate these attitudes into personal behavior." Helping such teenagers act according to the values they already hold may be more productive than trying to persuade adolescents with different attitudes to change their behavior (Zabin, Hirsch, Smith, & Hardy, 1984, p. 185).

Why do so many adolescents begin having sexual relations so early? Teenage girls (and, to a lesser extent, boys) often feel under pressure to engage in activities that they may not feel ready for. Social pressure was the chief reason given by 73 percent of the girls and 50 percent of the boys in the Harris poll who were asked why many teenagers do not wait for sex until they are older. One-fourth of the teenagers reported that they had felt pressured to go farther sexually than they wanted to. Both boys and girls also mentioned curiosity as a reason for early sex; more boys than girls cited sexual feelings and desires. Only 6 percent of the boys and 11 percent of the girls gave love as a reason.

Furthermore, the media present a distorted view of sex. On television, as opposed to real life, unmarried couples have sex from 4 to 8 times more often than married couples; contraceptives are almost never used, but women seldom get pregnant; and only prostitutes or homosexuals contract sexually transmitted diseases (STDs). Not surprisingly, then, adolescents who get their information about sex from television tend to accept the idea of premarital and extramarital intercourse with multiple partners and without protection against pregnancy or disease. This may change, since some television producers, responding to the AIDS epidemic and to pressure from public interest groups, are incorporating birth control and other evidence of responsible sexual behavior into both daytime and prime-time shows (J. D. Brown, Childers, & Waszak, 1988).

A major reason for concern about early sexual activity is the risk of pregnancy (discussed in the next section) and of STDs (see Chapter 10). Most adolescents do not plan ahead for their first intercourse: 85 percent of nonvirgins have not asked anyone about birth control or infection (American Academy of Pediatrics, AAP, Committee on Adolescence, 1986). Teenagers who can go to their parents or other adults with questions about sex have a better chance of avoiding some of the common problems associated with burgeoning sexual activity—and a better chance of achieving a mature sexual identity (see Box 11-2 on page 358).

## TWO PROBLEMS OF ADOLESCENCE

Although most young people weather adolescence well, some have serious problems. Two that can affect the rest of a young person's life are unplanned pregnancy and juvenile delinquency. Neither of these problems is "normal" or "typical." Both are signals that a young person is in trouble and needs help.

### TEENAGE PREGNANCY

The teenage pregnancy rate in the United States is one of the highest in the world. In 1984, 1 million teenage girls—10 percent of all teenage girls in the nation—became pregnant. About half had their babies, 13 percent miscarried, and 40 percent had abortions (National Research Council, NRC, 1987). A disproportionate number were from minority and disadvantaged groups (G. Adams, Adams-Taylor, & Pittman, 1989).

More than 9 out of 10 teenage mothers choose, at least at first, to keep their babies rather than give them up for adoption or place them in foster care. But caring for a baby is demanding, and these young mothers, barely more than children themselves, often cannot manage it. As a result, children of teenagers often enter the state's foster care system, and years may pass before a foster child's final status is settled (Alan Guttmacher Institute, 1981).

### Consequences of Teenage Pregnancy

The consequences of pregnancy are enormous for adolescent girls and boys, their babies, and society.

Teenage girls are more prone to such complications of pregnancy as anemia, prolonged labor, and toxemia (McKenry, Walters, & Johnson, 1979). They are twice as likely as older mothers to bear low-birthweight babies; to 3 times more likely to have babies who die in the first year; their children are twice as likely to have neurological defects (McKenry et al., 1979).

The health problems of teenage mothers and their children result from social causes rather than medical ones. Many of the mothers are poor, do not eat properly, and get inadequate prenatal care—or none at all (S. S. Brown, 1985). In two large-scale studies—one in the United States and one in Denmark—teenagers' pregnancies turned out better than those of women in any other age group, leading to the conclusion that "if early, regular, and high quality medical care is made available to pregnant teenagers, the likelihood is that pregnancies and deliveries in this age group will not entail any higher medical risk than those of women in their twenties" (Mednick, Baker, & Sutton-Smith, 1979, p. 17).

## COMMUNICATING WITH PARENTS ABOUT SEX

Parental attitudes toward teenagers' sexuality are more liberal than they used to be, and many parents do talk to their children about sex in helpful ways. An extensive survey of contemporary teenagers' views on, and experiences with, sex found that when parents give guidance, it is overwhelmingly positive. Only 3 percent of the teenagers recalled hearing from parents that sex was not normal and healthy (Coles & Stokes, 1985).

Yet communication about sex remains a problem. Most parents are still not giving their children enough information, and youngsters still get most of their information (including much misinformation) from friends (Conger, 1988). Parents often think that they have said more than their children have actually heard. One girl, already a mother at age 15, reported, "[My mother] told me that she'd told me to come to her when it was time for me to have sex and she'd get me some birth control, but she must have said it *very* softly" (Coles & Stokes, 1985, p. 37).

According to a recent survey (Louis Harris & Associates, 1986), 31 percent of American teenagers—28 percent of those who are sexually active—have never talked with their parents about sex, and 42 percent are nervous or afraid to bring it up. Furthermore, 64 percent have never discussed birth control at home. This is important, because sexually active teenagers who *have* had discussions with parents about sexual matters are more likely to use birth control consistently than those who have not. Teenagers' confusion and ignorance increase the risk of pregnancy. Boys, Hispanic teenagers, and teenagers whose parents are not college graduates are least likely to have talked about sex with their parents (Louis Harris & Associates, 1986).

Adolescents' ambivalence, however, makes it hard for parents to discuss sex with them. Although teenagers say that they would like to be open and frank with their parents about sexual behavior, they often resent being questioned, and they tend to consider their sexual activities nobody else's business. But when parents ignore obvious signs of sexual activity, young people sometimes become puzzled and angry. As one 16-year-old girl said, looking ahead to the time when *she* would be a parent:

I'm not going to pretend that I don't know what's happening. If my daughter comes in at five in the morning, her skirt backwards and wearing some guy's sweater, I'm not going to ask her, "Did you have a nice time at the movies?" . . . I don't plan to fail! (R. C. Sorensen, 1973, p. 61)

How, then, can parents help their children? Experts on adolescent behavior recommend the following:

- Be sensitive to your teenager's desire to talk to you, and give your undivided attention.
- Keep the door open on any subject. Be an "askable" parent.
- Reassure a teenager of your support and help in any kind of trouble.
- Be well informed yourself so that you can impart knowledge, or help your child find it.
- Listen calmly, and concentrate on hearing and understanding your teenager's point of view.
- Speak to your teenager as courteously as you would speak to a stranger.
- Try to understand feelings even if you don't always approve of behavior. Do not judge.
- Avoid belittling and humiliating your teenager and laughing at what may seem to you to be naive or foolish questions and statements.
- Listen—and then offer your own views as plainly and honestly as possible.

Even with the best care, however, and the best of physical outcomes, teenage mothers still have problems. They are less likely to finish high school than their age-mates who do not have babies, and many who do finish do so at a later age. In one study, 5 years after giving birth, only half of urban black adolescent mothers had graduated from high school; however, 10 years later, two-thirds had graduated (Furstenberg, Brooks-Gunn, & Morgan, 1987).

Teenage mothers are also likely to have money troubles; many receive public assistance, at least for a while. Furthermore, they are at high risk of repeat subsequent pregnancies. The risk is highest for those who drop out of school, remain sexually active, and do not use reliable means of birth control. These girls "may have resigned themselves to few options other than repeated childbearing" (McAnarney & Hendee, 1989, p. 76).

One of the worst consequences of teenage pregnancy is the tendency for girls to drop out of school and to drift into lifelong financial dependency. These girls go to a school in Fort Worth, Texas, especially oriented toward pregnant students aged 12 to 21. Some of the girls keep their babies; others release them for adoption. Either way, the mothers can continue their education.

Children of teenage parents are more likely than other children to have low IQ scores and to do poorly in school (Baldwin & Cain, 1980), and this likelihood increases over the years. As preschoolers, these children are often overactive, willful, and aggressive. In elementary school, they tend to be inattentive and easily distracted, and they give up easily. In high school, they are often low achievers (Brooks-Gunn & Furstenberg, 1986). However, a recent 20-year study that followed more than 400 teenage mothers in Baltimore found that two-thirds of their daughters did not become teenage mothers themselves, and most graduated from high school (Furstenberg, Levine, & Brooks-Gunn, 1990).

### Why Teenagers Get Pregnant

Why, in an age of improved methods of contraception, do so many adolescent girls become pregnant? Usually, it is because they use no method of contraception. Two-thirds of sexually active teenagers do not use birth control consistently, and one-fourth *never* use it.

Why don't teenagers use birth control? The most common reason they give is that they did not expect to have intercourse and therefore did not prepare for it. But when asked why their *peers* do not use contraceptives, many adolescents tell a different story. Nearly 40 percent say that young people either prefer not to use birth control, do not think about it, do not care, enjoy sex more without it, or want to get pregnant. Other reasons frequently mentioned are lack of knowledge about or access to birth control (25 percent), embarrassment about seeking contraception or fear that parents will find out that they are having sex (24 percent), and the belief that pregnancy "won't happen to me" (14 percent) (Louis Harris & Associates, 1986). This last reason is an example of the personal fable ("It can't happen to *me*!"), explained in Chapter 10.

Guilt feelings often underlie the explanation that sexual activity was unexpected. The saying "I'm not that kind of girl" sums up the attitude of some girls who do not use birth control (Cassell, 1984). These girls feel that sexual intercourse is wrong, and they preserve their self-respect by considering themselves swept away by love and unable to help themselves. Unpremeditated sex is acceptable; carefully planned sex is only for "bad" girls. The guiltier a girl feels about having premarital sex, the less likely she is to use an effective method of contraception (Herold & Goodwin, 1981). A girl who feels guilty is embarrassed to go to a birth control clinic and have an internal physical examination. She is less likely than a girl who does not feel guilty to read about birth control, and she is more likely to think that oral contraceptives are hard to get.

## BOX 11–3    WINDOW ON THE WORLD

# PREVENTING TEENAGE PREGNANCY

Why is the United States the only industrial nation in the world where teenage pregnancy is increasing? Several factors commonly offered as causes—the prevalence of sexual activity among teenagers, an unusually large population of poor African American teenagers, high unemployment among teenagers, and federal welfare programs that ease the financial pressure of teenage parenthood—fail to explain the trend (E. F. Jones et al., 1985).

Let's see why:

■ Rates of early intercourse are similar in the United States and the Netherlands, yet pregnancy and abortion rates for girls aged 15 to 19 are about 7 times higher in the United States. In Sweden, where girls become sexually active even earlier, rates of pregnancy and abortion are less than half the American rates.

■ Rates of pregnancy and abortion are far higher among both white and black American teenagers than they are for teenagers elsewhere.

■ Unemployment among teenagers is a serious problem in other industrial countries, too.

■ Industrial nations with more generous support programs for poor mothers have much lower rates of teenage pregnancy than the United States.

How, then, do other countries succeed in preventing teenage pregnancy?

■ *Easy availability of free or inexpensive contraceptives on a confidential basis.* Adolescents in Britain, France, the Netherlands, and Sweden can get contraceptives free or at low cost from doctors or clinics. In Sweden, parents cannot be told that their children have sought contraceptives; in the Netherlands, teenagers can request confidentiality (E. F. Jones et al., 1985). American teenagers say that making contraceptives free, keeping their distribution confidential, and making them easy to get would be the three most effective ways to encourage use of birth control. Teenagers suggest establishing clinics close to (but not in) schools to make access easier (Louis Harris & Associates, 1986).

■ *Sex education and information about sex.* In Sweden, sex education is compulsory at all grade levels. Dutch schools have no special sex education programs, but mass media and private groups in the Netherlands provide extensive information about birth control, and Dutch teenagers are well informed (E. F. Jones et al., 1985). Realistic, comprehensive educational programs that include information on various means of contraception and how to obtain them are related to getting teenagers to use birth control consistently and effectively (Alan Guttmacher Institute, 1981).

Delaying sexual activity is the most effective means of birth control. When parents talk about sex with children from an early age, communicate healthy attitudes, and are available to answer questions, the children are likely to wait longer for sex (Conger, 1988; Jaslow, 1982). Community programs can also help young people stand up against peer pressure to be more sexually active than they want to be (Howard, 1983). Peers can also influence teenagers to delay sex. In the United States, teenage girls tend to respond especially well to counseling by other girls close to their own age (Jay, DuRant, Shoffitt, Linder, & Litt, 1984). Girls (and boys) will often heed peers who say that having sex without birth control is foolish rather than romantic, when they might not pay attention to the same advice coming from an older person. The two arguments for delaying sex that teenagers find most convincing are the danger of getting STDs and the danger that a pregnancy will ruin a person's life (Louis Harris & Associates, 1986).

It seems clear that parents need support from communities to help prevent young people from becoming pregnant while they are still children themselves. Some school districts around the country have begun to provide such support, through programs of information and, increasingly, through distribution of condoms and other contraceptives (Barbanel, 1990). Perhaps steps like this, which other countries seem to use successfully, can also be effective in the United States.

## Who Is Likely to Get Pregnant?

Social factors affect both premarital sexual activity and the use of birth control. African American and Hispanic girls, girls who live with a single parent, and girls whose parents are relatively uneducated tend to use no birth control, or to use less effective methods than "the pill" or the diaphragm. On the other hand, girls who make high grades, have career aspirations, or are involved in sports or other activities *are* likely to use birth control effectively (Ford, Zelnick, & Kantner, 1979; Louis Harris & Associates, 1986).

Age, sexual knowledge, and experience are all major factors. The younger a girl is at first intercourse, the longer she is likely to wait before seeking help with contraception—and the more likely she is to become pregnant (Tanfer & Horn, 1985). The less she knows about sex, the less likely she is to protect herself (Louis Harris & Associates, 1986). And the newer she is to sexual activity, the more vulnerable she is. Half of first premarital pregnancies occur in the first 6 months of sexual activity, and 1 out of 5 occur in the first month (Zabin, Kantner, & Zelnik, 1979). Teenagers seldom seek advice about contraceptives until they have been sexually active for a year or more. Only about 40 percent use birth control for first intercourse (Louis Harris & Associates, 1986).

What is the boy's role? Studies done in the 1970s found that boys were less likely to take responsibility for preventing pregnancy than boys in previous generations (R. C. Sorensen, 1973). But more recent research shows that, though boys are less likely to use contraceptives than girls, 2 out of 5 girls who used birth control during recent intercourse relied on their partners' male methods—condoms or withdrawal (G. Adams et al., 1989). And the image of the irresponsible young man who abandons his pregnant sweetheart belies the amount of support supplied by many young fathers, especially in minority communities.

## Preventing Teenage Pregnancy

Since teenagers who are knowledgeable about sex are more likely to use birth control, parents and schools can help to lower the high level of teenage pregnancy by offering education about sex and parenthood—both the facts and the feelings (Conger, 1988). Many people fear that if teenagers know about sex, they will want to put this knowledge into practice, but community- and school-based sex education does not seem to result in more sexual activity by adolescents (Eisen & Zellman, 1987). Since the media are a powerful influence on adolescents' behavior, radio and television executives can mount campaigns to present sexual situations responsi-bly and to permit advertising of contraceptives. Since adolescents who have high aspirations for the future are also less likely to become pregnant, it is important to motivate young people in other areas of their lives and to raise their self-esteem. Programs that have focused on this approach rather than on the mechanics of contraception have achieved some success (Carrera, 1986). See Box 11-3 (opposite page) for other suggestions about how to prevent teenage pregnancy.

## Helping Pregnant Teenagers and Teenage Parents

Any pregnant woman needs to be reassured about her ability to bear and care for a child and about her continued attractiveness. She needs to express her anxieties and to receive sympathy and reassurance. The unmarried girl is especially vulnerable. Whatever she decides to do about her pregnancy, she has conflicting feelings. And just when she needs the most emotional support, she often gets the least. Her boyfriend may be frightened by the responsibility and turn away from her, her family may be angry with her, and she may be isolated from her school friends. Pregnant teenagers often benefit from talking to an interested, sympathetic, and knowledgeable counselor.

Programs that help pregnant girls stay in school can teach both job and parenting skills (Buie, 1987). Some high schools operate day care centers for the children of unmarried students, to help the mothers continue their schooling. They also offer courses in parenting for mothers and occasionally for fathers (Purnick, 1984).

The value of training young people to be parents showed up in one program in which 80 low-income teenage mothers learned either from a biweekly visit to their homes (by a graduate student and a teenage aide) or through paid job training as teachers' aides in the nursery of a medical school. The infants of both parent-training groups did better than babies in a control group. They weighed more, had more advanced motor skills, and interacted better with their mothers. The mothers who worked as teachers' aides and their children showed the most gains. These mothers had fewer additional pregnancies, more returned to work or school, and their babies made the best progress (T. M. Field, Widmayer, Greenberg, & Stoller, 1982).

The mother bears the major impact of teenage parenthood, but the young father's life is often affected as well. A boy who feels emotionally committed to the girl he has impregnated also has decisions to make. He may pay for an abortion. Or he may marry the girl, a move that will affect his educational and career plans. The father also needs someone to talk to, to help him sort out his own feelings so that he and the mother can make the best decision for themselves and their child.

## JUVENILE DELINQUENCY

There are two kinds of juvenile delinquents. One is the *status offender.* This is a young person who has been truant, has run away from home, has been sexually active, has not abided by parents' rules, or has done something else that is ordinarily not considered criminal—except when done by a minor. If Huckleberry Finn were alive and active today, he would fit perfectly into this category.

The second kind of juvenile delinquent is one who has done something that is considered a crime no matter who commits it—like robbery, rape, or murder. People under the age of 16 or 18 (depending on the state) are usually treated differently from adult criminals. Court proceedings are likely to be secret, the offender is more likely to be tried and sentenced by a judge rather than a jury, and punishment is usually more lenient. However, for some particularly violent crimes, minors may be tried as adults.

### Statistics

Teenagers are responsible for more than their share of certain kinds of crimes. Although people under age 18 constitute only about one-fourth of the total population, they account for about one-third of all crimes against property, including robbery, larceny, car theft and other kinds of theft, and arson (U.S. Department of Justice, Federal Bureau of Investigation, FBI, 1987).

Boys are much more likely than girls to get into trouble with the law. For years, 4 or 5 boys were arrested for every girl, though recently the ratio has dropped to 3.5 to 1. Still, girls' crime rates are similar to those of boys only for status offenses like running away from home, incorrigibility, and engaging in sexual intercourse. Boys commit more of almost all other offenses, especially violent ones, and account for more than 90 percent of juveniles in correctional institutions (U.S. Department of Justice, 1988). The increase among girls of such behaviors as drug use and running away from home apparently leads to activities that support them, like shoplifting, robbery, larceny, and prostitution (U.S. Department of Justice, FBI, 1987).

### Personal Characteristics of Delinquents

What makes one child get into trouble when another who lives on the same street or even in the same household remains law-abiding? Not surprisingly, children who get into trouble early in life are more likely to get into deeper trouble later on. Stealing, lying, truancy, and poor achievement in school are all important predictors of delinquency (Loeber & Dishion, 1983).

Socioeconomic status is the poorest predictor of delinquency (Loeber & Dishion, 1983). A study of 55 delinquents who had been patients at a psychiatric institute led to the conclusion that delinquency is not a class phenomenon but a result of emotional turmoil that affects young people from all levels of society. Delinquents from affluent families are frequently taken to psychiatrists, while those from poor families are more likely to be booked by the police (Offer, Ostrov, & Marohn, 1972).

In some cases, deliquency has been related to a history of physical and sexual abuse and to neurological and psychiatric problems (D. O. Lewis et al., 1988). Relating problems like these to delinquency may make it possible to treat some youthful offenders with such medications as anticonvulsants and antidepressants.

### The Delinquent's Family

Several family characteristics are associated with juvenile delinquency. In a 1987 study of 18,226 boys and girls under 18 in long-term state-operated correction institutes, more than half reported that a family member had also been imprisoned at least once, and nearly 3 out of 4 had not grown up with both parents (U.S. Department of Justice, 1988). Of course, these figures apply to young people who were arrested and convicted, and thus may reflect who gets caught up in the criminal justice system rather than who actually commits delinquent acts, since some young offenders' families have the resources to keep them out of jail.

The strongest predictor of delinquency is the family's supervision and discipline of the children. Antisocial behavior in adolescents is closely related to parents' inability to keep track of what their children do and with whom they do it. And parents of delinquent children are less likely to punish rule-breaking with anything more severe than a lecture or a threat (Patterson & Stouthamer-Loeber, 1984). The impact of ineffective parenting begins early in childhood. As we pointed out in Chapter 7, parents of delinquents often failed to reinforce their children's good behavior and were harsh or inconsistent or both in punishing misbehavior. And through the years they have not been closely involved in their children's lives in positive ways (Patterson, DeBaryshe, & Ramsey, 1989).

These findings support the discussion earlier in this chapter about adolescent rebellion. Much of the tension often considered a sign of such rebellion may arise over the conflict between adolescents' desire for instant gratification and parents' desire to socialize their children. When parents cannot or will not fill their role as socializers, their children may become problems for society.

## Dealing with Delinquency

How can we help young people lead productive, law-abiding lives? And how can we protect society? So far, the answers to both questions are unclear. Can we turn young offenders away from a life of crime by sentences that consider their youth, bolstered by social solutions like probation and counseling? Or would we have less crime if we treated young offenders as we treat adults, basing sentences on the seriousness of the crime rather than the age of the offender?

One study suggests that how young offenders are treated is less important in most cases than just letting them grow up. Except for a small group of "hard-core" offenders, it is almost impossible to predict which young people will commit crimes as adults (L. W. Shannon, 1982). In this study—a longitudinal analysis of police and court records, plus interviews with more than 6000 adults in Racine, Wisconsin—more than 90 percent of the men and 65 to 70 percent of the women had engaged in some adolescent misbehavior, although many had not been caught. But only 5 to 8 percent had been booked for felonies as adults. Why did most of these people become law-abiding? Fewer than 8 percent said that they were afraid of getting caught. Most said that they had realized that what seemed like fun in their early years was no longer appropriate.

Most adolescents, then, outgrow their "wild oats" as maturity brings valuable reappraisals of attitudes and behavior. But society must continue to explore ways to help those who cannot climb out of the morass of delinquency and alienation on their own.

## A POSITIVE VIEW OF ADOLESCENCE: THREE COHORT STUDIES

Fortunately, the great majority of adolescents neither become pregnant nor get into trouble with the law. With all its turbulence, normal adolescence is an exciting time, when all things seem possible. Teenagers are on the threshold of love, of their life's work, and of participation in adult society. They are getting to know the most interesting people in the world: themselves. And, according to a recent analysis of findings from three cohorts of adolescents, most of them manage very well during these years (Offer et al., 1989).

The data for this analysis came from three separate studies of adolescents—in the 1960s, the 1970s, and the 1980s. Although both similarities and differences showed up among the three cohorts, they were more alike than different. By and large, the findings were that most adolescents enjoy life, are happy with themselves most of the time, do not feel inferior to others, and do not have major problems with body image, physical development, or sexuality. They are usually relaxed and confident in new or challenging situations, and they take pleasure in doing good work.

Above all, most of the adolescents in the three groups did not show any evidence of either a "generation gap" or a "natural rebellion" against their parents. Instead, most got along well with their parents and did not see any major problems with them. Life may not always run smoothly at home, but apparently most teenagers like their families and are proud of them. As

With all its turbulence, normal adolescence is an exciting time of life. Teenagers are on the threshold of love, of life's work, and of participation in adult society. They are getting to know the most interesting people in the world: themselves. And most of them manage very well during these years.

these investigators point out, "the family serves as a first line of psychological defense" for typical teenagers (Offer et al., 1989, p. 735).

The differences that emerged for the three cohorts showed that teenagers in the 1960s were best off, and those in the 1970s worst off. What accounts for this? One theory involves "baby booms" and "baby busts" (Easterlin, 1980). It suggests that the higher the ratio of adolescents in a population, the more problems they have. Adolescents who were part of a "baby boom" have to compete more fiercely for jobs and college admission. Such pressures may help to explain differences in self-image between generations. The adolescents studied in the 1960s were at the end of a "baby bust" generation, those studied in the 1970s were in the middle of a "baby boom," and those in the 1980s were again in a "baby bust," offering some support for this theory.

Although high-risk groups like high school dropouts were not studied, this theory might help to explain the greater problems of disadvantaged populations, which tend to have higher proportions of young people than the population at large. In these studies, however, the data do not show systematic social class and racial differences (Offer et al., 1989).

The findings from a careful analysis like this one point to the importance of having an open mind about development. Instead of looking through the filter of a preconceived theory, it is essential to look at the facts. If people believe that adolescence is normally a time of stress and disturbance, the 20 percent of the teenage population with real problems may not get the help they need, as the adults around them stand back, waiting for them to "grow out" of adolescence and out of their problems. Adolescents who show by their behavior that they are disturbed can—and should—be helped at once. With support, more of them can recognize and build on their strengths as they enter adult life.

## SUMMARY

### UNDERSTANDING PERSONALITY DEVELOPMENT

■ G. Stanley Hall considered adolescence a time of storm and stress, marked by turbulent, contradictory emotions.

■ Margaret Mead concluded from studies of South Pacific cultures that much of the stress of adolescence in western societies may be the result of cultural influences.

■ According to Sigmund Freud, before adolescents enter the genital stage of mature adult sexuality, they must overcome their feelings of hostility toward their parents. Freud saw storm and stress as an inevitable part of adolescence.

■ Anna Freud expanded Sigmund Freud's work on defense mechanisms. Two that she found particularly important during adolescence are intellectualization and asceticism.

■ Erik Erikson's psychosocial crisis of adolescence is the conflict of identity versus identity confusion. The virtue that should arise from this crisis is fidelity.

■ The most important task during adolescence is the search for identity. Research by James Marcia, based on Erikson's theory, examined the presence or absence of crisis and commitment in identity formation. He identified four categories of identity formation: achievement, foreclosure, diffusion, and moratorium.

■ Marcia, Gilligan, and other researchers have found differences in how males and females achieve identity. Intimate relationships seem more important for females, and achievement seems more important for males.

### ASPECTS OF PERSONALITY DEVELOPMENT IN ADOLESCENCE

■ Although the relationship between adolescents and their parents is not always smooth, there is little evidence that a full-blown rebellion usually characterizes it. Parents and teenagers often hold similar values on major issues.

■ The effect of maternal employment on adolescents' development is filtered through other factors such as mothers' warmth and role satisfaction.

■ Adolescents spend most of their time with their peers, who play an important role in their development. Friendships become more intimate, and relationships develop with peers of the other sex.

■ Peer pressure influences some adolescents toward antisocial behavior, especially adolescents whose parents offer little supervision.

■ Adolescents' sexuality strongly influences their developing identity. Masturbation and occasional early homosexual experiences are common.

■ Sexual attitudes and behaviors are more liberal today than in the past. There is more acceptance of premarital sexual activity, and there has been a decline in the double standard.

■ Because of social pressure, many adolescents become sexually active sooner than they feel that they should. A majority have had intercourse by age 17.

■ Although many parents are more accepting of teenage sexuality than in the past, many adolescents have difficulty discussing sexual matters with their parents.

## TWO PROBLEMS OF ADOLESCENCE

■ Pregnancy is a major problem among adolescents today. The teenage pregnancy rate in the United States is one of the highest in the world.

■ Although many pregnant teenagers have abortions, 90 percent of those who have their babies keep them. Teenage pregnancy often has negative consequences for mother, father, child, and society.

■ Juvenile delinquents fall into two categories:

1 Status offenders, who commit acts (such as truancy and incorrigibility) that are not criminal for adults.
2 Young people (under age 16 or 18) who have been found guilty of an offense punishable by law.

■ People under age 18 account for more than their share of crimes, particularly crimes against property. However, the vast majority of youngsters who have juvenile police records grow up to be law-abiding.

## A POSITIVE VIEW OF ADOLESCENCE: THREE COHORT STUDIES

■ Even with all the difficulties of establishing a personal, sexual, social, and vocational identity, adolescence is typically an interesting, exciting, and positive threshold to adulthood.

## KEY TERMS

storm and stress (page 341)
genital stage (341)
libido (341)
reaction formation (342)
intellectualization (342)
asceticism (342)
identity versus identity confusion (343)

crisis (344)
commitment (344)
identity achievement (344)
foreclosure (344)
identity diffusion (345)
moratorium (345)

adolescent rebellion (346)
masturbation (355)
sexual orientation (355)
heterosexual (355)
homosexual (355)
status offender (362)

## SUGGESTED READINGS

**Apter, T. (1990).** *Altered loves: Mothers and daughters during adolescence.* New York: St. Martin's. This is an insightful study of changes in the mother-daughter relationship during adolescence. It is based on the author's interviews with mothers and daughters in England and the United States, and on recent psychological studies of family interaction.

**Hyde, J. (1990).** *Understanding human sexuality* (4th ed.). New York: McGraw-Hill. An exceptionally readable textbook covering a wide range of topics in the area of sexuality: physical and hormonal factors, contraception,

research on sex, variations in sexual behavior, sexual dysfunction, and the treatment of sex in religion, the law, and education.

**Steinberg, L., & Levine, A. (1990).** *You and your adolescent: A parent's guide for ages 10–20.* New York: Harper & Row. This informative book by a psychologist-writer team draws on current research (including the senior author's extensive investigations) to explain the physical and psychological changes of adolescence and to offer advice on communicating with teenagers and helping them through these years.

## PART FIVE

# FIVE

# YOUNG ADULTHOOD

People change and grow in many ways during the years from ages 20 to 40, the approximate boundaries by which we define *young adulthood*. During these two decades, they make many of the decisions that will affect the rest of their lives—their health, their happiness, and their success. It is in this stage of life that most people leave their parents' home, take their first job, get married, and have and raise children—all major transitions. No wonder many social scientists consider these years the most stressful in the life span!

■ How adults eat, how much they drink, whether they smoke, how much exercise they get, how they handle stress—all these choices involving lifestyle can have a major impact on both present and future physical functioning, as we see in **Chapter 12.** We also discuss here the ramifications of decisions about college and career, which are related to developments in intellectual functioning in early adulthood. And we see some ways in which adults' thought processes differ from those of younger people.

■ In **Chapter 13,** we discuss two different approaches to explaining social and emotional development in adulthood: Erik Erikson's age-related theory, which has inspired several intensive studies of adults; and the timing-of-events theory, which emphasizes life experiences more than chronological age in explaining why people feel and act as they do. With both theories as a background, it is easier to understand the events of young adulthood that relate to some core choices: to adopt a sexual lifestyle, to marry or remain single, to have children or not, and to make friends.

EARTH DAY 1990 WASHINGTON D.C.

# PHYSICAL AND INTELLECTUAL DEVELOPMENT IN YOUNG ADULTHOOD

If . . . happiness is the absence of fever then I will never know happiness. For I am possessed by a fever for knowledge, experience, and creation.

*DIARY OF ANAÏS NIN* (1931–1934),
WRITTEN WHEN SHE WAS BETWEEN 28 AND 31

- How do the lifestyles and behavior of young adults affect their physical health?
- How do intellectual functioning and moral reasoning develop in young adulthood?

- How does the college experience influence development?
- What impact do age, gender, and family have on career development and satisfaction with work?

For many people, the essence of young adulthood is captured in these words: "Time—there's never enough to do everything I want to do and everything I should do." A college senior is trying to fit in all the courses needed to prepare for medical school. A newly hired attorney works 80 hours a week while trying to find time to see her fiancé and her friends, run 5 miles a day, and occasionally relax. A middle-level management executive feels defensive when his boss questions his career commitment because he leaves work early enough to have dinner with his children. And a single mother, overwhelmed by the stresses of raising a baby alone and making ends meet, relieves her tensions by smoking too much and eating too little.

People set priorities every day of their lives. The important decisions made in these years affect health, careers, and personal relationships. And the people making them are still maturing in many important ways. At one time, developmentalists considered the years from the end of adolescence to the onset of old age as a relatively uneventful plateau, but research now confirms our own personal experiences that this is not so.

Actually, the adult years hold great potential for intellectual, emotional, and even physical development. Important advances occur during young adulthood (which we define here as the span between ages 20 and 40), throughout middle age (from age 40 to age 65), and through late adulthood (age 65 and over).

Some of these advances come about as the result of new and significant roles that many people assume in adulthood: worker, spouse, parent. These roles affect how people think and how they act. And how they think and act affects how they fill those roles—or whether they take them on at all.

The interactions among the various aspects of development—physical, intellectual, and social and emotional—are striking. We see how personality affects health when we look at factors that incline some people to smoke, drink, or exercise, or that increase the risk of heart attack. We examine such intellectual issues as the measurement of adult intelligence, whether there are adult stages of cognitive development, and whether men and women follow different routes to moral maturity. We also look at the college experience and the intellectual and personality development that occurs in college. We end this chapter with a discussion of one of the most important issues during this period of life, the choice of career, which will come up again in Chapter 13, when we explore personality development in adulthood and the choice of a personal lifestyle.

## PHYSICAL DEVELOPMENT

### SENSORY AND PSYCHOMOTOR FUNCTIONING

The typical young adult is a fine physical specimen. Strength, energy, and endurance are now at their peak. From the middle twenties, when most body functions are fully developed, until about age 50, declines in physical capabilities are usually so gradual that they are hardly noticed.

Today's 20-year-olds tend to be taller than their parents because of a secular trend in growth (see Chapter 10). Between ages 30 and 45, height is stable; then it begins to decline (Tanner, 1978).

The typical young adult is a good physical specimen—although few exhibit the kind of coordination, stamina, and endurance shown by the world's fastest woman runner, Florence Griffith Joyner. The Olympic gold medal winner is known to her fans as "Flo-Jo."

The peak of muscular strength occurs sometime around 25 to 30 years of age; it is followed by a gradual 10 percent loss of strength between ages 30 and 60. Most of the weakening occurs in the back and leg muscles, and slightly less in the arm muscles (Bromley, 1974). Manual dexterity is most efficient in young adulthood; agility of finger and hand movements begins to lessen after the mid-thirties (Troll, 1985).

The senses are also at their sharpest during young adulthood. Visual acuity is keenest at about age 20 and does not begin to decline until about age 40, when a tendency toward farsightedness makes many people put on reading glasses. A gradual hearing loss typically begins before age 25; after age 25, the loss becomes more apparent, especially for higher-pitched sounds. Taste, smell, and sensitivity to pain and temperature generally show no diminution until about age 45 to age 50 or later.

# HEALTH IN YOUNG ADULTHOOD
## HEALTH STATUS

Your favorite spectator sport may be tennis, basketball, figure skating, or football. Whatever it is, most of the athletes you root for are young adults, people in prime physical condition. Besides being at the peak of sensory and motor functioning, young adults are the healthiest age group in the United States. More than 90 percent of people aged 17 to 44 consider their health excellent, very good, or good (U.S. Department of Health and Human Services, USDHHS, 1990). People in this age group get far fewer colds and respiratory infections than they did as children; and when they do get a cold, they usually shake it off easily. They tend to have outgrown childhood allergies, and they have fewer accidents than children do. Many young adults are never seriously sick or incapacitated; fewer than 1 percent are limited in the ability to get around and do things because of chronic conditions or impairment.

About half of all acute conditions that young adults experience are colds, coughs, and other respiratory illness; about 20 percent are injuries. The most frequent chronic (long-lasting) conditions, especially in low-income families, are back and spine problems, hearing impairment, arthritis, and hypertension (high blood pressure). Young black adults are more likely than whites to suffer from hypertension (USDHHS, 1990). When young adults are hospitalized, it is most often because of childbirth, accidents, and diseases of the digestive and genitourinary systems (USDHHS, 1985).

Given the healthy state of most young adults, it is not surprising that in the United States, accidents (primarily automobile accidents) are the leading cause of death for people aged 25 to 34. Next comes cancer, followed by heart disease and suicide. Between the ages of 35 and 44, cancer and heart disease are the major killers. Age 35 represents a turning point—the first time since infancy when the chief cause of death is physical illness.

Gender, race, and ethnicity make a significant difference in both rates and the causes of death. Men aged 25 to 44 are twice as likely to die as women in the same age range; men are most likely to die in automobile crashes and women of cancer (USDHHS, 1990). Young African American adults are more than twice as likely to die as white people of the same age (the impact of race on health is discussed in more detail in Chapter 14). And Hispanic Americans have a variety of health problems, sometimes fatal, partly because they are less likely than any other ethnic group in the United States to have health insurance (Council on Scientific Affairs of the American Medical Association, 1991).

Killings per 100,000 men 15 through 24 years old for 1986 or 1987

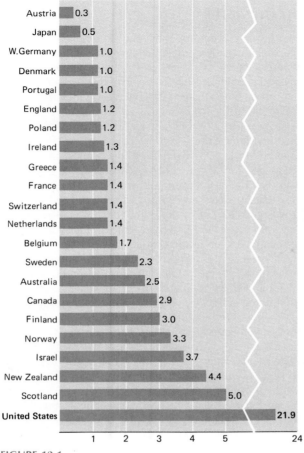

**FIGURE 12-1**
Young men at risk. Young American men are murdered at a rate 4 to 73 times that of other industrial nations. Are Americans more violent? Or is their greater accessibility to guns the reason for this high rate? (*Sources*: Fingerhut & Kleinman, 1990; *New York Times*.).

In the United States, murder is the fifth leading cause of death in young adulthood—and it is the *top* cause for young African American men and a major cause for Hispanic men. Young American men are slain at rates 4 to 73 times higher than the rates in other industrial nations (see Figure 12-1). Three-fourths of the killings in this country involve guns, compared with only one-fourth of those in other industrialized nations (Fingerhut & Kleinman, 1990). The high rate of murder might be a legacy of American frontier justice—a greater readiness to use violence. Or it may reflect the fact that the United States has no effective gun control legislation, as many other countries do. Of course, the first reason may explain the second.

## INFLUENCES ON HEALTH AND FITNESS

Good health is not just a matter of luck; it often reflects a way of life, a series of choices. Human beings are not passive victims or beneficiaries of their genes; they are to a remarkable degree the masters of their own destiny.

The Centers for Disease Control (1980) estimates that 50 percent of deaths from the 10 leading causes in the United States are linked to factors over which people have some control. Apart from such obviously risky or self-destructive behaviors as reckless driving, failing to use seat belts, associating with dangerous people, and suicide, many other things that people do from day to day can either expand or sap their vigor and extend or shorten their lives.

*Health,* as defined by the World Health Organization, is "a state of complete physical, mental, and social well-being and is not merely the absence of disease and infirmity" (Danish, 1983). People can seek health by pursuing some activities and refraining from others.

For example, a study of 7000 adults, aged 20 to 70, found that observing seven common habits (see Table 12-1 below) was directly related to health. People who followed all seven habits were the healthiest; the next-healthiest were those who followed six of the habits, then those who followed five, and so on (Belloc & Breslow, 1972). On the other hand, people who abuse drugs or alcohol and people who do not practice safe sex expose themselves to a heightened risk of disease (Pankey, 1983).

The link between behavior and health points up the interrelationship among the physical, intellectual, and emotional aspects of development. What people do af-

**TABLE 12–1**
SEVEN HEALTH HABITS

**Common Practices Directly Related to Health**

1   Eating breakfast
2   Eating regular meals and not snacking
3   Eating moderately to maintain normal weight
4   Exercising moderately
5   Sleeping regularly 7 to 8 hours a night
6   Not smoking
7   Drinking alcohol moderately or not at all

*Source:* Belloc & Breslow, 1972.

---

**BOX 12–1    PRACTICALLY SPEAKING**

# WHAT YOU CAN DO TO IMPROVE YOUR HEALTH

As research shows, people have a great deal of control over their health and longevity. How you feel and how long you live often depend on what you do. If you follow these recommendations, you will be doing your part to maximize good health and long life.

■ *Eat for health*. Eat breakfast, eat regular meals, and don't snack. Eat moderately to maintain normal weight. Eat a diet low in cholesterol to help prevent heart disease: fish and poultry (without skin) rather than red meats; almost no high-fat and smoked meats such as bacon and sausage; low-fat or skim milk and yogurt made from it; no more than two to four egg yolks a week; less butter and other fats; and low-fat cheeses like low-fat cottage cheese, low-fat ricotta, and low-fat mozzarella instead of hard and creamy cheeses. Eat foods associated with low rates of cancer: high-fiber fruits and vegetables and whole-grain cereals; citrus fruits and dark-green and yellow vegetables that are high in vitamin A, vitamin C, or both; and vegetables in the cabbage family (like cauliflower, broccoli, and brussels sprouts).

■ *Exercise regularly*. Find an exercise program that you will enjoy enough to stick with it. Try to find someone to exercise with you. It doesn't matter whether you run, bicycle, swim, walk briskly, or do aerobic dancing; what matters is working out for at least 20 minutes at a time three times a week. You need to get your pulse up to 70 to 85 percent of its theoretical maximum rate (estimated by subtracting your age from 220). If you're under 16 or over 35, see your doctor first. Build up gradually; continue to warm up gradually at the beginning of each session and cool down afterward.

■ *Use your seat belt*. It's very likely that at some time in your life you will be in an automobile accident. Your chance of being killed in a crash is 25 times higher if you are thrown out of your car. Your belt doubles your chance of surviving a crash (Engelberg, 1984).

■ *Don't smoke*. If you have never smoked, don't start. If you smoke now, stop. The sooner you stop, the better it will be for your health, the health of people around you, and the health of any children you may bear and raise in the future. You can go to one of a number of groups or professionals who offer support, or you can chew a gum specially designed for the purpose.

■ *Don't drink alcohol to excess*. If you don't drink, there's no reason to start. If you consume no more than two to three drinks a day (of whiskey, beer, or wine), and if your drinking has not caused any problems for you, there is probably no need to stop. But if you are drinking more than this—or if your drinking has gotten you into trouble on the job, at home, or with the law—your life and those of others may depend on your giving up alcohol altogether. Many people with drinking problems have found help from Alcoholics Anonymous, an organization which has chapters in communities around the world.

■ *Avoid drugs*. Drugs—especially if used heavily—can harm your health, affect your mind, weaken your motivation to work, and sour your relationships, as well as get you into trouble with the law. Pregnant women who use drugs endanger their unborn children.

■ *Learn how to cope with stress*. If you exhibit ''Type A'' behavior, make a deliberate effort to change your behavior patterns. Because hostility seems to be the harmful aspect of Type A behavior, look for a counseling program that can teach you to modify a hostile attitude.

■ *Lead a healthy sexual life*. Practice safe sex. Promiscuity has been linked to cervical cancer and to acquired immune deficiency syndrome (AIDS). Protect yourself from sexually transmitted diseases (see Box 10-2).

---

fects how they feel. But *knowing* the facts about good health habits is not enough. People's personalities, social settings, and emotional states often outweigh what they know they should do and lead them into unhealthy behavior.

Let's look at some of the behaviors that are strongly and directly linked with health (see also the practical tips in Box 12-1) and then at some factors that influence health indirectly: socioeconomic level, education, gender, and marital status.

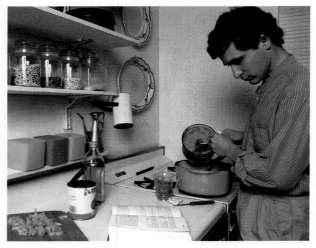

What people eat affects how they look, how they feel, and how likely they are to suffer from various diseases. This man's interest in cooking lentil soup may come from his knowledge that legumes are an excellent source of high-fiber, low-cholesterol protein. Or maybe he just likes the way it tastes.

## Diet

The saying "You are what you eat" sums up the importance of diet for physical and mental health. The first three of the seven health habits in Table 12-1 relate to diet. What people eat affects how they look, how they feel, and how likely they are to suffer from various diseases. Conditions like diabetes and gout, for example, are more common among people who eat rich foods.

### Diet and weight

In a society that values slenderness and judges people by their physical attractiveness, being overweight can lead to major emotional problems. It also carries physical risks—of high blood pressure, heart disease, and certain cancers.

The risk of being overweight is highest from ages 25 to 34, making young adults a prime target group for prevention (Williamson, Kahn, Remington, & Anda, 1990). Obesity is a serious health hazard; the National Institutes of Health (NIH, 1985) urges that the 34 million Americans who have medically significant obesity receive the same kind of attention given to patients with life-threatening disorders. Lower levels of overweight can also impair health, especially if other risk factors, like diabetes and hypertension, are present.

Research confirms the dangers of being fat. Among 8006 Japanese men aged 45 to 68, death rates were highest for the fattest and the thinnest. The thinnest men, however, had lost weight since their twenties, probably because of the illnesses they eventually died

from. People who are normally thin or who deliberately lose weight have a better prognosis than heavy people and people who lose weight as the result of ill health (Rhoads & Kagan, 1983).

The effort to lose weight is such a constant preoccupation for so many people that every year some new diet book becomes a best-seller. But although many overweight people do lose weight on fad diets, most gain it back almost immediately after resuming their usual eating patterns. The most effective way to lose weight is to eat less, use behavior modification techniques to change eating patterns, and exercise more.

### Diet and cholesterol

High levels in the bloodstream of a fatty substance called *cholesterol* pose a risk of heart disease. Cholesterol creates fat deposits in blood vessels throughout the body, sometimes narrowing those vessels so much that the blood supply to the heart can be cut off, leading to a heart attack.

The link between cholesterol and heart disease has been definitively established. In one large-scale study, almost 4000 middle-aged men with high cholesterol levels were observed for 7 years. All the men followed low-cholesterol diets, and some received a cholesterol-lowering drug. This study found that reducing cholesterol levels can lower the risk of heart disease and death (Lipid Research Clinics Program, 1984a, 1984b).

Since the most important determinant of cholesterol levels seems to be the kinds and amounts of food people eat, nine major voluntary and government health agencies have proposed a healthy American diet for everyone from age 2 up (American Heart Association, 1990). It emphasizes a variety of nutritionally sound foods, with less fat and salt, and more fiber and complex carbohydrates—cereals, grains, etc. (see Box 12-1).

### Diet and cancer

Extensive worldwide research points strongly to a link between diet and certain cancers. Japanese-American women in the United States, for example, have higher rates of breast cancer than women in Japan. But people in Japan have higher rates of cancer of the stomach and esophagus than Americans of Japanese descent. Breast cancer may be related to a high-fat diet, which is more common in the United States; and stomach and esophageal cancers are associated with pickled, smoked, and salted fish, which are more commonly eaten in Japan than in the United States (Gorbach, Zimmerman, & Woods, 1984). The new "healthy American diet" takes the risk of cancer into account, too (American Heart Association, 1990).

A moderate program of regular physical activity brings many benefits. It helps people feel and look good, builds muscles, strengthens heart and lungs, keeps weight down, and protects against various disorders.

## Exercise

After a distinctly nonathletic adolescence, each of the authors of this book joined one of the biggest trends of the past decade—regular exercise. Now Diane makes a point of taking a long brisk walk every day, and Sally jogs every morning. To our surprise, like many who have become more active in adulthood, we've found that exercise can be fun—even though it is good for us!

Today's "exercise boom" is highly visible; still, only about 8 percent of American adults regularly walk, swim, or do any other activity often enough and long enough to stay in good physical condition (Morbidity & Mortality Weekly Report, MMWR, 1989c). Those who

do—who jog or jump, dance or swim, bike or bounce—reap many benefits. Physical activity helps to maintain desirable body weight; build muscles; strengthen heart and lungs; lower blood pressure; protect against heart attacks, cancer, and osteoporosis (a thinning of the bones that tends to affect older women, causing fractures; see Chapter 14); relieve anxiety and depression; and possibly lengthen life (P. R. Lee, Franks, Thomas, & Paffenberger, 1981; McCann & Holmes, 1984; Notelovitz & Ware, 1983).

According to one study of more than 13,000 healthy men and women, the benefits of exercise are not reserved only for marathoners and aerobics fanatics (Blair et al., 1989; see Figure 12-2). These subjects fell into

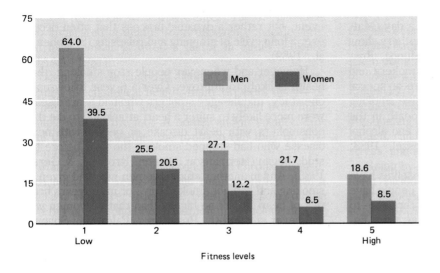

FIGURE 12-2
Death rates and fitness levels. In a study of adults at different levels of fitness, those at higher levels tended to live longer. The biggest difference showed up between the most sedentary group and the next higher level of fitness. (Note: Death rates are expressed as deaths per 10,000 person-years of follow-up.) (Source: Blair et al., 1989.)

**TABLE 12-2**
SOME TYPICAL LIFE EVENTS AND WEIGHTED VALUES

| Life Event | Value |
| --- | --- |
| Death of spouse | 100 |
| Divorce | 73 |
| Marital separation | 65 |
| Jail term | 63 |
| Death of close family member | 63 |
| Injury or illness | 53 |
| Marriage | 50 |
| Being fired at work | 47 |
| Marital reconciliation | 45 |
| Retirement | 45 |
| Change in health of family member | 44 |
| Pregnancy | 40 |
| Sex difficulties | 39 |
| Gain of new family member | 39 |
| Change in financial state | 38 |

*Source:* Adapted from T. H. Holmes & Rahe, 1976.

Holmes and Rahe's research is important in linking illness to stressful life events. But it has several shortcomings. First, it presents human beings as *react*ors rather than *act*ors and does not consider the significance of how a person interprets a particular event. For example, divorce affects a person who initiates it differently from one on whom it is imposed. Then, stress can also result from *lack* of change—boredom, inability to advance at work, or unrewarding personal relationships. Finally, their findings do not tell us *how* stress produces illness, or why some people get sick from stress while others thrive on it.

### Why does stress affect some people more than others?

*"Control" and stress*  One reason why the same event may be stressful for one person and not for another may have to do with control. When people feel that they can control stressful events, they are less likely to get sick. Research on human beings and animals has found links between stressful events perceived as uncontrollable and various illnesses, including cancer (Laudenslager, Ryan, Drugan, Hyson, & Maier, 1983; Matheny & Cupp, 1983; Sklar & Anisman, 1981).

Lack of control may also explain a finding based on a survey of 100 middle-class middle-aged Californians—that physical and psychological problems are more closely related to the irritations of everyday life than to major events (Lazarus, 1981). This might be because most people feel that they *should* be able to control the small things—avoiding traffic jams, keeping possessions from being lost or stolen, and getting along with other people. When these things turn out to be uncontrollable, people feel at fault.

Stress management workshops can teach people to control their reactions and to turn stress into an opportunity for constructive change. One program emphasizes "positive self-talk." For example, a mother who is upset by her son's poor report card can learn to stop blaming herself for failure as a parent and, instead, to tell herself that her son's grades are not within her control. Then she may be able to turn her attention to how she *can* influence her son: build communication with him or offer to help him improve his study skills. Such workshops frequently incorporate techniques like relaxation, meditation, and biofeedback.

*Personality and stress: Behavior patterns and heart disease*  How people experience stress or cope with it may reflect personality traits that have been implicated in heart disease. In one study of 227 middle-aged men, the 26 who had had heart attacks were more likely than the others to have worried and to have felt sad, anxious, tired, and lacking in sexual energy in the year before the attack (Crisp, Queenan, & D'Souza, 1984). And a study of 2320 men who survived heart attacks found that men who were socially isolated and under stress were more likely to die within 3 years after an attack than more sociable men who were under less stress (Ruberman, Weinblatt, Goldberg, & Chaudhary, 1984). It is possible that the state of mind of the high-risk men in both studies caused them to smoke more and to have unhealthy eating patterns and also affected their hormonal systems in ways that brought about heart disease.

Is a particular type of personality prone to heart attack? This is a controversial question. People who show what has been called the *"Type A" behavior pattern* are impatient, competitive, aggressive, and hostile. They act as if they are constantly racing against time and facing challenges. Those with the *"Type B" behavior pattern* are more relaxed, easygoing, and unhurried. They cope with their environment more realistically—they do not try to do the impossible; and, unlike Type A people, they do not regard everything (even leisure activities) as a challenge to their control. The doctors who coined these terms found that Type A people (mostly men) are more likely to suffer heart attacks in their thirties or forties, whereas Type B people almost never have heart attacks before age 70—even if they smoke, eat fatty foods, and do not exercise (Friedman & Rosenman, 1974).

Apparently because Type A people perceive their environment as challenging or threatening, their bodies react to even the mildest forms of stress by secreting excessive amounts of noradrenaline, an adrenaline-like hormone. These secretions may damage the lining of the coronary arteries and encourage cholesterol deposits; may cause abnormal heart rhythms, increased heart rate, and higher blood pressure; or may cause blood clots that lead to heart attacks (Rosenman, 1983).

However, recent research has found little evidence for a relationship between Type A behavior and heart disease. One line of study suggests that only one aspect of Type A behavior—hostility stemming from cynicism about other people's motives—seems to be related to heart disease (Barefoot, Dahlstrom, & Williams, 1983; R. B. Williams, Barefoot, & Shekelle, 1984). It seems that competitiveness, intensity, and other aspects of the classic Type A pattern are not harmful and that treatment should focus on reducing hostility. (Some specific suggestions are provided in Box 12-1.)

### Indirect Influences on Health

Clearly, what people do or refrain from doing, or how they respond to life's changes and challenges, affects their health directly. There are also indirect influences on health and health-related behavior: these include economic status, education, gender, and marital status.

#### Socioeconomic factors

Income is a major influence on health. More affluent people benefit both from access to better health care and from a healthier lifestyle. The association between poor living conditions and poor health helps to explain why the African American community, as well as other minority populations, has higher rates of sickness and death. But poverty is not the only reason.

#### Education

Adults who have not gone to college are at increased risk of developing chronic diseases like hypertension and heart disease. The less schooling people have had, the greater the chance that they will contract such a disease, that they will be seriously affected by it, and even that they will die of it. These findings—which hold true even when age, sex, race, and smoking or non-smoking are controlled—come from a survey of a representative national sample of 5652 working people aged 18 to 64 (Pincus, Callahan, & Burkhauser, 1987).

This does not mean, of course, that formal education *causes* good health. However, education is related to other factors that may be causative. The first, of

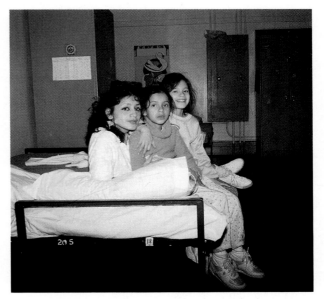

Income is a major influence on health. This family, living in a shelter for the homeless, may not be getting the nutrition and medical care needed for good health.

course, is income. Other such factors may include health habits (like diet) and the ability to solve problems (including problems about personal health). People with more education tend to come from families with more money, and so they can afford a healthier diet and better preventive health care and medical treatment. In addition, better-educated people tend to have learned and to practice sensible personal habits. They tend to exercise more and to eat better. Finally, education may help people to develop self-confidence and therefore to handle stress better.

#### Gender

Who are healthier—women or men? One problem in answering this question is that women have been excluded from a number of major studies, some of which were federally funded ones (Kolata, 1990). Thus much of what we know applies only to men. We do know that women have lower death rates throughout life. Yet women report being ill more often than men, and they use health services more often. What accounts for these differences?

***Biological differences*** Female hardiness at every stage of life has been attributed to the genetic protection given by the presence of two X chromosomes, and, in mature women, to the beneficial effects of female hormones. Also, menstruation and pregnancy tend to make women aware of the body and its functioning, and cultural standards encourage medical management of those processes. Women see doctors during pregnancy, while trying to become pregnant, and for routine tests like the Pap smear, which detects cervical cancer; and they are more likely to be hospitalized than men, most often for surgery in connection with the reproductive system (Nathanson & Lorenz, 1982).

Heart disease affects men to a much greater degree than women—or at least than women who have not reached menopause—possibly because of the hormonal protection women enjoy during the years their bodies are producing estrogen. This may be a major benefit of the menstrual cycle, a powerful regulator of hormones that fluctuate in a woman's body for some 40 years of her life—from about age 12 until about age 50.

To varying degrees, these hormones affect women's physiological, intellectual, and emotional states. For example, sight, hearing, smell, and touch operate differently at different phases of the menstrual cycle. Sight is keenest at the time of ovulation (usually midcycle), hearing peaks at the beginning of a menstrual period and again at ovulation, smell is most sensitive at midcycle and is reduced during menstruation, and sensitivity to pain is lowest just before a period. No reliable patterns have emerged for taste (Parlee, 1983). Women's cognitive abilities are only slightly influenced by the menstrual cycle, so slightly that their daily lives are not affected in any meaningful way (Kimura, 1989).

*Premenstrual syndrome (PMS)* is a disorder involving physical discomfort and emotional tension; symptoms may appear up to 2 weeks before a menstrual period and then decline during and after it. Up to one-third of women have PMS, and about 10 percent have symptoms severe enough to interfere with their normal activities (Wurtman & Wurtman, 1989).

Symptoms may include headaches, swelling and tenderness of the breasts, abdominal bloating, weight gain, anxiety, fatigue, depression, irritability, acne, constipation, and other discomforts (American Council on Science and Health, 1985; Harrison, 1982; R. L. Reid & Yen, 1981). These symptoms are not distinctive in themselves; it is their timing that identifies PMS. Women who think that they may have PMS should keep a diary to keep track of when their symptoms occur.

PMS is sometimes confused with *dysmenorrhea,* menstrual cramps. Cramps tend to afflict adolescents and young women; PMS is more typical in women in their thirties or older. Dysmenorrhea is caused by contractions of the uterus, which are set in motion by prostaglandin, a hormone-like substance; it can be treated with prostaglandin inhibitors.

The cause of PMS is not known: it may be related to hormonal and biochemical changes of the menstrual cycle; there may also be psychological causes.

Little information is available on the effectiveness of various treatments for PMS, and the Food and Drug Administration has not approved any particular drug. Some doctors prescribe progesterone; others recommend vitamins, minerals, a healthy diet, and exercise. Treatment may also target specific symptoms: for example, antidepressants for a woman who feels "blue" or diuretics for a woman who retains fluids. Since some women report relief after binge eating of carbohydrates, one research team suggests a high-carbohydrate diet (Wurtman & Wurtman, 1989). Treatment with a drug used to treat obesity has reduced some symptoms, apparently by affecting a transmitter chemical in the brain.

***Behavioral and attitudinal differences*** Women's more frequent visits to physicians reflect greater sensitivity to their bodies. Women generally know more than men about health, think more and do more about preventing illness, are more aware of symptoms and susceptibility, and are more likely to talk about their medical fears and worries (Nathanson & Lorenz, 1982). Gender-role stereotyping may also enter in: men may feel that illness is not "masculine" and thus may be less likely to admit that they do not feel well.

Thus the fact that women say more often than men that they are sick does not mean that women are in worse health, nor does it mean that they are imagining ailments or that they have an unhealthy preoccupation with illness. It may well be that the better care women take of themselves helps them to live longer than men.

As women's lifestyles have become more like men's, their vulnerability to illness has also become more like men's. Today more women than before are dying from lung cancer and heart attacks, probably because they are smoking more and drinking more and are under more stress.

Employment may be a factor in men's lower rates of reported illness. This may change, too, as more women join the work force. Employed women report less illness than homemakers, possibly because workers need to protect their jobs, their salaries, and their image as healthy producers (Nathanson & Lorenz, 1982).

The impact of gender-related behaviors and attitudes on physical health illustrates, once again, the relationship between the various domains of development. By and large, women are health-conscious not only for themselves but for their families—their husbands, their children, and (eventually) their aging parents. Now that women are under increasing pressures in the workplace, some observers are concerned that they will have less time and energy to monitor health, for themselves or for their families.

It will be interesting to see what changes occur as women's and men's roles keep moving closer to one another. Will the changing roles of men and women result only in women's picking up more of the ills that formerly fell more heavily on males? Or will men begin taking on such "feminine" habits as a heightened awareness of health and of what is necessary to keep it and restore it?

### Marital status

Marriage also enters the picture as a factor in health. Marriage seems to be healthful for both women and men, as we'll see in Chapter 13. But it is also possible that married people merely *seem* healthier, since family responsibilities discourage them from taking time off from work.

# INTELLECTUAL DEVELOPMENT

Common sense tells us that when we become adults, we think differently from the way we did as children, or as adolescents. We can hold different kinds of conversations, understand more complicated material, and solve harder problems. Common sense, of course, is not always correct. But in this case, new and exciting research confirms these beliefs.

In this section we'll look at what is now made possible by the leaps beyond earlier levels of thinking, and at what intellectual strengths we generally see in young adulthood. (We'll talk about intellectual functioning in later adulthood in Chapter 14 and Chapter 16, where we'll examine how psychologists have tested adults' intelligence and what distinctions they have made between two kinds of intelligence that psychometric tests have measured.)

## ADULT THOUGHT: THEORETICAL APPROACHES

Piaget held that cognitive progress from infancy through adolescence results from a combination of maturation and experience. What happens, then, in an adult? Experience plays an especially important role in intellectual functioning. But the experiences of an adult are different from and usually far broader than those of a child, whose world is defined largely by home and school. Because adults have such diverse experiences, it is very hard to generalize about the effects of experience on cognition in adults. Still, some developmentalists have looked at intellectual development in adulthood.

## K. WARNER SCHAIE: STAGES OF COGNITIVE DEVELOPMENT

As a teenager, Spencer liked to match wits with participants on television quiz shows. By his mid-twenties, he had become impatient with such "games" and concentrated on using his extensive knowledge to develop computer software for museums. By his late thirties, he was focusing on ways to expand the small company he had started, in order to provide for his family and the two employees who had been with him from the beginning.

Spencer illustrates a progression identified by K. Warner Schaie (1977–1978), who believes that intellectual development proceeds in relation to people's recognition of what is meaningful and important in their own lives. The five stages in Schaie's theory chart a series of transitions from "*what* I need to know" (acquisition of skills in childhood and adolescence), through "*how* I should use what I know" (integration of these skills into a practical framework), to "*why* I should know" (a search for meaning and purpose that culminates in the "wisdom of old age"). According to Schaie, real-life experiences are important influences on this progression.

The sequence of stages in Schaie's model of cognitive development is as follows (see also Figure 12-3 on page 382):

1 *Acquisitive stage (childhood and adolescence).* In the **acquisitive stage,** information and skills are learned mainly for their own sake, without regard for the context, as a preparation for participation in society. Children and adolescents perform best on tests that give them a chance to show what they can do, even if the specific tasks have no meaning in their own lives.

2 *Achieving stage (late teens or early twenties to early thirties).* In the **achieving stage,** people no longer acquire knowledge merely for its own sake but use what they know to become competent and independent. Now, they do best on tasks that are relevant to the life goals they have set for themselves.

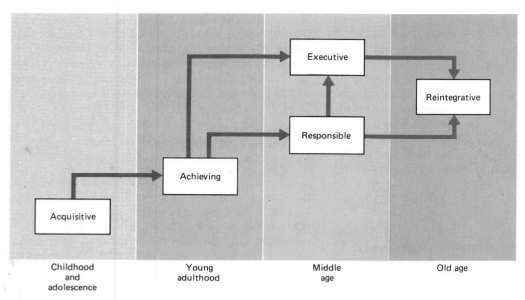

**FIGURE 12-3**
Stages of cognitive development in adults. (*Source:* Based on Schaie, 1977–1978.)

3 *Responsible stage (late thirties to early sixties).* In the **responsible stage,** people are concerned with long-range goals and practical real-life problems that are likely to be associated with their responsibilities to others (like family members or employees).

4 *Executive stage (thirties or forties through middle age).* People in the **executive stage** are responsible for societal systems (like governmental or business concerns) rather than just family units; they need to integrate complex relationships on several levels.

5 *Reintegrative stage (late adulthood).* Older adults—who have let go of some social involvement and responsibility, and whose cognitive functioning may be limited by biological changes—are more selective about what tasks they will expend effort on. In this **reintegrative stage,** they think about the purpose of what they do and bother less with tasks that have no meaning for them.

If adults do go through qualitative changes in intellectual functioning, traditional intelligence tests may be inappropriate for them (as we'll discuss further in Chapter 14). The challenge of developing new strategies to measure intellectual competence in adults will be, Schaie says , "no less than that faced by Binet in initially measuring the intelligence of school children" (1977–1978, p. 135).

## ROBERT STERNBERG: THREE ASPECTS OF INTELLIGENCE

Another way to think about thinking is in terms of the kinds of thought that become more important and more sophisticated in adult life. Let's look at an example involving three young women.

Alix, Barbara, and Courtney applied to graduate programs at Yale University. Alix had earned almost straight A's in college, scored very high on the Graduate Record Examination (GRE), and had excellent recommendations. Barbara's grades were only fair, and her GRE scores were low by Yale's high standards, but her letters of recommendation enthusiastically praised her exceptional research and creative ideas. Courtney's grades, GRE scores, and recommendations were good but not among the best.

Alix and Courtney were admitted to the graduate program. Barbara was not admitted to the program, but the psychology professor Robert Sternberg hired her as a research associate, and she took graduate classes on the side.

Alix did very well for the first year or so, but less well after that. Barbara confounded the admissions committee by doing work as outstanding as her letters of recommendation had predicted. Courtney's performance in graduate school was only fair, but she had the easiest time getting a good job afterward (Trotter, 1986).

What explains these three stories? According to Sternberg (1985b, 1987), the women represent three different aspects of intelligence. Everyone has each aspect to a greater or lesser extent, and each is particularly useful in specific kinds of situations:

1   *Componential element—how efficiently people process and analyze information.* The **componential element** is the *critical* aspect of intelligence. It tells people how to approach problems, how to go about solving them, and how to monitor and evaluate the results. Alix was strong in this area; thus she was good at taking intelligence tests and finding holes in arguments.

2   *Experiential element—how people approach novel and familiar tasks.* The **experiential element** is the *insightful* aspect of intelligence. It allows people to compare new information with what they already know and to come up with new ways of putting facts together—in other words, to think in original ways (as Einstein did, for example, when he developed his theory of relativity). Automatic performance of familiar operations (like recognizing words) facilitates insight, because it leaves the mind free to tackle unfamiliar tasks (like decoding new words). Barbara was strong in this area.

3   *Contextual element—how people deal with their environment.* The **contextual element** is the *practical* "real-world" aspect of intelligence. It becomes increasingly valuable in adult life—as in selecting a place to live or a field of work. It involves the ability to size up a situation and decide what to do: adapt to it, change it, or find a new, more comfortable setting. Courtney was strong in this area.

Alix's componential ability helped her to sail through tests in undergraduate school. But in graduate school, where original thinking is expected, it was Barbara's superior experiential intelligence—her fresh insights and innovative ideas—that began to shine. Courtney was strongest in practical, contextual intelligence—"street smarts." She knew her way around. She chose "hot" research topics, submitted papers to the "right" journals, and knew where and how to apply for jobs.

Psychometric tests measure componential (critical) intelligence rather than experiential (insightful) or contextual (practical) intelligence. Since experiential and contextual intelligence are very important in adult life, psychometric tests are much less useful in gauging adults' intelligence than in gauging children's.

An important component of contextual, or practical, intelligence is **tacit knowledge**—"inside information" or "savvy" which is not formally taught or openly expressed like knowing how to win a promotion or cut through red tape. (In the example above, Courtney was strong in tacit knowledge.)

Getting ahead in a career, for instance, often depends on tacit knowledge—*self-management* (understanding motivation and knowing how to organize time and energy), *management of tasks* (knowing how to write a grant proposal), and *management of others* (knowing when to reward subordinates). Job performance typically shows only a weak correlation with IQ and employment tests; but one study in which hypothetical work-related scenarios were presented to experts and novices in psychology and business management found a significant relationship between job performance and these three kinds of tacit knowledge (Wagner & Sternberg, 1986).

Getting a raise or a promotion, or achieving some other measure of success in business and professional life, often depends on tacit knowledge—practical, "inside" information about how things are done, which is not formally taught but must be gained from experience.

Further research may be able to answer questions like these: How and when is tacit knowledge acquired? Why do some people acquire it more efficiently than others? Are there ways to acquire it more quickly? Can it be taught directly, or is it best picked up by observing mentors?

## BEYOND JEAN PIAGET: POSTFORMAL THOUGHT

Mature thinking is even more complex than the use of formal logic in Piaget's stage of formal operations, which Piaget considered the highest level of thought. Thought in adulthood is flexible, open, and adaptive in new ways that go beyond logic. It is sometimes referred to as *postformal* thought.

A shift occurs in mature thought; as a result, mature thinkers combine both the *objective* (rational, or logical, elements) and the *subjective* (concrete elements, or elements based on personal experience). This shift helps people take their own feelings and experiences into account (Labouvie-Vief & Hakim-Larson, 1989). Wisdom can now flower, as more flexible thought enables people to accept inconsistency, contradiction, imperfection, and compromise so that they can solve real-life problems.

Thus mature thinking, or **postformal thought,** relies on subjectivity and intuition, as well as on the pure logic that is characteristic of formal operational thought (Labouvie-Vief, 1985, 1986; Labouvie-Vief & Hakim-Larson, 1989). Mature thinkers personalize their reasoning, using the fruits of their experience when they are called on to deal with ambiguous situations. In one study, for example, novice nurses stuck to the clearly defined rules they had learned for taking care of babies, but experienced nurses drew on their intuition to guide them in deciding when it was better *not* to be bound by rules (Benner, 1984). Experience, then, contributes to adults' superior ability to solve practical problems.

We can see how postformal thinking develops in a study that asked people from preadolescence through middle age to interpret a story (Labouvie-Vief, Adams, Hakim-Larson, Hayden, & DeVoe, 1987). The subjects in this study were asked to consider the following problem:

John is a heavy drinker, especially at parties. His wife, Mary, warns him that if he gets drunk once more, she will take the children and leave him. John does come home drunk after an office party. Does Mary leave John?

Children and most young adolescents said "yes"— Mary would leave John because she had said she would. Older adolescents saw that the problem was not so simple, but most of them still tried to approach it logically. However, the more mature adolescents and adults took into account the problem's "human dimensions." They realized that Mary might not go through with her threat, for a number of reasons. The *most* mature thinkers realized that there are a number of different ways to interpret the same problem, and that the way people look at such questions often depends on their individual life experiences.

In this study, that realization was partially age-related: it did not appear until late adolescence or early adulthood. In adulthood, however, age did not matter: people in their forties did not necessarily think more maturely than those in their twenties. What did matter in adulthood was that some people seemed better able to understand issues having to do with certainty and logical conclusions, and to integrate these issues with emotion.

Postformal thought is also characterized by a shift from polarization (right versus wrong, logic versus emotion, mind versus body) to an integration of concepts. This shift often occurs in college, as we'll see in the work of Perry (1970), whose studies of college students we discuss later in this chapter. One of its major effects is a new way of thinking about moral issues.

## ADULT MORAL DEVELOPMENT

According to both Piaget and Kohlberg, moral development depends on cognitive development—a shedding of egocentric thought and a growing ability to think abstractly. But at Kohlberg's fifth and sixth stages of moral reasoning—fully principled, postconventional morality—moral development is chiefly a function of experience. Not until their twenties, if ever, do people reach this level.

### HOW DOES EXPERIENCE AFFECT MORAL JUDGMENTS?

"Live and learn" sums up adult moral development. Experience leads people to reevaluate their criteria for judging what is right and fair. Experiences that promote such change are usually strongly colored by emotion, which triggers rethinking in a way that hypothetical, impersonal discussions cannot. People who undergo such experiences are more likely to see other people's points of view in social and moral conflicts.

BOX 12–2    WINDOW ON THE WORLD

# A CHINESE PERSPECTIVE ON MORAL DEVELOPMENT

Kohlberg's dilemma of "Heinz," who could not afford a drug for his sick wife (see Chapter 8), was revised for use in Taiwan: in the revision, a shopkeeper will not give a man food for his sick wife.

This version would seem unbelievable to Chinese villagers, who in real life are more accustomed to hearing a shopkeeper in such a dispute say, "You have to let people have things whether they have money or not" (Wolf, 1968, p. 21). In Kohlberg's format, subjects make an either-or decision based on their individual value systems. In Chinese society, people faced with such a dilemma discuss it openly, are guided by community standards, and try to find a way of resolving the problem to please as many parties as possible (Dien, 1982).

Other cultural differences are also involved here. In the west, even good people may be harshly punished if, under the force of circumstances, they break a law. The Chinese are unaccustomed to universally applied laws; they prefer to abide by the sound decisions of a wise judge. The Chinese outlook is that human beings are born with moral tendencies, and their moral development rests on intuitive and spontaneous feelings supported by society, rather than on the kind of analytical thinking, individual choice, and personal responsibility envisioned by Kohlberg. Kohlberg's philosophy is based on abstract principles of justice; the Chinese ethos leans toward conciliation and harmony.

How, then, can Kohlberg's theory, rooted in western values and reflecting western ideals, be applied to moral development in an eastern society that works along very different lines? Some say that it cannot be applied and that an alternative view is required—a view that measures morality by the ability to make judgments based on norms of reciprocity, rules of exchange, available resources, and complex relationships (Dien, 1982).

This viewpoint echoes the forceful protests of Carol Gilligan (1982, 1987), who has studied moral development in American women. Gilligan argues that Kohlberg's stages esteem only male-oriented values, such as justice and fairness, and ignore such female-oriented moral values as compassion and responsibility for the welfare of others.

These issues are important to American society as a whole, not only to women and to people from other cultures. If our leaders stress justice and rights (Kohlberg's values) rather than alternative values like care and responsibility, we may be encouraging our citizens to see morality as a rigid, either-or issue and to dismiss attempts to resolve conflicts in a care-focused way as "utopian, outdated, impractical," or even "the outworn philosophy of hippies" (Gilligan, 1987, p. 75). This, in fact, may help to explain the changes in our young people's values over the past two decades (see page 388). In the interest of national and global harmony, then, we need to rethink our concepts of morality.

For example, Bielby and Papalia (1975) noted that some adults spontaneously offer personal experiences as reasons for their answers to Kohlberg's moral dilemmas like Heinz's quandary (described in Chapter 8). People who have had cancer themselves, or whose family members or friends have had cancer, are more likely to condone a man's stealing an expensive drug to save his dying wife, and to explain this view in terms of their own experience.

Two experiences that advance moral development, Kohlberg believed, are encountering conflicting values away from home (as happens in college) and being responsible for the welfare of other people (as in parenthood—this is one reason why parenthood is such a major transition). According to Kohlberg (1973), cognitive awareness of higher moral principles develops in adolescence, but most people do not commit themselves to acting upon these principles until adulthood, when the crises and turning points of identity often revolve around moral issues.

With regard to moral judgments, then, a person's cognitive stage is not the entire story. Of course, someone whose thinking is still at the level of concrete operations is unlikely to make moral decisions at a postconventional level. But even someone who is at the stage of formal operations may not reach the highest level of moral thinking—unless experience catches up with cognition. Furthermore, experience is interpreted within a cultural context, affecting people differently in different countries or in different subcultures within the same country (see Box 12-2 above, for example).

## ARE THERE GENDER DIFFERENCES IN MORAL DEVELOPMENT?

The issue of gender differences in moral development is one of the hottest controversies in developmental psychology. Many critics have assailed Freud's idea that women, because of their biological nature, are morally inferior to men. Kohlberg's theory of moral reasoning has also been attacked as being based on male values and excluding female values.

Some studies of moral reasoning in adulthood have shown differences in the levels achieved by men and women, and these differences have consistently favored men. A review of the literature on moral development, however, found no significant gender differences in levels of moral reasoning across the life span (Walker, 1984). Only a few, inconsistent differences showed up in childhood and adolescence. Small differences in a few studies of adults did favor men, but the findings were not clearly gender-related, since the men were generally better educated and had better jobs than the women. The review therefore concluded that "the moral reasoning of males and females is more similar than different" (Walker, 1984, p. 687).

Still, men and women do seem to look at moral issues in different ways, to define morality differently, and to base their moral decisions on different values. One researcher who has focused on these differences is Carol Gilligan.

Gilligan (1982) maintains that Kohlberg's approach to moral development is oriented toward values that are generally more important to males than to females, and that it fails to take into account women's major concerns and perspectives. While our society expects from men assertiveness and independent judgment, it expects from women concern for the well-being of others and self-sacrifice to ensure that well-being. A woman's central moral dilemma is the conflict between herself and others, a conflict that does not emerge from Kohlberg's theory and testing methods.

**TABLE 12–3**
GILLIGAN'S LEVELS OF MORAL DEVELOPMENT IN WOMEN

| Stage | Description |
| --- | --- |
| Level 1: Orientation of individual survival | The woman concentrates on herself—on what is practical and what is best for her. |
| *Transition 1: From selfishness to responsibility* | The woman realizes her connection to others and thinks about what would be the responsible choice in terms of other people (such as the unborn baby), as well as herself. |
| Level 2: Goodness as self-sacrifice | This conventional feminine wisdom dictates sacrificing the woman's own wishes to what other people want—and will think of her. She considers herself responsible for the actions of others, while holding others responsible for her own choices. She is in a dependent position, one in which her indirect efforts to exert control often turn into manipulation, sometimes through the use of guilt. |
| *Transition 2: From goodness to truth* | She assesses her decisions not on the basis of how others will react to them but on her intentions and the consequences of her actions. She develops a new judgment that takes into account her own needs, along with those of others. She wants to be "good" by being responsible to others, but also wants to be "honest" by being responsible to herself. Survival returns as a major concern. |
| Level 3: Morality of nonviolence | By elevating the injunction against hurting anyone (including herself) to a principle that governs all moral judgment and action, the woman establishes a "moral equality" between herself and others and is then able to assume the responsibility for choice in moral dilemmas. |

*Source:* Adapted from Gilligan, 1982.

Gilligan examined women's reasoning about an area of their lives in which they have choices: the control of fertility. She interviewed and gave moral dilemmas to 29 women referred by abortion and pregnancy counseling services. These women talked about whether they would terminate or continue their pregnancies, and how they were arriving at their decisions. The women spoke "in distinct moral language whose evolution traces a sequence of development" (Gilligan, 1982, p. 73). They saw morality in terms of selfishness versus responsibility and as an obligation to exercise care and avoid hurting others. They viewed people who care for each other as the most responsible, and people who hurt someone else as selfish and immoral. Gilligan concluded that while men tend to think more in terms of abstract justice and fairness, women tend to think more about their responsibilities to specific people. (See Table 12-3 for Gilligan's description of moral development in women).

We see here a dramatic illustration of two contrasting concepts: Kohlberg's morality of rights and Gilligan's morality of responsibility. An example of the abstract morality of Kohlberg's stage 6 is the biblical story of Abraham and Isaac: Abraham was ready to sacrifice his son's life when God demanded it as a proof of faith. An example of Gilligan's person-centered morality can also be found in the Bible, in the story of the woman who proved to King Solomon that she was a baby's mother when she agreed to give the infant to another woman rather than see it harmed. Acknowledging the female perspective on moral development lets us appreciate the importance for both sexes of connections with other people and of the universal need for compassion and care.

## COLLEGE

*College* can mean anything from a 2-year community college stressing vocational training or a small 4-year liberal arts school to a large university with graduate divisions. Most colleges today are coeducational, but a few are still all-male or all-female. With such diversity, it is hard to generalize about the college experience.

### WHO GOES TO COLLEGE?

Today's college classrooms include many different kinds of students. Juanita, for example, entered college directly from high school, having already decided on a premedical program. Vince worked for 2 years after high school and is now taking courses in music and journalism, unsure which to follow as a career. Otis wants a

master's degree in business administration as the first step on his route to a six-figure salary. Marilyn came to college looking for a husband. Consuelo interrupted her education to marry and to raise three children; now that they are in college, she herself came back to get her degree. Toshio, retired from business after a lifetime of supporting a family, now has time to expand his intellectual horizons.

More than 13.5 million students are enrolled in American colleges and universities. Fifty-four percent are women, and an increasing proportion are age 35 and older (National Center for Education Statistics, NCES, 1989a; see Chapter 14 for a discussion of learning in midlife).

## INTELLECTUAL GROWTH IN COLLEGE

College can be a time of intellectual discovery and personal growth. For students of the traditional age—those in transition from adolescence to adulthood—college offers a chance to question assumptions held over from childhood and thus to mold a new adult identity. Sometimes this questioning may lead to an identity crisis and to serious problems: abuse of alcohol or drugs, eating disorders, risk taking, and even suicide. Fortunately, however, it more often fosters healthy development.

Students change in response to other students who challenge long-held views and values; to the student culture itself, which is different from the culture of society at large; to the curriculum, which offers new insights and new ways of thinking; and to faculty members, who often take a personal interest in students and provide new role models (Madison, 1969).

One avenue of self-discovery may be the exploration of new, more realistic career choices. For example, Lucas was first attracted to a career in astronomy; but after dipping into other academic disciplines, he decided that he really wanted to work with people.

The academic and social challenges of college often lead to intellectual and moral growth. In a study that has inspired much of the research on postformal thought, William Perry (1970) interviewed 67 Harvard and Radcliffe students throughout their undergraduate years and found that their thinking progressed from rigidity to flexibility and ultimately to freely chosen commitments:

■ As students encounter a wide variety of ideas, they accept the coexistence of several different points of view, and they also accept their own uncertainty. They consider this stage temporary, however, and expect to learn the "one right answer eventually."

- Next they see the relativism of all knowledge and values: they recognize that different societies, different cultures, and different individuals work out their own value systems. They now realize that their opinions on many issues are as valid as anyone else's, even if the other person is an authority figure.
- Finally they affirm their identity through the values and commitments they choose for themselves.

The values of today's college students seem very different from those of students in the 1960s, when activism prevailed (Conger, 1988). In 1986, students were almost twice as likely as those of a generation ago to rate highly "being very well off financially" and only about half as likely to consider "developing a meaningful philosophy of life" important. Few were interested in making a contribution to society, working to correct social and economic inequities, or keeping up with political affairs. Record lows were recorded for interest in taking part in cleaning up the environment or promoting racial understanding. Young people who were not in college had a similar outlook. The only values that seemed to have held up since the 1960s were self-fulfillment and self-expression.

It is possible, however, that a steadily growing awareness of the earth's fragility and a reaction against today's high levels of racial conflict will bring back some of the socially conscious attitudes that have been associated with youthful idealism. One college president referred to the 1990s as a decade when our society can "begin to deal with both the good values of the 1960s and the realities and frailties of human nature and society generally. The seeds sown in the youth of the 1960s may blossom in the mature leaders of the 1990s" (Guskin, 1990, pp. 12–13).

## GENDER DIFFERENCES IN ACHIEVEMENT IN COLLEGE

Looking around you at your own classmates, you can probably see many signs of the rapid change in women's roles—in college enrollment, in the courses women choose, and in their personal, educational, and occupational goals. In the 1970s, high school girls were less likely than boys to go to college and less likely to finish. Today, girls are *more* likely than boys to go to college and about as likely to aim for advanced degrees (NCES, 1989a).

And women are earning more degrees today than in the past. More than half of the bachelor's and master's degrees awarded in 1987–1988, and about half of the doctoral and professional degrees, were awarded to women (NCES, 1989b). From 1974 to 1984, the percentage of women among students of dentistry, medicine, veterinary medicine, and law took large leaps (Congressional Caucus for Women's Issues, 1987).

Yet as recently as the late 1970s, some of the same girls who had outshone boys throughout high school slipped behind in college. Even the ablest female students had lower self-esteem and more limited aspirations than males. Women were avoiding academic risks and steering away from mathematics (Sells, 1980). Many overprepared for class and took careful notes, but panicked over assignments and examinations and felt less confident than their male classmates about their preparation for graduate study (Leland et al., 1979). Even highly gifted women tended to go to less selective colleges than men and were less likely to go on to prestigious graduate schools and high-status occupations (Kerr, 1985).

These patterns may have resulted from gender socialization, since during adolescence girls become more focused on relationships and boys become more focused on careers (Kerr, 1985). Society gives girls messages that emphasize the roles of wife and mother and stress the difficulty or even impossibility of combining personal achievement with love and family. Young men are given no reason to feel that their roles as future husbands and fathers interfere with developing their career potential.

This may help to explain why gender-based differences still persist today. The great majority of engineering, architecture, and science students are boys, while girls account for most students of teaching, foreign languages, and home economics (Newhouse News Service, 1987).

## LEAVING COLLEGE

The *college dropout* is variously defined as a student who leaves a college and takes some time off before resuming studies at the same school ("stopping out"), or transfers to another school, or ends college studies altogether. About half of entering college students never get a degree at all (National Institute of Education, NIE, 1984).

There is no "typical" college dropout. Students leave school for many reasons—marriage, the desire to be close to a loved one, a change in occupational status, or dissatisfaction with their school. Ability may be a factor; able students are more likely than they were in the early 1970s to remain in college (U.S. Department of Education, 1987). But although most dropouts have lower average aptitude scores than those who stay in school, they are usually doing satisfactory work.

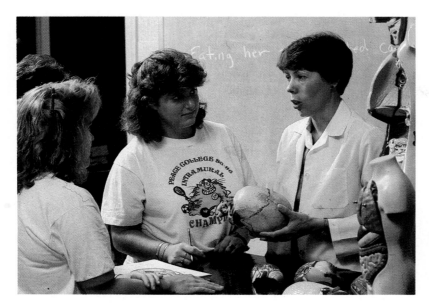

In the 1970s, high school girls were less likely than boys to go to college and less likely to finish. Today girls are *more* likely than boys to go to college and about as likely to aim for advanced degrees. Female college students may develop more interest and confidence in studying anatomy when taught by a female instructor who serves as a role model.

Leaving college temporarily is sometimes a positive step. Many students gain more by working for a while, enrolling at a more compatible institution, or just allowing themselves time to mature. After 2 years of academic work and 1 year of art school, for example, Sally's daughter Dorri took 2 years out to pursue a long-held dream of a career in rock music. She worked as a waitress and took music lessons while she was out of school—but then decided against following this route. Having learned more about herself, her goals, and the music business, she decided to go back to the school of design where she had been enrolled, which had allowed her to "stop out" for up to 2 years without having to reapply. Dorri majored in illustration, received her Bachelor of Fine Arts degree, and is now working as a graphic artist.

Many colleges make it easy for students to take leaves of absence, to study part time, and to earn credit for independent study, life experiences, and work done at other institutions. "Stopping out," then, is not a major problem; but students who drop out and never get degrees at all may limit their opportunities.

Formal education need not—and often does not—end in the early twenties. It can continue throughout adulthood. The trend toward lifelong learning can be seen in growing college enrollments over the past decade by people over 30, and especially by those over 35 (NCES, 1989b). We'll discuss the place of educational programs in the lives of mature adults in later chapters.

## STARTING A CAREER

On her way to becoming a professor of child development, Diane majored in psychology as an undergraduate and then went on to pursue a master's degree in child development and family relations, and a doctorate in life-span developmental psychology. Like many people, Diane embarked upon her first full-time job as a young adult. With her first faculty appointment, she carved out a major aspect of identity, earned financial independence, and showed the ability to assume adult responsibilities.

Long before that time, however, and long after it, work had and will continue to have a major role in her development, as it does for most people. Many a career is born in a child's dream (as a young girl, Diane pored over her parents' book on child development); adolescents struggle with thoughts of future vocations; people in midlife often change careers (sometimes voluntarily, sometimes not); and older adults face issues concerning retirement.

Work is entwined with all aspects of development. Intellectual factors, physical factors, social factors, and emotional factors affect the kind of work people do; and people's work can affect every other area of their lives. Let's look now at some important aspects of work: how age and gender affect attitudes and performance, and how working life and family life intersect. (Other work-related issues are discussed in Chapter 14 and Chapter 16.)

## WORK AND AGE

How does a person's stage of life affect the way he or she thinks about work and performs on the job? Age-related effects have been reported in an analysis of more than 185 studies (Rhodes, 1983).

### How Young Adults Feel about Their Jobs

By and large, workers under age 40, who are in the process of forming their careers, are less satisfied with their jobs overall than they will be later on, at least until age 60. They are less involved with their jobs, less committed to their employers, and more likely to change jobs than they will be in later life.

What accounts for the increase in "job satisfaction" with age? No one is sure. There are no clear age differences for some specific aspects of job satisfaction (like promotion, supervision, and coworkers), and findings about satisfaction with pay are mixed. The relationship between age and overall job satisfaction may reflect the nature of the work itself. The longer people work at an occupation, the more rewarding the work may be (Rhodes, 1983). Or it may be that younger people, who are still seeking the best path in life, know that they can change career directions more easily now than later. They may look at their jobs more critically than they will when they have made a stronger commitment.

Again, we have to be careful about differences that show up in cross-sectional studies. For example, older people have shown a greater belief in the *work ethic,* the idea that people should work hard to develop character. This is probably a difference in values between cohorts rather than an effect of how long people have lived. There may be more of a developmental difference, however, in personality needs associated with work. Younger workers, for example, are more concerned with how interesting their work is, with the opportunities it gives them to develop their abilities, and with their chances for advancement. Older workers care more about having friendly supervisors and coworkers and receiving help with their work.

### How Young Adults Perform on the Job

Findings about the relationship between age and performance at work are mixed. Studies on absenteeism, for example, give conflicting results. But if we break the findings down into *avoidable* absences (those which seem voluntary on the worker's part) and *unavoidable* absences (like those caused by sickness), we do see effects of age. Younger workers have more avoidable absences than older workers, possibly because of a lower level of commitment. Older workers have more

Age differences in performance on the job seem to depend largely on how performance is measured and on the demands of a specific kind of work. A job requiring quick reflexes and physical agility, like the work of a cable splicer, is likely to be done better by a young person.

unavoidable absences, probably because of poorer health and slower recovery from accidents.

When we look at how well people do their work, the picture again is not clear-cut. The key factor may be experience rather than age: when older people perform better, it may be because they have been on the job longer, not because they are older.

Many workers continue to be productive very late in life. In general, age differences in performance seem to depend largely on how performance is measured and on the demands of a specific kind of work. A job requiring quick reflexes is likely to be done better by a young person; a job that depends on mature judgment may be better handled by an older person.

## WORK AND GENDER

Today 1 out of every 3 economists, 1 out of every 3 computer programmers, and 1 out of every 6 mail carriers are women (Congressional Caucus for Women's Issues, 1987). Gender has less to do with vocational choice than it did 25 years ago, when most women—whatever their interests and talents—planned to devote most of their working lives to homemaking and child care. (This has rarely even been recognized as a vocational choice but has been seen as just something women are "supposed to do.")

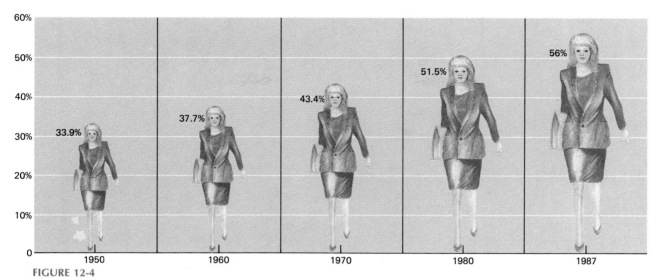

**FIGURE 12-4**

Percentage of American women in the labor force, 1950–1987. (*Source*: Matthews & Rodin, 1989.)

Even in the past, many women worked for pay outside of the home. Today, there are more women in the labor force than ever before: about 56 percent of women in 1987 (see Figure 12-4). More than 60 percent of mothers of children under age 18 and almost 60 percent of mothers with children under 6 are employed (Matthews & Rodin, 1989).

Like men, women work to earn money, to achieve recognition, and to fulfill personal needs. Many women need to work because they are single, divorced, widowed, separated, or married to men who do not earn enough to support the family. Trends toward later marriage, later childbearing, and smaller families have made it easier for many women to pursue ambitious career goals. And both men and women take advantage of alternative work patterns like part-time and flexible schedules and job sharing.

Laws mandating equal opportunity in employment are designed to give both sexes equal rights in hiring, pay, and promotion. But reality still falls far short of this ideal. For example, for every dollar that men earn, women earn only about 70 cents. This wage gap has narrowed slightly in the past few years—but that is not so much because women are paid more as because men's earnings have dropped with the disappearance of many highly paid manufacturing jobs (U.S. Bureau of Labor, 1989).

Although more women are getting better jobs these days (especially in business and the professions), a large proportion are still doing low-paid work that has traditionally been done by women (and that tends to remain low-paid largely *because* it is done by women). Almost half of all employed women are clerks, salespersons, and the like; very few have skilled craft or construction jobs. Many enter the labor force in low-paying entry-level jobs, and often they do not advance as rapidly as men. This is due partly to discrimination, and partly to the conflicts and problems of juggling work and family roles in a society that gives little support to families (see Box 12-3 on page 392). As one observer sees it, women are "stuck" (Kessler-Harris, 1987). Employers offer them low-level jobs because they believe women are unreliable workers whose primary commitment is to their families, but women who see that their employment options are limited figure that they might as well put more of their energies into their family lives than into their work.

New work patterns change day-to-day life for the whole family and bring new stresses and satisfactions. Once again, we see the interrelationship between different aspects of people's lives. In Chapter 13, we'll explore further the effects of both work and relationships on young men's and women's personality development.

BOX 12–3   THINKING CRITICALLY

# HOW DUAL-EARNER COUPLES COPE

Both authors of this book have been personally involved in a significant trend in American life: marriages in which husband and wife both hold jobs outside the home. This represents a major change from traditional family patterns and—as both research and our own personal experiences testify—it offers both pluses and minuses.

A major advantage, of course, is financial. Most first-time home buyers are two-earner families, for example, and a second income raises some families from poverty to middle-income status and makes others affluent. Many women who work in mills and factories contribute almost half of the family income (L. Thompson & Walker, 1989). Other benefits over the one-income household often include:

- More equal relationship between husband and wife
- Greater sense of integrity for the woman
- Closer relationship between a father and his children
- Greater capacity for each partner to function and develop in both work and family roles

But this way of life also creates many stresses. Working couples face extra demands on their time and energy, conflicts between work and family roles, possible rivalry between spouses, and anxiety and guilt over meeting children's needs.

One source of strain is the fact that husband and wife are part of three role systems—the wife's work system, the husband's work system, and the joint family system. Each role makes demands at different times, and partners have to decide which should take priority at each time. The family is most demanding when there are young children; careers are especially demanding, and especially stressful, when a worker is getting established or being promoted. And both kinds of demands frequently occur around the same time, often in young adulthood.

Because these sweeping changes in family patterns and career aspirations are so new, today's hard-working, family-oriented men and women have few role models—and few institutional supports from society. Couples must therefore work out their own solutions.

There have been some changes in how these couples divide work within the home. However, women who work outside the home continue to hold the primary responsibility for homemaking and child care—doing almost 80 percent of all housework (Berardo, Sheehan, & Leslie, 1987). Lower-income and minority-group husbands are most likely to do more at home, and men are most likely to "help out" with cooking or child care (L. Thompson & Walker, 1989). But still, mothers spend from 3 to 5 hours of active involvement with their children for every hour fathers spend, and mothers carry 90 percent of the burden of responsibility for child care (M. Lamb, 1987b).

The issue of who does what is not related to how much the wife earns, how many hours she works, or whether she is the dominant partner in the marriage. In fact, husbands who have more say about running the household do more of the chores (Kamo, 1988). So far, then, it is not clear what distinguishes marriages in which wage earning and family work are shared equitably from marriages in which they are not.

What kinds of changes could society institute to alleviate the strains on dual-earner families as more couples adopt this lifestyle? One possibility involves redesigning living and working environments so that people could pool domestic services and thus split their time more easily between home and workplace. Also, employers could structure more jobs on a part-time basis; communities and employers could provide more child-care services; the federal government could take a larger role in financing and offering tax incentives for child care, and in subsidizing new parents to let them postpone their return to work. Such changes would help parents, children, and society.

# SUMMARY

## SENSORY AND PSYCHOMOTOR FUNCTIONING

■ The typical young adult is in good condition; physical and sensory abilities are usually excellent.

## HEALTH IN YOUNG ADULTHOOD

■ Accidents are the leading cause of death for people from 25 to 34 years of age; cancer and heart disease, for people from 35 to 44.

■ Specific behavior patterns such as diet, exercise, smoking, drinking alcohol, and reactions to stress can affect health.

■ Good health is related to income, education, gender, and marital status.

■ Women are usually more likely than men to report being ill, to use health services, and to be hospitalized. Women are more health-conscious than men and tend to arrange for health services for the entire family.

■ Hormones of the menstrual cycle seem to affect at least some women physically and emotionally. The effect on cognitive abilities does not seem to influence daily functioning.

## ADULT THOUGHT: THEORETICAL APPROACHES

■ K. Warner Schaie has proposed five stages of cognitive development from childhood through late adulthood: acquisitive, achieving, responsible, executive, and reintegrative.

■ Robert Sternberg has proposed three aspects of intelligence: componential (critical), experiential (insightful), and contextual (practical). The experiential and contextual aspects develop and become particularly important during adulthood.

■ *Postformal thought* refers to thought in adulthood that is flexible, open, and adaptive, and goes beyond formal logic. It is characteristic of mature thinkers.

## ADULT MORAL DEVELOPMENT

■ According to Lawrence Kohlberg, moral development in adulthood depends primarily on experience; but, as before, moral thinking cannot exceed the limits set by cognitive development.

■ Women's moral development has been explored by Carol Gilligan, who proposes that women have concerns and perspectives that are not tapped in Kohlberg's theory and research. Whereas men tend to think more about justice and fairness, women are more concerned with reponsibilities to specific people.

## COLLEGE

■ The college experience affects intellect and personality, as college students question long-held assumptions and values.

■ In the past, girls often did better than boys in elementary school and high school, but that picture tended to change at the college level. Today, more women are going to college and are earning advanced degrees. The fields that men and women choose to study still differ markedly, however.

■ About 50 percent of college students never earn degrees.

## STARTING A CAREER

■ Career development is important during young adulthood. Younger workers are less committed to their present jobs than older workers.

■ Dual-earner families, in which both spouses work outside the home, are becoming more prevalent. Both society and the working couples have to make changes to alleviate the stresses associated with the potentially conflicting demands of work and family.

■ Women, like men, work for a variety of reasons—to earn money, to achieve recognition, and to fulfill personal needs. Women tend to earn less than men, and although more women are getting better jobs than in previous decades, most are still doing low-paid work. Today an increasing number of women are pursuing careers in business, law, medicine, and other traditionally male-dominated areas.

## KEY TERMS

stress (page 377)
"Type A" behavior pattern (378)
"Type B" behavior pattern (378)
premenstrual syndrome (PMS) (380)
acquisitive stage (381)

achieving stage (381)
responsible stage (382)
executive stage (382)
reintegrative stage (382)
componential element (383)

experiential element (383)
contextual element (383)
tacit knowledge (383)
postformal thought (384)

## SUGGESTED READINGS

**Belenky, M. F., Clinchy, B. McV., Goldberger, N. R., & Tarule, J. M. (1986).** *Women's ways of knowing: The development of self, voice, and mind.* New York: Basic Books. A lively and thought-provoking report of an in-depth survey of 135 women. The authors maintain that women think differently from men and that women's mode of thought, which combines objectivity with intuition and personal knowledge, is just as or more legitimate than traditional male models of dispassionate thinking. The book describes five common modes of women's thought, illustrates the findings with quotations and anecdotes, and explores implications for education.

**Gilligan, C., Ward, J. V., & Taylor, J. McL. (Eds.). (1988).** *Mapping the moral domain: A contribution of women's thinking to psychological theory and education.* Cambridge, MA: Harvard University Press. In 14 articles, researchers and theoreticians examine the different ways that males and females, from childhood through adolescence into adulthood, think about relationships, loyalty, responsibility, violence, and other moral issues.

**Sternberg, R. (1985).** *Beyond IQ.* Cambridge, MA: Cambridge University Press. Sternberg's statement of the triarchic theory of intelligence.

**Taylor, S. E. (1989).** *Positive illusions: Creative self-deception and the healthy mind.* New York: Basic Books. This provocative book by a social psychologist draws on a large body of research demonstrating that the best adjusted people are not, as has been traditionally believed, firmly in touch with reality. Instead, the healthy human mind seems to cope with life by replacing negative information with positive, often unrealistically optimistic, beliefs.

## CHAPTER 13

# PERSONALITY AND SOCIAL DEVELOPMENT IN YOUNG ADULTHOOD

Human beings are not born once and for all on the day their mothers give birth to them. . . . Life obliges them over and over again to give birth to themselves.

GABRIEL GARCIA MARQUEZ,
*LOVE IN THE TIME OF CHOLERA*, 1988

- Do adults' personalities develop in definite, predictable patterns, or does the course of development depend on what happens in people's lives?
- How is personality development alike and different for young men and women?
- How do young adults get along with their parents?
- What are the effects of such lifestyle choices as marriage, divorce, single life, cohabitation, parenthood, stepparenthood, and remaining childless?
- What do love, sexuality, and friendship mean to young adults?

Looking back, both authors of this book—one now in her early forties, and the other in her mid-fifties—would say, like most people at midlife, that they are very different from the people they were at age 20, when they entered young adulthood. And by age 60 or age 70, they are likely to have changed even more. It is difficult to realize, then, that until recently, students of human development paid very little attention to the social and emotional changes that take place during the 50 or more years of adult life.

Today, few people believe that the personality stops growing when the body does. Most developmentalists are now convinced that human beings can change and grow as long as they live. In this chapter and Chapters 14 through 17, we look at theories and research on adult development that have arisen over the past few decades.

Two main approaches to adult development are the normative-crisis model and the timing-of-events model. In this chapter, we look at research supporting both approaches. We also examine how young adults reach important decisions that frame their lives—decisions that revolve around love, sex, parenting, friendship, and work and career.

## PERSONALITY DEVELOPMENT IN YOUNG ADULTHOOD: TWO MODELS

### NORMATIVE-CRISIS MODEL

The **normative-crisis model** describes human development in terms of a definite sequence of age-related social and emotional changes. Those who follow this approach, like Erik Erikson and researchers whom he inspired, believe that everyone follows the same basic built-in "ground plan" for human development (see Table 13-1 on page 402). In this chapter we describe the changes of young adulthood; in Chapters 15 and 17 we discuss changes later in life.

### Erik Erikson: Crisis 6—Intimacy versus Isolation

The sixth of Erikson's eight crises—and what he considers the major issue of young adulthood—is **intimacy versus isolation**. Young adults, says Erikson, need and want intimacy; they need to make deep personal commitments to others. If they are unable or afraid to do this, they may become isolated and self-absorbed.

The ability to achieve an intimate relationship, which demands sacrifice and compromise, depends on the sense of identity, supposedly acquired in adolescence. A young adult who has a strong identity is ready to fuse it with that of another person.

Not until a person is ready for intimacy can "true genitality" occur. Until this point, people's sex lives have been dominated by the search for identity or by "phallic or vaginal strivings which make of sex-life a kind of genital combat" (1950, p. 264). Now, however, psychologically healthy people are willing to risk temporary loss of self in coitus and orgasm, very close friendships, and other situations requiring self-abandon.

The young adult, then, can aspire to a "utopia of genitality"—mutual orgasm in a loving heterosexual relationship, in which trust is shared and cycles of work, procreation, and recreation are regulated. The ultimate aim is to help the children of this union achieve all the stages of their own development. Erikson sees this not as a purely sexual utopia but as an all-encompassing achievement. He distinguishes sexual *intimacies*, which may take place in casual encounters, from *intimacy with a capital "I,"* characterized by mature mutuality that goes beyond sexuality (E. Hall, 1983).

The "virtue" that develops in young adulthood is the *virtue of love,* or *mutuality of devotion* between partners who have chosen to share their lives. People also need a certain amount of temporary isolation during this period in order to think about their lives on their own. As young adults resolve conflicting demands of intimacy, competitiveness, and distance, they develop an ethical sense, which Erikson considers the mark of the adult.

Intimacy, a major achievement of young adulthood, comes about through commitment to a relationship that may demand sacrifice and compromise. Erikson says that intimacy is possible only after each partner has achieved his or her own identity. But Gilligan and other researchers propose a different sequence for women, who, they say, often achieve intimacy first and then go on to find identity later, sometimes years later.

A decision not to fulfill the natural procreative urge has serious consequences for development, says Erikson. Thus he limits "healthy" development to loving heterosexual relationships that produce children. His exclusion of single, celibate, homosexual, and other childless lifestyles has been criticized, as has his focus on a male pattern of development. Also, his assertion that people establish their identity in adolescence is too narrow. Other research shows that the search for identity continues during adulthood.

## George Vaillant: Adaptation to Life

In adapting to life, people can change themselves, their surroundings, or both. What kinds of adaptations are healthiest, and how do various adaptations affect the quality of life?

In 1938, 268 eighteen-year-old Harvard undergraduates—self-reliant and emotionally and physically healthy—were selected for longitudinal research called the *Grant Study.* Reporting on the findings when the men were in their fifties and again in their sixties, Vaillant (1977; Vaillant & Vaillant, 1990) came to several important conclusions: that our lives are shaped not by isolated traumatic events but by the quality of sustained relationships with important people, that we change and develop throughout life, and that the mechanisms we use to adapt to circumstances determine our level of mental health.

### Vaillant's adaptive mechanisms

Vaillant identified four characteristic ways in which people adapt: (1) *mature* (such as using humor or helping others), (2) *immature* (such as developing aches and pains with no physical basis), (3) *psychotic* (distorting reality), and (4) *neurotic* (repressing anxiety, intellectualizing, or developing irrational fears). Men who used mature **adaptive mechanisms** were more successful in many ways. They were happier, were mentally and physically healthier, got more satisfaction from work, enjoyed richer friendships, made more money, and seemed better adjusted all around.

### Career consolidation and stages of development

The life histories of the men in the Grant Study support Erikson's progression, with the addition of a stage that Vaillant calls **career consolidation.** In this stage, somewhere between their twenties and their forties, people become preoccupied with strengthening a career. This stage would come after Erikson's sixth crisis (development of intimacy) and before the seventh (generativity, or guiding the next generation).

The timing of career consolidation—after intimacy but before generativity—may suggest why many marriages run into trouble by the seventh year. For one thing, either partner may turn away from the relationship to focus on a career. Also, problems loom largest for partners who are at different points: if, say, a wife is focused on intimacy and a husband on career; or if a wife is wrapped up in a career while the husband is ready to move on to generativity.

The ages when changes take place vary, but Vaillant (1977) saw a typical pattern. At age 20, many of the men he studied were still under parental dominance. (This finding has also surfaced in recent research, as indicated in Box 13-1 on page 400). During their twenties—and sometimes thirties—they won autonomy from parents, married, had and raised children, and deepened friendships begun in adolescence. Of the men who at age 47 were considered best adjusted, 93 percent had stable marriages before age 30 and were still married at 50.

Between ages 25 and 35, these men worked hard at consolidating their careers and devoted themselves to their families. They followed the rules, strove for promotions, accepted "the system," rarely questioning whether they had chosen the right woman or the right career. The excitement, charm, and promise they had radiated as students disappeared, so that in 1950 and 1952 they were described as "colorless, hardworking, bland young men in gray flannel suits" (Vaillant, 1977, p. 217).

BOX 13–1   THINKING CRITICALLY

# ESTABLISHING MATURE RELATIONSHIPS WITH PARENTS

When does a person leave adolescence to become a mature adult? According to new research, this transition usually occurs not in the teens but in the late twenties—at least for white middle-class high school graduates. A dramatic shift in psychological maturity typically occurs between ages 24 and 28; it can be tracked by measuring a young adult's relationship with his or her parents. Men and women mature differently, but whether a person is married or unmarried does not affect maturation.

These conclusions emerged from interviews with 78 women and 72 men between 22 and 32 years of age (Frank, Avery, & Laman, 1988). These 150 high school graduates from a midwestern suburb were assessed on their relationships with their parents, according to 10 different aspects of maturity. Five of the measures evaluated autonomy, including how well the young adults could make decisions and take responsibility for their own lives. Another five measures evaluated the relationships between the generations—how close they were, how they communicated, and how the young people felt about their parents. The researchers then described six major relationship patterns:

1 *Individuated.* Young adult (YA) feels respected by parents, freely seeks their advice and help, acknowledges their strengths, enjoys being with them, and has few conflicts with them. Yet YA feels separate from parents and is aware of and untroubled by a lack of intensity and depth in the relationship.

2 *Competent-connected.* YA is strongly independent, with life views that differ radically from parents' beliefs, but feels more empathic toward parents than individuated YA and often helps

parents resolve their own problems of health, drinking, or relationships. The mother may be seen as demanding and critical, but YA understands her limitations, keeps conflicts within limits, and stays close to her.

3 *Pseudoautonomous.* YA pretends not to care about conflicts with parents and disengages rather than confronting parents openly. Fathers are often seen as uninterested and mothers as intrusive; both are seen as unable to accept YA for himself or herself.

4 *Identified.* In this unusually open and intimate relationship, YA accepts parents' values and outlook on life, seeks advice on most major decisions, and feels secure in the parents' availability. There are few tensions, and parents are seen as nonjudgmental and supportive.

5 *Dependent.* YA cannot cope with ordinary life situations without parents' help, feels troubled by this but unable to change, and sees parents as overbearing and judgmental or emotionally detached and preoccupied with themselves. YA either goes along with parents' wishes or gets into childish power struggles. This pattern is equivalent to insecure or avoidant attachment.

6 *Conflicted.* This profile emerged only with fathers. YA sees the father as hot-tempered and incapable of a close relationship, feels constantly under attack, is ashamed of the father's inadequacies, and longs to be closer to him.

The profiles of young women's relationships with their parents—and thus of their psychological maturity, according to this model—differed from those of young men. Women were most likely to be "competent-connected" with their mothers and

"identified" or "conflicted" with their fathers. Men were most often "individuated" with both parents or "pseudoautonomous" with their fathers. And women were somewhat more likely than men to be "dependent" on their mothers.

For both sexes, age was important. About half of those over 28 years old felt that they could cope with most aspects of life without asking their parents for help, and only 1 in 5 had serious doubts that they could manage on their own. For people under 24, however, these proportions were reversed: only 1 in 5 felt that they could cope with most aspects of life independently, and half had serious doubts that they could manage on their own.

If findings like these are borne out by more broad-based research, developmentalists will need to take a new look at the timetable for the end of adolescence and the beginning of adulthood, and what this means for education, career planning, and relationships between the generations.

However, we need to look closely at the population groups involved. This new schedule for achieving adulthood probably reflects the fact that middle-class young people remain dependent on their parents for support longer today than they did in the past. Adulthood may come sooner for less affluent young people, who become economically independent at earlier ages. Adulthood may also come sooner for children who leave the nest earlier. Children who grow up in stepfamilies and single-parent families, especially when they have many siblings, are likely to leave home at younger ages (Mitchell, Wister, & Burch, 1989). Once again, we have to guard against drawing sweeping conclusions from relatively small, limited samples.

The stage of career consolidation ends when "at age 40—give or take as much as a decade—men leave the compulsive, unreflective busywork of their occupational apprenticeships, and once more become explorers of the world within" (Vaillant, 1977, p. 220).

## Daniel Levinson: Life Structure

In a smaller, biographical study, Daniel Levinson and his colleagues at Yale University (1978) interviewed in depth and gave personality tests to 40 men aged 35 to 45, equally divided among four occupations: hourly workers in industry, business executives, academic biologists, and novelists. The interviews covered education, work, religion, politics, leisure, and personal relationships. From this study, from biographical sources, from his (as of this writing) still unpublished studies of women, and from other research, Levinson constructed a theory of development in adulthood.

At the heart of Levinson's theory is the **life structure**—"the underlying pattern or design of a person's life at a given time" (Levinson, 1986, p. 6). It includes the people, places, things, institutions, and causes that a person finds most important, as well as the values, dreams, and emotions that make them so. Most people's life structures are built around work and family. Other elements may include race, religion, ethnic heritage, wars, economic depressions, and even influential books.

### Levinson's life eras

According to Levinson, people shape their life structures during four overlapping eras of about 20 to 25 years each, connected by transitional periods of about 5 years, when people appraise their structures and think about restructuring their lives (refer back to Table 13-1). They spend nearly half their adult lives in transition. Each era has its own tasks, and accomplishment of these tasks provides a strong foundation for the next era's life structure; failure to accomplish the tasks of one era may dangerously weaken the life structure of the next. But even the best structure will continue to change.

### Levinson's phases of early adulthood

Levinson divides early adulthood into two main phases, "novice" (ages 17–33) and "culminating" (33–45)* (again, see Table 13-1 for the tasks of each phase).

In the "novice" phase (ages 17 and 33), the first thing a man† needs to do is leave his parents' home and become financially and emotionally independent of them. Going to college or serving in the armed forces may provide a transition. Between age 22 and age 28, the emphasis is on relationships with friends and family, and with the other sex, usually leading to marriage and children; and on work, leading to choice of occupation.

Two important tasks of Levinson's "novice" phase involve the "dream" and the "mentor." A man's **dream** of the future is usually expressed in terms of his career: the vision of, say, winning a Nobel Prize spurs him on. (The eventual realization, which generally arrives in midlife, that a cherished dream will not come true may trigger an emotional crisis. The way men reassess their early goals and substitute more attainable ones determines how well they will cope with life.) Success during these apprenticeship years is influenced by a slightly older **mentor**—someone who offers guidance and inspiration, and passes on wisdom, moral support, and practical help in both career and personal matters. At about age 30, men reevaluate earlier commitments, or they make strong commitments for the first time. Some slide through this transition easily; others experience crises in their marriage or their work.

Then, in the second phase of young adulthood—Levinson's "culminating" phase—beginning at about age 33, men begin to settle down. They make deeper commitments, set goals (a professorship, for instance, or a certain level of income), and set a time for achieving their goals (say, by age 40). They anchor their lives in family, occupation, and community. But they continue to work at advancement—at improving and using their skills, becoming more creative, and contributing to society. Some of these tasks are mutually exclusive (people cannot advance if they remain stable, for example), and so they have to keep juggling and reordering their priorities.

A man now chafes under the authority of those with power and influence over him and wants to break away and speak with his own voice. He may now discard his mentor and be at odds with his wife, children, lover, boss, friends, or coworkers. How he deals with the issues of this phase will affect the midlife transition (this is discussed in Chapter 15).

---

*All ages are approximate.

†Levinson (1986) says that his conclusions apply to women, with some variations, but only his published studies of men are available at this writing.

**TABLE 13–1**
THREE NORMATIVE-CRISIS VIEWS OF PHASES IN ADULTS' DEVELOPMENT

| Erikson | Vaillant | Levinson |
|---|---|---|
| *Intimacy versus isolation (age 20 to age 40):*<br>Sense of identity, developed during adolescence, enables young adults to fuse their identity with that of others. Young adults resolve conflicting demands of intimacy, competitiveness, and distance, and develop an ethical sense. They are ready to enter into a loving heterosexual relationship with the ultimate aim of providing a nurturing environment for children. | *Age of establishment (age 20 to age 30):*<br>Moving from under the parents' dominance to autonomy; finding a spouse; raising children; developing and deepening friendships. | *Novice phase of early adulthood (age 17 to age 33):* Building a provisional life structure; learning its limitations.<br><br>**1** *Early adult transition (age 17 to age 22):* Moving out of the parents' home; becoming more independent.<br><br>**2** *Entry life structure for early adulthood (age 22 to age 28):* Building a first life structure; choosing an occupation; marrying; establishing a home and a family; joining civic and social groups; following a dream of the future and finding an older mentor to help find ways to achieve that dream. |
| | *Age of consolidation (age 25 to age 35):*<br>Doing what has to be done; consolidating career; strengthening marriage; not questioning goals. | **3** *Age-30 transition (age 28 to age 33):* Reassessing work and family patterns; creating the basis for the next life structure.<br><br>*Culminating phase of early adulthood (age 33 to age 45):* Bringing to fruition the efforts of early adulthood.<br><br>**1** *Culminating life structure for early adulthood (age 33 to age 40):*<br>a "Settling Down": Building a second adult life structure; making deeper commitments to work and family; setting timetables for specific life goals; establishing a niche in society; realizing youthful aspirations.<br>b "Becoming One's Own Man": Getting out from under other people's power and authority; seeking independence and respect; discarding the mentor. |
| | *Age of transition (around age 40):*<br>Leaving the compulsive busywork of occupational apprenticeships to examine the "world within." | **2** *Midlife transition (age 40 to age 45):* Ending early adulthood; beginning middle adulthood. |

*Sources:* Erikson, 1950; Levinson, 1978, 1986; Vaillant, 1977.

Finding a mentor—an older person who guides a younger person's career—is an important task of what Daniel Levinson calls the "novice" phase of life. The interest taken by this older doctor in the careers of his two younger colleagues may be a vital factor in their success.

### Women and Levinson's theory

Levinson (1986) believes that women go through the same kinds of age-linked changes as men. A review of four unpublished dissertations reporting in-depth interviews with very small samples of women supports his view in general but suggests some differences. The women handled tasks differently from men, and their lives were more conflicted and less stable (P. Roberts & Newton, 1987).

The four investigators interviewed a total of 39 women, from 28 to 53 years old. In one study (D. Adams, 1983), the eight respondents were all black attorneys. In the other three studies (Droege, 1982; Furst, 1983; W. Stewart, 1977), all were white, and from one-third to almost all were employed. At least half the women in each sample had been married at some time, and at least one-fourth were parents.

How did these women deal with four of Levinson's "novice" tasks?

**The dream**    All but 6 of the 39 women formed dreams, but theirs were vaguer, more complex, and less motivating than men's, and their life structures were more tentative and temporary. Most women's dreams were split between achievement and relationships; they defined themselves in relation to others— husbands, children, or colleagues.

Other research, too, points up a major difference between men's and women's paths to identity. Men "find themselves" by separating from their families of origin, becoming autonomous, and pursuing their own interests. Women seem to develop identity not by breaking away from others but through the responsibility and attachment that relationships involve (G. Baruch, Barnett, & Rivers, 1983; Chodorow, 1978; Gilligan, 1982).

**The love relationship**    All 39 women sought a "special man." Levinson envisions a "special woman" who helps a man pursue his dream; but these women mostly saw themselves as supporting a *man's* goals (rather than finding a "special man" to support their own). In fact, their husbands were the major obstacle to the individualistic part of their dreams. (The husband of one woman who considered applying for a Fulbright scholarship threatened to find another woman who would be more interested in marriage.)

**The mentor**    Many of the women identified role models during their twenties, but only four achieved a true mentor relationship. If a mentor is as important as Levinson believes, and if these women's pattern was typical, we would expect many women to be hampered in their occupations by lack of a mentor.

**Forming an occupation**    The task of forming an occupation stretched well into middle age for the women in these studies—both those who had raised children and then sought an occupation, and those who had formed career goals in their twenties but had postponed them.

At about age 30, many of the women reversed their career and family priorities, or at least paid more attention to the previously neglected aspect of their dream: either career or marriage and motherhood. (Diane's life, too, followed this pattern; first she established her academic career, and then, at age 29, she married.) They began making greater demands on their husbands to accommodate their interests and goals. Women who were unsatisfied with both their relationships and their occupational achievements during their twenties found the age-30 transition most stressful.

A longitudinal study of 132 college seniors found that women who committed themselves during their twenties to career, family, or both developed more fully than women who had no children and who chose work beneath their capabilities. Between age 27 and the early forties, women who had faced the challenges of career or parenthood became more disciplined, independent, hard-working, and confident and improved their "people skills." Compared with women who had made neither kind of commitment, they were more dominant, more motivated to achieve, more emotionally stable, more goal-oriented, and more interested in what was going on in the world (Helson & Moane, 1987). This research suggests that a range of satisfactory life structures is possible for young women who form dreams and set about making them come true.

### Evaluating the Normative-Crisis Approach*

The theory that there is a predictable sequence of age-related changes throughout adult life has been influential. But a universal pattern of development for adults is questionable. Children's ages are fairly indicative of their level or sequence of development, but for adults, individual personality and history reveal more about development than age does. People's unique experiences do much to shape their development. Personality characteristics, which show some stability over the years, also affect the course of people's lives. Furthermore, it is misleading to look at adult development as a series of stages, since many issues keep recurring.

It is also risky to generalize from studies with such limited samples. Both the Grant Study and Levinson's studies were based on small groups of mostly white middle-class to upper-middle-class men, all born in the 1920s or 1930s. Their development was undoubtedly influenced by societal events that did not affect earlier or later cohorts, by their socioeconomic status, by their race, and by their sex.

---

*We will offer a full critique of the normative-crisis approach in Chapter 15.

These pioneering studies of adult development are important mostly for their emphasis on how much development actually takes place after adolescence. Although limited, this research does help to identify developmental threads that run through the lives of many people.

## TIMING-OF-EVENTS MODEL

Instead of looking at adults' development as a function of age, the **timing-of-events model** views *life events* as markers of development. According to this model, which allows for more individual variation, people develop in response to specific events in their lives and to the times when these events occur. If life events occur as expected, development proceeds smoothly. If not, stress can result, affecting development. Stress may occur in response to an unexpected event (like losing a job), in response to an event that happens earlier or later than expected (like being widowed at age 35), or in response to the failure of an expected event to occur at all (like never being married). This model (which the gerontologist Bernice Neugarten supports) is concerned with age only as it relates to cultural norms regarding expected events.

### Types and Timing of Life Events

In childhood and adolescence, internal maturational events signal the transition from one developmental stage to another. For example, a baby says the first word, takes the first step, loses the first tooth; and the body changes at the onset of puberty.

In adulthood, however, people move from "a biological to a social clocking of adult development" (Danish & D'Augelli, 1980, p. 111). Physiological and intellectual maturation are now less important to growth than the effects of events like marriage, parenthood, divorce, widowhood, and retirement. For example, menopause is generally less important in a woman's life than a job change.

### *Normative versus nonnormative events*

Life events are of two types: those people expect (**normative life events**) and those they do not expect (**nonnormative life events**). Normative events include marriage and parenthood in early adulthood, and widowhood and retirement late in life. However, the events of people's lives are rarely orderly (Brim & Ryff, 1980); thus, people's lives are also typically punctuated by such nonnormative events as a traumatic accident, an unexpected promotion, the loss of a job, a lottery prize, or a notable achievement.

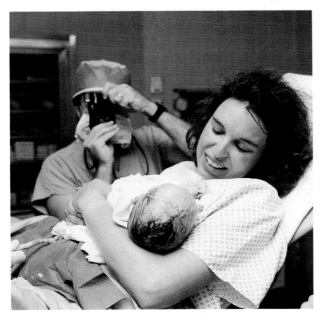

According to the timing-of-events model, the age at which people experience such major life events as a first baby can have an important influence on development. A normative event like parenthood, which most people expect during young adulthood, may become nonnormative and thus more difficult to deal with if it occurs earlier or later.

Whether or not an event is normative often depends on its timing. Most adults have strong feelings about the time in life when certain activities are acceptable (Neugarten, Moore, & Lowe, 1965). People are usually keenly aware of their own timing and describe themselves as "early," "late," or "on time" in marrying, having children, settling on a career, or retiring. Events that are normative when they are "on time" become nonnormative when they are "off time"; for example, marrying at 14 or 41 or retiring at 41 or 91 would be a nonnormative event.

In contrast to the normative-crisis school, the timing-of-events model holds that normative events that come at expected times are generally taken in stride; "it is the events that upset the expected sequence and rhythm of the life cycle that cause problems" (Neugarten & Neugarten, 1987, p. 33).

### Individual versus cultural events

An *individual event* happens to one person or one family (like pregnancy or a promotion). A *cultural event* shapes the context in which individuals develop; examples are an economic depression, an earthquake, a war, a famine, and an accident at a nuclear reactor or a chemical plant.

Cultural attitudes affect people's "social clocks." A timetable that seems right and proper to people in one age cohort may feel jarring to the next generation. And the typical timing of such events as marriage varies from culture to culture (see Box 13-2, page 407).

### The decline of age-consciousness

Over the past half-century, our society has become less age-conscious (Neugarten & Hagestad, 1976; Neugarten & Neugarten, 1987). The feeling that there is a "right time" to do certain things has become less widespread. In the 1950s, middle-aged middle-class people, when asked the "best age" for finishing school, marrying, and retiring, agreed far more than their counterparts two decades later (see Table 13-2 on page 406). Today people are more accepting of 40-year-old first-time parents and 40-year-old grandparents, 50-year-old retirees and 75-year-old workers, 60-year-olds in blue jeans, and 30-year-old college presidents.

Yet despite this "blurring of traditional life periods" (Neugarten & Neugarten, 1987, p. 32), there are still societal expectations about appropriate ages for events to occur, and people often try to time major life events (marriage, parenthood, job changes) by this social clock. For example, a young woman who puts off marrying to get a foothold on the career ladder may then "hurry to catch up with parenthood" (p. 33), perhaps having several children soon after marriage.

### Responding to Life Events

No matter which kind of event we are talking about, the key issue is how someone responds to it. An event that energizes one person may depress, or lead to illness in, another (see Chapter 12).

How a person reacts to events depends on both internal and external factors (Brim & Ryff, 1980; Danish & D'Augelli, 1980; Danish, Smyer, & Nowak, 1980). These include anticipation (level of preparation—for example, through classes for prospective parents or seminars for planning retirement), cognitive understanding (interpreting the event), physical health (including physical resources for handling stress), personality factors (flexibility and resilience), life history (past success in coping with stressful events), and social support (emotional support from others who understand what a person is going through).

In the next section, we look at important life events of young adulthood that revolve around intimate relationships like marriage and parenthood. We also examine some personal lifestyles in which some traditional events do not take place.

**TABLE 13–2**
THE "RIGHT TIME," FOR LIFE EVENTS AND ACTIVITIES

| Activity or Event | Appropriate Age Range | Late 1950s Study, % Who Agree | | Late 1970s Study, % Who Agree | |
|---|---|---|---|---|---|
| | | Men | Women | Men | Women |
| Best age for a man to marry | 20–25 | 80 | 90 | 42 | 42 |
| Best age for a woman to marry | 19–25 | 85 | 90 | 44 | 36 |
| When most people should become grandparents | 45–50 | 84 | 79 | 64 | 57 |
| Best age for most people to finish school and go to work | 20–22 | 86 | 82 | 36 | 38 |
| When most people should be ready to retire | 60–65 | 83 | 86 | 66 | 41 |
| When a man has the most responsibilities | 35–50 | 79 | 75 | 49 | 50 |
| When a man accomplishes most | 40–50 | 82 | 71 | 46 | 41 |
| When a woman has the most responsibilities | 25–40 | 93 | 91 | 59 | 53 |
| When a woman accomplishes most | 30–45 | 94 | 92 | 57 | 48 |

*Note:* Table shows the percentage of middle-aged middle-class people who agreed on a "right time" for major life events and achievements in two surveys, one taken in the late 1950s and the other in the late 1970s.

*Sources:* Adapted from Rosenfeld & Stark, 1987; adapted, in turn, from Passuth, Maines, & Neugarten, 1984.

## BOX 13–2    WINDOW ON THE WORLD

# THE MARRYING AGE

In eastern Europe people tend to marry early; Scandinavians are likely to marry late. Variations in the typical "marrying age" in different cultures tell us something about those cultures (Bianchi & Spain, 1986).

The statistical differences are striking. In Hungary, for example, 70 percent of women and 33 percent of men aged 20 to 24 have already married, whereas in Nordic countries, 85 percent of the women and 95 percent of the men in this age group have not. Like other eastern European nations, Hungary encourages births. In Scandinavia, cohabitation is popular among young adults. Although most Scandinavians eventually marry, they do not marry in their early twenties. Japan, too, has a high proportion of unmarried young adults. But young men and women in Japan do not cohabit, like those in Scandinavia; they tend to live at home with their parents longer than young adults in other cultures.

Industrialized nations, in which a growing number of women go to col-

A Japanese bride and groom are likely to be older than a bride and groom in eastern Europe and to have lived at home with their parents before marriage, rather than cohabiting as many unmarried couples do in Scandinavian countries.

lege and then to work, are seeing a trend toward later marriage. In the United States, for example, over half of the women and three-fourths of the men between ages 20 and 24 have not yet been married (see Table 13-4 later in this chapter).

## INTIMATE RELATIONSHIPS AND PERSONAL LIFESTYLES

During young adulthood, most people decide whether to marry, cohabit, or live alone, and whether or not to have children. Important relationships may include heterosexual or homosexual unions and kinship ties to members of an extended family—within and across generations.

From the late 1950s to the middle 1980s—especially during the 1960s and 1970s—major changes occurred in American society. Current norms no longer dictate that people must get married, stay married, have children, or maintain separate roles for men and women (Thornton, 1989). Today's rules for acceptable family behavior are more elastic than they were during the first half of this century. Still—now as then—for most

young adults, a loving relationship is a pivotal factor in their lives; and we begin our consideration of relationships and lifestyles with love.

### LOVE

Love has always been a favorite topic for poets, novelists, and songwriters. It has also become increasingly popular with social scientists, who have come up with some illuminating findings about "this thing called love."

Do opposites attract? Or do most people tend to fall in love with someone like themselves? Some element of self-love must be involved in selecting a loved one, since lovers and spouses tend to resemble each other in many traits: physical appearance and attractiveness, mental and physical health, intelligence, popularity, warmth, parents' marital and individual happiness, and

Lovers often resemble each other in appearance or personality, suggesting that a form of self-love plays a part in the choice of a partner. These two military cadets, for instance, have common career goals.

such other factors as socioeconomic status, religion, education, and income (Murstein, 1980). Sally and her husband, for example, have the same religious background, are both college graduates, and are enough alike physically that strangers have taken them for brother and sister.

On the other hand, many people choose partners whose qualities complement their own. Diane and her husband have different religious backgrounds and different countries of origin. Also, they feel differently about new situations and people: she prefers the comfort of the familiar; he is energized by the new. Still, Diane and Jonathan have much in common: they both have graduate degrees, and they have similar values on many issues.

An intriguing conceptualization is Robert J. Sternberg's *triangular theory of love* (1985a; Sternberg & Barnes, 1985; Sternberg & Grajek, 1984). In this view, love has three faces, or elements—intimacy, passion, and commitment. *Intimacy,* the emotional element, involves self-disclosure, which leads to connection, warmth, and trust. *Passion,* the motivational element, is based on inner drives that translate physiological arousal into sexual desire. And *commitment,* the cognitive element, is the decision to love and to stay with the beloved. In this theory, the degree to which these three elements are present affects the kind of love people feel, and mismatches of the elements lead to problems. The eight types of love relationships that result from different combinations of the elements are shown in Table 13-3.

Research on love has dispelled some of the myths about it. A cross-sectional study of 24 couples, ranging in age from the teens to the seventies and described by acquaintances as "very much in love" (Neiswender, Birren, & Schaie, 1975), found that:

- Married love is not different in kind from unmarried love. It is neither more realistic and mature nor less idealistic.
- Love is not only for the young. Although people of different ages experience love somewhat differently, older people love just as much as younger people.
- Physical intimacy becomes steadily more important from adolescence to middle age and then abruptly less so.
- Young and middle-aged adults are the most realistic about their lovers' strengths and weaknesses; both adolescents and older adults tend to idealize their loved ones.

The more evenly balanced the partners' contributions to a relationship are, the happier a couple tends to be. When two people think that one or the other is favored, they usually try to make things fairer (by demanding more or giving more), or talk themselves into believing that things are fairer than they seem, or end the relationship (Walster & Walster, 1978).

## MARRIAGE

Most adults marry, usually for the first time in young adulthood. But people have been marrying at later and later ages. In 1988, the median age of first-time bridegrooms was 25.9 and of first-time brides, 23.6 years, compared with 24.7 and 22 years, respectively, in 1980 (U.S. Bureau of the Census, 1988).

### Benefits of Marriage

The universality of marriage throughout history and around the world shows that it meets a variety of fundamental needs. Marriage is usually considered the best way to ensure orderly raising of children. Its economic benefits include providing for a division of labor and a consuming and working unit. Ideally, marriage also offers a source of intimacy, friendship, affection, sexual fulfillment, and companionship. It presents an opportunity for emotional growth through a bond that is more reciprocal than the bond with parents and more committed than bonds with siblings, friends, or lovers. (The high divorce rate shows how hard it is to attain these ideals, but the high remarriage rate shows how many people keep trying.)

**TABLE 13–3**
PATTERNS OF LOVING

| Type | Description |
| --- | --- |
| Nonlove | All three components of love—intimacy, passion, and commitment—are absent. This describes most of our personal relationships, which are simply casual interactions. |
| Liking | Intimacy is the only component present. This is what we feel in true friendship and in many loving relationships. There is closeness, understanding, emotional support, affection, bondedness, and warmth. Neither passion nor commitment is present. |
| Infatuation | Passion is the only component present. This is "love at first sight," a strong physical attraction and sexual arousal, without intimacy or commitment. This can flare up suddenly and die just as fast—or, given certain circumstances, can sometimes last for a long time. |
| Empty love | Commitment is the only component present. This is often found in long-term relationships that have lost both intimacy and passion, or in arranged marriages. |
| Romantic love | Intimacy and passion are both present. Romantic lovers are drawn to each other physically and bonded emotionally. They are not, however, committed to each other. |
| Companionate love | Intimacy and commitment are both present. This is a long-term, committed friendship, often occurring in marriages in which physical attraction has died down but in which the partners feel close to each other and have made the decision to stay together. |
| Fatuous love | Passion and commitment are present, without intimacy. This is the kind of love that leads to a whirlwind courtship, in which a couple make a commitment on the basis of passion without allowing themselves the time to develop intimacy. This kind of love usually does not last, despite the initial intent to commit. |
| Consummate love | All three components are present in this "complete" love, which many of us strive for, especially in romantic relationships. It is easier to reach it than to hold onto it. Either partner may change what he or she wants from the relationship. If the other partner changes, too, the relationship may endure in a different form. If the other partner does not change, the relationship may dissolve. |

*Source:* R. J. Sternberg, 1985a.

## Marriage and Happiness

Studies done from the 1950s to the 1970s found that married people were happier than singles. Either marriage brought happiness, or happy people tended to marry.

In one study of 2000 adults around the country, for example, married men and women of all ages reported more satisfaction than people who were single, divorced, or widowed. The happiest of all were married people in their twenties with no children—especially women. Young wives reported feeling much less stress after marriage, while young husbands, although happy, said that they felt more stress (A. Campbell, Converse, & Rodgers, 1975). Apparently marriage was still seen as an accomplishment and a source of security for a woman but as a responsibility for a man.

Women and men feel differently about marriage in other respects, too. Women see marriage as a place to express and talk about emotions; they consider the sharing of confidences a measure of intimacy. Men, however, define intimacy differently; they tend to express love through sex, giving practical help (like washing a wife's car), doing things together, or just being together (L. Thompson & Walker, 1989). As a result, men often get more of what is important to them, since women do the things that matter to men. Many men do not feel comfortable talking about feelings—or even listening to their wives talk about theirs—and this leaves their wives feeling dissatisfied.

The ability of marriage to bring happiness seems to be changing (Glenn, 1987). Although more married people than people who have never married call themselves "very happy," the gap has narrowed dramatically—among 25- to 39-year-olds, from 31 percentage points in the early 1970s to 8 points in 1986. Apparently, never-married people (especially men) are happier today, while married people (especially women) are less happy. One possible reason is that some benefits of marriage are no longer confined to wedlock. Single people can get both sex and companionship outside of marriage, and marriage is no longer the sole (or even the most reliable) source of security for women. Also, since most women now continue to work, marriage is likely to *increase* rather than decrease their stress.

## Marriage and Health

Marriage is a healthy state. Married people tend to be healthier than those who are separated, divorced, or widowed (Anson, 1989). Married people have fewer disabilities or chronic conditions that limit their activities; and when they go to the hospital, their stays are generally short. Married people live longer, too, according to a study going back to 1940 in 16 industrial countries (Hu & Goldman, 1990). Those who have never married are the next-healthiest group, followed by widowed people and then by people who are divorced or separated.

But we cannot conclude that marriage confers health. Healthy people may attract mates more easily, may be more interested in getting married, and may be better marriage partners. Or married people may lead healthier, safer lives than single people. Because spouses can take care of each other, they may be less likely to need care in hospitals or institutions. Even in less-than-ideal marriages, partners provide company for each other, offer emotional support, and do many things that ease day-to-day life. The loss of these supports through death or separation may make the widowed and divorced more vulnerable to mental and physical disorders (Doherty & Jacobson, 1982). This view is supported by a study of more than 25,000 women aged 18 to 55, which found that women who lived with another adult—whether married or not—were healthier than those who did not (Anson, 1989).

## Predicting Success in Marriage

What *is* success in marriage? To answer this question, researchers rely on people's ratings of their own marriages, on the absence of marital counseling, or on the number of years partners stay together. All these criteria are flawed: people are sometimes less than honest, even with themselves; some people acknowledge problems and seek help more easily than others; and some put up longer with unhappiness. Even so, these criteria are the best ones we have.

Age at marriage is a major predictor of success. Teenagers have high divorce rates: early marriage may affect career or educational ambitions, restrict both partners' potential, and lock a couple into a relationship neither one is mature enough to handle. People who wait until their late twenties or later to marry have the best chances for success. The marriage also has a better chance if the bride is not pregnant and has not had a baby before marrying. Those most likely to separate are people who have not completed their education and people whose parents were unhappily married or divorced (Glenn & Kramer, 1987; Kieren, Henton, & Marotz, 1975; Kimmel, 1980; A. J. Norton & Moorman, 1987; Troll, 1975).

Success in marriage is closely associated with the ways partners communicate, make decisions, and deal with conflict. One study found particular patterns that could predict the course of a marriage (Gottman & Krokoff, 1989). Whining, acting defensive, being stubborn, and withdrawing by walking away or not talking to the spouse are all signs of trouble. But arguing and showing anger (as a form of communication) seemed to be good for marriage. These authors suggest that wives who force confrontations of disagreement and anger will help their marriages—assuming that their husbands react without withdrawing, whining, or being stubborn, and that neither partner becomes defensive. The patterns set during young adulthood affect the quality of the marriage at midlife.

## Violence in Marriage

The kind of assault known as *wife battering* typically begins with a man's shoving or slapping a woman and then escalates into a beating. Wife battering leaves some women critically injured, some dead—and many others living in constant terror.

Violence is more common among young, poor, and unemployed couples, whether married or cohabiting (Lystad, 1975; Yllo & Straus, 1981). Lower levels of violence are fairly common early in relationships: 44 percent of women and 31 percent of men report pushing, shoving, or slapping their partners before marriage; and 36 percent of women and 27 percent of men in the first 18 months of marriage (O'Leary et al., 1989).

It is the violence committed by men against women that causes the most harm. Men who abuse women tend to be social isolates, to have low self-esteem, to be sexually inadequate, to be inordinately jealous, and to deny and minimize the frequency and intensity of their violence, usually blaming the woman (J.L. Bernard & Bernard, 1984; Bouza, 1990; R. Harris & Bologh, 1985).

Why do women stay with men who abuse them? As many as one-fourth of women and one-third of men whose spouses are regularly aggressive do not consider themselves unhappily married. Victims of aggression often minimize its importance; attribute it to alcohol, frustration, and stress; interpret it as a sign of love or of masculinity; and deny that their mates really mean to hurt them (O'Leary et al., 1989). Others have low self-esteem and feel that they deserve to be beaten.

Wife battering is least frequent in egalitarian marriages, more frequent in marriages with a dominant wife (a frustrated husband may see hitting his wife as the only way to exert power over her), and most frequent in marriages with a dominant husband (Yllo, 1984). Financially dependent wives are especially vulnerable; battered wives who return to their husbands are usually not employed and feel they have nowhere else to go (Kalmuss & Straus, 1982; Strube & Barbour, 1984). Some women are afraid to leave—a realistic fear, since some abusive husbands do track down and beat or even kill their estranged wives.

Abused women often feel that they have nowhere to turn. In many states, a wife cannot sue her husband for assault, and police officers called to break up a fight between husband and wife rarely arrest the husband. Yet men who are arrested for family violence are less likely to continue to abuse their families, and an increasing number of communities are now adopting this approach (Bouza, 1990; Sherman & Berk, 1984; Sherman & Cohn, 1989).

Today, more attention is being paid to the plight of abused wives. In many communities battered wives can go with their children to shelters for refuge and counseling, and they can get help from the legal system, including court orders to keep their husbands away. Programs are springing up to help abusive men stop their violent behavior, usually through group counseling (Bernard & Bernard, 1984; Feazell, Mayers, & Deschner, 1984). And family therapy, which treats the entire family together, can sometimes stop mild to moderate abuse before it becomes dangerous (Gelles & Maynard, 1987).

## DIVORCE

"I'm still trying to figure out what happened," said Gary, a man in his thirties who had been married for 8 years and was now in a support group for people going through separation and divorce. "In October my wife tells me she's unhappy and doesn't love me anymore. In November she hands me a letter saying she wants a divorce" (Ketcham, 1990).

The dissolution of marriage is largely a phenomenon of young adulthood. The "seven-year itch" is more than folklore; this is a peak time for divorce. The United States has one of the highest divorce rates in the world, with more than 1 million divorces a year (U.S. Bureau of the Census, 1989). Although the divorce rate, after a two-decade rise, seems to have leveled off since 1980, about 2 out of 3 first marriages are estimated to end this way (T. C. Martin & Bumpass, 1989).

Young adulthood is a peak time for divorce, but some couples work out problems and save their marriage with the help of counseling, like that given by the therapist Michele Weiner-Davis of Woodstock, Illinois. Counseling helps others to separate in the most positive way for everyone in the family.

## Why Divorce Has Increased

Divorce is more common now because society has changed in several ways. Women are less financially dependent on their husbands and so are less likely to stay in bad marriages. There are fewer legal obstacles to divorce, there is less religious opposition to it, and it carries less social stigma. Couples used to stay together "for the sake of the children"; today, that is not always considered the wisest course. And since more couples are childless today, it is easier to return to a single state (Berscheid & Campbell, 1981). Also, divorce rates are highest in times of national prosperity, when separated couples can afford the expense of keeping two households (Kimmel, 1980).

Furthermore, people now expect more from marriage. More people, who live far away from their extended families, want their spouses to be like parents and friends, as well as lovers—to enrich their lives, help them develop their potential, and be loving companions and passionate sexual partners. When this does not happen, few people consider it shameful or immoral to seek a divorce.

People today are are also more likely to recognize that staying in an unhappy marriage may well damage the personalities of both spouses and their children. Marriage counseling helps some couples to work out their problems and save the marriage; it helps other couples to separate in the most positive way for everyone.

## Reactions to Divorce

"You lose all your self-esteem," said one divorced wife. Said another," I never want to live through anything like that again. At the same time, I have grown so much; I feel so free and so optimistic that I can't say I'm sorry I'm where I am."

Ending even an unhappy marriage is always painful, especially when there are children. A divorce brings feelings of failure, blame, hostility, and self-recrimination. Divorce has many facets: emotional, legal, economic, parental (since the children's needs must be met), communal (since relationships with people and institutions outside the family will also change), and psychic (since both partners need to regain personal autonomy). In any one situation, some of these aspects will be more intense than others, but all of them cause stress.

Adjustment after divorce depends partly on how people feel toward themselves and their partners, and on how the divorce was handled. It also depends on other factors. After following 290 men and women—most of whom were white and well educated, and all of

whom were parents—for 2 years after divorce, researchers identified predictors of successful adjustment (Tschann, Johnston, & Wallerstein, 1989). Greater personal resources before the separation—like higher socioeconomic status for men and better psychological functioning for women—aided adjustment. Even in this advantaged group, money was important: people whose income dropped less adjusted better. Another important factor was the degree to which a person had detached from the former spouse, both positively and negatively. People who were still arguing with their former mates or who had not found a new lover or a new spouse had more trouble adjusting. For both sexes, an active social life helped people cut the emotional ties to their former spouses.

The person who takes the first step to end the marriage often feels a mixture of relief, sadness, guilt, apprehension, and anger. Nonetheless, she or he (more often she—women initiate divorce more often than men) is usually in better emotional shape in the early months of separation than the other partner, who feels the additional pain of rejection, loss of control, and powerlessness (J. B. Kelly, 1982; Pettit & Bloom, 1984). Anger, depression, and disorganized thinking and functioning are common after a divorce, but they are balanced by relief, a continuing attachment to the separated spouse, and the hope for a fresh chance in life (J. B. Kelly, 1982).

## Remarriage after Divorce

Most divorced people do not remain single. Until the late 1960s, the remarriage rate kept pace with the rising divorce rate; it declined sharply in the 1970s and more moderately in the 1980s, as more divorced adults cohabited outside of marriage or continued to live alone. Still, an estimated three-quarters of divorced women remarry, and men are even likelier to remarry than women. The more educated a woman is, the less likely she is to remarry, no matter how many children she has—perhaps because she has a better chance of supporting herself and her family. Redivorce, too, seems to have peaked in the late 1960s, when second marriages were more likely to dissolve than first marriages; now the incidence of redivorce is approaching that of first divorce (P. C. Glick, 1988, 1989; P. C. Glick & Lin, 1986b; A. J. Norton & Moorman, 1987).

Apparently, the high divorce rate is not a sign that people do not want to be married. Instead, it often reflects a desire to be *happily* married and a belief that divorce is like surgery—painful and traumatic, but needed to make a better life.

Single life is increasingly common among young adults, for a variety of reasons. This 30-year-old man with a master's degree in business administration returned to his Illinois farming community to manage land that has been in his family for a century. As a rural bachelor, he meets few eligible women; he spends his evenings reading by a wood-burning stove; and when he gets lonely, he takes his dog for a walk.

## SINGLE LIFE

The percentage of young men and women who have not yet married has increased dramatically during the past few decades in every age bracket from 20 to 39 (see Table 13-4). Some of these people will marry eventually, but it is possible that a growing number will never marry at all.

Some young adults postpone or avoid marriage because of a fear that it will end in divorce (P. C. Glick & Lin, 1986b). Postponement makes sense, since, as we have seen, the younger people are when they first marry, the worse the chances for success. And, by and large, single young adults like their status (Cargan, 1981).

Some people stay single so that they can be freer to take social, economic, and physical risks. They can decide more easily to move across the country or across the world, to take chances on new kinds of work, to further their education, or to do creative work, without having to worry about how their quest for self-fulfillment affects another person. Others just like being alone.

More than 60 single men and women, aged 22 to 62, told interviewers in one study about both the "pulls" (advantages of being single) and the "pushes" (disad-

vantages of being married) that made them opt for single life. Among the "pulls" they mentioned were career opportunities, mobility, self-sufficiency, sexual freedom, exciting lifestyles, freedom to change—and opportunities for sustained friendships, a variety of experiences, a plurality of roles, and psychological and social autonomy. Among the "pushes" were the restrictions of monogamy (these included feeling trapped, boredom, obstacles to self-development, unhappiness, anger, role-playing, and the need to conform to expectations), poor communication, sexual frustration, lack of friends, limited mobility, and limited availability of new experiences (Stein, 1976).

Single people's problems range from practical ones like finding a job, getting a place to live, and being totally responsible for themselves to the intangibles of wondering how they fit into the social world, how well friends and family accept them, and how being single affects their self-esteem.

Two common stereotypes—first, that single people are lonely and, second, that they have many different sexual partners—are not supported by research. When 400 never-married, divorced, and remarried Ohioans were interviewed, most of the never-married subjects did not express loneliness and fewer than 20 percent of them had multiple sexual partners (and this was even before the AIDS epidemic). In both respects, this study found that divorced people came closer to the stereotype than those who had never married (Cargan, 1981).

**TABLE 13–4**
PERCENT OF MEN AND WOMEN NEVER MARRIED AT VARIOUS AGES, 1970–1986

| Men | 1970 | 1980 | 1988 |
|---|---|---|---|
| 20–24 years | 54.7 | 68.8 | 77.7 |
| 25–29 years | 19.1 | 33.1 | 43.3 |
| 30–34 years | 9.4 | 15.9 | 25.0 |
| 35–39 years | 7.2 | 7.8 | 14.0 |

| Women | 1970 | 1980 | 1988 |
|---|---|---|---|
| 20–24 years | 35.8 | 50.2 | 61.1 |
| 25–29 years | 10.5 | 20.9 | 29.5 |
| 30–34 years | 6.2 | 9.5 | 16.1 |
| 35–39 years | 5.4 | 6.2 | 9.0 |

*Source:* U.S. Bureau of the Census, March 1989.

## COHABITATION

An increasingly common arrangement is **cohabitation,** in which a couple in a romantic and sexual relationship live together without being married. In 1988, there were about 2.6 million unmarried opposite-sex couples, compared with 523,000 in 1970 (U.S. Bureau of the Census, 1988).* According to one research team, living together outside of marriage has become so common that soon most adults will do it (Bumpass & Sweet, 1988).

Why do couples move in together without marrying? For one thing, the secular trend toward earlier maturation, along with the societal trend toward more education, creates a longer span between physiological maturity and social maturity. Many young people want close sexual relationships and yet are not ready for marriage. Living with someone helps some people know themselves better, helps them understand what an intimate relationship involves, and helps them clarify what they want in marriage and in a mate. Often the experience is a maturing one.

But living together is neither a trial marriage nor practice for marriage. It is like a modern equivalent of "going steady," and it does not last long: within a few years most cohabiting couples have either married or separated. People who lived together first do not have better marriages than those who did not. Furthermore, they are more likely to divorce within 10 years than those who did not live together beforehand (Bumpass & Sweet, 1988). This probably reflects the kind of people who decide to live together first rather than the effect of the cohabitation itself.

Some of the problems of cohabiting couples are like those of newlyweds: overinvolvement with the partner, working out a sexual relationship, perceived loss of personal identity, overdependency on the partner, and becoming distant from other friends. Other problems are specific to the nature of cohabitation: discomfort about the ambiguity of the situation, jealousy, and a yearning for a commitment.

Most newly married people seem satisfied with their premarital arrangement, whether they lived together or not; but when they do have regrets, women are more likely to regret having cohabited, while men are more likely to regret not having done so (R. E. L. Watson, 1983).

---

*Although the census data do not reveal the nature of these relationships (some of which may involve tenants or employees), a large percentage are assumed to be intimate ties.

## SEXUALITY

Underlying all these lifestyle decisions is the need to express sexuality. People entering their twenties face the tasks of achieving independence, competence, responsibility, and equality, all in relation to their sexuality. During the next few years, most people make major decisions about sexual lifestyles: whether they will engage in casual, recreational sex or be monogamous—and whether they will express their sexuality in heterosexual, homosexual, or bisexual activity. Many of the issues young adults face have a sexual aspect: the decision to marry, the decision to have a child, the foray into extramarital sex that often comes with the "seven-year itch," and the changes in sexual patterns following divorce.

### Sexual Activity among Unmarried People

The relaxation of strictures against premarital sex reflects a major change in attitudes. Among women aged 30 and older, the proportion who said that premarital sex was always or almost always wrong dropped from 62 percent in 1972 to 45 percent in 1986; a similar decline was seen among men (Thornton, 1989). Furthermore, actions are speaking as loud as—or louder than—words. Most Americans engage in premarital intercourse; the later they marry, the less likely they are to be virgins on the wedding day.

In one study, 82 percent of women in their twenties who had never been married had had intercourse, and more than half (53 percent) were currently sexually active (Tanfer & Horn, 1985). And surveys of women who visited a health service at a large private university in the northeast found that, despite the growing risks of sexually transmitted diseases (STDs), these women had changed only one aspect of their sexual behavior between 1975 and 1989: they were more likely to use condoms (25 percent in 1989, compared to 6 percent in 1975). Overall levels of sexual activity (88 percent were sexually experienced in 1975; 87 percent in 1986 and 1989) and such specific measures as numbers of sexual partners and frequency of fellatio, cunnilingus, and anal intercourse remained stable (DeBuono, Zinner, Daamen, & McCormack, 1990).

Among younger people, sexual activity is generally part of an affectionate relationship, and there is little promiscuity. There is more casual sex among older single people and separated and divorced people. Young adults who do *not* engage in premarital sex hold back for a number of reasons: moral or religious scruples, concern about how it will affect a future marriage, or fear of pregnancy, STDs, or public opinion. Women express such reservations more than men.

Married people of today seem to derive more pleasure from the sexual side of marriage than couples did in the past, as attitudes about sexual activity have become more open and more information is available.

## Sexual Activity in Marriage

It is surprising how little research exists about sex in marriage. We do know that most couples have sexual relations more frequently during the first year of marriage than they ever will again. And the more sexually active they are during that first year, the more active they are likely to be in the future. After 10 years of marriage, 63 percent of couples make love at least once a week and 18 percent three times a week or more, compared with 83 percent and 45 percent, respectively, for couples married less than 2 years (Blumstein & Schwartz, 1983).

Husbands and wives have intercourse more frequently than their counterparts in the same age brackets did in the past several decades. They also engage in more varied sexual activities. Most important, though, is that they now seem to derive more pleasure from the sexual side of marriage (M. M. Hunt, 1974).

This change has come about because of a societal evolution from Victorian attitudes about the "wickedness" of sex to an acceptance of sexual activity—especially in marriage—as normal, healthy, and pleasurable. More information about sex is available in the press, in professional journals, and from sex therapists. The greater reliability of contraceptives and the availability of legal and safe abortion have also contributed to this change, freeing husbands and wives from fears of unwanted pregnancy. And the feminist movement has helped many women to acknowledge their sexuality.

## Extramarital Sex

Some married people seek sex outside of marriage—especially after the first few years, when the excitement and novelty of sex with the spouse wear off or problems in the relationship surface. Either or both spouses may turn to other sex partners out of boredom or anger at the husband or wife, to recapture a remembered joy or to seek a more vital relationship, or from a desire for sexual emancipation.

It is hard to know just how common extramarital affairs are, because there is no way to tell how truthful people are about their sexual practices. Furthermore, some studies have used self-selected, skewed samples (like readers of such liberal magazines as *Cosmopolitan* and *Playboy*). However, it seems that more people, especially women, are having extramarital sex today than in the past, and that they are having it at younger ages.

In Kinsey's surveys done in the 1940s and 1950s, 51 percent of the men and 26 percent of the women reported extramarital intercourse (Kinsey, Pomeroy, & Martin, 1948; Kinsey, Pomeroy, Martin, & Gebhard, 1953). A more permissive attitude arose between 1965 and 1973, but after 1973 attitudes became more restrictive again, especially among people under age 30 (Thornton, 1989). Now, it is estimated that by age 40 or 50, between 50 and 75 percent of married men and between 34 and 43 percent of married women have extramarital sex (Nass, Libby, & Fisher, 1984; A. P. Thompson, 1983).

## PARENTHOOD

The birth of a baby marks a major transition in the parents' lives. Moving from an intimate relationship between two people to one involving a totally dependent third person changes individuals and changes marriages. Parenthood is a developmental experience, whether the children are biological offspring, are adopted, or are the children of only one spouse.

## Why People Have Children

Having children has traditionally been regarded as "the fulfillment of a marriage, if not the primary reason for marriage" (McCary, 1975, p. 289). In preindustrial societies, large families were a necessity: children helped with the family's work and eventually cared for their aging parents. And because the death rate in childhood was high, fewer children reached maturity. Because economic and social reasons for having children were so powerful, parenthood—and especially motherhood—had a unique aura.

Today, these considerations have lessened or have even been reversed. Because of technological progress, fewer workers are needed; because of modern medical care, most children survive; and because of

parents. Because advances in contraception and legalization of abortion have reduced the number of adoptable healthy white American babies, many adoptable children are disabled, beyond infancy, or (like Anna, Diane's daughter, who was born in Chile) of foreign birth. Adoptions are more likely to be arranged independently—through private attorneys and doctors—than through agencies.

Adoption is well accepted in the United States, but there are still prejudices and mistaken ideas about it, like the belief that all adopted children have problems because they have been deprived of their biological parents. Some negative views of adoption were reinforced by past studies that selected samples of adoptees from people seeking mental health services. However, some recent research has found that a difference between attitudes of adopted and nonadopted children favored the adoptees. Adopted children were more confident, viewed the world more positively, felt better able to control their lives, and saw their adoptive parents as more nurturing than the nonadopted children in a control group (Marquis & Detweiler, 1985).

That is not to say that adopting a child is easier than bearing one. To the contrary, besides the usual issues of parenthood, adoptive parents have extra challenges—acceptance of their infertility (if this is why they adopted), awareness that they are not repeating their own parents' experience, the need to explain the adoption to their children, and discomfort about their children's interest in the biological parents.

### New methods of becoming a parent

Couples can now have children that are genetically at least half their own, by four controversial methods.

**Artificial insemination** The first of these four methods, **artificial insemination,** involves injection of sperm directly into the woman's cervix. If a husband seems infertile, a couple may choose artificial insemination by a donor (AID), as do some 20,000 women a year. The donor may be matched with the husband for physical characteristics, and the husband's sperm may be mixed with the donor's so that the possibility exists that the husband is actually the biological father. Many couples who conceive in this way never tell the children or anyone else about the children's origins.

**In vitro fertilization** In 1978, headlines announced the birth of Louise Brown, the first "test-tube baby."*

---

*Actually, this popular term is a misnomer: the fertilization is seldom performed in a test tube. Even the term *in vitro* is wrong; it is Latin for "in glass," but most labs use plastic dishes.

After 12 years of trying to conceive, Louise's parents had authorized a gynecologist to extract an ovum from Mrs. Brown's ovary, allow it to mature in an incubator, and then fertilize it with Mr. Brown's sperm. The doctor then implanted the embryo in Mrs. Brown's uterus, where it grew in the normal way.

**In vitro fertilization,** fertilization that takes place outside the mother's body, is becoming increasingly common for women whose fallopian tubes are blocked or damaged. Usually several ova are fertilized and implanted, to increase the chances of success.

**Donor eggs** Women who cannot produce normal ova may use **donor eggs,** ova donated by fertile women—the female counterpart of AID. There are two ways of doing it. An ovum can be taken from a donor's body and fertilized in the laboratory, and the resulting embryo implanted in another woman's uterus (Lutjen et al., 1984). Or a donor egg can be fertilized by artificial insemination. The donor's uterus is flushed out a few days later, and the embryo is retrieved and inserted into the recipient's uterus (Bustillo et al., 1984). This procedure seems to be as effective with women 40 to 44 years old as with those under 35 (Sauer, Paulson, & Lobo, 1990).

**Surrogate motherhood** In **surrogate motherhood,** a woman is impregnated by the prospective father (usually artificial insemination). She carries the baby to term and gives the child to the father and his wife. The surrogate undergoes the entire pregnancy, with its risks and emotions. Since she is paid a fee—commonly $5000 to $15,000, plus medical expenses—some people consider the process a form of child buying. Surrogate motherhood is in legal limbo, partly as a result of the "Baby M" case, in which a surrogate mother changed her mind and wanted to keep the baby (Hanley, 1988a, 1988b; Shipp, 1988). She was not granted custody of the child, but she does have visiting rights.

**Technology and conception: Ethical issues** To many people, the most objectionable aspect of surrogacy, aside from the possibility of forcing the surrogate to relinquish the baby, is the payment of money (up to $30,000, including fees to a "matchmaker"). Payment for adoption is forbidden in about 25 states, but surrogate motherhood is not adoption, since the biological father is the social father. The idea of a "breeder class" of poor and disadvantaged women who carry the babies of the well-to-do strikes many people as wrong.

New and unorthodox means of conception raise other questions: Must people who use them be infertile, or should they be free to make such arrangements simply for convenience? Should single people and homosexual couples have access to these methods? Should the children know about their parentage? Should chromosome tests be performed on all prospective donors and surrogates? What is the risk that children fathered or mothered by the same donor or surrogate (genetic half siblings) might someday meet and marry, putting their children at risk of birth defects? Can handling an embryo outside the body injure it? If a test-tube baby is born with a major defect, is the physician liable? What happens if a couple who have contracted with a surrogate divorce before the birth?

One thing seems certain: as long as there are people who want children and who are unable to conceive or bear them, human ingenuity and technology will come up with new ways to satisfy their need.

## The Transition to Parenthood

Both women and men often feel ambivalent about becoming parents. Along with excitement, they usually feel some anxiety about the responsibility of caring for a child and about the permanence that a pregnancy seems to impose on a marriage. Pregnancy also affects a couple's sexual relationship, sometimes making it even more intimate, but sometimes creating barriers.

What happens in a marriage from the time of the first pregnancy until the child's third birthday? That varies considerably. One research team, Belsky and Rovine (1990), followed 128 middle- and working-class couples during this time; at the beginning of the study the husbands' ages averaged 29 years and the wives' 27 years. Although some marriages improved, many suffered overall, especially for the wives. Many spouses loved each other less, became more ambivalent about their relationship, argued more, and communicated less. This was true no matter what the sex of the child was and whether or not the couple had a second child by the time the first was 3 years old. But when the researchers looked, not at the *overall* quality of the marriage, but at such *individual* measures as love, conflict, ambivalence, and effort put into the relationship, at least half of the sample showed either no change on a particular measure or a small positive change.

What distinguishes marriages that deteriorate after parenthood from those that improve? This study found no single determining factor; rather, a number of different factors, related to both parents and child, seemed to influence the course of these marriages. In deteriorating marriages, the partners were more likely to be younger and less well educated, to earn less money, and to have been married for fewer years. One or both partners tended to have low self-esteem, and husbands were likely to be less sensitive (Belsky & Rovine, 1990). Other research has found that the more the division of labor in a marriage changes from egalitarian to traditional, the more marital happiness declines, especially for nontraditional wives (Belsky, Lang, & Huston, 1986).

Two surprising findings emerged from Belsky and Rovine's study. First, couples who were most romantic "pre-baby" had more problems "post-baby," perhaps because they had unrealistic expectations. Second, women who had planned their pregnancies were unhappier, possibly because they had expected life with a baby to be better than it turned out to be. (This second

These parents are obviously enjoying the fun and stimulation of having children. But by now they have undoubtedly realized that parenthood also has other aspects. The physical, psychological, and financial stresses of rearing children contribute to the parents' own development. One of the best things about parenthood is that it is never predictable: parents must constantly meet the challenges of their children's changing needs.

## BOX 13–3    PRACTICALLY SPEAKING

# IN STEP WITH THE BLENDED FAMILY

With today's high rate of divorce and remarriage, families made up of "yours, mine, and ours" are becoming more common. In 1987 there were 4.3 million such families and about 6 million stepchildren in the United States (P. C. Glick, 1989).

The stepfamily—also called the *blended,* or *reconstituted,* family—is different from a "natural" family. First, it has a larger supporting cast, including former spouses, former in-laws, and absent parents, as well as aunts, uncles, and cousins on both sides. Furthermore, it may be "contaminated with anger, guilt, jealousy, value conflicts, misperceptions, and fear" (Einstein, 1979, p. 64). It is, in short, burdened by much baggage not carried by an "original" family—and it cannot be expected to function in the same way.

Stepfamilies have to deal with the stress from losses (due to death or divorce) undergone by both children and adults, which can make them afraid to trust and to love. A welter of family histories can complicate present relationships. Previous bonds between children and their biological parents or loyalty to an absent or dead parent may interfere with forming ties to the stepparent—especially when children go back and forth between two households. Disparities in life experiences are also common, as when a father of adolescents marries a woman who has never had a child (E. Visher & Visher, 1983).

Stepfamilies cope in a number of ways. Some of the most successful strategies include the following (C. Berman, 1981; E. Visher & Visher, 1983; E. B. Visher & Visher, 1989):

▪ *Having realistic expectations.* Members of a stepfamily have to remember that it is different from a biological family. They have to allow time for loving relationships to develop. They need to see what is positive about their differences: instead of resisting the diversity in two households, for example, they can welcome it as a doubling of resources and experiences.

▪ *Developing new relationships within the family.* Stepfamilies need to build new traditions and develop new ways of doing things that will be right for them. They can plan activities to give the children time alone with the biological parent, time alone with the stepparent, and time with both parents—and activities that provide time alone for the couple. They can move to a new house or apartment, one that does not hold memories of a past life.

▪ *Understanding children's emotions.* Parents need to be sensitive and responsive to children's fears, hurts, and resentments at a time when the adults may be euphoric about building a new life together.

▪ *Maintaining a courteous relationship with the former spouse.* Children adjust best after divorce when they maintain close ties with both parents, when they are not used as weapons for angry parents to hurt each other, and when they are not subjected to the pain of hearing a parent or stepparent insult the absent parent. Parents can form "coparenting teams" to meet their children's needs.

▪ *Seeking social support.* Sharing feelings, frustrations, and triumphs with other stepparents and stepchildren often helps people to view their own situation more realistically and to benefit from the experiences of others.

For people who have been bruised by loss, the blended family has the potential for providing the same benefits as any family that cares about all its members. Achieving complete caring within the family is not easy (even for biological families), but it can be done.

---

with adults or think that they would not make good parents. Some want to retain the intimacy of their marriage, free from the emotional demands of parenting. Some do not want the financial burdens of parenthood. Some enjoy the freedom to travel or to make spur-of-the-moment decisions (F. L. Campbell et al., 1982).

In a study of 42 couples who had chosen either parenthood or childlessness, the two groups turned out to be very similar in family background and marital satisfaction, but different in their interaction with their spouses (H. Feldman, 1981). The childless couples had less traditional attitudes toward women and did more enjoyable activities together. (Parents may not need to do as much together, or even talk to each other as much, because being with their children meets some of their relational needs.)

Both groups in this study were happy in their marriages—a fact that may reflect their free choice of lifestyle. But some people who want children are discouraged by the costs and the difficulty of combining parenthood with employment. Better child care and other support services might help more couples make truly voluntary decisions (D. E. Bloom & Pebley, 1982).

## FRIENDSHIP

Young adults often feel as if they have too little time to be with friends. Friends, however, do play an important role in these years. In fact, one study of friendships across the life span found that newlyweds have more friends than adolescents, the middle-aged, or the elderly (Weiss & Lowenthal, 1975).

### Characteristics of Adult Friendship

How does a close friendship differ from a romantic tie? According to 150 people—two-thirds of them college students and one-third adults who were no longer in school—friendships involve trust, respect, enjoyment of each other's company, understanding and acceptance of each other, willingness to help and to confide in one another, and spontaneity, or feeling free to be oneself (K. E. Davis, 1985). Romantic bonds also have these aspects, plus sexual passion and extreme caring. However, these subjects saw "best friendships" as more stable than ties to a spouse or lover. Most people's close and best friends were of the same sex; only 27 percent listed members of the other sex as best friends.

### Benefits of Friendship

Friendships not only nourish the soul; they are also balm for the body. People who are isolated from friends and family are twice as likely to fall ill and to die as people who maintain social ties (House, Landis, & Umberson, 1988). The 10 to 20 percent of people who have close contact with others less than once a week and have no one with whom to share feelings are most at risk. The effect is greater for men, probably because women's relationships are generally more intimate—even if a woman has few ties with others, the ties she has may be very nurturing, making up in quality what they lack in quantity. These findings are supported by Anson's (1989) finding, cited earlier, that living with another person seems to enhance health.

What is it about social relationships that fosters good health—or about their absence that undermines health? Early theories suggested that emotional support from other people helps minimize the effect of stress. But more recent observers propose other possible reasons (House et al., 1988). Social ties may foster a sense of meaning or coherence in life. It is also possible that people who keep in touch with others are more likely to behave in healthy ways—sleeping and eating sensibly, getting enough exercise, avoiding substance abuse, and getting medical care when it is needed.

Broad social forces underlie both social ties and health. Older people, black people, and the poor tend to have fewer social bonds. And American adults today, compared with those of 30 years ago, are less likely to be married, more likely to be living alone, less likely to belong to voluntary organizations, and less likely to visit with others. It is ironic that just as we are discovering how important social interactions are for health, people seem to be engaging in them less often.

The bonds forged in young adulthood with friends and family often endure throughout life. These relationships continue to influence people through middle age and into old age; and the changes people experience in their more mature years affect their relationships, as we'll see in Parts Six and Seven.

## SUMMARY

### PERSONALITY DEVEOPMENT IN ADULTHOOD: TWO MODELS

■ Studies of adults show that development continues throughout life. In young adulthood, people develop as they confront the issues of leaving their parents' home, deciding on careers, establishing relationships and families, and setting life goals.

■ Two important perspectives on adulthood are the normative-crisis model and the timing-of-events model.

■ The normative-crisis model—exemplified by Erikson, Vaillant, and Levinson—proposes that there is a built-in plan for human development and that during each part of the life span, people face a particular crisis or task.

1 Erikson's sixth psychosocial crisis is intimacy versus isolation. To develop successfully, according to Erikson, young adults must fuse their identities in a close, intimate heterosexual relationship that leads to procreation. Negative outcomes that may result during this period are self-absorption and isolation.

2 In the Grant Study of Harvard men, Vaillant found that men who used "mature" defenses were more successful in many ways than those who used less mature adaptive techniques. This study also revealed a period of career consolidation that characterized men in their thirties.

3 According to Levinson, the goal of adults' development is building the life structure. In his studies of men, Levinson found periods of transition and periods of stability alternating throughout adulthood. Two important influences during young adulthood are the mentor and the dream.

■ Studies of women suggest gender differences in paths to identity. Males traditionally define themselves in terms of separation and autonomy; females seem to achieve identity through relationships and attachment.

■ The timing-of-events model proposes that adult development is influenced by the specific important events that occur in a person's life, and that the timing of an event affects the person's reaction to it.

■ Life events may be expected (normative) or unexpected (nonnormative). Timing can affect "normativeness." Events that are perceived as "off time" are generally more stressful than those that occur "on time."

■ Although our society has become less age-conscious, many people still try to time major life events such as marriage, occupational progression, and parenthood by "social clocks."

## INTIMATE RELATIONSHIPS AND PERSONAL LIFESTYLES

■ According to Robert Sternberg's triangular theory of love, love has three aspects: intimacy, passion, and commitment. These combine into eight types of love relationships.

■ During young adulthood, many people decide whether and whom to marry. Americans have been marrying later than in past generations. Marriage is related to happiness and health. Success in marriage is related to age of marriage and the way partners communicate.

■ The United States has one of the highest divorce rates in the world, with more than 1 million divorces each year. Although divorce usually entails a painful period of ad-justment (even for the spouse who has initiated it), most divorced people remarry.

■ Today more people feel free to remain single until a late age or never marry. Advantages of being single include career opportunities, travel, and self-sufficiency. Possible negative aspects include being totally responsible for oneself and finding social acceptance.

■ Cohabiting is in many ways a maturing experience, though there may be problems associated with it, such as dealing with the ambiguity of the situation, jealousy, and the desire for a commitment.

■ Most young adults make basic decisions about their sexual lifestyles. More young people today are having sexual experiences before marriage, and husbands and wives are having more frequent and more varied sexual activity than in previous generations. More married people, especially young married people, appear to be having sexual relationships outside of marriage.

■ Infertile couples may suffer adverse psychological effects. Adoption is becoming more difficult because of a decreased number of adoptable American babies, and more couples are trying artificial insemination, in vitro fertilization, donor eggs, and surrogate motherhood.

■ Having a child marks a major transition in a couple's life, from sharing reciprocal responsiblities to having total responsibility for a new life. Parenthood has a mixed impact on marriages.

■ Many couples today opt for fewer children or remain childless, and an increasing number of women, especially educated women, have children later in life.

■ Friendships are important during young adulthood. Social ties are important for health and well-being.

## KEY TERMS

normative-crisis model (page 398)
intimacy versus isolation (398)
adaptive mechanisms (399)
career consolidation (399)
life structure (401)
dream (401)

mentor (401)
timing-of-events model (404)
normative life events (404)
nonnormative life events (404)
triangular theory of love (408)
cohabitation (414)

infertility (417)
artificial insemination (418)
in vitro fertilization (418)
donor eggs (418)
surrogate motherhood (418)

## SUGGESTED READINGS

**Berger, G. S., Goldstein, M., & Fuerst, M. (1989).** *The couple's guide to fertility: How new medical advances can help you have a baby.* New York: Doubleday. A very readable and comprehensive guide.

**Block, J. (1990).** *Motherhood as metamorphosis: Change and continuity in the life of a new mother.* New York: Dutton. This examination of the psychological ramifications of becoming a mother explores how a woman's life is transformed in her baby's first year of life.

**Schnur, S. (1990).** *Daddy's home! Reflections of a family man.* New York: Crown. A book of sensitive and sometimes humorous essays that touch on many of the emotional issues of young adulthood.

**Tannen, D. (1990).** *You just don't understand: Women and men in conversation.* New York: Morrow. A fascinating and fun-to-read analysis of the differences in the ways men and women communicate. The author is an expert in linguistics.

# SIX

# MIDDLE ADULTHOOD

When does middle age begin? Is it at the birthday party when you have to summon up enough breath to blow out 40 candles? Is it the day your daughter demolishes you on the tennis court or the day your son announces his engagement? Is it the day when you notice that police officers are getting younger all the time? *Middle adulthood,* which we define in this book roughly as the years between ages 40 and 65, has many markers. In Chapters 14 and 15, we will see what sets these years apart from the years that come before and afterward.

■ In **Chapter 14,** we examine health in middle adulthood, looking at menopause, the male climacteric, and the physical changes that appear in both sexes. We also consider how thought processes continue to mature.

Finally, we examine the satisfactions that middle-aged people get from their work, as well as the effects of burnout, unemployment, and the challenge of changing careers at midlife.

■ The famous—or infamous—"midlife crisis" is discussed in **Chapter 15.** Should all middle-aged people get ready for it, or is it a figment of researchers' and journalists' imagination? Another controversial issue related to social and emotional development is whether personality is fixed early in adulthood or whether it changes over the years. Finally, we look at the relationships middle-aged adults have with important people in their lives: their spouses, their friends, and the generations on either side of them—their children and their parents. These are richly textured years.

## CHAPTER 14

# PHYSICAL AND INTELLECTUAL DEVELOPMENT IN MIDDLE ADULTHOOD

The primitive, physical, functional pattern of the morning of life, the active years before forty or fifty, is outlived. But there is still the afternoon opening up, which one can spend not in the feverish pace of the morning but in having time at last for those intellectual, cultural, and spiritual activities that were pushed aside in the heat of the race.

ANNE MORROW LINDBERGH,
*GIFT FROM THE SEA*, 1955

- What physical changes do men and women experience during the middle years, and how do they cope with them?
- How do the physical changes of midlife affect sexuality?

- Does intellectual functioning in middle adulthood have a distinctive character?
- Why do some people continue their education or change careers at midlife?
- What benefits do middle-aged people get from work?

The Spanish toast *Salud, amor, y pesetas—y el tiempo para gustarlos* ("Health, love, and money—and time to enjoy them") inspired the authors of a book about middle age to use it as a chapter title; they found it the "ideal summary of what middle age can offer" (B. Hunt & Hunt, 1974, p. 23).

What, though, *is* middle age? Since in this book we divide the life span chronologically, we define *middle age* as the years between ages 40 and 65. But it can also be defined contextually. One context is the family situation: a middle-aged person can be defined as one who has grown children or elderly parents (Troll, 1989).

A contextual definition may contradict a chronological one. In terms of chronology, both authors of this book are middle-aged. But contextually, Diane is a young adult. Although she is in her early forties, her child is only 5—hardly ready to leave the nest. Nor has she needed to assume the role of caregiver for her parents, who, in their late seventies, are active, fit, and intellectually alert (in a contextual sense, *they* fit more into middle age than into old age). By contrast, Sally in her early forties was the mother of three teenagers, one of whom was away at college; Sally had also assumed greater responsibility for helping her widowed mother, who at age 75 was in poor health.

Many people begin to feel middle-aged when they reach their fifties, a turning point that is often just as dramatic as adolescence. Younger colleagues call them "ma'am" or "sir," they suffer from arthritis or prostate trouble or some other physical condition associated with old age, sons go bald or daughters make them grandparents, they realize that they are the oldest people in the office, and they recognize more names in the obituaries.

Still, many people consider their middle years the best time of their lives. In general, middle-aged people are in good physical, financial, and psychological shape. They are likely to be in their peak earning years, and since their children are usually independent or nearly so, many are in the most secure financial position of their lives. Medical advances, awareness of preventive care, and fitness are keeping them, by and large, in good physical health. And one of the greatest strengths of midlife stems from having lived long enough to acquire valuable social and professional experience and having opportunities to use that experience.

This "prime time" of life has its stresses, too, of course. The middle-aged adult realizes that his or her body is not what it once was. In a youth-oriented and fitness-oriented society, wrinkles, sags, and stiff muscles are unwelcome signs of aging. Furthermore, signs of aging can hurt job seekers.

This last point is important because work strongly influences how people feel about midlife. This is a time of taking stock, a time of reevaluating earlier career aspirations and how well they have been fulfilled. Sometimes people respond by modifying their goals; sometimes they strike out in totally new directions.

Reevaluation—which extends to intimate relationships and other aspects of life—comes about because of a shift in people's orientation in time. Instead of thinking of their life span in terms of the years they have lived, people begin to think in terms of the time they have left to live (Neugarten, 1967). They realize that they cannot possibly do everything they want to do, and they are eager—sometimes desperately so—to make the most of their remaining years. This realization prompts some people to switch careers, some to leave their spouses, and some to retire.

In this chapter, we discuss physical and intellectual issues of middle age. We focus on sensory and psycho-motor functioning, on sexual expression, on health, and on the distinctive ways in which people think and learn at midlife. We look at adult education and the role of work, considering its satisfactions and stresses and the stimulating challenge of a change in career. (In Chapter 15, we will explore the social and emotional issues of midlife.)

# PHYSICAL DEVELOPMENT

From young adulthood through the middle years, biological changes generally take place so gradually that they are hardly noticed—until one day a 45-year-old man realizes that he cannot read the telephone directory without eyeglasses, or a 55-year-old woman has to admit that she is not as quick on her feet as she was.

Physical functioning and health are usually still good, though not at the peak level of young adulthood. Most people take changes in reproductive and sexual capacities—menopause and the male climacteric—in stride, and some experience a kind of sexual renaissance. Some, however—especially women—feel keenly a decline in physical attractiveness.

## PHYSICAL CHANGES OF MIDDLE AGE

### SENSORY AND PSYCHOMOTOR FUNCTIONING

Although changes in sensory and motor capabilities during midlife are real and affect people's concept of themselves and their interaction with others, these changes are usually fairly small, and most middle-aged people compensate well for them.

### Vision, Hearing, Taste, and Smell

Throughout life, the lens of the eye becomes progressively less elastic, so that its ability to focus is diminished; this process is usually noticed for the first time in middle age. Many people now need reading glasses for **presbyopia,** the farsightedness associated with aging. Bifocals—eyeglasses in which lenses for reading are combined with lenses for distant vision—help people make the adjustment between near and far objects. Middle-aged people also experience a slight loss in sharpness of vision; and because the pupil of the eye tends to become smaller, they need about one-third more brightness to compensate for the loss of light reaching the retina (Belbin, 1967; Troll, 1985). Near-sightedness, though, tends to level off in these years.

Many people become farsighted during middle age and now need reading glasses; but people who wore glasses for nearsightedness earlier in life sometimes find that they need their glasses less now.

There is also a gradual hearing loss during middle age, especially with regard to more high-pitched sounds; this condition is known as **presbycusis.** After about age 55, hearing loss is greater for men than for women (Troll, 1985). However, most hearing loss during these years is not even noticed, since it is limited to levels of sound that are unimportant to behavior. Hearing loss occurs at much later ages among some African tribespeople than it does in Europe and the United States, no doubt because people in western countries suffer the effects of an environment full of blaring auto horns, loud radios, jet airplanes, and other harsh noises (Timiras, 1972).

Taste sensitivity begins to decline at about age 50, particularly the ability to discriminate "finer nuances of taste" (Troll, 1985, p. 32). Since the taste buds become less sensitive, foods that may be quite flavorful to a younger person may seem bland to a middle-aged person (Troll, 1985).

Sensitivity to smell holds up well; it is one of the last senses to decline (Troll, 1985).

### Strength, Coordination, and Reaction Time

"Use it or lose it" is the motto of many middle-aged people, who have taken up jogging, racquetball, tennis, aerobic dancing, and other forms of physical exercise that often make them fitter, stronger, and more energetic than they were in their youth.

Although strength and coordination decline gradually during the middle years, the loss is so small that most people barely notice it (Spirduso & MacRae, 1990). A 10 percent reduction in physical strength from its peak during the twenties does not mean much to people who rarely if ever exert their full strength in daily life.

Of course, the less people do, the less they *can* do. People who lead sedentary lives lose muscle tone and energy, and so they become even less inclined to exert themselves physically. A sedentary lifestyle has recently emerged as the major correlate to deaths from heart attacks (J. Brody, 1990). People who become active early in life reap the benefits of more stamina and more resilience after age 60 (Spirduso & MacRae, 1990).

Simple reaction time (like the speed of lifting an index finger from a key) slows by about 20 percent, on the average, between ages 20 and 60 (Birren, Woods, & Williams, 1980). Complex motor skills (like those involved in driving), which increase during childhood and youth, gradually decline after people have achieved full growth. But the decline does not necessarily result in poorer performance. Driving, for instance, requires such skills as coordination, quick reaction time, and ability to tolerate glare. After the age of about 30 to 35, each of these abilities declines (DeSilva, 1938, in Soddy & Kidson, 1967); yet middle-aged drivers are typically better than younger ones (McFarland, Tune, & Welford, 1964). Also, 60-year-old typists are as efficient as 20-year-olds (Spirduso & MacRae, 1990). In these and other activities, the improvement that comes with experience more than makes up for the decrements that come with age. "Overpracticed" skills seem more resistant to the effects of age than skills that are used less.

Skilled industrial workers in their forties and fifties are often more productive than ever, partly because they are generally more conscientious and careful (Belbin, 1967). Furthermore, middle-aged workers are less likely than younger workers to suffer disabling injuries on the job—a result, no doubt, of experience and good judgment, which more than compensate for any lessening of coordination and motor skills (B. Hunt & Hunt, 1974).

## Physiological Changes

The most common physiological changes of midlife include a diminished ability to pump blood; reduced kidney functioning; less enzyme secretion in the gastrointestinal tract, leading to indigestion and constipation; weakening of the diaphragm; and, in the male, enlargement of the prostate gland (the organ surrounding the neck of the urinary bladder), which may cause urinary and sexual problems. Some of these changes are a direct result of aging. Still, behavioral factors and lifestyle, dating from youth, often affect their timing and extent. People age at different rates, and the decline of the body systems is gradual.

# SEXUALITY

## Sexual Activity

Myths about sexuality in midlife (many of which were believed by middle-aged people themselves) have often interfered with happiness. But recent advances in health and medical care, more liberal attitudes toward sex throughout society, and new studies are now making people more aware that sex can be a vital part of life during these—and even later—years. National surveys have found that middle-aged people are engaging in sexual activity more often and in more varied ways than ever before (Brecher & the Editors of Consumer Reports Books, 1984; B. D. Starr & Weiner, 1981).

In fact, freed from worries about pregnancy and blessed with more time to spend with their partners, many people find that their sexual relationship is better than it has been in years. This is usually so for people who consider a sexual relationship part of an overall sensual attachment. Lovers who hold and caress each other, both in and out of bed, without confining such touching to foreplay for genital sex, can experience a global kind of arousal that permeates a relationship. For such couples, midlife can be a time of heightened sexuality as part of a caring, close relationship. This holds true for homosexual as well as heterosexual couples (Weg, 1989).

Sexual activity is different during these years. Most men do not experience sexual tension as often as they did when they were younger: those who wanted intercourse every other day may now be content to go 3 to 5 days between orgasms. Their erections arrive less often of their own accord and more often only with direct stimulation. Their orgasms come more slowly and sometimes not at all. And they need a longer recovery time after one orgasm before they can ejaculate again. Also, after menopause, some women do not become aroused as readily as before, and some find intercourse painful because of thinning vaginal tissues and inadequate lubrication.

Very often, lessening of sexual activity is due to nonphysiological causes: monotony in a relationship, preoccupation with business or financial worries, mental or physical fatigue, depression, failure to make sex a high priority in the face of conflicting demands on one's time, and fear of failure to attain an erection. Physical causes include chronic disease, surgery, some medications, and too much food or alcohol (Masters & Johnson, 1966; Weg, 1989).

Couples who recognize the normal changes of middle age, and who can redesign their sex life around them, can find great satisfaction. In fact, the slower reactions of men can prove a boon: couples may enjoy longer, more leisurely periods of sexual activity; and women may find the longer period of arousal helpful in reaching orgasm—often by means other than intercourse. In one study of 160 middle-aged women, most reported having a better sex life than they had earlier (L. B. Rubin, 1982). They knew their own sexual needs and desires better, felt freer to take the initiative, and had a higher level of interest in sex.

## Reproductive and Sexual Capacity

One fundamental change of middle age—the decline of reproductive capacity—affects men and women differently. Women's ability to bear children comes to an end, and although men can continue to father children, they begin to experience lessened fertility and, in some cases, a decrease in potency.

### Menopause

The biological event of **menopause** occurs when a woman stops ovulating and menstruating and can no longer bear children. Menopause is generally considered to have occurred 1 year after the last menstrual period. For American women, this typically happens between ages 45 and 55, at an average age of 51 (Dan & Bernhard, 1989). Some women, however, begin to experience menstrual changes in their thirties, and others not until their sixties.

*Physical effects of menopause*  The time span of some 2 to 5 years during which a woman's body undergoes the various physiological changes that bring on the menopause is known technically as the **climacteric.** During the climacteric, a woman's body reduces its production of the female hormone **estrogen.** As a result, the woman usually menstruates irregularly, with either more or less bleeding than before and a shorter or longer time between cycles.

Some women—but not all—experience other physical effects. These may include hot flashes (sudden sensations of heat that flash through the body), thinning of the vaginal lining, or urinary dysfunction caused by tissue shrinkage (Weg, 1989). In 1 out of 4 postmenopausal women, the decrease in estrogen leads to **osteoporosis,** a condition in which the bones become thinner and more susceptible to fractures (see Box 14-1 on page 432).

*Managing menopause*  Troublesome physical effects of menopause, and other health problems like osteoporosis and a higher risk of heart disease, are linked to the lower levels of estrogen in a woman's body after menopause. Artificial estrogen is often prescribed—in a pill or in a slow-release skin patch—but not every woman needs estrogen-replacement therapy (ERT), and not every woman should get it.

Replacement of estrogen alone has been related to a higher risk of cancer of the lining of the uterus, but research suggests that when artificial progesterone is given along with the estrogen, the risk of developing this kind of cancer falls below the level for women who receive no hormone at all (Bush et al., 1983; Hammond, Jelovsek, Lee, Creasman, & Parker, 1979). However, the estrogen-progesterone combination has been linked to an increase in breast cancer. ERT is *not* advisable for women with a history of breast cancer or blood clots. The safety of long-term combined estrogen and progesterone treatment is hotly debated and is under study. Meanwhile, women need to examine their own situation and their family health history and, if they do get ERT, to stay in close touch with their physicians.

For most women, menopause is a psychological *non-event.* At one time, such problems as depression were blamed on menopause, but recent research shows no reason to attribute psychiatric illness to this normal event. In one classic study in which several hundred women from 21 to 65 years old were asked about their attitudes toward menopause, women who had been through it felt much more positive than women who had not (Neugarten, Wood, Kraines, & Loomis, 1963). A typical comment was, "I've been healthier and in much better spirits since the change of life. I've been relieved of a lot of aches and pains" (Neugarten, 1968, p. 200).

Psychological problems in midlife are more likely to be caused by attitude than by anatomy—especially by negative societal views of aging. In cultures that value older women, few problems are associated with menopause (Dan & Bernhard, 1989). Societal attitude toward aging seems to influence a menopausal woman's well-being far more than the level of hormones in her body does. Women who have problems or questions about menopause can often benefit from talking with postmenopausal women, who can reassure them and also pass on practical suggestions.

### The male climacteric

Although men can continue to father children till quite late in life, some middle-aged men experience a decrease in fertility and frequency of orgasm, and an increase in impotence (Beard, 1975). Furthermore, middle-aged men seem to have cyclic fluctuations in the production of hormones (Kimmel, 1980).

The **male climacteric** (sometimes inaccurately called the *male menopause*) is a period of physiological,

## BOX 14-1    PRACTICALLY SPEAKING

# PREVENTING OSTEOPOROSIS

Thinning of the bones—*osteoporosis*—is a major cause of broken bones in old age. This is largely a disorder of women, and it is most prevalent in white women, thin women, smokers, women who have early menopause, and women who get too little calcium or too little exercise.

Osteoporosis seems to be preventable if women take steps in youth and middle age. The most important preventive measures are getting more calcium and more exercise, avoiding smoking, and (for some women) taking hormone supplements (Dawson-Hughes et al., 1990; National Institutes of Health, NIH, 1984a).

Most American women drink little milk and eat few foods rich in calcium; those who have osteoporosis tend to consume even less of this important mineral. Women should get between 1000 and 1500 milligrams of calcium a day or even more, starting early in life. They can easily do so by consuming such calcium-rich foods as the following:

■ Dairy foods. Low-fat milk and low-fat yogurt provide the benefits of calcium without the cholesterol or the high calories of cream.
■ Canned sardines and salmon (if eaten with the bones); and oysters, canned or fresh.
■ Vegetables like broccoli; kale; and collard, dandelion, turnip, and mustard greens.

Exercise seems to stimulate bone growth: it should become part of the

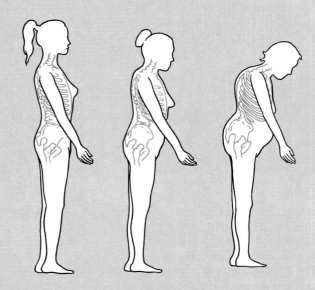

Osteoporosis. As osteoporosis weakens bones, fractures of vertebrae may cause women to become stooped from the waist up, and to lose 4 inches or more of height. (*Source*: Notelovitz & Ware, 1983; © 1982.)

daily routine early in life and should continue to some degree as long as possible throughout life. The best exercises for increasing bone density are weight-bearing activities like walking, running, jumping rope, aerobic dancing, and bicycling.

Some research suggests that extra supplements of calcium (in pills or fortified juices) can retard bone loss, but other studies have found no such effect. A recent study did find value in extra calcium intake by women over age 55 (Dawson-Hughes et al., 1990).

The National Institutes of Health 1984a) also recommend administra-

tion of estrogen to women at particularly high risk of developing osteoporosis, such as those who have had their ovaries removed. This step, however, is more controversial than the recommendations for diet and exercise, which can be safely followed by all women. Efforts to find a safe, effective treatment for osteoporosis are mounting; therapies now being tested include the hormone calcitonin (in the form of a nasal spray), a combined hormone therapy, and different kinds of calcium supplements (Dawson-Hughes et al., 1990; Skolnick, 1990).

emotional, and psychological change involving a man's reproductive system and other body systems. It generally begins about 10 years later than a woman's climacteric, and its physical effects vary (Weg, 1989). About 5 percent of middle-aged men experience depression, fatigue, lower libido, occasional impotence, and vaguely defined physical complaints (F. O. Henker, 1981; Weg, 1989). Since researchers have found no relationships between hormone levels and changes in mood (Doering, Kraemer, Brodie, & Hamburg, 1975), it is probable that most men's complaints are just as subject to nonphysiological pressures as women's are. Some problems may be related to such disturbing life events as illness, worries about work, children's leaving home, or the death of parents.

## APPEARANCE:
## THE DOUBLE STANDARD OF AGING

Although both sexes suffer from our society's premium on youth, women are especially oppressed because of a traditional double standard of aging. Gray hair, coarsened skin, and "crow's feet" are considered attractive in men, as indicators of experience and mastery; but in women they are regarded as telltale signs of being "over the hill." The ideal feminine look is "smooth, rounded, hairless, unlined, soft, unmuscled—the look of the very young; characteristics of the weak, of the vulnerable" (Sontag, 1972, p. 9). Once these signs of youth have faded, so (in many men's eyes) has a woman's value as a sexual and romantic partner and even as a prospective employee or business associate.

Of course, the existence of a double standard does not mean that men are completely unaffected when they begin to look old. Homosexual men may lose their physical appeal as they age (Berger, 1982). And even heterosexual men, who historically have escaped societal penalties for showing the natural effects of aging, are sometimes at a disadvantage in the job market as they reach midlife.

The different ways in which the double standard can affect husbands' and wives' sexual adjustment was shown dramatically by one study, which found that the physical changes of age are more likely to affect a husband's sexual responsiveness to his wife than vice versa (Margolin & White, 1987).

The pressures created by a society that believes in looking young, acting young, and being young—added to the real physical losses that people may suffer as they get older—may contribute to what has been called the *midlife crisis*. (This crisis is not inevitable, however, as discussed in Chapter 15.) Men and women who can withstand these pressures while staying as fit

Wrinkles and graying hair often imply that a man is "in the prime of life" but that a woman is "over the hill." This double standard of aging, which downgrades the attractiveness of middle-aged women but not of their husbands, can affect a couple's sexual adjustment.

as possible, and who can appreciate maturity as a positive achievement for both sexes, will be able to make the most of middle age—a time when both physical and intellectual functioning are likely to be at an impressively high level.

## HEALTH IN MIDDLE AGE

### HEALTH STATUS

The typical middle-aged American is quite healthy. In a recent government survey, about 82 percent of people 45 to 65 years old reported their health to be good, very good, or excellent (U.S. Department of Health and Human Services, USDHHS, 1990). Only about 8 percent of people in this age range are unable to carry out important activities because of poor health (USDHHS, 1990). College-educated people, wealthier people (those with an income of $35,000 or more), and white people rate their health better than less-educated, lower-income, and minority-group people; the differences probably reflect the benefits of good health care and habits set earlier in life (USDHHS, 1982, 1985, 1990).

The typical middle-aged American is quite healthy: about 82 percent of people 45 to 65 years old report their health as good, very good, or excellent. The healthiest are white and college-educated, with incomes over $35,000. Shown here is Sally Olds, who began to jog in her forties and now, in her fifties, jogs 3 miles a day.

## HEALTH PROBLEMS

### Diseases and Disorders

The most common chronic ailments of middle age are asthma, bronchitis, diabetes, nervous and mental disorders, arthritis and rheumatism, impaired sight and hearing, and malfunctions of the circulatory, digestive, and genitourinary systems. These ills do not necessarily appear in middle age, however; and while three-fifths of 45- to 64-year-olds have one or more of them, so do two-fifths of people between ages 15 and 44 (Metropolitan Life Insurance Company, in B. Hunt & Hunt, 1974; USDHHS, 1990).

One major health problem of midlife is **hypertension** (high blood pressure). This disorder, which often predisposes people to heart attack or stroke, affects 1 out of 5 adult Americans. It is particularly prevalent among black people and poor people (USDHHS, 1982, 1985, 1990). Blood pressure screening, a low-salt diet, and medication have prevented many deaths from heart disease and stroke (USDHHS, 1990).

Another health problem in this age group is AIDS, which now occurs more often in people over age 50 than in children under age 13. People over 50 now account for 10 percent of recorded cases. Although most cases occur in homosexual or bisexual men who contracted AIDS through sexual intercourse, about 17 percent of patients in this age group contracted it through contaminated blood transfusions before routine screening began in 1985. The disease seems to be more severe and to progress more rapidly in older people (Brozan, 1990).

Health problems in midlife are especially severe among Hispanic Americans because of poverty, low levels of education, and cultural and language barriers (Council on Scientific Affairs of the American Medical Association, 1991). Because their ailments tend to be diagnosed at a more advanced stage (since they often lack health insurance), they are less likely to benefit from treatment. This is a serious problem, since Hispanic Americans suffer disproportionately from high blood pressure, diabetes, kidney disease, certain cancers, AIDS, and lead poisoning.

### Death Rates and Causes of Death

Today, when people tend to live longer, death in middle age seems premature. It is not as unexpected as in earlier life stages, however. Beginning at age 35, the death rate at least doubles for each of the next two decades. Death is now more likely to come from natural causes than from accidents or violence. The three leading causes of death between ages 35 and 54 are cancer, heart disease, and accidents; between ages 55 and 64, the leading causes are cancer, heart disease, and strokes (USDHHS, 1982, 1990).

Since 1977, mortality has declined by 27 percent for people aged 25 to 64 (USDHHS, 1990). Today middle-aged people are less likely than they used to be to die of heart disease or stroke. But there are more fatal cancers. A 250 percent jump in deaths from lung cancer has offset a decline in deaths from all other kinds of cancer. Smoking is responsible for more than 80 percent of these deaths (USDHHS, 1990).

As in young adulthood, death rates are higher for men than for women and higher for black people than for white people. Men aged 45 to 64 are almost twice as likely to die as women in this age bracket. Men are 3 times more likely to die from heart disease and 25 to 30 percent more likely to die from cancer or stroke. The leading cause of death for women aged 45 to 64 continues to be cancer, mainly of the breast, genital organs, or lungs—the last, of course, is related to increased smoking by women (USDHHS, 1982, 1986, 1990).

## BOX 14–2   WINDOW ON THE WORLD

# THE IMPACT OF RACE ON HEALTH

In the United States as a whole, adults are healthier and can look forward to a longer life span than ever before. But one segment of our population—African-Americans who live in inner-city slums—is in as deplorable a state of health as people in some of the poorest and most backward nations in the world. Black men in New York's Harlem, for example, have a lower life expectancy than men in the third world country of Bangladesh. Overall death rates are considerably higher in inner-city African American communities than in some places that the government has designated "natural disaster areas" (McCord & Freeman, 1990). In Harlem, almost all the excess mortality involves people under age 65 (McCord & Freeman, 1990). What accounts for this catastrophe in the midst of a prosperous, highly developed country?

The largest single factor is poverty, which results in poor nutrition, substandard housing, inadequate prenatal care, and poor access to health care throughout life (Otten, Teutsch, Williamson, & Marks, 1990). Even when black people do have access to health care, they are less likely than white people to receive coronary bypass surgery, kidney transplants, and certain other treatments (Council on Ethical & Judicial Affairs, 1990).

Almost one-third (31 percent) of the excessive mortality of black peo-ple aged 35 to 54 can be accounted for by six risk factors: (1) high blood pressure, (2) high cholesterol, (3) overweight, (4) diabetes, (5) smoking, and (6) alcohol (Otten et al., 1990). The first four of these factors may be partly attributable to heredity, which also predisposes black people to sickle cell disease. But lifestyle also plays a part in these four factors, as well as in factors 5 and 6—smoking and drinking.

Ill health, as we have seen, is often directly linked to how people live from day to day—how much they smoke and drink, whether they abuse drugs, what and how much they eat. By practically every measure, lifestyle factors that contribute to ill health are epidemic in poor African American communities. Poor black people have high rates of cancer (especially lung cancer), high blood pressure, heart disease, and cirrhosis (liver disease) (Chissell, 1989; McCord & Freeman, 1990). Young black women are at risk of obesity; young black men are at risk of being murdered; black babies are at risk of being born too early and too small (McCord & Freeman, 1990; Wegman, 1989; Williamson, Kahn, Remington, & Anda, 1990).

African Americans also have another enemy to grapple with—racial prejudice. And some observers attribute the widening health gap between black and white Americans in part to the stress created by racism (Chissell, 1989; Lawler, 1990, in Goleman, 1990a). Research has shown, for example, that people who suppress their anger have abnormally high blood pressure. It is possible that constant racial discrimination and consistent suppression of anger combine, fatally, with a physiological predisposition of many black people to retain sodium in the kidneys while under emotional stress, a reaction that raises blood pressure (Goleman, 1990a). Some observers also point to the effects of low self-esteem, which leads some African Americans to early childbearing, violence, poor eating habits, overreacting to stress, and handling depression and frustration by smoking, drinking, and drug abuse (Chissell, 1989).

Although it is of course African Americans themselves who suffer most from these patterns, poor health and early death in the black population affect the entire society—in pressures on tax-supported institutions, in demands on medical care, and in crime rates. Government and communities must offer health education, access to basic health care, and employment that provides adequate income and decent housing—while eradicating racism from the body politic—if these trends are to be halted or reversed.

The death rate for middle-aged black people is 1.7 times that for white people (see Box 14-2). This is a smaller difference than that between black and white young adults, but 3 times as many black people as white people die of strokes, because more black people suffer from high blood pressure. In addition, death rates of black people are 50 percent higher than those of white people from heart disease, 40 percent higher from cancer, and 70 percent higher from cirrhosis of the liver (USDHHS, 1982, 1990).

# INTELLECTUAL DEVELOPMENT

Happily, the adage "You can't teach an old dog new tricks" does not apply to people. Middle-aged and older people can and do continue to learn new "tricks," new facts, and new skills, and they can remember those they already know well. There is no evidence of decline in many types of intellectual functioning before age 60, and there are even increases in such areas as vocabulary and general information. Middle-aged people can learn new skills—unless they think they cannot. Furthermore, they show a distinct advantage in solving the problems of everyday life, which is attributable to their ability to synthesize their knowledge and experience.

## ASPECTS OF INTELLECTUAL DEVELOPMENT IN MIDDLE ADULTHOOD

### INTELLIGENCE AND COGNITION

As we discuss intellectual functioning in maturity, we need to raise questions about the nature of intelligence and the way it is tested in adults: what standardized IQ tests can and cannot tell us about adults' intelligence, how appropriate these tests are for evaluating adults, and what kinds of intellectual abilities may improve through the years.

### Psychometrics: Does Intelligence Change in Adulthood?

For years, psychologists have tried to find out whether intelligence increases or declines during adulthood by giving adults psychometric tests like those used with children.

On such tests, young adults have done better than older adults in *cross-sectional* studies—that is, studies in which people of different ages were tested at the same time (Doppelt & Wallace, 1955; H. Jones & Conrad, 1933; Miles & Miles, 1932). But young people's superior performance in these studies may be due more to cohort differences than to their youth. That is, people born more recently may know more because they have had better or longer schooling, because they have learned more from television, because they are healthier, or for some other reason unrelated to aging.

By contrast, *longitudinal studies*—studies in which the same people are tested periodically over the years—

show an increase in intelligence at least until the fifties (Bayley & Oden, 1955; W. A. Owens, 1966). But these studies too present problems. Participants' higher scores on later tests may reflect "practice effects" like feeling more comfortable in the testing situation or remembering how similar problems were solved in earlier tests. Thus improvement may reflect better performance rather than better abilities. (The sequential approach of K. Warner Schaie is an attempt to overcome the drawbacks of both these methods of collecting data; we discuss Schaie's approach in Chapter 16, because the implications of an assumed decline in intelligence are especially relevant in late adulthood.)

Looking at adult intelligence is further complicated by the existence of different kinds of intellectual abilities. R. B. Cattell (1965) and J. L. Horn (1967, 1968, 1970) proposed one such distinction—between "fluid" and "crystallized" intelligence.

***Fluid intelligence*** is the capacity to apply intellectual ability in new situations. It involves the processes of perceiving relations, forming concepts, reasoning, and abstracting. Fluid intelligence is believed to depend on neurological development and to be relatively free from the influence of previous learning, education, or culture. It is assessed by tasks in which a problem is novel for everyone or else is an extremely common cultural element. Test-takers may be asked, for example, to group letters and numbers, to pair related words, or to remember a series of digits. Fluid intelligence is measured by tests like the Raven Progressive Matrices, in which a person is asked to select a pattern that best completes a series of patterns (see Figure 14-1 on the opposite page).

***Crystallized intelligence,*** on the other hand, is the ability to remember and use learned information. It depends on education and cultural background and is measured by tests of vocabulary, general information, and responses to social situations and dilemmas. Crystallized intelligence represents knowledge acquired over a lifetime.

Fluid intelligence requires the ability to process *new* information. Crystallized intelligence depends on the use of *stored* information and on how *automatic* a person's information processing has become, especially in complex tasks like reading, which call on a large number of mental operations.

Traditional tests suggest that pattern of intelligence persist into midlife: adults with relatively high IQ scores generally had high scores as children (they also tend to be healthier, better educated, and at higher socioeconomic levels than adults whose scores are lower).

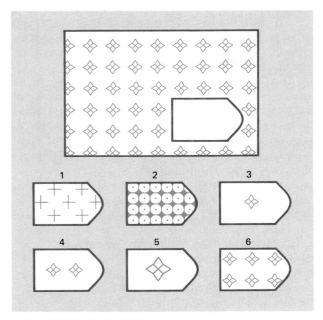

**FIGURE 14-1**
*Above:* Item from the Raven Progressive Matrices Test.
This test is a measure of fluid intelligence, since it represents a
novel task that does not ostensibly depend on knowledge.
Even without instructions, a test-taker can understand what
to do. However, people from a culture in which fill-in or
matching exercises are common may do better on tests like
these than people from other cultures. (*Source:* Raven,
1983.)

**FIGURE 14-2**
*Below:* Changes in "fluid intelligence" and "crystallized
intelligence" over the life span. While there is a decline in
fluid intelligence, there is a gradual increase in crystallized
intelligence. (*Source:* J. L. Horn & Donaldson, 1980.)

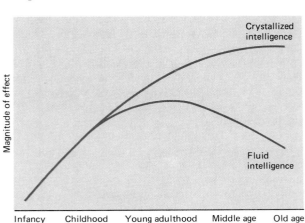

Standardized tests also show that performance on
some tasks improves during adulthood, with different
abilities peaking at different times. Performance on
tests of fluid intelligence seems to be highest in young
adulthood and to decline earlier than performance on
tests of crystallized intelligence (see Figure 14-2). People may continue to improve on tests of crystallized
intelligence through middle age, often until near the end
of life (J. L. Horn & Donaldson, 1980). For example,
verbal abilities rise, especially among people who use
their intellectual powers regularly, either on the job or
through reading or other mental stimulation.

So far, however, much of the research on fluid and
crystallized intelligence has been cross-sectional; thus
the results may reflect differences between cohorts
rather than changes with age. Furthermore, we have to
ask how valid traditional IQ tests are for adults. Many
of these tests were originally designed for children, and
adults often find the questions and tasks silly. In addition, adults may not be motivated to do their best.
Young people usually have a strong stake in performing
well, partly to prove themselves and partly because
they hope for some payoff, like admission to college.
Adults, especially older ones, rarely have so strong a
goal. Finally, we should ask whether these tests tap the
abilities that are most central to what intelligence
means in adulthood, like practicality and the ability to
function well in various situations. Although middle-
aged people may take somewhat longer than younger
people to do certain tasks and may not be as adept at
solving novel problems, they often compensate with
judgment developed from a wider range of experience.

K. Warner Schaie (whose stages of adult development are discussed in Chapter 12) has criticized the use
of conventional psychometric tests for adults. As he
points out, adults are usually more interested in using
knowledge for practical purposes than in acquiring
knowledge and skills for their own sake. In middle age,
according to Schaie's model (see Figure 12-2 on page
375), adults who are in either the "responsible" stage
or the "executive" stage use their intellectual abilities
to solve real-life problems associated with family, business, or societal responsibilities. This ties in with Erikson's belief (discussed in Chapter 15) that middle-aged
people are concerned with the task of generativity—
responsibility for establishing and guiding the next generation.

When adults do not perform well on psychometric
tests, then, it is not clear whether their memory or
reasoning ability is faltering or whether this kind of test
is simply not appropriate for their age group.

## Mature Thinkers:
## Does Cognition Change in Adulthood?

### Integrative thinking

Adults tend to think in an integrative way (see Chapter 12). Middle-aged people, in particular, tend to interpret what they read, see, or hear in terms of its personal and psychological meaning for them. Instead of accepting what they read at face value, for example, they filter it through their own life experience and learning, and interpret it accordingly. This, of course, has implications for every aspect of their lives.

In one series of studies, college students and older adults were asked to summarize stories (Labouvie-Vief & Hakim-Larson, 1989). One was a fable about a wolf who promises to reward a crane for removing a bone stuck in the wolf's throat (Labouvie-Vief, Schell, & Weaverdyck, 1982). The crane dislodges the bone with its beak—a maneuver that involves putting its head into the wolf's jaws—and then asks for the promised reward; the wolf replies that the crane's reward is to get away alive!

Both age groups recalled the story in detail, but they gave very different summaries. The students confined themselves to inferences from the text itself, while the older adults (their average age was 74) drew out moral and social meanings based on their own experiences and learning.

A similar study, built around a Sufi teaching tale, also included a middle-aged group (R. G. Adams, 1986). In this study, it was clear that the middle-aged adults were thinking on two levels at the same time: they integrated what was in the text with the psychological and metaphorical meaning the story held for them individually.

Integrative thinking has emotional and social implications. The ability to interpret events in a mature way enables many adults to come to terms with childhood events that once disturbed them, partly because of their earlier narrow interpretations (Schafer, 1980). Research has shown, for example, that women's adjustment in adulthood is related not to what actually happened between them and their mothers but to how they view their mothers' behavior toward them (Main, 1987).

Society benefits from this shift in adult thought. It is often middle-aged people who create inspirational myths and legends, who put truths about the human condition into symbols that younger generations can turn to for guidelines in leading their lives (Gutmann, 1977). People may need to be capable of integrative thought before they can become moral and spiritual leaders.

### Practical problem solving

Which do you think you would handle better—playing a game of "twenty questions" or figuring out what to do about a flooded basement?

In one study (Denney & Palmer, 1981), 84 adults between age 20 and age 79 were given two kinds of problems. One kind was like "twenty questions" (and like tasks on traditional intelligence tests): the subjects were shown 42 pictures of common objects and were told to figure out which one the examiner was thinking of, by asking questions that could be answered "yes" or "no." Scoring was based on how many questions it took to get the answer and what percentage of the questions eliminated more than one item at a time ("Is it an animal?") rather than only one item ("Is it the cow?").

In the second kind of problem, the subjects were asked what they would do in real-life situations like the following: your basement is flooding; you are stranded in a car during a blizzard; your 8-year-old child is 1½ hours late coming home from school. For these problems, scoring was based on the degree to which the solutions involved self-reliance rather than aid from other people.

The results confirmed our central point about intelligence in adulthood. The older the subjects were, the worse they did on "twenty questions"; but the *best* practical problem solvers were people in their forties and fifties, who based their answers on the experiences of everyday living. A follow-up study, which tried to give the elderly an advantage by posing problems with which they would be most familiar (concerning issues of retirement, widowhood, and ill health), found that people in their forties were better problem solvers than younger and older adults (Denney & Pearce, 1989).

After all, it is important to ask, What is the *purpose* of intelligence? Is it to play games, or to solve the real problems that face people every day? If the purpose of intelligence is to deal with real-life problems, then it is clear why middle-aged people are known as the *command generation,* and why this age group wields the most authority in virtually all institutions in society. Middle-aged people have not solved all our problems, of course, but no one else seems better qualified to bear this responsibility.

Thus even though middle-aged and older adults may not be as capable as younger people at solving novel problems, researchers are now beginning to discover the many complex strengths of mature thought that compensate for—and can often outweigh—any deficiencies.

This Spanish-speaking man and woman studying English are among the 14 percent of adults in the United States enrolled in part-time educational programs. Mature learners, who most often take classes for job-related reasons, tend to be more motivated than younger students.

## THE ADULT LEARNER

A woman marries at age 17, raises six children, and goes to college at 41 and to law school at 48; at 51 she is on the legal staff of the government of a major American city. A 56-year-old automotive mechanic takes a night course in philosophy. A 49-year-old physician signs up for a seminar on recent advances in endocrinology. These three people exemplify the boom in continuing education, the fastest-growing aspect of American education today.

Why do adults go to school? Almost two-thirds who take part-time classes do so for job-related reasons (U.S. Department of Education, 1986a). Some seek training to keep up with new developments in their fields. Many study in order to move up the career ladder or to prepare for different kinds of work. Some women who have devoted their young adult years to homemaking and parenting go back to school to embark on new careers. People close to retirement often want to expand their minds and skills to make more productive and interesting use of leisure. Some adults simply enjoy learning and want to keep on doing it throughout life.

Mature learners tend to be more motivated than those of traditional age. They have come to see that learning is not limited to the classroom but also occurs informally at home, on the job, and elsewhere. What they may lack in specific academic skills they make up for in the richness and variety of their life experiences, which they apply to the material they confront in school (Datan, Rodeheaver, & Hughes, 1987).

But adult learners are often more anxious and less self-confident than their younger classmates, who "know the ropes" because they have been going to school, usually without interruption, for the past 12 years or more. And older students often have special practical problems. They may have trouble fitting classes into busy schedules and juggling course work, parenting, and jobs. They may also have trouble just getting to class, and their friends and family are not always supportive.

To help meet their needs, a growing number of colleges are granting credits for practical life experience. They are also becoming more flexible in scheduling, letting more students matriculate part time and do much of their work independently.

In today's complex society, education is never finished. And although not all learning takes place in school, more and more people are finding that some sort of formal learning is important for developing their full intellectual potential, as well as for keeping up with the challenges and opportunities of the world of work.

# WORK IN MIDDLE ADULTHOOD

## OCCUPATIONAL PATTERNS

The typical middle-aged worker is likely to fit one of two descriptions. She or he may be at the peak of a career chosen in young adulthood—earning more money, exerting more influence, and commanding more respect than at any other period in life. Or a worker may be on the threshold of a new vocation, possibly spurred by the reevaluation that takes place during midlife—or by the need to seek a new line of work after being forced out of a job by cutbacks or for some other reason. A variation on the second pattern is that of some women, who enter or reenter the work force at this time of life, or move into more demanding work, because of the emptying of the nest or the need for money to send children to college.

### Pattern 1: Stable Careers

People who follow the pattern of a stable career are reaping personal benefits and also letting society benefit from their years of experience in a chosen field. Most of them continue to enjoy the work they have settled into. And because of their accumulated experience and wisdom, many reach positions of power and responsibility. Most business, academic, and political leaders, and many other prominent people in our society, tend to be in their middle years.

The top ranks of business, government, and the professions are still male-dominated, though women have made significant headway in these and other fields. In general, women still earn less than men and face barriers in both hiring and advancement.

Middle-aged men with stable careers tend to fall into two major categories: *workaholics* and the *mellowed* (Tamir, 1989). "Workaholics" may work at a frenzied pace either because of a last-ditch effort to reach financial security before they retire or because they find it hard to relinquish any of their authority.

The "mellowed" have come to terms with their level of achievement, even if they did not go as far in their careers as they had hoped. The best adjusted among the "mellowed" have a sense of relaxation rather than failure. They are often happier, less cynical, and steadier in temperament than their more successful counterparts (Bray & Howard, 1983). Although these middle-aged men want to do challenging work, they do not pin their emotional well-being on their jobs as much as they used to. These findings contradict Levinson's belief (see Chapter 13) that failure to achieve youthful goals will send a man into a midlife crisis.

## Pattern 2: Changing Careers

At age 40, the president of a multi-million-dollar corporation left his prestigious position to study architecture; eventually he opened his own architectural firm. At age 50, a homemaker who had held a variety of part-time jobs while her children were growing up enrolled in a school of social work; with her master's degree, she found a good job as a community organizer, which enabled her to draw on many of her past experiences.

Stories of midlife career changes abound these days, as people seek new careers for a variety of reasons. With longer life expectancies, many middle-aged people realize that they do not want to keep doing the same thing for the next 20 years and therefore strike out in totally new directions. Some are forced by unemployment to seek second careers. Some would rather change jobs than deal with competition from younger people moving up the career ladder. Some think, "I'm in a rut" or "I've gone as far as I can go with this company," and seek the challenge of a job that offers more opportunity for advancement or growth.

Common events of midlife can cause people to change careers. The emptying of the nest when the last child leaves home may change a woman's orientation from family to career and may also affect a man's outlook. People who have paid off the mortgage or put the last child through college may look for an easier work load, a job that pays less but is more satisfying, or a business venture that is risky but exciting. Others realize that they are ill-prepared for retirement and focus on accumulating a nest egg. And divorce or widowhood may create a need for more income.

How do career changers fare? The answer depends in part on whether the change is free or forced. People who freely choose to make a change often enjoy their lives more because they are contributing their valuable experience to new organizations or ventures; and they are often considered particularly valuable employees, since they are highly motivated and ambitious (Schultz & Schultz, 1986). But people who are forced to change careers may also do well, taking a layoff or forced retirement as an opportunity for growth.

Education and counseling can help people considering midlife career changes to see what possibilities are open to them and how they can make the most of those possibilities. The decision whether or not to stay in a job may hinge on the amount of intellectual and personal growth that the work provides.

People who follow this second pattern—changing careers—are getting considerable attention these days as part of a trend toward a lifetime of multiple careers. Many career changers are women. Although about half of middle-aged women now do paid work, compared with only about 20 percent in the 1920s (R. R. Bell, 1983), many have just entered the work force for the first time in their adult lives or have reentered it after "dropping out" to raise children. Such women not only face age and gender discrimination but are also handicapped by lack of experience, competing with people who may have a 20-year head start. Middle-aged men who change careers are more likely to have been in the work force throughout their adult life and thus are less often at such a disadvantage. This gender difference is likely to narrow, however, as the current generation of women, most of whom have been working straight through their child-rearing years, reach middle age.

We'll look next at some of the motivations that lead people to change jobs or careers, and then we'll see what kinds of work are most conducive to personal and intellectual growth.

## OCCUPATIONAL STRESS

When workers are dissatisfied with their jobs, it is often because of occupational stress. Table 14-1 lists major stressors, which are related to a number of physical and emotional complaints.

Certain patterns of stress are connected with certain occupations. Workers in low-status health care jobs (like technicians and aides) and personal service jobs (like waiters and telephone operators) have particularly high rates of admission to community mental health centers (Colligan, Smith, & Hurrell, 1977). These may be related to the strains of being in a subordinate position, in which workers experience pressure and authoritarian treatment but cannot respond to it (Holt, 1982).

Studies of 30- to 60-year-old men in a range of occupations also found that high psychological demands at work combined with little control resulted in "job strain" (Schnall et al., 1990). The men experiencing this kind of job strain were 3 times more likely to have high blood pressure and to show the changes in heart muscles that often precede heart attacks. This relationship held when the study controlled for smoking, alcohol, Type A behavior, and several other factors.

A major cause of daily stress on the job is conflict with supervisors, subordinates, and coworkers (Bolger, DeLongis, Kessler, & Schilling, 1989). Among 166 married couples who kept daily diaries for 6 weeks, the most upsetting stressors were arguments with other people. Dissension at work may be especially trying because people tend to suppress their anger instead of expressing it. Most reported incidents of stress had to do with work overloads: men felt more overloaded at

**TABLE 14–1**
SOURCES OF STRESS ON THE JOB

| Rank | Stressor |
| --- | --- |
| 1 | Lack of promotions or raises |
| 2 | Low pay |
| 3 | Monotonous, repetitive work |
| 4 | No input into decision making |
| 5 | Heavy work load or overtime |
| 6 | Supervision problems |
| 7 | Unclear job descriptions |
| 8 | Unsupportive boss |
| 9 | Inability or reluctance to express frustration or anger |
| 10 | Production quotas |
| 11 | Difficulty juggling home and family responsibilities |
| 12 | Inadequate breaks |
| 13 | Sexual harassment |

*Note:* Working conditions are listed in the order in which they were reported by 915 female office workers. In most cases the stressors are similar to those reported by workers in general, but there are some differences. Whereas these women rank low pay as the second greatest source of stress, this item is generally eighth or ninth in importance to men. Sexual harassment is almost always a woman's problem. One surprise is the low stress value given to "juggling work schedule with home and family responsibilities," which rates below elements of work life itself.
*Source:* Adapted from Working Women Education Fund, 1981, p. 9.

work, and women who worked outside the home felt overloaded both at home and at work.

***Burnout*** is a reaction to work-related stress; it involves emotional exhaustion, a feeling of being unable to accomplish anything on the job, and a sense of helplessness and loss of control. It is especially common among people in the helping professions (like teaching, medicine, therapy, social work, and police work) who feel frustrated by their inability to help people as much as they would like to. Burnout is usually a response to long-term stress rather than an immediate crisis. Its symptoms include fatigue, insomnia, headaches, persistent colds, stomach troubles, alcohol or drug abuse, and trouble getting along with people. A burned-out worker may quit a job suddenly, pull away from family and friends, and sink into depression (Briley, 1980; Maslach & Jackson, 1985).

Measures that seem to help burned-out workers include cutting down on working hours and taking breaks, including long weekends and vacations. Other standard stress-reducing techniques—exercise, music, and meditation—also help.

Unemployment can be devastating, bringing not only loss of a paycheck but loss of identity and self-esteem. Both men and women cope with unemployment better when they can draw on financial, psychological, and social resources. Some, in fact, develop both emotionally and professionally by seeing this forced change as an opportunity to do something new or as a challenge for growth.

## UNEMPLOYMENT

The greatest work-related stressor is sudden, unexpected loss of a job. Research on unemployment since the 1930s (concentrating almost entirely on men) has linked it to mental and physical illness and to problems in family functioning.

When people are unemployed, two major sources of stress are the loss of income (with its financial hardships) and the effect of this loss on their feelings about themselves. Workers who derive their identity from their work, men who define manhood as supporting a family, and people who define their worth in terms of their work's dollar value lose more than their paychecks when they lose their jobs. They lose a piece of themselves and their self-esteem (Voydanoff, 1983).

The ability to cope with unemployment depends on various factors. Those who cope best have some financial resources to draw on—savings, the earnings of other family members, and so on. They do not blame themselves for losing their jobs or see themselves as failures but assess their situation in more objective terms. They have the support of understanding, adaptable families and can draw on outside resources, like friends.

Women are as likely as men to feel distressed over loss of a job, as was shown by a study of former employees of a plant in Indiana that closed in 1982 (Perrucci & Targ, 1984). Both the women and the men who had lost their jobs reported such physical ailments as headaches, stomach trouble, and high blood pressure and felt less in control of their lives. The women's re-

sponses confirm another study, which found that a woman's sense of pride and power is more strongly related to her paid work than to her personal life (G. Baruch, Barnett, & Rivers, 1983).

A crucial factor in adjustment to losing a job is the context in which a person sees the situation. People who can look at such a forced change as an opportunity to do something else or as a challenge for growth can develop emotionally and professionally. They may change not only jobs but the entire direction of their careers.

## WORK AND INTELLECTUAL GROWTH

Do people change as a result of the kind of work they do? Research says "yes": people seem to grow in jobs that challenge their capabilities.

What specific aspects of work affect psychological functioning? In an examination of 50 different aspects of the work experience, from the pace of the work to relationships with coworkers and supervisors, the aspect that had the strongest impact was the **substantive complexity** of the work itself—"the degree to which the work, in its very substance, requires thought and independent judgment" (Kohn, 1980, p. 197). A sculptor's work, for example, is more complex than a ditchdigger's, a lawyer's work is more complex than a clerk's, and a computer programmer's work is more complex than a data processor's. (This "substantive complexity" may have something to do with creativity, discussed in Box 14-3.)

A combination of cross-sectional and longitudinal studies revealed a reinforcing interplay between the complexity of work and the worker's intellectual flexibility in coping with demanding situations. People with more complex work tend to become more flexible thinkers, not only on the job but in other areas of their lives. "They become more open to new experience. They come to value self-direction more highly. They even come to engage in more intellectually demanding leisure-time activities. In short, the lessons of work are directly carried over to nonoccupational realms" (Kohn, 1980, p. 204). At the same time, a person's intellectual flexibility influences the complexity of the work he or she will be doing 10 years down the road.

This circular relationship "may begin very early in life when children from culturally advantaged families develop skills and other qualities that result in their being placed in classroom situations and tracks that are relatively complex and demanding, which in turn contribute to further development of intellectual flexibility" (Smelser, 1980, p. 16). The circle continues in adult-

BOX 14–3   THINKING CRITICALLY

# CREATIVITY TAKES HARD WORK

At about age 40, Frank Lloyd Wright designed Robie House in Chicago, Louis Pasteur developed the germ theory of disease, and Woody Allen won three Oscars for the film *Annie Hall*. Charles Darwin was 50 when he presented his theory of evolution, Leonardo da Vinci was 52 when he painted the *Mona Lisa*, and Leonard Bernstein was 53 when he composed his *Mass* in honor of John F. Kennedy. At 48 the jazz singer Ella Fitzgerald began to record a 19-album series of nearly 250 popular classics; at 59 she finished it. These achievements are examples of the creative productivity possible in midlife.

Just what goes into the cognitive processes of highly creative minds is a puzzle that many researchers have tried to solve. The psychologist Howard Gruber (Gardner, 1981) has approached this question through intensive case studies of the intellectual lives of great scientists like Charles Darwin.

To find out how Darwin's mind worked, Gruber pored over Darwin's notebooks, trying to map the changes in his thinking during the 18 months after his return from a 5-year voyage of exploration in which he had meticulously recorded his observations of fossils, plants, animals, and rocks along the coast of South America and in the Pacific islands.

There is a commonly held idea that the creative act involves sudden insight. But Gruber was struck by how long it took Darwin to think through a new idea. Darwin had gone down at least one blind alley before he came upon an essay by the English economist Thomas Malthus, which described how natural disasters and wars keep population increases under control. After reading Malthus's description of the struggle for survival, it occurred to Darwin that some species—those whose characteristics were best adapted to the environment—would survive and others would not. But even then, it

A popular myth attributes creation to sudden flashes of inspiration, but the musician Leonard Bernstein, who at 53 composed his *Mass* in honor of John F. Kennedy, worked long, hard hours throughout his prolific career.

took Darwin several months after reading Malthus's essay to develop his principle of natural selection, which explains how adaptive traits are passed on through reproduction. And it was not until 2 decades later that he finally published his theory and the supporting evidence.

Although each mind works somewhat differently, Gruber found some common characteristics of highly creative people:

- They work *painstakingly and slowly* to master the knowledge and skills they need to solve a problem. Darwin studied barnacles for 8 years—until he probably knew more about them than anyone else in the world.
- They constantly *visualize* ideas. Darwin drew one particular image—a branching tree—over and over, as he refined his theory of how more complex, highly developed species evolve on the "tree" of nature.
- They are *goal-directed;* they have a strong "sense of purpose, a feel-

ing of where they are and where they want to go" (Gardner, 1981, p. 69).
- They have *networks* of *enterprises,* often juggling several seemingly unrelated projects or activities.
- They are *able to set aside problems* they have too little information to solve and go on to something else, or to adopt temporary working assumptions. Darwin did this when he got stuck on questions about heredity for which he had no reliable answers.
- They are *daring.* It took courage for Darwin to publish a theory that broke away from the entrenched ideas of his day.
- Rather than work in isolation (as they are often thought to do), they *collaborate* or discuss their ideas with others, by choosing peers and designing environments that nurture their work.
- They *enjoy turning over ideas* in their minds "and would not dream of doing anything else" (Gardner, 1981, p. 70). Darwin was reading Malthus's essay for amusement.
- Through hard work, they *transform themselves,* until what would be difficult for someone else seems easy for them.

This last point, in particular, is reminiscent of Kohn's belief (1980) that substantively complex work, requiring deep thought and independent judgment, can contribute to intellectual growth—not only in a Darwin but in anyone.

The challenge, then—for a society that depends on the creativity of its citizens—is how to encourage these characteristics. Are there, for example, ways to train people to visualize their ideas, to learn when to persist in pursuing a train of thought—and when to set aside a problem for the time being? In sum, how much of creativity can be expanded by what goes on in the home, the school, and the workplace?

hood, as people begin their careers—and the gap widens between flexible thinkers in complex jobs and less flexible thinkers in less complex jobs. The flexible thinkers tend to go into increasingly complex work, which in turn enables their thinking to become more and more flexible, qualifying them for even more complex work. People who show less flexibility at the outset and do less complex work grow more slowly or not at all (Kohn, 1980).

Why is the complexity of work tied so closely to intellectual growth? One reason may be that—in a society like ours, in which work plays a central role in people's lives—mastery of complex tasks affects people's sense of self; it gives them a feeling of competence and teaches them that they can manage the problems they encounter (Kohn, 1980).

What is most important, then, about work is not income or status but what people actually do. Research about work also confirms that people's minds do not stop developing at the end of adolescence or young adulthood. Thus we see again the links between intellectual development and the social and emotional aspects of personality, to which we turn in Chapter 15.

## SUMMARY

- Middle adulthood is a time of reevaluation. There is no single biological marker or behavioral sign denoting the beginning of middle age. In this book, *middle age* is defined as the period from 40 to 65 years of age.

### PHYSICAL CHANGES OF MIDDLE AGE

- Middle-aged adults experience some declines in sensory abilities and complex motor skills, but they can compensate for these declines with such aids as eyeglasses and with the application of experience and judgment.

- Middle-aged couples today are engaging in sexual relations more often and in more varied ways than their counterparts in the past. Sexual compatibility is not the most important factor in a happy marriage, but sexual activity and sexual satisfaction can and often do continue throughout middle age and the older adult years.

- Menopause, the cessation of menstruation and reproductive ability in women, typically occurs around age 50, when a decrease in the production of estrogen brings about the end of ovulation. It is associated with hot flashes, thinning of the vaginal lining, and urinary dysfunction. Osteoporosis, a condition in which bones become thinner and more susceptible to fractures, affects 1 out of 4 postmenopausal women. There is no reason to attribute psychological problems to menopause.

- Although men can continue to father children until late in life, in some men the male climacteric brings a decline in fertility and in frequency of orgasm, an increase in impotence, and other symptoms.

- The "double standard of aging" in American society causes women more than men to seem less desirable as they lose their youthful looks. For both sexes, the problems of getting older are often amplified by living in a society that places a premium on youth.

### HEALTH IN MIDDLE AGE

- Most middle-aged people are in good health. Three-fifths of middle-aged people suffer from chronic health conditions; however, two-fifths of young adults already have these conditions.

- Although death rates have declined in recent generations (especially death from heart disease and stroke), death rates increase throughout midlife. Death is more likely to occur in this period from natural causes than from accidents or violence. The leading causes of death are cancer, heart disease, accidents, and stroke. As in younger age groups, death rates are higher for males than for females and higher for black people than for white people.

### ASPECTS OF INTELLECTUAL DEVELOPMENT IN MIDDLE ADULTHOOD

- Performance on many standardized intelligence measures increases during adulthood, especially for verbal abilities and tasks involving stored knowledge. However, the appropriateness of conventional IQ tests for adults is questionable.

- Although middle-aged people may perform more slowly and may not be as adept at solving novel problems, some research suggests that the ability to solve practical problems based on experience peaks at midlife.

- Continuing education for adults is the fastest-growing area of education in the United States.

- Adults go to school for many reasons, but chiefly to improve their work-related skills and knowledge or to prepare for a change of career. Adult learners tend to be more motivated but less self-confident than young students.

## WORK IN MIDDLE ADULTHOOD

■ Many middle-aged people are at the peak of their careers, but others are involved in career changes that may be triggered by the self-evaluation process of midlife. For some, occupational stresses such as burnout, unemployment, and specific working conditions affect physical and emotional well-being.

■ The kind of work adults do affects the degree to which they grow intellectually. There seems to be a direct relationship between the complexity of the work a person does and that person's intellectual flexibility.

■ Some people do extremely creative work in middle age. Studies of scientists show that creativity appears to have more to do with slow, painstaking work than with sudden inspiration.

## KEY TERMS

presbyopia (page 429)
presbycusis (429)
menopause (431)
climacteric (431)

estrogen (431)
osteoporosis (431)
male climacteric (431)
hypertension (434)

fluid intelligence (436)
crystallized intelligence (436)
burnout (441)
substantive complexity (442)

## SUGGESTED READINGS

**Cooper, K. H. (1990).** *Preventing osteoporosis.* New York: Bantam. Showing that osteoporosis is not just a disease of the elderly and is not limited to women, Dr. Cooper explains how to develop bone density, investigates probable causes, and explains how to determine if you have osteoporosis or are at risk. The book includes complete diet and exercise plans that reduce the risk of developing this disease.

**Greenwood, S. (1989).** *Menopause, naturally: Preparing for the second half of life.* Volcano, CA: Volcano Press. This optimistic book by a woman doctor explains menopause in physical and psychological terms.

**Troll, L. E. (1985).** *Early and middle adulthood* (2d ed.). Monterey, CA: Brooks/Cole. A survey of research findings on physical status, personality, and intellectual functioning, by a leading developmental researcher.

## CHAPTER 15

# PERSONALITY AND SOCIAL DEVELOPMENT IN MIDDLE ADULTHOOD

What happens to a dream deferred?
Does it dry up
Like a raisin in the sun?
Maybe it just sags
Like a heavy load.
*Or does it explode?*

LANGSTON HUGHES,
*"MONTAGE OF A DREAM DEFERRED," 1951*

- How typical is the midlife crisis?
- Which aspects of personality typically change during middle adulthood, and which ones stay the same?
- How similar are women's and men's development at midlife?

- Do marriages become happier or less happy at midlife?
- How do middle-aged people cope with teenage children, the "empty nest," the care of aging parents, and the death of a parent?

When asked, "How are you?" a vivacious speech therapist replied, "I'm going to have my fortieth birthday in 2 weeks, and I can't talk to anyone without mentioning it. So I guess I'm having my midlife crisis. Isn't everybody?"

Changes in personality and lifestyle during middle adulthood are often attributed to the **midlife crisis,** a supposedly stressful period during the early to middle forties, which is triggered by a review and reevaluation of one's past life and which heralds the onset of middle age. This idea burst into public consciousness in the late 1970s, with the popularization of data from Daniel Levinson's studies and Erik Erikson's eloquent conceptualization of the normative-crisis approach to human development—the view that the human personality goes through a universal sequence of critical changes (which may or may not be upsetting) at certain ages.

Many psychologists talk about a *midlife transition,* which also may or may not involve upset. The term *midlife crisis,* however, implies a disturbing transition. It was coined by the psychoanalyst Elliott Jacques, and it has become a trendy catchphrase, which may pop up as an explanation for any bout of depression, extramarital affair, or career change. Such events are taken as signs of a shift from an outward orientation, a concern with finding a place in society, to an inward orientation, a search for meaning within the self (Jung, 1966). This inward turn may be unsettling; as people question their life goals, they may temporarily lose their moorings.

What brings on the midlife crisis, Jacques (1967) says, is awareness of mortality. The first part of adulthood is over, its tasks largely done. Most people have formed their families and are now tasting freedom from the daily responsibilities of child care. They have estab-lished their occupations and have, by and large, accepted their level of success. They have become independent of their parents, who may now be turning to *them* for advice and help. They are in the prime of life— but they now realize that their time has become shorter and they will not be able to fulfill all the dreams of their youth; or, if they have fulfilled their dreams, they realize that they have not found the satisfaction they had hoped for.

This realization is not necessarily traumatic. For many people, it is just one more of life's many transitions, and they adjust easily. People can emerge from this time of questioning with more awareness and understanding of themselves and of others; with more wisdom, strength, and courage; and with a greater capacity for love and enjoyment.

In one way, talking about a midlife crisis is helpful, because it calls attention to the dynamic nature of personality in middle age. In another way, it is not helpful, since it can lead to a rigid notion that everyone must undergo a crisis in order to develop emotionally during midlife.

Today, attention is shifting from the midlife crisis, and the normative-crisis model from which it springs, to the timing-of-events model (see Chapter 13). According to the timing-of-events model, personality development is influenced less by age than by the events in people's lives and when they occur. Twenty or thirty years ago, the occurrence and timing of such major events as marriage, first job, and the birth of children and grandchildren were fairly predictable, so that age may have been a generally adequate indicator of development. But today, lifestyles are more diverse, people's "social clocks" tick at different rates, and a "fluid life cycle" has washed out the old boundaries between

THE TERRIBLE FORTY-TWOS

The concept of a "midlife crisis" can lead to a rigid notion that everyone must have one. For many people, however, the transition to middle age is not particularly stressful. The timing and acuteness of the transition and the way people cope with it may reflect their circumstances and personalities more than their age. This disgruntled executive may be using the "midlife crisis" to excuse his temper tantrum.

youth and adulthood, and between middle age and old age (Neugarten & Neugarten, 1987). As a result, it may be more useful to consider development in terms of life events. The timing-of-events model also recognizes that societal changes affect the significance of events and their impact on personality. For example, when women's lives tended to revolve around bearing and rearing children, the end of the reproductive years meant something different from what it means now, when most women are only in their mid-thirties by the time their youngest child has started school. When people died earlier, survivors felt old earlier, since the death of friends, relatives, and public figures close to their own age reminded them that someday they too would die.

Whether or not an actual crisis takes place, however, a sharper awareness of life's limits often leads middle-aged people to recognize that if they want to change direction, they have to act quickly. Midlife is a time of stock taking, not only in regard to careers but also in intimate relationships.

In this chapter we look at midlife first through the prism of the normative-crisis model of development, and we also present a critique of that model. Then, we look at important events in relationships. As we examine changes in marriage, sexuality, sibling bonds, and friendship, as well as relationships with maturing children and with aging parents, we see variations in the shape and timing of these events.

# MIDLIFE: THE NORMATIVE-CRISIS APPROACH

## THEORIES AND RESEARCH

Much of the major theoretical and research work on adult development of the past few decades has taken a normative-crisis viewpoint. This is the perspective of Carl Jung's analysis of a necessary midlife transition, Erikson's stage of generativity versus stagnation, Robert Peck's expansion of Erikson's work, and Vaillant's and Levinson's research (introduced in Chapter 13). These views are summarized in Table 15-1 on the following page; they are discussed in the following sections, along with two studies of women's development; and then they are evaluated according to current psychological thought.

### Carl Jung: Balancing the Personality

Carl Jung was at one time a disciple of Freud but later broke with Freud over a number of issues. One of these issues was Jung's conviction that people grow and change throughout life—that their personalities are not unalterably set in childhood.

Jung (1953) emphasized the quest for meaning in life and the process of developing an individual personality. He considered the midlife transition very important in psychological development. Up till about age 40, according to Jung, women and men concentrate on their obligations to their families and to society, and they develop those aspects of personality that further these goals. Women emphasize expressiveness and nurturance; men emphasize an orientation toward achievement.

But when people's careers are established and their children are grown, both men and women are free to balance their personalities. They achieve a "union of opposites" by expressing those aspects of themselves that had been suppressed earlier. To do this, they need to pay more attention to their inner selves, often becoming preoccupied with the tasks of this stage. Two necessary tasks are giving up the image of youth and youthful lifestyles, and acknowledging eventual mortality. Since these tasks and the inner dialogue they call for involve threatening concepts, midlife is often stressful. But people who avoid the transition and do not reorient their lives appropriately will not make a good psychological adjustment at this stage or in the future.

**TABLE 15–1**
FIVE VIEWS OF DEVELOPMENT IN MIDDLE ADULTHOOD

| Jung | Erikson | Peck: Four Adjustments of Middle Age | Vaillant: Grant Study of Harvard Men | Levinson: Stages of Midlife Development in Men |
|---|---|---|---|---|
| *Midlife transition (about age 40):*<br><br>After child-rearing obligations have diminished, women and men can balance their personalities by expressing characteristics that had previously been suppressed. Women become more assertive and men become more emotionally expressive.<br><br>People become more inner-oriented and preoccupied with their inner world. They now need to give up the image of youth, adopt a more appropriate lifestyle, and acknowledge that their lives are finite. This inner work creates stress but is necessary for healthy adjustment. | *Crisis 7— Generativity versus stagnation*<br><br>The impulse to foster the development of the next generation leads middle-aged persons to become mentors to young adults. The wish to have children is instinctual, and so childless people must acknowledge their sense of loss and express their generative impulses in other ways, helping to care for other people's children directly or as protégés in the workplace. Some stagnation could provide a rest that leads to greater future creativity. Too much stagnation could lead to physical or psychological invalidism. | 1 *Valuing wisdom versus valuing physical powers:* People realize that the knowledge they have gained through the years, enabling them to make their life choices wisely, more than makes up for declining physical powers and youthful attractiveness.<br><br>2 *Socializing versus sexualizing in human relationships:* People appreciate the unique personalities of others as they learn to value them as friends rather than as sex objects.<br><br>3 *Emotional flexibility versus emotional impoverishment:* Deaths of parents and friends end meaningful relationships. People must develop the ability to shift their emotional investments from one person to another. Physical limitations can require a change in activities.<br><br>4 *Mental flexibility versus mental rigidity:* Flexibility enables people to use their past experiences as provisional guides to solving new issues. | *Midlife transition (age 40—"give or take a decade"):* Midlife is stressful, as adolescence is stressful, because of the demands of entrance into a new stage of life. Much of the pain comes from having the maturity to face pain that was suppressed for years. Many men reassessed their past, reordered their attitudes toward sexuality, and seized one more chance to find new solutions to old needs. The best-adjusted men were the most generative and found these years (from 35 to 49) the happiest of their lives.<br><br>*Tranquil fifties:*<br><br>Males become more nurturant and expressive. Sexual differentiation lessens. The fifties are a generally mellower time of life. | *Midlife transition (age 40 to age 45):* Questioning one's life—values, desires, talents, goals; looking back over past choices and priorities; deciding where to go now; coming to terms with youthful dreams; developing a realistic view of self.<br><br>*Entry life structure for middle adulthood (age 45 to age 50):* Reappraisal leads to a new life structure involving new choices. Some men retreat into a constricted—or well-organized, overly busy—middle age.<br><br>*Age-50 transition\* (age 50 to age 55):* Men who have not gone through their midlife crisis earlier may do so now. Others may modify the life structures they have formed in their mid-forties.<br><br>*Culminating life structure for middle adulthood\* (age 55 to 60):* Men complete middle adulthood; a time of great fulfillment.<br><br>*Late adult transition\* (age 60 to age 65):* Middle age ends; preparation for late adulthood begins. |

\*Projected.   *Sources:* Erikson, 1950; Jung, 1953; Levinson, 1978, 1986; Peck, 1955; Vaillant, 1977.

Coaching a Little League baseball team is one form of what Erikson calls *generativity*. Many middle-aged people fulfill this need to establish and guide the next generation by helping other people's children, in addition to or instead of their own.

## Erik Erikson: Crisis 7—Generativity versus Stagnation

Erikson also saw the years around age 40 as a critical time, when people go through their seventh normative crisis, **generativity versus stagnation.** *Generativity* is the concern of mature adults for establishing and guiding the next generation. Looking ahead to the waning of their own lives, people feel a need to participate in the continuation of life. If this need is not met, people become *stagnant*—inactive or lifeless.

The impulse to foster development of the young is not limited to guiding one's own children. It can be expressed through activities like teaching and *mentorship*—a mutually fulfilling relationship that satisfies a younger protégé's need for guidance as well as an older person's need for generativity. Generativity can also take the form of productivity or creativity (as in the arts) or of self-generation, the further development of personal identity. (Generativity corresponds to Schaie's "responsible" and "executive" stages of cognitive development in midlife, discussed in Chapters 12 and 14, which involve practical problem solving on behalf of others.)

As in all of Erikson's stages, it is the *balance* of one trait over its opposite that is important. Even the most creative person goes through stagnant or fallow periods, gathering energy for the next project; but too much stagnation can result in self-indulgence or even in physical or psychological invalidism. The "virtue" of this period is *care:* "a widening commitment to *take care of* the persons, the products, and the ideas one has learned *to care for*" (Erikson, 1985, p. 67).

Erikson (1985) believes that people who have not been parents do not easily achieve generativity. He urges childless adults to acknowledge a sense of loss, or "generative frustration," and to find other outlets for generative tendencies—as through helping children in developing countries, coaching a sports team, or leading a scout troop. However, many people who have cared for their own children for years may need to take care of themselves for a while before they can again focus on nurturing others. Furthermore, Erikson's view that childless people have trouble achieving generativity is considered narrow by many psychologists.

## Robert Peck: Four Adjustments of Middle Age

Expanding on Erikson's concepts, Peck (1955) sees four psychological developments as critical to successful adjustment in middle age:

1 **Valuing wisdom versus valuing physical powers.** *Wisdom,* defined as the ability to make the best choices in life, seems to depend largely on life experience and on opportunities for a wide range of relationships and situations. Sometime between the late thirties and the late forties, most well-adjusted people appreciate that their wisdom more than makes up for their diminished physical strength, stamina, and youthful appearance.

2 **Socializing versus sexualizing in human relationships.** People redefine the men and women in their lives, valuing them as individuals, as friends, and as companions rather than primarily as sex objects. Thus they can appreciate the unique personalities of others and can reach a greater depth of understanding.

3 **Emotional flexibility versus emotional impoverishment.** The ability to shift emotional investment from one person to another and from one activity to another becomes crucial during middle age. Parents, spouses, and friends are more likely to die, and children have matured and become independent. Also, middle-aged people may have to change their activities because of physical limitations.

4 **Mental flexibility versus mental rigidity.** By midlife, many people have worked out a set of answers to life's important questions. But when they let these answers control them rather than continue to seek out new answers, they become set in their ways and closed to new ideas. Those who remain flexible use their experiences and the answers they have already found as provisional guides to the solution of new problems.

None of these developments need wait until middle age; some may already have occurred in early adulthood. If they do not take place by midlife, however, Peck doubts that the person will be able to make a successful emotional adjustment.

## George Vaillant:
## Introspection and Transition

The longitudinal research reported by Vaillant and known as the *Grant Study* (introduced in Chapter 13), which followed male college students into later adulthood, identified a midlife transition at about age 40. After the stage of career consolidation, which usually occurred during the thirties, many of the men abandoned the "compulsive, unreflective busywork of their occupational apprenticeships and once more [became] explorers of the world within" (Vaillant, 1977, p. 220). Neugarten (1977), a prominent advocate of the timing-of-events model, also observed this tendency toward introspection in middle age; she calls it **interiority.** Introspection, or interiority, also echoes Jung's concept of turning inward as a necessity in middle age; but it seems to vary with personality. (This issue and the question of other personality changes in midlife are discussed in Box 15-1.)

The midlife transition may be stressful because of the demands made by a new stage of life, such as changing the parenting role to meet the needs of teenage children. Much of the pain of midlife, Vaillant says, is old, repressed pain, which surfaces now that men are mature and strong enough to deal with it. Once they have faced their repressed feelings, men can use the transition period as one more chance to find new solutions to old problems. Thus, many men reassess their past, come to terms with long-suppressed feelings about their parents, and reorder their attitudes toward sexuality.

However, as troubling as the transition years sometimes were for the men in the Grant Study, the transition rarely assumed crisis dimensions. These men were no more likely to get divorced, to be disenchanted with their jobs, or to become depressed at midlife than at any other time during the life span. By their fifties, the best-adjusted men in the group actually saw the years from 35 to 49 as the *happiest* in their lives.

The best-adjusted men were also the most generative, as measured by their responsibility for other people at work, their gifts to charity, and their children—whose academic achievements equaled those of their fathers. And in midlife the men were four times more likely to cope with life events in such mature ways as using altruism and humor than in immature ways like drinking or becoming hypochondriacs (Vaillant, 1989).

The fifties were a generally mellower and more tranquil time of life than the forties. Vaillant noted some of the same traits seen by others: a lessening of sexual differentiation with advancing age—which Brim (1974) calls the "normal unisex of later life"—and a tendency for men to become more nurturant and expressive.

## Daniel Levinson:
## Changing Life Structures

On the basis of studies of men,* Levinson and his associates (1978, 1980, 1986) describe midlife as a time when life structures "always" change appreciably, although in different ways and to different degrees. Most people become "senior members" of their "own particular worlds," responsible for the work of others and for guiding younger adults.

According to Levinson, sometime between age 40 and age 45, people go through a midlife transition. Of the 40 men in his sample, 32 found this a time of moderate or severe crisis, when they often felt upset and acted irrationally. Levinson believes that emotional turmoil is inevitable at this time of life, as people question previously held values. However, this reevaluation is healthy, helping people come to terms with their youthful dreams and allowing them to emerge with a more realistic view of themselves.

A man at midlife, Levinson says (echoing Jung), needs to deal with opposite tendencies. On the one hand, he must avoid clinging too much to youthful attitudes; but on the other hand, he must avoid thinking like an old person. He must also try to integrate the "masculine" and "feminine" parts of his personality—that is, his "masculine" need for separateness and his "feminine" need for attachment.

Between ages 45 and 50, men carve out new life structures, possibly by taking a new job or a new wife, or by changing patterns of work or relationships. Those who make no changes lead a boringly constricted life in middle age, or they are busy and well organized—but unexcited. Often those who do change their life structures find middle age the most fulfilling and creative time of life.

Levinson and his colleagues (1978) did not follow their original sample into their fifties and sixties, but Levinson made a number of projections concerning what would happen during those years. He predicted that men whose midlife transition had been fairly smooth would probably have a difficult time at about age 50; and that between ages 55 and 60, men would finish building the framework of middle adulthood. Those who could rejuvenate themselves and thus enrich their lives would find the fifties a time of great fulfillment. They would then experience another major turning point in the early sixties, when they were coming out of middle age and preparing for late adulthood.

---

*As noted earlier, Levinson's studies of women have still not been published.

BOX 15–1    THINKING CRITICALLY

# DOES PERSONALITY CHANGE IN MIDDLE AGE?

"I'm a completely different person now from the one I was twenty years ago," said the 47-year-old architect, as six friends, all in their forties and fifties, nodded vigorously in agreement.

Many people feel themselves changing at midlife. But are these changes deep-seated, or are they just on the surface? Is there a basic core of personality that remains stable throughout life?

These are controversial questions. For years, most psychologists believed that by young adulthood, personality is set like concrete. But in the 1970s, the image shifted to a seemingly limitless capacity for change throughout life (Z. Rubin, 1981). Now there are two camps. One believes that change will occur unless something interferes with development (Brim & Kagan, 1980); the other believes that personality will remain stable unless a specific event occurs to produce change (Costa & McCrae, 1981). The truth seems to be that people change in some ways and remain the same in others. Through experience and accomplishments, most adults gain in self-esteem and a sense of control over their lives, but basic temperament tends to remain constant (Brim & Kagan, 1980).

Longitudinal studies find that bubbly junior high schoolers grow up to be cheerful 40-year-olds, complaining adolescents turn into querulous

adults, assertive 20-year-olds become outspoken 30-year-olds, and people who cope well with problems of youth are equally able to handle problems of later life (J. Block, 1981; Costa & McCrae, 1981; Eichorn, Clausen, Haan, Honzik, & Mussen, 1981; Haan & Day, 1974; F. Livson, 1976; Noberini & Neugarten, 1975).

As people grow older, they tend to become more introverted and introspective. But people who were extroverts in their youth tend to remain more outgoing than other people. Extroversion, openness to new experience, and neuroticism (a mild emotional disturbance arising from anxiety) all remain quite stable throughout adulthood, according to the results of a nationwide cross-sectional study of more than 10,000 people 32 to 88 years old (Costa et al., 1986). Certain traits do seem to soften with maturity. For example, although impulsive children usually grow up to be restless, impatient adults, as adults they are less impulsive than they had been earlier (M. A. Stewart & Olds, 1973).

One common change in midlife is a tendency to take on characteristics associated with the other sex. Men often become more open about feelings, more interested in intimate relationships, and more nurturing; while women tend to become more assertive, self-confident, and achievement-oriented (Chiriboga &

Thurnher, 1975; Cytrynbaum et al., 1980; Helson & Moane, 1987; Neugarten, 1968). These findings support Jung's notion of "balancing" and suggest that middle-aged people who fail to develop the previously "disowned" parts of their personalities are more susceptible to emotional problems.

What causes this change? Some social scientists, citing historical observations of similar changes, suggest that the hormonal changes of midlife blur sexual distinctions (Rossi, 1980). Others offer a cultural explanation: at the same time that women are freer—because their children have grown up and left home—to develop nonmaternal abilities and to seek achievements in a career, men begin to wonder whether work is the most important thing in life after all (Gutmann, 1975, 1985). Now that younger women are more achievement-oriented and more likely to combine working with mothering, and younger men are more active in child rearing, we may no longer see this switch in personality at midlife. Indeed, the changes we have seen may have less to do with gender than with the questions middle-aged people ask themselves as they evaluate their lives: "Is this all there is to life? Shouldn't I try other options while I still have time?"

## Women's Development in Middle Adulthood: Two Studies

The normative-crisis models of Erikson, Levinson, and Vaillant have all been male-oriented in theory, in research samples, or in both. Other researchers who have examined women's experience at midlife have found some similarities to the male-based models, but they have also found some differences.

### Women and the midlife transition

Droege's dissertation (1982), analyzed by P. Roberts and Newton (1987—see Chapter 13), used Levinson's technique of biographical interviews with 12 women aged 44 to 53. In these subjects, the midlife transition was not a clear-cut dividing line; their lives continued to be unstable after the transition. Perhaps this was because they had not yet reached a point at which they could assess career achievements and make a definite change of direction.

Still, these women led different kinds of lives before and after midlife. In their late thirties, they began to identify themselves in a context beyond the family, taking on roles of community leadership. At midlife, they made changes in career and family commitments that seemed linked more to age, to the awareness of mortality, to shifting roles, and to a desire for self-expression than to any specific event. (The "emptying of the nest," for example, was a critical "marker" event only for women whose lives had been extremely family-centered.) Some took on paid or volunteer work; others reduced their work load. Some changed marital or other relationships or redefined basic values. This process seemed psychologically healthy: the women who took risks and made structural changes in their lives were less depressed and had higher self-esteem than those who did not build new structures for middle age.

### Mastery, pleasure, and women's adjustment

A much larger study, of almost 300 women between ages 35 and 55, points to factors that contribute to women's healthy adjustment in the middle years (Barnett, 1985; G. Baruch, Barnett, & Rivers, 1983). The investigators first interviewed 60 women, 10 from each of six groups: (1) employed women who had never married, (2) employed married women with children, (3) employed married women without children, (4) employed divorced women with children, (5) married homemakers with children, and (6) married homemakers without children. On the basis of what these women said about the pleasures, problems, and conflicts in their lives, the researchers drew up a questionnaire and gave it to a random sample of 238 other women in the six categories. On average, the subjects had 2 years' education beyond high school; their incomes ranged from $4500 to over $50,000.

Two main factors influenced these women's mental health: how much *mastery,* or control, they felt they had over their lives, and how much *pleasure* they got from life. Neither criterion was related to age: the older women felt just as good about themselves as the younger ones. There was no evidence of a midlife crisis. Nor did simple relationships show up between well-being and whether a woman was married, had children, or was pre- or postmenopausal. What did emerge as vitally important was the combination of a woman's work and her intimate relationships.

Paid work was the single best predictor of mastery; a positive experience with husband and children (including a good sex life) was the best predictor of pleasure; and the single best key to general well-being was a

A woman's well-being flourishes in multiple roles, which may include a positive experience with husband and children and a challenging, satisfying job. This mother is shown enjoying one of the pleasures of family life, one that may require her to redefine her role to reflect her children's independent status.

challenging job that paid well and gave opportunity to use skills and make decisions. The women who scored highest overall on both mastery and pleasure were employed married women with children; the lowest scorers were unemployed childless married women.

Women's well-being, then, seems to flourish in multiple roles, despite the stress that goes along with active involvement in several important areas of life. It is even more stressful, apparently, to be underinvolved—to have too little to do, to have a job that is not challenging enough, or to have too few personal and occupational demands. These findings support those of Helson & Moane (1987—see Chapter 13), that women who commit themselves to career, family, or both show more personality growth between early and middle adulthood than those who do not.

## EVALUATING THE NORMATIVE-CRISIS MODEL

Several questions can be asked about the normative-crisis model of adult development: How widely does it apply? Is the midlife crisis really typical? To what extent does adult development depend on age? Can the male model of development be considered "healthy"? Let's examine these issues.

## BOX 15–2   WINDOW ON THE WORLD

# A SOCIETY WITHOUT MIDDLE AGE?

The universality of the midlife crisis is questionable even in our culture. What, then, happens in nonwestern cultures that do not even have a clear concept of middle age? One such culture is that of the Gusii in Africa, a society of 1 million people in western Kenya, where people believe in witchcraft and men take several wives (R. Levine, 1980).

Among the Gusii, childbearing is not confined to young adulthood; people continue to reproduce as long as they are physiologically able. The Gusii do have a "life plan" with well-defined expectations for each stage, but this plan is very different from what is accepted as normal in the United States today.

The Gusii have no words meaning "adolescent," "young adult," or "middle-aged." A man goes through only one recognized stage of life—*omomura*, or "warrior"—between his circumcision, which takes place between ages 9 and 11, and the marriage of his first child, when he becomes an elder. Thus the *omomura* phase may last anywhere from 25 to 40 or more years. Women have an additional stage between being circumcised and becoming elders—*omosubaati*, or "married women"—

Many Gusii in western Kenya become ritual practitioners after their children are grown, seeking spiritual powers to compensate for their waning physical strength. For women like the diviner shown here, ritual practice may be a way to wield power in a male-dominated society.

emphasizing the greater importance of marriage in a woman's life.

Transitions in Gusii society, then, depend on life events, not on age. Status is gained from circumcision, from marriage (for women), from having children, and from becoming a parent of a married child (and thus a prospective grandparent). However, the Gusii have a "social clock," a set of expectations for when these events should normally occur. Women or men who are "off time"—who marry

and have their first child late or (worse) not at all—are subject to ridicule or ostracism.

Although the Gusii have no clearly labeled midlife transition, some of them do reassess their lives around the time they are old enough to be grandparents (typically by age 40). "Like their counterparts in our own society, middle-aged Gusii experience their lives and future performance as limited, and this can occasion a midlife crisis from which they emerge as ritual practitioners," or healers (R. Levine, 1980, p. 99). Their physical strength and stamina are waning, and they know that they will not be able to cultivate their land or herd their cattle indefinitely, and so they seek spiritual powers. The quest has a generative purpose, too: elders are responsible for protecting their children and grandchildren ritually from death or illness, even when the children are grown.

A disproportionate number of older women become either ritual practitioners or witches, seeking power either to help people or to harm them. Their motive may be to compensate for their lack of personal and economic power in a male-dominated society.

### Can the Findings of Normative-Crisis Research Be Generalized to Other Populations?

The subjects of these normative-crisis studies have been, for the most part, privileged white men born in the 1920s or 1930s. Vaillant's sample, for example, included no black people; and in Levinson's very small sample of 40 men, 30 were middle- or upper-class, and only 5 were black.

Let's look at the cohort issue. Many of the men in Vaillant's and Levinson's studies were born or grew up during the economic depression of the 1930s. They benefited from an expanding economy after World War II and may have succeeded at work far beyond their

early expectations—and then burned out early. Their development may, then, be unusual rather than typical (Rossi, 1980). Cohorts with different experiences may develop quite differently. For instance, if the pattern for future cohorts involves alternating periods of education, work, and leisure throughout life, as R. N. Bolles (1979) proposes, a midlife career change may be seen as routine, not as a sign of crisis.

Similarly, Levinson's findings cannot be generalized to men of other races or other socioeconomic levels—or to any women. Also, the theory has not been tested in other cultures, some of which do not even have a concept of middle age (see Box 15-2).

## How Typical Is the Midlife Crisis?

Many psychologists, challenging the notion that crisis is a hallmark of midlife, emphasize that "crisis, transition and change occur all through life" (Schlossberg, 1987, p. 74). They also hold that the transition to middle age may be stressful, but such stress does not necessarily amount to a crisis (Brim, 1977; Chiriboga, 1989; Farrell & Rosenberg, 1981; Haan, 1990; Rossi, 1980).

In one study, a group of men in their thirties who had achieved success quite young were already struggling with the kinds of issues commonly associated with middle age. They were asking themselves questions like "Was it worth it?" "What next?" and "What shall I do with the rest of my life?" (Taguiri & Davis, 1982, in Baruch et al., 1983).

Research that questions the universality of the midlife crisis also bears out the timing-of-events view that crises arise in response to events, not age. Events that used to characterize a certain time of life are no longer so predictable; and this unpredictability may bring on crises, catching people unprepared and unable to cope (Neugarten & Neugarten, 1987). Whether a transition turns into a crisis seems to be related less to age than to the circumstances of a person's life and how the person deals with them; "One person may go from crisis to crisis while another . . . experience[s] relatively few strains" (Schlossberg, 1987, p. 74).

Differences in how people handle the midlife transition may reflect their place in society, according to a large and socioeconomically diverse study (Farrell & Rosenberg, 1981) comparing 300 men at midlife with 150 younger men. These researchers found that only 12 percent of the older men experienced full-blown midlife crises, though about two-thirds had some adjustment problems. Unskilled laborers were much more likely to show stress than professional men or middle-class executives, but the lower-class men were more likely to deny or avoid their problems or to express them through an authoritarian attitude.

It seems, then, that although adults do go through a transition at midlife, they also experience transitions earlier and later; and the timing and acuteness of the midlife transition and the way people cope with it depends on their life circumstances and personalities rather than on their age.

## Is Adult Development Age-Linked?

The heart of the normative-crisis approach is the idea that development follows a definite age-linked sequence. Erikson and Vaillant assign ages to their stages (though rather sketchily), and Levinson is fairly rigid in this regard. Levinson admits that "individual lives unfold in myriad ways" (1986, p. 11) but argues (1980, 1986) that a view of adult development as a response to specific events is too limited—that there is an underlying order in the course of human life. This order derives from a series of tasks that everyone must work on, even though the forms of the tasks and the outcome of the work vary greatly.

But normative-crisis studies have been too limited to support this concept. For example, as we have seen, the developmental tasks in Levinson's scheme were derived from an intensive study of only 40 men from one cohort. Although he interviewed and tested all the subjects, he obtained little evidence from which to generalize, even about middle-aged men in the cohort sampled, let alone about other groups of men, or any women.

## How Healthy Is the Male Model?

Jung, Erikson, Peck, Vaillant, and Levinson all suggest that how men resolve developmental tasks tells us about their psychological health.

According to Levinson, for instance, the course of a man's life in middle age depends largely on the degree to which he realizes or modifies his early dream. A man values his relationships with his mentor and a "special woman" more as a means toward his goal than for their own sake. Not surprisingly, even the "healthiest" men in Levinson's study were unlikely to have close friendships with either men or women. In this model, healthy development is a matter mainly of personal achievement and separation from early relationships—not attachment. Not until middle age does a man even begin to concern himself with the need for attachment. Vaillant (1977), too, emphasizes work and deemphasizes relationships.

The men in the Grant Study and Levinson's study thus seem to present a picture of emotional constriction. If that picture is accurate, the model not only is inappropriate for women, whose lives typically involve a rich network of relationships, but also offers a dubious view of healthy male development (Gilligan, 1982).

It is ironic that, for many men, an increased interest in intimate relationships comes at midlife, when their children are about to leave home or have already done so and their wives may have adapted to a lack of intimacy in marriage by investing their emotions more deeply in other relationships. This late awareness of the need for intimacy may help to explain why, as we'll see, men seem more prone to greet the "empty nest" with regret while women welcome it with relief (L. B. Rubin, 1979). It may also explain why men and women so often have trouble communicating with each other.

Still, normative-crisis studies of adult development have captured both the professional and the public imagination, largely because of the main message of this age-oriented research—that adults continue to change, develop, and grow. Whether or not people grow in the specific ways suggested by the normative-crisis approach, it has challenged the notion that nothing important happens to personality in midlife or later.

## PERSONAL RELATIONSHIPS AND TIMING OF EVENTS IN MIDLIFE

The timing-of-events model suggests that adults' development hinges on the events in people's lives. If this is so, we need to look at some of the major changes likely to occur during the middle years—changes that often have to do with relationships. Just as the changes that go on within individuals affect their ties with others, changes in relationships affect individual personalities.

We'll examine the relationships middle-aged people have with people in their own generation—spouses or other sexual partners, siblings, and friends—with the next older generation, and with the next younger generation. Middle-aged people must often redefine their roles as parents to meet the changing needs of adolescent and young adult children and at the same time redefine what it means to be sons and daughters to their own parents, who may now need their help. We'll examine how people cope with being in the midlife "sandwich" between maturing children and aging parents.

### MARRIAGE AND DIVORCE

Midlife marriage today is very different from what it used to be. When life expectancies were shorter, with many women dying in childbirth, couples who remained together for 25, 30, or 40 years were rare. The most common pattern was for marriages to be broken by death and for the survivors to remarry. Households were usually filled with children. People had children early and late, had many of them, and expected them to live at home until they married. It was unusual for a middle-aged husband and wife to be alone together.

Today, more marriages end in divorce, but couples who manage to stay together can often look forward to 20 or more years of married life after the last child has left home.

#### Marital Satisfaction in Midlife

What happens to the quality of a longtime marriage? Marital satisfaction seems to follow a U-shaped curve. From an early high point, it declines until late middle age and then rises again through the first part of late adulthood (S. A. Anderson, Russell, & Schumm, 1983; Gilford, 1984; Gruber-Baldini & Schaie, 1986). The least happy time seems to be the period when most couples are heavily involved in child rearing and careers. *Positive* aspects of marriage (like cooperation, discussion, and shared laughter) seem to follow the U-shaped pattern, while *negative* aspects (like sarcasm, anger, and disagreement over important issues) decline from young adulthood through age 69 (Gilford, 1984; Gilford & Bengtson, 1979). This may be because many couples who are frequently in conflict divorce along the way.

Marriages are often affected by stressful events in midlife, as listed in Box 15-3 (page 458); but communication between partners can often mitigate such stress. The first part of the middle years, when many couples have teenage children making their way toward independence, tends to be stressful. The identity issues of midlife appear to affect wives' (but not husbands') feelings about their marriages; women become less satisfied with the marriage as child rearing makes fewer demands and their feelings of power and autonomy increase (Steinberg & Silverberg, 1987).

Typical personality changes of middle age, including women's tendency to take on "masculine" traits, can alter husbands' and wives' expectations and interactions. Their ability to adjust to each other's changing needs can affect their satisfaction with married life (Zube, 1982). For example, the husband of a woman who goes to work for the first time may have trouble accepting her new assertiveness and her involvement in an outside life that does not include him.

One 30-year study of 175 couples confirmed the U-shaped curve (Gruber-Baldini & Schaie, 1986), using a quasi-longitudinal method. It followed 22 couples for the entire time, and the rest for various lengths of time. This study found that the longer a couple were married, the more they resembled each other in their outlook on life and way of thinking—even in mathematical skills. But this tendency toward like-mindedness halted temporarily, with the dip in marital satisfaction, during the child-rearing years.

The years right after the children leave home, however, may bring as much contentment as the honeymoon (H. Feldman & Feldman, 1977). Husband and wife now have more privacy than they have had in years, the freedom to be spontaneous, fewer money worries, and a new chance to get to know each other as individuals. This "second honeymoon" may coincide with a "honeymoon stage" of retirement, but it may not last; another drop in marital satisfaction seems to occur after age 69 (Gilford, 1984; see Chapter 17).

## BOX 15-3   PRACTICALLY SPEAKING

# ENHANCING MARRIAGE AT MIDLIFE

Some of the normative events of midlife are likely to be stressful for one or both partners in a marriage. Whenever an individual is under stress, there is likely to be a ripple effect, so that people close to the stressed person are also affected. The one likely to be most affected is a spouse. As one husband commented, "When my wife is happy, I'm not always happy. But when she's unhappy, I'm sure to be unhappy, too."

Spouses can help each other deal with stress by showing their love and support and by helping each other understand what is happening and how to deal with it. One way to communicate about sources of anxiety is to do an exercise like the one below, suggested by the Cooperative Extension Service of The Pennsylvania State University, as part of its program "Strengthen Your Family."

In this exercise, each spouse looks

separately at each of the changes given in the following list, estimates how much stress it has already caused or might cause in the future, and checks off his or her responses. Then the couple look together at each item and talk about their answers, asking such questions as "Why did we rate the item the same or differently?" "How can we help each other deal with the stress?" and "Where else could we turn for help?"

| Husband | | | Wife | | | |
|---|---|---|---|---|---|---|
| **Estimated Stress:** | | | **Estimated Stress:** | | | |
| **Much** | **Some** | **Little** | **Much** | **Some** | **Little** | |
| ☐ | ☐ | ☐ | ☐ | ☐ | ☐ | Children leave home |
| ☐ | ☐ | ☐ | ☐ | ☐ | ☐ | Hair turns grey or falls out |
| ☐ | ☐ | ☐ | ☐ | ☐ | ☐ | Wife goes back to work or to school |
| ☐ | ☐ | ☐ | ☐ | ☐ | ☐ | You're no longer in the "young crowd" at work |
| ☐ | ☐ | ☐ | ☐ | ☐ | ☐ | Wrinkles multiply |
| ☐ | ☐ | ☐ | ☐ | ☐ | ☐ | You start to put on weight |
| ☐ | ☐ | ☐ | ☐ | ☐ | ☐ | A parent dies |
| ☐ | ☐ | ☐ | ☐ | ☐ | ☐ | Menopause begins |
| ☐ | ☐ | ☐ | ☐ | ☐ | ☐ | Your back aches |
| ☐ | ☐ | ☐ | ☐ | ☐ | ☐ | A son or daughter marries |
| ☐ | ☐ | ☐ | ☐ | ☐ | ☐ | You're passed over for promotion by a younger worker |
| ☐ | ☐ | ☐ | ☐ | ☐ | ☐ | You develop arthritis |
| ☐ | ☐ | ☐ | ☐ | ☐ | ☐ | A brother or sister has a heart attack |
| ☐ | ☐ | ☐ | ☐ | ☐ | ☐ | Your sex drive changes |
| ☐ | ☐ | ☐ | ☐ | ☐ | ☐ | You become a grandparent |
| ☐ | ☐ | ☐ | ☐ | ☐ | ☐ | You're bored with your job |

*Source:* B. W. Davis, undated.

The research on marital satisfaction has been criticized for its methodology. Much of the earlier research dealt with only the husband's or wife's attitude, not with both. Also, almost all studies have been cross-sectional; they show differences among couples of different cohorts rather than exploring changes in the *same* couples. In addition, samples have included only couples in intact marriages, omitting those who divorced (Blieszner, 1986).

## What Makes Middle-Aged Couples Divorce or Stay Together?

How a marriage fares in midlife may depend largely on its quality up to then. A marriage that has been basically good all along may be better than ever (Troll & Smith, 1976). The passionate love of newlyweds—the initial intense attraction with its wildly emotional ups and downs—may fade as day-to-day life together dispels the sense of mystery (Walster & Walster, 1978). But a strong marriage, even one of many years, may well fit Sternberg's definition of *consummate love* (1985a), which embodies passion, intimacy, and commitment (see Table 13-5).

In a shaky marriage, though, the "empty nest" may be a personal and marital crisis. With the children gone, a couple may realize that they no longer have much in common and may ask themselves whether they want to spend the rest of their lives together.

The divorce rate has gone up for middle-aged couples, as well as for younger ones. Current rates suggest that the first marriage of about 1 woman in 8 will end in divorce after she reaches age 40 (Uhlenberg, Cooney, & Boyd, 1990).

Middle-aged couples separate for many of the same reasons as younger ones—greater expectations for marriage, growing willingness to end an unsatisfactory relationship, increased acceptance of divorce, and less stringent divorce laws.

Divorce can be especially traumatic for middle-aged and older people, who expect their lives to be relatively settled. People over 50, particularly women, tend to suffer more than younger ones when going through divorce (Chiriboga, 1982). This may change, however, as midlife divorce becomes a more normative event (A. J. Norton & Moorman, 1987). Since divorce often seems preferable to living out a frustrating, conflict-filled rela-tionship, many people, even at this stage of life, end unhappy marriages.

Divorce has become so common that sociologists are now studying why some marriages do *not* break up. One survey asked 351 couples who had been married at least 15 years (300 said that they were happily married) to select from a list of 39 statements those that best explained why their marriages had lasted so long. The men's and women's responses were remarkably similar (see Table 15-2). The most common reasons were a positive attitude toward the spouse as a friend and as a person; commitment to marriage; belief in the sanctity of marriage; and agreement on aims and goals in life. Also, happily married couples spent as much time together as they could and shared many activities (Lauer & Lauer, 1985).

Although most of the happily married couples in this survey were generally satisfied with their sex life, that was not a primary reason for their happiness. Sexual compatibility was far down on the women's list of priorities and not much higher on the men's. Some respondents reported a decline in sexual activity; others said that their sex life had remained stable or had improved. Those whose sexual relations were less than ideal found other reasons to be happy in their marriages. These findings fit in with what we have learned since the 1960s regarding sexuality in middle adulthood (see Chapter 14).

**TABLE 15–2**
WHY SPOUSES STAY TOGETHER

| Men | Women |
|---|---|
| My spouse is my best friend. | My spouse is my best friend. |
| I like my spouse as a person. | I like my spouse as a person. |
| Marriage is a long-term commitment. | Marriage is a long-term commitment. |
| Marriage is sacred. | Marriage is sacred. |
| We agree on aims and goals. | We agree on aims and goals. |
| My spouse has grown more interesting. | My spouse has grown more interesting. |
| I want the relationship to succeed. | I want the relationship to succeed. |
| An enduring marriage is important to social stability. | We laugh together. |
| We laugh together. | We agree on a philosophy of life. |
| I am proud of my spouse's achievements. | We agree on how and how often to show affection. |
| We agree on a philosophy of life. | An enduring marriage is important to social stability. |
| We agree about our sex life. | We have a stimulating exchange of ideas. |
| We agree on how and how often to show affection. | We discuss things calmly. |
| I confide in my spouse. | We agree about our sex life. |
| We share outside hobbies and interests. | I am proud of my spouse's achievements. |

*Note:* These are the reasons given most often by 351 couples married for 15 years or more.
The reasons are listed in order of frequency.
*Source:* Lauer & Lauer, 1985.

## RELATIONSHIPS WITH SIBLINGS

After Margaret was widowed in her fifties, her brother, whom she had previously seen no more than once a month, made a point of seeing her every week. He helped her with home repairs and financial decisions, and he and his wife included her in their social activities.

Many middle-aged siblings stay in touch and stand ready to help each other. Relationships with siblings are the longest-lasting in most people's lives and become even more important as people grow older. Some 85 percent of middle-aged adults have at least one living brother or sister; the average person has two. Siblings usually get together at least several times a year—in many cases, once a month or more. It is unusual for them to lose touch completely (Cicirelli, 1980).

Although childhood rivalry may continue during adulthood, many siblings (especially sisters) become closer. More than two-thirds of people with siblings feel close or very close to their brothers and sisters and have good relationships with them; more than three-fourths say that they get along well or very well (Cicirelli, 1980). But issues may arise over the care of elderly parents and questions of inheritance, especially if the sibling relationship has not been good.

## FRIENDSHIPS

People sometimes devote less time and energy to friendship in midlife than in other stages of life. They tend to be heavily involved with family and busy with work, and they often want to spend their free time building up security for impending retirement. As a result, middle-aged people tend to have fewer friends than either newlyweds or people about to retire, and their friendships seem less complex.

Yet friendships do persist throughout middle age and are a strong source of emotional support and well-being (Baruch et al., 1983; House, Landis, & Umberson, 1988). Many of the friends of midlife are old friends, though people do make some new ones, often through organizations. Age is less of a factor in making friends now than is similarity in life stage, such as age of children, length of marriage, or occupational status (Troll, 1975). Diane, for example, has become friendly with other mothers of preschoolers, some of whom are several years younger than she is—and with professional colleagues who are several years older.

What midlife friendships lack in quantity, they often make up for in quality, as people turn to friends for emotional support and practical guidance—for example, to help them deal with maturing children and aging parents. As we noted in Chapter 13, close ties with others help to foster both mental and physical health (House et al., 1988).

Friends are a valuable source of companionship, support, and enjoyment in middle age. Being at the same stage of life and having similar interests are now the predominant factors in the choice of friends.

## RELATIONSHIPS WITH MATURING CHILDREN

Parenthood is a process of letting go. From the moment of birth, children's normal course of development leads to more and more independence from parents. During the parents' middle age, most families are in a definitive phase of this process.

### Adolescent Children: Issues for Parents

It is ironic that the people at the two times of life most popularly linked with emotional crises—adolescence and middle age—often live in the same household. It is usually middle-aged adults who are the parents of adolescent children. While dealing with their own special concerns, the parents have to deal daily with young people who are undergoing great physical, emotional, and social changes. Sometimes parents' own long-buried adolescent fantasies resurface as they see their children turning into sexual beings. Furthermore, seeing their children at the brink of adulthood makes some parents realize even more sharply how much of their own life is behind them. The contrast in life stages sometimes creates resentment and jealousy on the part

At the same time that middle-aged parents acknowledge their teenage children's need to become independent of them, most parents are happy when they can give help to their maturing adolescents—and when their children welcome that help.

of the parent—and an overidentification with the child's fantasies (H. Meyers, 1989).

An important task for parents is acceptance of children as they are—not as what the parents had hoped and dreamed they would be. In coming to terms with this reality, parents must realize that they do not have total control over their children, that they cannot make children into carbon copies or improved models of themselves. Parents have to face the fact that the directions their children choose may be very different from the ones the parents want them to follow.

This acceptance is so hard for many parents, and the need to break away is so strong for many young people, that the adolescent years can be hard on the whole family. The most frequent area of disagreement among the middle-aged couples interviewed in one study (Lowenthal & Chiriboga, 1972) was child rearing. As one father of three said, just after his youngest child had gone off to college, "They make the last couple of years at home so miserable that their going isn't a trauma—it's a relief!"

## When Children Leave: The "Empty Nest"

For years, people have talked about the *"empty nest"* crisis—a supposedly difficult transition, especially for women, when the last child leaves home. Research has shown, however, that although some women who have a heavy investment in mothering do have problems at this time, they are far outnumbered by those who find it liberating not to have children at home anymore (Barnett, 1985; Brecher & the Editors of Consumer Reports Books, 1984; L. B. Rubin, 1979). This stage may be harder on fathers, who often react to it with regret that they did not spend more time with their children when they were younger (L. B. Rubin, 1979). The empty nest also appears to be hard on parents whose children do not become independent when the parents expect them to (Harkins, 1978) and on women who have not prepared for it by reorganizing their lives through work or other involvements (Targ, 1979).

In one study of 54 middle- and lower-middle-class men and women whose youngest child was about to leave home, this transition stage represented the lowest point in life satisfaction for only three women and two men (Lowenthal & Chiriboga, 1972). And even among these five, none explained their low levels of happiness in terms of their children's imminent departure. Actually, 13 parents considered the most difficult period to be not the empty nest but their children's adolescence—when they had problems with the children or conflicts with their spouses over the children.

Many women, in fact, are freed by the empty nest from the "chronic emergency of parenthood" (Cooper & Gutmann, 1987, p. 347) and can now express such "masculine" qualities as assertiveness, aggression, and self-determination, which they had repressed for the sake of harmony in the home during their years of active mothering. One study of 50 women—25 "pre-empty nest" and 25 "post-empty nest"—found that the "post-empty nest" women had an active mastery style. This was shown partly by stories they told about ambiguous pictures. The "pre-empty nest" women tended to tell stories of emotionally conflicted leave-takings from home, of maternal warmth and nurturance, and of rescuing others; the "post-empty nest" women told stories of leaving home joyfully to realize a personal goal, of a mother as mentor more than nurturer, and of achievement done for the self (Cooper & Gutmann, 1987).

## When Children Stay or Return: The Not-So-Empty Nest

What happens if the nest does *not* empty when expected or is refilled by fledgling adults returning home to live? As the timing-of-events model would predict, this phenomenon sometimes leads to tension as parents are forced to adjust to the presence of full-grown off-spring (Lindsey, 1984).

The 1970s and 1980s, when the nation's economy slowed down, saw an increase in the numbers of young adults returning to live in their parents' homes (P. C. Glick & Lin, 1986a). Jobs were harder to get, housing costs climbed, couples were postponing marriage, divorce and unwed parenthood were on the rise, and many young people had trouble keeping up a household on a single income (Clemens & Axelson, 1985; P. C. Glick & Lin, 1986a).

Studies of parents whose young adult children were living with them found that the children were more welcome when they were under age 22 and were back for brief periods (Clemens & Axelson, 1985). Most of the parents were happy with the arrangement as a temporary one, appreciating help with household chores and with caring for younger children, and feeling closer to their grown children. But more than 4 out of 10 parents reported serious conflicts, often over the hours the young people kept or the way they took care of (or failed to take care of) the family home and car. Disagreements also arose over dress and lifestyle—particularly sex, alcohol, drugs, and choice of friends.

The situation creates a number of potential sources of conflict. Adults living with their parents may fall back into immature, dependent habits, expecting the parents to take care of them. Or the parents may infantilize adult children, treating them like younger children. The young adult is likely to feel isolated from peers and to have trouble establishing intimacy—the major Eriksonian task for this age—while the parents may have to continue to postpone renewing their own intimacy, exploring personal interests, and resolving marital issues that had been preempted by parental responsibilities.

Often, the parents' marriage is affected when adult children remain or return. Almost half of the still-married parents in one study complained of marital strain, particularly when the child was over 21 (Clemens & Axelson, 1985). But a study of 677 elderly couples in Boston whose children had been living with them for 1 to 44 years since becoming adults found little marital stress related to the presence, as such, of an adult child. Instead, it was the amount of conflict between parents and child that affected marital discord (Suitor & Pillemer, 1987, 1988). In these families, parent-child conflict was quite low—especially when the adult child was older, and when both parent and child had the same marital status—married, divorced, or widowed. The lower levels of conflict here may reflect the nature of the families that chose to live together; it may also reflect a desire by elderly parents to present the socially desirable appearance of family harmony.

Even after the years of active parenting are over, parents are still parents, who help their children in many ways. This grandmother is giving her daughter the peace of mind of knowing that her child will be lovingly cared for in her absence.

## Lifelong Parenting

The difficulty many parents have in treating their offspring as adults is illustrated by a story that Elliott Roosevelt used to tell about his mother, Eleanor. At a state dinner where she was seated next to him, she leaned over and whispered into his ear. When a friend later asked Elliott, then in his forties, what she had said, he answered, "She told me to eat my peas."

Even after the years of active parenting are over and all the children have flown the nest, parents are still parents. The midlife role of parent to young adults raises new issues and calls for new attitudes and behaviors. (This is also a time when the new role of grandparent is assumed, since the typical age for becoming a grandparent is the early fifties. But the role of grandparent often becomes more important later in life; we discuss it, therefore, in Chapter 17.)

Some studies show that young newly married adults (especially daughters) are closely tied to their middle-aged parents, who often help them financially or with such services as baby-sitting or helping them get their first homes in order. Parents and adult children often visit each other, and young couples spend a great deal of time talking about their parents.

Parents and adult children generally enjoy each other's company and get along well. Some keep harmony by avoiding touchy intergenerational issues—a strategy one researcher likens to the establishment of "demilitarized zones" (Hagestad, 1984).

Parents in the prime of life generally continue to give their children more than they get from them (Aldous,

1987; Troll, 1986, 1989; Troll, Miller, & Atchley, 1979). Their continuing support probably reflects the relative strength of middle-aged adults and the continuing needs of young adults, who are in what some psychologists consider the most stressful years in the life span (Pearlin, 1980). The balance of mutual aid tends to shift as the parents grow older.

## RELATIONSHIPS WITH AGING PARENTS

A 45-year-old woman says, "My mother is my best friend. I can tell her anything." A 50-year-old man visits his retired father every evening, bringing him news and asking his opinions about problems in the family business. A 40-year-old divorced mother sees her parents more often now than she did during her 15 years of marriage, and needs their help more now than at any time since her teens. A 55-year-old man, who cannot have a 10-minute conversation with his mother without an argument, says, "I wish she would die so I could feel guilty and get it over with." A couple in their early sixties find that the time they had hoped to spend traveling and playing with their grandchildren is being spent instead caring for both their widowed mothers.

Relationships between middle-aged people and their parents vary enormously, often reflecting the history of the bond (Leigh, 1982; Morgan, 1984). These ties are not static, however; they evolve constantly over the years. In middle age, many people can look at their parents objectively for the first time, neither idealizing them nor blaming them for mistakes and inadequacies. With maturity, it becomes possible to see parents as individuals with both strengths and weaknesses.

Something else happens during these years. One day a son or daughter looks at a mother or father—and sees an old person. The middle-aged child realizes that the parent is no longer a pillar of strength to lean on but is now starting to lean on the child. Older adults often seek their children's help in making decisions. The loss of physical faculties and earning power may make them dependent on their children for the performance of daily tasks and for financial support. If they become ill, infirm, or confused, their children may assume total responsibility for managing their lives.

### Contact with Parents

The picture that emerges from a growing body of research on middle-aged children and their elderly parents is one of a strong bond growing out of attachment earlier in life—and continuing as long as both generations live (Cantor, 1983; Cicirelli, 1980; Lang & Brody, 1983; B. Robinson & Thurnher, 1981). Parents and

By middle age, many people can look at their parents objectively, neither idealizing them nor exaggerating their shortcomings. This middle-aged daughter realizes that her mother is no longer a tower of strength but instead is beginning to lean on *her*. Mothers and daughters usually remain closer than any other combination of family members.

children see and speak to each other often and generally get along well, with relatively little strain. In one study, 91 percent of adult children with elderly parents felt close or very close to their mothers, and 87 percent to their fathers (Cicirelli, 1981).

Since both generations want to be independent, adults and elderly parents usually do not live together unless that arrangement becomes necessary because the parent is too poor or too ill to live alone and has no other good option. Most older people (even those in difficult circumstances) do not want to burden their families; fewer than 1 percent of those now living alone say that they would rather live with their children (Commonwealth Fund Commission on Elderly People Living Alone, 1986). With many people today living in smaller quarters, it can be inconvenient to absorb an extra person into a household, and everyone's privacy— and relationships—may suffer. Many older people do not want to live with their married children's families because it would be hard to keep from giving advice, which they know would rarely be welcomed (Lopata, 1973).

However, the two generations often live *near* each other and see each other frequently. One study found that 8 out of 10 older persons had seen at least one of their children within the past week (Rabushka & Jacobs, 1980). Mothers and daughters are more likely to stay in close contact than any other combination of family members (Troll, 1986; Troll et al., 1979).

## Mutual Help

Help flows back and forth between generations. "In general, parents give more services and money to their children throughout their life, and children give more emotional support, household help, and care during illness" (Troll, 1986, p. 23). Among working-class families, though, money is more likely to flow from child to parent (Troll et al., 1979).

Elderly parents tend to focus attention and aid on the child who needs them most. They may, for example, open their home to a child whose marriage has ended; and parents of handicapped children often maintain their protective roles as long as they live. Single adult children get more financial help and help with transportation from elderly parents than married adult children; divorced adult children are most likely to get emotional support and help with child care and housework (Aldous, 1987). Unhappily married, divorced, and widowed children often become closer to their parents, getting from them the support that they are not getting from their spouses.

## Caring for Parents

The generations get along best while parents are healthy and vigorous. When older people become infirm—especially if they suffer from mental deterioration or personality changes—the burden of caring for them may strain the relationship. Daughters, in particular, become distressed, because they are the ones who generally have this responsibility—most often for aging, ailing mothers (Troll, 1986). Today, the daughters are likely to be holding a full-time job, as well as having their own adolescent or young adult children (American Association of Retired Persons, AARP, 1989—see Table 15-3).

Even though mothers worry about losing their independence and being a burden on their children (Troll, 1986), the children are the ones to whom many elderly women turn first when in need of care. In one study, more than half of the adult children surveyed felt some strain, and one-third reported substantial strain, in connection with helping their elderly parents. The strain most often showed up as physical or emotional exhaustion and the feeling that a parent was impossible to satisfy (Cicirelli, 1980).

**TABLE 15–3**
CAREGIVERS

| Category | Percent Who Provide Care |
|---|---|
| *Gender* | |
| Female | 75 |
| Male | 25 |
| *Age* | |
| Under 35 | 28 |
| 35–49 | 29 |
| 50–64 | 26 |
| 65 and older | 15 |
| *Marital status* | |
| Married | 66 |
| Not married | 34 |
| *Children in household* | |
| Yes | 39 |
| No | 49 |
| *Current employment* | |
| Full-time | 42 |
| Part-time | 13 |
| Retired | 16 |
| Not employed or homemaker | 27 |

*Note:* A survey of 750 households found this profile of the people who provide unpaid care for an elderly relative or friend.

*Sources:* American Association of Retired Persons (AARP), 1989; "Juggling family," 1989, p. B8.

One common source of negative feelings is the disappointment, anger, and guilt that middle-aged people often feel when they realize that they, rather than their parents, now have to be the strong ones. In addition, their anxiety over the anticipated end of their parents' lives is tinged with worry about their own mortality (Cicirelli, 1980; Troll, 1986).

On a more practical level, there is also the burden of time, money, and energy that this "generation in the middle"—torn between obligations to their parents and the need to help launch their own children—must spend on aging parents. If they have full-time jobs, they may devote a large portion of nonworking hours to caring for parents, sometimes for years on end.

Strain also develops because the needs of aging parents seem to fall into the category of nonnormative, unanticipated demands. New parents expect to assume the full physical, financial, and emotional care of their babies, with the assumption that such care will gradually diminish as children grow up. Somehow, most people do not expect to have to care for their parents; they ignore the possibility of their parents' infirmity and rarely plan ahead for it; and when it cannot be denied, they perceive it as interfering with other responsibilities and plans. There is some historical justification for this attitude: caring for elderly parents used to be relatively rare. But now that the fastest-growing group in our population is aged 85 and over, many people in their fifties and sixties find themselves in that position.

Timing is another factor in these intergenerational strains. Parents who are looking forward to or are just experiencing the end of responsibility for their own children—and who now sense keenly that their own time on earth is limited—may feel that the need to care for their parents will deprive them of the chance to fulfill their own dreams. The sense of being "tied down," of not being able to take a vacation or make other plans, is, for some adult children, the hardest thing about caring for elderly parents (Robinson & Thurnher, 1981).

Still, children do care for their parents; they do not abandon them (Troll, 1986). Parents and children alike feel better when the care comes from feelings of attachment and not duty (Cantor, 1983; Robinson & Thurnher, 1981). Therefore, one psychologist who has studied intergenerational ties emphasizes that it is less effective to appeal to children's sense of obligation and more fruitful to encourage attachment behaviors like visiting and telephoning (Cicirelli, 1980). Children who are in touch with their parents can tell when help is needed, and they usually respond by giving it.

Even the most loving daughter or son may become frustrated, anxious, or resentful under the constant strain of meeting an older person's seemingly endless needs—especially if there is no one else to turn to—but there are ways to reduce the strain of caregiving.

The pressure of financial support for elderly parents has been greatly eased by such programs as social security, Supplemental Security Income, Medicare, and Medicaid. Other forms of support could be instituted and expanded—like free or low-cost programs where older people can go from morning till dinnertime, transportation and escort services, in-home services providing meals and housekeeping, and respite care, so that people whose elderly parents require daily attention can get away for a few days. Flexible work schedules would also benefit people with elderly dependents.

Counseling and self-help groups can offer emotional support, pass on information about community resources, and help sons and daughters develop skills with their aging parents. One such program, which helped daughters recognize the limits of their ability to meet their mothers' needs and the value of encouraging their mothers' own self-reliance, not only lightened the daughters' burden somewhat but actually improved their relationships with their mothers, so that the mothers became less lonely (Scharlach, 1987).

## Reacting to a Parent's Death

When Sally was 43 years old, her father, 76, died of a sudden heart attack. As the only surviving child, Sally then took a much more active role in her mother's life until, 3½ years later, after many bouts of illness, her 79-year-old mother also died. For months after her mother's death, Sally felt depressed. Despite her recognition that losing one or both parents is a normative experience of midlife, she had not been prepared for her deep feelings of loss. In this she was fairly typical.

A parent's death is difficult for offspring of any age, no matter what the relationship in life has been. But death may also help people deal with such developmental issues of middle age as coping with changes in the self, in social relationships, and in awareness of their own mortality (M. S. Moss & Moss, 1989).

With longer life expectancies, people are experiencing their parents' death at later ages, often in mid- to late middle age (Hagestad, 1984). Let's look at the ways a parent's death can affect the bereaved adult's handling of midlife issues.* (We discuss the grieving process itself in Chapter 18.)

### Personal changes

"Orphaned" middle-aged adults often experience a strengthening of the ego as they review a deceased parent's life and see it as relevant to their own. Their memories sometimes become selective, focusing on and identifying with the parent's good qualities. And for the first time they may be able to accept and forgive the parent's failures, especially those toward themselves.

In addition, people are often prompted to review their own lives and to evaluate and revise their goals and current activities. There is a new awareness—especially after the death of both parents—of being the "older generation," no longer a child but a mature adult in the senior ranks. This awareness can be empowering to those who see themselves as wise "elders," or frightening to those without a sense of purpose in life.

Some people become more self-assertive and autonomous when their parents die; others, especially those whose identity had been intertwined with the parent, may worry about their own future or feel despair over their lack of self-fulfillment. Some experience a surge of creativity as they work through their loss by editing a parent's diary or memoirs, or writing their own.

---

*This discussion is indebted to M. S. Moss & Moss, 1989.

### Changes in other relationships

"Death ends a life but it does not end a relationship" (R. Anderson, 1980, p. 110). Even very old people often mention their parents as the most influential persons in their lives, and even a dead parent can be an ongoing presence in a son's or daughter's life (Troll & Smith, 1976). But death of a parent often brings changes in other relationships.

If a child has been taking care of the parent, for example, the parent's death may free the child to spend time and emotional energy on relationships that had been temporarily neglected, like those with the child's spouse or with his or her own children or grandchildren.

Recognizing the finality of death and the impossibility of saying anything more to the deceased parent, some people are motivated to resolve any conflicts in their ties to the living—now, while there is still time. Generally, there is little or no change in sibling relationships, but sometimes siblings who have been estranged realize that the parent who provided a link between them is no longer there, and they try to mend the rift themselves. People may also be moved to reconcile with an adult child.

### Changes in attitudes toward time and death

A parent's death is inevitably a reminder of one's own mortality. It removes a "buffer" against death, leaving the child feeling older and unprotected. Many people, especially those whose parents died young, consider the parents' age at death significant for their own life span. Thus one man threw a large party for his fiftieth birthday, celebrating the fact that he had lived beyond his father's age. Other people are inspired to think about what they will do with their "bonus"—the extra years they have left to live.

The bond between parent and child, powerful in life, persists after death, becoming an "indelible legacy for later generations" (M. S. Moss & Moss, 1989, p. 110). This legacy is sometimes unhappy, if the parent's own life was unfulfilled. But adults who did not receive the kind of nurturing and guidance they would have liked from their own parents can often break the cycle and pass on more valuable gifts to their children.

As middle-aged adults enter the last stage of life, they often focus more on their legacy to their children and grandchildren. We'll see what these final years are like in Chapters 16 and 17.

## SUMMARY

- The "midlife crisis" is a stressful period during the early to middle forties that is triggered by a review and reevaluation of one's life. Research suggests that entering middle age does not necessarily result in a crisis; for many people this is just one of life's many transitions, and they adjust easily.

### MIDLIFE: THE NORMATIVE-CRISIS APPROACH

- Some personality traits remain stable in adulthood, but growth and change do occur. Middle-aged people tend to become more introspective, and both sexes tend to take on characteristics associated with the other sex.

- Carl Jung believed that people at midlife, freed from much of the obligation of child rearing, express personality characteristics that had previously been suppressed. Women become more assertive and men more emotionally expressive.

- Erikson's seventh psychosocial crisis, occurring during middle age, is generativity versus stagnation. The generative person is concerned with establishing and guiding the next generation. A person who fails to develop generativity suffers from stagnation, self-indulgence, and perhaps physical and psychological invalidism.

- Expanding on Erikson's concepts, Peck specified four psychological developments critical to successful adjustment during middle age: valuing wisdom versus valuing physical powers, socializing versus sexualizing, emotional flexibility versus emotional impoverishment, and mental flexibility versus mental rigidity.

- The Grant Study of Harvard men (reported by Vaillant) and Levinson's study of 40 males suggest that the early forties are a potentially stressful time of transition. Some people experience a "crisis," although midlife does not necessarily involve this.

- Normative-crisis research on middle-aged women suggests that women, too, go through midlife changes, but their subsequent lives are less settled than those of men.

- Mastery and pleasure are important elements of well-being for middle-aged women. Both challenging, well-paid work and family commitments contribute to women's psychological health.

- Because the Grant Study and Levinson's research focused mainly on privileged white men born in the 1920s or 1930s, their results may not be applicable to women, nonwhite people, and members of other cohorts and other cultures.

## PERSONAL RELATIONSHIPS AND TIMING OF EVENTS IN MIDLIFE

■ The timing-of-events model suggests that development depends on the occurrence and timing of important events, which are often changes that take place in relationships.

■ Research on the quality of marriage in middle age suggests a dip in marital satisfaction during the years of child rearing, followed by an improved relationship after the children leave home.

■ The most important factors in marital longevity seem to be positive feelings about the spouse, a commitment to long-term marriage, and shared aims and goals.

■ Bonds with siblings often become closer during middle age.

■ Middle-aged people tend to invest less time and energy in developing friendships than younger adults do, since their energies are devoted to family, work, and building up security for retirement.

■ Parents of adolescents need to come to terms with a loss of control over their children's lives.

■ The postparental years—when children have left—are often among the happiest. The "emptying of the nest"

may be stressful, however, for fathers who have not been involved with child rearing, for parents whose children have not become independent when expected, and for mothers who have failed to prepare for the event.

■ Today, more young adults are living with their parents, often for economic reasons. Conflict between the two generations can put strains on the parents' marriage.

■ Middle-aged parents tend to remain involved with their young adult children and continue giving them more than they get from them.

■ Relationships between middle-aged adults and their parents are usually characterized by a strong bond of affection. Although older parents typically do not live with their adult children, they generally maintain frequent contact and offer and receive assistance.

■ Middle-aged people, especially daughters, may have to become caregivers to ailing, aging parents. This can be a source of considerable stress. Various support programs can help relieve the strain of caregiving.

■ Reactions to parents' death are often profound and difficult. Death of a parent can precipitate changes in the self, in relationships with others, and in the personal meaning of time and of death.

## KEY TERMS

midlife crisis (page 448)
generativity versus stagnation (451)
valuing wisdom versus valuing physical powers (451)
socializing versus sexualizing in human relationships (451)
emotional flexibility versus emotional impoverishment (451)
mental flexibility versus mental rigidity (451)
interiority (452)
"empty nest" (461)

## SUGGESTED READINGS

**Edinberg, M. A. (1987).** *Talking with your aging parents.* Boston: Shambhala. The author, a clinical psychologist and director of the Center for the Study of Aging at the University of Bridgeport in Connecticut, suggests strategies for communicating with elderly parents about their special needs (for institutional care, extra help, and so on). The author also discusses how middle-aged children can cope with their own feelings of guilt regarding the burdens of family obligations.

**Klagsbrun, F. (1985).** *Married people: Staying together in the age of divorce.* New York: Bantam. A well-researched, sensitively written book that draws on pub-

lished research, interviews with happily married couples, and the author's exploration of her own long-term marriage to examine such topics as the transition from passionate to companionate love, competition between spouses, the influence of family (including children) and friends on a couple's relationship, and sexuality.

**Schreiber, L. A. (1990).** *Midstream: The story of a mother's death and a daughter's renewal.* New York: Penguin. A lovingly observed memoir by a 40-year-old journalist of her mother's illness and death. The book chronicles this difficult experience with hope, humor, and anger.

# SEVEN

# LATE ADULTHOOD

Development continues after age 65, as adults in the last phase of life face challenges, both old and new, in highly individual ways.

■ In **Chapter 16,** we look at some myths about aging, and at theories explaining the aging process. Most older people are in fairly good physical health, despite the changes that take place with age, and most are mentally sound as well. Some older persons do, of course, suffer physical or mental problems (or both), and we describe these problems, along with ways of preventing and treating them. We also examine the controversy over intellectual functioning in late life and conclude that although some abilities may diminish with age, there is a great deal of evidence that older

people who remain intellectually active retain their abilities and even increase their mental capacities in some ways.

■ In **Chapter 17,** we look at different patterns of aging, and we explore important relationships in late adulthood—with spouses, children, grandchildren, and siblings. We look at the ways people adjust to the loss of a spouse and at the role of sexuality in late life. We examine how older people live, either in the community or, for a small minority, in nursing homes. It becomes clearer than ever that—although there are certain common patterns in the human experience—each person is an individual, and that people's individuality becomes more pronounced in the later years of life.

## CHAPTER 16

# PHYSICAL AND INTELLECTUAL DEVELOPMENT IN LATE ADULTHOOD

Old age is rather like another country. You will enjoy it more if you have prepared yourself before you go.

B. F. SKINNER AND M. E. VAUGHAN,
*ENJOY OLD AGE,* 1983

One reason why these new categories are useful is that it is becoming harder to draw the line between the end of middle adulthood and the beginning of late adulthood. If, as the saying goes, "you're as old as you feel," how would we classify Sally's father-in-law, who at the age of 84 was still working as an engineer and talking about putting money aside for his "twilight years"? Middle-aged people and older people generally feel younger than the calendar would suggest (in contrast to teenagers, who feel older than they really are; or to young adults, who feel their own age—Montepare & Lachman, 1989).

Although retirement was traditionally a marker of old age, it is no longer a reliable guide. Sixty-five has long been the usual retirement age and the age when people become eligible for full social security benefits. But today many people keep working even into their nineties, and others retire by age 55 and then may start on new careers.

### The Graying of the Population

Not only is the older generation becoming "younger"; it is also becoming more numerous. By the year 2000, Americans aged 65 and over are expected to constitute 13 percent of the total population, compared with 7 percent in 1950 and 12½ percent in 1988 (American Association of Retired Persons, AARP, 1989; U.S. Bureau of the Census, 1989). By the year 2030, the proportion will have risen to 20 percent. The 30.4 million Americans aged 65 and older in 1988 represented about 1 in 8 Americans; this figure will be 1 in 5 in 2030 (see Figure 16-1). The fastest-growing age group are people 85 years old and older, who are now more than 1 percent

of the population (AARP, 1986; U.S. Bureau of the Census, 1983). These "oldest old" are discussed below.

The "graying" of the population has two basic causes. First is the high birthrates of the late 1800s and the early to mid-1900s, combined with the high immigration rates of the twentieth century. Second, medical advances have lengthened the average life expectancy. Fewer people now die young, and new medicines and procedures save many people who once would have succumbed to various illnesses.

As the "baby boom" generation (people born in the late 1940s and the 1950s) ages, the proportion of older Americans will peak about a third of the way through the twenty-first century, after which it will drop again.

### The Oldest Old

Since the number of healthy, vigorous people over age 65 is growing rapidly, we may soon begin to talk of old age as starting at 85. As we noted above, the age group over 85, which has been called the *oldest old,* is the fastest-growing segment of the United States population. It has increased by 165 percent in 22 years. In 1980, people over 85 numbered 2.3 million; in 2000, they are expected to reach 5.4 million; in 2040, 13 million (Longino, 1988).

Who are the oldest old? Where and how do they live? How is their health? What do they like to do? Some of the answers, based on 1980 census data (Longino, 1987, 1988) and on studies by the National Institute on Aging (NIA, 1986, in Meer, 1987), are predictable, but others are unexpected.

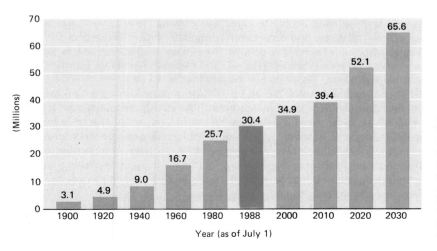

FIGURE 16-1
Population of the United States aged 65 and over, 1900–2030 (projected). Since the beginning of this century, the number of people aged 65 and over has continued to increase, both absolutely (as shown) and relative to the rest of the population. This trend is expected to continue through the aging of the "baby boom" generation. (Note: Increments in years on the horizontal scale are uneven.) (*Source:* American Association of Retired People, AARP, 1986.)

Because of men's lower life expectancy, almost 70 percent of the "oldest old" are women, and 82 percent of these women are widowed (compared with only 44 percent of the men). Since high schools were a new phenomenon when these people were young, it is not surprising that most of them never went beyond eighth grade.

A surprisingly large number of these oldest citizens need little medical care, but many do have health problems. At least one-fourth of those in the NIA studies were hospitalized in the previous year. Nationally, almost 10 percent are disabled and isolated—unable even to use public transportation (Longino, 1987, 1988). Costs of health care for the "oldest old" are expected to soar in the future; Medicare costs, for example, may well increase sixfold by 2040 because of the growth of this age group (Schneider & Guralnik, 1990). Successful containment of costs will depend on the ability to prevent or cure disorders of old age that entail the greatest need for long-term care.

Most people over 85 live in their own homes, and 30 percent live alone. One-fourth are in nursing homes, hospitals, or other institutions.

Their average household income topped $20,000 in 1985, but 1 in 6 are poor. Future generations will be both better educated and more affluent (Longino, 1988).

Most of the people in the NIA studies spend time with other people. More than half of a sample in Iowa belong to professional, social, recreational, or religious groups and go to religious services at least once a week. More than 3 out of 4 see their children or other close relatives once a month.

We see, then, that even at the last stage of life, it is misleading to generalize about people. What emerges is a picture not of "the elderly" but of individual human beings—some needy and frail, but most fairly independent, healthy, and involved.

## HOW CAN WE MAKE THE MOST OF THE LATER YEARS?

As older people become more of a presence, the need to help them make the most of their lives becomes more urgent, inspiring research in gerontology (as we noted above) and in *geriatrics,* the branch of medicine concerned with the aged and with aging. There is an especially strong need for support services for the frail elderly, many of whom have outlived their savings and cannot pay for their own care. As the older population becomes more influential at the polls and in the marketplace, we are likely to see changes in governmental programs, as well as in television programming, in new products, and in housing.

To serve this population, it is vital to combat misconceptions about aging. The list of inaccurate negative beliefs is long: that old people are poorly coordinated, feel tired most of the time, and easily fall prey to infections; that they have many accidents in the home and spend most of their time in bed; that they tend to live in hospitals, nursing homes, or other institutions for people with declining health and abilities; that they can neither remember the simplest things nor learn new facts and skills; that they have no interest in or desire for sexual relationships; that they are isolated from family and friends and spend their time mostly with television or radio; that they do not use their time productively; and that they are grouchy, self-pitying, touchy, and cranky.

Such ageist beliefs hurt older people in many ways. A physician who assumes that a 75-year-old heart patient is no longer interested in sex and thus does not bring up the subject denies the patient a source of fulfillment. A patronizing, overprotective adult child encourages an aging parent to become infantile. A social worker who accepts depression as expected in old age in effect abandons an elderly client. Such attitudes affect how older people live and how they feel about themselves—and many of the most ardent believers in myths about aging are the elderly themselves.

There are some positive stereotypes about old age, picturing it as a time of tranquillity—a "golden age" of peace and relaxation when people harvest the fruits of their lifelong labors—or as a carefree second childhood, spent idly on the golf course or at the card table. But these images are not much more helpful.

In fact, older people are an extremely diverse lot—not only statistically, as we've already seen, but personally, with individual strengths and weaknesses. Late adulthood is a normal period of the life span, with its own special nature and its own developmental tasks. In this chapter, we look at the physical and intellectual changes of this time of life, and at some of the implications these changes hold for social and emotional well-being, discussed in detail in Chapter 17.

Learning about late adulthood can prepare you for what to expect when you get there and can suggest what you can do now to ensure that your stay there will be as pleasant as possible. Knowing what the aging process is like can also help you get along with, and enrich the lives of, the older people in your life (see Box 16-2 on page 476).

## BOX 16–2   PRACTICALLY SPEAKING

# YOU AND THE OLDER PEOPLE IN YOUR LIFE

There is a wealth of recent research on late adulthood, with many findings that can be applied to daily life. The following suggestions might make the lives of your parents, your grandparents, or other older people you care about happier and more comfortable.

■ *For persons with hearing problems.* Speak somewhat more loudly than normal, but don't shout. Speak clearly and not too fast. Speak from a distance of 3 to 6 feet, in good light, so that your lip movements and gestures can be used as clues to your words. Don't chew, eat, or cover your mouth while you're speaking. Turn off the radio and the television while you're talking. If the listener doesn't understand what you have said, rephrase your idea in short, simple sentences.

■ *For persons with vision problems.* Install bright lighting at the top of staircases (most falls occur on the step at the top of the landing). Help to analyze lighting in work and reading areas to see that it is directed for greatest efficiency. Keep floor areas clutter-free, and don't rearrange furniture. Help get rid of unnecessary items in cupboards and bookshelves, and highlight often-used items with bright-colored markers. Good gifts include sunglasses (to be worn outside, so that less of an adjustment needs to be made upon coming indoors), a pocket or purse flashlight (for reading menus, theater programs, and the like), a magnifying glass to put in a pocket or hang on a chain, large-type reading matter, and a tape recorder and cassettes.

■ *Encourage physical activity.* Take part in shared activities that you both enjoy, like walking, bicycling, dancing, or skating. Make such activities a regular weekly event. Help by finding out what resources there are in the community—for example, at the local "Y." Good gifts are pool and "Y" memberships and exercise accessories.

■ *Help with memory.* When giving information, try to present it in more than one way (write it down and give it orally, too). Be patient and reassuring about memory lapses, remembering that younger people forget things, too. Learn and teach some memory tricks.

Good gifts are a pocket notebook and pen (for immediately jotting down thoughts and things to do), a calendar (for writing down appointments), and a note pad to keep near the phone or in the kitchen (or both).

■ *Encourage mental alertness.* Play games that require thought, such as word games, "twenty questions," and card games. Go to movies and plays together. Read a book together and discuss it. Find out what adult education courses are offered locally. Ask questions about subjects the older person knows about. Good gifts are games, books, and tickets.

■ *Enrich yourself through the older person's experience:* Tape-record interviews with the older person in which you ask about childhood memories, descriptions of family members, experiences, subjects about which the person is knowledgeable, and opinions about life. You will enrich your own knowledge and awareness, and the older person will be assured of the value of his or her wisdom and memories.

# PHYSICAL DEVELOPMENT

The onset of **senescence**—the period of the life span marked by declines in body functioning associated with aging—varies greatly. One 80-year-old man can hear every word of a whispered conversation, while another has trouble hearing words shouted at him. One woman in her seventies runs marathons, while another has trouble walking around the block.

The lengthening of life in modern times has not only swelled the older population but also focused attention on questions about aging. Why, for example, does senescence come earlier for some people than for others? In this section on physical development, we'll trace some historical changes in life expectancy, and then we'll consider two theories of why aging occurs. Then, we'll examine some physical changes often associated with aging and discuss what people can do to stay healthy and minimize physical losses.

# LONGEVITY AND THE AGING PROCESS

Eos, a mythological goddess, asked Zeus to allow Tithonus, the mortal she loved, to live forever. Zeus granted Tithonus immortality, and the lovers lived happily—but not forever after. Tithonus grew older and older until he became so infirm that he could not move. Yet he was denied the gift of death. To this day he lives on, where Eos finally put him away, a helpless, driveling vegetable. Eos had made a grievous error; she had forgotten to ask Zeus to grant eternal youth along with eternal life.

In recognition of the tragedy of life that is too long extended, the motto of the Gerontological Society is: "To add life to years, not just years to life." The goal of research on the aging is not just lengthening life but also lengthening the vigorous and productive years.

## LIFE EXPECTANCY

### Trends in Life Expectancy

Today, most people can expect to grow old. A large elderly population is, however, a relatively recent phenomenon. In 1900, babies born in the United States had a very low average life expectancy of about 47 years—in part because many died in infancy. By 1987, average life expectancy at birth had risen to 75 years (U.S. Department of Health and Human Services, USDHHS, 1990). An estimated 56,000 people are now over the age of 100 (U.S. Bureau of the Census, 1989). Life expectancy is expected to continue rising, to 82 years for women and 72.4 for men in 2020 and to 83.1 for women and 75 for men in 2040 (Schneider & Guralnik, 1990).

These gains result from two major avenues of medical progress. One is the dramatic decline in infant and child mortality during the first half of this century. The other is the development of new drugs and treatments for many illnesses that used to be fatal.

But this trend may now be ending: many gerontologists maintain that 110 years is about the upper limit of human longevity and that the average 80-year-old of today can expect to live only slightly longer than the 80-year-olds of previous centuries. Life expectancy at birth will probably never exceed 85 years in the absence of a breakthrough in the ability to control the basic rate of aging (Olshansky, Carnes, & Cassel, 1990).

**TABLE 16–1**

LIFE EXPECTANCY AT BIRTH BY SEX AND RACE, 1988, IN YEARS

|  | White | Black | All Nonwhite |
|---|---|---|---|
| Males | 72.1 | 65.1 | 67.4 |
| Females | 78.9 | 73.8 | 75.5 |

*Source:* U.S. Department of Health and Human Services, USDHHS, 1990

## Death Rates and Causes of Death

The dramatic increase in average longevity since the turn of the century reflects a sharp decline in death rates in the United States (the proportions of people of specific ages who die in a given year). Along with these declines have come changes in the leading causes of death. There have been fewer deaths from childbirth and infectious disease and more deaths from conditions related to age.

Heart disease remains by far the leading killer of people over 65, accounting for 45 percent of deaths despite a decline of 11 percent between 1978 and 1987 (USDHHS, 1990). Other major causes of death in this age group are cancer (20 percent, a 6 percent increase over previous years), stroke (11 percent, a 34 percent decrease), lung disease, pneumonia, influenza, hardening of the arteries, accidents, and diabetes (U.S. Bureau of the Census, 1983; USDHHS, 1990). If cancer were eliminated as a cause of death, the average life span would be increased by only 2 or 3 years, but if we could eliminate heart and kidney ailments, the increase would be more than 11 years (Fries & Crapo, 1981).

## Race, Gender, and Life Expectancy

On average, white Americans live longer than nonwhite Americans, and women live longer than men (see Table 16-1). But nonwhite women live longer than white men.

### Racial differences

In the United States, life expectancy is about 10 percent higher for white men than for black men, and about 7 percent higher for white women than for black women. A troubling aspect of this disparity is that life expectancy has not increased every year for black people as it has for white people. In fact, life expectancy for black people has declined from a peak of 69.7 years in

1984 to 69.4 in 1987 (Wegman, 1989). The decrease—although small—is a major public health concern; this is the only time in the twentieth century that life expectancy has decreased for black people while it increased for white people. Increases in death rates from several causes have affected the African American community disproportionately (refer back to Box 14-2).

### Gender differences

The vulnerability of males continues throughout life, with major implications for older people. In 1900, there was only a 2-year difference in life expectancy between the sexes; but because death rates for females have declined twice as much as death rates for males, the difference for babies born in 1985 was 7 years (U.S. Bureau of the Census, 1983; USDHHS, 1986). Among 65- to 69-year-olds, there are only 100 men to every 120 women; and for people 85 and older, the gap widens to 257 women for every 100 men (AARP, 1989).

Thus the problems of old age are largely problems of women: women are more likely than men to be widowed, to remain unmarried, and to have more years of poor health (Katz et al., 1983; U.S. Bureau of the Census, 1983). Far from being a bonus for women, their extra years are often years of illness, poverty, dependency, loneliness, and institutionalization. When we look at the quality of life, men have the advantage. They keep their health longer, have higher personal income, are more likely to be married, and so have more years of active life and independence (Katz et al., 1983; Longino, 1987). Our male-dominated society might handle the problems of aging differently if the people facing these problems late in life were more likely to be men.

## WHY PEOPLE AGE: TWO THEORIES

We do not know exactly why people's bodies function less efficiently as they age. We do know that aging is a complex process influenced by heredity, nutrition, health, and environmental factors. None of the many biological theories of aging is universally accepted, but most of them take one of two basic approaches—"programmed" aging or aging as "wear and tear."

### Programmed Aging

The ***programmed-aging theory*** maintains that bodies age according to a normal developmental pattern built into every organism; this program, present for each species, is subject to only minor modifications. Since each species has its own life expectancy and its own pattern of aging, this pattern must be predetermined and inborn.

Leonard Hayflick (1974), who studied cells of many different animals, found a limit on the number of times normal cells will divide—about 50 times for human cells. He holds that this limit controls the life span, which for humans seems to be about 110 years. People may have genes that become harmful later in life, causing deterioration. One area of deterioration may be the immune system, which seems to become "confused" in old age, so that it may attack the body itself.

Recent research transferred human chromosome 1 to hamsters and saw typical signs of aging, providing support for a cellular basis (Sugawara, Oshimura, Koi, Annab, & Barrett, 1990). Other research reversed some effects of aging by administering human growth hormone to 21 men aged 61 to 81, suggesting that a decline with age in this hormone is one factor that causes fat to collect, muscles to wither, and organs to atrophy (Rudman et al., 1990).

### Aging as Wear and Tear

The ***wear-and-tear theory*** holds that the body ages because of continuous use—that aging is the result of accumulated "insults" to the body. According to this theory, the human body is comparable to a machine, whose parts eventually wear out. For example, the cells of the heart and brain do not replace themselves, even early in life; when damaged, they die. The same thing seems to happen to other cells later in life: as they grow older, they are less able to repair or replace damaged components. Wear-and-tear theory suggests that internal and external stressors (including the accumulation of harmful materials, like chemical by-products of metabolism) aggravate the wearing-down process.

The difference between these two approaches is more than theoretical. If people are programmed to age, they can do little to retard the process; but if they age because of "insults" to the body, they may be able to live longer by eliminating stressors. Probably, the truth lies in a combination of the approaches: genetic programming may limit the length of life, but wear and tear may affect how closely a person approaches the limit.

Along the same lines, some gerontologists distinguish between ***primary aging,*** a gradual, inevitable process of bodily deterioration that begins early in life and continues through the years; and ***secondary aging,*** the results of disease, abuse, and disuse—factors that are often avoidable and under people's control (Busse, 1987; J. C. Horn & Meer, 1987). Older people may not be able to stop their reflexes from slowing down or their hearing from becoming less acute; but by eating sensibly and keeping physically fit, many can and do stave off the secondary effects of aging.

## PHYSICAL CHANGES OF OLD AGE

### SENSORY AND PSYCHOMOTOR FUNCTIONING

Although sensory and psychomotor abilities decline with age, there is a great degree of individual variation. Losses of vision or hearing have particularly strong psychological consequences, as they deprive people of activities, social life, and independence.

### Vision

Older adults report that they have trouble doing a variety of activities dependent on vision. Driving is most seriously affected (especially at night), because they cannot adapt as well to dim light, are more sensitive to glare, and have problems locating and reading signs. Also, it is often hard for them to read or do close work, shop for and cook food, and follow credits on a movie or television screen. Their problems stem from deficits in five areas: speed in processing what they see, near vision, light sensitivity, dynamic vision (reading moving signs), and visual search (locating a sign) (Kosnik, Winslow, Kline, Rasinski, & Sekuler, 1988).

Farsightedness usually stabilizes at about age 60, and with the help of glasses or contact lenses, most older people can see fairly well. After 65, however, serious visual problems that affect daily life are all too common. Many older adults have 20/70 vision or worse and have trouble perceiving depth or color. About 16 percent develop *cataracts,* cloudy or opaque areas in the lens of the eye that prevent light from passing through and thus cause blurred vision (AARP, 1989). Besides curtailing the activities of everyday life, these problems cause accidents in the home and outside it (Branch, Horowitz, & Carr, 1989).

Moderate vision problems can often be helped by corrective lenses, medical or surgical treatment, or changes in the environment (refer back to Box 16-2). New surgical techniques allow removal of cataracts; patients may use special glasses or contact lenses after cataract surgery, or they may have plastic lenses implanted during the operation.

At worst, visual disorders can result in blindness. Half of the legally blind people in the United States are over 65, and retinal disorders are the leading cause of blindness among the elderly (National Institute on Aging, NIA, undated a; White House Conference on Aging, 1971).

Glaucoma, another frequent cause of blindness, occurs when fluid pressure builds up, damaging the eye internally. If this disease (which seldom has early symptoms) is detected through routine vision checkups, it can be treated and controlled with eye drops, medicine, laser treatments, or surgery.

### Hearing

Hearing loss is very common late in life; about 3 out of 10 people between ages 65 and 74 and about half of those between 75 and 79 have it to some degree. More than 10 million older people in the United States are hearing-impaired (NIA, undated b). Because older people tend to have trouble hearing high-frequency sounds, they often cannot hear what other people are saying, especially when there is competing noise from radio or television or there is a buzz of several people talking at once.

The hearing aid in this man's ear makes it easier for him to understand his young granddaughter's high-pitched speech, but it may also magnify distracting background noise. More than 10 million older Americans have some degree of hearing loss, but only about 1 in 20 wears a hearing aid. Medical treatment, surgery, or special training can also help people with hearing problems.

## HEALTH IN OLD AGE

Despite these physical changes, most elderly people are reasonably healthy. According to a report by the U.S. Department of Health and Human Services published in 1990, about 71 percent of people 65 years old and older rate their health as good, very good, or excellent; slightly more than 29 percent describe their health as fair or poor.

Sixty percent of people over age 65 do not have to limit any of their major activities for health reasons (compared with 80 percent of 45- to 64-year-olds). Not until 85 and over do more than half the population report such limitations. Among noninstitutionalized people, most of those 85 and over, 75 percent of 75- to 84-year-olds, and 86 percent of 65- to 74-year-olds can take care of their personal needs (such as eating, using the toilet, dressing, and bathing) and home chores (such as cooking, shopping, and housework) without help (AARP, 1986; U.S. Bureau of the Census, 1983). Thus the stereotype of the helpless, ill old person is not based on reality—even for the very aged.

More affluent elderly people are likely to be healthier than the poor; rural residents are most likely to have chronic conditions (those of long duration) that limit their activity; and elderly white people tend to be healthier than elderly black people. Although little is known about elderly Hispanic Americans, their health status seems to fall between that of African Americans and whites (Markides, Coreil, & Rogers, 1989). These differences probably reflect differences in lifestyle, preventive care, and access to and affordability of good medical care (Petchers & Milligan, 1988; U.S. Bureau of the Census, 1983).

### INFLUENCES ON HEALTH AND FITNESS

Changes in the causes of death result from societal factors like better sanitation; immunization against childhood diseases that often used to be fatal; and the widespread use of antibiotics, which have made bronchitis, influenza, and pneumonia less dangerous. The American population as a whole has a higher standard of living, is eating better, and knows more about health.

But along with these positive changes have come some negative ones—increases in carcinogenic agents in foods, in the workplace, and in the air we breathe, which lead to more cases of cancer; and a faster pace of life, which contributes to hypertension and heart disease. The very fact of living longer increases the likelihood of contracting conditions and diseases that tend to occur late in life.

These enthusiastic square dancers are deriving the benefits of regular physical exercise in old age, along with having fun. They may well avoid some of the physical changes commonly—and apparently mistakenly—associated with "normal aging." Such changes are now thought to result from inactivity.

A person's chances of being reasonably healthy and fit in late life often depend on lifestyle—on the extent to which she or he has followed and continues to follow health practices like those listed in Box 12-1 on page 373.

Exercise is one very important health practice. For years Diane's father has been walking from 2 to 4 miles a day in sunshine, rain, and snow. Other older walkers, who prefer climate-controlled conditions, log their miles in indoor malls. Indoors or out, exercise is just as valuable in late adulthood as it is earlier in the life span. Because many of the physical changes commonly associated with "normal aging" are now thought to be caused by inactivity, the Council on Scientific Affairs of the American Medical Association (1984) recommends a lifelong program of exercise.

Regular exercise throughout adulthood seems to protect against both hypertension and heart disease. It also seems to help maintain speed, stamina, and strength, and such basic functions as circulation and breathing. It reduces the chance of injuries by making joints and muscles stronger and more flexible, and it helps prevent or relieve lower-back pain and symptoms of arthritis. It may also improve mental alertness and cognitive performance and may help relieve anxiety and mild depression (Birren et al., 1980; Blair, Goodyear, Gibbons, & Cooper, 1984; Bromley, 1974; Clarkson-Smith & Hartley, 1989; Pardini, 1984).

## HEALTH CARE AND HEALTH PROBLEMS

### Medical Conditions

Although most elderly people are in good health, chronic medical conditions do become more frequent with age and may cause disability. Most older people have at least one chronic condition: the most common are arthritis (48 percent); hypertension (37 percent); heart disease (30 percent); cataracts (16 percent); hearing impairments (30 percent); and impairments of the legs, hips, back, or spine (17 percent) (AARP, 1989). But people over 65 have fewer colds, flu infections, and acute digestive problems than younger adults. The danger with older people is that a minor illness—along with chronic conditions and loss of reserve capacity—may have serious repercussions.

Activity is usually cut back longer for an acutely ill older person than it would be for someone younger. Even so, this amounts to an average of only 30 days of curtailed activity (including 14 days sick in bed) in a year. Like younger workers, workers over 65 take off an average of only 4 or 5 days each year because of illness (AARP, 1989; Estes, 1969; U.S. Bureau of the Census, 1983; USDHHS, 1990).

Overall, older people need more medical care than younger ones. They go to the doctor more often, are hospitalized more frequently, stay in the hospital longer, and spend more than 4 times as much money (an average of $5360 a year) on health care. Medicare (part of the social security system, available to everyone over age 65), Medicaid (available only to low-income people), and other government programs cover about two-thirds of this cost. About one-fourth of the cost comes out of people's own pockets (or their relatives'); private insurance covers very little (AARP, 1989; Binstock, 1987).

Contrary to the stereotype of most elderly people as living in nursing homes, only a very small percentage are. Almost 99 percent of people under age 75 and 80 percent of those over 85 live in the community (USDHHS, 1990). We'll discuss the issues for the minority who do need institutional care in Chapter 17.

### Dental Health

Few people keep all their teeth until very late in life. This fact, and the fact that tooth and gum problems are common in these years, can have serious implications for nutrition. Since people with poor or missing teeth find many foods hard to chew, they tend to eat less and to shift to softer, sometimes less nutritious foods (Wayler, Kapur, Feldman, & Chauncey, 1982).

Dental health is related to inborn tooth structure and to lifelong eating and dental habits. In one interview study, more than half of those 65 and over had not seen a dentist for 2 years or more (USDHHS, 1990). Extensive loss of teeth—a condition which is especially serious among the poor—may reflect inadequate (or no) dental care more than effects of aging.

### Mental and Behavioral Disorders

As the family and friends of an 80-year-old man watched him go downhill mentally, they assumed that he was becoming senile. But his problem turned out to be the combined effects of several types of prescription drugs; when his medications were changed, his behavior returned to normal.

The confusion, forgetfulness, and personality changes sometimes associated with old age very often have physiological causes. The general term for such apparent intellectual deterioration is **dementia.** The word *senility,* frequently used to describe dementia in older people, is not a true medical diagnosis but a "wastebasket" term for a wide range of symptoms.

Contrary to another stereotype, dementia is not an inevitable part of aging. Although it does affect at least 3 million Americans, most older people are in good mental health. Moderate memory loss is not necessarily a sign of dementia. (When younger people cannot remember something, they usually shrug it off; when older people forget, they may become alarmed, afraid of deterioration in intellectual functioning.) Furthermore, while some dementias are irreversible, others can be reversed with the right treatment.

#### Reversible mental health problems

Many older people mistakenly believe that they can do nothing about mental and behavioral problems because "you can't turn back the clock." Actually, some 100 of these conditions—including about 15 percent of dementia cases—can be cured or alleviated with correct diagnosis and treatment. The most common are depression, delirium, intoxication caused by prescription drugs and over-the-counter drugs, and metabolic or infectious disorders; the next most common are malnutrition, anemia, alcoholism, low thyroid functioning, and head injury (NIA, 1980).

Unfortunately, many older people, especially those from minority groups and those who live in rural areas, do not get the help they need (Fellin & Powell, 1988; Roybal, 1988). Only a very small percentage of persons seen in psychiatric clinics are over age 60, and only a small percentage of people seen in community health centers are over 65 (Butler & Lewis, 1982).

*Treatment.* A great deal of research into Alzheimer's disease is going on. New drugs to improve memory are being tested (Fitten et al., 1990; Harbaugh, Roberts, Coombs, Saunders, & Reeder, 1984; Thal, Fuld, Masur, & Sharpless, 1983). Fetal brain tissue has been grafted into the brains of old, impaired rats (Gage, Bjorklund, Stenevi, Dunnett, & Kelly, 1984; M. B. Rosenberg et al., 1988). Drugs have been given to raise the levels of acetylcholine, a *neurotransmitter* (that is, a chemical needed to transmit information through the nervous system) whose concentration is lowered in the brains of patients with Alzheimer's disease (G. D. Cohen, 1987). However, at this point no cure has been discovered.

Patients with Alzheimer's disease may be helped by drugs that relieve their agitation, lighten their depression, or help them sleep. Proper nourishment and fluid intake are important, and exercise and physical therapy may help. Memory aids can help everyday functioning. Probably the biggest help to both patient and family is the social and emotional support that can come through professional counseling and support groups (Blieszner & Shifflett, 1990). Family members suffer, too, from Alzheimer's disease, since the patient's inability to reciprocate expressions of affection and caring robs relationships of intimacy, while at the same time imposing a major burden of caregiving (Blieszner & Shifflett, 1990).

***Other irreversible conditions***  About 80 percent of cases of dementia among older people are caused either by Alzheimer's disease or by a series of small strokes (NIA, 1980). When symptoms come on in several sudden steps, rather than gradually, stroke is the likeliest explanation. In cases of mixed dementia, changes like those seen with Alzheimer's disease and those with strokes both seem to occur (Reisberg, 1987). Small strokes can often be prevented by controlling hypertension through screening, a low-salt diet, and medication (NIA, 1984).

# INTELLECTUAL DEVELOPMENT

Most people do not deteriorate markedly in late adulthood. Do they, however, continue to learn and grow intellectually, or does intelligence now falter and decline? We'll examine this controversial question, and then we'll look at what happens to memory in normal, healthy adults. Finally, we'll see how some older people keep their minds sharp through continuing education and how they view work and retirement.

# ASPECTS OF INTELLECTUAL DEVELOPMENT

## DOES INTELLIGENCE DECLINE IN LATE ADULTHOOD?

When Sally's mother was 75, she was taken aback when a middle-aged neighbor told her how "alert" she seemed. Sally's mother considered the comment patronizing and gratuitous—as well she might.

### Two Views of Intelligence

Some psychologists argue that "general intellectual decline in old age is largely a myth" (Baltes & Schaie, 1974, p. 35, 1976; Schaie & Baltes, 1977). Others dismiss this view as rosy (J. L. Horn & Donaldson, 1976, 1977). To weigh these two points of view, we need to look at the results of intelligence tests that have been given to people of different ages, at the kinds of tests given, at the ways in which data have been collected, and at the kinds of intelligence being tested.

### *Fluid and crystallized intelligence: Which is more important?*

The distinction between *fluid* and *crystallized* intelligence (see Chapter 14) is crucial to this controversy.

Horn and his colleagues consider fluid abilities (which are called on to solve novel problems) to be at the heart of intelligence. They see the decline of these abilities in adulthood as the sign of a downhill slide. Schaie and Baltes, on the other hand, maintain that while some abilities (mostly fluid) decline, other important abilities (mostly crystallized abilities, the kind that depend on learning and experience) either hold their own or increase in later life. They stress the emergence of *new* abilities, like wisdom; cite studies suggesting that performance on fluid tests can be improved with training; and thus conclude that any assumption of an overall intellectual decline is unwarranted.

### *Fluid and crystallized intelligence: How are they tested?*

***Sequential testing***  To overcome the disadvantages of both cross-sectional and longitudinal tests (see Chapter 1) and to resolve discrepancies between the data yielded by these two types of research, Schaie and his colleagues employed a new approach for studying changes in intellectual functioning. Their approach—called *sequential testing* (see Chapter 1)—was designed to control cohort differences and practice effects (Baltes, 1985; Schaie, 1979, 1983; Schaie & Herzog, 1983; Schaie & Strother, 1968).

**TABLE 16–2**

TESTS OF PRIMARY MENTAL ABILITIES GIVEN IN SEATTLE LONGITUDINAL STUDY OF ADULT INTELLIGENCE

| Test | Ability Measured | Task | Type of Intelligence |
|---|---|---|---|
| Verbal meaning | Recognition and understanding of words | Find synonym by matching stimulus word with another word from multiple-choice list | Crystallized |
| Number | Applying numerical concepts | Check simple addition problems | Crystallized |
| Word fluency | Retrieving words from long-term memory | Think of as many words as possible beginning with a given letter, in a set time period | Part crystallized, part fluid |
| Spatial orientation | Rotating objects mentally in two-dimensional space | Select rotated examples of figure to match stimulus figure | Fluid |
| Inductive | Identifying regularities and inferring principles and rules | Complete a letter series | Fluid |

*Source:* Schaie, 1989.

In 1956, their now-classic sequential study began with a battery of tests given to 500 randomly chosen volunteers from Seattle (25 men and 25 women in each 5-year age interval from 20 to 70 years). Every 7 years, the original subjects were retested and new subjects were added to the study; by 1984, more than 2000 people had been tested on timed tasks of primary mental abilities (described in Table 16-2). They also measured subjects on their degree of rigidity or flexibility and on the complexity of their lives, and they took health histories.

The major findings are that older people's intellectual functioning is variable, that it changes in more than one direction, and that it is subject to cultural and environmental influences:

■ *Variability among people.* For some people, intellectual abilities begin to decline during their thirties; for others, the decline does not begin till their seventies; and about one-third of people over age 70 score higher than the average young adult. Women seem to decline earlier on fluid abilities, men on crystallized abilities. A person's functioning is influenced by such factors as health, work, and education. Most fairly healthy adults in the United States do not experience any significant mental loss until about age 60. If they live long enough, their intellec-

tual functioning will begin to decline at some point; but very few people decline on all, or even most, abilities. At age 81, less than half the subjects had declined consistently over the previous 7 years.

■ *Multidirectionality of change.* Fluid intelligence begins to decline in young adulthood, but crystallized intelligence remains stable or even increases into the seventies. After this time, crystallized intelligence also declines, but the decline may be due to older people's slower response time, not to their capacity.

■ *Cultural and environmental influences.* Different cohorts show different patterns of intellectual functioning in maturity (just as they do earlier in life), as a result of different kinds of life experiences. For example, people who grew up more recently in the United States have more formal education, on the average; they have been exposed to more information through television; they have taken more tests and have taken them more recently; they are in better health; and they are likely to have jobs that depend on thinking rather than on physical labor. All these factors contribute to differences among cohorts. More recent cohorts scored higher on inductive reasoning and verbal meaning, whereas the other abilities showed varying patterns (see Figure 16-2, page 488).

## The Three Memory Systems

Failing memory is often considered a sign of aging. The man who always kept his schedule in his head now has to write it in a calendar; the woman who takes several medicines now measures out each day's dosages and puts them where she is sure to see them.

Yet in memory, as in other respects, older people's functioning varies greatly. To understand why, we need to remember that there is no single capacity called *memory*. Memory involves three different storage systems—sensory memory, short-term memory, and long-term memory—each serving distinct purposes. Only one of these, long-term memory for recent events, is usually affected by aging (Poon, 1985).

### Sensory memory

Your brain records whatever you see, hear, smell, taste, or touch—anything that comes in through the senses—and places the information in a temporary storage called **sensory memory,** where it stays very briefly. Images in sensory memory fade quickly unless they are transferred to short-term memory.

Iconic (visual) memory seems to hold up fairly well in late adulthood (Poon, 1985). Without this ability to register visual images (like an array of letters), you would be unable to read or to make sense of anything you saw.

### Short-term memory

When you look up a telephone number before dialing, it goes into your **short-term memory,** which holds information for about 20 seconds. Researchers assess short-term memory by asking a subject to repeat a sequence of numbers, either in the order in which they were presented or in reverse order. How many digits a person can recall seems to be relatively unaffected by age, though it may take an older person slightly longer to respond (Craik, 1977; Poon, 1985).

### Long-term memory

**Long-term memory** is long-term storage of information. Older people's long-term memory for newly learned information is different from their memory for material learned in the more distant past. Memory for newly learned material drops off significantly with advancing age: over a period of hours or days, younger adults can remember such newly learned material as word pairs and paragraphs better than older people do (Craik, 1977; Poon, 1985). But the ability to recall long-ago events is not generally affected by advanced age (Poon, 1985).

## Explaining Why Memory Declines

Investigators have offered several hypotheses to explain age differences in memory, particularly in long-term memory for recent events.

### Biological hypotheses

Some researchers point to neurological changes and other physiological changes connected with aging. Thus, the more a person deteriorates physically, the more loss of memory will take place.

So far, the biological approach appears to be more useful in explaining memory impairment in people with brain damage or other pathological conditions than it is in explaining memory impairment in normal, healthy older adults (Poon, 1985). However, recent studies suggest that degeneration in the frontal lobes of the brain is related to a decline in episodic memory (memory for specific events) in old age.

### Processing hypotheses

A second approach focuses on the three steps required to process information in memory: encoding, storage, and retrieval. Older people seem to be less efficient than younger ones at encoding information—preparing and "labeling" it for storage so that it will be easier to retrieve when needed. Older people are not as likely to think of ways to organize material to make it easier to remember (like putting names in alphabetical order). But when given suggestions for organizing, older subjects remember just as well as younger ones (Hultsch, 1971; Poon, 1985).

Older people also often have trouble retrieving information from memory. In one study, older people had some trouble *recalling* items they had learned, though they did just as well as younger people in *recognizing* the items (Hultsch, 1971). In other words, if asked a question, they might not come up with the right answer; but if presented with multiple-choice answers, they could recognize the correct answer. But even though recognition memory seems to remain more stable with age than recall memory, it takes older people a longer time to search their memories (T. R. Anders, Fozard, & Lillyquist, 1972).

### Contextual considerations

How do "contextual" factors—factors determining how a particular person responds to a particular task—account for individual differences in memory? Such factors might include motivation, intelligence, learning habits, and degree of familiarity with test items, as well as the type of task.

The designers of one recent study reasoned that age differences in memory should be more pronounced when people are less intellectually able, flexible, and resourceful; when they receive little guidance in encoding and retrieval; or when the material is unfamiliar. The researchers compared three groups of 20 elderly volunteers (differing in socioeconomic status, verbal intelligence, and daily activity levels) with a group of 20 undergraduate students. All participants were tested individually on three verbal tasks, including recalling words from a list. The most intelligent, affluent, and socially active old people did best on all the tasks—about as well as the undergraduates. The least intelligent, least economically advantaged, and least active old people did worst. As expected, there was less difference in performance when the subjects were given cues to jog their memory than when they had to recall the words on their own (Craik, Byrd, & Swanson, 1987).

To speak of an across-the-board decline in memory, then, is seriously misleading. We need to ask: Which older people are we talking about? What tasks are they being asked to do? And how well prepared are they to do these tasks?

## LIFELONG LEARNING: ADULT EDUCATION IN LATE LIFE

One of the principal findings of research on intellectual functioning in late life is that the phrase "use it or lose it" is as applicable to mental ability as to physical ability. Continuing mental activity throughout life helps keep performance high, whether this activity takes the form of reading, conversation, crossword puzzles, games like bridge or chess or board games—or going back to school, as more and more mature adults are doing.

Qian Likun, a star student who walks to his classes on health care and ancient Chinese poetry, recently took part in a college-sponsored 2.3-mile foot race. This might not seem unusual, until you learn that Mr. Qian is 102 years old, one of thousands of students in China's network of "universities for the aged." More than 800 of these schools have been founded since the 1980s, demonstrating China's commitment to its elderly population—and older people's willingness and ability to learn everything from basic reading and writing skills to esoteric subjects (Kristof, 1990).

In the United States, too, many older people use their new bounty of time to educate themselves. Since people who were well educated in their youth are more

This Elderhostel group, visiting Christchurch, New Zealand, is among the growing number of older people who use their new bounty of time to educate themselves. Elderhostel offers low-cost 1- and 2-week minicourses, many of which are based on college campuses during school vacations. Colleges themselves often offer free or low-cost tuition to older people who want to attend regular academic courses.

likely to seek more education later in life, and since education rates have been rising steadily (U.S. Bureau of the Census, 1983), the number of older people who are enrolled in educational programs will probably grow.

Many colleges offer tuition-free courses for older students. Low-cost summer Elderhostel programs offer 1- or 2-week minicourses in Shakespeare, geography, early American music, and a wide variety of other subjects. Some vocational programs give special attention to the needs of older women who have never worked for pay and who now must do so for either financial or emotional reasons.

Older people can learn new skills and information, but they learn better when the materials and methods take into account the physiological, psychological, and intellectual changes that they may be going through. For example, they seem to learn best when material is presented slowly and over a longer period of time with intervals in between, rather than in concentrated form. And students with visual or hearing problems benefit from clear, easily understandable audiovisual materials.

## WORK AND RETIREMENT

At 79, Diane's father is still working full-time at his law practice. When Sally's father, a furniture salesman, was 73, he lost his job because of the death of his employer; he received three offers of employment, took one, and worked until the day he died, at 76.

Perhaps because older people doing productive paid work represent only 3 percent of the work force (Schick, 1986), they are less visible than the stereotyped carefree retirees "sallying forth from Florida condominiums every morning to frolic on the golf course" (Pollack, 1985, p. A27). Over the past 30 years, moreover, the proportion of elderly people seeking work has fallen considerably. In 1987, only 16.6 percent of men 65 and older, and 67 percent of those aged 55 to 64, were in the labor force, compared with 47.8 percent and 89.6 percent, respectively, in 1947 (U.S. Department of Labor, 1980, 1987). Mainly, this is because more men now retire early and fewer are self-employed. Most of the research in work and retirement in late adulthood has focused on older men (Ruhm, 1989), but with the increased role of work in women's lives, this imbalance is being corrected.

The proportion of older women who work has also decreased, but not as sharply—from about 10 percent to 7 percent. This probably reflects the fact that fewer women in this age group worked earlier in life and that those who did tended to retire as early as possible because the kinds of work they could do were limited (AARP, 1986; Bird, 1987).

Retirement does not necessarily mean stopping work altogether. Many healthy retirees work part time, and part-timers account for a little more than half of older workers. Although there are probably some people over age 65 in almost every occupation, 3 out of 4 older workers are white-collar and about 1 out of 4 are self-employed (AARP, 1986; Bird, 1987; Schick, 1986).

## WHY PEOPLE RETIRE

Most people leave their jobs by choice at or before the retirement age their employers set as mandatory. Although poor health is a factor in some of these decisions, a much more common basis for retiring is workers' economic status. Those who are still earning high wages are more likely to work longer. But lower-salary workers often retire when they feel they can afford to. And today, thanks to social security benefits (the most important source of income for the elderly) and private pension plans, more workers can retire and live relatively comfortably. (Issues related to income in late adulthood are discussed further in Chapter 17.)

Many private pension plans encourage early retirement by penalizing workers who are past their early sixties, and social security policies limit the income a recipient can earn. Changes in tax laws, pension plans, and company policies (like letting employees work part time at reduced pay) could encourage more older workers to stay on the job (Ruhm, 1989).

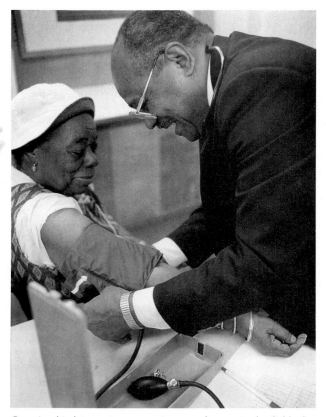

By using his leisure time to work as a volunteer in the field of health care, this retiree is helping not only the community but also himself. The self-esteem gained from using hard-won skills and from continuing to be a useful, contributing member of society is a valuable by-product of volunteer service.

## HOW PEOPLE FEEL ABOUT RETIREMENT

A favorite adage of Sally's father—"It's better to be rich and healthy than poor and sick"—sums up how people feel about retirement. To no one's surprise, retirees who are not worried about money and who feel well are happier in retirement than those who miss their income and do not feel well enough to enjoy their leisure (Barfield & Morgan, 1974, 1978; Streib & Schneider, 1971).

Use of time is also important, however. Many recent retirees relish the first long stretches of leisure time they have had since childhood. They enjoy spending time with family and friends and exploring new interests. After a while, though, they may begin to feel bored, restless, and useless. The most satisfied retirees tend to be physically fit people who are using their skills in part-time paid or volunteer work (Schick, 1986).

Retirement has little effect on physical health, but it sometimes affects mental health (Bossé, Aldwin, Levenson, & Ekerdt, 1987). Among 1513 older men surveyed in the Boston Veterans Administration Normative Aging Study (a cross-sectional study), retirees were more likely than workers to report depression, obsessive-compulsive behavior, and physical symptoms that had no organic cause. Those who had retired early (before age 62) or late (after age 65) reported the most symptoms.

Of course, poor mental health might have been the reason why some of these men retired. But it is also possible that the timing of retirement matters. Workers who are pressured to stop work before they want to may not have satisfying alternatives, or they may feel out of step with their peers. Workers who deferred retirement as long as possible because they enjoyed their work may now feel its loss; and those who continue working late may do so because they want to feel valued and needed.

On the other hand, some people's morale and life satisfaction remain stable through both working and retirement years, and some retirees have higher morale than some workers (M. L. Cassidy, 1983; Palmore, Fillenbaum, & George, 1984). Once again, we see that we cannot describe any single effect of such a complex change in people's lives.

## MAKING THE MOST OF RETIREMENT

Retirement is a major transition of old age. What can be done to help more people enjoy it? Two key elements are preparation before retirement and good use of time during retirement.

### Planning Ahead

Planning for retirement, which ideally should begin by middle age, includes structuring life to make it enjoyable and productive, providing for financial needs, anticipating physical or emotional problems, and discussing how retirement will affect a spouse. Help can come from preretirement workshops, self-help books on retirement, and company-sponsored programs.

### Using Leisure Time Well

Some retirees relish being able to sleep late, go fishing, or take in an afternoon movie. But many get more gratification from using the fruits of their experience in a more structured, "worklike" way, and programs have sprung up to tap this valuable resource. Retired business people share their experience with budding entrepreneurs, and retirees from many occupations tutor, counsel, and offer career advice to college students. Older persons serve as "foster" grandparents, and retired workers teach and supervise in such technical fields as drafting, automotive repairs, electronics, and computer technology.

Retirement could be made easier and more satisfying in the future by restructuring the course of life. Today, young adults usually plunge into education and careers, middle-aged people use most of their energy earning money, and older people have trouble filling their time. If people wove work, leisure, and study into their lives in a more balanced way at all ages, young adults would feel less pressure to establish themselves early, middle-aged people would feel less burdened, and older people would be more stimulated and would feel—and be—more useful.

## SUMMARY

### OLD AGE TODAY

■ Negative stereotypes about old people reflect *ageism*—prejudice or discrimination based on age. Today, many old people are healthy, vigorous, and active. These people can be referred to as the *young old,* and the frail and infirm as the *old old.*

■ People over 85 are the fastest-growing age group in the American population. They are largely widowed women.

■ The number and proportion of old people in the United States population are greater today than ever before.

This is due to high birthrates in the late eighteenth and early nineteenth centuries as well as high immigration rates.

■ Senescence, the period in the life span when people begin to grow old, begins at different ages for different people. The designation of age 65 as the beginning of late adulthood is based on the traditional age of retirement, even though many people now retire earlier (and some retire later).

■ Negative attitudes toward the elderly affect older people's feelings about themselves as well as society's treatment of them.

## LONGEVITY AND THE AGING PROCESS

■ Life expectancy has increased dramatically since 1900. American children born in 1987 have an average life expectancy of 75 years. Black people tend to die earlier than white people, and men tend to die younger than women.

■ The death rate for older people has declined. Today, heart disease, cancer, and stroke are the three leading causes of death for people over age 65.

■ Most theories of why people age physically fall into two categories: aging as a programmed process and aging as a result of wear and tear to the body. Most likely, both of these factors influence aging.

■ Some gerontologists distinguish between primary aging, an inevitable process of bodily deterioration; and secondary aging, which results from the way people use their bodies and thus is largely preventable.

## PHYSICAL CHANGES OF OLD AGE

■ Sensory and perceptual abilities decline during late adulthood, with vast individual differences in the timing and extent of decline.

■ Older people experience a general slowing down of responses and of information processing. This slowdown requires them to make adjustments in many aspects of their lives.

■ A number of other physical changes occur with advancing age, including some loss of skin coloring, texture, and elasticity; thinning and graying or whitening of hair; shrinkage of body size; and thinning of bones.

■ Most of the body systems generally continue to function fairly well, but the heart, in particular, becomes more susceptible to disease because of its decreased efficiency. The reserve capacity of the heart and other organs declines.

## HEALTH IN OLD AGE

■ Most older people are reasonably healthy, but incidence of illness and number of days of hospitalization are proportionally higher among older people than among younger people. Although most older people have one or more chronic conditions, many are not severely hampered by them.

■ Loss of teeth and gum problems are common in late adulthood, especially when dental care has been inadequate. Very few people keep all their teeth until late in life.

■ Most older people are in good mental health. Dementia, or intellectual deterioration, affects a minority of people of advanced age.

■ Some forms of dementia, such as those brought on by Alzheimer's disease or by multiple strokes, are irreversible; others, such as those caused by overmedication and depression, can be reversed with proper treatment.

## ASPECTS OF INTELLECTUAL DEVELOPMENT

■ A major controversy concerns whether intelligence declines in late adulthood. Fluid intelligence, the ability to solve novel problems, does appear to decline; but crystallized intelligence, which is based on learning and experience, tends to be maintained.

■ Early cross-sectional research using psychometric tests of intelligence indicated decline; longitudinal studies indicated stability up to age 60 or so. Schaie's sequential studies suggest a more complex picture: intellectual functioning in late adulthood is marked by variability, multidirectionality, and susceptibility to cultural and environmental influences.

■ Physical and psychological factors and test conditions can influence intellectual performance. Therefore, performance on intelligence tests may not be a precise measure of intellectual competence.

■ Older people show considerable cognitive plasticity (modifiability) in intellectual performance. Their positive response to an intellectually supportive environment demonstrates that they can and do learn.

■ Some aspects of intelligence seem to increase with age. Dixon and Baltes propose a dual-process model: the mechanics of intelligence often decline, but the pragmatics of intelligence (practical thinking, specialized knowledge and skills, and wisdom) continue to grow. Successful aging, according to this theory, involves selective optimization with compensation (using special abilities to compensate for losses).

■ While sensory, short-term, and remote long-term memory appear to be nearly as efficient in older adults as in younger people, long-term memory for recently learned information is often less efficient, probably because of problems with encoding (organization) and retrieval. Recognition is easier than recall.

■ Contextual factors—factors determining how a particular person responds to a particular task—may account for individual differences in recall. Like intelligence, memory functioning in older individuals varies greatly: more intelligent people may show little or no memory decline.

## LIFELONG LEARNING: ADULT EDUCATION IN LATE LIFE

■ Continuing mental activity may be critical to keep older people mentally alert. Adult education programs can be designed to meet their needs.

■ Learning and memory are interrelated. Older people can learn new skills and information provided that it is presented slowly and over a longer period of time with intervals between exposures.

## WORK AND RETIREMENT

■ Some older people continue to work for pay, but the vast majority are retired. There is a trend toward retirement before age 65. However, many retired people find part-time paid or volunteer work.

■ Retirement is a major transition of old age. It can be eased by planning for retirement and learning to use leisure time well.

## KEY TERMS

ageism (page 472)
gerontologists (472)
senescence (476)
programmed-aging theory (478)
wear-and-tear theory (478)
primary aging (478)
secondary aging (478)

reserve capacity (481)
dementia (483)
Alzheimer's disease (484)
terminal drop (488)
plasticity (489)
dual-process model (491)

mechanics of intelligence (491)
pragmatics of intelligence (491)
selective optimization with
    compensation (491)
sensory memory (492)
short-term memory (492)
long-term memory (492)

## SUGGESTED READINGS

**Dippel, R. L., & Hutton, J. T. (Eds.) (1991).** *Caring for the Alzheimer patient* (2d ed.). Buffalo, NY: Prometheus Books. This book is a compendium of articles by experts on Alzheimer's disease. It covers medical and physical aspects, environmental and behavioral problems, caregiver support, and ethical and legal issues.

**Jarvik, L., & Small, G. (1990).** *Parentcare: A compassionate, commonsense guide for children and their aging parents.* New York: Bantam. This comprehensive volume by two psychiatrists who specialize in geriatrics takes a commonsense approach to problem solving. Among the topics covered are mental and physical disabilities, common illnesses, legal questions, guilt, grief, commonly prescribed medications, and nutrition.

**Maddox, G. L. (Ed.) (1987).** *The encyclopedia of aging.* New York: Springer. A comprehensive, authoritative, concise reference on hundreds of topics related to late adulthood. Articles, arranged alphabetically, were written by prominent scholars in biology, medicine, nursing, psychology, psychiatry, sociology, and other fields.

## CHAPTER 17

# PERSONALITY AND SOCIAL DEVELOPMENT IN LATE ADULTHOOD

There is still today
And tomorrow fresh with dreams:
Life never grows old

RITA DUSKIN, ''HAIKU,''
*SOUND AND LIGHT*, 1987

# ASK YOURSELF:

- What important psychological tasks of late adulthood did Erikson and Peck identify?
- What personality and lifestyle patterns contribute to "successful aging"?

- How can society help older people deal with such issues as financial need and housing?
- How do relationships with family and friends provide emotional support to older people?

Dexter, 83, looks adoringly at his 81-year-old wife. "I always thought sunsets were more spectacular than sunrises, anyway," he says. "Now we're having some beautiful times in the evening of our lives." After each had been widowed and had lived alone, the two met at a senior citizens' dance. Now, after having been married for 2 years, Lizzie says, "This is the most well-rounded relationship I've ever had. Dexter and I are intellectual equals, and we have a lot of laughs together. Our story shows that it's never too late to find love and sex."

Love and sex are major social and personality issues throughout life. In late adulthood, they can go far to help people enjoy these years. The losses that Dexter and Lizzie suffered from widowhood are typical at this time of life—but so are the vigor and openness that let them begin a new relationship with each other.

Late adulthood is the developmental stage during which people clarify and find use for what they have learned over the years. People can continue to grow and adapt if they are flexible and realistic—if they learn how to conserve their strength, adjust to change and loss, and use these years productively. People now have a new awareness of time; and they want to use the time they have left to leave a legacy to their children or the world, pass on the fruits of their experience, and validate their lives as having been meaningful.

People who feel well, who can show their competence, and who feel in control of their lives are likely to have a strong enough sense of self to cope with losses like the death of loved ones, the relinquishing of work roles, and the diminution of bodily strength and sensory acuity. "Successful aging" *is* possible, and many people *do* experience the last stage of life positively.

In this chapter, we look at Erikson's and Peck's theories and at research on psychological development in late adulthood, and we examine some attempts to define *successful aging*. We discuss some social issues and how older people's lives are affected by how much money they have and where and how they live. Finally, we look at the ties between older people and their families and friends, which greatly influence the quality of these last years of life.

## THEORY AND RESEARCH ON PERSONALITY DEVELOPMENT

If I had my life to live over again, I'd try to make more mistakes the next time. I would relax. I would limber up. I would be sillier than I have been this trip. I know of very few things I would take seriously. I would be crazier. I would be less hygienic. I would take more chances. I would take more trips. I would climb more mountains, swim more rivers, and watch more sunsets. I would burn more gasoline. I would eat more ice cream and fewer beans. I would have more actual problems and fewer imaginary ones. (Stair, undated)

Nadine Stair—a participant in the Colorado Outward Bound School, which encourages adults of all ages to examine their lives and their values in the context of an outdoor experience—wrote these lines at the age of 85. In late adulthood, many people reexamine their lives, looking both backward and forward, and decide how to use the time left to them. Let's see what theory and research can tell us about this final phase of the search for self-knowledge.

Older people achieve a sense of integrity, according to Erik Erikson, when they gain a sense of the order and meaning of their lives within the larger social order—past, present, and future. Presiding at a family holiday dinner and thus carrying on a tradition across the generations is one way to arrive at acceptance of the life that has been lived.

## ERIK ERIKSON:
## CRISIS 8—INTEGRITY VERSUS DESPAIR

In his final crisis, ***integrity versus despair,*** Erikson sees older people as confronting a need to accept their lives—how they have lived—in order to accept their approaching death. They struggle to achieve a sense of integrity, of the coherence and wholeness of life, rather than give way to despair over inability to relive their lives differently (Erikson, Erikson, & Kivnick, 1986).

People who succeed in this final, integrative task—building on the outcomes of the seven previous crises—gain a sense of the order and meaning of their lives within the larger social order, past, present, and future. The "virtue" that develops during this stage is *wisdom,* an "informed and detached concern with life itself in the face of death itself" (Erikson, 1985, p. 61).

Wisdom, Erikson says, includes accepting the life one has lived, without major regrets over what could have been or what one should have done differently. It involves accepting one's parents as people who did the best they could and thus deserve love, even though

they were not perfect. It implies accepting one's death as the inevitable end of a life lived as well as one knew how to live it. In sum, it means accepting imperfection in the self, in parents, and in life. (This definition of *wisdom* as acceptance of one's life and imminent death, and thus as an important psychological resource, differs from Smith and Baltes's definition of *wisdom,* described in Chapter 16, as cognitive expertise in uncertain matters like life planning.)

People who do not achieve acceptance are overwhelmed by despair, realizing that time is too short to seek other roads to integrity. While integrity must outweigh despair if this crisis is to be resolved successfully, Erikson believes that some despair is inevitable. People need to mourn—not only for their own misfortunes and lost chances but for the vulnerability and transience of the human condition.

Yet Erikson also believes that late life is a time to play, to recapture a childlike quality essential for creativity. The time for procreation is over, but creation can still take place. Even as the body's functions weaken and sexual energy diminishes, people can enjoy "an enriched bodily and mental experience" (1985, p. 64).

## ROBERT PECK:
## THREE ADJUSTMENTS OF LATE ADULTHOOD

Peck (1955) expanded on Erikson's discussion of psychological development in late life, emphasizing three major adjustments that people must make. These adjustments allow them to move beyond concerns with work, physical well-being, and mere existence to a broader understanding of the self and of life's purpose.

Peck's three adjustments are:

**1** *Broader self-definition versus preoccupation with work roles.* The issue in this adjustment is the degree to which people define themselves by their work. Everyone has to ask: "Am I a worthwhile person only insofar as I can do a full-time job; or can I be worthwhile in other, different ways—as a performer of several other roles, and also because of the kind of person I am?" (Peck, 1955, in Neugarten, 1968, p. 90).

Retirees especially need to redefine their worth as human beings. People need to explore themselves and find other interests to take the place of the work (whether centered in the marketplace or the home) that had given direction and structure to life. People are more likely to remain vital if they can be proud of personal attributes beyond their work. They need to recognize that their ego is richer and more diverse than the sum of their tasks at work.

Older people, according to Robert Peck, need to find new interests and new sources of self-esteem to take the place of their former work roles and to make up for physical losses. An elderly person like the artist shown here, who can focus on relationships and absorbing activities, can often overcome physical discomforts.

**2** *Transcendence of the body versus preoccupation with the body.* Physical decline creates the need for a second adjustment: overcoming concerns with bodily condition and finding other sources of satisfaction. People who have emphasized physical well-being as the basis of a happy life may be plunged into despair by diminishing faculties or aches and pains. Those who focus on relationships and on activities that do not demand perfect health adjust better.

An orientation away from preoccupation with the body should be developed by early adulthood, but it is in late life that this orientation is critically tested. Throughout life people need to cultivate mental and social powers that can grow with age, along with attributes like strength and muscular coordination that are likely to diminish over the years.

**3** *Transcendence of the ego versus preoccupation with the ego.* Probably the hardest, and possibly the most crucial, adjustment for older people is to go beyond concern with themselves and their present lives and to accept the certainty of death.

How *can* people feel positive about their own death? They can recognize that they will achieve lasting significance through what they have done so far—through the children they have raised, the contributions they have made to society, and the personal relationships they have forged. They transcend the ego by contributing to the well-being of others—and this, Peck says, sets human beings apart from animals.

## GEORGE VAILLANT: FACTORS IN EMOTIONAL HEALTH

The Grant Study, a longitudinal study that began with college sophomores, was described in Chapters 13 and 15. The researchers in this study examined the physical and mental health of 173 of these men at age 65 (Vaillant & Vaillant, 1990). *Emotional health* at this age was defined as the "clear ability to play and to work and to love" (p. 31) and as having been happy over the previous decade.

It is surprising to see the very limited role that various factors played in emotional health. A happy marriage, a successful career, and a childhood free of such major problems as poverty or the death or divorce of parents were all unimportant in predicting good adjustment late in life. More influential was closeness to siblings at college age, suggesting a close family. Factors associated with poor adjustment at age 65 included major emotional problems in childhood and, before age 50, poor physical health, severe depression, alcoholism, and heavy use of tranquilizers.

Probably the most significant personality trait was ability to handle life problems without blame, bitterness, or passivity—or, in the researchers' terms, to use "mature defense mechanisms" (see Chapter 13). The subjects who, over the years, had not collected injustices, complained, pretended nothing was wrong, or become bitter or prejudiced—and could thus respond appropriately to crises—were the best adjusted at age 65. The best adjusted 65-year-olds had also been rated in college as well organized, steady, stable, and dependable; and they continued to show these traits (which were more important than being scholarly, analytic, or creative) throughout life.

But some characteristics linked with good adjustment in young adulthood—like spontaneity and making friends easily—no longer mattered. Possibly the men who were eccentric and isolated early in life improved their social skills over the years, while the extroverted men did not develop other abilities that may, in the long run, be more valuable (Vaillant & Vaillant, 1990).

## RESEARCH ON CHANGES IN PERSONALITY

Although basic personality traits (like extroversion, neuroticism, and openness to new experiences) are generally stable throughout life (see Box 15-1 on page 453), values and outlook do seem to change in ways like those Erikson proposed.

In studies by Carol Ryff and her associates (1982; Ryff & Baltes, 1976; Ryff & Heincke, 1983), men and women of various ages reported that they were most concerned with intimacy in young adulthood, with generativity in middle adulthood, and with integrity in late adulthood. They felt that other aspects of their personalities—like impulsiveness, humility, and orderliness—had not changed.

Between the middle and later years, many women's focus shifted from "doing" to "being," from *instrumental values* (like ambition, courage, and capability) to *terminal values* (such desirable end states of existence as a sense of accomplishment, freedom, and playfulness). Men did not show this kind of shift: middle-aged men were already focused on terminal values, possibly because in these cohorts, men may have changed their values earlier in life.

For some older people, the tendency toward introspection from middle age onward results in their becoming more preoccupied with meeting their own needs. This may be a reaction to a lifetime of caring for and about other people; it may also reflect the fact that personal needs are greater in old age.

## AGING

### APPROACHES TO "SUCCESSFUL AGING"

Is a person who tranquilly watches the world go by from a rocking chair on the front porch making as healthy an adjustment to aging as one who is busy and involved from morning till night? There is more than one way to age well, and the patterns that people follow vary with personality and life circumstances.

Let's look at two contrasting models of successful aging—activity theory and disengagement theory—and then at some personal definitions of successful aging. We'll then examine research findings about how people actually age.

### Activity Theory

After she retired from her job as principal of an inner-city school, Zora turned her attention and energy to community projects. She started a local chapter of the Gray Panthers, an intergenerational activist group; she became an area coordinator for help to the homeless; and she volunteered to teach in a literacy program for young adults. After her husband died, she resumed a relationship with a man she had known 50 years before, going to church, movies, and other events together.

Zora's life exemplifies *activity theory,* which holds that the more active older people remain, the better they age. In this model, people who are aging successfully act like middle-aged people, keeping up as many activities as possible and finding substitutes for activities lost through retirement or death of a spouse or

Maggie Kuhn, founder of the Gray Panthers, exemplifies successful aging as described by activity theory. In helping older people to become a powerful political force in the United States, she has developed her own leadership qualities and has continued to bring out new abilities in herself.

friends. In this view, a person's roles (worker, spouse, parent, and so on) are the major source of satisfaction in life; and the greater the loss of roles through retirement, widowhood, distance from children, infirmity, or other causes, the less satisfied the person will be.

### Disengagement Theory

Samuel followed a different pattern. He had been politically active as a younger man, and even after retirement from his job as a civil engineer he kept busy for a while—going to political meetings, writing for newsletters, and getting together for a weekly card game with old friends. But then he dropped out of one group after another; and eventually, he even gave up his weekly poker game. This is the pattern of *disengagement* (Cumming & Henry, 1961).

*Disengagement theory* sees aging as a process of mutual withdrawal. Older people voluntarily cut down their activities and commitments, while society encourages this by pressuring people to retire. Disengagement theory sees this pattern as normal. More preoccupation with the self and less emotional investment in others are also considered normal. This decline in social interaction theoretically helps older people to keep their balance and benefits both the individual and society. Disengagement theory predicts that as people disengage, their morale remains high.

So far, research has not proved that either of these models is more accurate than the other. Studies on activity theory have been inconclusive. Some studies found that activity in and of itself bore little relationship to satisfaction with life (Lemon, Bengtson, & Peterson, 1972). Later studies suggested that the *kind* of activity matters: that older people heavily involved in *informal* activities (doing things with friends and family) were happier than those pursuing *formal* (structured group) activities or *solitary* activities (reading, watching television, and hobbies) (Longino & Kart, 1982). But a subsequent meta-analysis indicated that how people feel about life is affected either not at all or only to the slightest degree by any kind of activity (M. A. Okun, Stick, Haring, & Witter, 1984). Furthermore, an analysis of the impact of activity on mortality over an 8-year period among 508 older Mexican Americans and Anglos found that when people died was not at all related to how active they had been, once other factors like age, health, and gender were taken into account (D. J. Lee & Markides, 1990).

Research on disengagement theory has not supported an overall relationship between disengagement and high morale, and it has not found disengagement to be inevitable, universal, or consistently sought by older people (Maddox, 1968; Reichard, Livson, & Peterson, 1962). Disengagement seems to be related less to age as such than to factors associated with aging, like poor health, widowhood, retirement, and poverty. It is influenced by the social environment. For example, when people work, they continue such work-related involvements as membership in trade unions, professional friendships, and reading in the field. When they lose or give up their jobs, they usually give up these activities. As we will see, other factors, like personality, help determine people's levels of activity—and their morale. Disengagement may be more common in people close to death. Researchers measured engagement levels in older people, followed them up, and found that those who had died in the interim had shown signs of disengagement 2 years before their death; the survivors had not. Thus disengagement may be a brief process, taking about 2 years rather than the 25 or 30 originally proposed (Lieberman & Coplan, 1970).

### Personal Definitions of Aging Successfully

Researchers in one study asked middle-aged adults (60 women and 9 men, with an average age of 52) and older adults (61 women and 41 men, average age 73) to evaluate their present lives; to describe how they had changed or stayed the same over the years; and to define "personal fulfillment," the "ideal person," "good" or "poor" adjustment for people their age, and "successful aging" (Ryff, 1989).

In both age groups, respondents defined "successful aging" mostly in terms of relationships with other people—unlike theorists, who emphasize self-oriented factors like confidence, self-knowledge, and self-acceptance. Middle-aged and older people seem to consider self-related attributes less important than caring about and getting along with others.

Differences between the two age groups showed up when people were asked what they were unhappy about and what they would change if they could. Middle-aged people were most unhappy about family problems and would, if they could, change themselves (as by exercising more) or accomplish more in schooling or careers. Older people, however, most commonly said that they were unhappy about nothing and would change nothing, although if they could change anything, it would be health.

The fact that middle-aged people emphasized continuous growth and older people emphasized acceptance suggests that people age best if they can initiate change themselves but accept the twists and turns of life—as long as they have good relationships with others.

## PERSONALITY AND PATTERNS OF AGING

How do people cope with the losses and other stresses of late life? They may use a number of strategies (such as the strategies listed in Table 17-1, and various strategies tied in with religious beliefs and practices, as described in Box 17-1 on page 506). But successful aging does not follow any single pattern. How people adapt in old age depends on their personalities and how they have adapted to situations throughout life.

One classic study analyzed styles of aging by looking at subjects' personality, their activity level, and their satisfaction with life (Neugarten, Havighurst, & Tobin, 1968). The researchers interviewed 159 men and women aged 50 to 90 and found four major personality types: *integrated, armor-defended, passive-dependent,* and *unintegrated.* They correlated these types with levels of activity in 11 social roles (such as parent; spouse; and club, church, or association member), rated the subjects by levels of life satisfaction, and identified patterns of aging.

Most of the subjects who had aged successfully were quite active, but less active styles were also associated with successful aging. As people aged, they tended to be less active and to fill fewer social roles. The four major personality types, with associated patterns of aging, were as follows:

1 *Integrated.* Integrated people were functioning well, with a complex inner life, a competent ego, intact cognitive abilities, and a high level of satisfaction. They ranged from being very active and involved, with a wide variety of interests, to deriving satisfaction from one or two roles to being self-contained and content.
2 *Armor-defended.* Armor-defended people were achievement-oriented, striving, and tightly controlled. Both those who stayed fairly active and those who limited their expenditures of energy, socializing, and experience showed moderate to high levels of satisfaction.
3 *Passive-dependent.* Passive-dependent people either sought comfort from others or were apathetic. Some, who depended on others, were moderately or very active and moderately or very satisfied. Others, who had been passive all their lives, did little and showed medium or low satisfaction.
4 *Unintegrated.* Unintegrated people were disorganized, with gross defects in psychological functioning, poor control over their emotions, and deteriorated thought processes. They managed to stay in the community, but with low activity and low satisfaction.

**TABLE 17–1**
SPONTANEOUSLY REPORTED EMOTION-REGULATING COPING STRATEGIES USED BY OLDER ADULTS DURING STRESSFUL EXPERIENCES[a]

| Rank order | Frequency of mention | |
|---|---|---|
| | *Number* | (%) |
| Religious | 97 | (17.4) |
| Kept busy | 84 | (15.1) |
| Accepted it | 63 | (11.3) |
| Support from family or friends | 62 | (11.1) |
| Help from professional | 34 | ( 6.1) |
| Positive attitude | 31 | ( 5.6) |
| Took one day at a time | 29 | ( 5.2) |
| Became involved in social activities | 19 | ( 3.4) |
| Planning and preparing beforehand | 15 | ( 2.7) |
| Optimized communication | 13 | ( 2.3) |
| Limited activities, didn't overcommit | 11 | ( 2.0) |
| Sought information | 8 | ( 1.4) |
| Exercised | 8 | ( 1.4) |
| Helped others more needy | 7 | ( 1.3) |
| Realized that time heals all wounds | 7 | ( 1.3) |
| Avoided situation | 6 | ( 1.1) |
| Experience of prior hardships | 5 | ( .9) |
| Carried on for others' sake | 5 | ( .9) |
| Ingested alcohol, tranquilizers | 5 | ( .9) |
| Carried on as usual | 4 | ( .7) |
| Took a vacation | 3 | ( .5) |
| Realized others in same situation or worse | 3 | ( .5) |
| Released emotion (cried or cursed) | 3 | ( .5) |
| Lowered expectations or devaluated | 3 | ( .5) |
| Miscellaneous | 31 | ( 5.6) |
| Totals | 556 | (100.6[b]) |

[a]100 older adults reported 556 coping behaviors for 289 stressful experiences.
[b]Due to rounding.
*Source:* Koenig, George, & Siegler, 1988, p. 306.

BOX 17–1    THINKING CRITICALLY

# RELIGION AND EMOTIONAL WELL-BEING IN LATE LIFE

Their health isn't what it was, they've lost old friends and beloved family members, they don't earn the money they once did, and their lives keep changing in countless stressful ways. Yet in general, older adults have fewer mental disorders and are more satisfied with life than younger ones. What accounts for this remarkable ability to cope?

In one study, interviewers asked 100 well-educated white men and women—aged 55 to 80, balanced for working-class and upper-middle-class status, and 90 percent Protestant—to describe the worst events in their lives and how they had dealt with them (Koenig, George, & Siegler, 1988). The respondents described 289 stressful events and 556 coping strategies.

Heading the list of the most frequent strategies (see Table 17-1) were behaviors associated with religion, cited by almost half the sample (45 percent—58 percent of the women and 32 percent of the men). Almost three-fourths of these religious strategies consisted of placing trust and faith in God, praying, and getting help and strength from God. Other religious sources of help included friends from church, church activities, the minister, and the Bible.

The next most common strategy involved taking one's mind off a problem by keeping busy—in work-related, social, recreational, and family activities; by reading or watching television; by working at hobbies; or by doing a variety of other things.

The third and fourth strategies involved acceptance—and other people. Many respondents were helped by the philosophy expressed in the "serenity prayer": "God grant me the serenity to accept things I cannot change, the courage to change those I can, and the wisdom to know the difference." These people would think about a problem and do everything they could to resolve it—but then would accept the situation and get on with their lives. Support and encouragement from family and friends also helped; when asked, most people said that others had aided them through the bad times. Relatively few of the respondents turned to a health worker; when they did, that person was four times more likely to be a personal physician than a mental health professional.

Other research has supported this finding that religion is a strong support for the elderly, especially for women, African Americans, and the oldest of the old. Possible explanations include the social support offered by a religious community, the perception gained from religion of a measure of control over life (as through prayer), and faith in God as a way of interpreting the stresses of life (believing, say, that one is part of a larger plan).

In a study of 836 older adults from two secular and three religiously oriented groups, morale was positively associated with three kinds of religious activity: organized (going to church or temple and taking part in the activities), informal (praying, reading the Bible), and spiritual (personal cognitive commitment to religious beliefs). The more religious people had higher morale and a better attitude toward aging, were more satisfied, and were less lonely. Women and people over 75 showed the strongest correlations between religion and well-being (Koenig, Kvale, & Ferrel, 1988).

The church has always been important to African Americans. During the 1960s, when church attendance began to decline among other groups, it remained strong in the black community, and religious leaders played a vital role in the civil rights movement. Among a representative sample of 2107 African American adults aged 18 to 75, the highest levels of religious involvement of all kinds were shown by women and people aged 65 and older. For all ages and both sexes, the most common religious activity was personal prayer (Chatters & Taylor, 1989).

Since almost all the research on religion in the lives of older Americans has been cross-sectional, it is possible that turning toward religion in old age is a cohort effect rather than a result of aging. It is also likely, however, that as people think about the meaning of their lives and about death as the inevitable end, they may focus more on spiritual matters.

In any case, people can help the elderly better—either on a personal or a professional basis—if they know the most effective strategies for coping with life's challenges. Old people are often reluctant to seek or accept help unless it is offered in a way that is comfortable for them. Since the major source of poor morale in old age is poor health, physicians are usually the first line of help for the elderly. Doctors can help older patients by, for example, tactfully suggesting such supports as congregational work or speaking to a member of the clergy. Religious institutions can institute programs to reach and serve older persons. And friends and family can respect the value of an older person's religious beliefs and activities.

Clearly, people differ greatly in how they live the later years of life. Older people (like young people) are influenced by health, work, money, and family status, and their personalities determine how they react to their situations. They choose activities that make them feel good about themselves—that fit in with their abilities or their values—and they have different capacities to cope with life's stresses.

Furthermore, people tend to react to life in old age much as they have always reacted to it. People who cope well early in life, for example, also cope well later on (Neugarten, 1968, 1973; Neugarten et al., 1968). As Bernice Neugarten writes, "Aging is not a leveler of individual differences except, perhaps, at the very end of life. In adapting to both biological and social changes, the aging person continues to draw upon that which he has been, as well as that which he is" (1973, p. 329).

## SOCIAL ISSUES RELATED TO AGING

The ability to cope with challenges may be sorely tested in late adulthood. On top of the physical problems that often accompany aging, the social circumstances of many older people are extremely trying, or even overwhelming. Two common issues are finances and living arrangements. A less common but growing problem is the abuse of elderly people.

### Income

Government programs—social security and Medicare— have allowed today's elderly people, on the whole, to be at least as well off financially as younger people (Hurd, 1989). In fact, the poverty rate is slightly less for people aged 65 and over than for younger people (Hurd, 1989).

Social security is the largest single source of income for older people in the United States. About 90 percent of them receive social security benefits, which account for 40 to 53 percent of older people's income. Pensions account for 14 percent; assets, 22 percent; and earnings from work, 23 percent (American Association of Retired Persons, AARP, 1986; Commonwealth Fund Commission on Elderly People Living Alone, 1986; Ruhm, 1989). Older people who live in family households are better off financially than those who live alone or with nonrelatives.

Still, about 3.5 million elderly people—more than one-fifth—are classified as poor or "near poor." Women (especially widows), minorities (see Box 17-2 on page 508), single people, and people who did unskilled or service jobs during their working years are likeliest to be poor (Hurd, 1989). Married couples rarely become impoverished after retirement, especially if they have pension benefits. A husband's death, however, is a major risk factor for his widow: she is 4 times as likely as a married person to fall below the poverty line (Burkhauser, Holden, & Feaster, 1988).

Although fewer older people live in poverty today than in the past few decades, many people face poverty for the first time in old age. Earlier in life, they could earn enough to meet their needs; but now they cannot work, and inflation has eroded their savings and pensions. Infirm or disabled people often outlive their savings at a time when their medical bills are soaring. Some get help from such public assistance programs as Supplemental Security Income, subsidized housing, Medicaid, and food stamps. Others, however, either are not eligible or for some other reason do not take part in these programs—often because they do not know what the programs offer or how to apply.

Our society's medical progress helps people to live longer; now we need to make economic progress to let them live better. To help the poor elderly who are simply continuing a lifelong pattern of poverty, we need social policies to address poverty for all age groups. To help those people who got by earlier in life but did not manage to save for their old age, we need insurance plans and programs to encourage saving. And to allay the risk of poverty resulting from the costs of long-term health care, we need a government-sponsored, self-supporting insurance program (Hurd, 1989).

### Living Arrangements

One stereotype pictures older people as living in institutions. On the contrary, almost 95 percent live in the community (U.S. Department of Health and Human Services, USDHHS, 1990). About two-thirds of these live in families—most with spouses, the rest with children or other relatives. (These last tend to be in poor health; they may have moved in with other family members because they cannot care for themselves.) The other one-third live alone or with nonrelatives. The probability of living alone rises with age (AARP, 1989; Commonwealth Fund Commission on Elderly People Living Alone, 1986) More women than men live alone (see Figure 17-1 on page 509).

The more than 8 million older people who live alone are at special risk. Almost 80 percent are women, 80 percent are widowed, and almost 50 percent have either no children or none living nearby. They are older and poorer on the average than elderly people who live with someone else. They are also more likely to be depressed and to worry about the future. Yet almost 90 percent value their independence and prefer to be on their own (Commonwealth Fund Commission on Elderly People Living Alone, 1986).

## BOX 17–2    WINDOW ON THE WORLD

# AGING AMONG AFRICAN AMERICANS, HISPANIC AMERICANS, AND OTHER AMERICAN MINORITY GROUPS

Many problems of aging are even more troublesome for African Americans and Hispanic Americans, who make up about 10 percent of the elderly population. First of all, they tend to be poorer. Almost one-third of older African Americans and one-fourth of older Hispanics have incomes below the poverty line (American Association of Retired Persons, AARP, 1986). They also tend to be sicker: they are more likely to fall ill and less likely to get treatment. They tend to be less educated, to have histories of unemployment or underemployment, to live in poorer housing, and to have a shorter life expectancy than white people (see Box 14-2). Although their need for social and medical services is greater, they often live in areas where services are least available.

A particular irony is that many minority-group workers do not get the social security and Medicare benefits they have earned. Often, after having contributed to these funds during their working years, they die too soon to collect benefits. This will become even more common after the year 2000, when social security benefits will not be available until age 67. Furthermore, since many jobs held by minority-group workers are not covered by social security, minority-group elderly people are more likely than others to be on Old Age Assistance.

Older people from various ethnic groups in the United States, and especially those who were born in other countries, often fail to take advantage of community and government services. They may not know what services are available; they may

be too proud to accept help because they think of it as charity; or they may not want, or may not have enough money, to seek services beyond their own neighborhoods. Also, they may feel uncomfortable dealing with people who do not understand their ways of doing things—their food, their family traditions, or their housing patterns. Agencies that serve older people, therefore, should be sensitive to these concerns and should reach out to the elderly in need when they do not seek help themselves (Gelfand, 1982).

Some minority subcultures differ from the dominant culture in patterns of family life and standards of behavior. Among Hispanic families, for example, older people have traditionally received a great deal of respect. In Hispanic families (as in African American families), grandparents have played an important role in child rearing and have exerted considerable influence over family decisions. In recent years, with assimilation, this pattern has been breaking down among Hispanic families, so that the relations between the generations are becoming more like those in the population as a whole. Still, Hispanic people show a strong extended-family pattern, and the position of the elderly remains relatively high. Mexican Americans, for example, have "strong helping networks with their children." But those who rely heavily on their children tend to have low levels of psychological well-being, possibly because of their dependency (Markides & Krause, 1986).

African American families also have extensive kinship networks,

through which the generations help each other with money, child care, advice, and other supports. This help usually adds to formal help from community and governmental agencies for the neediest family members (R. C. Gibson, 1986; Mindel, 1983).

Using data from the National Survey of Black Americans, a nationally representative cross-sectional sample aged 18 years and older, researchers analyzed answers from 581 respondents over age 55 on their state of well-being (Chatters, 1988). The happiest were, not surprisingly, those in better health, with higher incomes and more education, who were under relatively little stress from life problems. Married people were happier than widowed or separated people, but the health benefits of being married (seen in other studies) did not show up among these older African Americans. In this group, the oldest respondents were not, on the whole, less healthy than the youngest—a finding which may indicate a particularly robust cohort of very old black people. Perhaps reaching old age is in itself a test; those who do so demonstrate their hardiness. The women had more health problems but were no unhappier than the men, possibly because older women may expect and tolerate higher levels of disability.

Minority-group elderly people, then, are in many ways like the majority population. They do, however, have some special concerns, special needs, and special resources which policymakers and community service agencies need to keep in mind.

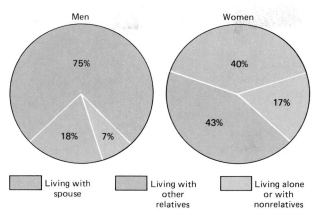

Men

75%

18%   7%

Women

40%

17%

43%

▨ Living with
spouse

▨ Living with
other
relatives

▨ Living alone
or with
nonrelatives

**FIGURE 17-1**
Living arrangements of noninstitutionalized people aged 65 and
over, 1988. (*Source*: American Association of Retired People,
AARP, 1989; based on data from U. S. Bureau of the Census.)

### Living independently

Fay's dream during the last years of her life, when she
was in a nursing home, was to live in a room in a private
home, so that she could regain her independence. But
because she needed a high level of care and her daughter could neither care for her herself nor find an appropriate house, Fay remained in the nursing home until
her death.

Most older people want to live in the community.
Those who do report higher levels of well-being than
those in institutions, even when their health is about
the same (Chappell & Penning, 1979). But living arrangements can become a major problem as people
age. A person may become too infirm to manage three
flights of rickety steps. A neighborhood may deteriorate, and frail-looking older people may become the
prey of young thugs. Mental or physical disability may
keep a person who lives alone from being able to manage.

Some older people in these situations go to an institution, but in recent years creative social planning has
enabled a growing number of older people to remain in
the community. Many elderly people do not need or
want to have their lives totally managed for them but
have an impairment that makes it hard, if not impossible, to manage entirely on their own. Relatively minor
forms of support—like meals, transportation, and
home health aides—can often help them stay in their
own homes. Older people usually want to stay in a familiar neighborhood, to be independent, to have privacy, to feel safe, and to have some social contacts (E.
M. Brody, 1978; Lawton, 1981).

A variety of living arrangements, some traditional
and some innovative, can help older people who fall between self-sufficiency and complete dependency (Hare
& Haske, 1983–1984; Lawton, 1981). These include:

- *Retirement and life-care communities.* Available
  only to well-off people, these often offer independent living units, with such services as cleaning,
  laundry, and meals. As residents age, they may use
  more extensive services, including health care in a
  nursing facility.
- *Sharing a house.* Social agencies match people who
  need a place to live with people who have houses or
  apartments with extra rooms. Each person usually
  has a private room but shares living, eating, and
  cooking areas.
- *Group homes.* A social agency that owns or rents a
  house brings together a small number of elderly residents and hires helpers to shop, cook, do heavy
  cleaning, drive the residents, and offer professional
  counseling. Residents care for their own personal
  needs and take some responsibility for day-to-day
  tasks.
- *Accessory housing.* Independent units ("granny
  flats") are created so that an older person can live in
  a remodeled single-family home or in temporary
  quarters set up on the property of a single-family
  home. These units provide privacy for both parties,
  cut travel time and expense for the caregivers, and
  offer security and care for the elderly residents.

Residents of group retirement homes enjoy socializing. They
also get help with shopping, cooking, and cleaning, while
caring for their own personal needs and maintaining a sense of
self-reliance. Such homes, usually run by social agencies, are
among an array of alternatives for elderly people who do not
need nursing care but are unable to be completely self-
sufficient.

BOX 17–3    PRACTICALLY SPEAKING

# VISITING SOMEONE IN A NURSING HOME

Visiting someone in a nursing home can be a wrenching experience. It is painful for family members to witness the deterioration of once-keen mental faculties, to hear complaints that may have less to do with what the resident is actually complaining about than with the physical and emotional losses she or he has suffered, and to feel the depths of the older person's depression. One survey of family visitors found that many of them enjoyed fewer than half of their visits, mostly for these reasons (York & Calsyn, 1977).

Visitors cannot change most of these realities, but they can do something about another major problem—a lack of anything to do. Even if nursing home residents have suffered mental and sensory losses, they can engage in stimulating and comforting activities. A visitor can adapt the following suggestions to a particular resident's level of functioning (B. W. Davis, 1985).

Visitors to residents of nursing homes can enliven their visits with stimulating activities that call on the older person's strengths, interests, and memories.

■ *Call on the older person's strengths.* Ask him or her for advice in an area of expertise, like cooking, fishing, or crafts.

■ *Provide the opportunity to make decisions.* Ask the resident where she or he wants to go if you are going out for lunch or for a drive; ask what she or he wants to wear; ask advice on a gift to buy for a family member.

■ *Be a good listener.* When the older person wants to talk, pay attention even if you have heard the stories before. Be patient. Do not judge or argue. Listen to the feelings beneath the words. Hear complaints as a sympathetic listener without feeling that you need to do anything about them.

■ *Call on the older person's reserves of memories.* A person who forgets what happened 5 minutes ago

may have vivid memories of the distant past. You might ask the resident to sing old songs with you; to tell you what his or her siblings were like; or to describe childhood celebrations, getting the first job, or meeting his or her spouse.

■ *Do a project together.* You could put together a scrapbook or a photo album, arrange flowers, make Christmas ornaments, do simple sewing or knitting, or do a jigsaw puzzle.

■ *Tape-record the older person.* You will be creating your own oral history to pass down to the older person's descendants. At the same time, the older person will probably appreciate the opportunity to review his or her life and to think about some of its high points. Questions you might ask could cover decisions and turning points in the person's life, achievements she or he is proud of, wisdom that can be passed along, and events that she or he experienced or witnessed.

■ *Stimulate the senses.* Enhance the older person's experience of the world. Wear and talk about bright colors. Bring in beautifully illustrated books and calendars, and put up seasonal decorations. Play favorite musical selections. Wear perfume or scented aftershave lotion and bring some for the resident. Bring favorite foods (that have been cleared with the nursing home staff). Most important—hug, hold hands, and touch the older person in comforting ways.

■ *Bring children to visit.* Older people are usually very happy to see young children, especially their own grandchildren or great-grandchildren. If you do bring children, take along something to keep them occupied.

Your visits are important to a person who lives in a nursing home, away from the familiar places and people of earlier life. You will enjoy them more yourself by following these guidelines.

Up to 40 percent of the people in nursing homes do not need nursing care but have no better way to manage (Baldwin, in Hinds, 1985). With the high cost of such care and the reluctance of people to enter nursing homes, there are both humane and economic reasons to explore alternative living arrangements.

### Living in institutions

The vast majority of older people do not live in institutions. Most do not want to, and most of their families do not want them to. Older people often feel that placement in an institution is a sign of rejection; and children usually place their parents reluctantly, apologetically, and with great guilt. Sometimes, though, because of an older person's needs or a family's circumstances, such placement seems to be the only solution.

***Who lives in nursing homes?*** Fewer than 1 out of 20 people over 65 live in nursing homes. This figure increases with age, however. Of people aged 65 to 74, only 1 in 80 are in nursing homes; but for people aged 75 to 84, the ratio increases to 1 in 17; and for people 85 and older, it soars to almost 1 in 4 (USDHHS, 1990). With the growing number of people over 85 in our population, the need for nursing homes and the costs of care in them will grow enormously in the coming years.

The single most important factor keeping people *out* of institutions is being married (Health Care Finance Administration, 1981). Most of the 1.5 million nursing home residents are widows, less than half can get around by themselves, more than half are mentally impaired, and one-third are incontinent (AARP, 1986; Moss & Halamandaris, 1977; Ouslander, 1989; U.S. Bureau of the Census, 1983). As the population ages and women's life expectancy continues to increase faster than men's, the number of nursing home residents is expected to swell. This will mean a need to build more homes and to finance them; nursing home care is very costly.

***What makes a good nursing home?*** One essential element in good care is opportunity for residents to make decisions and exert some control over their daily lives.

In one classic study, 91 nursing home residents were divided into two groups (Langer & Rodin, 1976). About half were told that they themselves were responsible for seeing that they got good care, for making decisions, and for changing things they did not like. They were also asked to choose and care for a plant. Those in the second group were told that the staff would care for them and make them happy. They were each handed a plant and told that the nurses would water and care for it. The results—judged by residents' questionnaires and nurses' ratings—were dramatic. In the group encouraged to take responsibility, 93 percent became more active, more alert, and happier. But in the group that had been encouraged to be passive, 71 percent became weaker and more disabled. These findings suggest that loss of control over one's life can lead to depression and even death.

Other essentials of a good nursing home are an experienced professional staff, specializing in care of the elderly; an adequate government insurance program; and a coordinated structure that can provide various levels of care as needed (Kayser-Jones, 1982). The ideal home should be lively, safe, hygienic, and attractive. It should offer stimulating activities and opportunities to socialize with people of both sexes and all ages. It should provide privacy so that (among other reasons) residents can be sexually active; and it should offer a full range of social, therapeutic, and rehabilitative services.

The best-quality care is provided by larger nonprofit facilities with a high ratio of nurses to nursing aides (Pillemer & Moore, 1989). Residents are happier in such places, and so are their visitors. (For suggestions on visiting someone in a nursing home, see Box 17-3 on the opposite page.)

***Problems in nursing homes*** In 1987, one-third of the nation's nursing homes did not meet minimum standards of legislation enacted that year, which could deny Medicare and Medicaid payments to nursing homes found substandard on three consecutive annual inspections.

A special horror is the abuse of elderly residents by staff members. In one telephone survey, 577 nurses and nurses' aides who worked in nursing homes told interviewers of many instances of abuse (Pillemer & Moore, 1989). More than one-third of the respondents (36 percent) had seen other staff members abusing patients physically—restraining them more than necessary; pushing, grabbing, shoving, pinching, slapping, hitting, or kicking them; or throwing things at them. Ten percent admitted having committed one or more of these acts themselves. Psychological abuse was even more common. Forty percent admitted committing it themselves, and eighty-one percent saw other staffers yell angrily at patients, insult them, swear at them, isolate them unnecessarily, threaten them, or refuse to give them food.

Furthermore, basic medical care is too often poor, with treatable conditions like depression and incontinence frequently misdiagnosed, drugs prescribed inappropriately, and patients kept oversedated and neglected. To improve care, more doctors need education in geriatrics, reimbursement policies are needed to offer incentives to health care workers for good long-term care, more mental health practitioners need to be involved, and systems should be set up to monitor prescription of medicines and other practices (Ouslander, 1989).

### Abuse of the Elderly

A shocking way for aging people to spend their final days is in the state of maltreatment known as **elder abuse**—neglect, or physical or psychological abuse, of dependent older persons. Although (as we describe above) it can occur in institutions, it is most often suffered by frail elderly people living with their spouses or their children.

Such abuse can take the form of neglect, as in the withholding of food, shelter, clothing, medical care, money, or other assets. It can involve psychological torment: tongue-lashings, insults, swearing, or threats of violence or abandonment. It can also take the form of actual physical violence—beating, punching, shoving, burning, or using weapons against old people who cannot protect themselves.

Because of problems in defining elder abuse, as well as in reporting it, estimates of the number of cases per year vary from 600,000 to over 1 million; it is believed to involve about 4 percent of the older population (Eastman, 1984). Elder abuse is probably as underreported as child abuse and violence between younger spouses; a study in the Boston area suggests that only 1 case in 14 reaches public attention (Pillemer & Finkelhor, 1988).

According to the findings of the Boston study, the typical victim is an old person in poor health who lives with someone. Elderly people living alone—whether widowed, divorced, or never married—are at low risk. The abuser is more likely to be a spouse than a child, reflecting the fact that more older people live with spouses than with children. Although many older men are abused, abuse against women inflicts more injuries. Rates of abuse are no higher for minority elderly people, the poor, or people over age 75.

One way to help these victims is, when appropriate, to recognize elder abuse as a type of domestic violence. Outsiders will then be more likely to identify cases of abuse, and the elderly themselves will be aware that they do not have to put up with mistreatment.

Both victim and abuser need treatment (Hooyman, Rathbone-McCuan, & Klingbeil, 1982; Pillemer & Finkelhor, 1988). Procedures have to be developed to identify and report abuse and to protect the victims by establishing safe places for them, perhaps in special apartments. Self-help groups may help victims acknowledge what is happening and find out how to stop it or get away from it. The abusers need treatment to recognize what they are doing and to reduce the stress of caregiving, especially when they are in poor health themselves. Some services offer caregivers education, emotional support, counseling, financial assistance, and substitute care to give them respite for a day, a weekend, or a week.

## PERSONAL RELATIONSHIPS IN LATE LIFE

Most older people's lives are enriched by the presence of people who care about them and to whom they feel close.

The family is still the primary source of emotional support, and the late-life family has its own special characteristics (Brubaker, 1983). First of all, it is likely to be multigenerational. Most older people's families include at least three generations; many span four or five. The presence of so many people is enriching but also creates special pressures. Second, the late-life family has a long history, which also has its pluses and minuses. Long experience of coping with stresses can give older people confidence in dealing with whatever life sends their way. On the other hand, many elderly people are still resolving unfinished business of childhood or early adulthood. Third, a number of life events are especially typical of (though not confined to) older families: becoming a grandparent or great-grandparent, retiring from work, and losing a spouse to death.

Personal relationships, especially with the family, continue to be important into very old age (past 85) (D. Field & Minkler, 1988). Let's look at the relationships older people have with people of their own generation—spouses, siblings, and friends—and with their children and grandchildren. We'll also examine the lives of older adults who are divorced or widowed, have never married, and are childless.

### MARRIAGE

"One wonderful thing about being married now," said Sylvia, 79, "is that Jake and I can have a 'show and tell' session every morning when we tell each other about our aches and pains and know that the other one really cares how we feel. Then we can go through the day without boring anyone else with them!"

The long-term marriage is a relatively novel phenomenon; most marriages, like most people, used to have a shorter life span. Many men lost one or more wives in childbirth; and both wives and husbands often succumbed young to disease. Today, fiftieth anniversaries are more common, though many marriages are still severed earlier by death or divorce. Because women usually marry older men and usually live longer than men, many more men than women live with their spouses (refer back to Figure 17-1, page 509).

## Marital Happiness

Married couples who are still together in their sixties are more likely than middle-aged couples to report their marriage as satisfying, and many say that their marriage has gotten better over the years (Gilford, 1986). One likely reason is that, since divorce has been easier to obtain for some years, spouses who are still together late in life have chosen to be together. The decision to divorce usually comes early in a marriage; partners who stay together despite difficulties are often able to work out their differences and eventually arrive at a mutually satisfying relationship. Another possible reason why older people report more satisfaction with marriage is that people of this age are more satisfied with life in general. Their satisfaction may stem from factors outside the marriage—work, the end of child rearing, or more money in the bank. Also, people may say that their marriage is happy as a conscious or unconscious justification for having stayed in it so long.

In a study of 17 marriages that had lasted from 50 to 69 years, nearly three-fourths were described—on the basis of interviews and observations over 50 years—as following one of two patterns: either basically happy over the years or happiest early and late with a dip in the middle (usually the child-rearing years). None of the marriages showed either a continuous increase or continuous decline in happiness (Weishaus & Field, 1988).

People over 70 consider themselves less happily married than those aged 63 to 69; perhaps advancing age and physical ills aggravate the strains on marriage. Also, women, who generally expect more warmth and intimacy from marriage than men do, tend to be less satisfied with marriage (Gilford, 1986).

## Strengths and Strains in Late-Life Marriage

Being in love is still important for successful marriage in late adulthood. Older spouses also value companionship and open expression of feelings, as well as respect and common interests. But problems may arise from differences in values, interests, and philosophies (Stinnett, Carter, & Montgomery, 1972).

Many couples who are still together late in life, especially in the middle to late sixties, say that they are happier in marriage now than they were in their younger years. The most rewarding aspects of marriage include companionship and the ability to express feelings. Romance, fun, and sensuality have their place, too, as this couple in a hot tub demonstrate.

A new freedom comes about as husband and wife shed the roles of breadwinner and child rearer, as they become more interested in each other's personality, and as they increasingly enjoy one another's company (Zube, 1982). Further, the ability of married people to handle the ups and downs of late adulthood with relative serenity may result from their mutual supportiveness. This reflects three important benefits of marriage: intimacy (both sexual and emotional), interdependence (sharing of tasks and resources), and the partners' sense of belonging to each other (Atchley, 1985; Gilford, 1986).

The success of a marriage in late life may depend on the couple's ability to adjust to the personality changes of middle age, which often lead women and men in opposite directions (Zube, 1982). As the husband becomes less involved with work and more interested in intimacy, the wife may be more interested in personal growth and self-expression. In changing roles, couples may argue over household chores or the like. And late-life marriages are often severely tested by one spouse's ill health. People who have to care for disabled spouses may feel isolated, angry, and frustrated, especially since they may be in poor health themselves (Gilford, 1986).

man, on his part, has to buy many of the services his wife provided. When both spouses have been employed, the loss of one income can be a major blow (Lopata, 1977, 1979). Women who have prepared themselves financially for widowhood—as by discussing pensions and insurance with their husbands—are better able to adjust after widowhood, partly, of course, because they understand their finances, but also because of the comforting feeling that their husbands loved them enough to help them plan for the future (O'Bryant & Morgan, 1989).

Like any life crisis, widowhood affects people differently, depending on personality and circumstances. It always takes time for the pain of loss to heal (see Chapter 18), but people can prepare better for widowhood (and for life in general) if they begin early to develop a strong sense of their own identity and a sturdy measure of self-sufficiency. A woman is less likely to be devastated by her husband's death if she is used to pursuing her own interests and knows how to manage the financial and practical details of her life. A man will cope better if he knows how to cook, do laundry, and make social plans.

### Living as a Widow or Widower

The people who adjust best to widowhood are those who keep busy, develop new roles (as by taking on new paid or volunteer work), or become more deeply involved in activities. They see friends often (which helps more than frequent visits with their children), and they take part in community programs like support groups for widows (Balkwell, 1981; C. J. Barrett, 1978; Vachon, Lyall, Rogers, Freedmen-Letofky, & Freeman, 1980).

Most widows, however, do not join organizations; they rely on their own informal support systems. The loneliest widows are those who have few or no children, who are in poor health, who lost their husbands suddenly or unexpectedly or at a relatively early age, who have been widowed for less than 6 years, or who have few friends or social activities (Lopata, Heinemann, & Baum, 1982).

Many studies have found older people to be better adjusted to widowhood than younger people, but often the investigators have not considered the length of time a person has been widowed. One study, which did take this factor into account, found that being widowed early does *not* generally have a long-term effect on morale. Nor is it easier or harder to lose a husband or wife at an earlier or a later age—grief is grief, no matter when the

Widowhood affects people differently, depending on personality and circumstances. It always takes time for the pain of loss to heal, but people who adjust best are those who have a sense of their own individual identity and a sturdy measure of self-sufficiency. The loneliness is still there, but the man who can, for example, keep house for himself and make social plans will be less disoriented by the loss of his wife.

loss occurs. Older widows and widowers interviewed did tend to have somewhat higher morale than younger ones, no matter how long they had been widowed; this led the investigator to suggest that the crucial factor might be availability of companions, especially widowed peers (Balkwell, 1985).

*Quality* of relationships may be more important than frequency of contact. Different relationships serve different purposes; a widow is more likely to seek out her children when she is worried or depressed but will turn to her brothers or sisters for financial help (T. B. Anderson, 1984).

## REMARRIAGE

After Norah's friend Alice died, Alice's widowed husband moved out of town. Some years later, back in town on a visit, he called on Norah, now widowed herself, and took her to lunch. She recalls:

> We began to write, and he called me up. Before I knew it, we decided to get married. I guess I didn't think I ever would [get married]. I didn't think I wanted to. [But] as he came, I kind of missed him when he didn't come, see? The more we saw of each other, the better we liked each other. It just worked into something. (Vinick, 1978, p. 361)

Norah's story is unusual—but her new husband's is not. Elderly widowers are more likely to remarry than widows, and men of any age are more likely than women to remarry after divorce. Men have more potential partners. Furthermore, they usually feel more need to remarry; women can handle their own household needs, are sometimes reluctant to give up survivors' pension rights, or do not want to end up caring for an infirm husband.

In one study of 24 older couples who had remarried when both partners were over 60, most had been widowed rather than divorced, and most had known each other during their first marriages or had been introduced by friends or relatives (Vinick, 1978). Why had these people decided to marry again? Men were more likely to mention companionship and relief from loneliness as reasons for remarrying, while women tended to mention their feelings toward their husbands or their husbands' personal qualities. Almost all these people—who had been remarried for 2 to 6 years—were happy. These marriages were calmer than marriages earlier in life; the partners had a "live and let live" attitude.

Besides enhancing married couples' lives, remarriage can make society's burden lighter, since older married people are less likely than older people living alone to need help from community agencies or to enter institutions. It would be wise on pragmatic as well as humanitarian grounds to encourage remarriage by letting people keep their pensions and social security benefits (or at least to encourage shared living like group housing).

## SINGLE LIFE: THE "NEVER MARRIEDS"

Only about 5 percent of older men and women have never married (see Figure 17-2). These people may constitute a "distinct type of social personality" that does not need or want such intimacy (Gubrium, 1975).

When 22 never-married people, aged 60 to 94, were interviewed about their attitude toward getting old, they expressed less loneliness than the typical person of their age. They also seemed to be less affected by aging; they were more independent, had fewer social relationships, and were generally satisfied with life.

Never-married women do not become lonely with the loss of friends and family, but they do feel lonely if they lose their health (Essex & Nam, 1987). Poor health undermines their sense of self-reliance and independence and may shove them into dependent relationships with relatives they would rather not be with.

## SEXUAL RELATIONSHIPS

Comments about sexuality in late life often reflect one of two attitudes: "Aren't they cute?" or "Dirty old man (or woman)." One of our most prevalent stereotypes has been that older people are sexless and should be sexless, and that those who are not are perverted. However, researchers who have studied older adults' sexual behavior have found that sexuality can be a vital force throughout life.

Human beings are sexual beings from birth until death; and even though illness or frailty may prevent older people from acting on sexual feelings, the feelings persist. People can express sexuality in many ways other than genital contact—in touching, in closeness, in affection, in intimacy. An active sexual relationship assures each partner of the other's love and affection and assures both of their own continuing vitality.

The physical aspect of sex was not scientifically recognized as a normal element of the lives of older people until the 1960s, with the pioneering research of William H. Masters and Virginia E. Johnson and the findings of the Duke University Longitudinal Study. More recent reports also indicate a rich diversity of sexual experience well into late adulthood (Brecher & the Editors of Consumer Reports Books, 1984; B. D. Starr & Weiner, 1981).

After interviewing men and women over age 60, Masters and Johnson (1966, 1981) concluded that people who have active sexual lives during their younger years are likely to remain sexually active in later life. The most important factor in maintaining sexuality is consistent sexual activity over the years. A healthy man who has been sexually active can usually continue some form of active sexual expression into his seventies or eighties, and women are physiologically able to be sexually active as long as they live. The major barrier to a fulfilling sexual life for older women is lack of a partner.

those who have an active circle of friends are happier (Babchuk, 1978–1979; Lemon et al., 1972).

Well into old age, even past 85, women continue to see their friends about as much, or more often, and feel the same way about them. Older men see friends less, see them more in group activities rather than on an intimate one-to-one basis, and consider friendship less important (D. Field & Minkler, 1988). Although family members provide more reliable emotional support, older people enjoy time spent with their friends more than time spent with their families.

In one study, 92 retired adults (52 women and 40 men) between ages 55 and 88 wore beepers for 1 week. At about 2-hour intervals, they were paged; then they filled out reports on what they were doing and with whom, and what they were thinking and feeling (Lar-

special flavor. Friends are a powerful source of *immediate* enjoyment, while the family provides a greater underlying sense of security and support.

Other studies have emphasized different aspects of friendship: common interests, social involvement, and mutual help (R. G. Adams, 1986). Intimacy is important to older adults, who need to know that they are still valued and wanted despite physical and other losses. This is especially true for formerly married women (Essex & Nam, 1987). Friends and neighbors often take the place of family members who are far away.

Friends are a bulwark against the impact of stress on physical and mental health (Cutrona, Russell, & Rose, 1986). People who can confide their feelings and thoughts and can talk about their worries and pain with friends deal better with the changes and crises of aging (Genevay, 1986; Lowenthal & Haven, 1968).

Older people often enjoy the time they spend with friends more than the time they spend with family members. The openness and excitement of relationships with friends help older men and women rise above worries and problems. Intimate friendships give older people a sense of being valued and wanted and help them deal with the changes and crises of aging.

Sexual relationships can be a vital part of life in late adulthood; they are by no means only a memory or an occasional foray into pleasures of the past. People who were sexually active when younger usually continue to be sexually active in late life, if partners are available. Sexuality can be expressed in closeness, touching, affection, and intimacy as well as sexual intercourse.

Sex is, of course, different in late adulthood from what it was earlier. Older people feel less sexual tension, usually have less frequent sexual relations, and experience less intensity. The sexual flush and increased muscle tone that accompany arousal are still present, but to a lesser degree. Older men take longer to develop an erection and longer to ejaculate and have lower levels of the male sex hormone testosterone than

ual functioning; and when such a drug must be taken, the patient should be alerted about its effects. Professionals should matter-of-factly discuss sexual activity—for example, with a heart patient who may be embarrassed to ask about it.

## RELATIONSHIPS WITH SIBLINGS

"When I die, don't you dare let my brother Pete come to my funeral," Sally's elderly mother told her daughter. "If he won't make up while I'm alive, I don't want him to do it after I'm dead." But another brother intervened as a peacemaker, and Leah and Pete reestablished the close ties they had known before a misunderstanding estranged them painfully for years. In their last years of life they were a source of great comfort to each other.

Sibling relationships are the longest-lasting ties in most people's lives. Since more than 75 percent of people aged 65 and older have at least one sibling, brothers and sisters play important roles in the support networks of older people (Scott & Roberto, 1981).

The small body of research on elderly siblings suggests that they have the same kinds of relationships they had in middle age: they see each other just as often and are just as involved (D. Field & Minkler, 1988). In fact, after establishing their own identities through career and family, they often become closer in early or middle adulthood than they were while growing up together. They often make special efforts to renew ties after their children leave home, and earlier rivalry is often offset by closeness and affection (Cicirelli, 1980; H. G. Ross, Dalton, & Milgram, 1980; Scott & Roberto, 1981).

Looking back, older people who feel close to their

---

In general, older people are less anxious about death than middle-aged people (Bengtson, Cuellar, & Ragan, 1975). Through the years, as people lose friends and relatives, they gradually reorganize their thoughts and feelings to accept their own mortality. Also, their physical problems and some of the other troubles of old age may diminish their pleasure in living. Those who feel that their lives have been meaningful are usually more able to accept the prospect of death than those who are still wondering about the point of having lived at all.

Some—like the 82-year-old woman who wrote the following lines within a few days before her second, and fatal, heart attack—have very complex feelings:

> . . . I refuse to believe I am a piece of dust scuttering through uncaring space. I believe I count—that I have work to do—that there is need of me. I have a place. I want to live. The moment is Now—Now is my forever. I am still somebody—somebody on whom nothing is lost. With my last breath, I sing a psalm. (Duskin, personal communication, February 1986)

Acknowledgment of death may be mixed with affirmation of the preciousness of the life that is slipping away.

## CONFRONTING ONE'S OWN DEATH

How do people face the approach of their own death? By what processes do they accept the fact that their life will soon end? What kinds of psychological changes do they undergo when death is imminent? Professionals have closely observed persons close to death and have evolved theories to explain some of the psychological changes that occur as death approaches.

### Changes Preceding Death

Psychological changes often begin to take place even before there are any physiological signs that a person is dying. In Chapter 16, we noted that a terminal drop in intellectual functioning often appears shortly before death. Other changes, too, may show up during the terminal period.

#### Personality changes

In one study, 80 people aged 65 to 91 were given batteries of psychological tests and followed over a 3-year period. Afterward, the researchers compared the scores of subjects who had died within a year after the last testing session with the scores of subjects who had lived an average of 3 years beyond that session (Lieberman & Coplan, 1970).

The subjects who had died within the year had lower scores on cognitive tests. They were also less introspective and more docile. Those who were dealing with some sort of crisis and were close to death were more afraid of and more preoccupied with death than people who were beset by similar crises but were not close to death. (Persons who were close to death but whose lives were relatively stable at the time showed neither special fear of death nor preoccupation with it.)

These observations suggest a psychosomatic relationship, in which physiological changes in the body are related to psychological changes, and vice versa. The changes are not simply effects of disease, since people who recovered from acute illnesses did not show the same pattern of personality decline as people who later died from the same kinds of illnesses. The people in this study talked quite freely about death. Many had worked out a personal meaning for death and had integrated it into their outlook on life.

#### Near-death experiences

Many people who have come close to death from drowning, cardiac arrest, or other causes have reported **near-death experiences.** These experiences often include a feeling of well-being, a new clarity of thinking, a sense of being out of one's body, and visions of bright lights. Three ways in which such experiences have been explained are as a prediction of a state of bliss after death (the *transcendental* theory); as a result of biological states that accompany the process of dying (the *physiological* theory); and as a response to the perceived threat of death (the *psychological* theory).

A recent study of such experiences, both in people who actually did come close to death and in others who only thought that they were close to death, found some support for all three theories (J. E. Owens, Cook, & Stevenson, 1990). Researchers studied the medical records and personal accounts of 28 hospital patients who would have died if doctors had not saved them, and of 30 who mistakenly thought they were in danger of dying. The two groups of patients had very similar sensations, a finding that lends support to the psychological theory. But those who had actually been near death reported near-death experiences more often—evidence for the physiological theory. And the researchers saw support for the transcendental theory in the fact that the dying patients reported clearer thinking, despite the likelihood that their brain functioning was in fact diminished. This intriguing area of research will probably be explored in more depth in the future.

# POSTPONING DEATH

Is there such a thing as a will to live? Can people postpone their own death so that they can celebrate a birthday, an anniversary, a grandchild's wedding, or some other meaningful event? Recent studies suggest that some people can. Researchers have looked at patterns of deaths around two important holidays, each of which appeals strongly to one ethnic group and not to others, who can thus serve as control groups.

One is the Jewish holiday of Passover, when more than 75 percent of American Jews attend a *seder* (a ceremonial dinner), usually conducted at home with close family members (D. P. Phillips & King, 1988). The other is the Chinese Harvest Moon Festival, when the senior woman of the house directs a ceremonial meal in her home (D. P. Phillips & Smith, 1990). This holiday emphasizes the symbolic importance of older women and is more important to them than to young women or to men of any age. Passover usually falls near Easter (the last supper of Jesus and the disciples is said to have been a seder), and the Harvest Moon Festival occurs in autumn. But the timing of each changes from year to year by as much as 4 weeks.

In two studies, both conducted in California, death rates from natural causes were lower just before the holiday for the people to whom the holiday meant most, and higher just afterward. It seems as if some people who are close to death put forth every ounce of psychological and physical strength to stay alive for just one more celebration.

Jewish people showed a death rate lower than expected just before Passover and a higher death rate just after it. The effect was strongest when Passover fell on a weekend, when more people were expected to celebrate it; it was not affected by the specific date of the holiday (D. P. Phillips & King, 1988). The same pattern held true for elderly Chinese women, whose death rate was unusually low before the Harvest Moon Festival and unusually high afterwards (D. P. Phillips & Smith, 1990). The pattern held for the three leading causes of death—heart disease, cancer, and stroke.

The "Passover effect" was especially strong among Jewish men, who have usually led the seder service. It was not found in African Americans, in Asians, or in Jewish infants (none of whom celebrate Passover). The

"Harvest Moon" effect did not appear among Jewish people or the general population, or among elderly Chinese men or younger Chinese women. It showed up only among women over age 75, the group to whom this holiday meant the most.

How might this effect work? It is not likely that stress or overeating causes high postholiday death rates, because these causes would not explain the very much lower death rates before the holidays. Perhaps psychosomatic processes let some people postpone death until they have reached an occasion important to them. In other words, they can will themselves to live just a little while longer.

A variant of this effect has also shown up in two former presidents of the United States who died on the Fourth of July. Thomas Jefferson's last words were "Is it the Fourth?"

If health professionals and family members can develop strategies to emphasize the importance of certain occasions or to create new occasions, patients may be inspired to set goals for living to meet future events.

## Stages of Dying:
## Elisabeth Kübler-Ross

Elisabeth Kübler-Ross, a psychiatrist who works with dying people, is widely credited with having inspired the current interest in the psychology of death and dying. She found that most patients welcome an opportunity to speak openly about their condition, and that most are aware of being close to death even when they have not been told how sick they are.

After speaking with some 500 terminally ill patients, Kübler-Ross (1969, 1970) outlined, and gave examples to illustrate, each of five stages in coming to terms with death: (1) denial (refusal to accept the reality of what is happening); (2) anger; (3) bargaining for extra time (see Box 18-1); (4) depression; and (5) ultimate acceptance (see Table 18-1 on pages 536–537). She also proposed a similar progression in the feelings of people facing imminent bereavement (Kübler-Ross, 1975).

## BOX 18-2 (CONTINUED)

■ By tearing their clothes (or wearing a symbolic strip of black cloth) before the funeral, mourners symbolize severing the relationship with the person who has died.

■ The funeral is not ostentatious; and it is realistic, to prevent mourners from denying the implications of death. The simple coffin (often a plain pine box) is kept closed. Children who were close to the deceased are likely to be there. The eulogy lets mourners

reflect on their loss and pour out their grief in tears.

■ At the cemetery, mourners shovel dirt into the grave themselves. This final act of love and concern helps put the loved one to rest.

■ The year of mourning corresponds roughly to the stages of grief: "three days of deep grief, seven days of mourning, thirty days of gradual readjustment, and eleven months of remembrance and healing" (A. Gordon, 1975, p. 51). As

they visit with each other and with friends throughout the week of *shiva*, mourners share memories of the deceased, talk about the death itself, and vent their emotions, while being reminded that life goes on. During the following year, the bereaved are gradually drawn back into the life of the community. At the end of the year, a ceremonial unveiling of the headstone signals the formal end of the mourning period.

### "Grief work": A three-phase pattern

Grieving usually (but not always) follows a fairly predictable pattern. The bereaved person must accept the painful reality of the loss, gradually let go of the bond with the dead person, readjust to life without that person, and develop new interests and relationships. This process of "grief work" generally takes place in three phases—though, as with Kübler-Ross's stages, they may vary (J. T. Brown & Stoudemire, 1983; Schulz, 1978):

1 *Shock and disbelief.* The initial phase, which may take several weeks (especially after a sudden or unexpected death), is shock and disbelief. This may protect the bereaved from intense reactions. Survivors often feel lost, dazed, and confused. Shortness of breath, tightness in the chest or throat, nausea, and a feeling of emptiness in the abdomen are common. As awareness of the loss sinks in, the initial numbness gives way to overwhelming feelings of sadness, often expressed by frequent crying.

2 *Preoccupation with the memory of the person who has died.* The second phase, preoccupation with memories of the dead person, may last 6 months or longer. The survivor tries to come to terms with the death but cannot yet accept it. Frequent crying continues; and insomnia, fatigue, and loss of appetite are common. A widow, for example, may relive her husband's death and their entire relationship, going over all the details in her mind and in conversation, in an obsessive search for the meaning of his death. From time to time, she may be seized by a feeling

that her dead husband is present: she will hear his voice, sense his presence in the room, even see his face before her. She may have vivid dreams of him. These experiences diminish with time, though they may recur—perhaps for years—on such occasions as the anniversary of the marriage or of the death.

3 *Resolution.* The final phase, resolution, has arrived when the bereaved person resumes interest in everyday activities—when memories of the dead person bring fond feelings mingled with sadness, rather than sharp pain and longing. A widower, for instance, may still miss his dead wife; but he knows that life must go on, and he becomes more active socially, getting out more, seeing people, resuming old interests, and perhaps discovering new ones. Many survivors feel a surge of strength and are proud to have recovered.

### Other patterns of grieving

Recently, mental health professionals have found considerable differences in people's reactions to bereavement. The resolution of grief does not necessarily follow a straight line from shock to resolution, and mourning may continue for years, surfacing on anniversaries or other dates that are important to the bereaved person.

In reviewing studies of reactions to a major loss—not only the death of a loved one but also a loss of a different nature, paralysis induced by spinal injury—one team of psychologists found that some common assumptions seem to be more myth than fact (Wortman & Silver, 1989).

Five common beliefs about loss are (1) that everyone who suffers a severe loss will be distraught and probably depressed; (2) that people who do not show such distress will have psychological problems later on; (3) that a bereaved person has to "work through" a loss by focusing on it and trying to make sense of it; (4) that the intense distress of mourning will come to an end within a fairly short period of time; and (5) that people will eventually accept a loss, both intellectually and emotionally. According to these researchers, none of these beliefs seems valid.

*First,* they say, depression is not universal. From 3 weeks to 2 years after their loss, only from 15 to 35 percent of widows, widowers, and victims of spinal cord injury showed signs of depression. *Second,* failure to show distress at the outset does not necessarily lead to problems later on. In fact, the subjects who were most upset immediately were likely to be most troubled up to 2 years later. *Third,* not everyone needs to work through a loss or will benefit from working through it. The subjects who worked through their loss intensely at the beginning sometimes had more problems later on. *Fourth,* not everyone returns to normal functioning soon. Various follow-up studies have found that many normal children whose fathers died in wars still showed emotional and behavioral problems 3½ years later; that parents of children killed by drunk drivers were likely to be functioning poorly up to 7 years later; and that more than 40 percent of widows and widowers showed moderate to severe anxiety up to 4 years after the spouse's death, especially if it had been sudden. *Fifth,* people cannot always resolve their grief and accept their loss. Parents and spouses of people who die in car accidents often have painful memories of the loved one even after many years. And when people paralyzed by a spinal injury were interviewed 38 years after the injury, many still thought about and missed the things they could no longer do (Wortman & Silver, 1989).

This research has found three main patterns of grieving. In the expected pattern, the mourner goes from high to low distress; in a second pattern, the mourner does not experience intense distress immediately or later; in a third pattern, the mourner remains distressed for a long time (Wortman & Silver, 1989).

## Helping People Deal with Dying and Bereavement

### Implications of research

Identifying the strengths—better coping styles, a particular religious or philosophical outlook, or other personal resources—that help some people mourn with less distress may help others to cope better with loss.

Also, it may be unnecessary and even harmful to encourage or try to force mourners to "work through" a loss by experiencing anger, guilt, and depression. And recognition that grief may have a very long life may enable long-term mourners to get help without being considered "sick." By respecting different patterns of grief, professionals and laypeople alike can help people deal with loss without imposing the additional burden of making them feel that their reactions are abnormal.

With the growing realization that people can face death better if they understand it and get help to deal with it, several movements have arisen to help make dying and bereavement more humane. These include programs of grief therapy and death education, hospices to care for the terminally ill, and support groups and services for dying people and their families.

### Grief therapy

Most bereaved people are able, with the help of family and friends, to work through their grief and to resume normal lives. For some, however, **grief therapy**—a program to help the bereaved cope with their losses—is indicated (Schulz, 1978).

Professional grief therapists focus on helping bereaved people express their sorrow and their feelings of loss, guilt, hostility, and anger. They encourage their clients to review their relationships with the deceased and to integrate the fact of the death into their lives so that they can be freed to develop new relationships and new ways of behaving toward surviving friends and relatives.

There are also organizations—such as Widow to Widow, Catholic Widow and Widowers Club, and Compassionate Friends (for parents of children who have died)—which provide nonprofessional grief therapy, emphasizing the practical and emotional help that one person who has lost someone close can give to another.

### Death education

"Why did my guinea pig die?" "When will it be alive again?" "How much should I tell terminally ill patients about their true situation?" These are just a few of the questions dealt with in **death education:** programs aimed at various age levels and groups to teach people about dying and grief and to help them deal with these issues in their personal and professional lives.

It is important for people to explore their own attitude toward death, to become familiar with the ways in which various cultures deal with death, and to be sensitive to its emotional ramifications, both for dying people and for survivors. Courses about death are offered to

ment to make children conform to a set standard of conduct. Compare with *authoritative parents* and *permissive parents*. (228)

**authoritative parents** In Baumrind's terminology, parents whose child-rearing style blends respect for a child's individuality with an effort to instill social values in the child. Compare with *authoritarian parents* and *permissive parents*. (228)

**autonomy** Independence; self-determination. (147)

**autonomy versus shame and doubt** According to Erikson, the second critical pair of alternatives in psychosocial development (from 12–18 months to 3 years), in which toddlers develop a balance of autonomous control (independence, self-determination) over shame and doubt. (147)

**autosomes** The 22 pairs of nonsex chromosomes. (42)

**avoidant attachment** Pattern of attachment in which an infant rarely cries when separated from the primary caregiver and avoids contact upon his or her return. (159)

**basic trust versus basic mistrust** According to Erikson's theory, the first critical balancing of alternatives in psychosocial development (from birth to 12–18 months), in which the infant develops a sense of whether or not the world can be trusted; the quality of interaction with the mother in feeding is a primary determinant of the outcome of this stage. (146)

**battered child syndrome** Pattern of child abuse and neglect first identified in 1962. (166)

**Bayley Scales of Infant Development** Standardized test for measuring the intellectual development of infants; the test consists of a mental scale and a motor scale, each of which yields a development quotient (DQ), computed by comparing what a particular baby can do at a certain age with the performance of a large number of previously observed babies at the same age. (119)

**behaviorism** School of psychology that emphasizes the study of observable behaviors and events and the role of environment in causing behavior. (27)

**behavior modification** Therapeutic approach using principles of learning theory to encourage desired behaviors or eliminate undesired ones; also called *behavior therapy*. (227)

**bereavement** Loss due to death, which leads to a change in the survivor's status (for example, from wife to widow). (538)

**birth trauma** Birth-related brain injury caused by oxygen deprivation, mechanical injury, or infection or disease at birth. (88)

**Brazelton Neonatal Behavioral Assessment Scale** Neurological and behavioral test to measure neonates' response to the environment; it assesses interactive behaviors, motor behaviors, physiological control, and response to stress. (88)

**bulimia nervosa** Eating disorder in which a person regularly eats huge quantities of food and then purges the body by laxatives or induced vomiting; most common in young women. (318)

**burnout** Syndrome of emotional exhaustion and a sense that one can no longer accomplish anything on the job, often experienced by people in the helping professions. (441)

**career consolidation** Stage, described by Vaillant, occurring between the twenties and forties and characterized by preoccupation with strengthening one's career. (399)

**case studies** Scientific studies, each covering a single case or life, based on notes taken by observers or on published biographical materials. (12)

**castration anxiety** Phenomenon described by Freud in which a male child, seeing that girls do not have a penis and overwhelmed by guilt about his Oedipal feelings and fear of his father's power, becomes fearful that he will be castrated by his father. (212)

**causality** Piagetian term for the recognition that certain events cause other events. (121)

**centration** In Piaget's theory, a limitation of preoperational thought that leads the child to focus on one aspect of a situation and neglect others, often leading to illogical conclusions. (190)

**cephalocaudal principle** Principle that development proceeds in a head-to-toe direction, i.e., that upper parts of the body develop before lower parts. (94)

**cerebral cortex** Upper layer of the brain, responsible for thinking and problem solving. (83)

**cesarean delivery** Delivery of a baby by surgical removal from the uterus. (72)

**child abuse** Maltreatment of a child involving physical injury, neglect, or psychological harm. (166)

**childhood depression** Affective disorder characterized by a child's inability to form and maintain friendships, have fun, concentrate, and display normal emotional reactions. (297)

**chorionic villus sampling** Prenatal diagnostic procedure in which tissue from villi (hairlike projections of the membrane surrounding the embryo) is analyzed for birth defects. (54)

**chromosomes** Segments of DNA that carry the genes, the transmitters of heredity; in the normal human being, there are 46 chromosomes. (43)

**circular reactions** In Piaget's terminology, processes by which the infant learns to reproduce desired occurrences originally discovered by chance. Piaget described three types of circular reactions: primary, secondary, and tertiary. (122)

**classical conditioning** Kind of learning in which a previously neutral stimulus (a neutral stimulus is one that does not elicit a particular response) acquires the power to elicit a response after the stimulus is repeatedly associated with another stimulus that ordinarily does elicit the response. (27, 114)

**climacteric** Period of 2 to 5 years during which a woman's body undergoes physiological changes that bring on menopause. (431)

**cognitive development** Changes in thought processes that result in a growing ability to acquire and use knowledge. (31, 120)

**cognitive play** Forms of play that reveal and enhance children's cognitive development. (234)

**cohabitation** Living together and maintaining a sexual relationship without being legally married. (414)

**cohort** People growing up in the same place at the same time. (8)

**commitment** Marcia's term for personal investment in an occupation or system of beliefs (one of two elements crucial in identity formation; see also *crisis*) (344)

**componential element** In Sternberg's triarchic theory, the analytic aspect of intelligence, which determines how efficiently people process information and solve problems. (383)

**concordant** In genetics, similar with respect to a trait. (56)

**concrete operations** Third stage of Piagetian cognitive development (approximately from age 5–7 to age 11), during which children develop logical but not abstract thinking. (248)

**conditioned response** In classical conditioning, a response that comes to be elicited by a conditioned stimulus. (28, 114)

**conditioned stimulus** In classical conditioning, an initially neutral stimulus that, after repeated pairing with an unconditioned stimulus, elicits a response similar to that elicited by the unconditioned stimulus. (28, 114)

**conservation** In Piaget's terminology, awareness that two objects of equal size remain equal in the face of perceived alteration (for example, a change in shape) so long as nothing has been added to or taken away from either object. (190, 249)

**contextual element** In Sternberg's triarchic theory, the practical aspect of intelligence, which determines how effectively people deal with their environment. (383)

**control group** In an experiment, a group of people who are similar to the people in the experimental group but who do not receive the treatment whose effects are to be measured. The results obtained with the control group are compared with the results obtained with the experimental group. (18)

**conventional morality** Kohlberg's Level II of moral reasoning, in which the standards of authority figures are internalized. (252)

**convergent thinking** Thinking aimed at finding the one "right" answer to a problem; traditional thinking. Compare with *divergent thinking*. (270)

**coregulation** Transitional stage during middle childhood in which parent and child share power over the child's behavior, the parent exercising general supervision and the child regulating his or her own specific activities. (287)

**correlational studies** Research that shows the direction and magnitude of relationships between variables but cannot establish cause-and-effect relationships. (15)

**crisis** Marcia's term for a period of conscious decision making (one of two elements crucial in identity formation; see also *commitment*). (344)

**critical period** Specific time during development when a given event will have the greatest impact. (9)

**cross-sectional study** Study design in which people of different ages are assessed on one occasion, providing comparative information about different age cohorts. Compare with *longitudinal study*. (20)

**cross-sequential study** Study design that combines cross-sectional and longitudinal techniques by assessing people in a cross-sectional sample more than once. (20)

**crystallized intelligence** Type of intelligence, proposed by Cattell and Horn, involving the ability to remember and use learned information; it is relatively dependent on education and cultural background. Compare with *fluid intelligence*. (436)

**culture-fair** Describing an intelligence test that deals with experiences common to various cultures, in an attempt to avoid placing test-takers at an advantage or disadvantage due to their cultural background. Compare with *culture-free*. (261)

**culture-free** Describing an intelligence test that, if it were possible to design, would have no culturally linked content. Compare with *culture-fair*. (261)

**data** Information that is obtained through research. (21)

**death education** Programs to educate people about dying and grief to help them deal with these issues in their personal and professional lives. (541)

**decenter** In Piagetian terminology, to consider all significant aspects of a situation simultaneously. Decentration is characteristic of operational thought. (191, 249)

**defense mechanisms** According to Freudian theory, ways in which people unconsciously combat anxiety by distorting reality. (23)

**deferred imitation** In Piaget's terminology, reproduction of an observed behavior after the passage of time by calling up a stored symbol of it. (126, 189)

**dementia** Apparent intellectual and personality deterioration sometimes associated with old age and caused by a variety of irreversible and reversible physiological conditions; sometimes called *senility*. (483)

**Denver Developmental Screening Test** Test given to children 1 month to 6 years old to determine whether or not they are developing normally; it assesses gross motor skills, fine motor skills, language development, and personal and social development. (102)

**deoxyribonucleic acid (DNA)** Genetic substance that controls the makeup and functions of body cells. (43)

**dependent variable** In an experiment, the factor that may or may not change as a result of manipulation of the independent variable. (17)

**depression** Emotional disturbance characterized by feeble responses to stimuli, low initiative, and sullen or despondent attitudes. (61, 152)

**discipline** The ways in which adults try to form a child's character, self-control, and moral behavior. (286)

**disengagement theory** Theory of aging that holds that successful aging is characterized by mutual withdrawal between the older person and society. Compare with *activity theory*. (504)

**divergent thinking** Thinking that produces a variety of fresh, diverse possibilities; creative thinking. Compare with *convergent thinking*. (270)

**dizygotic twins** Twins conceived by the union of two different eggs with two different sperm cells within a brief period of time; also called *fraternal*, or *two-egg*, *twins*. (41)

**dominant inheritance** Pattern of inheritance, described by Mendel, in which only the dominant trait of two competing traits is expressed. (44)

**donor eggs** Method of conception in which an ovum of a fertile woman is implanted in the uterus of a woman who cannot produce normal ova. (418)

**Down syndrome** Most common chromosomal disorder, usually caused by an extra twenty-first chromosome and characterized by mild or moderate mental retardation, and by such physical signs as a downward-sloping skin fold at the inner corners of the eyes. (51)

**dream** According to Levinson, the vision that spurs young adults and vitalizes their development; failure to fulfill the dream may precipitate a midlife crisis. (401)

**dual-process model** Model of intellectual functioning in late adulthood, proposed by Baltes, which identifies and seeks to measure two dimensions of intelligence: the mechanics of intelligence and the pragmatics of intelligence. (491)

**durable power of attorney** A legal instrument that appoints an individual to make decisions in the event of another person's incapacitation. (545)

**dyslexia** Common learning disability involving inability to learn to read or difficulty in doing so. (267)

**ecological approach** Bronfenbrenner's system of understanding development, which identifies four levels of environmental influence, from intimate to global. (9)

**ego** In Freudian theory, an aspect of personality that develops during infancy and operates on the reality principle, seeking acceptable means of gratification in dealing with the real world. (25)

**egocentrism** In Piaget's terminology, a characteristic of preoperational thought consisting of inability to consider another's viewpoint (000); a form of egocentrism is also characteristic of adolescents. (191)

**elaboration** A strategy for remembering items that involves linking them together in an imagined scene or story. (256)

**elder abuse**  Neglect or physical or psychological abuse of dependent older persons. (512)

**Electra complex**  According to Freudian theory, the female counterpart of the Oedipus complex, in which the young girl in the phallic stage feels sexual attraction for her father and rivalry toward her mother. (212)

**electronic fetal monitoring**  Monitoring of fetal heartbeat by machine in labor and delivery. (73)

**embryonic stage**  Second stage of gestation (2 to 8–12 weeks), characterized by rapid growth and development of major body systems and organs. (64)

**emotional flexibility versus emotional impoverishment**  One of four adjustments of middle age described by Peck. (451)

**emotions**  Subjective feelings such as sadness, joy, and fear, which arise in response to situations and experiences and are expressed through some kind of altered behavior. (148)

**empty nest**  Term for the transitional phase of parenting following the last child's leaving the parents' home. (461)

**enuresis**  Bed-wetting. (186)

**environmental influences**  Nongenetic influences on development that are attributable to experiences with the outside world. (8)

**equilibration**  In Piagetian terminology, the tendency to strive for equilibrium (balance) among cognitive elements within the organism and between it and the outside world. (33)

**estrogen**  Female hormone; its reduction during the climacteric may result in hot flashes, thinning of the vaginal lining, and urinary dysfunction. (431)

**executive stage**  Fourth of Schaie's cognitive stages, in which the middle-aged person responsible for societal systems integrates complex relationships on several levels. (382)

**experiential elements**  In Sternberg's triarchic theory, the insightful, creative aspect of intelligence, which determines how effectively people approach both novel and familiar tasks. (383)

**experiment**  Rigorously controlled, replicable (that is, repeatable) procedure in which the researcher manipulates variables to assess their effect on each other. (17)

**experimental group**  In an experiment, the group receiving the treatment under study; any changes in these people are compared with changes in the control group. (17)

**external aids**  A memory strategy that requires the use of something outside the person, such as a list. (256)

**extinction**  Cessation of a response, or its return to the baseline level, when the response is no longer reinforced. (29)

**fertilization**  Union of sperm and ovum to produce a zygote. (40)

**fetal alcohol syndrome (FAS)**  Mental, motor, and developmental abnormalities (including stunted growth, facial and bodily malformations, and disorders of the central nervous system) affecting the offspring of some women who drink heavily during pregnancy. (67)

**fetal stage**  Final stage of gestation (8–12 weeks to birth), characterized by increased detail of body parts and greatly elongated body size. (65)

**fluid intelligence**  Type of intelligence, proposed by Cattell and Horn, involving ability to perceive relations, form concepts, and reason abstractly. It is considered dependent on neurological development and relatively free from influences of education and culture and is thus tested by novel problems or tasks with common cultural elements. Compare with *crystallized intelligence*. (436)

**foreclosure**  Identity status described by Marcia in which a person who has not spent time considering alternatives (that is, has not been in crisis) is committed to other people's plans for his or her life. (344)

**formal operations**  According to Piaget, the final stage of cognitive development, reached by some adolescents, which is characterized by the ability to think abstractly. (324)

**gamete**  Sex cell (sperm or ovum). (40)

**gender**  Significance of being male or female. (211)

**gender constancy**  Realization that one's sex will always stay the same. Also called *gender conservation*. (214)

**gender differences**  Differences between males and females that may or may not be based on biological differences. (216)

**gender identity**  Awareness, developed in early childhood, that one is male or female. (214)

**gender roles**  Behaviors, interests, attitudes, and skills that a culture considers appropriate for males and females and expects them to fulfill. (217)

**gender schema**  In Bem's theory, a mentally organized pattern of behavior that helps a child sort out information about what it means to be male or female. (215)

**gender-schema theory**  Theory that children socialize themselves in their gender roles by developing the concept of what it means to be male or female. (215)

**gender stereotypes**  Exaggerated generalizations about male or female role behavior. (217)

**gender-typing**  Socialization process by which a child, at an early age, learns the appropriate gender role. (217)

**gene**  Basic functional unit of heredity, which determines an inherited characteristic. (43)

**generativity versus stagnation**  According to Erikson, the seventh critical alternative of psychosocial development, in which the mature adult develops a concern with establishing and guiding the next generation or else experiences stagnation (a sense of inactivity or lifelessness). (451)

**genetic counseling**  Clinical service that advises couples of their probable risk of having children with particular hereditary defects. (53)

**genetics**  Study of hereditary factors affecting development. (43)

**genital stage**  According to Freud, the psychosexual stage of mature sexuality, achieved during adolescence. (341)

**genotype**  Underlying genetic composition that causes certain traits to be expressed; may vary without causing changes in phenotype, because of the presence of recessive genes. (45)

**germinal stage**  First 2 weeks of prenatal development, characterized by rapid cell division and increasing complexity; the stage ends when the conceptus attaches itself to the wall of the uterus. (64)

**gerontologists**  Persons engaged in gerontology, the study of the aged and the process of aging. (472)

**giftedness**  Exceptional potential in any of the following areas: general intellectual ability, specific academic aptitudes, leadership, talent in the arts, creativity, psychomotor ability. (269)

**grief**  Emotional response of the bereaved to a death. (538)

**grief therapy**  Program to help the bereaved cope with loss. (541)

**habituation**  Simple type of learning in which familiarity with a stimulus results in loss of interest and reduces or stops the response. (100, 113)

**heredity**  Inborn influences on development, carried on the genes inherited from the parents. (8, 43)

**heterosexual**  Describing a person whose sexual orientation is toward the other sex. (355)

**heterozygous**  Possessing two dissimilar alleles for a trait. (44)

**holophrase**  Single word that conveys a complete thought; the typical speech form of children aged 12 to 18 months. (132)

**homosexual**  Describing a person whose sexual orientation is toward the same sex. (355)

**homozygous**  Possessing two similar alleles for a trait. (44)

**horizontal décalage**  Piagetian term for a child's inability to transfer learning about one type of conservation to other types, because of which the child masters different types of conservation tasks for the first time at different ages (for example, learning substance conservation before either weight conservation or volume conservation). (249)

**hospice care**  Warm, personal patient- and family-centered care for a person with a terminal illness. (543)

**human development**  Scientific study of quantitative and qualitative ways in which people change over time. (3)

**humanistic perspective**  View of humanity that sees people as having the ability to foster their own positive, healthy development through the distinctively human capacities for choice, creativity, and self-realization. (33)

**hypertension**  High blood pressure. (434)

**hypothesis**  Possible explanation for a phenomenon, used to predict the outcome of an experiment. (22)

**id**  In Freudian theory, the instinctual aspect of personality (present at birth) that operates on the pleasure principle, seeking immediate gratification. (25)

**ideal self**  Person's concept of who he or she would like to be; compare with *real self*. (277)

**identification**  Process by which a person acquires characteristics, beliefs, attitudes, values, and behaviors of another person or of a group; an important personality development of early childhood. (211)

**identity achievement**  Identity status, described by Marcia, which is characterized by commitment to choices made following a crisis period, or period spent in thinking about alternatives. (344)

**identity diffusion**  Identity status, described by Marcia, which is characterized by absence of commitment and may or may not follow a period of considering alternatives (crisis). (345)

**identity versus identity confusion**  According to Eriksonian theory, the fifth critical alternative of psychosocial development, in which an adolescent must determine his or her own sense of self (identity), including the role, she or he is to play in society. (343)

**imaginary audience**  Observer who exists only in an adolescent's mind and is as concerned with the adolescent's thoughts and actions as is the adolescent himself or herself. (326)

**imaginative play**  Play involving imaginary situations; also called *fantasy play, dramatic play,* or *pretend play.* (236)

**imprinting**  Instinctive form of learning in which, after a single encounter, an animal recognizes and trusts one particular individual. (156)

**independent segregation**  Mendel's law that hereditary traits are transmitted separately. (44)

**independent variable**  In an experiment, the variable over which the experimenter has control. Compare *dependent variable.* (17)

**industry versus inferiority**  In Erikson's theory, the fourth critical alternative of psychosocial development, occurring during middle childhood, in which children must learn the productive skills their culture requires or else face feelings of inferiority. (279)

**infantile autism**  Developmental disorder that begins within the first 2½ years of life and is characterized by lack of responsiveness to other people. (59)

**infant mortality rate**  Proportion of babies born who die in the first year of life. (88)

**infertility**  Inability to conceive after 12 to 18 months. (417)

**information-processing approach**  Study of intellectual development by analyzing the mental processes that underlie intelligent behavior: the manipulation of symbols and perceptions to acquire information and solve problems. (126)

**initiative versus guilt**  According to Erikson, the third crisis of psychosocial development, occurring between the ages of 3 and 6, in which children must balance the urge to form and carry out goals with their moral judgments about what they want to do. Children develop initiative when they try out new things and are not overwhelmed by failure. (212)

**integrity versus despair**  According to Erikson, the eighth and final critical alternative of psychosocial development, in which people in late adulthood either accept their lives as a whole and thus accept death or yield to despair that their lives cannot be relived. (501)

**intellectualization**  Defense mechanism typical of adolescence, described by Anna Freud, which is characterized by translation of sexual impulses into abstract intellectual discussions. (342)

**intelligent behavior**  Behavior that is goal-oriented (conscious and deliberate) and adaptive (used to identify and solve problems). (117)

**intelligence quotient (IQ) tests**  Tests used to assess *how much* a person has of certain abilities like comprehension and reasoning. (117)

**interiority**  In Neugarten's terminology, a concern with inner life (introversion or introspection), which generally increases as people grow older. (452)

**interview**  Research technique in which people are asked to state their attitudes, opinions, or histories. (15)

**intimacy versus isolation**  According to Erikson, the sixth critical alternative of psychosocial development, in which young adults either make commitments to others or face a possible sense of isolation and consequent self-absorption. (398)

**invisible imitation**  Imitation with parts of one's body that one cannot see, e.g., the mouth. (125)

**in vitro fertilization**  Fertilization of an ovum outside the mother's body. (418)

**irreversibility**  In Piaget's theory, a limitation on preoperational thinking consisting of failure to understand that an operation can be reserved, restoring the original condition. (190)

**karyotype**  Chart in which photomicrographs of a person's chromosomes are arranged according to size and structure to reveal any chromosomal abnormalities. (53)

**laboratory observation**  Research method in which all subjects are placed in the same situation, the laboratory, where the surroundings are under the researcher's control. (14)

**language acquisition device (LAD)**  In Noam Chomsky's nativist theory, an inborn mental structure that enables children to build linguistic rules by analyzing the language they hear. (130)

**lanugo**  Fuzzy prenatal body hair, which drops off within a few days after birth. (81)

**latency period**  In Freudian theory, a period of relative psychosexual calm that occurs during middle childhood after the Oedipus or Electra complex has been resolved and the superego has developed. (279)

bodies age in accordance with a normal development pattern built into every organism of a particular species; compare with *wear-and-tear theory of aging*. (478)

**Project Head Start** Compensatory preschool education program begun in the United States in 1965. (203)

**prosocial behavior** Behavior intended to help others without external reward. (225)

**proximodistal principle** Principle that development proceeds from within to without, i.e., that parts of the body near the center develop before the extremities. (94)

**psychoanalytic perspective** View of humanity concerned with the unconscious forces motivating human behavior. (23)

**psychological maltreatment** Action or failure to act that damages children's behavioral, cognitive, emotional, or physical functioning and may keep children from realizing their full potential as adults. (300)

**psychometric approach** Study of intellectual development by attempting to measure quantitatively the factors that appear to make up intelligence. (117)

**psychosexual development** In Freudian theory, an unvarying sequence of stages of personality development during childhood and adolescence, in which gratification shifts from the mouth to the anus and then to the genitals. (25)

**psychosocial-development theory** Theory of Erikson that societal and cultural influences play a major part in healthy personality development. According to this theory, development occurs in eight maturationally determined stages throughout the life span, each revolving around a particular crisis or turning point in which the person is faced with achieving a healthy balance between alternative positive and negative traits. (26)

**puberty** Process by which a person attains sexual maturity and is able to reproduce. (308)

**punishment** In operant conditioning, a stimulus that, when administered following a particular behavior, decreases the probability that the behavior will be repeated. (28)

**qualitative change** Change in kind, structure, or organization, such as the nature of a person's intelligence or the way the mind works. (3)

**quantitative changes** Change in number or amount of something, such as height, weight, or vocabulary. (3)

**random sample** Type of sample that ensures representativeness because each member of the population has an equal chance to be selected. (18)

**reaction formation** In Freudian theory, a defense mechanism characterized by the replacement of an anxiety-producing feeling by the expression of its opposite. (342)

**real self** Person's concept of who he or she actually is. Compare with *ideal self*. (277)

**recall** Ability to reproduce material from memory without being presented with it again. Compare with *recognition*. (187)

**recessive inheritance** Expression of a recessive (nondominant) trait, which, according to Mendel, occurs only if the offspring receives the same recessive gene from both parents. (44)

**recognition** Ability to identify previously learned material when presented with it again; tested by asking a person to choose the correct answer from among several possibilities. Compare with *recall*. (187)

**reflex behaviors** Automatic responses to external stimulation. Reflexes—by their presence or disappearance—are early signs of an infant's neurological growth. (85)

**rehearsal** Mnemonic device consisting of conscious repetition. (255)

**reinforcement** In operant conditioning, a stimulus that, when administered following a particular behavior, increases the probability that the behavior will be repeated. (28, 115)

**reintegrative stage** Fifth of Schaie's cognitive stages, in which older people choose to focus energy on tasks that have meaning for them. (382)

**reliability** Consistency of a test in measuring performance. (117)

**reliable** Describing a test that is consistent in measuring performance. (117)

**representational ability** Capacity to remember (mentally represent) objects and experiences without needing a stimulus, largely through the use of symbols. (121)

**reserve capacity** Ability of body organs and systems to put forth 4 to 10 times as much effort as usual in times of stress or dysfunction; also called *organ reserve*. (481)

**responsible stage** Third of Schaie's five cognitive stages, in which middle-aged people are concerned with long-range goals and practical problems often related to their responsibility for others. (382)

**role-taking** Ability to imagine another person's situation or point of view. (250)

**sample** In an experiment, the group of subjects chosen to represent the entire population under study. (18)

**scaffolding** The temporary support that parents give a child to do a task. (198)

**scheme** In Piaget's terminology, a basic cognitive structure that an infant uses to interact with the environment; an organized pattern of thought and behavior. (32, 122)

**schizophrenia** Psychological disorder characterized by loss of contact with reality and such symptoms as delusions, hallucinations, and thought disturbances. (59)

**school phobia** Unrealistic fear of school, probably reflecting separation anxiety. (297)

**scientific method** System of established principles of scientific inquiry, including careful observation and recording of data, testing of alternative hypotheses, and widespread dissemination of findings and conclusions so that other scientists can learn from, analyze, repeat, and build on the results. (12)

**secondary aging** Aging processes that result from disease and bodily abuse and disuse, factors that may be subject to the person's own control. Compare with *primary aging*. (478)

**secondary circular reactions** An infant's intentional repetition of actions to reproduce desired effects discovered in the environment outside the body; characteristic of the third substage of the sensorimotor stage described by Piaget. (122)

**secondary sex characteristics** Physiological characteristics of the sexes which develop during adolescence (and do not involve the sex organs), including breast development in females, broadened shoulders in males, growth of body hair in both sexes, and adult skin and adult voices of men and women. See *primary sex characteristics*. (312)

**secular trend** Trend that can be seen only by observing several generations. A secular trend toward earlier attainment of adult height and sexual maturity began a century ago and appears to have ended in the United States. (311)

**secure attachment** Attachment pattern in which an infant can separate readily from the primary caregiver and actively seeks out the caregiver upon return. (158)

**selective optimization with compensation** In the dual-process model of Baltes, the ability of older people to maintain or enhance their intellectual functioning through the use of special abilities to compensate for losses in other areas. (491)

**self-awareness** Realization, beginning in infancy, of separateness from other people and things, allowing reflection on one's own actions in relation to social standards. (149, 276)

**self-care children** Children who regularly care for themselves at home without adult supervision. (289)

**self-concept** Sense of self, including self-understanding and self-control or self-regulation. (276)

**self-control** Child's ability to alter or delay an action when the caregiver is not present, on the basis of knowing what behavior is socially acceptable. (147)

**self-definition** External and psychological characteristics by which a person describes himself or herself. (277)

**self-esteem** Person's self-evaluation or self-image. (278)

**self-fulfilling prophecy** Expectation or prediction of behavior that tends to come true because it leads people to act as if it were already true. (265)

**self-recognition** Children's ability to recognize their own physical image; occurs at about 18 months. (149, 276)

**self-regulation** Child's independent control of behavior to conform to understood social expectations. (147)

**self-schema** According to the information-processing approach, the self-concept; a set of knowledge structures, or hypotheses, based on social experience, which organize and guide the processing of information about the self and help children decide how to act and imagine what they may become. (280)

**senescence** Period of the life span during which people experience decrements in bodily functioning associated with aging; begins at different ages for different people. (476)

**sensorimotor stage** First of Piaget's stages of cognitive development, when infants (from birth to 2 years) learn through their developing senses and motor activities. (120)

**sensory memory** Fleeting awareness of images or sensations, which disappears quickly unless transferred to short-term memory. (492)

**separation anxiety** Distress shown by an infant, usually beginning in the second half of the first year, when a familiar caregiver leaves; it is commonly a sign that attachment has occurred. (164)

**separation anxiety disorder** Condition involving excessive anxiety for at least 2 weeks, concerning separation from people to whom a child is attached. (296)

**sex chromosomes** Pair of chromosomes that determines sex: XX in the normal female, XY in the normal male. (42)

**sex differences** Physical differences between males and females. (216)

**sex-linked inheritance** Pattern of inheritance in which certain characteristics carried on the sex chromosomes (usually the X chromosome) are transmitted differently to males and females. (45)

**sexual abuse** Any kind of sexual contact between a child and an older person, or any sexual activity between adults to which one of the participants has not consented. (166)

**sexually transmitted diseases (STDs)** Diseases transmitted by sexual contact; also called *venereal diseases*. (320)

**sexual orientation** Sexual interest either in the other sex (heterosexual orientation) or in the same sex (homosexual orientation), usually first expressed during adolescence; also called *sexual preference*. (355)

**shaping** In operant conditioning, a method of bringing about a new response by reinforcing responses that are progressively more like it. (29)

**short-term memory** Working memory, the active repository of information currently being used; its capacity is limited but increases rapidly during middle childhood and is relatively unaffected by aging. Material in short-term memory disappears after about 20 seconds unless transferred to long-term memory. (492)

**small-for-date babies** Babies whose birth weight is less than that of 90 percent of babies of the same gestational age, as a result of slow fetal growth. (90)

**socialization** Process of learning the behaviors considered appropriate in one's culture. (156)

**social-learning theory** Theory, proposed chiefly by Bandura, that behaviors are learned by observing and imitating models and are maintained through reinforcement. (30)

**social play** Play in which children interact with other children, commonly regarded as a sign of social competence. (234)

**social referencing** Understanding an ambiguous situation by seeking out another person's perception of it. (151)

**social speech** Speech intended for a listener. (196)

**socializing versus sexualizing in human relationships** One of four adjustments of middle age described by Peck. (451)

**spontaneous abortion** Natural expulsion from the uterus of a conceptus that cannot survive outside the womb; also called *miscarriage*. (65)

**standardized norms** Standards for determining mental age of persons who take an intelligence test, obtained from scores of a large, representative sample of children who took the test while it was in preparation. (117)

**Stanford-Binet Intelligence Scale** Individual intelligence test used primarily with children to measure practical judgment, memory, and spatial orientation. (197)

**states** Periodic variations in an infant's daily cycles of wakefulness, sleep, and activity. (95)

**status offender** Juvenile charged with committing an act that would not be considered criminal if the offender were older (for example, being truant, running away from home, or engaging in sexual intercourse). (362)

**storm and stress** In Hall's terminology, the idea that adolescence is necessarily a time of intense, fluctuating emotions; see *adolescent rebellion*. (341)

**strange situation** Research technique used to assess the attachment between a mother and her infant. (158)

**stranger anxiety** Phenomenon that often occurs during the second half of a child's first year (in conjunction with separation anxiety), when the infant becomes wary of strange people and places; commonly a sign that attachment has occurred. (164)

**stress** The organism's physiological and psychological reaction to demands made on it. (377)

**substantive complexity** Degree to which a person's work requires thought and independent judgment. (442)

**sudden infant death syndrome (SIDS)** Sudden and unexpected death of an apparently healthy infant. (93)

**superego** According to Freudian theory, the aspect of personality representing values that parents and other agents of society communicate to a child. It develops around the age of 5 or 6 as a result of resolution of the Oedipus or Electra complex. (25, 212)

**surrogate motherhood** Method of conception in which a woman who is not mar-

Treat TV with T.L.C. One-page flyer. Newtonville, MA: Author.

Adams, D. (1983). *The psychosocial development of professional black women's lives and the consequences of careers for their personal happiness.* Unpublished doctoral dissertation, Wright Institute, Berkeley, CA.

Adams, G., Adams-Taylor, S., & Pittman, K. (1989). Adolescent pregnancy and parenthood: A review of the problem, solutions, and resources. *Family Relations, 38,* 223–229.

Alemi, B., Hamosh, M., Scanlon, J. W., Salzman-Mann, C., & Hamosh, P. (1981). Fat digestion in very low-birth-weight infants: Effects of addition of human milk to low-birth-weight formula. *Pediatrics, 68*(4), 484–489.

Allore, R., O'Hanlon, D., Price, R., Neilson, K., Willard, H. F., Cox, D. R., Marks, A., & Dun, R. J. (1988). Gene encoding the B subunit of S100 protein is on chromosome 21: Implications for Down syndrome. *Science, 239,* 1311–1313.

(1991). *Immunization protects children.* Brochure.

American Academy of Pediatrics (AAP) Committee on Accident and Poison Prevention. (1990). Bicycle helmets. *Pediatrics, 85*(1), 229–230.

American Academy of Pediatrics Committee on Adolescence. (1986). Sexuality, contraception, and the media. *Pediatrics, 78*(3), 535–536.

American Academy of Pediatrics (AAP) Committee on Adolescence. (1987).

ried to a man agrees to bear his baby and then give the child to the father and his wife. (418)

**symbol**    In Piaget's terminology, an idiosyncratic mental representation of a sensory experience. (189)

**symbolic function**    In Piaget's terminology, ability to learn by using mental representations (symbols or signs) to which a child has attached meaning: this ability, char-

events is expected or unexpected. Compare with *normative-crisis model.* (404)

**transduction**    In Piaget's terminology, a preoperational child's tendency to mentally link particular experiences without the use of inductive or deductive logic, sometimes resulting in false conclusions. (191)

**transitional objects**    Objects—commonly soft, cuddly ones—used repeatedly at

**valuing wisdom versus valuing physical powers**    One of four adjustments of middle age described by Peck. (451)

**vernix caseosa**    Oily substance on a neonate's skin that protects against infection; it dries within a few days after birth. (81)

**visible imitation**    Imitation with parts of one's body that one can see, such as the hands and the feet. (125)

Alcohol use and abuse: A pediatric concern. *Pediatrics, 79*(3), 450–453.

**American Academy of Pediatrics (AAP) Committee on Drugs. (1978).** Effects of medication during labor and delivery on infant outcome. *Pediatrics, 62*(3), 402–403.

**American Academy of Pediatrics (AAP) Committee on Children with Disabilities and Committee on Drugs. (1987).** Medication for children with an attention deficit disorder. *Pediatrics, 80*(5), 758–760.

**American Academy of Pediatrics (AAP) Committee on Drugs. (1982).** Psychotropic drugs in pregnancy and lactation. *Pediatrics, 69*(2), 241–243.

**American Academy of Pediatrics (AAP) Committee on Fetus and Newborn. (1986).** Use and abuse of the Apgar score. *Pediatrics, 78*(6), 1148–1149.

**American Academy of Pediatrics (AAP) Committee on Fetus and Newborn. (1987).** Neonatal anesthesia. *Pediatrics, 80*(3), 446.

**American Academy of Pediatrics (AAP) Committee on Nutrition. (1981).** Nutritional aspects of obesity in infancy and childhood. *Pediatrics, 68*(6), 880–883.

**American Academy of Pediatrics (AAP) Committee on Nutrition. (1986).** Prudent life-style for children: Dietary fat and cholesterol. *Pediatrics, 78*(3), 521–525.

**American Academy of Pediatrics (AAP) Committee on Pediatric Aspects of Physical Fitness, Recreation, and Sports. (1981).** Competitive athletics for children of elementary school age. *Pediatrics, 67*(6).

**American Academy of Pediatrics (AAP) Committee on Sports Medicine and Committee on School Health. (1989).** Organized athletics for preadolescent children. *Pediatrics, 84*(3), 583–584.

**American Academy of Pediatrics (AAP) Task Force on Blood Pressure Control in Children. (1987).** Report of the second task force on blood pressure control in children. *Pediatrics, 79*(1), 1–25.

**American Academy of Pediatrics (AAP) Task Force on Circumcision. (1989).** Report on the task force on circumcision. *Pediatrics, 84*(4), 388–390.

**American Academy of Pediatrics (AAP) Task Force on Infant Mortality. (1986).** Statement on infant mortality. *Pediatrics, 78*(6), 1155–1160.

**American Association of Retired Persons (AARP). (1986).** *A profile of older Americans.* Brochure. Washington, DC: Author.

**American Association of Retired Persons (AARP). (1989, March).** *Working caregivers report.* Washington, DC: Author.

**American Cancer Society. (1985).** *1985 cancer facts and figures.* Pamphlet. Washington, DC: Author.

**American Cancer Society. (1988).** *Cancer statistics, 1988. Cancer Journal of Clinicians, 38*(1), 21.

**American Council on Science and Health. (1985).** *Premenstrual syndrome.* Pamphlet. Summit, NJ: Author.

**American Foundation for the Prevention of Venereal Disease (AFPVD). (1986).** *Sexually transmitted disease (STD): Prevention for everyone* (13th ed.). Pamphlet. New York: Author.

**American Heart Association. (1990).** *The healthy American diet.* Dallas: Author.

**American Medical Association Council on Scientific Affairs. (1984).** Exercise programs for the elderly. *Journal of the American Medical Association, 252*(4), 544–546.

**American Psychological Association (APA). (1982).** *Ethical principles in the conduct of research with human participants.* Washington, DC: Author.

**American Psychological Association (APA). (1985, February 22).** *Psychologists warn of potential dangers in TV violence.* Position statement. Washington, DC: Author.

**Anand, K. J. S., & Hickey, P. R. (1987).** Pain and its effect in the human neonate and fetus. *The New England Journal of Medicine, 317*(21), 1321–1329.

**Anastasi, A. (1958).** Heredity, environment, and the question "how?" *Psychological Review, 65*(4), 197–208.

**Anastasi, A. (1988).** *Psychological testing* (6th ed.). New York: Macmillan.

**Anders, T., Caraskadon, M., & Dement, W. (1980).** Sleep and sleepiness in children and adolescents. In I. Litt (Ed.), Adolescent medicine. *Pediatric Clinics of North America, 27*(1), 29–44.

**Anders, T. R., Fozard, J. L., & Lillyquist, T. D. (1972).** Effects of age upon retrieval from short-term memory. *Developmental Psychology, 6*(2), 214–217.

**Anderson, R. (1980).** I never sang for my father. In R. G. Lyell (Ed.), *Middle age, old age* (pp. 55–110). New York: Harcourt Brace Jovanovich.

**Anderson, S. A., Russell, C. S., & Schumm, W. R. (1983).** Perceived marital quality and family life-cycle categories: A further analysis. *Journal of Marriage and the Family, 45*, 127–139.

**Anderson, T. B. (1984).** Widowhood as a life transition: Its impact on kinship ties. *Journal of Marriage and the Family, 46*, 105–114.

**Andrews, S. R., Blumenthal, J. B., Johnson, D. L., Kahn, A. J., Ferguson, C. J., Lasater, T. M., Malone, P. E., & Wallace, D. B. (1982).** The skills of mothering—a study of parent-child development centers. *Monograph of the Society for Research in Child Development, 47*(6, Serial No. 198).

**Angier, N. (1990, March 8).** Gene implant therapy is backed for children with rare disease. *The New York Times,* pp. A1, B9.

**Anson, O. (1989).** Marital status and women's health revisited: The importance of a proximate adult. *Journal of Marriage and the Family, 51*, 185–194.

**Anthony, E. J., & Koupernik, C. (Eds.). (1974).** *The child in his family: Children at psychiatric risk.* (Vol. 3). New York: Wiley.

**Antonarakis, S. E., & Down Syndrome Collaborative Group. (1991).** Parental origin of the extra chromosome in trisomy 21 as indicated by analysis of DNA polymorphisms. *New England Journal of Medicine, 324*, 87–876.

**Apgar, V. (1953).** A proposal for a new method of evaluation of the newborn infant. *Current Research in Anesthesia and Analgesia, 32*, 260–267.

**Arend, R., Gove, F., & Sroufe, L. A. (1979).** Continuity of individual adaptation from infancy to kindergarten: A predictive study of ego-resiliency and curiosity in preschoolers. *Child Development, 50*, 950–959.

**Ariès, P. (1962).** *Centuries of childhood.* New York: Vintage.

**Ash, P., Vennart, J., & Carter, C. (1977, April).** The incidence of hereditary disease in man. *The Lancet,* pp. 849–851.

**Asher, J. (1987).** Born to be shy? *Psychology Today, 21*(4), 56–64.

**Asher, S., Renshaw, P., Geraci, K., & Dor, A. (1979, March).** *Peer acceptance and social skill training: The selection of program content.* Paper presented at the meeting of the Society for Research in Child Development, San Francisco.

**Aslin, R. N., Pisoni, D. B., & Jusczyk, P. W. (1983).** Auditory development and speech perception in infancy. In P. H. Mussen (Ed.), *Handbook of child psychology* (4th ed., pp. 573–687). New York: Wiley.

**Atchley, R. (1985).** *Social forces and aging* (4th ed.). Belmont, CA: Wadsworth.

**Aylward, G. P., Pfeiffer, S. I., Wright, A., & Verhulst, S. J. (1989).** Outcome studies of low birth weight infants published in the last decade: A metaanalysis. *Journal of Pediatrics, 115*, 515–520.

**Babchuk, N. (1978–1979).** Aging and primary relations. *International Journal of Aging and Human Development, 9*(2), 137–151.

**Babson, S. G., & Clark, N. G. (1983).** Relationship between infant death and maternal age. *Journal of Pediatrics, 103*(3), 391–393.

**Backett, K. (1987).** The negotiation of fatherhood. In C. Lewis and M. O'Brien (Eds.), *Reassessing fatherhood: New observations on fathers and the modern family.* London: Sage.

**Baillargeon, R. (1987).** Object permanence in 3½- and 4½-month-old infants. *Developmental Psychology, 23*(5), 655–664.

**Baird, P. A., & Sadovnick, A. D. (1987).** Life expectancy in Down syndrome. *Journal of Pediatrics, 110,* 849–854.

**Bakwin, H. (1970, August 29).** Sleepwalking in twins. *The Lancet,* pp. 446–447.

**Bakwin, H. (1971a).** Car-sickness in twins. *Developmental Medicine and Child Neurology, 13,* 310–312.

**Bakwin, H. (1971b).** Constipation in twins. *American Journal of Diseases of Children, 121,* 179–181.

**Bakwin, H. (1971c).** Enuresis in twins. *American Journal of Diseases of Children, 121,* 222–225.

**Bakwin, H. (1971d).** Nail-biting in twins. *Developmental Medicine and Child Neurology, 13,* 304–307.

**Baldwin, W., & Cain, V. S. (1980).** The children of teenage parents. *Family Planning Perspectives, 12,* 34.

**Balkwell, C. (1981).** Transition to widowhood: A review of the literature. *Family Relations, 30,* 117–127.

**Balkwell, C. (1985).** An attitudinal correlate of the timing of a major life event: The case of morale in widowhood. *Family Relations, 34,* 577–581.

**Baltes, P. B. (1985).** *The aging of intelligence: On the dynamics between growth and decline.* Unpublished manuscript.

**Baltes, P. B., Reese, H. W., & Lipsitt, L. (1980).** Life-span developmental psychology. *Annual Review of Psychology, 31,* 65–110.

**Baltes, P. B., & Schaie, K. W. (1974).** Aging and IQ: The myth of the twilight years. *Psychology Today, 7*(10), 35–38.

**Baltes, P. B., & Schaie, K. W. (1976).** On the plasticity of intelligence in adulthood and old age. Where Horn and Donaldson fail. *American Psychologist, 31,* 720–725.

**Bandura, A. (1960).** *Relationship of family patterns to child behavior disorders* (Progress report, USPHS, Project No. M-1734). Stanford, CA: Stanford University.

**Bandura, A., & Huston, A. (1961).** Identification as a process of incidental learning. *Journal of Abnormal and Social Psychology, 63*(12), 311–318.

**Bandura, A., Ross, D., & Ross, S. A. (1961).** Transmission of aggression through imitation of aggressive models. *Journal of Abnormal and Social Psychology, 63,* 575–582.

**Bandura, A., Ross, D., & Ross, S. A. (1963).** Imitation of film-mediated aggressive models. *Journal of Abnormal and Social Psychology, 66*(1), 3–11.

**Barbanel, J. (1990, Sept. 26).** Chancellor has plan to distribute condoms to students in New York. *The New York Times,* pp. A1, B3.

**Bardouille-Crema, A., Black, K. N., & Feldhusen, J. (1986).** Performance on Piagetian tasks of black children of differing socioeconomic levels. *Developmental Psychology, 22*(6), 841–844.

**Barefoot, J. C., Dahlstrom, W. G., & Williams, R. B. (1983).** Hostility, CHD incidence, and total mortality: A 25-year follow-up study of 255 physicians. *Psychosomatic Medicine, 45*(1), 59–63.

**Barfield, R. E., & Morgan, J. N. (1974).** *Early retirement: The decision and the experience and a second look.* Ann Arbor, MI: Institute for Social Research.

**Barfield, R. E., & Morgan, J. N. (1978).** Trends in satisfaction with retirement. *Gerontologist, 18*(1), 19–23.

**Barnes, A., Colton, T., Gunderson, J., Noller, K., Tilley, B., Strama, T., Townsend, D., Hatab, P., & O'Brien, P. (1980).** Fertility and outcome of pregnancy in women exposed in utero to diethylstilbestrol. *The New England Journal of Medicine, 302*(11), 609–613.

**Barnes, K. E. (1971).** Preschool play norms: A replication. *Developmental Psychology, 5*(1), 99–103.

**Barnett, R. (1985, March 2).** *We've come a long way—but where are we and what are the rewards?* Presentation at conference, Women in Transition, New York University's School of Continuing Education, Center for Career and Life Planning, New York.

**Barr, H. M., Streissguth, A. P., Darby, B. L., & Sampson, P. D. (1990).** Prenatal exposure to alcohol, caffeine, tobacco, and aspirin: Effects on fine and gross motor performance in 4-year-old children. *Developmental Psychology, 26*(3), 339–348.

**Barrett, C. J. (1978).** Effectiveness of widows' groups in facilitating change. *Journal of Counseling and Clinical Psychology, 46*(1), 20–31.

**Barrett, D. E., Radke-Yarrow, M., & Klein, R. E. (1982).** Chronic malnutrition and child behavior: Effects of early caloric supplementation on social and emotional functioning at school age. *Developmental Psychology, 18,* 541–556.

**Baruch, G. K., & Barnett, R. C. (1986).** Fathers' participation in family work and children's sex-role attitudes. *Child Development, 57,* 1210–1223.

**Baruch, G., Barnett, R., & Rivers, C. (1983).** *Lifeprints.* New York: McGraw-Hill.

**Bass, J. L., Brennan, P., Mehta, K. A., & Kodzis, S. (1990).** Pediatric problems in a suburban shelter for homeless families. *Pediatrics, 85,* 33–38.

**Bass, M., Kravath, R. E., & Glass, L. (1986).** Death-scene investigation in sudden infant death. *The New England Journal of Medicine, 315,* 100–105.

**Bassuk, E., & Rubin, L. (1987).** Homeless children: A neglected population. *American Journal of Orthopsychiatry, 57*(2), 279–286.

**Bassuk, E. L., & Rosenberg, L. (1990).** Psychosocial characteristics of homeless children and children with homes. *Pediatrics, 85*(3), 257–261.

**Bates, E., O'Connell, B., & Shore, C. (1987).** Language and communication in infancy. In J. D. Osofsky (Ed.), *Handbook of infant development* (2d ed.). New York: Wiley.

**Battelle, P. (1981, February).** The triplets who found each other. *Good Housekeeping,* pp. 74–83.

**Bauer, D. (1976).** An exploratory study of developmental changes in children's fears. *Journal of Child Psychology and Psychiatry, 17,* 69–74.

**Baughman, E. E. (1971).** *Black Americans.* New York: Academic.

**Baumrind, D. (1968).** Authoritarian vs. authoritative control. *Adolescence, 3,* 255–272.

**Baumrind, D. (1971).** Harmonious parents and their preschool children. *Developmental Psychology, 41*(1), 92–102.

**Baumrind, D. (1977).** Some thoughts about childrearing. In S. Cohen & T. Comiskey (Eds.), *Child development: Contemporary perspectives.* Itasca, IL: Peacock.

**Baumrind, D., & Black, A. E. (1967).** Socialization practices associated with dimensions of competence in preschool boys and girls. *Child Development, 38*(2), 291–327.

**Bayley, N. (1933).** Mental growth during the first three years. *Genetic Psychology Monographs, 14,* 1–93.

**Bayley, N. (1965).** Comparisons of mental and motor test scores for age 1-15 months by sex, birth order, race, geographic location, and education of parents. *Child Development, 36,* 379–411.

**Bayley, N. (1969).** *Bayley scales of infant development.* New York: Psychological Corporation.

**Bayley, N., & Oden, M. (1955).** The maintenance of intellectual ability in gifted adults. *Journal of Gerontology, 10,* 91–107.

**Beard, R. J. (1975).** The menopause. *British Journal of Hospital Medicine, 12,* 631–637.

**Beautrais, A. L., Fergusson, D. M., & Shannon, F. T. (1982).** Life events and childhood morbidity: A prospective study. *Pediatrics, 70*(6), 935–940.

**Beckwith, L., & Cohen, S. E. (1989).** Maternal responsiveness with preterm infants and later competency. In M. H. Bornstein (Ed.), Maternal responsiveness: Characteristics and consequences. *New Directions for Child Development,* No. 43. San Francisco: Jossey-Bass.

**Behrman, R. E. (1985).** Preventing low birth weight: A pediatric perspective. *Journal of Pediatrics, 107*(6), 842–854.

*the first year of life.* Unpublished manuscript.

**Bracken, M., Holford, T., White, C., & Kelsey, J. (1978).** Role of oral contraception in congenital malformations of offspring. *International Journal of Epidemiology, 7*(4), 309–317.

**Bradley, R., & Caldwell, B. (1982).** The consistency of the home environment and its relation to child development. *International Journal of Behavioral Development, 5,* 445–465.

**Bradley, R., Caldwell, B., & Rock, S. (1988).** HOME environment and school performance: A ten-year follow-up and examination of three models of environmental action. *Child Development, 59,* 852–867.

**Bradley, R. H. (1989).** Home measurement of maternal responsiveness. In M. H. Bornstein (Ed.), Maternal responsiveness: Characteristics and consequences. *New Directions for Child Development,* No. 43. San Francisco: Jossey-Bass.

**Bradley, R. H., et al. (1989).** Home environment and cognitive development in the first 3 years of life: A collaborative study involving six sites and three ethnic groups in North America. *Developmental Psychology, 25*(2), 217–235.

**Braine, M. (1976).** Children's first word combinations. *Monographs of the Society for Research in Child Development, 41* (1, Serial No. 164).

**Branch, L. G., Horowitz, A., & Carr, C. (1989).** The implications for everyday life of incident of self-reported visual decline among people over age 65 living in the community. *Gerontologist, 29*(3), 359–365.

**Brand, D. (1987, August 31).** The new whiz kids. *Time,* pp. 42–51.

**Bray, D. W., & Howard, A. (1983).** The AT&T longitudinal study of managers. In K. W. Schaie (ed.). *Longitudinal studies of adult psychological development.* New York: Guilford.

**Brazelton, T. B. (1973).** *Neonatal behavioral assessment scale.* Philadelphia: Lippincott.

**Brecher, E., & the Editors of Consumer Reports Books. (1984).** *Love, sex, and aging: A Consumers Union report.* Boston: Little, Brown.

**Bremner, W. J., Vitiello, M. V., & Prinz, P. N. (1983).** Loss of circadian rhythmicity in blood testosterone levels with aging in normal men. *Journal of Clinical Endocrinology and Metabolism, 56,* 1278–1281.

**Brewster, A. B. (1982).** Chronically ill hospitalized children's concepts of their illness. *Pediatrics, 69,* 355–362.

**Bridges, K. M. B. (1932).** Emotional development in early infancy. *Child Development, 3,* 324–341.

**Briley, M. (1980, July-August).** Burnout stress and the human energy crisis. *Dynamic Years,* pp. 36–39.

**Brim, O. G. (1974).** *Theories of the male mid-life crisis.* Address at the Annual Convention of the American Psychological Association, New Orleans.

**Brim, O. G. (1977).** Theories of the male mid-life crisis. In N. Schlossberg & A. Entine (Eds.), *Counseling adults.* Monterey, CA: Brooks/Cole.

**Brim, O. G., & Kagan, J. (Eds.). (1980).** *Constancy and change in human development.* New York: Wiley.

**Brim, O. G., & Ryff, C. D. (1980).** On the properties of life events. In P. B. Baltes & O. G. Brim (Eds.), *Life-span development and behavior* (Vol. 3). New York: Academic.

**Brittain, C. (1963).** Adolescent choices and parent-peer cross-pressures. *American Sociological Review, 28,* 385–391.

**Brodbeck, A. J., & Irwin, O. C. (1946).** The speech behavior of infants without families. *Child Development, 17,* 145–156.

**Brody, E. B., & Brody, N. (1976).** *Intelligence.* New York: Academic.

**Brody, E. M. (1978).** Community housing for the elderly. *Gerontologist, 18*(2), 121–128.

**Brody, J. (1990, October 11).** Sedentary living, not cholesterol, is the nation's leading culprit in fatal heart attacks. *The New York Times,* p. B12.

**Brody, L. R., Zelazo, P. R., & Chaika, H. (1984).** Habituation-dishabituation to speech in the neonate. *Developmental Psychology, 20,* 114–119.

**Bromley, D. B. (1974).** *The psychology of human aging* (2d ed.). Middlesex, England: Penguin.

**Bronfenbrenner, U. (1979).** *The ecology of human development.* Cambridge, MA: Harvard University Press.

**Bronfenbrenner, U., Alvarez, W. F., & Henderson, C. R. (1984).** Working and watching: Maternal employment and parents' perceptions of their three-year-old children. *Child Development, 55,* 1362–1378.

**Bronfenbrenner, U., Belsky, J., & Steinberg, L. (1977).** Daycare in context: An ecological perspective on research and public policy. Review prepared for Office of the Assistant Secretary for Planning and Evaluation, U.S. Department of Health, Education, and Welfare.

**Bronfenbrenner, U., & Crouter, A. (1982).** Work and family through time and space. In S. B. Kamerman & C. D. Hayes (Eds.), *Families that work: Children in a changing world.* Washington, DC: National Academy.

**Bronson, F. H., & Desjardins, C. (1969).** Aggressive behavior and seminal vesicle function in mice: Differential sensitivity

to androgen given neonatally. *Endocrinology, 85,* 871–975.

**Bronstein, P. (1988).** Father-child interaction: Implications for gender role socialization. In P. Bronstein & C. P. Cowan (Eds.), *Fatherhood today: Men's changing role in the family.* New York: Wiley.

**Brooks-Gunn, J. (1988).** Pubertal processes and the early adolescent transition. In W. Damon (Ed.), *Child development today and tomorrow.* San Francisco: Jossey-Bass.

**Brooks-Gunn, J., & Furstenberg, F. F. (1986).** The children of adolescent mothers: Physical, academic, and psychological outcomes. *Developmental Review, 6,* 224–251.

**Brophy, J. E., & Good, T. L. (1974).** *Teacher-student relationships.* New York: Holt.

**Brown, B. B., Clasen, D. R., & Eicher, S. A. (1986).** Perceptions of peer pressure, peer conformity dispositions, and self-reported behavior among adolescents. *Developmental Psychology, 22,* 521–530.

**Brown, E. F., & Hendee, W. R. (1989).** Adolescents and their music: Insights into the health of adolescents. *Journal of the American Medical Association, 262*(12), 1659–1663.

**Brown, J., LaRossa, G., Aylward, G., Davis, D., Rutherford, P., & Bakeman, R. (1980).** Nursery-based intervention with prematurely born babies and their mothers: Are there effects? *Journal of Pediatrics, 97*(3), 487–491.

**Brown, J. D., Childers, K. W., & Waszak, C. S. (1988, June).** *Television and adolescent sexuality.* Paper presented at the conference on "Television and Teens: Health Implications," Manhattan Beach, CA.

**Brown, J. E. (1983** *Nutrition for your pregnancy.* Minneapolis: University of Minnesota Press.

**Brown, J. H. (1979).** Suicide in Britain: More attempts, fewer deaths, lessons for public policy. *Archives of General Psychiatry, 36,* 1119–1124.

**Brown, J. L. (1987).** Hunger in the U.S. *Scientific American, 256*(2), 37–41.

**Brown, J. T., & Stoudemire, A. (1983).** Normal and pathological grief. *Journal of the American Medical Association, 250,* 378–382.

**Brown, P., & Elliott, H. (1965).** Control of aggression in a nursery school class. *Journal of Experimental Child Psychology, 2,* 103–107.

**Brown, R. (1973a).** Development of the first language in the human species. *American Psychologist, 28*(2), 97–106.

**Brown, R. (1973b).** *A first language: The early stages.* Cambridge, MA: Harvard University Press.

**Brown, R., Cazden, C. B., & Bellugi, U. (1969).** The child's grammar from I to III. In J. P. Hill (Ed.), *Minnesota symposia on child psychology* (Vol. 2). Minneapolis: University of Minnesota Press.

**Brown, S. S. (1985).** Can low birth weight be prevented? *Family Planning Perspectives, 17*(3), 112–118.

**Browne, A., & Finkelhor, D. (1986).** Impact of child sexual abuse: A review of research. *Psychological Bulletin, 99*(1), 66–77.

**Brozan, N. (1990, November 29).** Less visible but heavier burdens as AIDS attacks people over 50. *The New York Times,* pp. A1, A16.

**Brubaker, T. (1983).** Introduction. In T. Brubaker (Ed.), *Family relationships in later life.* Beverly Hills, CA: Sage.

**Bryer, J. B., Nelson, B. A., Miller, J. J., & Krol, P. A. (1987).** Childhood sexual and physical abuse as factors in adult psychiatric illness. *American Journal of Psychiatry, 144*(11), 1426–1430.

**Buie, J. (1987, April 8).** Pregnant teenagers: New view of old solution. *Education Week,* p. 32.

**Bukowski, W. M., & Kramer, T. L. (1986).** Judgments of the features of friendship among early adolescent boys and girls. *Journal of Early Adolescence, 6,* 331–338.

**Bullen, B. A., Skrinar, G. S., Beitins, I., von Mering, G., Turnbull, B. A., & McArthur, J. W. (1985).** Induction of menstrual disorders by strenuous exercise in untrained women. *The New England Journal of Medicine, 312,* 1349–1353.

**Bumpass, L. L., & Sweet, J. A. (1988).** *Preliminary evidence on cohabitation.* NSFH Working Paper No. 2. Center for Demography and Ecology, University of Wisconsin-Madison.

**Burgess, A. W., Hartman, C. R., & McCormack, A. (1987).** Abused to abuser: Antecedents of socially deviant behaviors. *American Journal of Psychiatry, 144*(11), 1431–1436.

**Burkhauser, R. V., Holden, K. C., & Feaster, D. (1988).** Incidence, timing, and events associated with poverty: A dynamic view of poverty in retirement. *Journal of Gerontology, 43*(2), S46–52.

**Bush, T. L., Cowan, L. D., Barrett-Connor, E., Criqui, M. H., Karon, J. M., Wallace, R. B., Tyroler, H. A., & Rifkind, B. M. (1983).** Estrogen use and all-cause mortality: Preliminary results from the Lipid Research Clinics program follow-up study. *Journal of the American Medical Association, 249*(7), 903–906.

**Busse, E. W. (1987).** Primary and secondary aging. In G. L. Maddox (Ed.), *The encyclopedia of aging* (p. 534). New York: Springer.

**Bustillo, M., Buster, J. E., Cohen, S. W., Hamilton, F., Thorneycroft, I. H., Simon, J. A., Rodi, I. A., Boyers, S., Marshall, J. R., Louw, J. A., Seed, R., & Seed, R. (1984).** Delivery of a healthy infant following nonsurgical ovum transfer. *Journal of the American Medical Association, 251*(7), 889.

**Butler, R. (1961).** Re-awakening interests. *Nursing Homes: Journal of American Nursing Home Association, 10,* 8–19.

**Butler, R., & Lewis, M. (1982).** *Aging and mental health* (3d ed.). St. Louis: Mosby.

**Butterfield, E., & Siperstein, G. (1972).** Influence of contingent auditory stimulation upon nonnutritional suckle. In J. Bosma (Ed.), *Oral sensation and perception: The mouth of the infant.* Springfield, IL: Thomas.

**Cahan, S., & Cohen, M. (1989).** Age versus schooling effects on intelligence development. *Child Development, 60,* 1239–1249.

**Cain, V. S., & Hofferth, S. L. (1989).** Parental choice of self-care for school-age children. *Journal of Marriage and the Family, 51,* 65–77.

**Calderone, M. S., & Johnson, E. W. (1981).** *The family book about sexuality.* New York: Harper & Row.

**Calvert, S. L., & Huston, A. C. (1987).** Television and children's gender schemata. In L. S. Liben & M. L. Signorella (Eds.), *Children's gender schemata.* San Francisco: Jossey-Bass.

**Campbell, A., Converse, P. E., & Rodgers, W. L. (1975).** *The quality of American life: Perceptions, evaluations, and satisfactions.* New York: Russell Sage Foundation.

**Campbell, F. L., Townes, B. D., & Beach, L. R. (1982).** Motivational bases of childbearing decisions. In G. L. Fox (Ed.), *The childbearing decision: Fertility, attitudes, and behavior.* Beverly Hills, CA: Sage.

**Campos, J., Bertenthal, B., & Benson, N. (1980, April).** *Self-produced locomotion and the extraction of form invariance.* Paper presented at the meeting of the International Conference on Infant Studies, New Haven.

**Campos, J. J., Langer, A., & Krowitz, A. (1970).** Cardiac responses on the visual cliff in prelocomotor human infants. *Science, 170,* 196–197.

**Cantor, M. H. (1983).** Strain among caregivers: A study of experience in the United States. *Gerontologist, 23*(6), 597–604.

**Capute, A. J., Shapiro, B. K., & Palmer, F. B. (1987).** Marking the milestones of language development. *Contemporary Pediatrics, 4*(4), 24.

**Cargan, L. (1981).** Singles: An examination of two stereotypes. *Family Relations, 30,* 377–385.

**Carlson, B. E. (1984).** The father's contribution to child care: Effects on children's perceptions of parental roles. *American Journal of Orthopsychiatry, 54*(1), 123–136.

**Carlton-Ford, S., & Collins, W. A. (1988, August).** *Family conflict: Dimensions, differential reporting, and developmental differences.* Paper presented at the annual meeting of the American Sociological Association, Chicago.

**Carpenter, M. W., Sady, S. P., Hoegsberg, B., Sady, M. A., Haydon, B., Cullinane, E. M., Coustan, D. R., & Thompson, P. D. (1988).** Fetal heart rate response to maternal exertion. *Journal of the American Medical Association, 259*(20), 3006–3009.

**Carrera, M. A. (1986, April 11).** *Future directions in teen pregnancy prevention.* Talk presented to the annual meeting of the Society for the Scientific Study of Sex, Eastern Region.

**Carroll, J. L., & Rest, J. R. (1982).** Moral development. In B. Wolman (Ed.), *Handbook of developmental psychology.* Englewood Cliffs, NJ: Prentice-Hall.

**Carter, D., & Welch, D. (1981).** Parenting styles and children's behavior. *Family Relations, 30,* 191–195.

**Carton, R. W. (1990).** The road to euthanasia. *Journal of the American Medical Association, 263*(16), 2221.

**Casey, P. H., Bradley, R., & Wortham, B. (1984).** Social and nonsocial home environment of infants with nonorganic failure-to-thrive. *Pediatrics, 73*(3), 348–353.

**Casey, R. J., & Berman, J. S. (1985).** The outcome of psychotherapy with children. *Psychological Bulletin, 98*(2), 388–400.

**Cassell, C. (1984).** *Swept away.* New York: Simon & Schuster.

**Cassidy, J. (1986).** The ability to negotiate the environment: An aspect of infant competence as related to quality of attachment. *Child Development, 57,* 331–337.

**Cassidy, M. L. (1983).** The effect of retirement on emotional well-being: A comparison of men and women. *Dissertation Abstracts International, 43*(9-A), 3118.

**Cattell, R. B. (1965).** *The scientific analysis of personality.* Baltimore: Penguin.

**Celis, W. (1990).** More states are laying school paddle to rest. *The New York Times,* pp. A1, B12.

**Centers for Disease Control. (1980).** Risk factor update. Atlanta: U.S. Department of Health and Human Services.

**Centers for Disease Control. (1983).** *CDC Surveillance Summaries* (Vol. 32). Atlanta: Author.

**Centers for Disease Control. (1986).** Statistical information. Atlanta: Author.

**Chance, P., & Fischman, J. (1987).** The magic of childhood. *Psychology Today, 21*(5), 48–58.

**Chapman, A. H. (1974).** *Management of emotional problems of children and adolescents* (2d ed.). Philadelphia: Lippincott.

**Chappell, N. L., & Penning, M. J. (1979).** The trend away from institutionalization. *Research on Aging, 1*(1), 161–187.

**Charness, M. E., Simon, R. P., & Greenberg, D. A. (1989).** Ethanol and the nervous system. *The New England Journal of Medicine, 321*(7), 442–454.

**Chasnoff, I. J., Griffith, D. R., MacGregor, S., Dirkes, K., & Burns, K. A. (1989).** Temporal patterns of cocaine use in pregnancy: Perinatal outcomes. *Journal of the American Medical Association, 261*(12), 1741–1744.

**Chatters, L. M. (1988).** Subjective well-being evaluations among older blacks. *Psychology and Aging, 3*(2), 184–190.

**Chatters, L. M., & Taylor, R. J. (1989).** Age differences in religious participation among black adults. *Journal of Gerontology, 44*(5), S183–189.

**Chavez, G. F., Mulinare, J., & Cordero, J. F. (1989).** Maternal cocaine use during early pregnancy as a risk factor for congenital urogenital anomalies. *Journal of the American Medical Association, 262*(6), 795–798.

**Chen, C., & Stevenson, H. W. (1989).** Homework: A cross-cultural examination. *Child Development, 60,* 551–561.

**Cherlin, A., & Furstenberg, F. F. (1986).** Grandparents and family crisis. *Generations, 10*(4), 26–28.

**Chervenak, F. A., Isaacson, G., & Mahoney, M. J. (1986).** Advances in the diagnosis of fetal defects. *The New England Journal of Medicine, 315*(5), 305–307.

**Chess, S. (1983).** Mothers are always the problem—or are they? Old wine in new bottles. *Pediatrics, 71*(6), 974–976.

**Chess, S., & Thomas, A. (1982).** Infant bonding: Mystique and reality. *American Journal of Orthopsychiatry, 52*(2), 213–222.

**Child Welfare League of America. (1986).** *Born to run: The status of child abuse in America.* Washington, DC: Author.

**Chilman, C. S. (1980).** *Adolescent sexuality in a changing American society: Social and psychological perspectives* (NIH Publication No. 80–1426). Bethesda, MD: National Institutes of Health.

**Chira, S. (1988, July 27).** In Japan, the land of the rod, an appeal to spare the child. *The New York Times,* pp. A1, A10.

**Chiriboga, D. A. (1982).** Adaptation to marital separation in later and earlier life. *Journal of Gerontology, 37,* 109–114.

**Chiriboga, D. A. (1989).** Mental health at the midpoint: Crisis, challenge, or relief. In S. Hunter & M. Sundel (Eds.), *Midlife myths.* Newbury Park, CA: Sage.

**Chiriboga, D. A., & Thurnher, M. (1975).** Concept of self. In M. F. Lowenthal, M. Thurnher, & D. A. Chiriboga & Associates (Eds.), *Four stages of life: A comparative study of women and men facing transitions.* San Francisco: Jossey-Bass.

**Chisholm, J. S. (1983).** *Navajo infancy: An ethological study of child development.* New York: Aldine.

**Chissell, J. T. (1989, July 16).** Paper delivered at symposium on race, racism, and health at National Medical Association's 94th annual convention, Orlando, Florida.

**Chodorow, N. (1978).** *The reproduction of mothering.* Berkeley: University of California Press.

**Chomsky, C. S. (1969).** *The acquisition of syntax in children from five to ten.* Cambridge, MA: Massachusetts Institute of Technology (MIT) Press.

**Chomsky, N. (1972).** *Language and mind* (2d ed.). New York: Harcourt Brace Jovanovich.

**Chumlea, W. C. (1982).** Physical growth in adolescence. In B. B. Wolman (Ed.), *Handbook of developmental psychology.* Englewood Cliffs, NJ: Prentice-Hall.

**Cicirelli, V. G. (1976a).** Family structure and interaction: Sibling effects on socialization. In M. McMillan & S. Henao (Eds.), *Child psychiatry: Treatment and research.* New York: Brunner/Mazel.

**Cicirelli, V. G. (1976b).** Siblings teaching siblings. In V. L. Allen (Ed.), *Children as teachers: Theory and research on tutoring.* New York: Academic.

**Cicirelli, V. G. (1977).** Relationship of siblings to the elderly person's feeling and concerns. *Journal of Gerontology, 12*(3), 317–322.

**Cicirelli, V. G. (1980, December).** *Adult children's views on providing services for elderly parents.* Report to the Andrus Foundation.

**Cicirelli, V. G. (1981, April).** *Interpersonal relationships of siblings in the middle part of the life span.* Paper presented at the biennial meeting of the Society for Research in Child Development, Boston.

**Cicirelli, V. G. (1989).** Feelings of attachment to siblings and well-being in later life. *Psychology and Aging, 4*(2), 211–216.

**Clark, R. A., & Gecas, V. (1977).** *The employed father in America: A role competition analysis.* Paper presented at the Annual Meeting of the Pacific Sociological Association.

**Clarke-Stewart, A. (1977).** *Child care in the family: A review of research and some propositions for policy.* New York: Academic.

**Clarke-Stewart, K. A. (1987).** Predicting child development from day care forms and features: The Chicago study. In D. A. Phillips (Ed.), Quality in child care: What does the research tell us? *Research Monographs of the National Association for the Education of Young Children.* Washington, D.C.: National Association for the Education of Young Children.

**Clarke-Stewart, K. A. (1989).** Infant day care: Maligned or malignant. *American Psychologist, 44*(2), 266–273.

**Clarkson-Smith, L., & Hartley, A. A. (1989).** Relationship between physical exercise and cognitive abilities in older adults. *Psychology and Aging, 4*(2), 183–189.

**Clemens, A. W., & Axelson, L. J. (1985).** The not-so-empty nest: Return of the fledgling adult. *Family Relations, 34,* 259–264.

**Clinton, H. R. (1990, April 7).** In France, day care is every child's right. *The New York Times,* p. 25.

**Cobrinick, P., Hood, R., & Chused, E. (1959).** Effects of maternal narcotic addiction on the newborn infant. *Pediatrics, 24,* 288–290.

**Cohen, G. D. (1981).** *Depression and the elderly.* (DHHS Publication No. ADM 81–932). Washington, DC: U.S. Government Printing Office.

**Cohen, G. D. (1987).** Alzheimer's disease. In G. L. Maddox (Ed.), *The encyclopedia of aging* (pp. 27–30). New York: Springer.

**Cohen, S., Lichtenstein, E., Prochaska, J. O., Rossi, J. S., Gutz, E. R., Carr, C. R., Orleans, C. T., Schoenbach, V. J., Biener, L., Abrams, D., DiClemente, C., Curry, S., Marlatt, G. A., Cummings, K. M., Emont, S. L., Grovino, G., & Ossip-Klein, D. (1989).** Debunking myths about self-quitting: Evidence from 10 prospective studies of persons who attempt to quit smoking by themselves. *American Psychologist, 44*(11), 1355–1365.

**Cohn, J. F., & Tronick, E. Z. (1983).** Three-month-old infants' reaction to simulated maternal depression. *Child Development, 54,* 185–193.

**Coie, J. D., & Kupersmidt, J. B. (1983).** A behavioral analysis of emerging social status in boys' groups. *Child Development, 54,* 1400–1416.

**Colby, A., Kohlberg, L., Gibbs, J., & Lieberman, M. (1983).** A longitudinal study of moral development. *Monographs of the Society for Research in Child Development, 48*(1–2, Serial No. 200).

**Cole, C., & Rodman, H. (1987).** When school-age children care for themselves: Issues for family life educators and parents. *Family Relations, 36,* 92–96.

**Coleman, J. (1980).** Friendship and the peer group in adolescence. In J. Adelson (Ed.), *Handbook of adolescent development.* New York: Wiley.

**Coles, R., & Stokes, G. (1985).** *Sex and the*

*American teenager*. New York: Harper & Row.

Colligan, M. J., Smith, M. J., & Hurrell, J. J. (1977). Occupational incidence rates of mental health disorders. *Journal of Human Stress, 3*, 34–39.

Collins, R. C., & Deloria, D. (1983). Head Start research: A new chapter. *Children Today, 12*(4), 15–19.

Collins, W. A. (Ed.). (1984). *Development during middle childhood: The years from six to twelve*. Washington, DC: National Academy.

Collins, W. A. (1990). Parent-child relationships in the transition to adolescence: Continuity and change in interaction, affect, and cognition. In R. Montemayor, G. R. Adams, & T. P. Gullotta (Eds.), *From childhood to adolescence: A transitional period?* Newbury Park, CA: Sage.

Commonwealth Fund Commission on Elderly People Living Alone. (1986). Problems facing elderly Americans living alone. New York: Louis Harris & Associates.

Condon, W., & Sander, L. (1974). Synchrony demonstrated between movements of the neonate and adult speech. *Child Development, 45*, 456–462.

Condry, J. C., & Condry, S. (1974). *The development of sex differences: A study of the eye of the beholder*. Unpublished manuscript, Cornell University, Ithaca, NY.

Condry, J. C., Siman, M. L., & Bronfenbrenner, U. (1968). Characteristics of peer- and adult-oriented children. Unpublished manuscript, Cornell University, Department of Child Development, Ithaca, NY.

Conger, J. J. (1988). Hostages to fortune: Youth, values, and the public interest. *American Psychologist, 43*(4), 291–300.

Conger, J. J., & Petersen, A. C. (1984). *Adolescence and youth*. New York: Harper & Row.

Congressional Caucus for Women's Issues. (1987). *The American woman, 1987–88*. Washington, DC: Author.

Connecticut Early Childhood Education Council (CECEC). (1983). *Report on full-day kindergarten*. Author.

Conners, C. K. (1988). Does diet affect behavior and learning in hyperactive children? *Harvard Medical School Mental Health Letter, 5*(5), 7–8.

Coons, S., & Guilleminault, C. (1982). Development of sleep-wake patterns and non-rapid eye movement sleep stages during the first six months of life in normal infants. *Pediatrics, 69*(6), 793–798.

Cooper, K. L., & Gutmann, D. L. (1987). Gender identity and ego mastery style in middle-aged, pre- and post-empty nest women. *Gerontologist, 27*(3), 347–352.

Coopersmith, S. (1967). *The antecedents of self-esteem*. San Francisco: Freeman.

Corbin, C. (1973). *A textbook of motor development*. Dubuque, IA: Brown.

Correa, P., Pickle, L. W., Fontham, E., Lin, Y., & Haenszel, W. (1983, September 10). Passive smoking and lung cancer. *The Lancet*, pp. 595–597.

Costa, P. T., & McCrae, R. R. (1981). Still stable after all these years: Personality as a key to some issues in adulthood and old age. In P. B. Baltes & O. G. Brim (Eds.), *Lifespan development and behavior* (Vol. 3). New York: Academic.

Costa, P. T., McCrae, R. R., Zonderman, A. B., Barbano, H. E., Lebowitz, B., & Larson, D. M. (1986). Cross-sectional studies of personality in a national sample: 2. Stability in neuroticism, extraversion, and openness. *Psychology and Aging, 1*(2), 144–149.

Costanzo, P. R., & Shaw, M. E. (1966). Conformity as a function of age level. *Child Development, 37*, 967–975.

Costello, A. J., Edelbrock, C., Burns, B. J., Dulcan, M. K., Brent, D., & Janiszewsku, S. (1988). Psychiatric disorders in pediatric primary care. *Archives of General Psychiatry, 45*(12), 1107–1116.

Coster, W. J., Gersten, M. S., Beeghly, M., & Cicchetti, D. (1989). Communicative functioning in maltreated toddlers. *Developmental Psychology, 25*(6), 1020–1029.

Council on Ethical and Judicial Affairs. (1990). Black-white disparities in health care. *Journal of the American Medical Association, 263*, 2344–2346.

Council on Scientific Affairs of the American Medical Association. (1984). Exercise programs for the elderly. *Journal of the American Medical Association, 252*(4), 544–546.

Council on Scientific Affairs of the American Medical Association. (1989). Dyslexia. *Journal of the American Medical Association, 261*(15), 2236–2239.

Council on Scientific Affairs of the American Medical Association. (1991). Hispanic health in the United States. *Journal of the American Medical Association, 265*(2), 248–252.

Courchesne, E., Yeung-Courchesne, R., Press, G. A., Hesselink, J. R., & Jernigan, T. L. (1988). Hypolasia of cerebellar vermae lobules VI and VII in autism. *The New England Journal of Medicine, 318*, 1349–1354.

Cousins, N. (1979). *Anatomy of an illness as perceived by the patient*. New York: Norton.

Covey, H. C. (1988). Historical terminology used to represent older people. *Gerontologist, 28*(3), 291–297.

Cowan, M. W. (1979). The development of the brain. *Scientific American, 241*, 112–133.

Cox, J., Daniel, N., & Boston, B. O. (1985). *Educating able learners: Programs and promising practices*. Austin: University of Texas Press.

Craik, F. I. M. (1977). Age differences in human memory. In J. E. Birren & K. W. Schaie (Eds.), *Handbook of the psychology of aging*. New York: Van Nostrand Reinhold.

Craik, F. I. M., Byrd, M., & Swanson, J. M. (1987). Patterns of memory loss in three elderly samples. *Psychology and Aging, 2*(1), 79–86.

Cratty, B. (1979). *Perceptual and motor development in infants and children* (2d ed.). Englewood Cliffs, NJ: Prentice-Hall.

Crisp, A. H., Queenan, M., & D'Souza, M. F. (1984). Myocardial infarction and the emotional climate. *The Lancet, 1*(8377), 616–618.

Croake, J. W. (1973). The changing nature of children's fears. *Child Study Journal, 3*(2), 91–105.

Crockett, L. J., & Petersen, A. C. (1987). Pubertal status and psychosocial development: Findings from the Early Adolescent Study. In R. M. Lerner & T. T. Foch (Eds.), *Biological-psychosocial interactions in early adolescence: A life-span perspective*. Hillsdale, NJ: Erlbaum.

Csikszentmihalyi, M., & Larson, R. (1984). *Being adolescent: Conflict and growth in the teenage years*. New York: Basic Books.

Cumming, E., & Henry, W. (1961). *Growing old*. New York: Basic Books.

Cummings, E. M., Iannotti, R. J., & Zahn-Waxler, C. (1989). Aggression between peers in early childhood: Individual continuity and developmental change. *Child Development, 60*, 887–895.

Cunningham, N., Anisfeld, E., Casper, V., & Nozyce, M. (1987, February 14). Infant carrying, breast feeding, and mother-infant relations. *The Lancet*, p. 379.

Curtiss, S. (1977). *Genie*. New York: Academic.

Cutrona, C., Russell, D., & Rose, J. (1986). Social support and adaptation to stress by the elderly. *Journal of Psychology and Aging, 1*(1), 47–54.

Cytrynbaum, S., Bluum, L., Patrick, R., Stein, J., Wadner, D., & Wilk, C. (1980). Midlife development: A personality and social systems perspective. In L. Poon (Ed.), *Aging in the 1980s*. Washington, DC: American Psychological Association.

Damon, W. (1984). Peer education: The untapped potential. *Journal of Applied Developmental Psychology, 5*, 331–343.

Dan, A. J., & Bernhard, L. A. (1989). Menopause and other health issues for midlife women. In S. Hunter & M. Sundel (Eds.), *Midlife myths*. Newbury Park, CA: Sage.

Daniels, D., & Plomin, R. (1985). Origins of individual differences in infant shyness. *Developmental Psychology, 21*(1), 118–121.

**Danish, S. J. (1983).** Musings about personal competence: The contributions of sport, health, and fitness. *American Journal of Community Psychology, 11*(3), 221–240.

**Danish, S. J., & D'Augelli, A. R. (1980).** Promoting competence and enhancing development through life development intervention. In L. A. Bond & J. C. Rosem (Eds.), *Competence and coping during adulthood.* Hanover, NH: University Press of New England.

**Danish, S. J., Smyer, M. A., & Nowak, C. A. (1980).** Developmental intervention: Enhancing life-event processes. In P. B. Baltes & O. G. Brim (Eds.), *Life-span development and behavior* (Vol 3). New York: Academic.

**Datan, N., Rodeheaver, D., & Hughes, F. (1987).** Adult development and aging. *Annual Review of Psychology, 38,* 153–180.

**Davidson, J. E., & Sternberg, R. J. (1984).** The role of insight in intellectual giftedness. *Gifted Child Quarterly, 28*(2), 58–64.

**Davidson, R. J., & Fox, N. A. (1989).** Frontal brain asymmetry predicts infants' response to maternal separation. *Journal of Abnormal Psychology, 98*(2), 127–131.

**Davis, B. W. (1985).** *Visits to remember: A handbook for visitors of nursing home residents.* University Park: Pennsylvania State University Cooperative Extension Service.

**Davis, B. W. (undated).** *Celebrate your marriage* (Marriage Strength Builder No. 4, Learn-at-Home Program). University Park: Pennsylvania State University Cooperative Extension Service.

**Davis, K. E. (1985, February).** Near and dear: Friendship and love compared. *Psychology Today, 19,* 22–30.

**Davis, S. (1985, Summer).** Pop lyrics: A mirror and molder of society. *Et cetera,* 167–169.

**Dawson-Hughes, B., Dallal, G. E., Krall, E. A., Sadowski, L., Sahyoun, N., & Tannenbaum, S. (1990).** A controlled trial of the effect of calcium supplementation on bone density in postmenopausal women. *The New England Journal of Medicine, 323,* 878–883.

**Deaux, K. (1985).** Sex and gender. *Annual Review of Psychology, 36,* 49–81.

**DeBuono, B. A., Zinner, S. H., Daamen, M., & McCormack, W. M. (1990).** Sexual behavior of college women in 1975, 1980, and 1989. *The New England Journal of Medicine, 322,* 821–825.

**DeCasper, A., & Fifer, W. (1980).** Newborns prefer their mothers' voices. *Science, 208,* 1174–1176.

**DeCasper, A. J., & Spence, M. J. (1986).** Prenatal maternal speech influences newborns' perception of speech sounds. *Infant Behavior and Development, 9,* 133–150.

**Decker, M. D., Dewey, M. J., Hutcheson, R. H., & Schaffner, W. (1984).** The use and efficacy of child restraint devices. *Journal of the American Medical Association, 252*(18), 2571–2575.

**DeFrain, J., & Ernst, L. (1978).** The psychological effects of sudden infant death syndrome on surviving family members. *Journal of Family Practice, 6*(5), 985–989.

**DeFrain, J., Montens, L., Stork, J., & Stork, W. (1986).** *Stillborn: An invisible death.* Lexington, MA: Heath.

**DeFrain, J., Taylor, J., & Ernst, L. (1982).** *Coping with sudden infant death.* Lexington, MA: Heath.

**DeFries, J. C., Fulker, D. W., & LaBuda, M. C. (1987).** Evidence for a genetic etiology in reading disability of twins. *Nature, 329,* 537–539.

**Denney, N. W. (1972).** Free classification in preschool children. *Child Development, 43,* 1161–1170.

**Denney, N. W., & Palmer, A. M. (1981).** Adult age differences on traditional and practical problem-solving measures. *Journal of Gerontology, 36*(3), 323–328.

**Denney, N. W., & Pearce, K. A. (1989).** A developmental study of practical problem solving in adults. *Psychology and Aging, 4*(4), 438–442.

**Dennis, W. (1960).** Causes of retardation among institutional children: Iran. *Journal of Genetic Psychology, 96,* 47–59.

**Denny, F. W., & Clyde, W. A. (1983).** Acute respiratory tract infections: An overview. In W. A. Clyde & F. W. Denny (Eds.), *Workshop on acute respiratory diseases among children of the world. Pediatric Research, 17,* 1026–1029.

**deRegt, R. H., Minkoff, H. L., Feldman, J., & Schwartz, R. H. (1986).** Relation of private or clinic care to the cesarean birth rate. *The New England Journal of Medicine, 315,* 619–624.

**deVos, S. (1990).** Extended family living among older people in six Latin American countries. *Journal of Gerontology, 45*(3), S87–94.

**DeVries, M. W., & Sameroff, A. J. (1984).** Culture and temperament: Influence on infant temperament in three East African societies. *American Journal of Orthopsychiatry, 54*(1), 83–96.

**DeVries, R. (1969).** Constancy of generic identity in the years three to six. *Monographs of the Society for Research in Child Development, 34*(3, Serial No. 127).

**Deykin, E. Y., Alpert, J. J., & McNamarra, J. J. (1985).** A pilot study of the effect of exposure to child abuse or neglect on adolescent suicidal behavior. *American Journal of Psychiatry, 142*(11), 1299–1303.

*Diagnostic and statistical manual of mental disorders* **(3d ed., rev.) (DSM III-R).**

**(1987).** Washington, DC: American Psychiatric Association.

**Dickson, W. P. (1979).** Referential communication performance from age 4 to 8: Effects of referent type, context, and target position. *Developmental Psychology, 15*(4), 470–471.

**Dickstein, S., & Parke, R. D. (1988).** Social referencing in infancy: A glance at fathers and marriage. *Child Development, 59,* 506–511.

**Dien, D. S. F. (1982).** A Chinese perspective on Kohlberg's theory of moral development. *Developmental Review, 2,* 331–341.

**Dietz, W. H., & Gortmaker, S. L. (1985).** Do we fatten our children at the television set? Obesity and television viewing in children and adolescents. *Pediatrics, 75,* 807–812.

**DiMaio, M. S., Baumgarten, A., Greenstein, R. M., Saal, H. M., & Mahoney, M. J. (1987).** Screening for fetal Down's syndrome in pregnancy by measuring maternal serum alpha-fetoprotein levels. *The New England Journal of Medicine, 317,* 342–346.

**Dion, K. K., Berscheid, E., & Walster, E. (1972).** What is beautiful is good. *Journal of Personality and Social Psychology, 24,* 285–290.

**Dixon, R. A., & Baltes, P. B. (1986).** Toward life-span research on the functions and pragmatics of intelligence. In R. J. Sternberg & R. K. Wagner (Eds.), *Practical intelligence: Nature and origins of competence in the everyday world.* New York: Cambridge University Press.

**Doctors rule out transplant from organs of hanged boy. (1984, November 23).** *The New York Times,* p. A26.

**Dodge, K. A. (1983).** Behavioral antecedents of peer social status. *Child Development, 54,* 1386–1399.

**Doering, C. H., Kraemer, H. C., Brodie, H. K. H., & Hamburg, D. A. (1975).** A cycle of plasma testosterone in the human male. *Journal of Clinical Endocrinology and Metabolism, 40,* 492–500.

**Doherty, W. J., & Jacobson, N. S. (1982).** Marriage and the family. In B. Wolman (Ed.), *Handbook of developmental psychology.* Englewood Cliffs, NJ: Prentice-Hall.

**Doka, K. J., & Mertz, M. E. (1988).** The meaning and significance of great-grandparenthood. *Gerontologist, 28*(2), 192–197.

**Doppelt, J. E., & Wallace, W. L. (1955).** Standardization of the Wechsler Adult Intelligence Scale for older persons. *Journal of Abnormal and Social Psychology, 51,* 312–330.

**Dore, J. (1975).** Holophrases, speech acts, and language universals. *Journal of Child Language, 2,* 21–40.

**Dornbusch, S. M., Ritter, P. L., Leiderman,**

P. H., Roberts, D. F., & Fraleigh, M. J. (1987). The relation of parenting style to adolescent school performance. *Child Development, 58,* 1244–1257.

Doty, R. L. (1984, December). Smell identification ability: Changes with age. *Science, 226,* 1441–1443.

Dove, J. (undated). *Facts about anorexia nervosa.* Bethesda, MD: National Institutes of Health, Office of Research Reporting, National Institute of Child Health and Human Development.

Dreyer, P. H. (1982). Sexuality during adolescence. In B. B. Wolman (Ed.), *Handbook of developmental psychology.* Englewood Cliffs, NJ: Prentice-Hall.

Droege, R. (1982). *A psychosocial study of the formation of the middle adult life structure in women.* Unpublished doctoral dissertation, California School of Professional Psychology, Berkeley, CA.

Dunn, J. (1983). Sibling relationships in early childhood. *Child Development, 54,* 787–811.

Dunn, J. (1985). *Sisters and brothers.* Cambridge, MA: Harvard University Press.

Dunn, J., & Kendrick, C. (1982). *Siblings: Love, envy and understanding.* Cambridge, MA: Harvard University Press.

DuPont, R. L. (1983). Phobias in children. *Journal of Pediatrics, 102*(6), 999–1002.

Durlak, J. A. (1973). Relationship between attitudes toward life and death among elderly women. *Developmental Psychology, 8*(1), 146.

Dutta, R., Schulenberg, E., & Lair, T. J. (1986, April). *The effect of job characteristics on cognitive abilities and intellectual flexibility.* Paper presented at the annual meeting of the Eastern Psychological Association, New York.

DuVerglas, G., Banks, S. R., & Guyer, K. E. (1988). Clinical effects of fenflivramine on children with autism: A review of the research. *Journal of Autism and Developmental Disorders, 18*(2), 297–308.

Dyslexia. (1989, September 23). *The Lancet,* pp. 719–720.

Easterbrooks, M. A. (1989). Quality of attachment to mother and to father: Effects of perinatal risk status. *Child Development, 60,* 825–830.

Easterbrooks, M. A., & Goldberg, W. A. (1984). Toddler development in the family: Impact of father involvement and parenting characteristics. *Child Development, 55,* 740–752.

Easterlin, R. A. (1980). *Birth and fortune.* New York: Basic Books.

Eastman, P. (1984). Elders under siege. *Psychology Today, 18*(1), 30.

Eckerman, C. O., Davis, C. C., & Didow, S. M. (1989). Toddlers' emerging ways of achieving social coordination with a peer. *Child Development, 60,* 440–453.

Eckerman, C. O., & Stein, M. R. (1982). The toddler's emerging interactive skills. In K. H. Rubin & H. S. Ross (Eds.), *Peer rela-*

*tionships and social skills in childhood.* New York: Springer-Verlag.

Edwards, C. P. (1977). The comparative study of the development of moral judgment and reasoning. In R. Monroe, R. Monroe, & B. B. Whiting (Eds.), *Handbook of cross-cultural human development.* New York: Garland.

Egbuono, L., & Starfield, B. (1982). Child health and social status. *Pediatrics, 69*(5), 550–557.

Egeland, B., & Farber, E. A. (1984). Infant-mother attachment: Factors related to its development and changes over time. *Child Development, 55,* 753–771.

Egeland, B., & Sroufe, L. A. (1981). Attachment and early maltreatment. *Child Development, 52,* 44–52.

Egertson, H. A. (1987, May 20). Recapturing kindergarten for 5-year-olds. *Education Week,* p. 28, 19.

Ehrhardt, A. A., & Money, J. (1967). Progestin induced hermaphroditism: I.Q. and psychosocial identity. *Journal of Sexual Research, 3,* 83–100.

Eichorn, D. H., Clausen, J. A., Haan, N., Honzik, M. P., & Mussen, P. H. (1981). *Present and past in midlife.* New York: Academic.

Eiger, M. S., & Olds, S. W. (1987). *The complete book of breastfeeding* (rev. ed.). New York: Workman.

Eimas, P. (1985). The perception of speech in early infancy. *Scientific American, 252*(1), 46–52.

Eimas, P., Siqueland, E., Jusczyk, P., & Vigorito, J. (1971). Speech perception in infants. *Science, 171,* 303–306.

Einstein, E. (1979, April). Stepfamily lives. *Human Behavior,* pp. 63–68.

Eisen, M., & Zellman, G. L. (1987). Changes in incidence of sexual intercourse of unmarried teenagers following a community-based sex education program. *Journal of Sex Research, 23*(4), 527–544.

Eisenberg, A., Murkoff, H. E., & Hathaway, S. E. (1984, 1986). *What to expect when you're expecting* (2d ed.). New York: Workman.

Eisenberg, L. (1980). Adolescent suicide: On taking arms against a sea of troubles. *Pediatrics, 66,* 315–320.

Eisenberg, L. (1986). Does bad news about suicide beget bad news? *The New England Journal of Medicine, 315,* 705–706.

Eisenberg, N., Fabes, R. A., Schaller, M., & Miller, P. A. (1989). Sympathy and personal distress: Development, gender differences, and interrelations of indexes. In N. Eisenberg (Ed.), Empathy and related emotional responses. *New Directions in Child Development, 44.* San Francisco: Jossey-Bass.

Elkind, D. (1981). *The hurried child.* Reading, MA: Addison-Wesley.

Elkind, D. (1984). *All grown up and no place to go.* Reading, MA: Addison-Wesley.

Elkind, D. (1987a). *Miseducation.* New York: Knopf.

Elkind, D. (1987b). Superkids and super problems. *Psychology Today, 21*(5), 60–61.

Ellis, L., & Ames, M. A. (1987). Neurohormonal functioning and sexual orientation: A theory of homosexuality-heterosexuality. *Psychological Bulletin, 101*(2), 233–258.

Emery, R. E. (1989). Family violence. *American Psychologist, 44*(2), 321–328.

Emmerick, H. (1978). The influence of parents and peers on choices made by adolescents. *Journal of Youth and Adolescence, 7*(2), 175–180.

Engelberg, S. (1984, September 26). Why motorists won't buckle up. *The New York Times,* pp. C1, C8.

Epstein, J. L. (1984, May). Single parents get involved in children's learning [Summary]. *CSOS Report.* Baltimore, MD: Johns Hopkins University Center for Social Organization of Schools (CSOS).

Epstein, L. H., & Wing, R. R. (1987). Behavioral treatment of childhood obesity. *Psychological Bulletin, 101*(3), 331–342.

Erikson, E. H. (1950). *Childhood and society.* New York: Norton.

Erikson, E. H. (1964). *Insight and responsibility.* New York: Norton.

Erikson, E. H. (1968). *Identity: Youth and crisis.* New York: Norton.

Erikson, E. H. (1973). The wider identity. In K. Erikson (Ed.), *In search of common ground: Conversations with Erik H. Erikson and Huey P. Newton.* New York: Norton.

Erikson, E. H. (1985). *The life cycle completed.* New York: Norton.

Erikson, E. H., Erikson, J. M., & Kivnick, H. Q. (1986). *Vital involvement in old age.* New York: Norton.

Eron, L. D. (1980). Prescription for reduction of aggression. *American Psychologist, 35*(3), 244–252.

Eron, L. D. (1982). Parent-child interaction, television violence, and aggression in children. *American Psychologist, 37*(2), 197–211.

Espenschade, A. (1960). Motor development. In W. R. Johnson (Ed.), *Science and medicine of exercise and sports.* New York: Harper & Row.

Essex, M. J., & Nam, S. (1987). Marital status and loneliness among older women: The differential importance of close family and friends. *Journal of Marriage and the Family, 49,* 93–106.

Estes, E. H. (1969). Health experience in the elderly. In E. Busse & E. Pfeiffer (Eds.), *Behavior and adaptation in late life.* Boston: Little, Brown.

Evans, D. A., Funkenstein, H., Albert, M. S., Scherr, P. A., Cook, N. R., Chown, M. J., Hebert, L. E., Hennekens, C. H., & Taylor, J. O. (1989). Prevalence of Alzheimer's disease in a community population of older persons: Higher than previously reported. *Journal of the American Medical Association, 262*(18), 2551–2556.

Evans, G. (1976). The older the sperm . . . *Ms., 4*(7), 48–49.

Evans, J., & Ilfeld, E. (1982). *Good beginnings: Parenting in the early years.* Ypsilanti, MI: High/Scope.

Evans, R. I. (1967). *Dialogue with Erik Erikson.* New York: Harper & Row.

Eveleth, P. B., & Tanner, J. M. (1976). *Worldwide variation in human growth.* London: Cambridge University Press.

Eysenck, H. J., & Prell, D. B. (1951). The inheritance of neuroticism: An experimental study. *Journal of Mental Science, 97,* 441–466.

Fagan, J. F. (1982). Infant memory. In T. M. Field, A. Huston, H. Quay, L. Troll, & G. Finley (Eds.), *Review of human development.* New York: Wiley.

Fagan, J. F., & McGrath, S. K. (1981). Infant recognition memory and later intelligence. *Intelligence, 5,* 121–130.

Fagan, J. W. (1984). Infant's long-term memory for stimulus color. *Developmental Psychology, 20*(3), 435–440.

Fagan, J. W., Morrongiello, B. A., Rovee-Collier, C., & Gekoski, M. J. (1984). Expectancies and memory retrieval in three-month-old infants. *Child Development, 55,* 936–943.

Fahey, V. (1988). The gene screen: Looking in on baby. In *Health,* May/June, 68–69.

Falbo, T., & Polit, D. F. (1986). Quantitative review of the only child literature: Research evidence and theory development. *Psychological Bulletin, 100*(2), 176–189.

Fallot, M. E., Boyd, J. L., & Oski, F. A. (1980). Breast-feeding reduces incidence of hospital admissions for infection in infants. *Pediatrics, 65*(6), 1121–1124.

Fantuzzo, J. W., Jurecic, L., Stoval, A., Hightower, A. D., Goiins, C., & Schachtel, D. (1988). Effects of adult and peer social initiations on the social behavior of withdrawn, maltreated preschool children. *Journal of Consulting and Clinical Psychology, 56*(1), 34–39.

Fantz, R. L. (1963). Pattern vision in newborn infants. *Science, 140,* 296–297.

Fantz, R. L. (1964). Visual experience in infants: Decreased attention to familiar patterns relative to novel ones. *Science, 146,* 668–670.

Fantz, R. L. (1965). Visual perception from birth as shown by pattern selectivity. In H. E. Whipple (Ed.), New issues in infant development. *Annals of the New York Academy of Science, 118,* 793–814.

Fantz, R. L., Fagen, J., & Miranda, S. B. (1975). Early visual selectivity. In L. Cohen & P. Salapatek (Eds.), *Infant perception: From sensation to cognition:*

*Vol. 1. Basic visual processes* (pp. 249–341). New York: Academic.

Fantz, R. L., & Nevis, S. (1967). Pattern preferences and perceptual-cognitive development in early infancy. *Merrill-Palmer Quarterly, 13,* 77–108.

Farrell, M. P., & Rosenberg, S. D. (1981). *Men at midlife.* Boston: Auburn.

Farrow, J. A., Rees, J. M., & Worthington-Roberts, B. S. (1987). Health, developmental, and nutritional status of adolescent alcohol and marijuana abusers. *Pediatrics, 79*(2), 218–223.

Feagans, L. (1983). A current view of learning disabilities. *Journal of Pediatrics, 102*(4), 487–493.

Feazell, C. S., Mayers, R. S., & Deschner, J. (1984). Services for men who batter: Implications for programs and policies. *Family Relations, 33,* 217–223.

Feifel, H. (1977). *New meanings of death.* New York: McGraw-Hill.

Fein, G. (1981). Pretend play in childhood: An integrative review. *Child Development, 52,* 1095–1118.

Feinberg, I. (1982). Schizophrenia: Caused by a fault in programmed synaptic elimination during adolescence. *Journal of Psychiatric Research, 17,* 319–334.

Feinberg, M., Smith, M., & Schmidt, R. (1958). An analysis of expressions used by adolescents at varying economic levels to describe accepted and rejected peers. *Journal of Genetic Psychology, 93,* 133–148.

Feinman, S., & Lewis, M. (1983). Social referencing at ten months: A second-order effect on infants' responses. *Child Development, 54,* 878–887.

Feldman, H. (1981). A comparison of intentional parents and intentionally childless couples. *Journal of Marriage and the Family, 43*(3), 593–600.

Feldman, H., & Feldman, M. (1977). *Effect of parenthood at three points on marriage.* Unpublished manuscript.

Feldman, H., Goldin-Meadow, S., & Gleitman, L. (1979). Beyond Herodotus: The creation of language by linguistically deprived deaf children. In A. Lock (Ed.), *Action, gesture and symbol: The emergence of language.* New York: Academic.

Feldman, R. D. (1982). *Whatever happened to the quiz kids: Perils and profits of growing up gifted.* Chicago: Chicago Review Press.

Fellin, P. A., & Powell, T. J. (1988). Mental health services and older adult minorities: An assessment. *Gerontologist, 28*(4), 442–446.

Fergusson, D. M., Horwood, L. J., & Shannon, F. T. (1986). Factors related to the age of attainment of nocturnal bladder control: An 8-year longitudinal study. *Pediatrics, 78,* 884–890.

Fetterly, K., & Graubard, M. S. (1984, March 23). Racial and educational fac-

tors associated with breast-feeding— United States, 1969 and 1980. *Morbidity and Mortality Weekly Report,* (MMWR), pp. 153–154.

Field, D. (1977). The importance of the verbal content in the training of Piagetian conservation skills. *Child Development, 52,* 326–334.

Field, D. (1981). Can preschool children really learn to conserve? *Child Development, 52,* 326–334.

Field, D., & Minkler, M. (1988). Continuity and change in social support between young-old and old-old or very-old age. *Journal of Gerontology, 43*(4), P100–106.

Field, T. M. (1978). Interaction behaviors of primary versus secondary caretaker fathers. *Developmental Psychology, 14,* 183–184.

Field, T. M. (1986). Interventions for premature infants. *Journal of Pediatrics, 109*(1), 183–190.

Field, T. M. (1987). Interaction and attachment in normal and atypical infants. *Journal of Consulting and Clinical Psychology, 55*(6), 853–859.

Field, T. M., & Roopnarine, J. L. (1982). Infant-peer interaction. In T. M. Field, A. Huston, H. C. Quay, L. Troll, & G. Finley (Eds.), *Review of human development.* New York: Wiley.

Field, T. M., Sandberg, D., Garcia, R., Vega-Lahr, N., Goldstein, S., & Guy, L. (1985). Pregnancy problems, postpartum depression, and early mother-infant interactions. *Developmental Psychology, 21*(6), 1152–1156.

Field, T. M., Widmayer, S., Greenberg, R., & Stoller, S. (1982). Effects of parent training on teenage mothers and their infants. *Pediatrics, 69*(6), 703–707.

Field, T. M., Woodson, R., Greenberg, R., & Cohen, D. (1982). Discrimination and imitation of facial expressions by neonates. *Science, 218,* 179–181.

Fielding, J. E., & Phenow, K. J. (1988). Health effects of involuntary smoking. *The New England Journal of Medicine, 319*(22), 1452–1460.

Fingerhut, L. A., & Kleinman, J. C. (1990). International and interstate comparisons of homicide among young males. *Journal of the American Medical Association, 263*(4) 3292–3295.

Fitness Finders. (1984). *Feelin' good.* Spring Arbor, MI: Author.

Fitten, L. J., Perryman, K. M., Gross, P. L., Fine, H., Cummins, J., & Marshall, C. (1990). Treatment of Alzheimer's disease with short and long-term oral THA and lecithin: A double-blind study. *American Journal of Psychiatry, 147,* 239–242.

Fivush, R., Hudson, J., & Nelson, K. (1983). Children's long term memory for a novel event: An exploratory study. *Merrill-Palmer Quarterly, 30,* 303–316.

Flavell, J. H. (1970). Cognitive changes in adulthood. In L. R. Goulet & P. B. Baltes (Eds.), *Life-span developmental psychology: Research & theory.* New York: Academic.

Flavell, J. H., Beach, D., & Chinsky, J. (1966). Spontaneous verbal rehearsal in a memory task as a function of age. *Child Development, 37,* 283–299.

Flavell, J. H., Speer, J. R., Green, F. L., & August, D. L. (1981). The development of comprehension monitoring and knowledge about communication. *Monographs of the Society for Research in Child Development,* 46(5, Serial No. 192).

Fomon, S. J., Filer, L. J., Anderson, T. A., & Ziegler, E. E. (1979). Recommendations for feeding normal infants. *Pediatrics,* 63(1), 52–59.

Ford, J., Zelnik, M., & Kantner, J. (1979, November). *Differences in contraceptive use and socioeconomic groups of teenagers in the United States.* Paper presented at the meeting of the American Public Health Association, New York.

Forman, M. R., Graubard, B. I., Hoffman, H. J., Beren, R., Harley, E. E., & Bennett, P. (1984). The Pima infant feeding study: Breast feeding and gastroenteritis in the first year of life. *American Journal of Epidemiology,* 119(3), 335–349.

Francoeur, R. T. (1985). Reproductive technologies: New alternatives and new ethics. *SIECUS Report, 14,* 1–5.

Frank, S. J., Avery, C. B., & Laman, M. S. (1988). Young adults' perception of their relationships with their parents: Individual differences in connectedness, competence, and emotional autonomy. *Developmental Psychology,* 24(5), 729–737.

Frankenburg, W. K. (1967, 1978). Denver developmental screening test. Denver: University of Colorado Medical Center.

Frankenburg, W. K., Dodds, J. B., Fandal, A. W., Kazuk, E., & Cohrs, M. (1975). *The Denver developmental screening test: Reference manual.* Denver: University of Colorado Medical Center.

Frankl, V. (1965). *The doctor and the soul.* New York: Knopf.

Freedman, D. G. (1979, January). Ethnic differences in babies. *Human Nature,* pp. 15–20.

Freeman, D. (1983). *Margaret Mead and Samoa.* Cambridge, MA: Harvard University Press.

Freud, A. (1946). *The ego and the mechanisms of defense.* New York: International Universities Press.

Freud, S. (1953). *A general introduction to psychoanalysis* (J. Riviere, Trans.). New York: Perma-books.

Freud, S. (1959). An autobiographical study. In J. Strachey (Ed. and Trans.), *The standard edition of the complete psychological works of Sigmund Freud* (Vol. 20).

London: Hogarth, 1959. (Original work published 1925)

Frezza, M., DiPadova, C., Pozzato, G., Terpin, M., Baraona, E., & Lieber, C. S. (1990). High blood alcohol levels in women: The role of decreased gastric alcohol dehydrogenase activity and first-pass metabolism. *The New England Journal of Medicine, 322,* 95–99.

Fried, P. A., Watkinson, B., & Willan, A. (1984). Marijuana use during pregnancy and decreased length of gestation. *American Journal of Obstetrics and Gynecology, 150,* 23–27.

Friedman, M., & Rosenman, R. H. (1974). *Type A behavior and your heart.* New York: Knopf.

Fries, J. F., & Crapo, L. M. (1981). *Vitality and aging.* San Francisco: Freeman.

Frisch, H. (1977). Sex stereotypes in adult-infancy play. *Child Development, 48,* 1671–1675.

Fromkin, V., Krashen, S., Curtiss, S., Rigler, D., & Rigler, M. (1974). The development of language in Genie: Acquisition beyond the "critical period." *Brain and Language,* 15(9), 28–34.

Frueh, T., & McGhee, P. (1975). Traditional sex role development and amount of time spent watching television. *Developmental Psychology,* 11(1), 109.

Fuchs, D., & Fuchs, L. S. (1986). Test procedure bias: A meta-analysis of examiner familiarity effects. *Review of Educational Research, 56,* 243–262.

Fuchs, F. (1980). Genetic amniocentesis. *Scientific American,* 242(6), 47–53.

Fuchs, L. S., & Fuchs, D. (1986). Effects of systematic formative evaluation of student achievement: A meta-analysis. *Exceptional Children, 53,* 199–205.

Furman, W. (1982). Children's friendships. In T. M. Field, A. Huston, H. C. Quay, L. Troll, & G. E. Finley (Eds.), *Review of human development.* New York: Wiley.

Furman, W., & Bierman, K. L. (1983). Developmental changes in young children's conceptions of friendship. *Child Development, 54,* 549–556.

Furman, W., & Buhrmester, D. (1985). Children's perceptions of the personal relationships in their social networks. *Developmental Psychology,* 21(6), 1016–1024.

Furry, C. A., & Baltes, P. B. (1973). The effect of age differences in ability-extraneous performance variables on the assessment of intelligence in children, adults, and the elderly. *Journal of Gerontology,* 28(1), 73–80.

Furst, K. (1983). *Origins and evolution of women's dreams in early adulthood.* Unpublished doctoral dissertation, California School of Professional Psychology, Berkeley, CA.

Furstenberg, F. F., Brooks-Gunn, J., & Mor-

gan, S. P. (1987). Adolescent mothers and their children in later life. *Family Planning Perspectives, 19,* 142–152.

Furstenberg, F. F., Levine, J. A., & Brooks-Gunn, J. (1990). The children of teenage mothers: Patterns of early childbearing in two generations. *Family Planning Perspectives,* 22(2), 54–61.

Gaensbauer, T., & Hiatt, S. (1984). *The psychobiology of affective development.* Hillsdale, NJ: Erlbaum.

Gaertner, S. L., Mann, J., Murrell, A., & Dovidio, J. F. (1989). Reducing intergroup bias: The benefits of recategorization. *Journal of Personality and Social Psychology,* 57(2), 239–249.

Gage, F. H., Bjorklund, A., Stenevi, U., Dunnett, S. B., & Kelly, P. A. T. (1984). Intrahippocampal septal grafts ameliorate learning impairments in aged rats. *Science, 22,* 533–536.

Galambos, N. L., Petersen, A. C., & Lenerz, K. (1988). Maternal employment and sex typing in early adolescence: Contemporaneous and longitudinal relations. In A. D. Gottfried and A. W. Gottfried (Eds.), *Maternal employment and children's development: Longitudinal research.* New York: Plenum.

Gamble, T. J., & Zigler, E. (1986). Effects of infant day care: Another look at the evidence. *American Journal of Orthopsychiatry,* 56(1), 26–42.

Garcia, R. E., & Moodie, D. S. (1989). Routine cholesterol surveillance in childhood. *Pediatrics,* 84(5), 751–755.

Garcia-Coll, C., Kagan, J., & Reznick, J. S. (1984). Behavioral inhibition in young children. *Child Development, 55,* 1005–1019.

Gardner, H. (1979, March 29). Exploring the mystery of creativity. *The New York Times,* pp. C1, C17.

Gardner, H. (1981, July). [Interview with Howard Gruber]. Breakaway minds. *Psychology Today,* pp. 64–71.

Gardner, H. (1983). *Frames of mind: The theory of multiple intelligences.* New York: Basic Books.

Gardner, H. (1989, December). Learning, Chinese-style. *Psychology Today,* pp. 54–56.

Garfield, C., & Clark, R. (1978). The Shanti Project: A community model of psychosocial support for patients and families facing life-threatening illness. In C. Garfield (Ed.), *Psychosocial care of the dying patient* (pp. 355–364). New York: McGraw-Hill.

Garland, J. B. (1982, March). *Social referencing and self-produced locomotion.* Paper presented at the meeting of the International Conference on International Studies, Austin, TX.

Garmezy, N. (1983). Stressors of childhood. In N. Garmezy & M. Rutter. (Eds.),

*Stress, coping and development in children.* New York: McGraw-Hill.

Garrison, E. G. (1987). Psychological maltreatment of children: An emerging focus for inquiry and concern. *American Psychologist, 42*(2), 157–159.

Garrison, W. T., & Earls, F. J. (1986). Epidemiological perspectives on maternal depression and the young child. In E. Z. Tronick & T. Field (Eds.), *Maternal depression and infant disturbances.* San Franciso: Jossey-Bass.

Gavotos, L. A. (1959). Relationships and age differences in growth measures and motor skills. *Child Development, 30,* 333–340.

Geber, M. (1962). Longitudinal study and psychomotor development among Baganda children. *Proceedings of the Fourteenth International Congress of Applied Psychology, 3,* 50–60.

Geber, M., & Dean, R. F. A. (1957). The state of development of newborn African children. *The Lancet, 1,* 1216–1219.

Gelfand, D. E. (1982). *Aging: The ethnic factor.* Boston: Little, Brown.

Geller, E., Ritvo, E. R., Freeman, B. J., & Yuwiler, A. (1982). Preliminary observations of the effect of fenfluramine on blood serotonin and symptoms in three autistic boys. *The New England Journal of Medicine, 307*(3), 165–169.

Gelles, R. J., & Maynard, P. E. (1987). A structural family systems approach to intervention in cases of family violence. *Family Relations, 36,* 270–275.

Gelman, R., Bullock, M., & Meck, E. (1980). Preschoolers' understanding of simple object transformations. *Child Development, 51,* 691–699.

Gelman, R., Spelke, A., & Meck, E. (1983). [Work on animism in children].

General Mills, Inc. (1977). *Raising children in a changing society.* Minneapolis, MN: Author.

General Mills, Inc. (1981). *The General Mills American family report 1980–81: Families at work: Strengths and strains.* Minneapolis, MN: Author.

Genevay, B. (1986). Intimacy as we age. *Generations, 10*(4), 12–15.

Gesell, A. (1929). Maturation and infant behavior patterns. *Psychological Review, 36,* 307–319.

Getzels, J. W. (1964). Creative thinking, problem-solving and instruction. In *Yearbook of the National Society for the Study of Education* (Part I, pp. 240–267). Chicago: University of Chicago Press.

Getzels, J. W. (1984, March). *Problem-finding and creativity in higher education* [The Fifth Rev. Charles F. Donovan, S.J., Lecture]. Boston College, School of Education, Boston.

Getzels, J. W., & Jackson, P. W. (1962). *Creativity and intelligence: Explorations with gifted students.* New York: Wiley.

Gewirtz, H. B., & Gewirtz, J. L. (1968). Caretaking settings, background events, and behavior differences in four Israeli childrearing environments: Some preliminary trends. In B. M. Foss (Ed.), *Determinants of infant behavior* (Vol. 4). London: Methuen.

Gibson, E. J., & Walk, R. D. (1960). The "visual cliff." *Scientific American, 202,* 64–71.

Gibson, R. C. (1986). Older black Americans. *Generations, 10*(4), 35–39.

Gil, D. G. (1971). Violence against children. *Journal of Marriage and the Family, 33*(4), 637–648.

Gilford, R. (1984). Contrasts in marital satisfaction throughout old age: An exchange theory analysis. *Journal of Gerontology, 39,* 325–333.

Gilford, R. (1986). Marriages in later life. *Generations, 10*(4), 16–20.

Gilford, R., & Bengtson, V. (1979). Measuring marital satisfaction in three generations: Positive and negative dimensions. *Journal of Marriage and the Family, 41,* 387–398.

Gilligan, C. (1982). *In a different voice: Psychological theory and women's development.* Cambridge, MA: Harvard University Press.

Gilligan, C. (1987). Adolescent development reconsidered. In C. E. Irwin (Ed.), *Adolescent social behavior and health.* San Francisco: Jossey-Bass.

Ginsburg, H., & Miller, S. M. (1982). Sex differences in children's risk-taking behavior. *Child Development, 53,* 426–428.

Ginsburg, H., & Opper, S. (1979). *Piaget's theory of intellectual development* (2d ed.). Englewood Cliffs, NJ: Prentice-Hall.

Ginzberg, E., et al., (1951). *Occupational choice: An approach to a general theory.* New York: Columbia University Press.

Gladue, B. A., Green, R., & Hellman, R. E. (1984). Neuroendocrine response to estrogen and sexual orientation. *Science, 225,* 1496–1499.

Glass, R. B. (1986). Infertility. In S. S. C. Yen & R. B. Jaffe (Eds.), *Reproductive endocrinology: Physiology, pathophysiology, and clinical management* (2d ed.). Philadelphia: Saunders.

Gleitman, L. R., Newport, E. L., & Gleitman, H. (1984). The current status of the motherese hypothesis. *Journal of Child Language, 11,* 43–79.

Glenn, N. D. (1987). Marriage on the rocks. *Psychology Today, 21*(10), 20–21.

Glenn, N. D., & Kramer, K. B. (1987). The marriages and divorces of the children of divorce. *Journal of Marriage and the Family, 49,* 811–825.

Glenn, N. D., & McLanahan, S. (1981). The effects of offspring on the psychological well-being of older adults. *Journal of Marriage and the Family, 43*(2), 409–421.

Glick, J. (1975). Cognitive development in cross-cultural perspective. In F. Horowitz (Ed.), *Review of child development research* (Vol. 4, pp. 595–654). Chicago: University of Chicago Press.

Glick, P. C. (1988). Fifty years of family demography: A record of social change. *Journal of Marriage and the Family, 50,* 861–873.

Glick, P. C. (1989). Remarried families, stepfamilies, and stepchildren: A brief demographic profile. *Family Relations, 38,* 24–27.

Glick, P. C., & Lin, S.-L. (1986a). More young adults are living with their parents: Who are they? *Journal of Marriage and the Family, 48,* 107–112.

Glick, P. C., & Lin, S.-L. (1986b). Recent changes in divorce and remarriage. *Journal of Marriage and the Family, 48*(4), 737–747.

Goedert, J. J., Mendez, H., Drummond, J. E., Robert-Guroff, M., Minkoff, H. L., Holman, S., Stevens, R., Rubinstein, A., Blattner, W. A., Willoughby, A., & Landesman, S. H. (1989, December 9). Mother-to-infant transmission of human immunodeficiency virus type 1: Association with prematurity or low anti-gp 120. *The Lancet,* 1351–1354.

Golbus, M., Loughman, W., Epstein, C., Halbasch, G., Stephens, J., & Hall, B. (1979). Prenatal genetic diagnosis in 3000 amniocenteses. *The New England Journal of Medicine, 300*(4), 157–163.

Gold, D., & Andres, D. (1978a). Developmental comparison between adolescent children with employed and non-employed mothers. *Merrill-Palmer Quarterly, 24,* 243–254.

Gold, D., & Andres, D. (1978b). Relations between maternal employment and development of nursery school children. *Canadian Journal of Behavioral Science, 10,* 116–129.

Gold, D., Andres, D., & Glorieux, J. (1979). The development of Francophone nursery-school children with employed and nonemployed mothers. *Canadian Journal of Behavioral Science, 11,* 169–173.

Gold, M., & Yanof, D. S. (1985). Mothers, daughters, and girlfriends. *Journal of Personality and Social Psychology, 49*(3), 654–659.

Goldberg, E. L., Comstock, G. W., & Harlow, S. D. (1988). Emotional problems in widowhood. *Journal of Gerontology, 43*(6), S206–208.

Golden, M., Birns, B., & Bridger, W. (1973). *Review and overview: Social class and cognitive development.* Paper presented at the meeting of the Society for Research in Child Development, Philadelphia.

Goldschmid, M. L., & Bentler, P. M. (1968). The dimensions and measurement of conservation. *Child Development, 39,* 787–815.

Goldsmith, M. F. (1989). 'Silent epidemic' of 'social disease' makes STD experts raise their voices. *Journal of the American Medical Association, 261*(24), 3509–10.

Goleman, D. (1990a, April 24). Anger over racism is seen as a cause of blacks' high blood pressure. *New York Times,* p. C3.

Goleman, D. (1990b, May 10). Why girls are prone to depression. *New York Times,* p. B15.

Gopnick, A., & Meltzoff, A. N. (1987). Relations between semantic and cognitive development in the one-word stage: The specificity hypothesis. *Child Development, 57,* 1040–1053.

Gorbach, S. L., Zimmerman, D. R., & Woods, M. (1984). *The doctors' antibreast cancer diet.* New York: Simon & Schuster.

Gordon, A. (1975). The Jewish view of death: Guidelines for mourning. In E. Kübler-Ross (Ed.), *Death: The final stage of growth.* Englewood Cliffs, NJ: Prentice-Hall.

Gordon, D., & Young, R. (1976). School phobia: A discussion of etiology, treatment, and evaluation. *Psychological Bulletin, 39,* 783–804.

Gortmaker, S. L., Dietz, W. H., Sobol, A. M., & Wehler, C. A. (1987). Increasing pediatric obesity in the United States. *American Journal of the Diseases of Children, 141,* 535–540.

Goslin, D. A. (ed.). (1969). *Handbook of Socialization Theory and Research.* Skokie, IL, Rand-McNally.

Gottesman, I. I. (1962). Differential inheritance of the psychoneuroses. *Eugenics Quarterly, 9,* 223–227.

Gottesman, I. I., & Shields, J. (1966). Schizophrenia in twins: 16 years consecutive admission to a psychiatric clinic. *British Journal of Psychiatry, 112,* 809–818.

Gottesman, I. I., & Shields, J. (1982). *Schizophrenia: The epigenetic puzzle.* Cambridge: Cambridge University Press.

Gottman, J. M., & Krokoff, L. J. (1989). Marital interaction and satisfaction: A longitudinal view. *Journal of Consulting and Clinical Psychology, 57*(1), 47–52.

Gould, J. B., Davey, B., & Stafford, R. S. (1989). Socioeconomic differences in rates of cesarean section. *New England Journal of Medicine, 321*(4), 233–239.

Graubard, S. G. (1988, January 29). Why do Asian pupils win those prizes? *The New York Times,* p. A35.

Graziano, A. M., & Mooney, K. C. (1982). Behavioral treatment of "nightfears" in children: Maintenance and improvement at 2½ to 3-year follow-up. *Journal of Counseling and Clinical Psychology, 50*(4), 598–599.

Greenberg, J., & Becker, M. (1988). Aging parents as family resources. *Gerontologist, 28*(6), 786–790.

Greenberg, M., & Morris, N. (1974). Engrossment: The newborn's impact upon the father. *American Journal of Orthopsychiatry, 44*(4), 520–531.

Greenberger, E., & Steinberg, L. (1986). *When teenagers work.* New York: Basic Books.

Greenfield, P. M., Bruzzone, L., Koyamatsu, K., Satuloff, W., Nixon, K., Brodie, M., & Kingsdale, D. (1987). What is rock music doing to the minds of our youth? A first experimental look at the effects of rock music. *Journal of Early Adolescence, 7,* 315–329.

Greenhouse, L. (1990, June 26). Justices find a right to die, but the majority sees need for clear proof of intent. *The New York Times,* pp. A1, A18, A19.

Gribben, K., Schaie, K. W., & Parham, I. A. (1980). Complexity of life style and maintenance of intellectual abilities. *Journal of Social Issues, 36,* 47–61.

Grief, E. B., & Ulman, K. J. (1982). The psychological impact of menarche on early adolescent females: A review of the literature. *Child Development, 53,* 1413–1430.

Gross, R. T., & Duke, P. (1980). The effect of early versus late physical maturation on adolescent behavior. In I. Litt (Ed.), Symposium on adolescent medicine. *Pediatric Clinics of North America, 27*(1), 71–78.

Grotevant, H., & Durrett, M. (1980). Occupational knowledge and career development in adolescence. *Journal of Vocational Behavior, 17,* 171–182.

Gruber-Baldini, A., & Schaie, K. W. (1986, November 21). *Longitudinal-sequential studies of marital assortativity.* Paper presented at the annual meeting of the Gerontological Society of America, Chicago.

Gruen, G., Korte, J., & Baum, J. (1974). Group measure of locus of control. *Developmental Psychology, 10*(5), 683–686.

Gualtieri, T., & Hicks, R. E. (1985). An immunoreactive theory of selective male affliction. *Behavioral and Brain Sciences, 8,* 427–441.

Gubrium, F. F. (1975). Being single in old age. *International Journal of Aging and Human Development, 6*(1), 29–41.

Guidubaldi, J., & Perry, J. D. (1985). Divorce and mental health sequelae for children: A two year follow-up of a nationwide sample. *Journal of the American Academy of Child Psychiatry, 24*(5), 531–537.

Guilford, J. P. (1959). Three faces of intellect. *American Psychologist, 14,* 469–479.

Guskin, A. E. (1990, Spring). State of the college address. *The Antiochian, 60,* 10–13.

Gutmann, D. (1975). Parenting: A key to the comparative study of the life cycle. In N. Datan & L. H. Ginsberg (Eds.), *Life-span developmental psychology: Normative life crises.* New York: Academic.

Gutmann, D. (1977). The cross-cultural perspective: Notes toward a comparative psychology of aging. In J. Birren & K. W. Schaie (Eds.), *Handbook of the psychology of aging.* New York: Van Nostrand Reinhold.

Gutmann, D. (1985). The parental imperative revisited. In J. Meacham (Ed.), *Family and individual development.* Basel: Karger.

Alan Guttmacher Institute. (1981). *Teenage pregnancy: The problem that hasn't gone away.* New York: Viking.

Haan, N. (1990). Personality at midlife. In S. Hunter & M. Sundel (Eds.), *Midlife myths.* Newbury Park, CA: Sage.

Haan, N., & Day, D. (1974). A longitudinal study of change and sameness in personality development: Adolescence to later adulthood. *International Journal of Aging and Human Development, 5*(1), 11–39.

Hadeed, A. J., & Siegel, S. R. (1989). Maternal cocaine use during pregnancy: Effect on the newborn infant. *Pediatrics, 84*(2), 205–210.

Hadley, J. (1984, July–August). Facts about childhood hyperactivity. *Children Today,* pp. 8–13.

Hagestad, G. O. (1978). *Patterns of communication and influence between grandparents and grandchildren in a changing society.* Paper presented at the meeting of the World Conference of Sociology, Uppsala, Sweden.

Hagestad, G. O. (1982). *Issues in the study of intergenerational continuity.* Paper presented at the National Council on Family Relations Theory and Methods Workshop, Washington, DC.

Hagestad, G. O. (1984). *Family transitions in adulthood: Some recent changes and their consequences.* Paper presented at the annual meeting of the Gerontological Society of America, San Antonio, TX.

Haith, M. M. (1986). Sensory and perceptual processes in early infancy. *Journal of Pediatrics, 109*(1), 158–171.

Hall, E. (1983). A conversation with Erik Erikson. *Psychology Today, 17*(6), 22–30.

Hall, E. G., & Lee, A. M. (1984). Sex differences in motor performance of young children: Fact or fiction? *Sex Roles, 10,* 217–230.

Hall, G. S. (1916). *Adolescence.* New York: Appleton. (Original work published 1904.)

Hall, G. S. (1922). *Senescence: The last half of life.* New York: Appleton.

Hamilton, S., & Crouter, A. (1980). Work and growth: A review of research on the impact of work experience on adolescent development. *Journal of Youth and Adolescence, 9*(4), 323–338.

those at risk of dropping out, an enduring program that works. *The New York Times*, p. B9.

Werner, E. E. (1985). Stress and protective factors in children's lives. In A. R. Nichol (Ed.), *Longitudinal studies in child psychology and psychiatry*. New York: Wiley.

Werner, E. E. (1989). Children of the garden island. *Scientific American, 260*(4), 106–111.

Werner, E. E., Bierman, L., French, F. E., Simonian, K., Connor, A., Smith, R., & Campbell, M. (1968). Reproductive and environmental casualties: A report on the 10-year follow-up of the children of the Kauai pregnancy study. *Pediatrics, 42*(1), 112–127.

Werner, J. S., & Siqueland, E. R. (1978). Visual recognition memory in the preterm infant. *Infant Behavior and Development, 1*, 79–94.

Werts, C. E. (1966). Social class and initial career choice of college freshmen. *Sociology of Education, 39*, 74–85.

Werts, C. E. (1968). Paternal influence on career choice. *Journal of Counseling Psychology, 15*, 48–52.

West Berlin Human Genetics Institute. (1987). Study on effects of nuclear radiation at Chernobyl on fetal development.

Whiffen, V. E., & Gotlib, I. H. (1989). Infants of postpartum depressed mothers: Temperament and cognitive status. *Journal of Abnormal Psychology, 98*(3), 274–279.

Whisnant, L., & Zegans, L. (1975). A study of attitudes toward menarche in white middle class American adolescent girls. *American Journal of Psychiatry, 132*(8), 809–814.

White, B. L. (1971, October). *Fundamental early environmental influences on the development of competence*. Paper presented at the Third Western Symposium on Learning: Cognitive Learning, Western Washington State College, Bellingham, WA.

White, B. L., Kaban, B., & Attanucci, J. (1979). *The origins of human competence*. Lexington, MA: Heath.

White, K. R. (1982). The relation between socioeconomic status and academic achievement. *Psychological Bulletin, 91*(3), 461–481.

White, N., & Cunninghamn, W. R. (1988). Is terminal drop pervasive or specific? *Journal of Gerontology, 43*(6), P141–144.

White House Conference on Aging. (1971). *Aging and blindness*. Special Concerns Session Report. Washington, DC: U.S. Government Printing Office.

Whitehurst, G. J., Falco, F. L., Lonigan, C. J., Fischel, J. E., DeBaryshe, B. D., Valdez-Menchaca, M. D., & Caulfield, M. (1988). Accelerating language development through picture book reading.

*Developmental Psychology, 24*(4), 552–559.

Whitehurst, G. J., Fischel, J. E., Lonigan, C. J., Valdez-Menchaca, M. C., DeBaryshe, B. D., & Caulfield, M. B. (1988). Verbal interaction in families of normal and expressive-language-delayed children. *Developmental Psychology, 24*(5), 690–699.

Whitson, J. S., Selkoe, D. J., & Cotman, C. W. (1989). Amyloid B protein enhances survival of hippocampal neurons in vitro. *Science, 243*, 1488–1490.

Wideman, M. V., & Singer, J. F. (1984). The role of psychological mechanisms in preparation for childbirth. *American Psychologist, 34*, 1357–1371.

Wilcox, A. J., Weinberg, C. R., O'Connor, J. F., Baird, D. D., Schlatterer, J. P., Canfield, R. E., Armstrong, E. G., & Nisula, B. C. (1988). Incidence of early loss of pregnancy. *The New England Journal of Medicine, 319*(4), 189–194.

Williams, E. R., & Caliendo, M. A. (1984). *Nutrition: Principles, issues, and applications*. New York: McGraw-Hill.

Williams, J., Best, D., & Boswell, D. (1975). The measurement of children's racial attitudes in the early school years. *Child Development, 46*, 494–500.

Williams, R. B., Barefoot, J. C., & Shekelle, R. B. (1984). The health consequences of hostility. In M. A. Chesney, S. E. Goldston, & R. H. Rosenman (Eds.), *Anger: Hostility and behavior medicine*. New York: Hemisphere/McGraw-Hill.

Williams, T. M. (1978). *Differential impact of TV on children: A natural experiment in communities with and without TV.* Paper presented at the meeting of the International Society for Research on Aggression, Washington, DC.

Williamson, D. F., Kahn, H. S., Remington, P. L., & Anda, R. F. (1990). The 10-year incidence of overweight and major weight gain in U.S. adults. *Archives of Internal Medicine, 150*, 665–672.

Willis, S. L., & Baltes, P. B. (1980). Intelligence in adulthood and aging. In L. W. Poon (Ed.), *Aging in the 1980s*. Washington, DC: American Psychological Association.

Willis, S. L., Blieszner, R., & Baltes, P. B. (1981). Intellectual training research in aging: Modification of performance on the fluid ability of figural relations. *Journal of Educational Psychology, 73*, 41–50.

Wilson, G., McCreary, R., Kean, J., & Baxter, J. (1979). The development of preschool children of heroin-addicted mothers: A controlled study. *Pediatrics, 63*(1), 135–141.

Wilson, R. S. (1983). The Louisville twin study: Developmental synchronies in behavior. *Child Development, 54*, 298–316.

Winick, M. (1981, January). Food and the fetus. *Natural History*, pp. 16–81.

Winick, M., Brasel, J., & Rosso, P. (1972). Nutrition and cell growth. In M. Winick (Ed.), *Nutrition and development*. New York: Wiley.

Wittrock, M. C. (1980). Learning and the brain. In M. C. Wittrock (Ed.), *The brain and psychology*. New York: Academic.

Wolf, M. (1968). *The house of Lim*. Englewood Cliffs, NJ: Prentice-Hall.

Wolfe, D. A. (1985). Child-abusive parents: An empirical review and analysis. *Psychological Bulletin, 97*(3), 462–482.

Wolfe, D. A., Edwards, B., Manion, I., & Koverola, C. (1988). Early intervention for parents at risk of child abuse and neglect: A preliminary investigation. *Journal of Consulting and Clinical Psychology, 56*(1), 40–47.

Wolff, P. H. (1963). Observations on the early development of smiling. In B. M. Foss (Ed.), *Determinants of infant behavior* (Vol. 2). London: Methuen.

Wolff, P. H. (1966). The causes, controls, and organizations of behavior in the newborn. *Psychological Issues, 5*(1, Whole No. 17), 1–105.

Wolff, P. H. (1969). The natural history of crying and other vocalizations in early infancy. In B. M. Foss (Ed.), *Determinants of infant behavior* (Vol. 4). London: Methuen.

Wood, D. (1980). Teaching the young child: Some relationships between social interaction, language, and thought. In D. Olson (Ed.), *The social foundations of language and thought*. New York: Norton.

Wood, D., Bruner, J., & Ross, G. (1976). The role of tutoring in problem solving. *Journal of Child Psychiatry and Psychology, 17*, 89–100.

Woodruff, D. S. (1985). Arousal, sleep and aging. In J. E. Birren & K. W. Schaie (Eds.), *Handbook of the psychology of aging*. New York: Van Nostrand Reinhold.

Working Women Education Fund. (1981). *Health hazards for office workers*. Cleveland, OH: Author.

Wortman, C. B., & Silver, R. C. (1989). The myths of coping with loss. *Journal of Consulting and Clinical Psychology, 57*(3), 349–357.

Wright, A. L., Holberg, C. J., Martinez, F. D., Morgan, W. J., & Taussig, L. M. (1989, October 14). Breast-feeding and lower respiratory tract illness in the first year of life. *British Medical Journal, 299*, 946–949.

Wright, J. T., Waterson, E. J., Barrison, I. G., Toplis, P. J., Lewis, I. G., Gordon, M. G., MacRae, K. D., Morris, N. F., & Murray Lyon, I. M. (1983, March 26). Alcohol consumption, pregnancy, and low birthweight. *The Lancet*, pp. 663–665.

**Wurtman, R. J., & Wurtman, J. J. (1989).** Carbohydrates and depression. *Scientific American, 260*(1), 68–75.

**Yamamoto, K., Soliman, A., Parsons, J., & Davies, O. L. (1987).** Voices in unison: Stressful events in the lives of children in six countries. *Journal of Child Psychology and Psychiatry, 28*(6), 855–864.

**Yamazaki, J. N., & Schull, W. J. (1990).** Perinatal loss and neurological abnormalities among children of the atomic bomb. *Journal of the American Medical Association, 264,* 605–609.

**Yarrow, M. R. (1978, October 31).** *Altruism in children.* Paper presented at the program, Advances in Child Development Research, New York Academy of Sciences, New York.

**Yllo, K. (1984).** The status of women, marital equality, and violence against women: A contextual analysis. *Journal of Family Issues, 5,* 307–320.

**Yllo, K., & Straus, M. A. (1981).** Interpersonal violence among married and cohabiting couples. *Family Relations, 30,* 339–347.

**Yogman, M. J. (1984).** Competence and performance of fathers and infants. In A. MacFarlane (Ed.), *Progress in child health.* London: Churchill Livingston.

**Yogman, M. J., Cooley, J., & Kindlon, D. (1988).** Fathers, infants, and toddlers: A developing relationship. In P. Bronstein & C. P. Cowan (Eds.), *Fatherhood today: Men's changing roles in the family.* New York: Wiley.

**Yogman, M. J., Dixon, S., Tronick, E., Als, H., & Brazelton, T. B. (1977, March).** *The goals and structure of face-to-face interaction between infants and their fathers.* Paper presented at the meeting of the Society for Research in Child Development, New Orleans.

**York, J. L., & Calsyn, R. J. (1977).** Family involvement in nursing homes. *Gerontologist, 17*(6), 500–505.

**Young, K. T., & Zigler, E. (1986).** Infant and toddler day care: Regulations and policy implications. *American Journal of Orthopsychiatry, 56*(1), 43–55.

**Zabin, L. S., Hirsch, M. B., Smith, E. A., & Hardy, J. B. (1984).** Adolescent sexual attitudes and behavior: Are they consistent? *Family Planning Perspectives, 15,* 16, 185.

**Zabin, L. S., Kantner, J. F., & Zelnik, M. (1979).** The risk of adolescent pregnancy in the first months of intercourse. *Family Planning Perspectives, 11*(4), 215–222.

**Zakariya, S. B. (1982, September).** Another look at the children of divorce: Summary report of the study of school needs of one-parent children. *Principal,* pp. 34–37.

**Zametkin, A. J., Nordahl, T. E., & Gross, M., et al. (1990).** Cerebral glucose metabolism in adults with hyperactivity of childhood onset. *New England Journal of Medicine, 323,* 1361–1366.

**Zelazo, P. R., Kotelchuck, M., Barber, L., & David, J. (1977, March).** *Fathers and sons: An experimental facilitation of attachment behaviors.* Paper presented at the meeting of the Society for Research in Child Development, New Orleans.

**Zelnik, M., Kantner, J. F., & Ford, K. (1981).** *Sex and pregnancy in adolescence.* Beverly Hills, CA: Sage.

**Zelnik, M., & Shah, F. K. (1983).** First intercourse among young Americans. *Family Planning Perspectives, 15*(2), 64–72.

**Zeskind, P. S., & Iacino, R. (1984).** Effects of maternal visitation to preterm infants in the neonatal intensive care unit. *Child Development, 55,* 1887–1893.

**Zeskind, P. S., & Ramey, C. T. (1981).** Preventing intellectual and interactional sequelae of fetal malnutrition: A longitudinal, transactional, and synergistic approach to development. *Child Development, 52,* 213–218.

**Zigler, E. F. (1987).** Formal schooling for four-year-olds? *North American Psychologist, 42*(3), 254–260.

**Zimmerman, I. L., & Bernstein, M. (1983).** Parental work patterns in alternate families: Influence on child development. *American Journal of Orthopsychiatry, 53*(3), 418–425.

**Zube, M. (1982).** Changing behavior and outlook of aging men and women: Implications for marriage in the middle and later years. *Family Relations, 31*(1), 147–156.

**Zuckerman, B. S., & Beardslee, W. R. (1987).** Maternal depression: A concern for pediatricians. *Pediatrics, 79*(1), 110–117.

**Zuckerman, B., Frank, D., Hingson, R., Amaro, H., Levenson, S. M., Kayne, H., Parker, S., Vinci, R., Aboagye, K., Fried, L., Cabral, H., Timperi, R., & Bauchner, H. (1989).** Effects of maternal marijuana and cocaine use on fetal growth. *The New England Journal of Medicine, 320*(12), 762–768.

**Zuckerman, D. M., & Zuckerman, B. S. (1985).** Television's impact on children. *Pediatrics, 75*(2), 233–240.

**Zylke, J. W. (1989).** Sudden infant death syndrome: Resurgent research offers hope. *Journal of the American Medical Association, 262*(12), 1565–1566.

# PERMISSIONS AND CREDITS

## CHAPTER 1

### Figures

Figure 1-4: Maslow, A. (1954). "Hierarchy of Needs" from *Motivation and Personality* by Abraham Maslow. Copyright 1954 by Harper & Row, Publishers, Inc. Copyright © 1970 by Abraham H. Maslow. Reprinted by permission of HarperCollins Publishers.

### Photos

Chapter 1 opening photo: Anthony Jalandoni/Monkmeyer, Page 3: Erika Stone. 5: AP/Wide World. 9: John Vachon/Library of Congress. 11: Musée des Beaux Arts de Rennes. 14: Roe DiBona. 18: James Kilkelly/DOT. 25: Mary Evans/Sigmund Freud Copyrights. 26: UPI/Bettmann Newsphotos. 30: Frank Siteman/The Picture Cube. 32: Yves DeBraine/Black Star.

## CHAPTER 2

### Boxes

Box 2-3: Eisenberg, A., Murkoff, H.E., & Hathaway, S.E. (1986). *What to Expect When You're Expecting.* Copyright © 1986 by A. Eisenberg, H. E. Murkoff, & S. E. Hathaway. Reprinted by permission of Workman Publishing. All Rights Reserved.

### Figures

Figure 2-9: March of Dimes Birth Defects Foundation. (1987). *Genetic counseling: A public health information booklet* (rev. ed.). Adapted by permission.

Figure in Box 2-1: Fuchs, F. (1980). Genetic amniocentesis. *Scientific American, 242*(6), 47–53. Copyright © 1980 by Scientific American, Inc. All rights reserved.

Figure 2-11: Tellegen, A., Lykken, D. T., Bouchard, T. J., Wilcox, K. J., Segal, N. L., & Rich, S. (1988). Personality similarity in twins reared apart and together. *Journal of Personality and Social Psychology.* Copyright 1988 by the American Psychological Association. Reprinted by permission.

Figures 2-13 and 2-14: Lagercrantz, H., & Slotkin, T. A. (1986). The stress of being born. *Scientific American, 245*(40), 104–105. Copyright © 1986 by Scientific American, Inc. All rights reserved.

Figure 2-15: Norton, F. C., Placek, P. J., & Taffel, S. M. (1987). Comparisons of national cesarean-section rates. Reprinted by permission of *The New England Journal of Medicine, 316,* 386–389, 1987.

### Tables

Table 2-1: Fahey, V. (1988). The gene screen: Looking in on baby. *In Health,* formerly *Hippocrates,* May/June 1988, 68–69. Research by Valerie Fahey. Excerpted from *In Health.* Copyright © 1988.

### Photos

Chapter 2 opening photo: Randy Masser/International Stock Photo. Page 41: top, Petit Format/Science Source/Photo Researchers; bottom, AP/Wide World. 52: Tony Mendoza/The Picture Cube. 55: J. Pavlovsky/Sygma. 56: Bob Sacha. 59: Mark Olds. 60: Rick Fiedman/Black Star. 62: First and second, Petit Format/Nestle/Science Source/Photo Researchers; third, Lennart Nilsson, *A Child Is Born.* English translation © 1966, 1977 by Dell Publishing Co. Inc.; fourth, J. S. Allen/Daily Telegraph/International Stock; fifth, James Stevenson/Photo Researchers. 63: Sixth, Lennart Nilsson, *Being Born;* seventh and eighth, Petit Format/Nestle/Science Source/Photo Researchers; ninth, Ronn Maratea/International Stock Photo. 68: Steve Leonard/Black Star. 69: Joel Gordon. 72: Ken Biggs/International Stock Photo.

## CHAPTER 3

### Figures

Figure 3-1: Restak, R. (1984). "Fetal Development," from *The Brain* by Richard Restak, M.D. Copyright © 1984 by Educational Broadcasting Corporation and Richard M. Restak, M.D. Used by permission of Bantam Books, a division of Bantam Doubleday, Dell Publishing Group, Inc.

Figure 3-3: Copyright © 1990 by The New York Times Company. Reprinted by permission.

### Tables

Table 3-1: Timiras, P. (1972). Reprinted with permission of Macmillan Publishing Company from *Developmental Physiology and Aging* by Paola Timiras. Copyright © 1972 P. S. Timiras.

Table 3-3: Apgar, V. (1953). A proposal for a new method of evaluation of the newborn infant. *Current Researches in Anesthesia and Analgesia, 32,* 260–267. Reprinted by permission of International Anesthesia Research Society.

Table 3-4: Brown, S. S. (1985). Can low birth weight be prevented? *Family Planning Perspectives, 17*(3). Adapted by permission of Alan Guttmacher Institute and the author.

Table 3-5: Wolff, P. H. (1966). The causes, controls, and organizations of behavior in the newborn. *Psychological Issues, 5*(1, Whole No. 17), 1–105. Adapted by permission of International Universities Press, Inc.

Table 3-6: Frankenburg, W. K., & Dodds, J. B. (1967). Denver developmental screening test. *Journal of Pediatrics, 71,* 181–191. Copyright © 1967, William K. Frankenburg, M.D., and Josiah B. Dodds, Ph.D. Adapted by permission.

### Photos

Chapter 3 opening photo: Alex Low/International Stock Photo. Page 81: Joseph Nettis/Photo Researchers. 85: top left, Kathryn Abbe; top center, Lew Merrim/Monkmeyer; top right, Laura Dwight/Black Star; bottom left, center and right, Elizabeth Crews. 87: Rick Browne/Stock, Boston. 93: Joseph Nettis/Photo Researchers. 97: Erika Stone. 100: Left and right, J. Guichard/Sygma. 101: Innervisions. 104: Erika Stone. 106: Sybil Shackman/Monkmeyer.

## CHAPTER 4

**Boxes**

Box 4-1: Gardner, H. (1989). Learning, Chinese-style. *Psychology Today*, December 1989, 54–56. Copyright © 1989 (Sussex Publishers, Inc.)

**Photos**

Chapter 4 opening photo: Erika Stone. Page 113: James Kilkelly/DOT. 114: Mary Ellen Mark. 116: David Schaefer/The Picture Cube. 119: Courtesy of Safra Nimrod. 120: John Coletti/Stock, Boston. 125: Enrico Ferorelli. 127: Richard Howard. 132: Elizabeth Crews. 136: Larry Lawfer/The Picture Cube.

## CHAPTER 5

Chapter-opening quotation: Hartford, J. *Life Prayer*. Copyright © 1968 by Ensign Music Corporation.

Table 5-3: Thomas, A., & Chess, S. (1984). Genesis and evolution of behavioral disorders: From infancy to early adult life. *American Journal of Psychiatry, 141*(1), 1–9. Copyright 1984 American Psychiatric Association. Adapted by permission.

**Photos**

Chapter 5 opening photo: Jean-Claude Lejeune. Page 146: Laura Dwight/Black Star. 147: Gary Gladstone/The Image Bank. 151: Bob Krist/Black Star. 156: Michal Heron/Woodfin Camp & Associates. 157: Harry Harlow Primate Laboratory/University of Wisconsin. 160: Jonathan Finlay. 163: Courtesy of Safra Nimrod. 166: James Nachtwey/Magnum. 167: Newsday. 170: Sean Sprague/UNICEF.

## CHAPTER 6

**Figures**

Figure 6-1: Brown, J. L. (1987). Hunger in the United States. *Scientific American, 256*(2), 37–41. Copyright © 1987 by Scientific American, Inc. All rights reserved.

Figure 6-4: Gelman, R., Bullock, M., & Meck, E. (1980). Preschoolers' understanding of simple object transformations. *Child Development, 51*, 691–699. © The Society for Research in Child Development, Inc.

Figure 6-5: Field, D. (1977). The importance of the verbal content in the training of Piagetian conservation skills. *Child Development, 52*, 326–334. © The Society for Research in Child Development, Inc.

**Tables**

Table 6-1: American Academy of Pediatrics. (1991). Reprinted with permission from "Immunization Protects Children." Copyright © 1991 American Academy of Pediatrics.

Table 6-2: Corbin, C. B. (1973). Adapted with permission from Charles B. Corbin, *A Text of Motor Development*. Copyright © 1973 by William C. Brown Publishers, Dubuque, Iowa.

Table 6-3: Bolles, E. B. (1982). Excerpted from *So Much to Say* by Edmond Blair Bolles. Copyright © 1982 by Edmund Blair Bolles. Published by St. Martin's Press, Inc.

Table 6-4: Tobin, J. J., Wu, D. Y. H., & Davidson, D. H. (1989). *Preschools in Three Cultures: Japan, China, and the United States, 190–191*. Reprinted by permission of Yale University Press.

**Photos**

Chapter 6 opening photo: Barbara Kirk/The Stock Market. Page 179: Elliott Varner Smith/International Stock Photo. 184: top left, B. Mitchell/The Image Bank; top right, Bob Daemmrich: bottom left, Miro Vintoniv/Stock, Boston; bottom right, Tom McCarthy/The Image Bank. 188: Suzanne Haldane. 189: Erika Stone. 194: Charles Gupton/Stock, Boston. 196: Alan Carey/The Image Works. 198: Gregory K. Scott/Photo Researchers. 202: Jon Feingersh/The Stock Market.

## CHAPTER 7

**Photos**

Chapter 7 opening photo: Jeffrey W. Myers/The Stock Market. Page 211: Mimi Cotter/International Stock Photo. 213: Anthony Jalandoni/Monkmeyer. 215: Both, Sandra Lipsitz Bem. 218: Erika Stone. 221: Bill Stanton/International Stock Photo. 222: Michal Heron/Monkmeyer. 226: Peter Vandermark/Stock, Boston. 229: Bill Stanton/International Stock Photo. 230: Markova/The Image Bank. 232: Bill Foley/Black Star. 236: Bill Stanton/International Stock Photo.

## CHAPTER 8

**Figures**

Figure 8-1: Otis, A. L., & Lennon, R. T. (1967). Otis-Lennon Mental Ability Test. Copyright © 1967 by Harcourt Brace Jovanovich, Inc. Reproduced by permission. All rights reserved.

**Tables**

Table 8-1: Cratty, B. J. (1979). *Perceptual & Motor Development in Infants and Children*, 2e, © 1979, p. 222. Adapted by permission of Prentice Hall, Englewood Cliffs, New Jersey.

Table 8-2: From L. Kohlberg, "The Development of Moral Character and Moral Ideology," in *Review of Child Development Research*, Vol. I, M. L. Hoffman and L. W. Hoffman, editors. © Russell Sage Foundation, 1964. Used with permission of the Russell Sage Foundation.

Table 8-3: Selman, R. L. (1973). A structural analysis of the ability to take another's perspective. Paper presented at meeting of the Society for Research in Child Development, March 1973. © The Society for Research in Child Development, Inc.

Table 8-4: Kohlberg, L. (1969). Stage and sequence: The cognitive-developmental approach to socialization. In D. A. Goslin (ed.), *Handbook of Socialization Theory and Research*. Reprinted by permission of the author.

Table 8-5: Chomsky, C. S. (1969). *The Acquisition of Syntax in Children from Five to Ten*. Copyright © 1969. Reprinted by permission of MIT Press.

**Photos**

Chapter 8 opening photo: Richard Hutchings/Photo Researchers. Page 243: Bob Daemmrich/The Image Works. 245: Michal Heron/Woodfin Camp & Associates. 248: George Ancona/International Stock Photo. 256: Charles Gupton/Stock, Boston. 257: F.E. O'Neal/Taurus. 262: Peter Dublin/Stock, Boston. 265: George Ancona/International Stock Photo. 269: Will McIntyre/Photo Researchers. 270: The National Gallery, London.

## CHAPTER 9

Chapter-opening quotation: "The Absentees" from *Verses From 1929 On* by Ogden Nash. Copyright 1942 by Ogden Nash. First appeared in *The Saturday Evening Post*. By permission of Little, Brown and Company.

**Tables**

Table 9-2: Selman, R. S., & Selman, A. P. (1979). Children's ideas about friendship. *Psychology Today 13*(4), 71–80, 114. Copyright © 1979 (Sussex Publishers, Inc.)

Table 9-3: Matthews, K. A., & Rodin, J. (1989). Women's changing work roles: Impact on health, family, and public policy. *American Psychologist, 44*(11), 1389–1393. Copyright 1989 by the American Psychological Association. Reprinted by permission.

**Photos**

Chapter 9 opening photo: Mark Bolster/International Stock Photo. Page 277: Elliott Varner Smith/International Stock Photo 278: Elyse Lewin/The Image Bank. 279: Paul Conklin/Monkmeyer. 280: Larry Kolvoord/The Image Works. 283: Ida Wyman/International Stock Photo. 286: Lawrence Migdale/Photo Researchers. 288: Blair Seitz/Photo Researchers. 295: top, Erika Stone; bottom, Cary Wolinsky/Stock, Boston. 297: Mimi Cotter/International Stock Photo. 298: Michal Heron/Monkmeyer.

**CHAPTER 10**

**Figures**

Figure 10-1: Gortmaker, S. L., Dietz, W. H., Sobol, A. M., & Welher, C. A. (1987). Increasing pediatric obesity in the United States. *American Journal of the Diseases of Children, 141,* 535–540. Copyright 1987, American Medical Association.
Figure 10-2: Copyright © 1990 by The New York Times Company. Reprinted by permission.

**Photos**

Chapter 10 opening photo: Will and Deni McIntyre/Photo Researchers. Page 309: Bill Gillette/Stock, Boston. 312: Larry Miller/Photo Researchers. 313: left, Andy Levin/Black Star; right, Mieke Maas/The Image Bank. 315: Sybil Shackman/Monkmeyer. 317: Patt Blue. 320: Louis Fernandez/Black Star. 325: Mimi Forsyth/Monkmeyer. 326: Richard Hutchings/InfoEdit. 333: Billy E. Barnes/Stock, Boston.

**CHAPTER 11**

**Boxes**

Box 11-1: Brown, E. F., & Hendee, W. R. (1989). Adolescents and their music: Insights into the health of adolescents. *Journal of the American Medical Association, 262*(12), 1659–1663. Copyright 1989, American Medical Association.

**Figures**

Figures 11-1, 11-2, and 11-3: Csikszentmihalyi, M., & Larsen, R. (1984). From *Being Adolescent: Conflict and Growth in the Teenage Years,* by Mihaly Csikszentmihalyi and Reed Larson. Copyright © 1984 by Basic Books, Inc. Reprinted by permission of Basic Books, a division of HarperCollins Publishers.

**Tables**

Table 11-2: Marcia, J. E. (1966). Development and validation of ego identity status. *Journal of Personality and Social Psychology, 3*(5), 551–558. Copyright 1966 by the American Psychological Association. Adapted by permission.
Table 11-3: Montmeyer, R. (1983). Parents and adolescents in conflict. *Journal of Early Adolescence, 3,* 83–103. Copyright © 1983. Reprinted by permission of Sage Publications, Inc.

**Photos**

Chapter 11 opening photo: Maratea/International Stock Photo. Page 340: Dario Perla/International Stock Photo. 341: Library of Congress. 342: Barton Silverman/NYT Pictures. 345: Harvard University News Office. 346: Erika Stone. 348: Ruth Duskin Feldman. 350: Richard Hutchings/Photo Researchers. 353: D. Fineman/Sygma. 354: Tony Mottram/Retna. 356: Bob Daemmrich/The Image Works. 359: D. Fineman/Sygma. 363: Myrleen Ferguson/Photo Edit.

**CHAPTER 12**

**Figures**

Figure 12-1: Copyright © 1990 by The New York Times Company. Reprinted by permission.
Figure 12-2: Blair, S. N., Kohl, H. W., Paffenberger, R. S., Clark, D. G., Cooper, K. H., & Gibbons, L. W. (1989). Physical fitness and all-cause mortality: A prospective study of healthy men and women. *Journal of the American Medical Association, 262,* 2395–2401. Copyright 1989, American Medical Association.
Figure 12-3: Schaie, K. W. (1977–1978). Toward a stage theory of adult cognitive development. *International Journal of Aging and Human Development, 8*(2), 129–138. © 1977–1978 by Baywood Publishing Company, Inc.

**Tables**

Table 12-1: Belloc, N. B., & Breslow, L. (1972). Relationship of physical health status and health practices. *Preventive Medicine, 1*(3), 409–421. Reprinted by permission of Academic Press.
Table 12-2: Holmes, T. H., & Rahe, R. H. (1976). The social readjustment rating scale. *Journal of Psychosomatic Research, 11*(213). Copyright 1976, Pergamon Press plc.
Table 12-3: Gilligan, C. (1982). *In a Different Voice: Psychological Theory and Women's Development.* Reprinted by permission of Harvard University Press.

**Photos**

Chapter 12 opening photo: Michael McGovern/The Picture Cube. Page 371: Rich Clarkson/Time Magazine. 374: Margot Granitsas/The Image Works. 375: Jim Wilson/Woodfin Camp & Associates. 376: Drawing by W. B. Park; © 1988 The New Yorker Magazine, Inc. 379: Yvonne Hemsey/Gamma-Liaison. 383: Gabor Demjen/Stock, Boston. 389: Charles Gupton/Stock, Boston. 390: Tom Myers/Photo Researchers.

**CHAPTER 13**

**Figures**

Figure 13-1: Graph designed by Dorri Olds.

**Tables**

Table 13-2: Passuth, P., Maines, D., & Neugarten, B.L. (1984). Age Norms paper. Reprinted by permission of the authors.
Table 13-3: Sternberg, R. J. (1985). A triangular theory of love. Paper presented at the annual meeting of American Psychological Association, Los Angeles, 1985. Reprinted by permission of the author.

**Photos**

Chapter 13 opening photo: Sepp Seitz/Woodfin Camp & Associates. Page 399: Julie Houck/Stock, Boston. 403: Henley & Savage/The Stock Market. 405: Vince Streano/The Stock Market. 406: Eiji Miyazawa/Black Star. 408: Robert Kristofik/The Image Bank. 411: Ralf-Finn Hestoft/Saba. 413: Paul L. Merideth/Click/Chicago. 415: Arlene Collins/Monkmeyer. 417: Erika Stone. 419: Michal Heron/Woodfin Camp & Associates. 421: Palmer Brilliant/The Picture Cube.

**CHAPTER 14**

**Figures**

Figure in Box 14-1: Notelovitz, M., & Ware, M. (1982). *Stand Tall: The Informed Woman's Guide to Preventing Osteoporosis.* Illustration © 1982 by Triad Publishing Company.
Figure 14-1: Raven, J. C. (1983). Raven progressive matrices test. A5 from the Raven *Standard Progressive Matrices.* Reproduced by permission of J. C. Raven Ltd.
Figure 14-2: Horn, H. J., & Donaldson, G. (1980). Changes in fluid and crystalizated intelligence. In O. G. Brim and J. Kagan (eds.), *Constance and Change in Human Development.* Reprinted by permission of Harvard University Press.

## Tables

Table 14-1: 9 to 5, Working Women Education Fund. (1981). *Warning! Health Hazards for Office Workers,* 9. Reprinted by permission of 9 to 5, Working Women Education Fund.

## Photos

Chapter 14 opening photo: Gabe Palmer/ The Stock Market. Page 429: David Ycung-Wolff/PhotoEdit. 433: Gabe Palmer/The Stock Market. 434: Mark Olds. 439: Blair Seitz/Photo Researchers. 442: Gilles Peress/Magnum. 443: Doug Bruce/Picture Group.

## CHAPTER 15

Chapter-opening quotation: Hughes, L. "Dream Deferred" from *The Panther and the Lash* by Langston Hughes. Copyright 1951 by Langston Hughes. Reprinted by permission of Alfred A. Knopf, Inc.

## Tables

Table 15-2: Lauer, J., & Lauer, R. (1985). Marriages made to last. *Psychology Today,* 19(60), 22–26. Copyright © 1985 (Sussex Publishers, Inc.)

Table 15-3: Copyright © 1989 by The New York Times Company. Reprinted by permission. AARP. (1989). *National Survey of Caregivers.* Copyright 1989, American Association of Retired Persons. Reprinted with permission.

Table in Box 15-3: Reprinted by permission of Pennsylvania State University Cooperative Extension Service.

## Photos

Chapter 15 opening photo: Bob Daemmrich/The Image Works. Page 449: Drawing by M. Twohy; © 1990 The New Yorker Magazine, Inc. 451: Bob Daemmrich/Stock, Boston. 454: Miriam White/ The Stock Market. 455: Levine/Anthro-Photo. 460: Randy Taylor/Sygma. 461: Erika Stone. 462: Sybil Shackman/ Monkmeyer. 463: Phil Huber/Black Star.

## CHAPTER 16

### Boxes

Box 16-1: Martin, L. G. (1988). The aging of Asia. *Journal of Gerontology: Social Sciences,* 43(4), S99–S113. Copyright by The Gerontological Society of America. Used with permission.

### Figures

Figure 16-2: Schaie, K. W. (1989). The hazards of cognitive aging. *The Gerontologist,* 29(4), 484–493. Copyright by The Gerontological Society of America. Used with permission.

### Tables

Table 16-1: AARP. (1986). *A Profile of Older Americans.* Copyright 1986, American Association of Retired Persons. Reprinted with permission.

Table 16-2: Schaie, K. W. (1989). The hazards of cognitive aging. *The Gerontologist,* 29(4), 484–493. Copyright by The Gerontological Society of America. Used with permission.

Table 16-3: Smith, J., & Baltes, P. B. (1990). Wisdom-related knowledge: Age/cohort differences in response to life-planning problems. *Developmental Psychology,* 26(3), 494–505. Copyright 1990 by the American Psychological Association. Reprinted by permission.

### Photos

Chapter 16 opening photo: Sybil Shelton/ Peter Arnold. Page 473: Eastcott/ Momatiuk/Woodfin Camp & Associates. 479: Barbara Kirk/The Stock Market. 480: Cotton Coulson/Woodfin Camp & Associates. 482: Frank Fisher/Gamma-Liaison. 484: Bill Gillette/Stock, Boston. 485: NYT Pictures. 489: James Balog/Black Star. 493: Jim Harrison/Stock, Boston. 494: Joel Gordon.

## CHAPTER 17

Chapter-opening quotation: Haiku. In *Sound and Light.* Copyright 1987 Ruth Duskin Feldman and Bunny L. Shuch.

### Boxes

Box 17-4: DeVos, S. (1990). Extended family living among older people in six Latin American countries. *Journal of Gerontology: Social Sciences,* 45(3), S87–S94. Copyright by The Gerontological Society of America. Used with permission.

## Tables

Table 17-1: Koenig, H. G., George, L. K., & Siegler, I. C. (1988). The use of religion and other emotion-regulating coping strategies among older adults. *The Gerontolotist,* 28(3), 303–310. Copyright by The Gerontological Society of America. Used with permission.

Table 17-2: Hamon, R. R., & Blieszner, R. (1990). Filial responsibility expectations among adult child–older parent pairs. *Journal of Gerontology: Psychological Sciences,* 45(3), P110–P112. Copyright by The Gerontological Society of America. Used with permission.

### Photos

Chapter 17 opening photo: Junebug Clark/ Photo Researchers. Page 501: George Ancona/International Stock Photo. 502: Nilo Lima/Photo Researchers. 503: Dennis Brack/Black Star. 509: Blair Seitz/Photo Researchers. 510: Blair Seitz/ Photo Researchers. 513: Paul Fusco/ Magnum. 516: Gary M. Roberts/The Picture Cube. 518: Bill Pierce-Time/Sygma. 519: Leonard Freed/Magnum. 520: Elliott Varner Smith/International Stock Photo. 523: Jonathan L. Barkan/The Picture Cube.

## CHAPTER 18

Chapter-opening quotation: Kübler-Ross, E. (1969). Adapted with permission of Macmillan Publishing Company from *On Death and Dying* by Elisabeth Kübler-Ross. Copyright © 1969 Elisabeth Kübler-Ross.

### Tables

Table 18-1: Kübler-Ross: (1969). Adapted with permission of Macmillan Publishing Company from *On Death and Dying* by Elisabeth Kübler-Ross. Copyright © 1969 Elisabeth Kübler-Ross.

### Photos

Chapter 18 opening photo: Dennis Stock/ Magnum. Page 532: Alan Carey/The Image Works. 533: Mary Ellen Mark. 538: Laurence Nelson/Black Star. 539: Nathan Benn/Woodfin Camp & Associates. 542: Bill Binzen/Photo Researchers. 543: James D. Wilson/Woodfin Camp & Associates. 548: Ted Kirk. 551: William Strode/Woodfin Camp & Associates.

# INDEXES

## NAME INDEX

# SUBJECT INDEX